A Normative Foucauldian

Educational Futures

RETHINKING THEORY AND PRACTICE

Series Editor

Michael A. Peters (*Beijing Normal University, P.R. China*)

Editorial Board

Michael Apple (*University of Wisconsin-Madison, USA*)
Miriam David (*Institute of Education, London University, UK*)
Cushla Kapitzke (*Queensland University of Technology, Australia*)
Simon Marginson (*UCL Institute of Education, London, UK*)
Mark Olssen (*University of Surrey, UK*)
Fazal Rizvi (*University of Melbourne, Australia*)
Susan Robertson (*University of Cambridge, UK*)
Linda Tuhiwai Smith (*University of Waikato, New Zealand*)
Arun Kumar Tripathi (*Indian Institute of Technology, Mandi, Himachal Pradesh, India*)

VOLUME 74

The titles published in this series are listed at *brill.com/edfu*

A Normative Foucauldian

Selected Papers of Mark Olssen

By

Mark Olssen

BRILL

LEIDEN | BOSTON

All chapters in this book have undergone peer review.

The Library of Congress Cataloging-in-Publication Data is available online at https://catalog.loc.gov

Typeface for the Latin, Greek, and Cyrillic scripts: "Brill". See and download: brill.com/brill-typeface.

ISSN 2214-9864
ISBN 978-90-04-46443-8 (paperback)
ISBN 978-90-04-46444-5 (hardback)
ISBN 978-90-04-46445-2 (e-book)

Copyright 2021 by Koninklijke Brill NV, Leiden, The Netherlands, except where stated otherwise.
Koninklijke Brill NV incorporates the imprints Brill, Brill Nijhoff, Brill Hotei, Brill Schöningh, Brill Fink, Brill mentis, Vandenhoeck & Ruprecht, Böhlau Verlag and V&R Unipress.
All rights reserved. No part of this publication may be reproduced, translated, stored in a retrieval system, or transmitted in any form or by any means, electronic, mechanical, photocopying, recording or otherwise, without prior written permission from the publisher. Requests for re-use and/or translations must be addressed to Koninklijke Brill NV via brill.com or copyright.com.

This book is printed on acid-free paper and produced in a sustainable manner.

To the memory of James R. Flynn

Contents

Foreword: Critique, Ethics, Learning   XIII
    Stephen J. Ball
Series Editor's Foreword: Mark Olssen: Foucauldian Social Democrat   XXIII
    Michael A. Peters
Preface   XXVI

PART 1
Michel Foucault

1 Foucault and the Imperatives of Education   3
   1 Introduction   3
   2 Foucault and Kant   4
   3 Rejecting Kantian Foundationalism   6
   4 Critique as a Historicophilosophical Practice   9
   5 Critique as How Not to Be Governed   12
   6 Criticism as Practical Politics   13
   7 Foucault and Critique in Education: Some Illustrations   15
   8 Critique in a Non-Foundational World: A Question of Method   17

2 Discourse, Complexity, Normativity: Tracing the Elaboration of Foucault's Materialist Concept of Discourse   29
   1 A Brief Introduction to Foucault's Methods   29
   2 From the Early to the Late Foucault   34
   3 An Incorporeal Materialism   37
   4 Resisting Hegelian Assumptions of Unity   39
   5 Foucault's Poststructuralism   42
   6 Foucault Contra Habermas: Overcoming Relativism by Adding the Concept of Life   51

PART 2
Foucault, Marx, Hegel

3 Foucault and Marxism: Rewriting the Theory of Historical Materialism   67
   1 Introduction   67

2 Marxist Preliminaries: A Brief Summation   68
3 Reconceptualising Determination   73
4 Change and Determination   75
5 Monism and Pluralism   78
6 Complexity, Chance, Pluralism: Appropriating Nietzsche to Correct Marx   86
7 Complexity and Openness   94
8 The Nature of Identity   97
9 Difference and Community   98
10 Conclusion   102

4 Marx, Education and the Possibilities of a Fairer World: Reviving Radical Political Economy through Foucault   115
  Mark Olssen and Michael A. Peters
  1 Introduction   115
  2 Marx's Radical Political Economy   118
  3 Foucault's Radical Political Economy   121
  4 Governmentality Studies   125
  5 Neoliberalism and the Birth of Biopolitics   128
  6 Towards a Possible Foucauldian Politics   133
  7 From Governmentality to the Hermeneutics of the Self as Education   134

5 In Conversation with Mark Olssen: On Foucault with Marx and Hegel   147
  Rille Raaper and Mark Olssen

PART 3
Social Democracy in the 21st Century

6 From the Crick Report to the Parekh Report: Multiculturalism, Cultural Difference and Democracy: The Re-visioning of Citizenship Education   177
  1 Introduction: The Crick Report   177
  2 Iris Marion Young and the Politics of Cultural Difference   179
  3 The Crick Report and the Politics of Cultural Difference   181
  4 The Parekh Report on the Future of Multi-Ethnic Britain: Multi-Ethnic Citizenship   183
  5 Adding the Parekh Report to the Crick Report   190

7 In Defence of the Welfare State and Publicly Provided Education: A New Zealand Perspective   194
  1 Neoliberalism and New Zealand Education   196

2　The Failure of Market Theories　199
　　3　Alternatives　211
　　4　Conclusion　223

8　Education Policy, the Cold War and the "Liberal–Communitarian" Debate　229
　　1　Introduction　229
　　2　Classical Liberalism　231
　　3　Classical Economic Liberalism　232
　　4　Utilitarianism　233
　　5　The Moment of Equality in Liberal Theory: John Rawls　234
　　6　The Unsatisfactory Basis of Rawls's Theory　238
　　7　The Communitarian Response to Liberal Frameworks　240
　　8　Communitarianism and the Philosophers of the Cold War　250
　　9　Communitarianism and School Choice　255
　　10　Conclusion　258

9　Social Democracy, Complexity and Education: Perspectives from the Writings of John Atkinson Hobson and John Maynard Keynes　266
　　1　The Philosophy of John Atkinson Hobson　266
　　2　Complexity Theories　268
　　3　Hobson and Keynes　272
　　4　Complexity and Education　274

PART 4
Neoliberal Governmentality

10　Neoliberalism and Laissez-Faire: The Retreat from Naturalism　283
　　1　The Problem of Laissez-Faire in Neoliberal Thought　283
　　2　Foucault, Röpke and Neoliberalism　287
　　3　Hayek and Neoliberalism　289
　　4　Planning and the Rule of Law　290
　　5　A Critique of Hayek's Concept of Planning　291
　　6　Knowledge and Planning　292
　　7　Lars Cornelissen on Hayek and Democracy　297
　　8　Education　298

11　Neoliberal Competition in Higher Education Today: Research, Accountability and Impact　307
　　1　Introduction　307

2 Research and Accountability   311
   3 From Bad to Worse: The REF and the Impact of Research   314
   4 Neoliberalism and Democracy   318

12 Foucault and Neoliberalism: A Response to Recent Critics and a New Resolution   328
   1 Introduction   328
   2 Criticisms of Foucault   329
   3 Rescuing Foucault   333
   4 Neoliberal "Biopower" as a Form of "Positive" State Power   336
   5 A Possible Resolution: Adam Ferguson and the Concept of Civil Society as a Category in Governmentality   340
   6 Conclusion   349

PART 5
Complexity, Democracy, Ethics

13 Foucault as Complexity Theorist: Overcoming the Problems of Classical Philosophical Analysis   359
   1 Introduction   359
   2 Complexity and Openness   372
   3 The Nature of Identity   375
   4 Holism–Particularism, Uniqueness and Creativity   376

14 Exploring Complexity through Literature: Reframing Foucault's Research Project with Hindsight   385

15 Complexity and Learning: Implications for Teacher Education   396
   1 An Introduction to the Science of Complexity   396
   2 The Normative Consequences of Complexity for Learning and Teacher Education   401
   3 A Possible Ethical Theory for a Complex Global Society   405

PART 6
Political Theory in the 21st Century

16 Globalisation, the Third Way and Education Post-9/11: Building Democratic Citizenship   413
   1 Introduction   413

CONTENTS   XI

    2   Neoliberalism, Globalisation and the Move to the "Third Way"   414
    3   What Is Globalisation?   417
    4   A New Political Settlement?   419
    5   Totalitarianism   423
    6   Rights Talk   427
    7   A New Multicultural Cosmopolitanism   428
    8   Democracy   429
    9   Deepening Democracy through Education   431

17 Totalitarianism and the "Repressed" Utopia of the Present: Moving beyond Hayek and Popper with Foucault   439
    1   Introduction   439
    2   Hayek and Popper: Utopianism, Planning and Holistic Engineering   441
    3   Karl Popper: "Utopian" and "Piecemeal" Engineering   444
    4   Utopianism and the Totalitarian State   447
    5   The Poverty of the Liberal Critique of Totalitarianism   450
    6   Foucault and Totality   454
    7   Reconceptualising Utopianism Post-9/11   458
    8   Conclusion   463

18 Wittgenstein and Foucault: The Limits and Possibilities of Constructivism   470
    1   Introduction   470
    2   Social and Individual Constructions   470
    3   Idealism   471
    4   Objectivity, Truth and Relativism   474
    5   The Centrality of Language and Discourse   477
    6   Foucault as Constructivist   480
    7   Conclusion   485

19 Invoking Democracy: Foucault's Conception (with insights from Hobbes)   488
    1   Introduction   488
    2   Liberty, Ethics and Domination   489
    3   Rights as a Historico-Political Discourse   494
    4   Contestation and Deliberation   499
    5   Extending Foucault and Democracy Post-9/11   503

FOREWORD

Critique, Ethics, Learning

Stephen J. Ball

Charles Taylor begins an essay on Foucault with the words "Foucault disconcerts" (1986, p. 69). That is the point of Foucault.

I want to say something here about how Foucault is read and used in the social sciences and explore a distinction between those who simply "read" Foucault as against those who "use" Foucault in an active and constructive fashion to "do" social science. There are then two sorts of writers who address themselves to Foucault's work. There are those who present themselves as Foucauldian scholars, who seek to identify exactly what it was that Foucault meant when he wrote or spoke at any point. They display "a persistence that borders on stubbornness" (Foucault, 1980a, p. VII) to know the *true* Foucault, and in doing so often make little attempt to grasp the style and attitude of his work. Their engagement is almost exclusively textual. Then there are those who "use" Foucault, and take seriously the attitude and orientation of his intellectual and political challenges to make things not as necessary as all that (Foucault, 1991a, p. 76). Mark Olssen is very much one of the latter. "Everything I do", Foucault said, "I do in order that it may be of use" (Defert & Ewald, 2001, pp. 911–912). The usefulness of Foucault lies in the application and development of his ideas and methods and concepts in relation to specific "enterprises" of "problematisation" (Foucault, 1984a, p. 3) as the starting point from which to begin to think differently. This is what Mark Olssen is doing in many of the papers in this book. As he signals: not simply going into Foucault but going beyond him: "This is going well beyond Foucault as he developed his position, of course" (Chapter 2, this volume).

Olssen uses Foucault for "cutting"—as Foucault said: "Knowledge is not made for understanding; it is made for cutting" (Foucault, 1984a, p. 88) and the task each day, he suggested, is to decide that which is of the greatest danger. He went on to explain: "My point is not that everything is bad, but that everything is dangerous, which is not exactly the same as bad. If everything is dangerous, then we always have something to do. So my position leads not to apathy but to a hyper- and pessimistic activism" (Foucault, 1983a, pp. 231–232). That activism joins up the intellectual with the political in complex ways (see Hoffman, 2015).

Over and against this, I would argue, much writing "about" Foucault both misunderstands and misrepresents him. Misunderstands in the sense of failing to grasp the method and raison d'être of his endeavours and concomitantly the status of his statements. Perhaps the most egregious example of this is the Zamora and Behrent (2016) collection *Foucault and Neoliberalism*. As Vogelmann (2016) notes in his review of the book: "By consistently refusing to reflect on how Foucault reads and by neglecting to reflect on their own way of reading Foucault, the authors of this collection obstruct further discussion by obscuring rather than criticising Foucault's analysis of neoliberalism". Vogelmann goes on to point out that the argument for Foucault's neoliberal sympathies proceeds by "simply referring to a sentence or two where it suits their particular aim, without any attention to their conceptual status or their context within the lectures". Johanna Oksala (2015) responds to Zamora, as others have done, by arguing that he and Behrent are asking the wrong questions:

> The only relevant question the academic left should be asking regarding Foucault's analyses of neoliberalism is whether they provide us with any useful tools that can be successfully deployed against the current neoliberal hegemony. And I believe that the answer to this question is, significantly, also a yes.

Zamora's particular argument (p. 70) is that the politics implied by Foucault's analysis—implies mind you, what ever that means—involves the displacement of struggles over the redistribution of power and against exploitation and for equality with a politics of identity. Aside from the fact that Foucault was concerned with subjectivity and not identity, surely what this illustrates is a profound inability to understand Foucault and particularly to understand *governmentality* as a form of power and an art of governing. It also displays a studied neglect of Foucault's views on political struggle and his own political militancy.

> Nowadays, the struggle against the forms of subjection—against the submission of subjectivity—is becoming more and more important, even though the struggles against forms of domination and exploitation have not disappeared. Quite the contrary. (Foucault, 1982, p. 213)

While Foucault does reject any utopian impulse revolving around the laws of economic development or the role of the proletariat in history, the question Foucault raises in his work on neoliberalism is what kind of self, what kind of subject have we become, and how might we be otherwise? Or more succinctly: "Maybe the target nowadays is not to discover what we are but to refuse what we are" (Foucault, 1982, p. 785) and perhaps "refusing, changing and ridding ourselves are only the ethical conditions, made possible by genealogical work, of creation, innovation and invention" (Cremonesi et al., 2016, p. 14). This is hardly a commitment to the subject Homo economicus as the one possible way of being within the neoliberal episteme. Rather this is a particular form of what Foucault called in his Dartmouth Lectures (2016, p. 15) a "politics of ourselves". That is to say, "All those on whom power is exercised to their detriment, all who find it intolerable, can begin the struggle on their own terrain and on the basis of their proper activity (or passivity)" (Foucault, 1977, p. 216). That is, a modern form of politics for a modern form of government. Struggle on this terrain is an engagement with and can involve *a refusal of neoliberal governmentality in its own terms*—a combative relationship to oneself and others not some kind of accommodation to or celebration of neoliberal sensibilities.

For Foucault, as the earlier quotation illustrates, philosophy was not a body of knowledge; rather, it was a critical practice, a relentless questioning of dogmatic beliefs and intolerable practices in contemporary society, a practice of "insolent assertion". He did not set out to develop a general theory of society, or adopt a specific political strategy but rather to identify a set of "problems" and to outline some methods of analysis (archaeology and genealogy, in particular) and develop a set of tools, a toolbox of concepts, which he hoped others would use and develop further in the struggle to be freer than we think we are. "My role" he said, "is to show people that they are much freer than they feel" (Martin, Gutman, & Hutton, 1988, p. 10), but he goes on to say: "whether our freedom is liberating or not is something that is not guaranteed to us" (May, 2011, pp. 80–81). This does not come with the promise of an end point of freedom.

The other point about the many attempts to pigeon-hole Foucault, or to capture the true Foucault—neoliberal, nihilist, hedonist, structuralist or whatever—is the failure to come to grips with the modalities and method of his intellectual practice. That is to say, his body of work consists of a set of incomplete forays and false starts. His writing is always "work in progress, and it is not certain when or even if the work will be conclusive—or to what degree it has even begun" (Kromann & Andersen, 2011, p. 230); he is "continuously analysing, developing and displacing concepts" (p. 230). When asked in a 1982 interview if he was a philosopher, historian, structuralist, or Marxist, Foucault replied, "I don't feel that it is necessary to know exactly what I am. The main interest in life and work is to become someone else that you were not in the beginning" (Martin, Gutman, & Hutton, 1988, p. 9). In other words, he was always moving on rather than taking up fixed positions. Furthermore, perhaps disingenuously at times, Foucault expressed many doubts about the clarity and coherence of his work. He saw himself as experimenting with ideas and possibilities that often led to what he regarded as dead ends.

> None of it does more than mark time. Repetitive and disconnected, it advances nowhere. Since indeed it never ceases to say the same thing, it

perhaps says nothing. It is tangled up into an indecipherable, disorganised muddle. In a nutshell, it is inconclusive. (Foucault, 1980b, p. 78)

We can think about Foucault's oeuvre in the same way he characterised the problems of historical analysis, to be understood as: "discontinuity, rupture, threshold, limit, series, and transformation" (1972, p. 21). Foucault (1997a, p. 180) described his methodological shifts as "auto-critique". The shifts, the dead ends, the unstable use of terms and concepts in Foucault's work are all the more evident, and all the more irrelevant in themselves in as much that a great deal of what we now read of Foucault was never intended for publication, never intended to be read and poured over. The Collège de France lectures in particular which have been endlessly interrogated and dissected by Foucauldian scholars were very much works in progress and opportunities to try out ideas, some of which were disavowed or altered from one lecture to the next, but which are now often read in isolation as definitive statements. Foucault's "final book" recently published, *The History of Sexuality, Volume 4: Confessions of the Flesh* (2021), is also a case in point. Foucault was editing and revising the manuscript in hospital in the weeks before his death and specified in his will that he did not want this work to be published after his death. The now published text was "drawn together" from hand-written notes by the editor. But it will no doubt come to be read, like other posthumous publications, as a finished and fixed book, whereas Foucault saw his books as a means of clarifying his thinking and then moving beyond: "I write a book only because I still don't know what to think about this thing I want so much to think about, so that the book transforms me and transforms what I think" (Foucault, 2000, pp. 239–240). Foucault was preoccupied with writing, and described it as "like a game that invariably goes beyond its own rules and transgresses it limits" (Foucault, 1998, p. 206). He attributed great importance to the act of writing as a practice of freedom and in a very late paper explored the possibilities of what he called "self writing" (Foucault, n.d.), that is a process of self-shaping through the production of texts. "When I write I do it above all to change myself and not to think the same thing as before" (Foucault, 1991b, p. 27). His text do not refer to or report some prior thinking but gesture towards new possibilities of thought. In this way he was clear about how he approached intellectual problems and approached writing. He regarded his intellectual endeavours as a way of working on himself; he was always a work in progress, always unfinished, restless, and bellicose. There is no singular and definitive Foucault to be found on the surfaces of his texts. Indeed, more generally, Foucault was suspicious of the book as an original single-authored text—which we know that *Confessions* is not. "The frontiers of a book are never clear-cut: beyond the title, the first lines, and the last full stop, beyond its internal configuration and its autonomous form, it is caught up in a system of references to other books, other texts, other sentences: it is a node within a network" (Foucault, 1972, p. 23).

How then does Olssen read and use Foucault? Olssen's Foucault is a political Foucault, in a numbers of senses, and relatedly he is a materialist Foucault. And Olssen's Foucault is read in relation to a network of other thinkers—Marx, Wittgenstein, Keynes, Hegel, Nussbaum, Hobbes, Sartre, Althusser, Heidegger, Nietzsche, and Spinoza. Through the engagements and dialogues with these interlocutors offered in Olssen's papers we get a sense of the way Foucault's thought was shaped and influenced by many philosophers almost all of whom he disagreed with, deviated from, subjected to criticism but made use of. His relation to them is one he seeks to encourage among his readers, not to agree with him but to use him, question him and to move on. These engagements are starting points for thinking otherwise. Olssen's Foucault is also very contemporary—a Foucault of globalisation, of neoliberal political economy, of citizenship and complexity and democracy. He is a pragmatic and practical Foucault. Olssen uses Foucault in particular to explore issues of education. Olssen's Foucault is not a lonely nihilist but a troubled provocateur who encourages in us toward the political project of self-formation—our relation to ourselves and always, to others.

Crucially, as Olssen (2007, p. 207) makes clear, such 'ethical action is not, for Foucault, an individual affair but presupposes a certain political and social structure with respect to liberty". The "care of the self" Olssen argues, is set against the performative individualism of modernity and rests in contrast on what he calls "thin" communitarianism, which "has no common goal or bond but comprises of a minimal structure of agreements, rules, practices, and understandings necessitated to permit a social ontology of difference" (Olssen, 2009, p. 489) and he goes on to say "freedom, in this sense, is a historically and politically constructed space" (p. 491). Thus, "far from being a lonely and selfish process, self-care fosters generosity and solidarity, enables stronger and more meaningful ties with others" (Sicilia-Camacho & Fernandez-Balboa, 2009, p. 455). Ethics here concern the kind of relation one has to oneself and others and indicate a different form of self-government, structuring and shaping the field of possible action of subjects.

Olssen (2009, p. 267) suggests, drawing on Sen and Nussbaum in particular, that all of this presupposes "a range of capabilities" that education must develop and he goes on to offer a list of requirements for such an education.

> Taking Foucault's emphasis on "self-creation" as fundamental, we can say that a number of things are clearly required. These include: (1) basic material and institutional supporting structures and resources, (2) training and knowledge, (3) non-humiliation, respect and dignity, (4) a protected

space where freedom can be practised, (5) structures that permit dialogue and communication.

These he also calls "agentic skills", such as "the capacity to understand and access global knowledge systems; the awareness of multi-perspectival orientations to self and culture, based upon an understanding of diverse human experiences, as well as the ability to construct new ideas" (p. xx). Education in these terms involves a commitment to fostering ethical learners with a healthy suspicion of the present, while at the same time being able to acknowledge their own fallibility, and the adoption of a critical stance that moves through experiments in living intended to re-create ourselves, and the world. Olssen (2017) suggests that this has parallels with Dewey's sense of learning as "a cooperative and collaborative activity centred upon experiential, creative responses to contingent sets of relations to cope with uncertainty in a never-ending quest". Learning thus becomes an exploration of limits—mapping, testing and crossing them when possible. The work done "at the limits of ourselves", must always be experimental, we may never be able "both to grasp the points where change is possible and desirable, and to determine the precise form this change should take" (Foucault, 2000).

Foucault's project of critique is not a particular and specific set of actions it is a permanent orientation of scepticism, it is "a mode of relating to contemporary reality" (Foucault, 1984b, p. 39). This involves both "a critique of what we are saying, thinking, and doing" (ibid., p. 45) and experiments with "the possibility of moving beyond" (ibid., p. 47). This is not just a "gesture of rejection" rather we have to move beyond the outside-inside alternative; we have to be at the frontiers" (ibid., p. 45). In relation to this, Foucault studiously avoids the prescription of particular actions that should be employed in order to escape or oppose the phenomena of being governed. Instead, he asserts that criticism is comprised of "analyzing and reflecting upon limits" (ibid., p. 45). This is a stance of liminality that is intended to address specific transformations in "our ways of being and thinking, relations to authority, relations between the sexes, the way in which we perceive insanity or illness" (ibid., pp. 46–47).

The "limit attitude" is a means by which a subject can positively resist power, through "counter-conducts" and creative strategies of resistance that "open up processes of "autonomous and independent" subjectivation, that is, "possibilities for the constitution of oneself" (Lazzarato, 2009, p. 114). This requires that we cultivate "the art of voluntary insubordination, and a practice of reflective intractibility" (Foucault, 1997c, p. 32). "In this sense, critique aims to free us from the historically transitory constraints of contemporary consciousness as realised in and through discursive practices" (Olssen, 2003, p. 73). Drawing on Nietzsche, Foucault sought to displace the humanist/progressive traditions of

Western philosophy, with their promise of personal well-being and collective progress, and which require us to search for and link our essential qualities to inherent abstract principles, and instead set the challenge "of creatively and courageously authoring one's ethical self" (Pignatelli, 2002, p. 158). The task is to avoid fixity in order to become "a stylist, an ironist, a hero by taking oneself as object of a complex and difficult elaboration" (Foucault, 1986, p. 166), to take responsibility for the *form* of one's life and character, the constitution of oneself as a subject. The question is "How is one to live?" and the response is an "aesthetics of existence", an appeal to beauty as a weapon "which can be used to bring down the tyranny of modern morality" (O'Leary, 2002, p. 1). The task of giving style to character in this way is always unfinished.

This is a *negative ethics*, not a matter of asserting ideals, but rather an imaginative creativity. This is ethics as a practice rather than a plan, as "the kind of relationship you ought to have with yourself" (Foucault, 1984c, p. 352). It is the cultivation of a self that is both a product and a disruption of various discourses that requires one to practice the art of living well. It is creating a space within which it is possible to make oneself thinkable in a different way—"to become other than how you find yourself" (Foucault, 1983b). This is very different from and indeed opposed to some kind of grand design for a new world of experience; it is rooted in local situations and specific incidents. It is about the relation between knowing and acting, rather than some kind of inner state or planned alternative. Self-formation is an active and engaged process, based on learning from the immediate and quoditian, forming and testing at the same time; an "exercise of oneself in the activity of thought" (Foucault, 1992, p. 9), over and against or redeploying the techniques of *governmentality*. There is a dynamic interplay here between what it is one does not want to be and what one might become. Nonetheless, and without resort to a traditional code-based morality, Olssen's Foucault is a normative Foucault—but this is a certain sort of normativity, a kind of consequentialist normativity that rests on the concept of life and well-being, and from which a politics of possibility might be constructed. This turns on a commitment to the interests of survival and continuance of all as a basis the basis for ethical judgement and politics.

Following from all of this, as noted, Olssen argues that education can contribute to the development of ethical skills and sensibilities, but only if it is itself a form of ethical practice:

> Learning must be seen, in this sense, as a goal-directed activity, related to the evolution and survival of life. It involves a qualitatively different type of thinking, one that recognises uncertainty, unpredictability, novelty, openness, a balance between order and disorder, and which represents discursive elements, such as concepts and words, as conventional and

historical. Due to human fallibility and limitations, the type of knowledge that complex learning results in is bereft of the arrogance of the Enlightenment claim to know (*aude sapere*) according to the newfound faith in reason. Rather, it is more modest, humble, less self-assured, recognising "partial knowledge", "human error", and limited cognition. At the same time, it also encompasses processes of creativity and of possibilities of unexpected developments within situations. Complex education implies, say Trueit and Doll (2010, p. 138), a view of "education as a journey into the land of the unknown taken by ourselves but with others". (Chapter 15, this volume)

What Olssen does is to deploy Foucault to address a set of fundamental contemporary social and political problems. He takes up Foucault's conceptions of power, of freedom, of self-creation and makes these into a very practical framework for thinking differently about community and about democracy. And in relation to this education becomes a very relevant concern, a particular site at which capabilities and "agentic skills" for self-creation and for community building can be elaborated. Whereas many commentaries focus on "the relation to oneself" and neglects "and to other", and conceive of self-formation as a lonely process of self-discipline, Olssen puts ethics firmly into a collective context, a political context. Olssen starts from and goes beyond Foucault to begin to envision another form of life, a militant life, beyond discipline and security, "a struggle against and for self, against and for others" (Foucault, 2011, p. 283). Olssen offers directions in which we might go, "lines of flight" if you will.

References

Cremonesi, L., Davidson, A. I., Irrera, O., Lorenzini, D., & Tazzioli, M. (2016). Introduction. In M. Foucault, *About the beginning of the hermeneutics of the self: Lectures at Dartmouth College, 1980* (pp. 1–18).

Defert, D., & Ewald, F. (Eds.). (2001). *Dits et Écrits 1954–1988. Vol. II, 1976–1988 Michel Foucault*. Gallimard.

Foucault, M. (1972). *The archaeology of knowledge*. Tavistock.

Foucault, M. (1977). Intellectuals and power. In Bouchard, D. F. (Ed.), *Language, counter-memory, practice: Selected essays and interviews* (D. F. Bouchard & S. Simon, Trans.; pp. 205–217). Cornell University Press.

Foucault, M. (1980a). *Herculine Barbin: Being the recently discovered memoirs of a nneteenth-century French hermaphrodite* (R. McDougall, Trans.). Pantheon Books.

Foucault, M. (1980b). Two lectures (K. Soper, Trans.). In C. Gordon (Ed.), *Power/ knowledge: Selected interviews and other writings 1972–1977* (pp. 78–108). Harvester Press.

Foucault, M. (1982). The subject and power. *Critical Inquiry, 8*(4), 777–795.

Foucault, M. (1983a). On the genealogy of ethics: An overview of work in progress. In H. Dreyfus & P. Rabinow (Eds.), *Michel Foucault: Beyond structuralism and hermeneutics* (pp. 229–252). University of Chicago Press.

Foucault, M. (1983b). Why study power: The question of the subject. In H. Dreyfus & P. Rabinow (Eds.), *Michel Foucault: Beyond structuralism and hermeneutics* (pp. 212–221). University of Chicago Press.

Foucault, M. (1984a). Interview with Michel Foucault (conducted by Catherine Baker). *Actes, 45–46*, 3–6.

Foucault, M. (1984b). What is enlightenment? In P. Rabinow (Ed.), *The Foucault reader* (pp. 32–50). Penguin.

Foucault, M. (1984c). On the genealogy of ethics: An interview of work in progress. In P. Rabinow (Ed.), *The Foucault reader* (pp. 340–372). Pantheon.

Foucault, M. (1986). *Death and the labyrinth: The world of Raymond Roussel* (C. Ruas, Trans.). Introduction by J. Ashberry. Doubleday.

Foucault, M. (1991a). Questions of method. In G. Burchell, C. Gordon, & P. Miller (Eds.), *The Foucault effect: Studies in governmentality* (pp. 73–86). Harvester/Wheatsheaf.

Foucault, M. (1991b). *Remarks on Marx: Conversations with Duccio Trombadori.* Semiotext(e).

Foucault, M. (1992). *The history of sexuality, volume 2: The use of pleasure* (R. Hurley, Trans.). Penguin.

Foucault, M. (1997a). Subjectivity and truth. In S. Lotringer (Ed.), *The politics of truth* (pp. 171–198). Semiotext(e).

Foucault, M. (1997b). What is enlightenment? In P. Rabinow (Ed.), *Essential works of Foucault, 1954–1984, vol. 1: Ethics* (pp. 303–319). Penguin.

Foucault, M. (1997c). What is critique. In M. Foucault, *The politics of truth* (S. Lotringer, Ed.; pp. 23–82). Semiotext(e).

Foucault, M. (1998). What is an author? (J. V. Harari, Trans.). In J. D. Faubion (Ed.), *Essential works of Foucault, 1954–1984, vol. 2: Aesthetics, method, epistemology* (pp. 205–222). The Free Press.

Foucault, M. (2000). Interview with Michel Foucault. In J. D. Faubion (Ed.), *Essential works of Foucault, 1954–1984, Vol. 3: Power* (R. Hurley et al., Trans., pp. 239–297). London: Penguin.

Foucault, M. (2011). *The courage of truth: Lectures at the Collège de France 1983–84.* Palgrave Macmillan.

Foucault, M. (2016). *About the beginning of the hermeneutics of the self. Lectures at Dartmouth College, 1980* (G. Burchell, Trans.). University of Chicago Press.

Foucault, M. (2021). *The history of sexuality, volume 4: Confessions of the flesh* (R. Hurley, Trans.; F. Gros, Ed.). Penguin Random House.

Foucault, M. (n.d.). Self-writing. itsy.co.uk/archive/sisn/Pos/green/Foucault.doc

Hoffman, M. (2015). *Foucault and power: The influence of political engagement on theories of power.* Bloomsbury.

Kromann, J., & Andersen, T. (2011). Parrêsia: The problem of truth. *Ephemera. Copenhagen, 11*(2), 225–230.

Lazzarato, M. (2009). Neoliberalism in action: Inequality, insecurity and the reconstitution of the social. *Theory, Culture & Society, 26*(6), 109–133. https://doi.org/10.1177/0263276409350283

Martin, L. H., Gutman, H., & Hutton, P. H. (Eds.). (1988). *Technologies of the self: A seminar with Michel Foucault*. Tavistock.

May, T. (2011). Foucault's conception of freedom. In D. Taylor (Ed.), *Michel Foucault: Key concepts* (pp. 71–84). Acumen.

Oksala, J. (2015, January 4). Never mind Foucault: What are the right questions for us? *An und für sich*. https://itself.blog/2015/01/04/foucault-and-neoliberalism-aufs-event-johanna-oksala-never-mind-foucault-what-are-the-right-questions-for-us/

O'Leary, T. (2002). *Foucault and the art of ethics*. Continuum.

Olssen, M. (2003). Foucault and critique: Kant, humanism and the human sciences. In M. Peters, M. Olssen, & C. Lankshear (Eds.), *Futures of critical theory: Dreams of difference* (pp. 73–102). Rowman and Littlefield.

Olssen, M. (2007). Invoking democracy: Foucault's conception (with insights from Hobbes). In M. A. Peters & T. A. C. Besley (Eds.), *Why Foucault? New directions in educational research* (pp. 205–226). Peter Lang.

Olssen, M. (2009). *Toward a global thin community: Nietzsche, Foucault, and the cosmopolitan commitment*. Paradigm.

Olssen, M. (2017). Complexity and learning: Implications for teacher education. In M. A. Peters, B. Cowie, & I. Menter (Eds.), *A companion to research in teacher education* (pp. 507–519). Springer Nature. http://dx.doi.org/10.1007/978-981-10-4075-7_34

Pignatelli, F. (2002). Mapping the terrain of Foucauldian Ethics: A response to the surveillance of schooling. *Studies in Philosophy and Education, 21*(1), 157–180.

Sicilia-Comacho, A., & Fernandez-Balboa, J. M. (2009). Reflecting on the moral bases of critical pedagogy in PETE: Towards a Foucauldian perspective on ethics and the care of the self. *Sport Education & Society, 14*(4), 443–463.

Taylor, C. (1986). Foucault on freedom and truth. In D. C. Hoy (Ed.), *Foucault: A critical reader* (pp. 152–183). Blackwell.

Trueit, D., & Doll, W. E. (2010). Thinking complexly. In D. Osberg & G. Biesta (Eds.), *Complexity theory and the politics of education* (pp. 135–152). Sense Publishers.

Vogelmann, F. (2016). Reading practices: How to read Foucault? *Krisis: Journal for Contemporary Philosophy, 2*. https://archive.krisis.eu/reading-practices-how-to-read-foucault/

Zamora, D., & Behrent, M. Z. (Eds.). (2016). *Foucault and neoliberalism*. Polity.

SERIES EDITOR'S FOREWORD

Mark Olssen: Foucauldian Social Democrat

Michael A. Peters

Mark Olssen is a political theorist who specialises in education and political sociology with an accent on the theory of social democracy. He is also an internationally acknowledged expert on Foucault whose philosophical ideas inform his work on neoliberalism. His work critiques neoliberalism both as a mode of governmentality, as well as an alternative social democratic conception of politics and education for the 21st century. His recent work utilises Foucault and complexity as the basis of a new ontology in order to escape deterministic views of history and society, associated with Marx and Hegel. Together, these elements ground a new conception of social democracy where public education, and the social basis of citizenship, will once again play a major role.

Actually, I based this description on an official statement that Mark Olssen uses to succinctly summarise the value of his intellectual labours for the New Zealand performance-based assessment framework (Performance Based Research Fund, PBRF) that monitors and determines institutional and research rankings. It tells us precisely where he locates himself in relation to Foucault and Marx and what he is working toward—a social democratic theoretical account of public education as the basis of social citizenship. It also tells us how he regards Foucault and what use he wants to make of his work. These essays organised into six parts—(1) Michel Foucault, (2) Foucault, Marx, Hegel, (3) Social Democracy in the 21st Century, (4) Neoliberal Governmentality, (5) Complexity, Democracy, Ethics, and (6) Political Theory in the 21st Century—show us the trajectory and progression of Olssen's work. Without doubt he is one of the leading theorists working in this area and his work is widely cited and justly so.

I invited Mark to contribute to my book series because I thought it would be useful to have a comprehensive approach to his papers organised into a coherent whole that guides the reader through the theoretical debates and issues that he has engaged over many years. I have known Mark Olssen for over 20 years from when he was at Otago University in New Zealand in the 1980s, where he was a voice in the wilderness. He had stronger ties and shared theoretical interests with Jim Marshall and me at Auckland University during the 1990s, and with a small group of scholars interested in the work of Michel Foucault that Marshall Olssen and I helped introduce to New Zealand scholars, especially in educational studies. The reception of critical sociology in New

Zealand had been held up until relatively recently with the ascendency of Karl Popper, who occupied a position at the University of Canterbury in the period from 1937 to 1943. Even when Popper was debating with Adorno in the positivistic disputes of German sociology in the late 1950s and early 1960s—a dispute between the critical rationalists and the Frankfurt School—little of it rubbed off on sociology of education in New Zealand. Philosophy of science in New Zealand was dominated by Popper, perhaps rightly so, given the influence of *The Logic of Scientific Discovery*, originally published in 1934, and rewritten and published in English in 1959. Little did the University of Canterbury in the late 1930s appreciate Popper's work nor did they much appreciate the concept of "research", loading Popper up with teaching about which he complained bitterly.

Mark, well read in the work of the Frankfurt School, I imagine, would have sided with Habermas and the Frankfurt School that collectively held that critical sociology could not been cut off from its base in metaphysics with the consequence that all empirical questions are in some sense anchored in philosophical issues. I think Mark would also hold on to this proposition. And I suspect also that he, like Foucault, does not see any deep contradiction between the Frankfurt School and Foucault.

At the University of Otago in New Zealand philosophy was dominated by Alan Musgrave, who edited with Imre Lakatos the wonderful book *Criticism and the Growth of Knowledge* (1970). He became Head of the Philosophy Department at Otago in 1970 and only retired in 2005. The atmosphere was not very receptive to Foucault. James Flynn in the Department of Politics, where Olssen studied as a student, managed to combine moral and political philosophy with psychology to write about issues of race, class and IQ, as well as issues of social and political concern. I know that Olssen and Flynn were on good terms.

The problem was really an Education Department committed to empiricism and psychology that did not try to make room for other approaches, and like education more broadly in New Zealand, in the main drew up firm disciplinary borders between educational psychology and sociology. And yet at the same time the reception of Foucault in educational studies was a major influence on his reception in New Zealand. The downside is that now there are a large group of PhD students who want to use discourse analysis and theory who have never read "The Order of Discourse", Foucault's inaugural lecture at the Collège de France in 1970. Mark Olssen certainly changed the intellectual landscape in sociology of education and in relation the concept of social democracy, always with a policy orientation. He also worked closely with his colleagues at Massey University, including John Codd and Anne-Marie O'Neill in 2001

He left Otago for the Politics Department at the University of Surrey, where he focused on his project of developing approach to Foucault's ethics and elaborating Foucault's normative approach to education. He has been there ever since but also took an adjunct role as professorial chair in higher education at the Auckland University of Technology, for the period of the 2018 PBRF. The result of his life's work is a strong vision of social democracy and a coherent account of education's role within it. Olssen is a thinker. He is a meticulous scholar and a creative writer.

I have had the good fortune to work and collaborate with Mark and I count him as a friend and colleague, so it is with great pleasure that I am able to offer this collection to his readers and to the academic community at large.

Preface

The following papers represent a selection of academic articles that I have published over the last 25 years. The themes I have chosen to guide my selection include Michel Foucault, Marxism, neoliberalism, complexity theory, social democracy, and political theory. All of these themes are related and indeed are highly interconnected in my own mind to the intellectual project I embarked upon and which I improvised and altered over the course of my academic career. Essentially, I have followed Michel Foucault in his opposition to Marxism and Hegelianism, in his pluralistic endorsement of democracy and freedom, and in the need to rethink much of the project of Western liberalism in relation to its views on philosophy, science, reason, history, the subject, and democracy.

Foucault's work has guided my thinking specifically in relation to all of these themes. When I was in my first academic position, at Otago University in New Zealand, I initially started lecturing on what was termed by my department, the "social foundations of education". I lectured on Plato, John Dewey, Antonio Gramsci, Pierre Bourdieu, and Michael Foucault. I also taught a course in the sociology of education, where I dealt with what in those times were called "the new sociology of education", which included debates over the nature of knowledge and what counts as knowledge by academics such as Michael Young, Basil Bernstein, Michael Apple, Stephen Ball, Henry Giroux, and many others. The discovery of Foucault came as a bombshell in the sense that here was a thinker intent on sidestepping the traditional problematic of Marxism, concerned as it was with the perennial issue of base and superstructure and the interminable difficulty of how to present a model of the social structure which explained how all the elements of the superstructure—cultural, political, ideological, scientific—could both reflect and yet maintain independence from the central role of the economic base. Foucault was interesting in that he retained a view of historical materialism as a broad theory of change which stressed the integral role of both history and social construction, while not becoming encumbered with the problems of economic determinism, of a closed totality, or of the inevitability of historical progress towards a communist utopia.

Since those early days of my first academic appointment my academic programme has continued to be influenced by Foucault in important respects. With Foucault I found a liberation from the prison house of received opinions and conventional social science verities. Foucault managed to look back at history and ask whether it was necessary that our received understandings and institutions were in fact strictly necessary or whether they could have been different if certain events in history had only occurred in a different way. While in that we are, like other living beings, constituted in history, and some things will be necessary if we are to survive, the way these become organized and structured within any complex social whole at any time will also express contingent patterns of power and hierarchy which give to any social structure a particular relativity. The sense in which Foucault is a historical materialist is that he sees the evolving structures of society as dynamically affected by and changing in relation to incremental changes of their parts. Rather than a theory of dynamics which is linear and deterministic, in the tradition of Newton, Kant, or Hegel and Marx, as was characteristic of the Enlightenment, what Foucault effects is a post-quantumization of history and of the social, now characterized by uncertainty, non-linearity, non-predictability, openness, and chance. In this new non-Hegelian version of holism–particularism, history implies the relativity of all established orders, whether social or discursive, whether of societies, institutions, systems, or concepts.

That such a relativity creates problems for truth and morality can be acknowledged as the hard issues, and I quickly recognized, as did Foucault, that there is little prospect of confronting and solving the issues head-on, in any simplistic manner. Yet, in my books, as well as my articles, I express concern and awareness of these issues, and indeed, the inclusion of articles within this volume can be seen to contain insights as to how best these issues can be tackled. While truth and ethics must be seen to operate as necessary codes in terms of such a historical materialism, what is important to understand is how what is necessary and what is relative mutually coexist and implicate each other, without cancelling each other out, and without turning into incoherence. It is how truth and ethics manifest themselves and are justified, or warranted, within a contingently assembled social order that generates the most interesting and most difficult issues to understand.

Relativity also applies to knowledge and the disciplines themselves irrespective of any verities revealed. The emergence of the disciplines of science themselves reflected the imperatives of particular social structures and particular historical changes. Facts were incomplete, partial, mixed with other values and perspectives, represented from a particular point of view. It is no accident that psychology emerged with the Enlightenment and reflected the new-found position of man at the center of the universe, even of the cosmos. In this sense, psychology could be represented as an apparatus (*dispositif*) of power itself constructed as a means of disciplining and positioning individuals within a new hierarchy of life. Although several articles on educational psychology are not reproduced within this volume of papers (see Olssen, 1991, 1993), the Kantian emphasis upon autonomy is referred to in Chapter 1. In this article, Kant's emphasis on autonomy is briefly subjected to a Foucauldian critique. Foucault is useful for questioning normative axes and beliefs that have become embedded in modernist culture, such as autonomy. In the Kantian tradition, autonomy serves to indicate both rationality and moral independence or self-sufficiency of each individual in the face of the moral law. Such a view reflects the arrogance of the Enlightenment. Kant is able to recognize such an autonomous nature by abandoning all contingency, including situationally specific constraints, or context specific imperatives, that serve to constrain or bear down on each individual making the fact of any moral adjudication much more fraught and uncertain than merely implementing some universal maxim. To the extent that individuals can be represented as autonomous it is only as the effect or outcome of complex historical–institutional developments and supports. The individual and their capacities are in this sense the product of the social conditions of existence. Foucault sees the world as characterized by multiple and conflicting demands and, in this sense, much more complicated than did Kant. In that individuals can be said at all to achieve autonomy it presupposes, I argue, elaborate historical–institutional, social and educational pre-conditions. To the extent that these pre-conditions unleash mature forms of critical reflection and thinking as possible, mankind can still never be certain, which is to say that it is never vouchsafe, that reason stands "clear and distinct", or separate from falsehood and superstition. Indeed, the legacy of the Enlightenment would suggest that it does not offer any comfort in this regard. While we are certainly moving forward it is not clear that we are moving uphill in a progressive direction, or that we are going anywhere in particular. To the extent that good sense and reason are possible, however, they presuppose complex social, political, and institutional structures, which underscore not so much the autonomy of each individual, but their interdependency and interconnectedness in networks and structures of social support and facilitation. The individual, in this sense, is not "self-made" or responsible for their own good fortune, for they are dependent upon institutional structures of social and historical support which have made their development possible. Similarly, individuals do not reason autonomously, based upon their own cognitive faculties. For it is the shared dimension of life that typifies the social, in its essential feature, and it is the integral feature of the social that renders decision-making and judgement as capable of being mature. The classical liberal view of knowledge and autonomy is thus overly individualistic and overly arrogant in obscuring and misrepresenting the social supports to knowledge and reason, as well as the extent of the fallibility of knowledge, limited cognition or partial knowledge, uncertainty, as well as the need for cautiousness, tentativeness and humility in our attitudes and dispositions.

Foucault was also influential in terms of my understanding of the political. Firstly, his conception of critique was important. If Descartes's axiom that reason can be separated from superstition is false, that the *Evil Genius* of the *First Meditation* cannot be evacuated from the process of knowledge, then critical interrogation and scrutiny become epistemologically necessary to unmasking the real conditions of existence. Critique in this sense becomes pivotal to understanding the world, both in terms of epistemology and in terms of ethics. Perhaps Foucault's concepts of "limit-experience" and "transgression" establish the conditions for partially overcoming relativism and establishing certain degrees of confidence that we are encountering the real world of the pre-discursive. Testing limits seems to be Foucault's answer, not just in science, but in all of the domains of experience. Hence, in science, via falsifications, as Popper devised; in politics, via "intolerability", as mobilized prisoners in their protests, or peasants in their revolutions, or Black Lives Matter advocates in their marches, manifest; via the body or the other, as in sexuality, or the erotic; via new forms of understanding or communication, as in literature. Ultimately, testing limits secures the primordial character of affects in asking what it is that our actions and thoughts do, what forces do they unleash, what truths do they necessitate, what lies do they conceal. Testing limits for Foucault is the only way to establish footholds.

Foucault was also important in terms of his opposition to Hegel and Marx, or perhaps, to express the point better, in terms of the particular way in which he opposes Hegel and Marx. I have included three chapters on my writings or reflections on Marx and/or Hegel. These express how I have read Foucault, and what for me Foucault articulates. All of these express different aspects of Foucault's relation to Marxism, and serve to highlight, or illustrate, the senses in which Foucault draws on Marx and Hegel, and the senses in which he stands opposed to Marx and Hegel. "Foucault and Marxism: Rewriting the Theory of Historical Materialism", published in *Policy Futures in Education*, serves to suggest the particular nature of Foucault's own form of historical materialism in contrast to Marx's historical materialism. The article with my New Zealand compatriot, Michael A. Peters, "Marx, Education and the Possibilities of a Fairer World: Reviving Radical Political Economy through Foucault", was initially published in a book edited by Anthony Green, Glenn Rikowski and Helen Raduntz, *Renewing Dialogues in Marxism and Education* (Olssen & Peters, 2007), and subsequently revised and republished in the journal *Linguistic and Philosophical Investigations* (Olssen & Peters, 2015), and it is this later version that appears here. The interview with Rille Raaper sets out clearly the senses in which Foucault stands opposed to Marx and Hegel, as well as his incorporation of Nietzsche as a means of displacing Hegel, in addition to addressing many related issues in poststructuralist thought, including the issue of relativism. What emerges overall is that to the extent that Foucault is a historical materialist, his is a profoundly non-Marxist version of that doctrine. In essence, his version is simply a theory of change which characterizes how changes in one part of the system or structure interact with and affect changes in other parts, and on the structure overall. Foucault's historical materialism is profoundly pluralist in its nature. While this may be thought to eclipse a central or foundational role for the economy, as in Marxism, Foucault seems to argue in lecture courses such as *The Birth of Biopolitics* (2008) that the economic and the governmental must be viewed as a couple, contingently articulated differently in different historical contexts.[1] My own view of Foucault paints him also as a social democrat, a thin communitarian, and as a post-quantum complexity theorist. The papers included in this volume that deal with the subject of social democracy take off in this light. When I started writing on Foucault, that he could be located as a realist interested in radically retheorizing the historical and the domain of the social, together with the post-quantum insights unleashed by Henri Poincaré[2] and later by Ilya Prigogine,[3] regarding indeterminacy and chance, as well as being an advocate of a form of radical social democracy, complete with a radical conception of pluralism, was to say the least, uncommon. Such a view is now standard. I still stand by every element of this view, and indeed, also included in this volume, is a paper in the Italian journal *Materiali Foucaultiani* (Olssen 2018), which argues that his lecture notes on neoliberalism, *The Birth of Biopolitics*, incorporate the last chapter on Adam Ferguson because Ferguson's model of civil society represents Foucault's preferred model, essentially articulating a conception of the economic within the political. By utilizing Foucault to undergird a conception of social democracy also unburdens traditional conceptions as in the work of writers such as Bosanquet, Green and Bradley, of Hegelian assumptions, or at least, those Hegelian assumptions that are most objectionable, those that stress unity and "thick" conceptions of community which place too much emphasis on conformity. As the traditional theories of the welfare state were spearheaded by the English Hegelians over the latter part of the 19th century, up until the ascendency of logical positivism in the 20th century, Foucault enables a retheorization of social democracy, incorporating post-quantum onto-epistemology with respect to uncertainty, interconnectedness, interdependency, indeterminacy, nonpredictability and chance. Accepting Foucault's radical critique of neoliberalism and the present, social democracy should, if practice followed theory perfectly, be ascendant once again. I believe that this sort of articulation puts Foucault's scholarship on a better and more assured footing than those that would falsely represent him as a neoliberal, a libertarian, or anarchist, or as neutral and agnostic with regard to all things political. My articles on neoliberalism included in this volume incorporate many of the insights of Foucault's 1978 course at the Collège de France, *The Birth of Biopolitics*.[4] My major insights on neoliberalism, however, are developed in specific regard to the university, or to education generally. It is interesting in this respect to extend Foucault's approach to neoliberalism with respect to a specific institutional site within society, as the importation of neoliberal technologies to higher education represents a dismantlement of the traditional liberal conception and stands in marked contrast with the earlier model of the liberal university as conceptualized by both John Henry (Cardinal) Newman and Max Weber. The self-governing status and professionalism of academics has been undermined and supplanted under neoliberal governmentality and has witnessed at the same time the professionalization of a new breed of recruits: *Managers*. The consequences of such a marketization process are explored in the three papers that are included in this volume.[5]

Finally, I have maintained an interest throughout my work on Foucault on normative political theory, especially in relation to ethics and education. While in the early and middle period of his writing, Foucault took a view of the subject as constructed and shaped by power, in his later writings, from 1978, after the publication of *The History of Sexuality, Volume 1*, he sought to develop a more ethical sense of the subject. Although, as is well known, Foucault eschewed advice-giving and shied away from facing the conundrums associated with normative justification. To my mind this avoidance, together with the perceived absence of ethical foundations within his work, constitute limitations to what is in all other respects a powerful correction to the lacunae and omissions of the Western intellectual tradition, from Plato to Kant, and from Kant to Nietzsche. How could his work inspire an ethics and an education if it was solely concerned with genealogy? The insight that power is ubiquitous and constitutes both a limitation and enabling condition of action and thought is just one insight which until the 20th century only thinkers like Nietzsche and Marx took seriously. The insight that it is people who make history but under conditions given and transmitted from the past is another. While neither of these insights are, in themselves, therefore novel, with Foucault they are assembled in relation to a new theory, one which manages to avoid the determinism of Hegel and Marx, and which permits the incorporation of conceptions of liberty, pluralism, and power, compatible with liberalism itself.

I have sought to develop a normative conception for Foucault from within the body of Foucault's later work, a conception which is set out more fully in another book, *Constructing Foucault's Ethics: A Poststructuralist Moral Theory for the 21st Century*, published in June 2021 by Manchester University Press. Hopefully this book will dispel the view that Foucault's system necessarily constitutes a quagmire of ethical and moral relativism. Here, in this collection, however, the attentive reader will be able to discern the early echoes of my interest in the issue of normativity within Foucault, especially in the articles such as, "Foucault and the Imperatives of Education: Critique and Self-creation in a Non-foundational World" (Chapter 1), "Totalitarianism and the 'Repressed' Utopia of the Present: Moving beyond Hayek and Popper with

Foucault" (Chapter 17), and "Invoking Democracy: Foucault's Conception (with insights from Hobbes)" (Chapter 19).

Taken as a whole, these essays represent a selection of my published work between 1995 and 2020. Although minor edits have been performed in several chapters, these have only been undertaken for the purposes of resolving ambiguities, correcting errors in the original, or clarifying textual comprehension. In addition to these minor edits, some textual repetition occurs across the different chapters. This applies to repetition in quotes, sentences, paragraphs, or to longer sections, which while occurring only in a few instances, have been retained in this volume in the interests of accuracy and completeness so that the integrity of each original published work is preserved. The original publishers are acknowledged as each chapter merely reproduces the initial article, and the title and co-authors are retained in the order as originally published. Here I would like to thank the co-authors and publishers of the originals for the reproduction in this context. I hope that this book makes their work as well as mine more accessible to a wider public. I would like to thank Michael Jones for assistance with bibliographical querries. I would also like to thank Jolanda Karada, Henriët Graafland, and John Bennett for steering this project so efficiently to its conclusion. I would also like to thank Michael Peters for inviting me to compile this volume, and to him and Stephen J. Ball for the respective forewords that they have so kindly written for it.

Notes

1 See especially the April 4th Lecture where Adam Ferguson's model of civil society is discussed, a model which revolves around both the economic and governmental as linked.
2 Poincaré was important for the topographical conception of the social and physical realms, a mathematical formulation which echoes in important ways Spinoza's field metaphysic, as well as his resolution to the "three body problem" as always defying determinism. Importantly, this makes Poincaré the father of chaos theory.
3 Prigogine is important in his contributions to chaos theory and for his formulations relating to chance, that is, to constraint and necessity, in scientific terms.
4 See note 1.
5 My most significant journal article on neoliberalism, co-authored with Michael Peters, published in the *Journal of Education Policy* in 2005, is not included in this volume (Olssen & Peters, 2005). Not only is this a very long article, comprising almost 20,000 words, but it has already been republished numerous times. This article, titled "Neoliberalism, Higher Education and the Knowledge Economy: From the Free Market to Knowledge Capitalism", was also constructed in an unusual way, where I constructed it by simply adding my article first, followed by Michael's article following on. The entire first part, up until the subheading "Knowledge as the new form of capital under neoliberalism", was written by me, Mark Olssen, and Michael Peters wrote the latter part from and including that subheading. That this article was actually constructed in a highly unusual fashion can be accepted, and it is partly for this reason, together with the fact that it is easily available that I have decided not to reproduce it again in this volume.

PART 1

Michel Foucault

CHAPTER 1

Foucault and the Imperatives of Education
Critique and Self-Creation in a Non-Foundational World

Abstract

This article outlines Foucault's conception of critique in relation to his writings on Kant. In that Kant saw enlightenment as a process of release from the status of immaturity in that we accept someone else's authority to lead us in areas where the use of reason is called for, it is claimed in this article that Foucault's notion of critique reveals his own conception of maturity. Whereas Kant sees maturity as the rule of self by self through reason, Foucault sees it as an attitude towards ourselves and the present through a historical analysis of the limits, and the possibility of transgression, of going beyond. Critique is thus a permanent interrogation of the limits, an escape from normalization, and a facing-up to the challenges of self-creation while seeking to effect changes in social structures on specific regional issues of concern. The article concludes by suggesting that the problem of historical and epistemological relativism, which a conception of total critique gives rise to, may not be as insurmountable as some critics of Foucault have claimed.

1 Introduction

Critique, for Foucault, aims at identifying and exposing the unrecognized forms of power in people's lives, to expose and move beyond the forms in which we are entrapped in relation to the diverse ways that we act and think. In this sense, critique aims to free us from the historically transitory constraints of contemporary consciousness as realized in and through discursive practices. Such constraints impose limitations which have become so intimately a part of the way that people experience their lives that they no longer experience these systems as limitations but embrace them as the very structure of normal and natural human behaviour. Within these limits, seen as both the limits of reason and the limits of nature, freedom is subordinated to reason, which is subordinated to nature, and it is against such a reduction of reason to nature that Foucault struggles. His commitment is to a form of "permanent criticism" which must be seen as linked to his broader programme of freedom of thought. It is the freedom to think differently than what we already know. Thought and life achieve realization through an attitude of "permanent criticism" which does not have as its aim an objective of absolute emancipation, or absolute enlightenment, but rather aims at limited and partial operations on the world as well as acts of aesthetic self-creation framed within a critical ontology of ourselves and supported by an ethics and aesthetics of existence.

2 Foucault and Kant

This article seeks to outline and defend a non-foundational conception of critique as representing the core of Foucault's distinctive approach. Critique, for Foucault, is the basis of his own conception of maturity. Whereas Kant sees maturity as the rule of self by self through reason, Foucault sees it as an attitude towards ourselves and the present through a historical analysis of the limits, and the possibility of transgression, of going beyond. Critique is thus a permanent interrogation of the limits, an escape from normalization, and a facing-up to the challenges of self-creation while seeking to effect changes in social structures on specific regional issues of concern.

Much of Foucault's approach to critique stems from his radicalization of the Kantian approach to critique, As James Miller (1993, p. 138) notes, "Foucault never ceased to consider himself a kind of Kantian". In *The Order of Things*, Foucault (1970, p. 384) tells us that Kantian critique forms an essential part of "the immediate space of our reflection. We think in that area". Further, as Miller (1993, p. 138) notes, in an essay completed shortly before his death for a French dictionary of philosophy,[1] Foucault also situates his own work within the critical tradition of Kant. This tradition, says Foucault, entails "an analysis of the conditions under which certain relations of subject and object are formed or modified" and a demonstration of how such conditions "are constitutive of a possible knowledge" (cited in Miller, 1993, p. 138).[2]

In Foucault's view, Kant founded the two great critical traditions between which modern philosophy has been divided. On the one hand, Kant laid down and founded that critical tradition of philosophy which defines the conditions under which a true knowledge is possible, of which a whole area of modern philosophy since the 19th century has been presented and developed on that basis as an analytic of truth; on the other hand, he initiated a mode of critical interrogation that is immanent in the movement of the Enlightenment and which directs our attention to the present and asks "what is the contemporary field of possible experience?" It is to this latter emphasis, starting with Hegel and leading through Nietzsche, Weber and the Frankfurt School, that Foucault locates his own work.

Foucault sees in Kant's essay "An Answer to the Question: What Is Enlightenment?"[3] (see Kant, 1970) of 1784 the origin of a critical ontology of the present.

Foucault summarises Kant's definition of the concept "enlightenment" as a measure of man's "release from his self-incurred tutelage" (Kant, 1784/1992, p. 90). Kant defines enlightenment, says Foucault (1984a, p. 34), "in an entirely negative way, as an *Ausgang*, an 'exit' or 'way out'. ... [H]e is looking for a difference: what difference does today introduce with respect to yesterday?" In this, Foucault discovers Kant as "an archer", as Habermas (1986, p. 165) has put it, "who aims his arrow at the heart of the most actual features of the present and so opens the discourse of modernity". As Foucault puts it:

> The question which seems to me to appear for the first time in this text by Kant is the question of the present, of the contemporary moment. What is happening today? What is happening now? And what is this "now" which we all inhabit, and which defines the moment in which I am writing? ... Now it seems to me that the question Kant answers ... has to do with what this present is. ... The question is: [W]hat is there in the present which can have contemporary meaning for philosophical reflection[?] (Foucault, 1986, pp. 88–89)[4]

In considering the Enlightenment, what also must be taken into account, says Foucault (1986, p. 89) is that it was "the *Aufklärung itself* which named itself the *Aufklärung*". In this, it was "a cultural process of indubitably a very singular character, which came to self-awareness through the act of naming itself, situating itself in relation to its past and its future, and in prescribing the operation which it was required to effect within its own present". Thus, as Foucault (1984a, p. 34) summarizes it, Kant indicates in his essay that the "way out" that characterizes the Enlightenment is a process that releases us from the status of our own immaturity, an immaturity in which we accept someone else's authority to lead us in areas where the use of reason is called for.

Kant links the process of release from immaturity to man himself. He notes that "man himself is responsible for his immature status ... that he is able to escape from it by a change that he himself will bring about in himself". Hence Kant's motto for the Enlightenment: *aude sapere* (dare to know) (1984a, p. 34). It is in this sense, says Foucault (1984a, p. 35), that the Enlightenment for Kant is both a *collective process*, as well as an *act of personal courage*. As integral to the conditions for escape from immaturity, Kant seeks to distinguish the realm of obedience and reason. Hence one must obey as a condition of being able to reason freely. (Kant gives the example of paying one's taxes while being free to reason about the system of taxation in operation.) Thus central to the Enlightenment in Kant's view is the public use of reason which "must be free ... [for] it alone can bring about enlightenment among men" (Kant, 1784/1992, p. 92). To resolve the issue as to how the public use of free reason can coexist with obedience to the law, Kant proposes his famous contract with Frederick II. This, as Foucault puts it, "might be called the contract of rational despotism with free reason: the public and free use of autonomous reason will be the best guarantee of obedience, on condition, however, that the political principle that must be obeyed itself be in conformity with universal reason" (Foucault, 1984a, p. 37).

There is a connection, in Foucault's view, between the brief article "What Is Enlightenment?" and Kant's three Critiques, for Kant describes the Enlightenment as the moment when humanity is going to put its own reason to use, without subjecting itself to any authority. It is precisely at this moment, however, that critique is necessary since, as Foucault (1984a, pp. 37–38) puts it, "its role is that of defining the conditions under which the use of reason is legitimate. … The Critique is, in a sense, the handbook of reason that has grown up in the Enlightenment; and, conversely, the Enlightenment is the age of the Critique". Thus, Kant's short essay on the Enlightenment constitutes "a reflection … on the contemporary status of his own enterprise" (1984a, p. 37). It is in this sense, as Foucault maintains (1984a, p. 38), that "this little text is located … at the crossroads of critical reflection and reflection on history".

3   Rejecting Kantian Foundationalism

In that Kant established the limits beyond which reason could not transgress, for Foucault (1977b, p. 38) Kant ends "by closing this opening when he ultimately relegated all critical investigations to an anthropological question". In that Kant's transcendentalism is underpinned by an anthropological conception of the subject, Foucault opposes Kantian humanism in the same way he opposed the Cartesian conception of the atomized and disembodied *Cogito* at the centre of the universe. For Foucault, the Cartesian conception of an autonomous and rational subject who is set apart from history depends upon a distinction between mind and body setting up a dualism of inner/outer. In this model, while the body is subject to the determinations of the laws of nature, mind is autonomous unto itself. In such a conception, knowledge is seen as grounded upon an incorrigible and indubitable foundation. Following Heidegger and Nietzsche, humanism, for Foucault, has a specific meaning, which refers to the philosophical centrality or priority of the subject whose rational capacities, which are asocial and ahistorical, serve as a foundation anchoring objectivity and truth. As Nancy Fraser (1994, p. 191) states, humanism "is the project of making the subject pole triumph over the object pole", representing man as constitutor, as free, as all knowing, and as master of their fate and destiny. Foucault's conception of the subject, influenced by Nietzsche, sees it as having no "unity", "essence" or integral identity.

It is in the cause of theoretical anti-humanism that Foucault (1960) presents his reading of Kant's *Anthropology from a Pragmatic Point of View*, arguing that this work is much more important to Kant's overall project than has commonly been represented.[5] By "anthropology" Kant meant the actual empirical study of the human being, and in his *Logic* Kant suggests that anthropology might be regarded as the fundamental issue in philosophy, as all of the questions that he was centrally concerned with stem from the more basic question, "What is Man?" In his introduction to Kant's *Anthropology*,[6] Foucault suggests that Kant's own conception of the person's choice grows out of the network of social practices which constitute them. Yet in order to establish knowledge as secure Kant distinguished between the empirical and the transcendental, positing specific laws of cognition in order to ground objectivity against sceptical attack. Thus central to Kant's Copernican Revolution were (1) the establishment of lawful cognitive regularities to anchor objectivity, (2) the establishment of free will as a transcendental practice, and (3) the representation of human beings as constructing their moral and political worlds for themselves through the utilization of the capabilities of reason. Although Kant believed that such a constructivism, if carried out according to the dictates of reason, would vindicate the traditional Christian idea of God, in Foucault's view the consequences of his transcendental critique was to establish human beings as having much greater creative capabilities than Kant had supposed. Hence, for Foucault (1960, p. 17), as Miller (1993, p. 140) recounts, "the world appears as a city to be built, rather than as a cosmos already given".

What Kant's *Anthropology* also reveals, in Foucault's view, is the contextual historical character of the categories, which take root in, and develop in the social and historical customs and practices of a specific society. In this context, the role of the philosopher is to understand the historical nature of the a priori through a detailed examination of the social and historical practices (customs, language, habits, discourses, institutions, disciplines) from which a particular style of reasoning emerges and develops. It is in this sense, for Foucault, as Miller (1993, p. 140) puts it, Kant's *Anthropology*, far from being "a piece of crackpot pseudo-science opens up an important new philosophical horizon". For Foucault, the unresolved tension of Kant's philosophical project is that he fails to appreciate the contingent and historically contextualized character of all truth claims, i.e., to advocate a notion of critique which claims to transcend specific historical conditions through the exercise of cognitive faculties (of understanding, reason, and judgement) deduced a priori as timeless structures. The transcendental character of Kant's argument resides in positing a priori categories which are deduced to constitute the consciousness of the human subject, as that which organizes perception as a timeless and universal structure. In this sense, Foucault rejects Kant's claims to have established the universal grounds for the conditions of possibility of human knowledge, and Kant's claims for transcendental reason are replaced for Foucault by a principle of permanent contingency. By extension, Foucault disputes Kant's claim to have established a secure foundation by which to differentiate different types of knowledge claims, relating to science, practical reason or aesthetics. The objective is to switch from a conception of critique as being transcendentally grounded, to a conception of critique which conceives it as practical and as historically specific. Thus, as Foucault says:

> criticism is no longer going to be practiced in the search for formal structures with universal value, but rather as an historical investigation into the events that have led us to constitute ourselves and to recognize ourselves as subjects of what we are doing, thinking, saying. In that sense, this criticism is not transcendental, and its goal is not that of making metaphysics possible: it is genealogical in its design and archaeological in its method. (Foucault, 1984a, pp. 45–46)

Foucault's genealogical project is then a critique of reason whereby he seeks to introduce, to use Thomas McCarthy's (1994, p. 249) phrase "a socio-historical turn" into the practice of philosophy. Foucault thus adapts Kant to support his socio-historical conception through which individuals are constituted in relation to a world of already given practices of a determinate historical terrain. In drawing on Nietzsche's method of genealogy, institutions and practices are historically investigated in order to trace the forms of power and lines of opposition between and amongst them. For Nietzsche our habitual modes of action and thought have a historical origin and bare the marks of conflicting individual wills to power of people, groups and classes in history. In *On the Genealogy of Morals*, Nietzsche shows how our dominant moral codes emerged from the battle of classes and groups (e.g., Romans and Jews) in the past. Genealogy seeks to trace the lines of the battles that have gone into making the world, as we know it in the present. In this sense it contributes to problematizing our taken-for-granted beliefs and conceptions about the way the world is.

It is in the context of this "socio-historical turn" that Foucault rejects humanism. The rejection of humanism, however, cannot be seen as a relativistic rejection of ethics, freedom, or the possibilities of self-creation. Rather, Foucault explicitly advocates for a non-humanist ethical paradigm, which can be extrapolated for him, from his later works on ethics, to answer the charge, in Fraser's (1994, p. 196) terms, of why we should challenge a fully panopticized society. Although for Foucault, as for Spinoza, "the body forgets nothing",[7] in that it is subject to external determinations, as for Spinoza, it also has its own momentum or force for acting on the world. In opposing humanism, Foucault is not thereby rejecting agency or freedom for, like Spinoza, he sees the subject as possessing both *passive* and *active* dimensions.[8] It is not then that no humanist values are worthy of protection, but that modernist humanism radically misconceives them. If this argument is valid, then Foucault's rejection of modernity and its values is not a rejection *tout court*, but only of some aspects of it. Likewise, in rejecting humanism, he is rejecting a specific theoretical, philosophical discourse. The rejection of humanism, then, does not entail the rejection of *humane values*, despite historical associations between thinkers like Heidegger or Nietzsche with political movements like Nazism.[9]

4   Critique as a Historicophilosophical Practice

For Foucault because the Enlightenment has not evacuated the problems and dangers of earlier periods in history, the implications of his criticisms of Kant mean that the basis to critique must be as a form of permanent interrogative thinking:

> The thread that may connect us with the Enlightenment is not faithfulness to doctrinal elements, but rather the permanent reactivation of an attitude—that is, of a philosophical ethos that could be described as a permanent critique of our historical era. (Foucault, 1984a, p. 42)

In that the Enlightenment emphasizes "permanent critique", it is not a doctrine, or theory, or period, but rather an *ethos* or *attitude*. It emphasizes a form of philosophical interrogation which "simultaneously problematizes man's relation to the present, man's historical mode of being, and the constitution of the self as an autonomous subject", says Foucault (1984b, p. 42). In his article "C'est-ce-que critique", written in 1978, Foucault (1996) refers to this as a *historicophilosophical practice* which "finds itself in a certain privileged relation to a certain empirically determinate epoch" (1996, p. 392). Such a practice asks:

> What am I then, I who belong to this humanity, perhaps to this fringe, to this moment, to this instant of humanity that is subjected to the power of truth in general and of truths in particular? To desubjectify the philosophical question by referring to its historical component, to liberate the

historical contents questioning the effects of power from the truth which they are supposed to restore, this is, if you will, the first characteristic of this historicophilosophical practice.

In historicophilosophical critique one examines the relations "among power, truth, and the subject". One has to have a "procedure of analysis" (p. 393) which is "an inquiry into the legitimacy of the historical modes of knowing ... more simply still, what false idea did knowledge make of itself, and to what excessive use was it found exposed, to what domination consequently was it found tied" (p. 393). Such an inquiry is an *inquiry into power* which "is a matter of describing the nexus of knowledge and power that allows one to grasp what constitutes a systems acceptability, be it the system of mental illness, of punishment, of delinquency, of sexuality, and so on" (p. 394). An inquiry into power involves what Foucault calls *eventalization* which contains a number of elements. First, it treats all objects of knowledge as historical *events*. Second, it refers to a "pluralization of causes" (Foucault, 1987, p. 104). In addition, says Foucault (1987, p. 104), eventalization refers to the rediscovery of the "connections, encounters, blockages, plays of forces, strategies, etc. that at a given moment establish what consequently comes to count as being self-evident, universal and necessary". In this sense, it constitutes a "breach of self-evidence", i.e.: "it means making visible a *singularity* at places where there is a temptation to invoke historical constants, an immediate anthropological trait, or an obviousness that imposes itself uniformly on all. To show that things "weren't as necessary as all that". In this sense, eventalization opposes the evidences upon which knowledge sequences and practices rest. Because it focuses on a particular historical ensemble of truths, in an analysis of the knowledge–power nexus, it works at the level of *archaeology* aiming to bring out "the conditions of acceptability of a system and following the lines of rupture that mark its emergence" (1996, p. 395). Such phenomena are analysed, not as *universals*, *essences*, or *species*, but as "pure singularities" related to "simple conditions of acceptability".

In addition to this, they must not be analysed by reducing them to a single cause but rather by considering them in their complexity. This introduces *genealogy* which looks to the multiple descents to account for the conditions of appearance of a singularity from "multiple determining elements" (1996, p. 397). Such a critical procedure avoids the principle of closure, asserting an always open procedure focusing on interactions and relations between individuals and groups. In focusing on power, Foucault (1996, p. 397) is not thus understanding power as domination or mastery but:

> as a relation in a field of interactions, it is a matter of thinking it in an inseparable relation with forms of knowledge, and it is always a matter of

thinking it in such a way that one sees it associated with a domain of possibility and consequently of reversibility. ... You see, ... the question is no longer: through what error, illusion, forgetting, by what lack of legitimacy does knowledge come to induce effects of domination[?] ... The question would rather be this: How can the inseparability of knowledge and power in a game of multiple interactions and strategies induce at once regularities that fix themselves on the basis of their conditions of acceptability, ... that make them fragile, that make them impermanent, that make of these effects events—nothing more, nothing less than events[?]

For Foucault, *Aufklärung* comprises a set of events and complex historical processes located at a certain point in the development of European societies. It represents a particular critical attitude, a state of maturity, and entails courage. It is not necessary to see it only as Kant does, as a particular period without a fixed date, for one can define it just as well "by the formation of capitalism, the constitution of the bourgeois world, the establishment of the state system, the foundation of modern science with all its correlative techniques" (p. 392). Criticism thus entails some understanding of the limits of knowledge and of reason—of "how far you can reason without danger?" (1996, p. 387).

This creates the necessity for a double conception of critique. On the one hand, it must proceed genealogically through an examination of the historical a prioris of all possible experience; on the other, it must seek to explore the possible limits to experience by exorcizing the transcendental freedom which Kant himself established as an essential foundation for critique. In this sense, the philosophical ethos of critique may be characterized as a *limit-attitude*, but in a different sense to that suggested by Kant:

> Criticism indeed consists of analysing and reflecting upon limits. But if the Kantian question was that of knowing what limits knowledge must abstain from transgressing, it seems to me that the critical question today has to be turned back into a positive one: in what is given to us as universal, necessary or obligatory, what part is taken up by things which are actually singular, contingent, the product of arbitrary constraints? The point, in brief, is to transform critique conducted in the form of necessary limitations into a practical critique that takes the form of a possible transgression. (Foucault, 1984a, p. 46)

Rather than accepting pre-established limits to reason based on Kant's transcendental analysis, the theoretical task becomes testing the limits which establish to what extent we can move beyond them. Foucault defines transgression as "an action which involves the limit. ... [T]he experience of transgression brings to light this relationship of finitude to being, this moment of the limit which anthropological thought, since Kant, could only designate from the distance and from the exterior through the language of dialectics" (1977b, pp. 33, 49). Such transgressive behaviour thus makes visible the limits to reason and in that it takes thought to its limit it serves as an arm in the critique of reason. As Biesta (1998, p. 9) notes, "limits are both enabling and constraining. We only know that there are limits because acts of transgression illustrate their location, revealing how far it is possible to go". Yet the limits to transgression are unsurpassable, as there is no neutral ground beyond power/knowledge from which critique could establish itself. As Foucault (1984a, p. 47) expresses it, "we have to give up hope of ever acceding to a point of view that could give us access to any complete knowledge of what may constitute our historical limits. ... [W]e are always in a position of beginning again".

5 Critique as How Not to Be Governed

It is in this sense of rejecting humanism and establishing critique as a *historicophilosophical* practice that Foucault claims it is a method of problematizing existence and of rejecting or questioning the present constellations of representations. In this context, Foucault (1996, p. 384) links the critical attitude directly to *governmentalization*. This is meant in the broad sense. More specifically, he says, it is about "how not to be governed":

> I do not mean ... "We do not want to be governed, and we do not want to be governed *at all*". What I mean is that in the great anxiety surrounding the way to govern and in the inquiries into modes of governing, one detects a perpetual question which would be: "How not to be governed *like that*, by that, in the name of these principles, in view of such objectives and by the means of such methods, not like that, not for that, not by them?" (p. 384)

It is in this sense that critique takes on a slightly altered sense. Not being governed in a particular way embodies a practical refusal of a certain form or type of subjectivity, encompassing a refusal to define ourselves to ourselves and to others in a particular way; to liberate ourselves from certain conceptions about ourselves. Such a refusal becomes a new form of "virtue" (Butler, 2002).

But whether as a form of refusal of a certain way of being, or as mature judgement, or enlightenment, critique has taken various forms: *biblical*, in relation to challenging Scripture; *juridical*, as concerned from the 16th century with the "limits to the right to govern" (Natural Law). Finally, not wanting to be governed is "to reject what authority tells you is true'. In sum, says Foucault (1996, p. 386):

> Critique is a movement through which the subject gives itself the right to question truth concerning its power effects and to question power about its discourses of truth. Critique will be the art of voluntary inservitude, of reflective indocility. The essential function of critique would be that of desubjectification in a game of what one could call, in a word, the politics of truth.

It is in this political sense that critique performs a function of challenging conventional authority whether governmental, religious, social, theoretical, or conceptual, as well as a refusal to define oneself as a particular kind of subject. The role of critique is thus personal and political. Without a critique of the immediate concepts in which each epoch thinks through its history, one remains prisoner of its illusions and myths. In this sense, critique implies a relativity of every established system or order, whether of ways of thinking, ways of ordering, or ways of being governed.

6   Criticism as Practical Politics

In a methodological sense, Foucault's conception of critique seeks to expose the unrecognized operations of power in social practices. This is why Foucault's conception of critique differs from that of Marxism, the Frankfurt School and Habermas. His aim is not the realization of a rational society, but more pragmatically orientated to revealing the contemporary limits of the necessary. Models such as Marxism, the Frankfurt School, and Habermas presuppose, in Foucault's view, the revelation of some concealed emancipatory truth about our "real" natures, just as much as they do about the real nature and limits to reason. It is the absence of some implicit or explicit ultimate measure or standard by which truth is assessed that explains why Foucault terms his own form of critical interrogation as "practical". In this sense, its most immediate and central concern is to sound a warning on the dangers of power, and this becomes the main function of philosophy. As Foucault (1991a, p. 20) states, "on the critical side ... philosophy is precisely the challenging of all phenomena of domination at whatever level or whatever form they present themselves—political, economic, sexual, institutional, and so on".

In that the task of criticism is not linked to the objective of absolute or total emancipation, the commitment is part of a broader programme of freedom of the thinker which involves an ascetical moment of self-creation. In this sense, critique for Foucault involves both work on oneself and responding to one's time. In relation to the former, Foucault developed new forms of relating to the self, most clearly expressed in his ethical theories designed to resist the constraints of normalization in an "ecstatic transcendence of any history which asserts its necessity" (Bernauer, 1991, p. 70). As a modern example of work on oneself, Foucault points to Baudelaire whose "consciousness of modernity is widely recognized as one of the most acute in the 19th century" (Foucault, 1984a, p. 39). Baudelaire defines modernity as "the will to 'heroize' the present". Modern man is the man who tries to invent himself through an ascetic elaboration of self. For Baudelaire this can only be produced through art. In *The Care of the Self* and *The Use of Pleasure*, however, Foucault recognizes various forms of self-creation drawing variously on the Greeks, the Romans, and the Renaissance (Jacob Burckhardt) as well as contemporary models.

In that it is related to aesthetics, criticism also functions in relation to the *transformation of the real-world structures*, "Criticism", says Foucault (1988a, p. 155), "is absolutely indispensable for any transformation. ... [A]s soon as one can no longer think things as one formerly thought them, transformation becomes both very urgent, very difficult, and quite possible". Such criticism can only be carried out in a free atmosphere. This gives a programmatic role for the "specific intellectual" and for "thought". His role, since he works specifically in the realm of thought, is to see how far the liberation of thought can make these transformations urgent enough for people to want to carry them out:

> Out of these conflicts, these confrontations, a new power relation must emerge, whose first, temporary expression will be a reform. If at the base there has not been the work of thought upon itself and if, in fact, modes of thought, that is to say modes of action, have not been altered, whatever the project of reform, we know that it will be swamped, digested by modes of behaviour and institutions that will always be the same. (1988a, p. 156)

Thought, then, is a crucial factor in the process of criticism. It is something which is often hidden but which always animates everyday behaviour (1988a, pp. 154–155).

Problematization operates for a very long time before thought intervenes. A critique is not simply a question of criticizing things as not being right as they are. Rather, says Foucault (1988a, p. 154), it functions as a consequence of problematizations:

> [I]t is a matter of pointing out what kinds of assumptions, what kinds of familiar, unchallenged, unconsidered modes of thought the practices

that we accept rest. ... Criticism is a matter of flushing out that thought and trying to change it: to show that things are not as self-evident as one believed, to see that what is accepted as self-evident will no longer be accepted as such. Practicing criticism is a matter of making facile gestures difficult. (1988a, p. 154)

Critique, then, is practical, in that it is through the arm of critique that Foucault wants to change our world, not simply our idea of it. The role of the intellectual in this process is to challenge power. As Foucault (1977b, p. 208) explains to Gilles Deleuze:

The intellectual's role is no longer to place himself "somewhat ahead and to the side" in order to express the stifled truth of the collectivity; rather, it is to struggle against the forms of power that transform him into its object and instrument in the sphere of "knowledge", "truth", "consciousness", and "discourse". In this sense theory does not express, translate, or serve to apply practice: it is practice. But it is local and regional ... and not totalizing. This is a struggle against power, a struggle aimed at revealing and undermining power where it is most invisible and insidious. It is not to "awaken consciousness" that we struggle ... but to sap power, to take power; it is an activity conducted alongside those who struggle for power, and not their illumination from a safe distance. A "theory" is the regional system of this struggle.

7 Foucault and Critique in Education: Some Illustrations

Amongst writers in the field of education studies there have been a large number of authors utilizing Foucault's insights. Stephen Ball's (1990) edited volume *Foucault and Education* includes a number of authors examining educationally significant topics, in order to "unmask the politics that underlay some of the apparent neutrality of educational reform" (p. 7). And in a number of papers and books spanning several years, James Marshall (1989, 1990, 1995, 1996a, 1996b) has presented a Foucauldian analysis of liberal education principles focusing upon (1) personal autonomy, (2) notions of identity, (3) the adequacy of the liberal concept of authority, and (4) the notion of the improvement or progress of human beings through education or in society.

Maintaining the Foucauldian thesis that the autos or self has been constructed politically by power/knowledge, Marshall critiques the view that education is involved in the pursuit of personal autonomy, or that rational autonomy is the aim of education. For Foucault, says Marshall, the pursuit of personal autonomy in such Enlightenment terms is a social construction and is destined to fail because it masks the fact that any such persons have been constituted by political acts. As he puts it (1996a, p. 113), "the notion of a self able to deliberate upon and accept laws so as to act autonomously as opposed to following laws heteronomously is a fiction, furnished upon the Western world post-Kant as the basis for moral action but, for Foucault in the cause of governmentality". Rather, for Foucault, says Marshall, our conception of ourselves as "free agents" is an illusion, and he argues that liberal educators like Kenneth Strike, R. F. Dearden, Paul Hirst and R. S. Peters who advocated personal autonomy as a fundamental aim of education do not understand how modern power, through the technologies of domination and the technologies of the self, has produced individuals who are governable. As Marshall states (1996b, p. 70):

> For [R. S.] Peters education becomes essentially the development of mind through the search for truth, essentially in the traditional academic disciplines. ... In thinking rationally a person thinks on their own, autonomously. This person, the autos, is the source of law, the nomos.

For Marshall, the very concepts which we use to construct our identities are such as to make independence and autonomy illusory. Hence education via governmentality effects the production of a new form of subject—one who believes they are free. Such an education simply introduces a new form of social control and socialisation and new and more insidious forms of indoctrination where a belief in our own authorship binds us to the conditions of our own production and constitutes an identity that makes us governable. In that "selves" do emerge it is as "pathologized" into certain types of human beings which are discursively constructed. As Marshall (1996b, p. 83) puts it, "to believe that personal autonomy in modern times is liberating is mistaken—according to Foucault ... its pursuit leads to unfreedom". According to Marshall, "from Foucault's perspective the political has become *masked* and the true nature of this alleged autonomy and its role in governmentality hidden" (p. 85).

In this sense, arguments for autonomy conceal a political agenda: that of limiting the state's role in co-ordinating collective aspirations and goals of communities by accentuating the *responsibilization* of individuals and families as a general strategy of governance. Such proposals also disguise the sense in which in arguing for autonomy they result also in greater inequality, which is a direct (but often unstated) effect of policies of individualisation and privatisation. In this sense the advocation of autonomy is in accord with neoliberal governmentality. On the "individualization–totalization" spectrum, it can be said that to advocate autonomy as an educational aim, in fact, undermines the traditional welfare state, as well as all other strategies of collective action which are necessary to human survival and well-being.

In a related sense, utilizing Foucault's concept of governmentality, Marshall (1995, 1996a, b) and Peters and Marshall (1996) examine the neoliberal notion of the autonomous chooser as embodying a particular conception of human nature, as a model of the security of the state, and as a particular model of surveillance and control. Focusing upon the extensive neoliberal changes in political policies regarding education, as well as other social services, which have taken place in countries such as America, Britain, Australia and New Zealand since the late 1970s, he develops a Foucauldian analysis of the reforms in terms of notions such as "choice", "quality", "freedom", and "autonomy". In a way similar to his analysis of autonomy as a liberal educational goal, what is presupposed in the notion of the "autonomous chooser", says Marshall, is that the notion of autonomy needed to make choices and the notion of needs and interests entailed as a result, have not been manipulated or imposed in some way upon the chooser, but are the subject's own. A Foucauldian critique rejects such a possibility.

In his own right, Michael Peters (2001) has applied Foucauldian notions of governmental reason to assessing contemporary neoliberal models of governance in education. In his book *Poststructuralism, Marxism and Neoliberalism* (2001) Peters summarizes the applicability of Foucault to neoliberalism, governance, and welfare, in terms of the effects on educational restructurings over the last 30 or so years.

My own work, with John Codd and Anne-Marie O'Neill, (2004) has also developed a Foucauldian critique of neoliberal governmentality critiquing the assumptions underpinning classical and contemporary versions of liberal theory. In *Education Policy: Globalization, Citizenship & Democracy*, we seek to outline the parameters of a Foucauldian approach to policy studies and specify its application in relation to liberal and neoliberal theory, establishing a genealogy of neoliberalism in relation to the various different forms (public choice theory, monetarism, agency theory, transaction-cost economics, Nozackian political philosophy) that it has taken.

8 Critique in a Non-Foundational World: A Question of Method

Richard Bernstein (1994, p. 220) notes Jürgen Habermas's criticism that when critique is totalized it is caught in a contradiction as it has no standard. As Habermas (1987, pp. 275–276) put it, genealogy "is overtaken by a fate similar to that which Foucault had seen in the human sciences". If this criticism of Foucault's critical method is valid, then it will offer us little. Yet Bernstein seeks to defend Foucault's position by relating critique to the exigencies of the environment, not in terms of truth, but in terms of the ever-present dangers in which people in history face. What is dangerous is that "everything becomes a target for normalisation".[10] Furthermore, Foucault's "archaeological–genealogical analyses of problematiques are intended to specify the changing constellation of dangers" (Bernstein, 1994, p. 227). And, of course, for Foucault (1984d, p. 343), "everything is dangerous" and "if everything is dangerous, then we always have something to do". As Bernstein (1994, p. 230) argues, this makes Foucault "the great sceptic of our times ... sceptical about dogmatic unities and philosophical anthropologies" as well as about the verities and axioms of the human sciences.

Bernstein's point that Foucault is a sceptic enables us to clarify a number of issues in relation to relativism, realism, and essentialism. For Foucault, critique recognizes no fixed concepts and no moulds into which to pour experience. In this sense, there can be no "pure" or fixed method that hovers around, above and outside of the events of history, waiting to be applied. As Foucault (1985) himself noted in the "Introduction" to *The History of Sexuality, Volume 2*, the appropriate theoretical methods required different tools depending upon the topic of enquiry.[11] The task of critique is not "pure" except in the sense that critique constitutes "a tool-box[12] out of which any number of useful conceptual tools ... may emerge to enable a critical perspective in the present milieu" (Mackenzie, 2004, pp. 54, 108).

For those, like Habermas, who criticize Foucault for strong forms of epistemological relativism, it can be noted that Foucault himself claimed always to be a realist, even a materialist, who recognized the "necessities" of the world as "there". It is not the world Foucault doubts; it is what is assumed in our approach to understanding it; that which presumes a model of the subject, of reason, of mind–world interrelations, of how causation works, which insist on being applied in all contexts, at all times, which fail to consider it in its complexity, its contingency, or in relation to power. What Foucault accepts is the relativity of all theoretical and conceptual forms, of all systems of order, of societies and of systems of institutions. His is a critique of the fixity of the concept and of the intellect.

While Foucault rejects foundationalism, he may not necessarily disagree with the broad thrust of Martha Nussbaum's soft version of Aristotelian essentialism which involves some version of appeal to a "determinate account of the human being, human functioning, and human flourishing" (Nussbaum, 1995, p. 450). This is not to accept a particular, essential or ahistorical conception of human beings, but rather to accept an "essentialism of a kind: for a historically sensitive account of the basic human needs and human functions" (Nussbaum, 1995, p. 451). Nussbaum's account is a "historically grounded empirical essentialism" which she calls "internalist essentialism". Yet what is important to understand is that Nussbaum's conception does not constitute an essentialism as traditionally understood, as pertaining to an entelechy or nature which constitutes a ground. For all that is essential in her constructivist conception are the capabilities necessary to continue life. This specifies contingently relevant "capabilities" or "the most important functions of human beings in terms of which human life is defined" (p. 456).

In Nussbaum's conception, such a conception of the good is concerned "with the overall shape and content of the human form of life" (p. 456). Such a conception, she says, is "vague, and this is deliberately so ... for it admits of much multiple specification in accordance with varied local and personal conceptions. The idea is that it is better to be vaguely right than precisely wrong" (p. 456). Such a conception is not metaphysical in that it does not claim to derive from a source exterior to human beings in history. Rather, it is as "universal as possible" and aims at "mapping out the general shape of the human form of life, those features that constitute life as human wherever it is" (p. 457). Nussbaum calls this her "thick, vague conception ... of the human form of life" (p. 457). Hence, her list of factors constitutes a set of general concepts without substantive content, allowing for difference or variation within each category, defined solely in relation to their efficacy for the future. Amongst the factors are (1) mortality: all human beings face death; (2) various invariant features of the human body, such as "nutritional, and other related requirements" regarding hunger, thirst, the need for food and drink and shelter; (3) cognitive: "all human beings have sense perception ... the ability to think"; (4) early development, (5) practical reason, (6) sexual desire, (7) affiliation with other human beings, and (8) relatedness to other species and to nature (pp. 457–460).

As a list of purely indicative characteristics or generic "species" characteristics, which can admit to cultural and historical variation, Foucault, in my view, could agree with the general tenor of Nussbaum's list, although he may wish to enter qualifications or caveats on specific features (sexual desire?). Of course, in that Nussbaum claims to be influenced by Aristotle, there is a clear difference with Foucault, who was influenced by Nietzsche and Heidegger and Spinoza. Thus Foucault would reject the essentialist teleological conception of the subject as "realizing" their *ends* or *destiny*, in preference for a more Nietzschean emphasis on "self-creation", or the Spinozian concept of "constitutive praxis". Both represent the subject as "free standing" as opposed to the Aristotelian conception of the subject of pre-given essences and ends. But beyond this, it can be claimed that self-creation presupposes certain "capabilities" in the way Nussbaum claims. Also, the models of social relations, and specifically of the ontological priority of the social to the individual, are similar in both traditions.[13]

In that such a list of factors Nussbaum identifies are universal, it is in terms of reach, rather than validity. That they correlate with certain necessary laws or characteristics need not be denied, of course. Foucault himself says that universal forms may well exist. In "What Is Enlightenment?" (Foucault, 1984a, pp. 47–48), he suggests there may possibly be universalizing tendencies at the root of Western civilization, which include such things as "the acquisition of capabilities and the struggle for freedom" as "permanent elements". Again, more directly, in the "Preface to *The History of Sexuality*, Volume II" (Foucault, 1984b, p. 335), he says that he is not denying the possibility of universal structures:

> Singular forms of experience may perfectly very well harbor universal structures; they may well not be independent from the concrete determinations of social existence. ... [T]his thought has a historicity which is proper to it. That it should have this historicity does not mean it is deprived of all universal form, but instead that the putting into play of these universal forms is itself historical.

So the fact of necessary laws does not deny the inevitability of a historically contingent component in knowledge. Discursive mediation and structuration constitute ineradicably contingent components of knowledge. In saying this, Foucault is not denying the existence of necessities, and even that there are some forms of determinate structure to the way things are, but he would argue that most structures (economies, languages, social structures) would be shaped and modified in the process of history.[14] He could accept, as well, that while general human characteristics may be transformed or modified in history, the process of change would occur at a different (i.e., slower) rate than most discursive or cultural phenomena. Further discursive and cultural phenomena themselves change at different rates, and some (maths) have achieved remarkable stability, thus enabling comparisons between older and newer institutions and discourses. While in this sense there are still no foundations or invariant structures outside of the flux of history, this need not lead to an impasse of relativism in there being no ground on which to stand.

From her point of view, Nussbaum also claims to be anti-foundationalist. She claims (1995, p. 455), for instance:

> When we get rid of the hope of a transcendent metaphysical grounding for ... judgements—about the human being as about anything else—we

are not left with the abyss. We have everything that we always had all along: the exchange of reasons and arguments by human beings within history, in which, for reasons that are historical and human but not the worse for that, we hold some things to be good and others bad, some arguments to be sound and others not sound. Why indeed should the relativist conclude that the absence of a transcendent basis for judgement—a basis that, according to them, was never there anyway—should make us despair of doing as we have done all along, distinguishing persuasion from manipulation.

Habermas of course may still not be happy, yet he fails to see the import of Bernstein's point, that although the lack of foundations and the inseparability of knowledge from the context of its production causes difficulties in epistemology, it does not leave us without any normative guideposts, for in a world of dangers, there is always some sense of direction. To recognize danger suggests we understand what we need to do to survive. To recognize survival is to recognize the conditions of our own well-being. When Foucault (1991) talks of "domination", when he talks of "ethics", and the requirement for fluid relations of power and for freedom, he is mindful of continuing to survive, of continuing to persevere, of self-preservation and of well-being. As in Deleuze, with Foucault, there is a Spinozist inspiration here: of *conatus*, of the *univocity of being*, of the *play of difference*, of *constitutive praxis*, and of the centrality of *power* and of *freedom*. It is my own view that Aristotle is a burden to Nussbaum, and that the tasks she sets could better be done by Spinoza, Nietzsche and Foucault. A Spinozist/Nietzschean reading of Foucault presents "weak" grounds, located not in the subject, or reason, or the Enlightenment, but in survival.[15]

This sort of "capabilities" approach constitutes a new analytics of finitude as providing some temporary "anchorage" in history, and of providing a horizon for education. Such an approach has not only been advanced by Nussbaum but also by Amartya Sen (1979, 1985, 1992, 1993). It is also in my view compatible with Foucault's general emphasis in his later works on self-creation.[16] Foucault's emphasis on self-creation can be held to presuppose a range of capabilities. Such an approach, as Nussbaum argues, enables both international comparisons and concentrates on the actual conditions which provide for the functional needs of individuals and groups. Such an approach also provides for education, for a politics based on the capabilities approach presupposes that a society provides necessary public education by which capabilities can be developed. Under such an approach it is the business of education to provide for the production of such capabilities. Indeed, inspired by Nussbaum's propensity for "creating lists", and by Foucault's emphasis on the creation of the self, we can say, in a very preliminary way, that a number of things are clearly required, including: (1) basic material and institutional supporting structures and resources, (2) training and knowledge, (3) nonhumiliation and respect for the dignity of persons, (4) a protected space where freedom can be practised, (5) structures that permit dialogue and communication, and (6) an equalization of access to wealth and resources. For Foucault, as there is no natural self, these things must be provided for through collective agency. Unlike Nussbaum, who sees Rawls as a major influence, the great advantage of Foucault is that he provides for a non-liberal conception of education and development, yet one which protects traditional liberal ideals as regards liberty and freedom. By stressing "capabilities" such an approach is not advocating a pure "virtue-based" ethics, nor a traditional "rights-based" approach, nor a teleology of functioning in the Aristotelian sense, but simply focuses on the collective and individual arrangements wherein development and self-creation can take place.

Such an approach can be represented as a new "analytics of finitude", beyond the human subject, at this juncture in history. Rather than view such capabilities as a definitive list, by orientating critique to the tasks of survival, it could be construed as constituting a new analytics of finitude, beyond the subject, concerned in Bernstein's sense with "avoiding dangers". Such a frame, which is of great relevance post-9/11, and in an age of nuclear terrorism, climate change, AIDS, SARS, MERS, and COVID-19, constitutes an analytics of finitude which evacuates the over-optimism of the Enlightenment and takes us beyond the solitary subject to a concern with humanity at large. Humanity constitutes a collective subject which must understand that it lives in a world without any foundations, and without any guarantees. In this sense—a sense that I would claim is compatible with the general spirit of Foucault's work and in terms of which we can extend his analysis—such an analytics of finitude generates a new strategic complex of power relations which can take on board those traditional liberal concerns of importance—freedom, well-being, a right to life—and yet dispense with a theory of the subject for whom foundations and relativism constitute a central stultifying anxiety. In that they constitute "grounds", they are of course only temporary grounds, although they contain in them at the same time a quest for well-being and freedom as the new genuinely *social* contract made by all of the motley social subjects—i.e., "us"—who face this new horizon at this point in time.

Acknowledgement

This chapter originally appeared as Olssen, M. (2006), Foucault and the imperatives of education: Critique and self-creation in a non-foundational world,

Studies in Philosophy and Education, 25, 245–271, https://doi.org/10.1007/s11217-006-0013-0. Reprinted here, with minor edits, with permission from the publisher.

Notes

1. See Foucault (1984). Foucault used the pseudonym "Maurice Florence" for this article.
2. His interest in Kant is continuous throughout his academic career and begins with his translation of Kant's *Anthropology from a Pragmatic Point of View* into French in 1960 as his *thèse complémentaire*—a smaller supplement to his major thesis of publishable quality, *Madness and Civilization*. Foucault submitted his translation of Kant's *Anthropology* to the Sorbonne jury in 1960 along with a commentary of 128 typescript pages (see Foucault, 1960). Kant is also considered in depth in *The Order of Things* (Foucault, 1970) as the introducer of humanism to the human sciences. Again, Kant is considered in "Qu'est ce-que la critique" (Foucault, 1978a), translated as "What Is Critique?" (Foucault, 1996); in the 1983 essay "What Is Enlightenment?" (Foucault, 1984a); in 1984 in "Un cours inedit" in *Magazine littéraire* (see Foucault, 1984), translated by Colin Gordon as "Kant on Enlightenment and Revolution" in *Economy and Society* (Foucault, 1986). In addition, Foucault gives a brief discussion on Kant in his introduction to the English translation of Georges Canguilhem, *The Normal and the Pathological* (see Foucault, 1978b); in his interview with Gerard Raulet, "How Much Does It Cost for Reason to Tell the Truth", published in *Foucault Live* (see Foucault, 1989, pp. 240–243), and in his essay "The Subject and Power", printed as an afterword in Hubert L. Dreyfus and Paul Rabinow (1983, pp. 215–216), *Michel Foucault: Beyond Structuralism and Hermeneutics*. Also, as Hacking (1996, pp. 238–239) notes, Foucault read Kant at the Sorbonne under the Heidegger scholar Jean Beufret. He also comments that the discussion of Kant in *The Order of Things* had its origin in Foucault's doctoral thesis.
3. See Kant (1970).
4. A different translation of the same article appears in Foucault (1988c).
5. Foucault translated this work into French for the first time and submitted it as part of his doctorate in 1960 (see Foucault, 1960. This was the first translation into French. It was only translated into English in 1978. The work has traditionally been seen either as crackpot or marginal to Kant's central philosophical enterprise (see Miller, 1993, p, 137).
6. My own analysis and interpretation of Kant's Anthropology has been substantially influenced by that of James Miller (1993).
7. The phrase is taken from Michele Bertrand (1983, p. 66) who applies it to Spinoza.
8. Spinoza's conception of *conatus* incorporates the notion that our bodies, as well as being shaped by external determinants, also have a force or momentum of a positive sort. See Spinoza's Ethics, Part III "On the Origin and Nature of the Emotions" (Spinoza, 1960).
9. Nietzsche did not give any direct support to the Nazis, although as Davies (1997, p. 33) states, his sister Elizabeth became in her later years an enthusiastic disciple of the Fuhrer. It is also true that the Nazis appropriated a number of Nietzschean themes and tropes—the Übermensch, or "blond beast" into their own repertoire. It is also now well documented that Martin Heidegger committed himself to Nazism and also wrote approvingly about Nietzsche. Such documented associations make an additional comment important, however. The existence of support for fascist causes by a thinker such as Heidegger, or the appropriation of several Nietzschean themes for the support of Nazi policies, cannot be seen as undermining or discrediting the thinkers entire philosophical ouvre. Nor can it suggest that themes such

as genealogy, or the priority of the social over the individual, could be represented as lending support to such causes, directly or indirectly, in spite of the fact that Nietzsche (like Wagner) was appropriated to the Nazi campaign. In this sense, as Davies (1997, p. 34) states, it is: "'worth stressing that what is at stake in the Nietzschean critique ... is not the endorsement of some protofascist brutality and humiliation but the analysis of one of the central myths of 19th century civilization, its "religion of humanity", among whose monstrous offspring Nazism itself can be numbered'". Neither is it possible to see how Foucault's philosophical anti-humanism could plausibly be linked to such themes. Rather, it denotes Foucault's attempt to expunge a metaphysical remnant from the enlightenment. In this sense, then, it is a limited. technical discourse which signifies his affinity with structuralism as it "kicks away the twin pillars of humanism; the sovereignty of rational consciousness and the authenticity of individual speech. Thought and speech, which for the humanist had been the central substance of identity, are located elsewhere, and. the self is a vacancy. 'I' as the poet Rimbaud put it, 'is an other'" (Davies, 1997, p. 60).

10 Bernstein is citing Hiley (1988, p. 103).
11 I am indebted to McKenzie (2004, p. 54) for this point.
12 The "tool box" metaphor is from "Intellectuals and Power: A conversation between Michel Foucault and Gilles Deleuze, Language, Counter-Memory, Practice", p. 208 (Mackenzie, 2004, p. 108).
13 It should also be noted that Nussbaum has been challenged on her dependence on Aristotle (see Arneson, 2000; Mulgan, 2000). In her defence of locating herself in an Aristotelian tradition, she maintains that she is inspired by the basic ontological postulates, but not the detailed arguments, of Aristotle, and she admits that her identification as "Aristotelian" has a great deal to do with her own biography and early philosophical commitments and training. (See Nussbaum, 2000b)
14 Foucault advances what today would be called a version of complexity theory, which I have documented elsewhere (Olssen, 2005, chapter 11).
15 This reading of Foucault is what I think of as the "Spinozist crutch", in that by locating Foucault in reference to Spinoza's themes of survival, preservation and well-being provides a "crutch" for him to offset Habermas's criticisms. I call this a "reading" for it is not customary to link Foucault and Spinoza in this way. However, Foucault clearly knew his Spinoza. See, for instance, Foucault's essay "Truth and Juridical Forms", originally published in May 1973, where he summarizes Spinoza in relation to Nietzsche (Foucault, 2001, pp. 11–12); again, Foucault refers to Spinoza in the debate with Chomsky (Foucault, 1997, p. 136); in "Theatrum Philosopicum" (Foucault, 1998, pp. 359–360 and 366–367); and in "Afterword to *The Temptation of St Anthony*" (1998, p. 105), just to name a few. It is also noteworthy that Deleuze was influenced by Spinoza (indeed wrote a book on Spinoza), as Deleuze had a strong influence on Foucault. See Paul Veyne (1997, pp. 63–64), "Foucault Revolutionizes History". Also see index entries to Deleuze and Guattari (1987), Deleuze (1990, 1994) and others. Like Deleuze, Foucault (1998, p. 364) at times uses Spinozist concepts to express his views. For example: "'The univocity of being, its singleness of expression, is paradoxically the principal condition that permits difference to escape the domination of identity, frees it from the law of the Same as a simple opposition within conceptual elements'".
16 By "self-creation", as I have explained elsewhere (Olssen 1999, 2005), Foucault does not mean that each individual creates of and for him/herself as in the liberal conception of the subject. As he states (1977, p. 30): "the man described for us ... is already himself the effect of a subjection much more profound than himself". Rather the individual uses the existing "practices of the self" that are "proposed, suggested and imposed upon him by his culture" (1991, p. 12).

References

Arneson, R. J. (2000). Perfectionism and politics. *Ethics, 111*(1), 37–63.
Ball, S. (Ed.). (1990). *Foucault and education: Disciplines and knowledge*. Routledge.
Biesta, G. (1998). Pedagogy without humanism: Foucault and the subject of education. *Interchange, 29*(1), 1–16.
Bernauer, J. (1991). Michel Foucault's ecstatic thinking. In J. Bernauer & D. Rasmussen (Eds.), *The final Foucault* (pp. 45–82). MIT Press.
Bernstein, R. J. (1994). Foucault: Critique as a philosophical ethos. In M. Kelly (Ed.), *Critique and power: Recasting the Foucault/Habermas debate* (pp. 211–241). MIT Press.
Bertrand, M. (1983). *Spinoza et l'imaginaire*. PUF.
Butler, J. (2002). Was ist Kritik? Ein Essay über Foucaults Tugend. *Deutsche Zeitschrift für Philosophie, 50*(2), 249–265.
Dreyfus, H. L., & Rabinow, P. (1983). *Michel Foucault: Beyond structuralism and hermeneutics* (2nd ed.). University of Chicago Press. (With an afterword and interview with Michel Foucault)
Foucault, M. (1960). *Introduction à l'anthropologie de Kant*. (thèse complémentaire). (Typescript available in the Libraire Philosophique J. Vrin; in the Bibliothèque de la Sorbonne, and photocopy available in the Centre Michel Foucault, Paris)
Foucault, M. (1963). Preface a transgression. *Critique, 195–196*(August–September), 751–770.
Foucault, M. (1970). *The order of things: An archaeology of the human sciences*. Vintage.
Foucault, M. (1977a). *Discipline and punish: The birth of the prison* (A. Sheridan, Trans.). Pantheon.
Foucault, M. (1977b). A preface to transgression. In D. F. Bouchard (Ed.), *Language, counter-memory, practice: Selected essays and interviews* (D. F. Bouchard & S. Simon, Trans.; pp. 29–52). Cornell University Press.
Foucault, M. (1978a). Qu'est-ce-que la critique. Compte rendu de la séance du 27 mai 1978. *Bulletin de la société française de philosophie, 84*(1990), 35–63.
Foucault, M. (1978b). Introduction. In G. Canguilhem (Ed.), *The normal and the pathological* (C. R. Fawcett, Trans.; R. S. Cohen, Ed.). D. Reidel.
Foucault, M. (1978c). *The history of sexuality, volume 1: An introduction* (R. Hurley, Trans.). Pantheon.
Foucault, M. (1980a). Georges Canguilhem: Philosopher of error (G. Burchell, Trans.). *Ideology & Consciousness, 7*(Autumn), 51–62.
Foucault, M. (1980b). *Power/knowledge: Selected interviews and other writings 1972–1977* (C. Gordon, Ed.). Harvester Press.
Foucault, M. (1980c). Two lectures (K. Soper, Trans.). In C. Gordon (Ed.), *Power/knowledge: Selected interviews and other writings 1972–1977* (pp. 78–108). Harvester Press.
Foucault, M. (1984). Michel Foucault. In D. Huisman (Ed.), *Dictionnaire des philosophes* (p. 941). Paris. (Written under the pseudonym Maurice Florence)

Foucault, M. (1984a). What is enlightenment? (C. Porter, Trans.). In P. Rabinow (Ed.), *The Foucault reader* (pp. 32–50). Pantheon.

Foucault, M. (1984b). Preface to *The history of sexuality, volume II* (W. Smock, Trans.). In P. Rabinow (Ed.), *The Foucault reader* (pp. 333–339). Pantheon.

Foucault, M. (1984c). Un cours inedit. *Magazine littéraire, 207,* 35–39.

Foucault, M. (1984d). On the genealogy of ethics: An interview of work in progress. In P. Rabinow (Ed.), *The Foucault reader* (pp. 340–372). Pantheon.

Foucault, M. (1985). *The history of sexuality, volume 2: The use of pleasure* (R. Hurley, Trans.). Penguin.

Foucault, M. (1986). Kant on enlightenment and revolution (C. Gordon, Trans.). *Economy and Society, 15*(1), 88–96.

Foucault, M. (1987). Questions of method. In K. Baynes, J. Bonman, & T. McCarthy (Eds.), *After philosophy: End or transformation* (pp. 101–117). MIT Press.

Foucault, M. (1988a). Practicing criticism. In M. Foucault (Ed.), *Politics, philosophy, culture: Interviews and other writings, 1977–1984* (A. Sheridan et al., Trans.; L. D. Kritzman, Ed.; pp. 152–158). Routledge.

Foucault, M. (1988b). (Auto)biography: Michel Foucault 1926–1984. (J. Ursala, Trans.). *History of the Present, 4*(Spring), 13–15.

Foucault, M. (1988c). The art of telling the truth. In M. Foucault (Ed.), *Politics, philosophy, culture: Interviews and other writings, 1977–1984* (A. Sheridan et al., Trans.; L. D. Kritzman, Ed.; pp. 86–95). Routledge.

Foucault, M. (1989). *Foucault live* (J. Johnson, Trans.; S. Lotringer, Ed). Semiotext(e).

Foucault, M. (1991). The ethic of care for the self as a practice of freedom: An interview (J. D. Gauthier, Trans.). In J. Bernauer & D. Rasmussen (Eds.), *The final Foucault* (pp. 1–20). MIT Press.

Foucault, M. (1994). Two lectures. In M. Kelly (Ed.), *Critique and power: Recasting the Foucault/Habermas debate* (pp. 17–46). MIT Press.

Foucault, M. (1996). What is critique? In J. Schmidt (Ed.), *What is enlightenment? Eighteenth-century answers to twentieth-century questions.* University of California Press.

Foucault, M. (1998). Theatrum philosophicum. In J. D. Faubion (Ed.), *Essential works of Foucault, 1954–1984, vol. 2: Aesthetics, method, epistemology* (pp. 343–368). Penguin.

Foucault, M. (2008). *The birth of biopolitics: Lectures at the Collège de France, 1978–79* (G. Burchell, Trans.; M. Senellart, Ed.). Palgrave Macmillan.

Fraser, N. (1994). Michel Foucault: A "young conservative"? In M. Kelly (Ed.), *Critique and power: Recasting the Foucault/Habermas debate* (pp. 185–210). MIT Press.

Guess, R. (1981). *The idea of a critical theory: Habermas & the Frankfurt School.* Cambridge University Press.

Habermas, J. (1986). Taking aim at the heart of the present. In D. Couzens Hoy (Ed.), *Foucault: A critical reader* (pp. 103–108). Blackwell.

Habermas, J. (1987). *The philosophical discourse of modernity* (F. Lawrence, Trans.). MIT Press.

Habermas, J. (1994). Some questions concerning the theory of power: Foucault again. In M. Kelly (Ed.), *Critique and power: Recasting the Foucault/Habermas debate* (pp. 79–108). MIT Press.

Hacking, I. (1996). Self-improvement. In D. Couzens Hoy (Ed.), *Foucault: A critical reader* (pp. 235–240). Blackwell.

Hiley, D. R. (1985). Foucault and the question of enlightenment. *Philosophy and Social Criticism, 11,* 63–83.

Hiley, D. R. (1988). *Philosophy in question: Essays on a Pyrrhonian theme.* University of Chicago Press.

Jameson, F. (1984). Foreword. In J.-F. Lyotard (Ed.), *The postmodern condition: A report on knowledge* (G. Bennington & B. Massumi, Trans.; pp. vii–xxi). University of Minnesota Press.

Kant, I. (1970). An answer to the question: What is enlightenment? In *Kant's political writings* (H. B. Nisbet, Trans.; H. Reiss, Ed.; pp. 54–60). Cambridge University Press.

Kant, I. (1992). An answer to the question: What is enlightenment? In P. Waugh (Ed.), *Postmodernism: A reader.* Edward Arnold. (Original work published 1784)

Mackenzie, I. (2004). *The idea of pure critique.* Continuum.

Marshall, J. (1989). Foucault and education. *Australian Journal of Education, 2,* 97–111.

Marshall, J. (1990). Foucault and educational research. In S. J. Ball (Ed.), *Foucault and education: Discipline and knowledge.* Routledge.

Marshall, J. (1995). Skills, information and quality for the autonomous chooser. In M. Olssen & K. Morris Matthews (Eds.), *Education, democracy and reform* (pp. 44–59). New Zealand Association for Research in Education (NZARE)/Research Unit for Maori Education (RUME), University of Auckland.

Marshall, J. (1996a). Personal autonomy and liberal education: A Foucauldian critique. In M. Peters, W. Hope, J. Marshall, & S. Webster (Eds.), *Critical theory, post-structuralism and the social context* (pp. 106–126). Dunmore Press.

Marshall, J. (1996b). *Michel Foucault: Personal autonomy and education.* Kluwer Academic.

Miller, J. (1993). *The passion of Michel Foucault.* Flamingo.

Mulgan, R. (2000). Was Aristotle an "Aristotelian social democrat"? *Ethics, 111*(1), 79–101.

Nussbaum, M. (1995). Human functioning and social justice: In defense of Aristotelian essentialism. In D. Tallack (Ed.), *Critical theory: A reader* (pp. 449–472). Harvester Wheatsheaf.

Nussbaum, M. (1996). *For love of country.* Beacon Press.s

Nussbaum, M. (1997). *A classical defence of reform in liberal education.* Harvard University Press.

Nussbaum, M. (2000a). *Women and human development: The capabilities approach.* Cambridge University Press.

Nussbaum, M. (2000b). Aristotle, politics, and human capabilities: A response to Antony, Arneson, Charlesworth, and Mulgan. *Ethics, 111*(1), 102–140.

Olssen, M. (1991). Producing the truth about people: Science and the cult of the individual in educational psychology. In J. Morss & T. Linzey (Eds.), *Growing up* (pp. 188–209). Longman Paul.

Olssen, M. (1993). Science and individualism in educational psychology: Problems for practice and points of departure. *Educational Psychology: An International Journal of Experimental Educational Psychology, 13*(2), 155–172.

Olssen, M. (2006). *Michel Foucault: Materialism and education*. Paradigm.

Olssen, M. (2018). Foucault and neoliberalism: A response to recent critics and a new resolution. *Materiali Foucaultiani, 7*(13–14), 28–55. http://www.materialifoucaultiani.org/images/02olssen.pdf

Olssen, M., Codd, J., & O'Neill, A.-M. (2004). *Education policy: Globalization, citizenship & democracy*. Sage.

Olssen, M., & Peters, M. A. (2005). Neoliberalism, higher education and the knowledge economy: From the free market to knowledge capitalism. *Journal of Education Policy, 20*(3), 313–345. https://doi.org/10.1080/02680930500108718

Olssen, M., & Peters, M. A. (2008). Marx, education and the possibilities of a fairer World: Reviving radical political economy through Foucault. In A. Green, G. Rikowski, & H. Raduntz (Eds.), *Renewing dialogues in Marxism and education: Openings* (pp. 151–179). Palgrave/Macmillan.

Olssen, M., & Peters, M. A. (2015). Marx, education and the possibilities of a fairer world: Reviving radical political economy through Foucault. *Linguistic and Philosophical Investigations, 14*, 39–69.

Peters, M. (1996). Habermas, poststructuralism and the question of postmodernity. In M. Peters, W. Hope, J. Marshall, & S. Webster (Eds.), *Critical theory, poststructuralism and the social context* (pp. 33–56). Dunmore Press.

Peters, M. (2001). *Poststructuralism, Marxism and neoliberalism*. Rowman & Littlefield.

Peters, M., & Marshall, J. (1996). *Individualism and community. Education and social policy in the postmodern condition*. Falmer Press.

Rajchman, J. (1985). *Michel Foucault: The freedom of philosophy*. Columbia University Press.

Spinoza, B. (1960). *The ethics* (R. H. M. Elwes, Trans.). In *The rationalists: Descartes, Spinoza, Leibniz* (pp. 179–405). Anchor/Doubleday.

CHAPTER 2

Discourse, Complexity, Normativity

Tracing the Elaboration of Foucault's Materialist Concept of Discourse

Abstract

In this article, I want to suggest that it is through the elaboration of the concept of discourse that the differences between Foucault and thinkers like Habermas, Hegel and Marx can best be understood. Foucault progressively develops a conception of discourse as a purely historical category that resists all reference to transcendental principles of unity—whether of substance or form—but sees the emergence of discursive frameworks as precarious and contested assemblages characterized by indeterminacy, complexity, openness, uncertainty and contingency. His approach thus enables a reconciliation of difference and commonality, or the particular and the general, in a distinctive and viable way.

1   A Brief Introduction to Foucault's Methods

In his book *The Archaeology of Knowledge*, originally published in 1968 to encapsulate the methods used in his earlier works (*Madness and Civilisation*; *The Birth of the Clinic*; *The Order of Things*), Foucault distinguishes between the discursive and pre-discursive levels of reality and seeks to present an account of the emergence and constitution of discourse as a purely historical assemblage (Foucault, 1970, 1972). A discourse is defined in terms of statements (*énoncés*) of "things said". Statements are events of certain kinds at once tied to a historical context and capable of repetition. The position in discourse is defined as a consequence of their functional use. Hence, statements are not equivalent to propositions or sentences; neither are they phonemes, morphemes, or syntagms. Rather, as Foucault (1972, p. 114) states:

> In examining the statement what we have discovered is a *function* that has a bearing on groups of signs, which is identified neither with grammatical "acceptability" nor with logical correctness, and which requires it to operate: *a referential* (which is not exactly a fact, a state of things, or even an object, but a principle of differentiation); *a subject* (not the speaking consciousness, nor the author of the formulation, but a position that may be filled in certain conditions by various individuals); *an*

associated field (which is not the real context of the formulation, the situation in which it was articulated, but a domain of coexistence for other statements); *a materiality* (which is not only the substance or support of the articulation, but a status, rules of transcription, possibilities for use and re-use).

Foucault is interested in serious statements comprising that subset that have some autonomy, which contain truth claims and which are differentiated and individuated according to a single system of formation. A "discursive formation" comprises the regularity that obtains between "objects, types of statement, concepts, or thematic choices" (Foucault, 1972, pp. 38, 107). It is "the general enunciative system that governs a group of verbal performances" (p. 117).

Central to understanding Foucault's concept of discourse, it is important to understand his approach to methods. Methodologically Foucault's works utilize two approaches: that of *archaeology*, concerned to describe the historical presuppositions of a given system of thought, and *genealogy*, concerned to trace the historical process of *descent* and *emergence* by which a given thought system or process comes into being and is subsequently transformed. Archaeological analysis is centrally concerned to uncover the rules of formation of discourses, or discursive systems. In a technical sense, proceeding at the level of statements (*énoncés*), it searches for rules that explain the appearance of phenomena under study. It examines the forms of regularity, i.e., the discursive conditions, which order the structure of a form of discourse and which determine how such orders come into being. It is not analysis of that which is claimed to be true in knowledge but an analysis of "truth games". Discourse is thus analysed in terms of the operation of rules which bring it into being. Thus, in his archaeological studies, Foucault attempts to account for the way discourses are *ordered*. As he states, "my object is not language but the archive, that is to say, the accumulated existence of discourses. Archaeology, as I intend it, is kin neither to geology (or analysis of the sub-soil) nor to genealogy (as description of beginnings or sequences); it is the analysis of discourse in its modality of archive" (1989a, p. 25). As such, archaeology focuses attention on the link between perception and action and why at different periods specialists in knowledge perceive objects differently. The core of archaeology is thus an attempt to establish the discursive practices and rules of formation of discourses through asking "how is it that a particular statement appeared and not another" (Foucault, 1972, p. 27). As Manfred Frank (1992, p. 107) says, "As such, he is more interested in the conditions which make it possible for the structures to arise than in the structures themselves … for Foucault the foundation of the constitution of an order is never a subject, but yet another order: in the last instance this would be the order of the discourse with its *regard déjà codé* (already coded look)".

In *The Order of Things*, for example, Foucault seeks to uncover the regularities which accounted for the emergence of the sciences of the 19th century by comparing forms of thought across different historical periods (Renaissance, classical, and modern). Archaeology here constitutes a method for examining the historicity of science by describing rules which undergird ways of looking at the world. These rules are regularities that determine the systems of possibility of discourse as to what is considered as true and false, and they determine what counts as grounds for assent or dissent, as well as what arguments and data are relevant and legitimate. These deeper "structures of thought" are termed *epistemes*. An "episteme" refers to "the total set of relations that unite, at a given period, the discursive practices. ... The episteme is not a form of knowledge ... or type of rationality which, crossing the boundaries of the most varied sciences, manifests the sovereign unity of a subject, a spirit, or a period; it is the totality of relations that can be discovered for a given period, between the sciences when one analyses them at the level of discursive regularities" (Foucault, 1972, p. 191).

Robert Machado (1992, p. 14) characterizes an episteme as defined by two features. The first is its depth; an "episteme" relates to the nature of "deep" knowledge (*savoir*) and to the specific order or configuration which such knowledge assumes in a given period. This is to say that an episteme is governed by a principle prior to and independent of the ordering of discourse such as science, which is constituted of "surface" knowledge (*connaissance*). The second is its general global nature. In any culture, at a particular point in time, there is only one episteme which defines the conditions of possibility of all theoretical knowledge (see Foucault, 1970, p. 179). Archaeology is a historical analysis of this theoretical knowledge attempting to trace links between the different domains of "life, work, and language", revealing relationships that are not readily apparent. In doing so it seeks to expose the "historical a priori" of the episteme as it manifests itself in the body of discourses under study.

In this sense, Foucault insists that *epistemes* are not transcendental in the Kantian sense; neither are they origins or foundations. Rather, they are a practice to be encountered, i.e., they are time-bound and factual. Notwithstanding such a caveat, Foucault was to stop using the concept of episteme after *The Order of Things*, and it is noteworthy that the word is not mentioned in *The Archaeology of Knowledge*, first published in 1968. In his review of *The Archaeology*, Dominique Lecourt (1970) saw this as a positive step forward, for concepts such as "historical a priori", "discursive practise" and "archive" have more direct empirical reference to the historicity and materiality of the discursive order, in that they imply links with institutions, as well as economic and political processes. Such concepts thus more effectively resist transcendental imputation. As Foucault says in *The Archaeology*, they "[do] not constitute, above events, and in an unmoving heaven, an atemporal structure. ... [T]hese rules are not imposed from the outside on the elements that they relate together; they are caught up in the very things they connect" (1972, p. 127). Hence the process of the birth of discourse is itself historical. Initially clusters of statements achieve a certain identity as grouped, characterizing their separateness, autonomy, or distinctness according to their functioning in space and time. It is here that Foucault says, using Hegel's concept of "positivity", that discursive practices cross a "threshold of positivity", which "characterizes its unity throughout time" (p. 126). It is once the "positivity" is established that the archive constitutive of the discursive formation takes root as a historical a priori. Far from being something static or unified, such a system is constantly being reproduced and transformed through use. The archive is "the system that governs the appearance of statements as unique events. ... [I]t defines at the outset the *system of its enunciability*" (p. 129). It is in this sense, says Foucault, "it is that which defines the mode of occurrence of the statement-thing; it is *the system of functioning*. ... It is *the general system of the formation and transformation of statements*" (pp. 129–130).

In contract to archaeology, genealogical analysis aims to explain the existence and transformation of elements of theoretical knowledge (*savoir*) by situating them within power structures and by tracing their descent and emergence in the context of history. As such, it traces an essential, historically constituted tie between power and knowledge, and provides a causal explanation for change in discursive formations and epistemes. Because it is more historical it helps Foucault avoid succumbing to the temptations of structuralism. Yet, like archaeology, it avoids reference to a philosophical conception of the subject, radicalizing Nietzsche's and Heidegger's opposition to the post-Cartesian and Kantian conceptions. Like archaeology, too, it is limited and justified as a method in terms of the fruitfulness of its specific applications.

Genealogy thus asserts the historical constitution of our most prized certainties about ourselves and the world in its attempts to de-naturalize explanations for the existence of phenomena. It analyses discourse in its relation to social structures and has an explicit focus on power and bodies. It is interested in institutional analysis and technologies of power aiming to isolate the mechanisms by which power operates. Through its focus on power, also, it aims to document how culture attempts to normalize individuals through increasingly rationalized means, by constituting normality, turning them into meaningful subjects and docile objects. Power relations are thus pivotal. Genealogy thus shifts the model for historical understanding from Marxist science and ideology, or from hermeneutical texts and their interpretation, to a Nietzschean-inspired analysis of strategies and tactics in history.

As a Nietzschean strategy, Foucault (1977, p. 142) is clear that genealogy opposes itself to the search for origins (*Ursprung*) or essences. To search for origins is to attempt to capture the exact essence of things which Foucault sees as reinstating Platonic essentialism. Such a search assumes the existence of "immobile forms that precede the external world of accident and succession". Such a search, says Foucault assumes the existence of a:

> primordial truth fully adequate to its nature, and it necessitates the removal of every mask to ultimately disclose an original identity. However, if the genealogist refuses to extend his faith in metaphysics, if he listens to history, he finds that there is "something altogether different" behind things: not a timeless and essential secret, but the secret that they have no essence or that their essence was fabricated in piecemeal fashion from alien forms. (Foucault, 1977, p. 142)

Rather than trace origins (*Ursprung*), genealogy traces the process of *descent* and *emergence*. Descent (*Herkunft*) is defined by Foucault as pertaining to practices as series of events: "To follow the complex course of descent is to maintain passing events in their proper dispersion; it is to identify the accidents, the minute deviations—or conversely, the complete reversals—the errors, the false appraisals, and the faulty calculations that gave birth to these things that continue to exist and have value for us" (Foucault, 1977, p. 146).

Unlike the continuities traced by those historians who search for origins, genealogy traces the jolts and surprises of history in terms of the effects of power on the body. Following Nietzsche's nominalism, Foucault's genealogies of the subject constitute an investigation into how we have been fashioned as ethical subjects. Hence, it attaches itself to the body: that "inscribed surface of events ... and volume in perpetual disintegration" (Foucault, 1977, p. 148). It reveals how history "inscribes itself on the nervous system, in temperament, in the digestive apparatus ... in faulty respiration, in improper diets, in the debilitated and prostrate body of those whose ancestors committed errors" (p. 147). In contrast to descent, emergence (*Entstehung*) traces "the movement of arising" (p. 148). "Emergence is thus the entry of forces; it is their eruption, the leap from wings to center stage, each in its youthful strength" (pp. 149–150).

In summary then, while archaeology examines the unconscious rules of formation which regulate the emergence of discourse, genealogical analysis focuses on the specific nature of the relations between discursive and non-discursive practices, and on the material conditions of emergence of practices and of discursive systems of knowledge. Genealogical analysis is thus essentially a method for looking at the historical emergence in the search for antecedents. While archaeology examines the structure of discourse, genealogy gives a greater weight to practices, power, and institutions.

2 From the Early to the Late Foucault

As is now accepted, while Foucault's use of archaeology characterized his earlier works, up to the original publication of *The Archaeology of Knowledge* in 1968, the Nietzschean inspired use of genealogy became of central importance after *The Archaeology* and characterized the studies of the 1970s and 1980s. Most of those who have examined the issue of continuity of his work, from the early to the later periods, see this change in his treatment of discourse as representing more of "change of emphasis" rather than marking an "abrupt reversal", or even a serious abandonment of his earlier positions, however. According to Mark Poster (1984), Dreyfus and Rabinow (1983), Barry Smart (1985) and Michèle Barrett (1988), while in his earlier archaeological investigations Foucault held that the deep structures of human life and culture were explicable in relation to the structures of language, after 1968 he carried out a reorientation and reclassification of his ideas that altered the direction of his work in important respects. As Poster puts it, "after 1968 [the] structuralist concern with language and its autonomy that was paramount in *The Order of Things* (1966) gave way to an ill-defined but suggestive category of discourse/practice in which the reciprocal interplay of reason and action were presumed. … This subtle yet ill-defined sense of the interplay of truth and power, theory and practice, became the central theme of Foucault's investigations" (Poster, 1984, p. 9).

Dreyfus and Rabinow (1983) argued similarly that Foucault changed his emphasis over time, attempting to adopt a more realist position. They maintain that Foucault's continued dissatisfaction with the achievements of *The Archaeology of Knowledge* led him to shift emphasis from archaeology to Nietzsche's concept of genealogy as a dominant method. The idea of genealogy, claim Dreyfus and Rabinow, places a much greater emphasis on practices and social institutions and on the relations between discursive and extra-discursive dimensions of reality.

A similar thesis is maintained by Barrett (1988). According to Barrett, in his earlier works Foucault elaborated a view of the "production of things by words" (Barrett, 1988, p. 130), and she claims that Foucault as archaeologist was phenomenologically and epistemologically detached from the discursive formations studied (p. 130). It is only Foucault's later works—*Discipline and Punish* and *The History of Sexuality*—where "practice is favoured over theory" and where "discourse is understood as a way of organising practices" (p. 134). The shift from archaeology to genealogy means essentially that Foucault no longer regards himself as detached from the social practices he studies. Indicative of the transition, says Barrett, is the fact that Foucault "discovered the concept of power" (p. 135). In this she cites Foucault to support her case:

> When I think back now, I ask what else it was that I was talking about in *Madness and Civilization* or *The Birth of the Clinic* but power. Yet I am perfectly aware that I scarcely even used the word and never had such a field of analysis at my disposal. (Cited in Barrett, 1988, p. 135)

Smart also agrees with this highly qualified sense in which Foucault's work changed, seeing the methodological approach of *The Archaeology of Knowledge* as altered only as a matter of focus or topic area by Foucault's shift to genealogy. In the shift from archaeology to genealogy, the major emphasis of the latter constitutes an expressed commitment to realism, equivalent to a form of historical materialism, and as Smart puts it, "a change in Foucault's value relationship to his subject matter" from the "relative detachment" of archaeology to a "commitment to critique characteristic of genealogy" (Smart, 1985, p. 48). While for Smart this:

> represented a change of emphasis and the development of new concepts ... such shifts and transformations as are evident do not signify a rapid change or "break" between earlier and later writings, rather a re-ordering of analytic priorities from the structuralist-influenced preoccupation with discourse to a greater and more explicit consideration of institutions. (Smart, 1985, pp. 47–48)

Thus, while Foucault's later analysis adopts new methods and strategies, and explores new problems, there is no repudiation of the central theoretical insights of *The Archaeology of Knowledge*. There are shifts of emphasis as well as in the problems of interest, and he becomes more manifestly materialist in the sense that he elaborates a theory of power, but there is no fundamental disqualification of the epistemological or ontological insights of *The Archaeology*—only a putting them to use for different purposes. It is in this sense that, while there is a clear shift at the level of method, of the types of issues investigated, and the abandonment of the use of certain concepts,[1] the later methods should not be seen as excluding the earlier ones. As Foucault explains to Raymond Bellour, in answer to a question concerning the "break" that *The Order of Things* establishes, "there is no reason for describing this autonomous layer of discourse except to the extent that one can relate it to other layers, practices, institutions, social and political relations, etc. It is this relationship that has always haunted me" (Foucault, 1989a, p. 23). My view supports those authors who concur with this view. Minson (1985, p. 115) argues that a full understanding of Foucault's later genealogies *requires* an understanding of archaeology. For Arnold Davidson, too, archaeology is quite compatible with genealogy and is in fact required to give genealogy its full expression. As Davidson states bluntly: "Genealogy does not so much displace archaeology as widen the kind of analysis to be pursued. It is a question, as Foucault put it in his last writings, of different axes whose 'relative importance ... is not always the same for all forms of experience'" (Davidson, 1986, p. 227).

It is in the context of his later genealogical studies, and especially the later two volumes of *The History of Sexuality*, that Foucault represents the self in more active terms as something that makes and cares for itself. On this view, however, he is interested to theorize a more active self within a purely social constructionist frame of reference. As he comments in a lecture given at Dartmouth College in 1983, his interest in the governmentality of the self "has been my obsession for years because it is one of the ways of getting rid of a traditional philosophy of the subject" (Foucault, 1997a, p. 199). In *Madness and Civilization*, it was a matter, he says, of how one "governed" "the mad"; in the later works on the care of the self, it is a matter of how one "governs" oneself (Foucault, 1989b, p. 457).[2] In addition, as he states:

> If I am now interested ... in the way in which the subject constitutes himself in an active fashion, by the practices of the self, these practices are nevertheless not something that the individual invents by himself. They are patterns that he finds in his culture and which are proposed, suggested and imposed upon him by his culture, his society and his social group. (Foucault, 1991, p. 11)[3]

Agency is protected and enabled for Foucault because subjects appropriate historically constituted discourses for their own ends in novel and contingent ways as they struggle to survive and be more.[4] It is in this sense that subjects are both the passive bearers and active creators of history. In terms of his tripartite ontology of labour, life and language, Foucault makes it clear that subjects appropriate and utilize actual historical practices, comprising both discursive and non-discursive, rather than simply systems of information or language. As he states:

> So it is not enough to say that the subject is constituted in a symbolic system. It is not just in the play of the symbolic that the subject is constituted. It is constituted in real practices—historically analyzable practices. There is a technology of the constitution of the self which cuts across symbolic systems while using them. (Foucault, 1997b, p. 277)

3 An Incorporeal Materialism

For Foucault, then, language, discourse, and thought were always theorized as belonging to an autonomous realm, separate from the being of the physical world. As he tells us in *The Order of Things*, "it would be necessary to dismiss as fantasy any anthropology in which there was any question of the being of language, or any conception of language or signification which attempted to connect with, manifest, and free being proper to man" (Foucault, 1970, p. 339). Hence, for Foucault, the object of knowledge, or the other person, while independent of the knower, is known only in relation to a historically constituted discourse. This is to say that discourse, for Foucault, does not directly represent nature in the sense of an exact copy. Foucault presents the history of knowledge as a quest for representation from the classical age to modernity. The quest of modernity was the production of a subject that would think itself as the fount of reason, and think thought as directly reflecting nature. Modernity, for Foucault, was representational only in the sense that it patterned itself as a copy of nature. It thus sought to deny the being of language, which operated through power, but represented it as an inert reflection, or translucent medium.

The concern to represent the world faithfully became central to the modernist Enlightenment's modality of the claim to know. Signification became represented as a copy of the world, rather than acknowledging its positivity as an autonomous domain. This led to a different understanding of discursive construction. Foucault's concept of discourse pertained, as he put it in *The Archaeology of Knowledge*, neither to words nor things, but to the regularities internal to discourse. A discourse is defined in terms of statements, of "things said". Language is part of discourse, but not equivalent to it. A discourse represents a particular regularity of language, with its own truth conditions, schemas of perception, hierarchy of practices, modes of institutionalized inclusion and exclusion, criteria of acceptability for speaking, and so on. Discourse circulates with power and thus is *active*. That is, it maintains its own *positivity*. It produces, limits, excludes, frames, hides, scars, cuts, distorts, and juxtaposes distorted and illusory images alongside knowledge of the present. Between language and being there is an infinite chasm. Language is perpetually inadequate to its task of representation and being is forever inaccessible, infinitely receding. Words, as Faubion (2004, p. IX) states, are "bad actors which botch their roles". They express not a perfect or even adequate correspondence with being but rather they distort being in a way that reflects the contingent imperatives of time, place, and power. Discourses therefore manifest the relativity of every system—institutional or theoretical, of structures, theories, concepts, and practices of the self. The conditions which enable discourses, and define the limits for thought, constitute for Foucault the historical a priori of the episteme of an era. While not usually completely impenetrable, Foucault explains in the "Preface" to *The Order of Things*, the "stark impossibility of thinking *that*", in reference to the way animals are classified in Borges's "Chinese encyclopaedia".[5]

In "Theatrum philosophicum" (Foucault, 1998b), his review of Deleuze's books *The Logic of Sense* and *Difference and Repetition*, Foucault refers to Deleuze's position as expressing an "incorporeal materialism". Here Foucault allies himself with Deleuze in recognizing the level of phantasms and the event. Deleuze acknowledges the role of the Stoics in the origination of this way of conceiving of being, as being the first to reverse a tradition that he tells us has dominated since Plato. Deleuze then cites Émile Bréhier (1928) from his book on Stoic thought:

> [The Stoics distinguished] radically two planes of being, something that no one had done before them: on the one hand, real and profound being, force; on the other, the plane of facts, which frolic on the surface of being, and constitute an endless multiplicity of incorporeal beings. (Cited in Deleuze, 2004, p. 8)

In his review, Foucault reiterates the importance of this insight:

> *The Logic of Sense* should be read as the boldest and most insolent of metaphysical treatises—on the simple condition that instead of denouncing metaphysics as the neglect of being, we force it to speak of extrabeing. Physics: discourse dealing with the ideal structure of bodies, mixtures, reactions, internal and external mechanisms; metaphysics: discourse dealing with the materiality of incorporeal things—phantasms, idols, and simulacra. (Foucault, 1998b, p. 347)

For Foucault and Deleuze, this approach rejects all logics of Identity, or the Same; it is a pure theory of differences, based on a conception of the "event". As Foucault expresses it:

> To consider a pure event, it must first be given a metaphysical basis. But we must be agreed that it cannot be a metaphysics of substances, which can serve as a foundation for accidents; nor can it be a metaphysics of coherence, which situates these accidents in the entangled nexus of cause and effects. The event—a wound, a victory, defeat, death—is always an effect produced entirely by bodies colliding, mingling, or separating, but this effect is never of a corporeal nature; it is the intangible, inaccessible battle that turns and repeats itself a thousand times. (Foucault, 1998b, p. 349)

Previous philosophers have failed to grasp the importance of the event, because they have sought to constrain the field of differences, seeing in nature, or the Devine, some tendency to order or equilibrium. Metaphysics must be conceptualized as difference and recurrence, without dialectical contradiction, negation or synthesis. Such a present "as the recurrence of difference, as repetition giving voice to difference, affirms at once the totality of chance" (Foucault, 1998b, p. 366). In such a model, "[d]ifference recurs: and being, expressing itself in the same manner with respect to difference, is never the universal flux of becoming; nor is it the well-centred circle of the identical" (p. 366). Rather, "[b]eing is a Return freed from the curvature of the circle: it is Recurrence" (p. 366).

4 Resisting Hegelian Assumptions of Unity

Notwithstanding the changes he made as he sought to adopt a more realist position, Foucault consistently conceptualized the discursive as an ontologically autonomous domain which interacts with the practices of the non-discursive. In this sense, he stresses the materiality of the discursive systems, both in themselves, and in their relations to the non-discursive, and characterizes the theoretical choices and forms of exclusion that constitute them as suggested by "the function that the discourse … must carry out in a field of non-discursive practices" (Foucault, 1972, p. 68). A diagrammatic model of the relationship between discursive and extra-discursive is set out in Figure 2.1.[6] The importance of the non-discursive is emphasized in the *Archaeology* to reaffirm Foucault's commitment to a more materialist analysis. In this, but more notably in his later studies, Foucault allows for the duality of articulation between discourse and material forms as well as distinguishing between both the *discursive* and *pre-* or *extra-discursive* levels of reality. Mark Gottdiener (1995, p. 70) cites Deleuze (1986, p. 124) who expresses the point in different terms when he notes that:

> Foucault's general principle is that every form is a compound of relations between forces. Given these forces, our first question is with what forces from outside they enter into a relation, and then what form is created as a result.

In *Discipline and Punish* (1977), for example, Foucault observes how punishment cannot be derived solely from the force of the discourse, for torture, machines and dungeons are material things, and have meaning because of the discourse of punishment. But we cannot derive the resultant forms solely from the discourse, or the law, although they are clearly related. Rather, the social forms of discipline and punishment represent a synthetic and relatively autonomous compound of knowledge and technique and material objects. The developments of the prison, the clinic, the mental asylum, are thus the outcomes of this multiple articulation. Foucault can be distinguished in this from other poststructuralist and postmodern writers, such as Baudrilliard and Derrida, who, as Gottdiener (1995, p. 73) says, "have ignored the interrogation of material forms" in the same way as Western sociologies like Symbolic Interactionism have done.

Although it was not until *Discipline and Punish* and *The History of Sexuality, Volume 1*, that he would examine the empirical interactions between discursive and non-discursive and incorporate the dimension of power as an explicit category, in *The Archaeology of Knowledge* he was interested in formulating the theoretical dimensions of the relations between the two domains, and also in the iterative conditions for the repeatability of the statement (see Figure 2.1). In a way similar to Derrida, as he formulated the conditions for iterability in the text, discourse for Foucault is both located in, and yet exceeds its context, at least in relation to its unrepeatability. Thus, as for Derrida, while all knowledge is through description, an alternative description of any situation is always possible. Yet, in a way different from Derrida, for Foucault, it is *history*, and not merely *text*, which constitutes the conditions for non-repeatability. In historical terms this helps understand novelty and creativity, and assists also with a theory of agency, for every practice in time is in a certain sense new and irreversible. The statement is, says Foucault, "an unrepeatable event". It has "a situated and dated uniqueness" (1972, p. 101).

Also characteristic of Foucault's conception of discourse and its constitution, emanating from his philosophical dependence on Heidegger and

Discursive
Language, discourse, culture, thought.
Elements embedded in configurations which depend on time and place (therefore infinite possibilities of configurative form and articulation).

Pre-discursive
Life/non-life necessities, practices.
Non-discursive materialities: facts, things, events, regularities (e.g., birth, death, finite regularities technologies, etc.).

FIGURE 2.1   Non-linear system of open articulation

Nietzsche, is its anti-Hegelianism. It is as a consequence of this that it resists any transcendental imputations of unity. Yet, some authors have difficulty in accounting from exactly where discursive relations of unity or coherence are achieved or constituted. Charles Larmore (1981, p. 117) makes this point against Heidegger, for instance, accusing him of letting certain familiar resonances of Hegel in through the back door:

> Behind Heidegger's notion that all our background beliefs hang together systematically according to principles understood ... in advance, stands the old Hegelian idea that history divides into epochs, each epoch putting into practice a single basic conception of man and the world. The Hegelian influence becomes manifest in the later writings, where Heidegger speaks of *Seinsepochen*, delimitable historical periods guided by a single thought.

This sounds similar to the concept of *episteme*, used by Foucault in *The Order of Things*, or to those of *discursive formation*, *historical a priori*, and *archive*, utilized in *The Archaeology of Knowledge*. For Larmore, clearly, the idea of *Seinsepochen*, as used by Heidegger, introduces the structure of unity (a "single thought"), which in his view, derives from Hegel, or at least reinstates the Hegelian idea of unity as a metaphysical postulate derived from his teleology. Without getting into an argument as to the correct interpretation of Heidegger on the point, as Foucault is very careful to elaborate in *The Archaeology*, the unity introduced by such conceptions as "discursive formation", "archive", or "a priori", resists any sort of transcendentalism which could constitute the statements of a discourse as having any "formal unity" separate from their historical occurrence and use (Foucault, 1972, p. 117). Contra Larmore, then, the unity of discourse derives exclusively from history. As Foucault says:

> Discourse, in this sense, is not an ideal, timeless form that also possesses a history; the problem is not therefore to ask oneself how and why it was able to emerge and become embodied at this point in time; it is, from beginning to end, historical—a fragment of history, a unity and discontinuity in history itself, posing the problem of its own limits, its divisions, its transformations, the specific modes of its temporality rather than its sudden irruption in the midst of the complicities of time. (p. 117)

Hence, structures like the a priori and the archive "must take account of statements in their diversity" (p. 127). In speaking of the a priori, Foucault claims that in no way does it represent an atemporal structure; nor is it imposed from the outside by any ahistorical foundation. Rather, the unity of the a priori is a consequence of a constellation moving in time. As such "[t]he *a priori* of positivities is not only the system of temporal dispersion; it is itself a transformable group" (1972, p. 127).

As for the earlier concept of *episteme*, the concepts of *discursive formation*, *archive*, and *a priori* are historically specific relations and frames which anchor and make possible more immediate discourse in terms of its functioning. They do not express any pre-ordained plan or programme. As purely contingent and empirical phenomena, the unity they forge is always *a posteriori*—and as such, always precarious, contested, forever being made, lost, fought over, and (possibly) re-won.

It is not necessary, then, to draw conclusions as to the unity of such beliefs within a culture or period or that they delimit in advance its possible forms of expression or articulation in the way Larmore claims with regard to Heidegger. A frame of reference can itself arise historically and permit a great deal of diversity within it. While the idea of unity as a transcendental category which holds out against history might have been central to Hegel, it was not for Nietzsche, Heidegger and Foucault.

5   Foucault's Poststructuralism

Foucault's historical analysis of discourse gives a further insight into his method and his difference to writers like Habermas. In his lecture notes from the Collège de France, published in *Dits et écrits* (1994a), Foucault presents a variety of statements on method which denote a rejection of, or departure from, either the dialectical methodologies of the Marxists, or of the types of causal analysis of the modernist Enlightenment thinkers. His approach bares striking affinities, in various senses, to contemporary complexity theory approaches based on notions such as irreversability, self-organization, emergence and non-linearity. In addition to such initiatives, Foucault argues for the importance of analytic method in relation to the philosophy of language for the analysis of discourse.[7] In one essay, "La philosophie analytique de la politique" (1994b), initially delivered in 1978 in Japan, Foucault spells out the superiority of analytical methods as used in Anglo-American philosophy compared to dialectical methodology. The particular dimension of analytic methods that caught his attention was its concern not with the "deep structures" of language, or the "being" of language, but with the "everyday use" made of language in different types of discourse.

By extension, Foucault argues that philosophy can similarly analyse what occurs in "everyday relations of power", and in all those other relations that "traverse the social body". Such an approach can therefore be utilized in relation to his approach to discourse. Just as language can be seen to underlie thought, so there is a similar grammar underlying social relations and relations of power. Hence, Foucault argues for what he calls an "analytico-political philosophy". Similarly, rather than seeing language as revealing some eternal buried truth which "deceives or reveals", the metaphorical method for understanding that Foucault utilizes is that of a game: "Language, it is played". It is, thus, a "strategic" metaphor, as well as a linguistic metaphor that Foucault utilizes to develop a critical approach to society freed from the theory of Marxism: "Relations of power, also, they are played; it is these games of power (*jeux de pouvoir*) that one must study in terms of tactics and strategy, in terms of order and of chance, in terms of stakes and objectives" (Foucault, 1994b, pp. 541–542).[8]

Foucault's dependence on structural linguistics is also central to understanding the nature of his analysis and method. Traditionally, the rationality of analytic reason, he says, has been concerned with causality in a model that implied determinism. In structural linguistics, however, the concern is not with causality, but in revealing multiple relations that Foucault calls in his 1969 article "Linguistique et sciences sociales" "logical relations" (see Foucault, 1994c, p. 824). While it is possible to formalize one's treatment of the analysis of relations, it is, says Foucault (1994c, p. 824), in a grappling toward the themes of complexity analysis, the discovery of the "presence of a logic that is not the logic of causal determinism that is currently at the heart of philosophical and theoretical debates".

Foucault's reliance on the model of structural linguistics provides him with a method which avoids both methodological individualism and being trapped by a concern with causalism. Structural linguistics is concerned with "the systematic sets of relations among elements" (Davidson, 1997, p. 8), and it functions for Foucault as a model to enable him to study social reality as a logical structure or set of logical relations revealing relations that are not transparent to consciousness. The methods of structural linguistics also enable Foucault to analyse change. For just as structural linguistics undertakes synchronic analysis seeking to trace the necessary conditions for an element within the structure of language to undergo change, a similar synchronic analysis applied to social life asks the question "in order for a change to occur what other changes must also take place in the overall texture of the social configuration" (Foucault, 1994c, p. 827). Hence, Foucault seeks to identify logical relations where none had previously been thought to exist or where previously one had searched for causal relations. This form of analysis becomes for Foucault a method of analysing previously invisible determinations (see Davidson, 1997, pp. 1–20).

The methodological strategies common to both archaeology and genealogy were also developed in response to Marxism, which is characterized by a specific narrow conception of causality (*un causalisme primaire*) and a dialectical logic that has very little in common with the logical relations that Foucault is interested in. Thus he maintains: "what one is trying to recover in Marx is something that is neither the determinist ascription of causality, nor the logic of a Hegelian type but a logical analysis of reality" (Foucault, 1994c, pp. 824–825). Such a difference with Marxism foreshadows Foucault's greater commitment to insights from complexity and non-linear dynamics. For whereas Marxism echoed modernist conceptions of a closed universe and conceptions of determination as based on traditional linear models of cause and effect, Foucault sees his own approach as premised on an open system of articulation, characterized by variable, or complex, forms of determination. Hence although archaeology functions to "reveal ... relations between discursive and non-discursive domains" (Foucault, 1972, p. 162), its mode of analysis is quite different to the way that Marxism or any other form of causal analysis would analyse such relations:

> A causal analysis ... would try to discover to what extent political changes, or economic processes, could determine the consciousness of scientists—the horizon and direction of their interest, their system of values, their way of perceiving things, the style of their rationality. ... Archaeology situates its analysis at another level. ... It wishes to show not how political practice has determined the meaning and form of medical discourse, but how and in what form it takes part in its conditions of emergence, insertion and functioning. (Foucault, 1972, p. 163)

For archaeology, in comparison to Marxism, then, the aim is not to "isolate mechanisms of causality", but to establish "how the rules of formation that govern it may be linked to non-discursive systems; it seeks to define specific forms of articulation" (Foucault, 1972, p. 162). Arnold Davidson (1997), points out that it is through such methodological strategies that Foucault proceeds to advance a non-reductive, holist, analysis of social life. As he puts it, "this kind of analysis is characterised, first, by anti-atomism, by the idea that we should not analyse single or individual elements in isolation but that one must look at the systematic relations among elements; second, it is characterised by the idea that the relations between elements are coherent and transformable, that is, that the elements form a structure" (Davidson, 1997, p. 11). Thus Foucault seeks to describe the relations among elements as structures which change as the component elements change, i.e., he endeavours to establish the systematic sets of relations and transformations that enable different forms of knowledge to emerge.

There is a similarity in terms of approach, here, to that of Ludwig Wittgenstein in that the central focus is on language. While Foucault focuses on serious formal statements in order to accurately chart the historically constituted discursive frame, Wittgenstein, at least in his later work, concentrated on ordinary language and common sense as a form of life.[9] As for Wittgenstein, for Foucault language is not seen as an expression of inner states, but as a historically constituted system, which is social in its origins as well as in its uses. In abandoning the phenomenological subject, the dualism of mind and world is surpassed, as well as the intractable difficulties as positing the world as a product of mind. The rules of language were themselves seen as a bundle of interactional and public norms. Meaning is generated within the context of the frame of reference (for Wittgenstein, a game; for Foucault a discourse). Hence to understand a particular individual we must understand the patterns of their socialization, the nature of their concepts, as well as the operative norms and conventions that constitute the context for the activity and the origin of the concepts utilized. If mind operates, not as a self-enclosed entity, as Descartes held, attaching words to thoughts, as if they were markers, but rather operated in terms of publicly structured rule-systems, then meanings are in an important sense public.[10]

It is related to the discursive nature of meaning and the publicity of language that practices can be seen to be intelligible only in relation to existence as communal. Existence is communal in the sense that meanings are public. A communal context defines a group of beings collectively adapting public resources for their use. Yet, the implications of this are far reaching. If meanings are linguistic, and language is public, and being public relates to individuals together, i.e., in communities, then as Hacking (2002, p. 131) says, "we are not talking only about language, but about high politics, about the person and the state, about individual rights, about the self, and much else". The thesis here is that the social nature of practices defines a community context in one very important sense, a sense which is fundamentally inescapable. Such a theoretical revolution, which has largely developed in the 20th century, has rendered the liberal conception of the autonomous self-interested individual as obsolete. Todd May, in his discussion of the work of Jean-Luc Nancy, expresses the sense in which a conception of the social nature of practices presupposes a conception of community:

> An instance of a single-practice community would be people working in a particular political campaign. They are engaged in a common task, recognize their compatriots as being so engaged, and are bound by this engagement, this recognition, and the norms of their practice. Everyday talk reflects the use of term "community" in this way: we speak of political, religious, and even economic communities in referring to communities comprising specific practices. (May, 1997, p. 57)

In most cases, however, May explains that it is multiple, or what he calls "overlapping practices" that constitute a community (May, 1997, p. 57). May notes that in the Continental tradition, Michel Foucault, Gilles Deleuze, and Jean-François Lyotard represent such a social theory of practice. In Anglo-American philosophy, Wittgenstein, Wilfred Sellars and Robert Brandom (p. 51). The central claim is that "a community is defined by the practices that constitute it" (p. 52). This defines, he says, what it means to be in community. Practice, he defines as "a regularity or regularities of behaviour, usually goal directed, that are socially and normatively governed" (p. 52). While, in this sense, practices are "rule governed", such rules need not be formal, or even explicit. A second feature of practices is that their normative governance is social, which is to reject the idea of a private language. This is to say that not only is the *governance* of practices social, but the *practices* are also social. Even solitary practices, like diary writing are social in this sense. As such says May (p. 53) "the concept of practice lies at the intersection of individuality and community". Thirdly, he says, "practice ... involves a regularity in behaviour. In order to be a practice, the various people engaged in it must be said to be "doing the same thing" under some reasonable description of their behaviour" (p. 54). As a consequence of these three definitions, says May, practices must be seen as discursive, meaning that they involve the use of language (p. 55). This entails:

> some sort of communication between participants in order that they may either learn or coordinate the activities that the practice involves ... Moreover, this communication must be potentially accessible to non-participants, since without such accessibility the practice would cease to exist when its current participants dropped out. The communication required by a practice, then, must be linguistic. The idea of linguistic communication can be broadly constructed here, needing only a set of public signs with assignable meanings. (p. 55)

Such a theory of practice, says May (p. 55) "is akin to Wittgenstein's idea that language games are central components of forms of life". The central theoretical point concerning practices is that they embody actions organized according to rules which are both linguistic and cultural. As Theodore R. Schatzki (2001a, p. 48) points out, "practices are organized nexuses of activity", and constitute "a set of actions ... constituted by doings and sayings". In this sense, he says (p. 45), "the social order is instituted within practices". Schatzki defines the social order as "arrangements of people, and the organisms, artefacts, and things through which they coexist" (p. 43). They coexist within what Schatzki (2001b, p. 2) calls "a field of practices" which constitutes "the total nexus of interconnected human practices". Such practices are 'embodied, materially mediated arrays of human activity centrally organized around shared practical understanding". Referring to Foucault, Schatzki (p. 2) notes how "bodies and activities are "constituted" within practices". It can be said, further, echoing Foucault in *The Archaeology of Knowledge*, that the practices that make up the social order comprise both "discursive" and "extra-discursive" elements. In this way, the idea of practices highlight "how bundled activities interweave with ordered constellations of nonhuman entities" (p. 3). In this sense, says Schatzki, "practice approaches promulgate a distinct social ontology: the social is a field of embodied, materially interwoven practices centrally organized around shared practical understandings" (p. 3).

A similar thesis is made at the level of language by J. L. Austin (1962) and John Searle (1969, 1995), who note the "performative" dimensions of language use within a community.[11] As performative, language is also constitutive and derives its meaning in relation to a "form of life". It is in this sense that possible language usage is never constrained by the actual system of rules that operate. Such a model allows for the possibility of contingency and novelty. Building on Wittgenstein in the *Philosophical Investigations*, language does not have a "fixed and unequivocal use" (1953, p. 37) at all times and places. Names, thus, do not have fixed meanings but depend on their *use*. This recalls the principle of contingency where things are not determined by prior causes, in the natures of things, but depend on context, and are historical, and hence, in classical parlance, *could have been otherwise*. As Wittgenstein (1953) says:

> the application of a word is not everywhere bounded by rules. ... What does a game look like that is everywhere bounded by rules? Whose rules never let a doubt creep in, but stop up all the cracks where it might? (s. 4, p. 39)

Austin's speech act theory both drew on and further developed a broad system of philosophical pragmatism building on a tradition including William James, Charles Horton Cooley, John Dewey, George Herbert Mead, Charles Sanders Pierce, and Alfred Schultz, all who introduced in different but related ways notions of the relative autonomy of language and the interactional character of self and society.[12]

In this context, it is worth noting the parallel between Foucault's systemic conception of change in discursive and non-discursive assemblages, linked closely to a system of open possibilities or variations, and what is now known as complexity theory. Although having roots in ancient Chinese and Greek thought, versions of complexity theory are a relatively new field of scientific enquiry and are perhaps one of the most notable new developments since the advent of quantum theory in the early 1900s. Such theories are not only compatible with materialism, but are systemic, or holist, in that they account for diversity and unity in the context of a systemic field of complex interactional changes. Chaos theory is one version of complexity. Partly with origins in computing technology, and partly in the development of new non-Euclidean structures of fractal geometrical mathematics, chaos theory became concerned to explain "the qualitative study of unstable aperiodic behaviour in deterministic non-linear dynamical systems" (Sardar & Abrams, 1999, p. 9).[13] It is complexity theory more broadly, however, that has drawn off poststructuralist methods, and establishes them as a form of critical realism.[14]

In the recent history of science, the work of Ilya Prigogine (1980, 1994, 1997, 2003; Prigogine & Stengers, 1984; Prigogine & Nicolis, 1989) has advanced the field of post-quantum complexity analysis at the macroscopic and microscopic levels, based in non-equilibrium physics, linked to the significant work of the Solvay Institutes for Physics and Chemistry. Prigogine received a Nobel Prize in 1977. Like Nietzsche and others before him, he translated the effects of a theory of becoming, based on an Heraclitean idea of ceaseless change, providing a post-quantum understanding of the universe in terms of dimensions of chance, bifurcation, self-organization, unpredictability, uncertainty, chaos, non-equilibrium systems, and change. Prigogine's central contribution was to non-equilibrium statistical mechanics and thermodynamics and the probabilistic analysis of complex systems (2003, pp. 45, 82). His main ideas (expressed non-mathematically) were that "nature leads to unexpected complexity" (p. 8); that "self-organization appears in nature far from equilibrium" (p. VII); that "the universe is evolving" (p. 9); that the messages of Parmenides (that nothing changes) must be replaced by those of Heraclitus (that everything always changes) (pp. 9, 56); that "time is our existential dimension" (p. 9); that "the direction of time is the most fundamental property of the universe" (p. 64); that nothing is predetermined (p. 9); that non-equilibrium, time-irreversibility, and non-integration are features of all systems, including evolution, which is to say that our universe is full of non-linear, irreversible processes (p. 59); that life creates evolution (pp. 61, 65), and that everything is historical (p. 64).[15] Writing at the same time as Foucault, but seemingly unaware of each other's work,[16] he was concerned to analyse *irreversible processes* that generate successively higher levels of organizational complexity, where the complex phenomena are not reducible to the initial states from which they emerged. His work was especially important for understanding changes within open systems,[17] for theorizing time as a real dimension,[18] and for theorizing interconnectedness as a "characteristic feature of nature" (Prigogine, 2003, p. 54).[19] Of especial relevance, his work theorizes the possibilities of chance as the outcome of system contingencies.[20]

In his book *Complexity and Postmodernism*, Paul Cilliers (1998, pp. VIII–IX) defines complexity in the following way:

> In a *complex* system ... the interaction among constituents of the system, and the interaction between the system and its environment, are of such a nature that the system as a whole cannot be fully understood simply by analysing its components. Moreover, these relationships are not fixed, but shift and change, often as a result of self-organisation. This can result in novel features, usually referred to in terms of *emergent properties*.

Cilliers presents a useful contemporary summary and update of complexity research as it has emerged from the early works of Gregory Bateson,[21] Heinz von Foerster,[22] the Macy Conferences,[23] as well as writings of Paul Watzlawick in the 1960s,[24] and Nikolas Luhmann in the 1970s and 1980s.[25] The usefulness of Cilliers's approach is that he presents a distinctly poststructuralist conception of complexity. Poststructuralism, says Cilliers, has introduced a new conception of complexity based on "distributed" or "relational" representation, following Saussure.[26] Such a system is complex in relation to the fact that it has a large number of elements which interact dynamically in a non-linear and asymmetrical manner. Interactions take place in open systems through "self-organization" by adapting dynamically to changes in both the environment and the system. Self-organization is an emergent property of the system as a whole. An emergent property is a property that is constituted due to the combination of elements in the system as a whole. As such it is a property possessed by the system but not by its components.[27] Cilliers (1998, p. 90) defines "self-organization" as "the capacity of complex systems which enables them to develop or change internal structure spontaneously and adaptively in order to cope with or manipulate the environment". Such systems are not in equilibrium because they are constantly changing as a consequence of interaction between system and environment. As well as being influenced by external factors, they are also influenced by the history of the system (1998, p. 66). Cilliers identifies social systems, the economy, the human brain, and language as complex systems.[28]

Hence one could characterize Foucault's conception of societies as "non-equilibrium systems", where no general laws can predict the detailed behaviour of such systems. As what develops does so as a consequence of emergence, life is created as a consequence of the collective interactions of parts. This entails not only the limitless possibility of combinations that can occur in open environments, but also that as the collectivity possesses properties and energies not possessed by the parts, but through which change can take place, new forms and patterns can develop. Relatively small changes in initial conditions can trigger major changes throughout the system, in part or whole. The view of history as pluralist and not accounted for within a context of causal, "iron law" determinism was thus important in Foucault's debt to Nietzsche, and also contributes background to understanding the affinities with complexity theory. Whereas Hegel adopted a totalistic programme of seeking to explain the whole by understanding the interrelations between its component parts, for Foucault the totality always eluded analysis or understanding in terms of a harmonic science of structure, but rather was characterized by *incompleteness, indeterminacy, complexity* and *chance*. This was the core of his nominalism. As Foucault says, "though it is true that these discontinuous discursive series each have, within certain limits, their regularity, it is undoubtedly no longer possible to establish links of mechanical causality or of ideal necessity between the elements which constitute them. We must accept the introduction of the *aléa* [chance] as a category in the production of events" (Foucault, 1981, p. 69).[29] In seeking to characterize the nature of this "pluralism" and how it effects the analysis of discourse as operating through complex laws, Foucault (1978, p. 11) explains how he "substitutes the analysis of different types of transformation for the abstract, general, and monotonous form of "change" in which one so willingly thinks in terms of succession". In this, he seeks to define with the greatest care the transformations which have constituted the change, replacing the general theme of *becoming* by the analysis of the transformations in their specificity, an examination of "the diversity of *systems* and the play of discontinuities into the history of *discourse*" (1978, p. 15).

In this conception, there are many similarities between Foucault and systems theorists such as Nikolas Luhmann (1990, 1995). Although Foucault does not use the language of systems theory, like Luhmann he is committed to a conception of open systems where the parts comprise assemblages (*dispositifs*) of dynamic and contingent relations. Like Luhmann, too, the rejection of foundationalism results in a conception where elements and relations are mutually conditioned, where linear models of causality give way to dynamical models, and where complexity, contingency, risk, and multiple constitution are central features of open environments (Grant, 2007, pp. 109–110). The importance of contingency is central to the work of both theorists, whether as non-repeatability, unpredictability, irreversibility, uncertainty, or relations of contingent dependence. For both, too, as for Bergson, time is represented as a real dimension. "[D]uration is irreversible. ... Each of its moments is something new added to what was before. ... It is no longer *thought*, it is something *lived*" (Bergson, 1998, pp. 6, 10). As with Bergson, "Life ... progresses and *endures* in time" (p. 51).

6 Foucault Contra Habermas: Overcoming Relativism by Adding the Concept of Life

In asserting the inseparability of power from knowledge or discourse, we must be sure to understand wherein the central differences between someone like Foucault and a thinker like Habermas reside. What power/knowledge signals, indeed, is that between these two thinkers is a difference in fundamental philosophical epistemology. Habermas (1984–1987), in seeing communicative action as based on the "force of the better argument", commits himself to a view which sees reason and knowledge as potentially separable from power and history, and is thus, like Kant, an inheritor of the Cartesian tradition which sees the theoretical possibility of excluding distorting aspects, or the insidious affects of *Evil Geniuses*, from the process of knowledge acquisition. For Habermas, then, truth, or reason, serves as a ground or foundation which underpins communication, and which accounts for the coherence or unity of discourse. The model is thoroughly modern. Knowledge in this model is simply the product of "clear and distinct" ideas where all distorting or ideological features are conveniently held at bay. Hence, the knowledge process for Habermas rests on the possibility of achieving truth derived through argumentation or communication, where all distorting effects can be conveniently bracketed or excluded from the process. This also reveals a commitment to certain Hegelian views concerning the possibility of progression in history culminating in the realization of greater objectivity in knowledge as we go toward the Absolute, or in the Habermasian sense, of emancipation.

For Foucault, however, the interlinking of power/knowledge means that there is no assuredness that communication is not itself ideological, and that the so-called "force of the better argument" does not win out based purely on epistemological criteria but is rather justifiable only in relation to power. Not only does power trap truth, through such practices as agenda-setting, controlling processes of inclusion/exclusion, intimidation and bullying, or similar practices, but for Foucault, in an even more profound sense, truth and ideology, communication and distortion, can coexist, and circulate together. The truth can assume certain masks which are themselves ideological. Even worse, more often than not, the so-called truth fails to recognize itself as such, or be able to distinguish itself from ideology. If this is so, then it is impossible to know whether purely communicative action, which fulfils the conditions of the ideal speech situation, has truth as its outcome, or simply conforms to the "fashion" of the day, the outcome that is "preferred" by the most powerful interests, or the "most respectable" view. We are all aware of this happening in our regular day-to-day existences, whether at home or the office. Habermasians have to play "make believe" in the very claim to distinguish the strategic from the communicative.[30]

In Foucault's view, in it is possible to have access to the truth, it will invariably be seen through various distorting lens. For in Foucault's view, Descartes *Evil Genius* is not evacuated by the simple cognisance of what appear like "clear and distinct ideas". Truth and ideology circulate together, as Derrida has famously noted (2001, pp. 36–76). Even more, truth sometimes appears *within* ideology. When this happens, it may be possible to work out the grain of some important truth within the mystifying shell of its ideological representation, but the evidence will be more in the way of "judgement", than through experimental, or direct empirical test.[31] While life's immanent quest for survival and continuance to the future permit certain objective and cross-cultural assessments, the context-relatedness of discourse, and its irreducible contingency mean that the tasks of evaluation and privileging must be through "weighing" or "judging" in both an individual and collective sense.

How, then, is objectivity, or reason, possible? How can a pernicious relativism be avoided? It is only through the multiple voices of competing perspectives in relation to real life forces that objectivity is achieved and a pernicious relativism avoided. The extent and manner of such objectivity will be different in relation to different domains, and different types of claims. In suggesting such an answer we must go beyond Foucault, of course, for he studiously avoided such questions concerning what should we do. As is well known, in his own work he actively dissented from undertaking normative types of enquiry, preferring to confine himself to genealogies of power investigating historical forms of rationality around sexuality, discipline, governmentality and morality. Partly his objections to undertaking normative studies in an academic sense were associated to his dislike of acting as an "advice giver" by advising people what to do. For Foucault the two were closely associated. As he told Foulek Ringelheim in December of 1983: "I have always insisted on not playing the role of the prophet intellectual who tells people in advance what they must do" (Foucault, 1989c, p. 424).

My own answer to the problem of normativity in Foucault seeks a basis for politics and communication by appeal to a philosophy of life. This is one of my concerns in my book *Toward a Global Thin Community: Nietzsche, Foucault, and the Cosmopolitan Commitment* (Olssen, 2009, chapter 6) where I maintain that the problems associated with contextualism, such as relativism and solipsism, are overcome in part at least once one considers the immanent forces of life which works in and through discourse.[32] The concept of life, on which Foucault wrote on several occasions, generates immanent forces to survive and continue, and achieve well-being and introduces a normative force which can salvage a certain conception of objectivity and the good, and can thus function as a constructed and variable ground for a politics of hope and a politics of the future. It is life which "endures in time", as Bergson (1998, p. 51) stated, and which modulates itself contingently in different times and places through a multiplicity of perspectives. At the individual level this is what supports egoism; at the societal level, it motivates a concern for the public good. Although some may argue that this is so obvious as to not need stating, the recognition that life itself is defined by its immanent quest to survive and continue, without presupposing any vital force or entelechy, enables a greater awareness of why we act in certain ways, and why we make the judgements we do. Such forces, which vary in different contexts in relation to different constellational imperatives, are in the varying ways they express themselves semantic, semiotic, syntactical, and pragmatic.[33]

The concept of life, thus, potentially helps resolve the impasse associated with normativity in Foucault. It can thus help him to answer the Habermasian challenge. The Habermasian critic can quite rightly ask how Foucault can justify one set of choices or criteria, or practices of self, over others. If not through the "force of the better argument", then what? Foucault can answer, "It is for life". It is always an estimation of the best life in the best circumstances. In this way, life can partially answer the question as to what the "better argument" is better for. While there is no rationally single right way to act; there are, however, many different ways that better enable life to survive and continue. This is why the committee was constituted as it was; this is why the prisoner was denied bail; this is why the teacher was sacked because he was a menace to the continuance and survival of the school children. The only answer that we can give to what is right and proper is that which enables life to best survive and continue in contingent circumstances. The abstractness and generality of the concept constitute its strength. That certain maxims might be applicable time and time again, or generally useful or relevant, as Kant argued was the case universally, is countered when contingent circumstances make the general rule redundant or ridiculous. The answer always is: because life could not best be continued under those circumstances. Or because life could not be fairly continued under conditions which respect the dignity and integrity of each element; i.e., which give to each element its due consideration. Continuance then is what the judge appeals to when she proscribes for the general good; it is what the politician appeals to when she proscribes policy; or it is what the foreign secretary appeals to when she says what the country intends to do. It is always at the base of our judgments when we say, "That is not right!" For by "right" we mean here adequate to the appropriate functioning between the part(s) and the whole; that is, adequate to how each individual human agent ought to act in relation to their community, or nation, or to the global polis. Why is this notion, which applies to both public and private actions, important? Because the idea that life has an immanent force for continuance enables us to explain behaviours in all times and places in a way that is both beyond social convention and historical relativism. In this sense, it serves to reconcile the universal and the particular, but in a way that is distinctively nominalist. Indeed, as we can plausibly argue that what is really best for the continuance of all can be (more or less) objectively ascertained—in terms of nutrition, health, security, or liberty—we can go a certain way to defeating the subjectivist in ethics.[34] To go even further, we can say that the extent to which an individual's actions correlate with what is in the interests of the survival and continuance of all could possibly be adjudged to constitute a basis for a theory of ethics, as well as politics.[35]

This is going well beyond Foucault as he developed his position, of course. Although Foucault rejected the role of "advice giver" and showed no interest in serious normative enquiry himself, there are evident normative assumptions that do operate within his work and which manifest themselves quite readily if one looks for them. Certainly, Foucault left these "buried", as if the reader may not notice, but certain assumptions operate nevertheless. In his "uncommon view of Michel Foucault", James Johnson (1999) notes how egalitarian assumptions about power reveal themselves through his major work *Discipline and Punish* (Foucault, 1977). Foucault implicitly assumes throughout *Discipline and Punish*, for instance, that an absence of reciprocity and symmetry of power relations is what characterizes oppressive structures, or "states of domination". He talks about power relations that are "asymmetrical" and "non-reciprocal", and "incapable of reversibility", in many of his works. He also speaks of "states of domination", which might seem to imply that some state of liberation just might be possible (see Foucault, 1991, p. 3).

The existence of latent normative assumptions in Foucault's work should not surprise us, as it is indeed epistemologically and ethically difficult to undertake critical historical enquiries, of the sort Foucault does, and not to presuppose, if even only as an absent presence, some sort of normative vision. In his political activism Foucault revealed his political and ethical commitments as recounted in nearly every interview he did. In a sense, it is because power factors are always co-present in knowledge processes that, from the perspective of normative politics, an equality of power in society and globally could be seen as the best strategy to maximize the possibility of ensuring the "best" outcome overall. Hence, the view that Foucault is committed to a rough equality of agonistic social and political relations clearly seems warranted by his thesis of the irremovability of power from epistemological processes. So, while Foucault may well support the communicative speech situation, he does not see the force of the better argument as the inevitable outcome, or that the advantages are in relation to truth. It may lead to a possible rapprochement over Habermas's concept of *Diskurs*, if interpreted pragmatically, i.e., not as a form of intersubjective communication subtended by norms of truth, but where consent is produced from differences and conflict through a mutual exchange of different viewpoints. Such an exchange, in that it facilitates the ongoing continuance and survival of the project that is life, and hence is related to a conception of the good for mankind, could indeed be termed rational in that particular sense. For Foucault, the idea of consensus, although not a "regulative principle", was a "critical idea to maintain at all times" (Foucault, 1984, p. 379). For policymakers, in Foucault's view, the degree of "nonconsensuality" is related to the broader issue of the distribution of power in terms of its symmetry and reciprocity.

Given this situation, the question that must be asked is whether there is any way out for Foucault? To postulate further is inevitably to go even further beyond Foucault, although I would claim that the seeds of his own alternative approach to Habermas are already latent within his general approach. For Foucault it would be necessary to ask, as I have suggested above, what the better argument was better *for*. The idea that there exists some "pure rationality" independent of particular ends or goals, pace Habermas, is for Foucault akin to the positivist dream of a pure observation language. Reasons always have to be relative to an *end* or *goal* which must be specified. This is not a teleology, but a constructivism. It can never be assumed in advance to define the process or outcome of a dialogic encounter, however. The "best" outcome is perhaps one that "suits" all parties, and gives them a stake in the future, enables them *to continue life*. Certainly this answer would be consistent with Nietzsche's emphasis on *life*. The outcome is not assured solely with relation to truth, but "suitable", "warranted" and the "best estimate" within the current configuration of life and discourse, in relation to life or survival.

Central to such a conception of the normative is, consistent with Foucault's analysis, an analysis that enquires into the minimal conditions for mutual coexistence, survival and well-being as a future strategy given the conditions of the present. It will involve an analysis that does not seek, as previous approaches have sought to do, timeless values or rules which constitute the truth of the human being. It does not assume an ideal communicative context either. Rather, starting from the present, it asks instead, given the impossibility of knowing any truth in any ultimate sense, or working out what the better argument is in a way that is certain, how can human continuance be constructed in our present horizon under conditions that are fair to all. Consistent with Nietzsche, Heidegger, and Foucault, such a commitment to continue, to survive, to achieve well-being, would be seen not as grounded in a fixed conception of nature (*conatus*), but represented simply as a decision based upon a *will to survive*. In this situation, the "better argument" is simply that which best assures our future under the horizon of the present. The case for a conception of fairness and equality in this sense is based purely upon the negative argument that no one has any greater justification to privilege, at least in a fundamental moral sense, than anyone else.

Acknowledgement

This chapter originally appeared as Olssen, M. (2014), Discourse, complexity, normativity: Tracing the elaboration of Foucault's materialist concept of discourse, *Open Review of Educational Research*, 1(1), 28–55, https://doi.org/10.1080/23265507.2014.964296. Reprinted here, with minor edits, with permission from the publisher.

Notes

1 The concept of "episteme" which Foucault used in *The Order of Things*, was not used in his later studies, and it is noteworthy that it is not mentioned in *The Archaeology of Knowledge*. For Foucault, the episteme referred to deeper structures of thought that gave unity to the various discursive systems of a particular era. In his review of *The Archaeology*, Dominique Lecourt (1970) sees abandonment of the use of the concept as a positive step forward, consistent with Foucault's concern to become more materialist, for concepts such as "historical a priori", "discursive practice" and "archive", which Foucault began to use instead, have a more direct empirical reference to the historicity and materiality of the discursive order, in that they imply links with institutions, as well as economic and political processes. However, the new concepts, like that of episteme, effectively performed a crucial similar function for Foucault in that they similarly resisted transcendental imputation.
2 This statement was made by Foucault (1989b) to François Ewald first published in *Magazine Littéraire*, May 1984.
3 This statement was made by Foucault (1991) on 20 January 1984 in an interview with Raul Fornet-Betancourt, Helmut Becker, and Alfredo Gomez-Muller.
4 To consider how Foucault theorizes the agency of the subject would require a consideration of his writings on life, which is both parasitic on, and productive of discourse. See Olssen (2009, especially chapter 5).
5 The classification reads: "(a) belonging to the Emperor; (b) embalmed, (c) tame, (d) sucking pigs, (e) sirens, (g) fabulous, (f) fabulous, (h) stray dogs, (i) frenzied, (j) innumerable, (k) drawn with a very fine camelhair brush, (l) etcetera, (m) having just broken the water pitcher, (n) that from a long way off look like flies" (1970, p. xv). Foucault says, "[t]he fundamental codes of a culture—those governing its language, its schemas of perception, its exchanges, its techniques, its values, the hierarchy of its practices—establish for every man, from the very first, the empirical orders with which he will be dealing and within which he will be at home" (1970, p. xx).
6 The point of this figure is both to graphically represent the duality of systems in terms of which discourse operates in relation to the world. Hence, while he recognizes a "superabundance of signifiers", to use a term from Levi-Strauss, which permits signifiers endless creativity, signification operates both in relation to the historical system of concepts and discursive structures as well as real-world practices, which also permit endless discursive strategies in relation to real-world events.
7 Complexity theory, so-called, encompasses a broad alignment of different approaches which will be elaborated further later.
8 Foucault was, of course, indebted to Wittgenstein, especially for his use of the concept of "game".
9 I have in mind the *Philosophical Investigation*, and not the *Tractatus*, or the *Philosophical Grammar*.
10 Although meaning systems are public, the agent can be seen as active and volitional in relation to the fact that life is independent of the discursive, and appropriates, utilizes, and manipulates existing discursive options specific to the concerns and purposes of life in particular times and places. Unlike the systems theorists, for Foucault the structures of life, labour and language operate in history as coterminous with the environment.
11 Austin's key distinction was between "locutionary acts", "illocutionary acts" (which are performative), and "perlocutionary" effects of actions (which are also performative).

12 The possible list could be extended, and could include systems theorists like Luhmann, as well as writers like Garfinkel (1989), Bakhtin (1998), Putnam (1997), and many more.
13 For other accounts of chaos theory, see Swinney (1983), Holden (1985), Gleick (1987), Sappington (1990), Ayers (1997).
14 Chaos theory and complexity theories are distinct although chaos theory can be seen as one type of complexity theory, which emphasizes the importance of sensitivity to initial conditions. This is not so important with complex systems in general, which stresses the interaction of a large number of components (see Cilliers, 1998, p. ix).
15 Prigogine mostly applies these ideas to physical systems but does sometimes demonstrate their applicability to the social and human world. Discussing his theories of time and irreversibility, he notes how they apply potentially to all events (e.g., "a marriage is an irreversible event" [2003, p. 67]). The consequence of irreversibility is that "it leads to probabilistic descriptions, which cannot be reduced to individual trajectories or wave functions corresponding to Newtonian or Quantum mechanics" (p. 75).
16 Prigogine's publications date from 1964 until shortly before his death in 2003.
17 This involves a different description at the level of physics of elementary processes and a reversal of classical physics which saw systems as integrable, leading to determinism, and premised on time reversibility and equilibrium (as from Newton to Poincaré). Prigogine's approach replaces classical and Quantum mechanics in a concern for thermodynamics and probability and emphasizes variables such as noise, stochasticity, irreversibility. Such an approach suggests distinct limits to reductionism. It amounts to a different conception of reality, giving a different account of the emergence of events.
18 In this, he differs from Einstein who saw time as an illusion, as well as from classical mechanics. He acknowledges debts to Bergson (Prigogine, 2003, pp. 19–20); to Heidegger (Prigogine, 2003, p. 9), and to Heraclitus (Prigogine, 2003, pp. 9, 10). Time is seen as a real dimension which endures, and the universe is evolving. Foucault's Nietzschean view of history is highly compatible with this.
19 Interconnectedness means that "individualities emerge from the global" and counters the idea that "evolution is independent of environment" (Prigogine, 2003, p. 54).
20 Pomian (1990) discusses issues such as determinism and chance in relation to Prigogine's work. Also see Prigogine (1997).
21 See Bateson (1972).
22 See Foerster (1984, 2003).
23 The Macy Conferences spanned 1945–1954, and five proceedings were published. See Foerster, Mead, and Teuber (1949–1955). Also see Wiener (1948) and Heims (1991).
24 See Watzlawick et al. (1967).
25 See Luhmann (1990, 1995).
26 Meaning is conferred not by one-to-one correspondence with the world but by relationships between structural components of the system. See Cilliers (1998, p. 81). His analysis of poststructural complexity is based on Saussure's well-known analysis in the *Course in General Linguistics* (1974). Having said this, it is interesting that Cilliers translates poststructural philosophy into Western analytic schemas rather than elaborate his thesis in relation to difference theory as elaborated by Foucault or Deleuze. I have done the same here simply to convey something of the tenor of the poststructural innovation.
27 For other forms of emergentist materialism in Western thought, see Bunge (1977), Haken (1977, 1990), Rapp et al. (1986) or Skarda and Freeman (1990). Although such theories are broadly analogous to Foucault's materialism, the emphasis in poststructuralism on the open and incomplete character of the totality presents new insights into issues like determination and chance. Again, see Cilliers (1998).

28 For another view of complexity theory, see Kauffman (1991, 1993, 1995). Kauffman suggests that while events can be seen as having antecedent conditions which explain them, in open environments the possible combinations are unpredictable. Other characteristics of complex systems are that they do not operate near equilibrium; the relationships between components are non-linear and dynamic; elements do not have fixed positions; the relationships between elements are not stable; and there are always more possibilities than can be actualized.

29 In his review of two of Deleuze's books, Foucault (1998b, p. 366) reinforces the importance of chance: "The present as the recurrence of difference, as repetition giving voice to difference, affirms at once the totality of chance. The univocity of being in Duns Scotus led to the immobility of an abstraction, in Spinoza it led to the necessity and eternity of substance; but here it leads to the single throw of chance in the fissure of the present. If being always declares itself in the same way, it is not because being is one but because the totality of chance is affirmed in the single dice throw of the present".

30 This can be applied to the traditional context of policymaking, of course. For example, how is it possible when seeking, for instance, to try to decide the case for humanitarian intervention in, say, Kosovo, for the Habermasian to differentiate communicative from political criteria over such issues as who shall be included and excluded from the negotiating process, or, what matters should be eligible for inclusion on the agenda for determination, and which will not, and so on?

31 As in the model of a "fable", when it is said, for instance, that there is a "grain" of truth in it.

32 The concept of "Labour, Life and Language" famously denotes Foucault's tripartite ontology (see Foucault, 1970, chapter 8). For specific writings on the concept of life, see Foucault (1980, 1998a).

33 Thus there is no irreducible semantic core which operates consistently in all times and places, as for instance in the model advanced by Cappelen and Lepore (2005). However, common material necessities will undoubtedly be recognizable beyond the culturally specific forms of their articulation.

34 This is a well-known tradition in Anglo-American philosophy. See, for instance, Mackie (1977).

35 Lest I be accused of being Hegelian here, although the shadow of continuance goes before us in the sense of being immanent in everything we do, and why we do it, and also links individuals to the whole, at ever-increasing expanding circles, continuance is not the absolute idea, or progressive toward any predefined telos.

References

Austin, J. L. (1962). *How to do things with words*. Clarendon Press.
Ayers, S. (1997). The application of chaos theory to psychology. *Theory and Psychology*, 7(3), 373–398.
Bakhtin, M. M. (1998). *The dialogic imagination: Four essays* (C. Emerson & M. Holquist, Trans.; M. Holquist, Ed.). University of Texas Press.
Barrett, M. (1988). *The politics of truth*. Polity.
Bateson, G. (1972). *Steps to an ecology of mind*. Ballantine.
Bergson, H. (1998). *Creative evolution*. Dover.

Bunge, M. (1977). Emergence and the mind: Commentary. *Neuroscience, 2*, 501–509.
Cappelen, H., & Lepore, E. (2005). *Insensitive semantics: A defence of semantic minimalism and speech act pluralism*. Blackwell.
Cilliers, P. (1998). *Complexity and postmodernism: Understanding complex systems*. Routledge.
Davidson, A. I. (1986). Archaeology, genealogy, ethics. In D. Couzens Hoy (Ed.), *Foucault: A critical reader* (pp. 221–234). Blackwell.
Davidson, A. I. (Ed.). (1997). *Foucault and his interlocutors*. University of Chicago Press.
Deleuze, G. (1986). *Foucault* (S. Hand, Trans.). University of Minnesota Press.
Deleuze, G. (2004). *The logic of sense*. Continuum.
Derrida, J. (2001). Cogito and the history of madness. In J. Derrida (Ed.), *Writing and difference* (pp. 36–76). Routledge.
Dreyfus, H. L., & Rabinow, P. (1983). *Michel Foucault: Beyond structuralism and hermeneutics* (2nd ed.). University of Chicago Press. (With an afterword and interview with Michel Foucault)
Faubion, J. (2004). General introduction. In M. Foucault (Ed.), *Death and the labyrinth* (pp. vii–xxii). Continuum.
Foerster, H. von. (1984). *Observing systems* (2nd ed.). Intersystems Publications.
Foerster, H. von. (2003). *Understanding understanding: Essays on cybernetics and cognition*. Springer.
Foerster, H. von, Mead, M., & Teuber, H. L. (Eds.). (1949–1954). *Cybernetics: Circular causal and feedback mechanisms in biological and social systems* (Vols. 6–10). Josiah Macy Jr Foundation.
Foucault, M. (1970). *The order of things*. Random House.
Foucault, M. (1972). *The archaeology of knowledge* (A. Sheridan, Trans.). Tavistock.
Foucault, M. (1977). *Discipline and punish: The birth of the prison* (A. Sheridan, Trans.). Pantheon.
Foucault, M. (1978). Politics and the study of discourse (C. Gordon, Trans.). *Ideology and Consciousness, 3*(Spring), 7–26.
Foucault, M. (1980). Georges Canguilhem: Philosopher of error (G. Burchell, Trans.). *Ideology & Consciousness, 7*(Autumn), 51–62.
Foucault, M. (1981). The order of discourse (I. McLeod, Trans.). In R. Young (Ed.), *Untying the text: A post-structuralist reader* (pp. 48–78). Routledge & Kegan Paul.
Foucault, M. (1983). Structuralism and poststructuralism: An interview with Michel Foucault (with G. Raulet). *Telos, 55*, 195–211.
Foucault, M. (1984). Politics and ethics: An interview (C. Porter, Trans.). In P. Rabinow (Ed.), *The Foucault reader* (pp. 373–380). Pantheon.
Foucault, M. (1989a). The discourse of history. In S. Lotringer (Ed.), *Foucault live: Interviews, 1966–1984* (pp. 11–34). Semiotex(e).

Foucault, M. (1989b). Concern for truth. In S. Lotringer (Ed.), *Foucault live: Interviews, 1966–1984* (J. Johnston, Trans., pp. 455–464). Semiotext(e).

Foucault, M. (1989c). What calls for punishment? In S. Lotringer (Ed.), *Foucault live: Interviews, 1966–1984* (pp. 423–431). Semiotext(e).

Foucault, M. (1991). The ethic of care for the self as a practice of freedom: An interview (J. D. Gauthier, Trans.). In J. Bernauer & D. Rasmussen (Eds.), *The final Foucault* (pp. 1–20). MIT Press.

Foucault, M. (1994a). *Dits et écrits: 1954–1988* (D. Defert & F. Ewald, Eds., with J. Lagrange; 4 Vols.). Éditions Gallimard.

Foucault, M. (1994b). La philosophie analytique de la politique. In D. Defert & F. Ewald (Eds.) with J. Lagrange, *Dits et écrits, 1954–1988* (4 Vols., Vol. 3, No. 232, pp. 534–551). Éditions Gallimard.

Foucault, M. (1994c). Linguistique et sciences sociales. In D. Defert & F. Ewald (Eds.) with J. Lagrange, *Dits et écrits: 1954–1988* (4 Vols, Vol. 1, No. 70, pp. 821–842). Éditions Gallimard.

Foucault, M. (1997a). *The politics of truth* (S. Lotringer & L. Hochroth, Eds.). Semiotext(e).

Foucault, M. (1997b). On the genealogy of ethics: An overview of work in progress. In P. Rabinow (Ed.), *Essential works of Foucault, 1954–1984, vol. 1: Ethics* (pp. 253–280). Penguin.

Foucault, M. (1998a). Life, experience, science. In J. D. Faubion (Ed.), *Essential works of Foucault, 1954–1984, vol. 2: Aesthetics, method, epistemology* (pp. 465–478). Penguin.

Foucault, M. (1998b). Theatrum philosophicum. In J. D. Faubion (Ed.), *Essential works of Foucault, 1954–1984, vol. 2: Aesthetics, method, epistemology* (pp. 343–368). Penguin.

Frank, M. (1992). On Foucault's concept of discourse. In T. J. Armstrong (Ed. and Trans.), *Michel Foucault: Philosopher* (pp. 99–116). Harvester Wheatsheaf.

Garfinkel, H. (1989). *Studies in ethnomethodogy*. Polity.

Gleick, J. (1987). *Chaos: Making a new science*. Abacus.

Gottdiener, M. (1995). *Postmodern semiotics: Material culture and forms of postmodern life*. Basil Blackwell.

Grant, C. B. (2007). *Uncertainty and communication: New theoretical investigations*. Palgrave/Macmillan.

Grant, C. B. (Ed.). (2010). *Beyond universal pragmatics: Studies in the philosophy of communication*. Peter Lang.

Habermas, J. (1984–1987). *The theory of communicative action* (T. McCarthy, Trans.; 2 Vols.). Beacon.

Hacking, I. (2002). *Historical ontology*. Harvard University Press.

Haken, H. (1977). *Synergetics: An introduction*. Springer.

Haken, H. (1990). Synergetics as a tool for the conceptualization and mathematization of cognition and behaviour: How far can we go? In H. Haken & M. Stadler (Eds.), *Synergetics of cognition* (pp. 2–31). Springer.

Heims, S. J. (1991). *The cybernetics group*. MIT Press.

Holden, A. (1985). Chaos is no longer a dirty word. *New Scientist, 106*(1453), 12–15.

Johnson, J. (1999). Communication, criticism, and the postmodern consensus: An unfashionable interpretation of Michel Foucault. *Political Theory, 25*(4), 559–583. https://doi.org/10.1177/0090591797025004004

Kauffman, S. A. (1991, August). Antichaos and adaptation. *Scientific American*, pp. 64–70.

Kauffman, S. A. (1993). *The origins of order: Self-organisation and selection in evolution*. Oxford University Press.

Kauffman, S. A. (1995). *At home in the universe: The search for laws of complexity*. Viking Press.

Larmore, C. (1981). The concept of a constitutive subject. In C. McCabe (Ed.), *The talking cure* (pp. ?–?). Macmillan.

Lecourt, D. (1970). Sur l'archaéology du savoir. *La pensée, 152*, 69–78.

Luhmann, N. (1990). The cognitive program of constructivism and a reality that remains unknown. In W. Krohn, G. Kuppers, & H. Nowotny (Eds.), *Selforganization: Portrait of a scientific revolution* (pp. 64–85). Kluwer.

Luhmann, N. (1995). *Social systems* (J. Bednarz Jr., with D. Baecker, Trans.). Stanford University Press.

Machado, R. (1992). Archaeology and epistemology. In. J. Armstrong (Ed. and Trans.), *Michel Foucault: Philosopher* (pp. 3–19). Harvester Wheatsheaf.

Mackie, J. L. (1977). *Ethics: Inventing right and wrong*. Penguin.

May, T. (1997). *Reconsidering difference: Nancy, Derrida, Levinas, and Deleuze*. Pennsylvania State University Press.

Minson, J. (1985). *Genealogies of morals*. St Martin's Press.

Olssen, M. (2009). *Toward a global thin community: Nietzsche, Foucault, and the cosmopolitan commitment*. Paradigm.

Pomian, K. (Ed.). (1990). *La querelle du determinisme. Philosophie de la science aujourd'hui*. Gallimard/Le Debat.

Poster, M. (1984). *Foucault, Marxism, history: Mode of production vs mode of information*. Polity.

Prigogine, I. (1980). *From being to becoming*. W. H. Freeman and Co.

Prigogine, I. (1994). *Time, chaos and the laws of chaos*. Ed. Progress.

Prigogine, I. (1997). *The end of certainty: Time, chaos and the new laws of nature*. The Free Press.

Prigogine, I. (2003). *Is future given?*. World Scientific.

Prigogine, I., & Nicolis, G. (1989). *Exploring complexity*. W. H. Freeman and Co.

Prigogine, I., & Stengers, I. (1984). *Order out of chaos*. Bantam.

Putnam, H. (1997). *Mind, language, reality, volume 2: Philosophical papers*. Cambridge University Press.

Rapp, P. E., Zimmerman, I. D., Albano, A. M., DeGuzman, G. C., Greenbaun, N. N., & Bashore, T. R. (1986). Experimental studies of chaotic neural behaviour: Cellular activity and electroencephalographic signals. In H. G. Othmer (Ed.), *Nonlinear oscillations in biology and chemistry* (pp. 175–205). Springer.

Sappington, A. A. (1990). Recent psychological approaches to the free will versus determinism issue. *Psychological Bulletin, 108*, 19–29.

Sardar, Z., & Abrams, I. (1999). *Introducing chaos*. Icon Books.

Saussure, F. de. (1974). *Course in general linguistics*. Fontana.

Schatzki, T. R. (2001a). Practice mind-ed orders. In T. R. Schatzki, K. Knorr Cetina, & E. von Savigny (Eds.), *The practice turn in contemporary theory* (pp. 42–55). Routledge.

Schatzki, T. R. (2001b). Introduction: Practice theory. In T. R. Schatzki, K. Knorr Cetina, & E. von Savigny (Eds.), *The practice turn in contemporary theory* (pp. 1–14). Routledge.

Searle, J. R. (1969). *Speech acts: An essay in the philosophy of language*. Cambridge University Press.

Searle, J. R. (1995). *The construction of social realty*. Penguin.

Skarda, C. A., & Freeman, W. J. (1990). Chaos and the new science of the brain. *Concepts in Neuroscience, 1*, 275–285.

Smart, B. (1985). *Michel Foucault*. Routledge.

Swinney, H. L. (1983). Observations of order and chaos in nonlinear systems. *Physica, 7*, 3–15.

Watzlawick, P., Bavelas, J. B., & Jackson, D. D. (1967). *Pragmatics of human communication: A study of interactional patterns, pathologies, and paradoxes*. Norton.

Wiener, N. (1948). *Cybernetics; or, control and communication in the animal and machine*. MIT Press.

Wittgenstein, L. (1953). *Philosophical investigations* (3rd ed.; G. E. M. Anscombe, Trans.). Blackwell.

PART 2

Foucault, Marx, Hegel

CHAPTER 3

Foucault and Marxism
Rewriting the Theory of Historical Materialism

Abstract

This article explores the relationship of Foucault to Marxism. Although he was often critical of Marxism, Foucault's own approach bears striking parallels to Marxism, as a form of method, as an account of history, and as an analysis of social structure. Like Marxism, Foucault represents social practices as transitory and all knowledge and intellectual formations as linked to social relations and power. In this he asserts the historical relativity of all systems and structures—of society, of thought, of theory and of concepts, while at the same time not denying a materialism of physical necessities. Yet while Foucault's approach reveals these important similarities to Marxism, the differences, claims the author, are fundamental. These concern his rejection of Hegel's conceptions of history and society as a unified developing totality, his rejection of essences and teleology, and his rejection of any utopian impulse revolving around the laws of economic development or the role of the proletariat in history. Foucault's own conception of change, in fact, is represented in ways that are altogether different to Marx's approach, and ultimately supports localistic forms of resistance and specific forms of democratic incrementalism, rather than revolutionary or totalistic strategies as the basis of transforming society.

1 Introduction

> Gérard Raulet: "But does this reference ... mean that, in a certain way, Marx is at work in your own methodology?" Michel Foucault: "Yes, absolutely". (Foucault, 1988, p. 46)

> I have never been a Freudian, I have never been a Marxist, and I have never been a structuralist. (Foucault, 1988, p. 22)

This article explores the relationship of Foucault to Marxism. Although he was often critical of Marxism, Foucault's own approach bears striking parallels to Marxism, as a form of method, as an account of history, and as an analysis of social structure. If Foucault's worldly poststructuralism can be represented, as Poster (1984), Rabinow (1984), and I (Olssen, 1999) have argued, as a form of both historical and materialist analysis, the questions I will start this article with are, how does Foucault's form of historical materialism differ from that of Marx, and, to the extent he does differ, what alternative conceptions does he embrace?

2   Marxist Preliminaries: A Brief Summation

> Marx's economic discourse comes under the rules of formation of the scientific discourses that were peculiar to the nineteenth century. ... Marxist economics—through its basic concepts and the general rules of its discourse—belongs to a type of discursive formation that was defined around the time of Ricardo. (Foucault, 2001, p. 269)

In the Marxist conception of historical materialism, discourse is represented as part of the superstructure which is split from material practice (the economic base) and subordinated to it. In the same way, the mental operations of consciousness are represented as derivative from the material base of society. The most famous expression of Marx's conception is from the Preface of *A Contribution to the Critique of Political Economy* (1904, pp. 11–12):

> In the social production which men carry on they enter into definite relations that are indispensable and independent of their will; these relations of production correspond to a definite stage of development of their material powers of production. The sum total of these relations of production constitutes the economic structure of society—the real foundation, on which rise legal and political superstructures and to which correspond definite forms of social consciousness. The mode of production in material life determines the general character of the social, political and spiritual processes of life. It is not the consciousness of men that determines their existence, but on the contrary, their social existence determines their consciousness. At a certain stage of their development, the material forces of production in society come in conflict with the existing relations of production, or—what is but a legal expression for the same thing—with the property relations within which they had been at work before. From forms of development of the forces of production these relations turn into their fetters. Then comes a period of social revolution. With the change of the economic foundation the entire immense superstructure is more or less rapidly transformed. In considering such transformations the distinction should always be made between

> the material transformation of the economic conditions of production which can be determined with the precision of natural science, and the legal, political, religious, aesthetic, or philosophic—in short, ideological forms in which men become conscious of this conflict and fight it out. ... No social order ever disappears before all the productive forces, for which there is room in it, have been developed; and new higher relations of production never appear before the conditions of their existence have matured in the womb of the old society. Therefore, mankind always takes up only such problems as it can solve; since, looking at the matter more closely, we will always find that the problem itself arises only when the material conditions necessary for its solution already exist or are at least in the process of formation.

That Marx's formulation led to charges of economic determinism is evident from the political debates of his own day. Joseph Bloch had levelled such a charge, and in replying to Bloch's accusations in 1890 Engels (1978, pp. 760–761) sought to defend Marx's conception:

> According to the materialist conception of history, the ultimately determining element in history is the production and reproduction of real life. More than this neither Marx nor I have ever asserted. Hence if somebody twists this into saying that the economic element is the only determining one, he transforms that proposition into a meaningless, abstract, senseless phrase. The economic situation is the basis, but the various elements of the superstructure: political forms of the class struggle and its results, to wit: constitutions established by the victorious class after a successful battle, etc., juridical forms, and then even the reflexes of all these actual struggles in the brains of the participants, political, juristic, philosophical theories, religious views and their further development into systems of dogmas, also exercise their influence upon the course of the historical struggles and in many cases preponderate in determining their form. There is an interaction of all these elements in which, amid all the endless host of accidents ... the economic movement finally asserts itself as necessary.

In the 20th century one of the central issues addressed by Western Marxists has been an attempted resolution and reconceptualisation of the nature of the relation between the economic base and the cultural superstructure of society. In the classical Marxist model both the character of a society's culture and institutions, as well as the direction set for its future development, are determined by the nature of the economic base, which can be defined as the mode of production at a certain stage of development (Williams, 1980, p. 33).

The simplest nature of this relation, as Williams (1980, p. 33) tells us, was one of "the reflection, the imitation, or the reproduction of the reality of the base in the superstructure in a more or less direct way"; that is, a relation in which the economic base and specifically the forces of production constituted the ultimate *cause* to which the social, legal and political framework of the society can be traced back.

In the attempt to reformulate Marxism in the 20th century the economic determinist conception was challenged by those who saw Marxism as granting rather more "independence" or "autonomy" to the superstructures of society. Hence a "dialectical" notion of the relation was stressed, suggesting a relation of reciprocal influence. It was argued that, although the base *conditions* and *affects* the superstructure, it is in turn *conditioned* and *affected* by it. In all cases, however, in order to remain as Marxists, the ultimate priority of the economic base as the causal determinant of the social character of a society was safeguarded by maintaining that the economic factor is "determining in the last instance". Hence, it was maintained that the superstructure had only a "relative autonomy", and the theory of "relative autonomy", as a shorthand designation of the base–superstructure relation, became a central concept of 20th-century Marxism.

There were, of course, other attempted formulations of the process of determination and of the relations or mode of interaction between economic and cultural phenomena in a society. Some of these sought to replace, or go beyond, the topographical metaphor of base and superstructure with its suggestion of a definite dichotomous spatial relationship, and conceptualise the issue of determination in altogether different ways. In his own summary of the qualifications and amendments introduced by 20th-century Marxists, usually claiming to clarify Marx's true and original intentions, Williams (1980, pp. 32–33) points out that:

> The first kind of qualification had to do with delays in time, with complications, and with certain direct or relatively distant relationships. ... The second stage was related but more fundamental in that the process of the relationship itself was more substantially looked at. This was the kind of reconsideration which gave rise to the notion of "mediation", in which something more than simple reflection or reproduction—indeed something radically different from either reflection or reproduction—actually occurs. In the later twentieth century there is the notion of "homologous structures", where there may be no direct or easily apparent similarity,

and certainly nothing like reflection or reproduction, between the superstructural process and the reality of the base, but in which there is an essential homology or correspondence of structures, which can be discovered by analysis. This is not the same notion as "mediation", but it is the same kind of amendment in that the relationship between the base and the superstructure is not supposed to be direct, nor simply operationally subject to lags and complications and indirectnesses, but that of its nature it is not direct reproduction.

In his own attempted reformulation, Williams (1980, p. 34) argues that:

> We have to revalue "determination" towards the setting of limits and the exertion of pressure and away from a predicted, prefigured and controlled content. We have to revalue "superstructure" towards a related range of cultural practices, and away from a reflected, reproduced or specifically dependent content. And, crucially, we have to revalue "the base" away from the notion of a fixed economic or technological abstraction, and towards the specific activities of men in real social and economic relationships, containing fundamental contradictions and variations and therefore always in a state of dynamic process.

Notions of "totality" (associated with Lukács), or of "hegemony" (associated with Gramsci), or of society as a "complex whole" (associated with Althusser), constitute attempts to move beyond simple dichotomous models of base and superstructure. In Althusser's conception, the social structure, represented as a "complex whole structured in dominance" is characterised by a series of *levels of practices*, including the level of science or theoretical practice, the level of ideological practice, the level of political practice, and the level of economic practice. Althusser argues for the *primacy of practice* "by showing that all the levels of social existence are the sites of distinct practices" (Althusser, 1970, p. 58) and claims that Marx's achievement was to found "a historico-dialectical materialism of praxis: that is ... a theory of the different specific *levels* of *human practice*" (Althusser, 1969, p. 169; emphasis in original).

The determination of events and processes was theorised using the concept of *overdetermination*, a concept which Althusser borrowed from Freud, and which indicates a process of the *complex* and *multiple causation* of events whereby a causal contribution is made by all of the levels, the relative importance of any level in any particular instance varying according to time and place. Theorised in this way, Althusser argues that the non-economic practices have a *specific effectivity* which means that they are determining as well as determined, just as economic practices are determining as well as determined. What it also means is that every aspect or part contributes in its own right to determining the character of the overall whole of which it is a part, as well as being shaped by it in turn. In the same way, rather than characterising contradictions as singularly concerned with the economic forces and relations of production, there is in Althusser's conception a multiplicity of contradictions occurring at all levels of the social formation. In this sense, determination is never simple, but rather, complex and multiple. Again, however, in order to retain his link to Marxism, and to differentiate his own theory of social structure from non-Marxist theories of systems functionalism, Althusser argues that economic practice is fundamental and is "determining in the last instance". Although the economy is "determining in the last instance", it is not always the dominant structure, however. The apparent paradox is explained because the economy determines which of the other elements will be dominant. That is, it determines for the non-economic levels their respective degrees of autonomy or dependence in relation to each other and to itself, and thus the different degrees of effect that each will have. It can determine itself as dominant or non-dominant at any particular time. At a particular juncture one element may displace another to assume the dominant role. In addition, different elements can be dominant in different societies, or at different times. Hence, this is what Althusser intends when he refers to the social formation as a *structure in dominance*.

After 1968, says Poster, Foucault attempted to come to grips with Marxist scholarship, and while the positions he adopted in some cases resembled those of Western Marxists, generally he went beyond those positions towards a new formulation of critical theory. Although Foucault rejects Marxism as a specific theory of the mode of production, as a critique of political economy, or as a dialectical method, he advances a critical view of domination which, like historical materialism, takes all social practices as transitory, and all intellectual formations as indissociably connected with power and social relations (Poster, 1984, pp. 39–40). Poster explains what he sees as Foucault's greater relevance than Marxism in terms of a shift from 19th- and early-20th-century forms of capitalism based upon the "mode of production" to new forms of later 20th-century capitalism based upon the "mode of information". These changes were associated, says Poster, with changes in the nature of the economy, an increase in the service and white collar sectors, the increasing development of information technology, developments in electronic communications, together with new possibilities that these developments generate for a decentralisation of political power. While Marxism's focus on labour and the central causal priority of the economy may have had heuristic value in the age of ascendant capitalism, in an era of "information capitalism" historical materialism finds its premise in power that is the effect of "discourse/practice". Thus, according to Poster:

> the couplet discourse/practice ... enables [Foucault] to search for the close connection between manifestations of reason and patterns of domination. Foucault can study the way in which discourse is not innocent, but shaped by practice, without privileging any form of practice such as class struggle. He can also study how discourse in turn shapes practice without privileging any form of discourse. (Poster, 1984, p. 12)

Foucault thus rejects Marx's conception of historical materialism as a mechanism by which discourse is split from material (non-discursive) practice and by which the former is then subordinated to the latter. By representing the mental operations of consciousness as derivative from the material base of society, Marx, for Foucault, remains firmly fixed within a traditional Enlightenment problematic (Poster, 1984, pp. 16–18).

3 Reconceptualising Determination

Foucault rejects Marxist models of a determining economic base and a determined superstructure as well as refinements based on conceptions of totality by Marx's 20th-century successors. Like Bourdieu and Althusser, he retains a concept of practice, however, and utilises the concept of strategies to understand how practice is operationalised and how people act on their environments. To some extent, the concept enabled Foucault to distance himself from structuralism and to see practice as something not entirely the result of rational calculation. As a series of strategies, Foucault sees power as mobilised, and he utilises the strategic metaphor of the game, in reference to both language and power: "Language it is played. ... Relations of power, also, they are played; it is these games of power (*jeux de pouvoir*) that one must study in terms of tactics and strategy, in terms of order and of chance, in terms of stakes and objectives" (Foucault, 1994a, pp. 541–542). The game is a useful metaphor for Foucault. In a game one is both free and constrained. Players find themselves at points where they must respond (e.g., when the ball that has been kicked by the opponent lands). In addition, movements in a game are infinitely variable. While players are confined by rules, indefinite number of possibilities and options exist within them. In addition, through effective strategies players can utilise the rules to their own advantage; they can invent and improvise; within a system of constraints moves are numerous.

Foucault is not interested in accounting for such practices in terms of a model of economic determination. Although, like Althusser, he utilises a model of complex and multiple causation and determination within the social structure, the specific elements and mechanisms of such processes, as elaborated by Foucault, differ in important, indeed crucial, respects. In Foucault's materialism, explaining the relations between discursive formations and non-discursive domains (institutions, political events, economic practices and processes) is recognised as the ultimate objective, at least from the time of *The Archaeology of Knowledge*. For archaeology, in comparison to Marxism, however, "The *rapprochements* are not intended to uncover great cultural continuities, nor to isolate mechanisms of causality ... nor does it seek to rediscover what is expressed in them ... it tries to determine how the rules of formation that govern it ... may be linked to non-discursive systems: it seeks to define specific forms of articulation" (Foucault, 1972, p. 162). Unlike Marxists, he sees no one set of factors as directing human destiny. Rather, the forms of articulation and determination may differ in relation to the relative importance of different non-discursive (material) factors in terms of both place and time. In the shift from a purely archaeological to a genealogical mode of enquiry, Foucault's concern with the relation between discursive and non-discursive domains is given a more historical and dynamic formulation, although the concern with synchronic analysis is not abandoned. Throughout, however, as Mark Poster (1984, pp. 39–40) explains, Foucault's central aim is to provide a version of critical theory in which the economic base is not the totalising centre of the social formation, whereby Hegel's evolutionary model of history is replaced by Nietzsche's concept of genealogy, and where causes and connections to an imputed centre or foundation are rejected in favour of exposing the contingency and transitory nature of existing social practices. In Poster's (1984, pp. 39–40) view, this presents us with a crucial decision. In comparing Foucault and Althusser, he maintains that "the theoretical choice offered by these two theorists is dramatic and urgent. In my opinion Foucault's position in the present context is more valuable as an interpretative strategy ... Foucault's position opens up critical theory more than Althusser's both to the changing social formation and to the social locations where contestation actually occurs". While having a generally historicised view of the nature and development of knowledge, Foucault rejects the possibility of any "absolute" or "transcendental" conception of truth "outside of history" as well as of any conception of "objective" or "necessary" interests which could provide a necessary "Archimedean point" to ground either knowledge, morality or politics. Read in this way, historical materialism is about the systematic character of society and how it might change. It is about the processes of change internal to social systems. It holds that societies are to varying extents integrated systematically through their material practices and discursive coherences and break down and change as the component elements of the system change.

4   Change and Determination

The notion of change is central to the difference between Foucault and Marxism, for the understanding of change is linked closely to the issue of the status of causal explanations. For Marxism, in the main, with the partial exception of Althusser's structuralist version, the conception of change is that of Newton and the Enlightenment, which had been applied to both the natural and the social sciences. Although Althusser developed a model of complex causation, whereby the specific effectivity of structures depended upon specific historical conditions, the fact that he underwrote his theory with a conception of the economic as the final ultimate determinant made his own approach consistent with this Enlightenment view. This was a linear and individualist conception of cause and effect between objects whose self-determined essences collide and interact with predictable consequences. For Foucault, such an approach not only implied a conception of change and causality which he found problematic, but with respect to Marxism specifically, it was associated by topographical and architectural metaphors, between deep/surface or base/superstructure which sat uncomfortably with his own preference for analysing the micropractices of lived experience.

Foucault's approach to structuralism and change led him to question the central importance of humanism or the individual human subject as a means by which to understand change. While political liberals may well seek to account for change in terms of voluntary theory of human agency, for Foucault, what was significant about structuralism was the analysis of the internal laws of structures. As he puts it in "Interview avec Michel Foucault" of 1968, reproduced in *Dits et écrits* (Foucault, 1994c, p. 654):

> In a positive manner, we can say that structuralism investigates above all an unconscious. It is the unconscious structures of language, of the literary work, and of knowledge that one is trying at this moment to illuminate. In the second place, I think that one can say that what one is essentially looking for are the forms, the system, that is to say that one tries to bring out the logical correlations that can exist among a great number of elements belonging to a language, to an ideology (as in the analyses of Althusser), to a society (as in Lévi-Strauss), or to different

fields of knowledge; which is what I myself have studied. One could describe structuralism roughly as the search for logical structures everywhere that they could occur.

Structural linguistics thus served as a model for his analysis of the human sciences. His major work on linguistic method and the methodology of the social sciences appears in his 1969 article "Linguistique et sciences sociales", reproduced in *Dits et écrits*, where he discusses the epistemological issues concerned with the social sciences. In opposing the linear notions of determination dominant in the Enlightenment, and in Marxism, structural linguistics, he says (1994b, p. 824), is concerned with "logical relations" between elements. These "logical relations" are essentially "multiple relations". They are ontologically separate from the elements to which they pertain, and they derive from the collective interactions between elements. Hence, he says (1994b, p. 824), it is the "presence of a logic that is not the logic of causal determinism that is currently at the heart of philosophical and theoretical debates".

Foucault's reliance on the model of structural linguistics provides him with a method which avoids both methodological individualism and being trapped by a concern with causalism. Structural linguistics is concerned with "the systematic sets of relations among elements", and it functions for Foucault as a model to enable him to study social reality as a logical structure, or set of logical relations revealing relations that are not transparent to consciousness. The methods of structural linguistics also enable Foucault to analyse change. For just as linguistics undertakes synchronic analysis seeking to trace the necessary conditions for an element within the structure of language to undergo change, a similar synchronic analysis applied to social life asks the question, in order for a change to occur, what other changes must also take place in the overall texture of the social configuration (Foucault, 1994b, p. 827). Hence, Foucault seeks to identify logical relations where none had previously been thought to exist or where previously one had searched for causal relations. This form of analysis becomes for Foucault a method of analysing the multifaceted yet invisible determinations within the social structure.

The methodological strategies common to both archaeology and genealogy were also developed in response to Marxism, which is characterised by a specific narrow conception of causality (*un causalisme primaire*) and a dialectical logic that has very little in common with the logical relations that Foucault is interested in. Thus, he maintains, "what one is trying to recover in Marx is something that is neither the determinist ascription of causality, nor the logic of a Hegelian type but a logical analysis of reality" (Foucault, 1994b, pp. 824–825). To seek to uncover "logical relations" instead of linear, atomistically conceived cause–effect determinations is to provide a major rupture from Marxist analysis of base and superstructure, especially with respect to articulating the nature of the determinations present. Foucault is adamant that his concern with analysing logical relations is qualitatively different to the sorts of causal analysis that characterises Marxist and dialectical logics, even those analysed by Althusser.

Arnold Davidson (1997), in a review of *Dits et écrits* to which my own analysis is indebted, points out that it is through such methodological strategies that Foucault proceeds to advance a non-reductive, holist, analysis of social life. As he puts it (1997, p. 11), "this kind of analysis is characterised, first, by anti-atomism, by the idea that we should not analyse single or individual elements in isolation but that one must look at the systematic relations among elements; second, it is characterised by the idea that the relations between elements are coherent and transformable, that is, that the elements form a structure". In this sense, says Davidson (1997, p. 10):

> [t]he status of causal explanations is connected to the problem of how to account for change. ... As Foucault points out, we should not identify history with the dimension of the successive since "the simultaneity of two events is no less an historical fact than their succession". Moreover, according to Foucault, the synchronic analysis done by linguists is in reality an analysis "of the conditions of change" where the dimension of change must not be confused with that of cause. ... Foucault always insisted that causal relations represented only one kind of change and that one should not collapse the different types of changes into a single level. Foucault claimed that it was the humanist Marxists, like Sartre and Roger Garaudy, who insisted that one speak exclusively of causality and who therefore wanted to impose a reduction of "the field of exploration". ... Furthermore, in practice the search for causality always risked losing itself in "a more or less magic fog"; ... notions like the spirit of the times, influence, social change, crisis, interest, all of which were supposed to have some causal force, seemed to Foucault to provide explanations "for the most part, more magic than real". ... As Foucault indicated, causal explanations aside, "change can be an object of analysis in terms of structure".

This sort of approach accounts for one of the major differences between Foucault and Marxism, and also from individualist traditions in Anglo-American social science. Thus, in his dissertation on the knowledge of heredity as a system of thought, submitted as part of his application for his position at the

Collège de France, Foucault seeks to describe the changes, transformations, and conditions of possibility that made genetics possible, that constituted it as a science based on a series of discourses concerning breeding, just as in *The Order of Things* he had done for natural history and biology. What factors led to the emergence of these fields as sciences? What elements changed to make such developments possible? What made them possible as systems of thought? Thus, Foucault seeks to describe the relations among elements as structures which change as the component elements change, i.e., he endeavours to establish the systematic sets of relations and transformations that enable different forms of knowledge to emerge.

5 Monism and Pluralism

In as much as Foucault was influenced by structuralism, he of course adamantly denied being a structuralist, and it is the sense in which he departs from structuralism that reinforces his commitments to a less deductive, more pluralist mode of approach, inspired by Nietzsche. There are a number of senses. First, Foucault rejected the notion central to structuralism of a system of universal rules, or laws, or elementary structures, that underpinned history and explained its surface appearances. When it is noted in the final dialogue of *The Archaeology of Knowledge* (1972, pp. 199–200) that "throughout this book, you have been at great pains to dissociate yourself from structuralism", the other Michel says, "I reject a uniform model of temporalization, in order to describe, for each discursive practice, its rules of accumulation, exclusion, reactivation, its own forms of derivation, and its specific modes of connexion over various successions". Foucault always stood opposed to a marked tendency among structuralist writers to prioritising the structure over the parts, whereby the units could be explained once the essence of the structure is uncovered. The failure to theorise adequately the historicity of structures was in fact common to both structuralists and Marxists, as both adopted ahistorical and uniform models of temporalisation and change. In retrospect, one can see that even when Foucault's methodological focus privileged archaeology, prior to the 1970s, it was *within* the context of historically constituted *epistemes*, and the difference of his position to structuralism was already manifest in relation to several key dimensions—the thesis which is set out explicitly in *The Archaeology of Knowledge*.

Closely related to the senses in which Foucault rejected structuralism, a central element of his critique of Marxism relates to the notion of "totalisation". Essentially, for Foucault, Marxism was not just a "deterministic" but a "deductivistic" approach. That is, it directs attention not just to the primacy of the economy but it seeks to explain the parts of a culture as explicable and decodable parts of the whole totality or system. Marxism, claims Foucault, seeks to ascertain "the principle of cohesion or the code that unlocks the system explaining the elements by deduction" (Thompson, 1986, p. 106). This is an approach which seeks to analyse history and society in terms of "totality", where the parts are an "expression" of the whole—hence the notion of an "expressive totality".

Of central importance in Hegel is the conception of society as a closed and bounded totality. For Hegel this was an expressivist notion where society expresses the inner essence of its subject in a process of continuous unfolding by which reason realises itself in history. The essence manifests its appearance in different ways at different times, becoming more exposed in the process of history. In this model there is a tendency to conceptualise society as a potentially unified subject with a unified will and, thus, considerations of pluralism in any of its forms—social, political, or cultural—become problematic. Similarly, there is too much reliance in Marxism on forms of analysis, particularly class analysis, in establishing the causes and conditions of oppression in existing social orders. Further, both Hegel and Marx subscribed to a philosophy of history that underplayed the roles of contingency, locality, chance and identity in struggles against oppressive power. As a consequence, for Marxism, every aspect of capitalist society—every institution, social form, or relationship—becomes an expression of the inner essence.

In countering this Hegelian emphasis, Foucault (1972, pp. 9–10) draws a distinction between "total history" and "general history". The central differences are:

> The project of total history is one that seeks to reconstitute the overall form of a civilization, the principle—material or spiritual—of a society, the significance common to all the phenomena of a period, the law that accounts for their cohesion. ... A total description draws all phenomena around a single centre—a principle, a meaning, a spirit, a world-view, an overall shape. ... [I]t is supposed that between all the events of a well-defined spatiotemporal area, between all the phenomena of which traces have been found, it must be possible to establish a system of homogeneous relations: a network of causality that makes it possible to derive each of them, relations of analogy that show they symbolize one another or how they all express one and the same central core; it is also supposed that one and the same form of historicity operates upon economic structures, social institutions and customs ... and subjects them all to the same

> type of transformation; lastly, it is supposed that history itself may be articulated into great units—stages or phases—which contain within themselves their own principle of cohesion. ... [G]eneral history, on the contrary, would deploy the space of dispersion. ... [I]t speaks of series, divisions, limits, differences of level, shifts, chronological specificities, particular forms of rehandling, possible types of relation. ... The problem ... which defines the task of general history is to determine what form of relation may be legitimately described between these different series.

Whereas total history seeks to explain all phenomena in relation to a single centre, general history employs the space of dispersion. It represented a "new history" (1972, p. 9) characterised by "a general theory of discontinuity, of series, of limits, unities, specific orders and differentiated autonomies and dependences" (p. 12), in contrast to "history in its traditional form" (p. 7) which is based on a model of "the continuous chronology of reason" and the correlative founding function of the subject (p. 12). The methodological task for general history is the empirical establishment of interconnections in order to "determine what form of relation may be legitimately described between these different series" (p. 10).

For Foucault, the explanatory quest is not to search for the organising principle of a cultural formation—whether the "economy", or the "human subject" or the "proletariat". Rather, Foucault is interested in advancing a polymorphous conception of determination in order to reveal the "play of dependencies" in the social and historical process. As he puts it in an article written in 1968 and translated and printed in English in 1978, "I would like to substitute this whole play of dependencies for the uniform simple notion of assigning causality and by suspending the indefinitely extended privilege of the cause, in order to render apparent the polymorphous cluster of correlations" (Foucault, 1978, p. 13).

For Foucault (1978, p. 13), there were three aspects to the play of dependencies: firstly, the *intradiscursive*, which concerns relations between objects, operations and concepts within the discursive formation; secondly, the *interdiscursive*, which concerns relations between different discursive formations; and, thirdly, the *extradiscursive*, concerning the relations between a discourse and the whole play of economic, political and social practices. Rather than seek to find the articulating principle of a cultural complex, Foucault was interested in discerning how cultural formations were made to appear "rational" and "unified", how particular discourses came to be formed, and what rules lay behind the process of formation. In doing so he sought to produce accounts of how discursive formations like 19th-century psychopathology came to be formed, how it constituted its scientific legitimacy and shaped the thinking of a particular period. Thus, in the case of 19th-century psychiatry and psychopathology, Foucault shows how the term "madness" came to be applied to certain types of behaviour, and how, in its very designation by what it wasn't, it helped establish our conceptions of "the rational" and "the sane".

What Foucault resists, however, in all of these studies, is the temptation to try to explain the development of particular discursive formations as a result of any single cause or principle. In opposition to the themes of totalising history, with its notions of "the progress of reason" and "the sprit of a century", Foucault (1978, p. 10) substitutes what he calls a differentiated analysis:

> Nothing, you see, is more foreign to me than the quest for a sovereign, unique and constraining form. I do not seek to detect, starting from diverse signs, the unitary spirit of an epoch, the general form of its consciousness: something like a Weltanschauung. Nor have I described either the emergence and eclipse of formal structure which might reign for a time over all the manifestations of thought: I have not written the history of a syncopated transcendental. Nor, finally, have I described thoughts or century-old sensitivities coming to life, stuttering, struggling and dying out like great phantoms—ghosts playing out their shadow theatre against the backdrop of history. I have studied, one after another, ensembles of discourse; I have characterised them; I have defined the play of rules, of transformations, of thresholds, of remanences. I have established and I have described their clusters of relations. Whenever I have deemed it necessary I have allowed systems to proliferate.

It is the attempt to "individualise" discourses that defines Foucault's methodological imperative: specifying their systematic and specific character; searching for the rules of formation for all of the concepts, methods, and theoretical postulates; examining the conditions of transformation which are effective, at a precise time, for the operations, concepts, and theories to be formed, or discarded, or modified; and ascertaining their specific existence in relation to other types of discourse.

It is interesting that in the "Introduction" to *The Archaeology of Knowledge*, Foucault (1972, p. 13) exonerates Marx himself from such a totalising approach to history. Marx is credited as being an exponent of an early (pre-Nietzschean) version of general history involving a "decentring" based on "the historical analysis of the relations of production, economic determinations, and the class struggle" (p. 13), whereby Marx sought to identify and analyse "specific series", "levels and limits" and "the whole interplay of differences" in their uniqueness and autonomy (p. 13). But, says Foucault, Marx's own approach "gave place, towards the end of the nineteenth century, to the search for a total history" (p. 13) whereby "one is led to anthropologize Marx, to make him a historian of totalities, and to recover in him the meaning of humanism" (p. 13).

In a normative sense, Foucault clearly opposed both political policies and academic approaches that erode difference or diversity. This explains his distaste for Hegelian conceptions of community whereby identity (individual or collective) becomes a shadow of the whole and reducible to it, thus eclipsing individuality, producing a sterile conformity, and eradicating difference. It was for this reason that Foucault opposed utopian theorising, as in Habermas. In Habermas there is the notion of a rationality premised, as Jameson (1984, p. VII) has put it, on the idea of a "noisefree, transparent, fully communicational society". As Foucault (1991a, p. 18) states, in relation to this issue:

> [In Habermas's work] there is always something which causes me a problem. It is when he assigns a very important place to relations of communication and also to functions that I would call "utopian". The thought that there could be a state of communication which would be such that the games of truth could circulate freely, without obstacles, without constraint, and without coercive effects, seems to me to be Utopia. It is being blind to the fact that relations of power are not something bad in themselves, from which one must free oneself. I don't believe there can be a society without relations of power. ... The problem is not of trying to dissolve them in the utopia of a perfectly transparent communication, but to give oneself the rules of law, the techniques of management, and also the ethics, the ethos, the practice of self, which would allow these games of power to be played with a minimum of domination.

For Foucault, "strategic" action, conceived broadly as politically or ideologically distorted dialogue, necessarily supervenes on "communicative" action. It is always the question of maintaining the correct "balance of power relations in the present rather than seeking to exclude all forms of power from the world in the search for a different order of society. Hence Foucault rejects the idea, that he sees in Habermas, Marxism, and the Frankfurt School, of conceiving history as a single rational trajectory along which humanity fulfils its essential nature, arriving ultimately at a utopia of "pure existence" freed from the realities of power or conflict. For Foucault, following Nietzsche, power is more ubiquitous, diffuse, and corporeal; it infiltrates the fine textures of social existence as well as self-identity, and hence it is impossible to know one's true humanity apart from power's distorting effects.

Foucault also gives only qualified support to consensus models of policy-making for the same reasons. The issue was put to him in 1983 by a group of interviewers including Paul Rabinow, Charles Taylor, Martin Jay, Richard Rorty, and Leo Lowenthal (Foucault, 1984a, p. 379):

Q.   If one can assume that the consensus model is a fictional possibility, people might nonetheless act according to that fiction in such a way that the results might be superior to the action that would ensue from the bleaker view of politics as essentially domination and repression, so that although in an empirical way you may be correct and although the utopian possibility may never be achievable, nonetheless, pragmatically, it might in some sense be better, healthier, freer, whatever positive value one uses, if we assume that the consensus is a goal still to be sought rather than one that we simply throw away and say it's impossible to achieve.
M.   F. Yes, I think that is, let us say, a critical principle ...
Q.   As a regulatory principle?
M. F.   I perhaps wouldn't say regulatory principle, that's going too far, because starting from the point where you say regulatory principle, you grant that it is indeed under its governance that the phenomenon has to be organised, within limits that may be defined by experience or the context. I would say, rather, that it is perhaps a critical idea to maintain at all times: to ask oneself what proportion of nonconsensuality is implied in such a power relation, and whether that degree of nonconsensuality is necessary or not, and then one may question every power relation to that extent. The farthest I would go is to say that perhaps one must not be for consensuality, but one must be against nonconsensuality.

It is linked to such views that in the 1970s he advocated "localistic" analyses. The issue became contested by Marxist writers who saw in this a certain circumscription of analytical capacity and an inability to deal with the political level. The inability to conceptualise change in a way that transcends localistic issues and links the individual to groups and collective politics is taken up by Duccio Trombadori in his interviews with Foucault in 1978 (see Foucault, 1991b). Trombadori asks:

One of the observations that could be made of the way in which you confront the theme of power is this: the extreme fragmentation or "localization" of the questions ends up impeding the transition from a dimension that we might even call "corporate" to a vision of the totality within which the particular problem is inserted. (Foucault, 1991b, p. 150)

Foucault gives a long answer in which he says:

> Yes, the problems that I pose are always concerned with local and particular issues. ... [H]ow could one do otherwise? (pp. 150–151)

To this Trombadori raises an objection:

> Perhaps I didn't explain myself. I do not dispute the need to raise local problems, even in a radical way, if it is necessary. Moreover, I am sensitive to what you say about intellectual work. Nevertheless, it seems to me that that way of confronting problems by particularizing them ends up inhibiting the possibility of their coordination in relation to other problems in the general understanding (vision) of a determinate historical and political situation. (p. 152)

To this Foucault responds:

> Localizing problems is indispensable for theoretical and political reasons. But that doesn't mean that they are not, however, general problems. After all, what is more general in a society than the way in which it defines the relation to madness. (p. 152)

Trombadori is still not satisfied, however:

> When I spoke of a general understanding (vision), I was referring essentially to the political immersion of a problem and to the necessity of its articulation in a wider action or program that at the same time is linked to certain historico-political conditions. (p. 153)

To this Foucault responds:

> The generality that I try to make apparent is not of the same type as others. And when I am blamed for localizing problems, confusion is created between the local character of my analyses and an idea of generality similar to the one usually discussed by historians, sociologists, economists etc. I don't advance problems that are less general than those usually proposed by political parties or by certain great theoretical systems. (p. 153)

Somewhat frustrated, Trombadori endeavours to restate the problem:

> What you say is perfectly acceptable. But you seem to confirm a certain closure, or unwillingness to open your discourse clearly onto the level of the "political". (p. 154)

He continues to elaborate in an effort to clarify:

> For every local problem one always faces the need to find solutions—even if provisional and temporary ones—in political terms. From this arises the need to shift one's way of seeing things from a particular analysis to the examination of real possibilities, within which a process of change and transformation can advance. It is in this balance between the local situation and the general picture that the "political" function is at stake. (pp. 156–157)

To which Foucault says:

> I would respond in this way: for reasons that essentially pertain to my political choice, in the widest sense of the term, I absolutely will not play the part of one who prescribes solutions. I hold that the role of the intellectual today is not that of establishing laws or proposing solutions or prophesying, since by doing that one can only contribute to the functioning of a determinate situation of power that to my mind must be criticized. (p. 157)

Trombadori remains unsatisfied, however, and asks Foucault whether "in the long run", by evading in some way the "political dimension", his proposal "risks representing a kind of 'distraction', considering the contingent and complex stakes in question that are placed in society but have their immediate reflection on the level of institutions and parties" (p. 164).[1]

It is noteworthy that it was after this interview that Foucault developed the concept of "governmentality" in the early 1980s in response to criticisms that his conception of power was too "localistic" and "regional" and did not take the formation of national and international hegemonies into account, and developed the concept of the "strategic reversibility of power relations" at the same time, to seek to explain how individuals exert *agency* drawing on the very discursive systems through which they have been constructed.

In terms of the sociological implications of the principle of totality as utilised by Marxism, Balibar (1992, p. 44) notes that it conveys "the idea that in the social 'whole', the 'parts' or the 'cells' are necessarily similar to the whole itself". Foucault's objection to this principle on a practical level, i.e., in terms of its implications for actual historical and social research, can be seen in regard to any number of institutional sectors. Balibar gives the example of the family which Foucault analyses in *The History of Sexuality, Volume 1*. While, typically, Marxists had considered the family reductively as the consumption-hub of bourgeois society, i.e., as purely reproductive of capitalist class relations, for Foucault, the family has more positive functions. As Balibar (1992, p. 44) points out:

> Foucault stresses the strategic role of the family (its moralisation and its medicalisation) in the apparatus of the regulation of populations which forms one of the essential powers of the "bourgeois" State; also it is important for him to show that the family is simultaneously the locus of institutional perversion ... the hysterisation of the women's body ... the space which is the opposite to psychiatric space ... the central concern in the competition between holders of professional knowledge about man ... the means of socialising reproductive activity and, in particular, the locus of the juridical "recoding" of bodily techniques in general into forms of alliance or kinship. ... It is for all these reasons that the family *cannot* be considered as the reduced *image* of the global society.

Hence, the family does not reproduce society and the society does not imitate the family. As Balibar states (1992, p. 44), it is "not a monad *pars totalis* of 'the society'" and its strategic importance lies not in its resemblance but in the specific nature of its difference. Foucault's criticism of the Marxist use of the concept of power is also related to totalism in that the power of dominant groups is seen in Marxism to *"echo through successive amplifications"* throughout the whole social body (Balibar, 1992, p. 44).

6   Complexity, Chance, Pluralism: Appropriating Nietzsche to Correct Marx

The dissociation between structuralism and Marxism, and Foucault's own position became more apparent after Foucault's turn to genealogy and Nietzsche at the close of the 1960s. With his growing interest in genealogy, Foucault became more concerned with power and history, and the historical constitution of knowledge. In this process there was, however, no integrative principle or essence. If the genealogist studies history "he finds that there is 'something altogether different' behind things: not a timeless and essential secret, but the secret that they have no essence or that their essence was fabricated in a piecemeal fashion from alien forms" (Foucault, 1977b, p. 142).

Foucault's objection to elements of Marxism explicitly reflects his Nietzschean heritage and his belief that certain aspects of Marxism distorted the liberatory potential of the discourse.

> The interest in Nietzsche and Bataille was not a way of distancing ourselves from Marxism or communism—it was the only path towards what we expected from communism. (Foucault, 2001, p. 249)

It was in terms of the philosophy of difference and Nietzsche's conception of multiplicities through a rejection of Platonic hierarchies that Foucault enunciates a theory of discursive formations and rejects Marxist and Hegelian conceptions of history. The utilisation of Nietzsche signalled a rupture from Marxism in relation to a series of interrelated conceptual, theoretical and methodological percepts, including power, knowledge and truth, the subject, and the nature of historical change and determination.

Nietzsche focused on power in an altogether different way to Marx. In "Prison Talk", Foucault (1980a, p. 53) states:

> It was Nietzsche who specified the power relation as the general focus, shall we say, of philosophical discourse—whereas for Marx it was the production relation. Nietzsche is the philosopher of power, a philosopher who managed to think of power without having to confine himself within a political theory in order to do so.

Power, for Nietzsche, was conceived as a relation of forces within an analytics of power/knowledge/truth, which became important for Foucault to understand in the later 1960s after the publication of *The Archaeology of Knowledge* and his growing friendship with the Parisian Nietzschean Gilles Deleuze. Foucault accredits Nietzsche as the source of his interest in the question of truth and its relation to power. As he states in "Truth and Power" (Foucault, 1980b, p. 133), "The political question ... is not error, illusion, alienated consciousness or ideology; it is truth itself. Hence, the importance of Nietzsche". Nietzsche's importance to Foucault can be seen as "correcting Marx", especially in relation to the linkage between power/knowledge/truth, and the functioning of knowledge as an instrument of power. As Alan Schrift (1995, p. 40) notes, Nietzsche's influence drew attention away from "substances, subjects and things, and focused attention instead on the *relations between* these substantives". In a related way, Foucault "draws our attention away from the substantive notion of power and directs our attention instead to the multifarious ways that power operates through the social order" (Schrift, 1995, p. 40). For Nietzsche, such relations were relations of forces. Foucault thus focused on new relations as the relations of forces that existed and interacted within social systems as social practices. These were forces of repression and production that characterised the disciplinary society; forces that enable and block, subjugate and realise, and normalise and resist. In this model, power is not a thing, but a process, a becoming.

Beyond these concerns with power/knowledge/truth, and language and discourse, Foucault acknowledges the influence of Nietzsche in reference to the decentring of the subject, and the constitutive ethics of self-creation. In the *Genealogy of Morals* (1967) Nietzsche traces the processes of descent or provenance (*Herkunft*) and emergence (*Entstehung*), but distinguishes these from a concern with origins (*Ursprung*) or essences (*Wesen*). Nietzsche's thesis is that the subject is historically constituted and does not exist as something given metaphysically in advance. This is what Nietzsche (1967, pp. 1, 13) means when he says "there is no 'being' behind doing, effecting, becoming; 'the doer' is merely the fiction added to the deed—the deed is everything". For Foucault, accepting this view of the subject, he sees it as an ideological product, an effect of power, whose identity is defined in relation to the functionality of discourse.

The view of history as pluralist and not accounted for within a context of causal iron-law determinism was also important in Foucault's debt to Nietzsche. Whereas Marxists like Althusser adopted a structuralist programme of seeking to explain the whole by understanding the interrelations between its component parts, for Foucault the totality always eluded analysis or understanding in terms of structure, but rather was characterised by *incompleteness, indeterminacy, complexity* and *chance*. As Foucault says:

> though it is true that these discontinuous discursive series each have, within certain limits, their regularity, it is undoubtedly no longer possible to establish links of mechanical causality or of ideal necessity between the elements which constitute them. We must accept the introduction of the *aléa* [chance] as a category in the production of events. (Foucault, 1981, p. 69)[2]

In seeking to characterise the nature of his "pluralism" and how it affects the analysis of discourse, Foucault (1978, p. 11) explains how he "substitutes the analysis of different types of transformation for the abstract, general, and monotonous form of 'change' in which one so willingly thinks in terms of succession". In this, he seeks to define with the greatest care the transformations which have constituted the change, replacing the general theme of *becoming* ("general form, abstract element, primary cause, and universal effect") by the analysis of the transformations in their specificity, an examination of "the diversity of *systems* and the play of discontinuities into the history of *discourse*" (1978, p. 15). This involves, says Foucault (1978, pp. 11–12), within a given discursive formation, (1) detecting the changes which affect the operations, objects, theoretical choices, etc.; (2) detecting the changes which affect the discursive formations themselves (e.g., changes in the boundaries that define the field); and (3) changes which affect simultaneously several discursive formations (e.g., reversal of the hierarchy of importance, as happened, for instance, in the classical period when the analysis of language lost the "directing role" that it had in the first years of the 19th century to biology, which in turn led to the development of new concepts such as "organism", "function", "organisation", etc., which in turn affected other sciences). All of these types of changes, says Foucault, characterise changes to both individual discourses and effect modifications in the episteme itself: its "redistributions", i.e., "the different transformations which it is possible to describe concerning ... states of a discourse".

In opposition to totalising models, Foucault sees his own analysis as more limited: to searching for the empirical historical grounds for discursive consistency or coherence; to recognising in discourse its empirical worldly features—"the work of the author. And why not?—His juvenilia or mature work, the patterns of a linguistic or rhetorical model (an idea, a theme)"; and acknowledging that the transformatory operations are all carried out "prior to discourse and outside of it" (1978, p. 17).

In his later reflections on method, in response to interviews on the subject of *Discipline and Punish*, Foucault (1977b) asserts the "pluralist" nature of his project through his use of concepts like "eventalization"; that "specific events" ("*événements signuliers*") cannot be integrated or decoded simply as an application of a uniform and universal regularity. In this non-unified sense, the analytic of discourse effects a non-unified method. As Foucault (1972, p. 8) explains it:

> It has led to the individualization of different series, which are juxtaposed to one another, follow one another, overlap and intersect, without one being able to reduce them to a linear schema. Thus, in place of the continuous chronology of reason, which was invariably traced back to some inaccessible origin, there have appeared scales that are sometimes very brief, distinct from one another, irreducible to a single law, scales that bear a type of history peculiar to each one, and which cannot be reduced

to the general model of a consciousness that acquires, progresses, and remembers.

The notion of "eventalization" itself contains a number of elements. First, it treats all objects of knowledge as historical *events*. Second, it refers to a "pluralization of causes" (Foucault, 1987, pp. 104–105):

> Causal multiplication consists in analysing an event according to the multiple processes that constitute it. ... "[E]ventalization" thus works by constructing around the singular event analysed as process a "polygon" or rather a "polyhedron" of intelligibility, the number of whose faces is not given in advance and can never properly be taken as finite. One has to proceed by progressive, necessarily incomplete saturation. And one has to bear in mind that the further one decomposes the processes under analysis, the more one is enabled, and indeed obliged to construct their external relations of intelligibility.

In addition, says Foucault (1987, p. 104) eventalization refers to the rediscovery of the "connections, encounters, blockages, plays of forces, strategies, etc. that at a given moment establish what consequently comes to count as being self-evident, universal and necessary". In this sense, it constitutes a "breach of self-evidence", i.e.:

> it means making visible a *singularity* at places where there is a temptation to invoke historical constants, an immediate anthropological trait, or an obviousness that imposes itself uniformly on all. To show that things "weren't as necessary as all that"; that it wasn't a matter of course that mad people came to be regarded as mentally ill; it wasn't self-evident that the only things to be done to a criminal were to lock him up, it wasn't self-evident that the causes of illness were to be sought through the individual examination of bodies; and so on.

In this sense, eventalization opposes the evidences upon which knowledge sequences and practices rest. Its theoretical quest is endlessly open. It operates, in Foucault's (1987, p. 105) view, "as a procedure for lightening the weight of causality".

Alongside the concept of *singular events* are those of *exteriority/interiority*, which Foucault (1972, pp. 120–122, 125, 140) discusses in *The Archaeology of Knowledge* as well as in his inaugural lecture at the Collège de France (see Foucault, 1981), and in his essay on Blanchot (Foucault, 1990). What Foucault means by "exteriority" is that the being of discourse resides in the "pure dispersion" of the socio-historical processes of reproduction and change; in the "particular events, regularities, relationships, modifications and systematic transformations", which constitute an "autonomous (although dependent)" domain, and "which can be described at its own level" (1972, pp. 121–122). As expressed in his essay on Blanchot (1990, p. 15), it is "the breakthrough to a language from which the subject is excluded ... the being of language only appears for itself with the disappearance of the subject". This places the emphasis on "speech" rather than on the Cartesian Cogito. As he states (1990, p. 13):

> "I speak" runs counter to "I think". "I think" led to the indubitable certainty of the "I" and its existence; "I speak", on the other hand, distances, disperses, effaces that existence and lets only its empty emplacement appear. Thought about thought, an entire tradition wider than philosophy, has taught us that thought leads us to the deepest interiority. Speech about speech leads us, by way of literature as well as perhaps by other paths, to the outside in which the speaking subject disappears. No doubt that is why Western thought took so long to think the being of language: as if it had a premonition of the danger that the naked experience of language poses for the self-evidence of the "I think".

Manfred Frank emphasises the ontological and methodological functions of exteriority. What Foucault means by exteriority, he says (1992, p. 108) is that each individual element in discourse is irreducible "to the unified discursive principle, or to an internal core of meaning to be found in the discourse". As he continues:

> What the rule of exteriority of discourse means then, is: "not moving from the discourse towards its internal, hidden core, towards the heart of the thought or the meaning, which is manifest in it". So the procedure of the analytic of discourse is external because it wishes to leave the series (*série*) of single events, mutually irreducible (in terms of a deductive or teleological principle), just as they are "external" to any totalizing general concept.

In a methodological sense, in that events and instances are individualised, "individualised" means here, as Frank (1992, p. 110) states it, "not predictable from the point of view of their structure, and contingent with respect to the way they happen to be". What is important in terms of the analytics of discourse is not seeking such a reduction: hence the analytics of discourse is *external* to the process of analysis. What is important to Foucault (1990, pp. 15–16) is that:

thought stands outside subjectivity, setting its limits as though from without, articulating its end, making is dispersion shine forth, taking only its invincible absence; and that at the same time stands at the threshold of all positivity, not in order to grasp its foundation or justification but in order to regain the space of its unfolding, the void serving as its site, the distance in which it is constituted and into which its immediate certainties slip the moment they are glimpsed—a thought that, in relation to the interiority of our philosophical reflection and the positivity of our knowledge, constitutes what in a word we might call "the thought from the outside".

As well as referring to consciousness, interiority thus refers also to any foundation or centre to the social formation which the events or parts echo or reflect. Hence, again, this can also be seen as consistent with, and expressing, his opposition to the notion of a determined causality embodied in the Hegelian conception of an "expressive totality" and, by derivation, also embodied in the notion of a primary causal necessity (*un causalisme primaire*) which he sees as central to Marxism. In this sense, the analytics of discourse must resist interiorisation, "forsaking the wordy interiority of consciousness", as well appeal to a centre or foundation, and become, as in Bataille, the "discourse of the limit" (1990, p. 18).

What Foucault, following Nietzsche, Blanchot and Bataille, also elaborates as a theme is the "uniqueness" and "unpredictability" of the singular historical instance, however. What he seeks to do is introduce conceptions of *indeterminacy, irregularity, openness, complexity* and *uniqueness* as integral to his conception of the historical process. In *The Archaeology of Knowledge* (1972, p. 101) examples abound: it takes the form of establishing the spatio-temporal coordinates that ensure the novel aspect of the "statement" (*énoncé*): "The enunciation is an unrepeatable event; it has situated and dated uniqueness that is irreducible. Yet this uniqueness allows of a number of constants—grammatical, semantic, logical—by which we can, by neutralising the moment of enunciation and the co-ordinates that individuate it, recognise the general form". Or again (1972, pp. 146–147), "every statement belongs to a certain regularity—that consequently none can be regarded as pure creation, as the marvellous disorder of genius. But we have also seen that no statement can be regarded as inactive and be valid as the scarcely real shadow or transfer of the initial statement. The whole enunciative field is both regular and alerted: it never sleeps". This fact that the future never simply reproduces the past, but adds always elements of novelty, means that the self is never simply the reproduced habitus of its socialisation, but due to its necessarily distinct location in time and space and culture, as well as its progressively growing capacity for agency, is characterised by elements of difference and uniqueness. Similarly, it means that ethical values can never simply be expressed merely as *repeatable* rules of conduct, which increases, rather than decreases, our sense of ethical responsibility in action.

Such a conception also expresses an "internalist" view of history. There is no guiding principle underlying structures or their emergence. Difference, then, is historical, and resists transcendence in all its forms, whether God, Cogito, Forms, Economy. There is nothing outside of history. Although such a conception does not adopt a uniform ahistorical model of temporalisation, or prioritise one element (economy) over others, neither does it deny that invariant necessities may exist which can express themselves through the different discursive lens of a particular historical periods. In this sense, as Joseph Margolis (1993, p. 204) notes, Foucault does not deny a world of "things", he:

> does not dismiss de re necessities of this or that episteme; they are rightly recognised there as the necessities they are. But they are also not enshrined as universal, changeless structures of any kind (regarding world or reason). [Rather,] [w]e are always invited to "test" for the "limits" that we may go beyond. That's to say: the invariances of any proposed transcendental limits of reason may be tested by exploring whether we can alter such a model of coherence convincingly, in a way that rests on historical change.

Like Heidegger, in *Being and Time*, Foucault manifests a pragmatic anti-foundationalism. Such an approach bears a similarity to parallel developments in Western Anglo-American philosophy to writers like Dewey, Quine, Davidson, Putnam, Kuhn and Goodman, and in the continental tradition to writers like Habermas, Bourdieu and Apel. While all developed versions of historicism, all denied any total pernicious form of relativism and all claimed a measure of objectivity. For Foucault, the maxim that "everything is historical" means that while we remain forever imprisoned by contingency, non-correspondence, relativity and ideological prejudice, there are some "footholds", even if they do not lead easily to a uniform consensus. Foucault's anti-essentialism places him alongside a possible (pragmatic) reading of Popper, who also rejected essentialist ontologies, in that there is nothing that prevents testing and attempted falsifications in order to "take a bearing", or "check the situation out". While this will give a certain form of confidence on some issues, on others, the conditions of what constitutes falsifiability will not be so easy to foresee.[3] Foucault's realism holds to the view that correspondence or synchronisation of discourse and reality is not required. Rather than correspondence, we must speak of isomorphism. There is no assurance, pace Kant, either, of transcendentally valid and universally reliable cognitive schemata, for such a conception relies on a conception of a subject posited prior to history. What justified Kant's cognitive schemata depends on various historically contingent conditions within what Heidegger would call the "horizon" within which they appear. This doesn't mean there are no historical justifications (survival), nor does it mean there are no footholds of any sort. But with Heidegger, Foucault's thesis of the historicity of existence would deny that there is any eternal "point of view".

Although Foucault acknowledges a debt to Nietzsche, it would be an error to represent his approach as simply Nietzschean and would misrepresent his relation to Marx and to radical politics. As well as Nietzsche, Foucault has debts to Heidegger, and Herbert Dreyfus (1992, pp. 80–81) claims that "it was through Heidegger that Foucault came to appreciate Nietzsche". As Foucault (1985, p. 9) says, "it is possible that if I had not read Heidegger, I would not have read Nietzsche. I had tried to read Nietzsche in the fifties but Nietzsche alone did not appeal to me—whereas Nietzsche and Heidegger, that was a philosophical shock". One of the central themes which Foucault shared with Heidegger and Nietzsche, as well as with the French Marxist, Althusser, was their challenge to the Cartesian and Kantian conceptions of the subject. He was also influenced by Heidegger in terms of the understanding of Being as indicating the presuppositions, things, tools, language, institutions, shared understandings, and other people, which determines what is deemed possible or impossible, or what counts as important or unimportant, or meaningful or unmeaningful. Like Heidegger, Foucault came to reject the view of a constant, ahistorical, universal truth, which came to influence his rejection of essentialism and other forms of foundationalism, thereby influencing the precise nature of his materialism. Yet another writer that Foucault has cause to refer to is Spinoza, whom he refers to and summarises in several of his papers over the course of his writing career.[4] While Spinoza cannot be represented as a direct influence, his detailed understanding of Spinoza is suggestive in that Spinoza's concepts of *conatus*, the univocity of being, power, politics, constitutive praxis, and the general fit with a theory of republican constitutionalism can, if suitably modified according to the dictates of difference, be rendered broadly compatible with Foucault's approach.

7 Complexity and Openness

In that Foucault talks of "chance" and "unpredictability", such a conception of historical openness is not technically incompatible with deterministic Newtonian physics, in the sense that events and outcomes are still the result of antecedent conditions. Causation, in Foucault's view, however, is conceived of *systemically*, in terms of a model of holism–particularism, or complex causation, which makes events, which are the outcomes of system interactions in open systems, *effectively* unpredictable, in that the full range of possible combinations or effects cannot be specified in advance. Complex systems, moreover, are contingent and dynamic, whereby the structure of the system is continuously transformed through the interaction of the elements and which are not explainable in reference to any external principle, origin, or foundation. In this process, says Cilliers (1998, pp. 107–108), "no complex system, whether biological or social, can be understood without considering its history. ... To be more precise, the history of a system ... co-determines the structure of a system". In this theory, while change is understood as the outcome of contingent complex activity, human agency is understood as an emergent property of the historical and social system.[5]

In insisting on the open nature of the historical system, Foucault's approach to understanding history parallels Derrida's critique and revision of Saussure's in stressing the open and incomplete character of the totality of social relations. In Foucault, however, the analysis proceeds beyond the textual to an analysis of the historical relations between the discursive and pre-discursive, whereas for Derrida and Saussure the analysis is synchronic and confined to language. Throughout his career, in fact, it can be said that Foucault maintains a distinction between the discursive and the pre-discursive. In his early period, prior to *The Archaeology of Knowledge*, written in 1968, Foucault sees discourses formed on the basis of *epistemes*, that provide a unified view of intellectual life during a particular period or age. After his turn to genealogy, he developed such an approach more directly in relation to how the practices discursive and pre-discursive were related. As a consequence, in retaining the poststructural emphasis on the open and incomplete nature of the totality, but applied to history and social relations, rather than language, Foucault's more materialist approach has radical implications for our understanding of concepts like determinism, predictability, and the future.

In this context, it is worth noting the parallel between Foucault's systemic conception of change, linked closely to a system of open possibilities or variations, and what is now known as complexity theory. Although having roots in ancient Chinese and Greek thought, versions of complexity theory are a relatively new field of scientific enquiry and are perhaps one of the most notable new developments since the advent of quantum theory in the early 1900s. Such theories are not only compatible with materialism, but are systemic, or holist, in that they account for diversity and unity in the context of a systemic field of complex interactional changes. Chaos theory is one version of complexity.

Partly with origins in computing technology, and partly in the development of new non-Euclidean structures of fractal geometrical mathematics, chaos theory became concerned to explain "the qualitative study of unstable aperiodic behaviour in deterministic non-linear dynamical systems" (Sardar & Abrams, 1999, p. 9).[6] It is complexity theory more broadly, however, that has drawn off poststructural methods, and establishes them as a form of critical realism.[7]

In his book *Complexity and Postmodernism*, Paul Cilliers (1998, p. VIII) defines complexity in the following way:

> In a complex system ... the interaction constituents of the system, and the interaction between the system and its environment, are of such a nature that the system as a whole cannot be fully understood simply by analysing its components. Moreover, these relationships are not fixed, but shift and change, often as a result of self-organisation. This can result in novel features, usually referred to in terms of emergent properties. The brain, natural language and social systems are complex.

Poststructuralism, says Cilliers, has introduced a new conception of complexity based on "distributed" or "relational" representation, following Saussure.[8] Such a system is complex in relation to the fact that it has a large number of elements which interact dynamically in a non-linear and asymmetrical manner. Interactions take place in open systems through "self-organisation" by adapting dynamically to changes in both the environment and the system. Self-organisation is an *emergent* property of the system as a whole. An emergent property is a property that is constituted due to the combination of elements in the system as a whole. As such, it is a property possessed by the system but not by its components.[9] Cilliers (1998, p. 90) defines "self-organisation" as "the capacity of complex systems which enables them to develop or change internal structure spontaneously and adaptively in order to cope with or manipulate the environment". Such systems are not in equilibrium because they are constantly changing as a consequence of interaction between system and environment, and as well as being influenced by external factors are influenced by the history of the system (1998, p. 66). Cilliers identifies social systems, the economy, the human brain, and language as complex systems.[10]

Hence one could characterise Foucault's conception of societies as "non-equilibrium systems", where no general laws can predict the detailed behaviour of such systems. As much that develops does so as a consequence of emergence, life is created as a consequence of the collective interactions of parts. This entails not only the limitless possibility of combinations that can occur in open environments, but also that as the collectivity possesses properties and energies not possessed by the parts, but through which change can take place, new forms and patterns can develop. Relatively small changes in initial conditions can trigger major changes throughout the system, in part or whole. Such a perspective gives a new insight to the "contradictions of capitalism".[11] Although for Foucault, the economy cannot be represented as a transhistorical foundation permitting an understanding of change in history, it can be analysed internally, i.e., a genealogy of capitalism in terms of the history of economic structures, and the effects they engender throughout the social structure. Although I realise that this brief account cannot possibly do justice to the topics of complexity theory, emergence, chance or critical realism, it is broadly in this direction that Foucault's historical materialism leads.

8   The Nature of Identity

Given that structural linguistics seeks to define identity relationally, Saussure (1974, p. 120) argued that it cannot posit a theory of identity as a substantive entity, or as a concrete "positive" unique particularity. This was retained by Derrida in his revision of Saussure's view, seeing identities as constituted by the series of *traces* of the differences in the system.[12] But if one conceives of identity in purely relational terms, as Mark Currie (2004, p. 13) notes, "it could be said that the concept of difference is no respecter of difference". As he continues, in explaining Saussure's view:

> A theory of subjectivity, or personhood, for example, might locate identity not in the body of the individual but in the relations between that person and others. In other words a person might not be defined by inherent characteristics, but like Saussure's train or chess piece, be understood as an identity only because of the relationships that person has with other people, in a system of family, friendship and social relations. This would be referred to as a relational view of personal identity. The same might be said of collective identities. It might be argued for example, that a national identity is not one that is made up of inherent qualities (of "positive terms" in Saussure's language) but of relational ones concerned with how a nation distinguishes itself from other nations.

For Nietzsche, Deleuze and Foucault, difference operates historically and has a dynamic quality that the theories of Saussure and Derrida lack. On this basis there is no reason why the traces that infuse identity could not be seen as leaving a residue or mark, developing into a positive conception of self constituted through complex interactions in the to and from of the historical process. The stress on historical praxis creates a more enduring sense of identity in this sense. While this still leaves identity as relational in terms of its constitution, an identity which can be represented as positive and substantial (in the sense of it being irrepressible or non-reducible) is the outcome of self-creation or constitutive praxis in history.[13]

Such a view has the advantage over Saussure's and Derrida's view in that it can account for a substantial conception of the self, and explain, in the context of historical and social constructionist views of the self, how identities can emerge that are both *distinct* and *unique*,[14] which are non-reversible, and irreducible to the social whole.[15] For Nietzsche and Deleuze, following Duns Scotus, Spinoza and Hume, identities are constituted in experience, which is defined in terms of complex effects and relations, as practices (or for Deleuze, *haecceities*) whose complex modes of operation are *individuating* (but not personalising or privatising). For Deleuze (1985; Deleuze & Guattari, 1987, chapter 1), such patterns show parallels to nomadology or rhizomatic (rather than arborescent) development. For Foucault (1990), it is "outside thought"; for Nietzsche, "gay science". In 20th-century Marxist thought, Althusser's conception of structural causality, as outlined at the start of this article, partly fits such a model.[16] Similar models of organisation and development are also evident in Spinoza's "ethics", as what Spinozian interpreters like Damasio (2003, p. 37) call "nesting" theories of development, where the "parts of simple reactions [are] incorporated as components of more elaborate ones, a nesting of the simple within the complex".[17] Yet other approaches utilising complex models, although in somewhat variable ways, are cybernetics, or the early theories of Gregory Bateson (see Bateson, 1972).

9 Difference and Community

That Foucault identifies pluralism as a central principle on which Marxism fails has affinities with liberal criticisms of Marxism and Hegelianism. Foucault's opposition to utopianism and his unease regarding consensus models of policymaking parallel liberal sentiments as well. Yet to what extent this represents a failure to face up to the issue of collective politics might well be asked. Given also a marked reluctance to theorise the role of the state, one could ask whether Foucault doesn't implicitly fall back on some conception of the invisible hand of a beneficent nature with respect to the coordinative tasks of human collectivities.

If his conception of difference is not to merely result in an atomistic retreat to individualism, it must within it, or in relation to it, build in a notion of community. Because this is not normally the way Foucault or poststructuralist conceptions are stated, it is necessary to further articulate the justifications for such a designation. Central to my argument is that Foucault's notion of difference presupposes a "minimal universalism", which in turn necessitates a certain conception of community. Just as people are marked by their difference, they also have commonalities between them. While aspects of race or culture may separate them, they will be linked in their common aspirations (food, shelter and support). To say this is to say that difference must be paired with commonality in a way where neither is reducible to the other. As Deleuze might say, while any structures manifest *segmentarity*, the point that also needs to be made is that proliferating segmentarities are also characterised by *structure*.

My own way of representing this is to say that that differences must be underpinned by a minimal universalism. By this I mean a limited and conditional universalism which does not "overarch" or "ground" difference, but which must be seen as always "co-present" with difference, and which permits of variations in degree in different times and places. It is not a Kantian universalism in relation to reason but rather a Nietzschean and Spinozian universalism conditional upon the will of the human species to survive. To the extent that there is such a will to survive, then there are certain implications for democratic politics and the equalisation of power, and certain shared concerns. The argument is that a concordance of difference and unity is a requirement of Foucault's thought if it is not to suffer from self-contradiction. While Foucault supports a conception of the politics and philosophy of difference in the sense that he opposes the unitaristic tendencies inherent in Hegelianism, Marxism, and other Enlightenment discourses as well, it is important that he does not privilege difference over unity, or to the exclusion of unity.

This perspective, which entails that difference can only be articulated in the context of a concept of community, stands opposed to the perspective of some poststructuralist writers. My own argument places greater emphasis upon the complementary nature of difference and community. It is based both on an analysis of the concept of difference in Western philosophical ontology and on Foucault's representation of difference as dialogical or relational, presupposing strategies to equalise power relations, involving, not isolation or separateness, but an open-ended process of negotiation and debate. Since the time of the Greeks, and certainly in Marxism and Hegelianism, difference has been articulated in relation to unity. While Marxism has always refused to make the theme of difference its organising principle, it has always found a place for difference in relation to unity. What the poststructuralist correction involves, then, is altering their ontological weightings of "unity" and "difference" within the context of the theory as a whole. As Milton Fisk (1993, p. 326) observes:

> The materialist interpretation of history is certainly in the tradition of the theme of difference-in-unity, for it attempts to organise the different aspects of a society around its economy considered as a unity. ... Post Marxists of the poststructuralist sort claim that privileging gets us into difficulty since it is inherently reductionist of differences.

The central argument here—that Foucault must be adjudged a "thin" communitarian—relates to the sub-arguments that difference cannot constitute a structuring ontological principle on its own, but must always be seen in relation to unity. While difference will affect the sort of communitarianism that Foucault could be adjudged as subscribing to, it nevertheless constitutes the ordering principle of a community. The central point here is that, as Fisk (1993) observes, the ontological postulates of difference and unity have to be kept in balance, which is to say that the principle of difference cannot plausibly explain social relations on its own (Fisk, 1993, p. 324). This is why in classical philosophy the theme of otherness, which underpins difference, was always paired with that of unity or identity. To try to make one's philosophical orientation work solely on the grounds of difference neglects equally strong arguments for "unity". For to try to define objects solely in terms of differences neglects equally compelling reasons for considering them as objects of certain kinds. Similarly, if, as the poststructuralist insists, a final synthesis is not possible to achieve, this doesn't mean, nor should it entail, that all unities or identities simply collapse into differences, or that social life is simply a process of endless, vicious regress. In short, as Fisk (1993, p. 325) argues, unless the theory of difference is to result in incoherence, there must be a minimal kind of unity. This is perhaps the major reason for considering Foucault as a "thin" communitarian.

To represent this argument in political terms, it can be said that pushing the principle of difference too far results in contradiction. While Foucault, like Deleuze, wants to celebrate multiplicity and a decentred polis, the fundamental ambiguity results from the fact that respecting the autonomy of different groups—whether based on religion, race, gender, or ethnicity—is only possible within certain bounds unless difference is to be elevated as a new universal. This paradoxically lets Kant in through the back door: "act always so as to respect the difference of the other".

Todd May (1994, pp. 39–40) develops a similar argument in relation to Deleuze, which applies equally well to Foucault. As he expresses the point:

> Thus Deleuze asks us to think difference as constitutive all the way, and of unity as a product of the play of difference. But if difference is to be thought of as constitutive, this is in order to rid philosophy not of unities,

but of unifying forces or principles that either preclude difference or relegate it to a negative phenomenon.

Part of the point here is that difference cannot be reduced to a logic outside of history or injected with metaphysical serum. Thus, for Foucault, neither difference nor unity can be seen as primary. As May (1994, pp. 46–47) puts the point:

> If meaning were merely the product of difference, there would be no meaning, only noises unrelated to each other. In order for meaning to occur, identity must exist within difference, or better, each must exist within the other. To speak with Saussure, if language is a system of differences, it is not only differences but system as well; and system carries with it the thought of identity ... to posit a concept whose function is to be given primacy to difference is to violate the necessary chiasmic relationship between unity and difference.

Like Deleuze, Foucault utilizes difference to create a context to shape a way of thinking for a general perspective. Central here is how the concept of difference is to function, and for Foucault the principle functions to undermine the unity of being that has reigned supreme from Plato to Hegel, to introduce a new way of thinking philosophically. Yet difference and commonality exist in relation to each other: in that people all manifest the commonality of needing nutrition, they manifest difference in relation to that single goal. In Foucault's pluralism, systems are not unities but compositions of series, each defined on the basis of difference.

In this sense, it is necessary to modify poststructuralist thought in several senses, for difference cannot explain identity on its own. It cannot explain diversity either, for if all were simply different there would be unintelligible communities who could not relate to each other. In this sense, as Philip Pettit (1997, p. 249) explains with respect to the "politics of difference":

> that while it requires partial forms of civility in order to be effective, it also requires a disposition on the part of people, even people of quite different perspectives, to display a civility that relates to the society as a whole. Let people cease to countenance society-wide norms in their enthusiasm for more local affiliations, and the republic will degenerate into a battlefield of rival interest fields.

Thus, while we may accept Deleuze's and Foucault's Spinozist position seeing difference as constitutive of reality but seeing unities and commonalities as the contingent outcome (assemblages, apparatuses, hegemonies), or in Spinoza's sense, as the "expression" of historical practice, pluralism cannot be seen as founded on a metaphysical atomism but must be seen as describing a world of interconnections and relations linked to the inevitability of commonalities, or of totalising episodes. What should thus be noted with respect to Deleuze and Foucault is that neither necessarily sees difference as metaphysically *detached* from commonalities/unities, or as one set being reducible to the other.

It is also important to distinguish "unity" from "commonality", however. To say that communities must have common features is not to say they need be highly unified or consensual. A community may have commonality (of concerns, interests, features) without having an excessively high degree of unity, or even without having a centre, hence giving rise to the possibility of an *acentred community*.[18] In addition to this, we may also characterise communities as varying in their degree of unity, i.e., as displaying different relations of unity/difference at different historical periods. In terms of historical practice, in particular societies at particular times, we might also distinguish processes of *convergence* (or what Foucault called *totalization*) as opposed to processes of *deconvergence* (*individualization*). Processes of *decovergence* allow for greater difference, whereas processes of *convergence* stress unity. Nazism represents a supreme example of convergence in the recent normative history of states. Some societies may encourage unity, or uniformity, however, if the overall tasks of survival and well-being are being threatened.[19]

The political problem, not adequately addressed by either Marx or Foucault, is one of reconciling the collective with the particular. If Hegel's theism defines the limits at which unity is imposed, then the permissibility of difference (diversity) will be very confined, and Hegel has been rightly criticised on this ground.[20] If the limits on diversity are in accord with species survival and well-being, however, given optimal historical circumstances, they may be much wider, as this is a broad criterion potentially permitting of a wide range of styles of life.[21] At a social ontological level, these are always in tension, and are historically variable, in terms of society's or humanity's relation to survival and well-being. At a political/normative level, as Marx suggestively pointed out in his critique of Hegel, they are tensions which only democracy can reconcile.[22] And clearly it is appropriate that difference is an entitlement to the extent that the survival (of individuals, groups, and humanity) is not threatened.

10   Conclusion

While Foucault's project thus marks a break with Marxism's central postulates, there is, as Balibar (1992, p. 56) observes, a partial usage of Marxist tenets as well. Like Marx, Foucault asks questions of the same order, concerning philosophy and philosophy of history, and concerning the nature of historical investigations. Both writers can be represented as "historical materialists", *albeit, in quite different senses*. As Balibar (1992, pp. 54–55) notes:

> Inasmuch as it is true that the *shift* in philosophy as practised by Marx and by Foucault involves, in a nutshell, the need which has existed for a century to move from a philosophy *of* history to a philosophy *in* history, it is necessary, in the rigorous form of a series of dilemmas (*either* Marx *or* Foucault), that the main lines of tension of a theoretical field should become apparent and, eventually, definable. This field must, in some form, *already* exist, and it must already have been traversed and particularised. Nonetheless it must remain to a large extent *to be discovered* and defined cartographically. Perhaps it could be referred to as the field of "historical materialism". ... Central to this ... is the concept of social relations or contradictions as a structure internal to power relations. This is what sustains the Marxian notion of historical materialism. This then is what, more and more explicitly, Foucault questions. At the (provisional) point of his evolution on this question ... he developed ideas which it would not be wrong to refer to by the name of "historical materialism", but in a way which is opposed, in each of the ways in which it is meant, to Marx: *materiality* is seen not as the materiality of "social relations" but as the materiality of the apparatus and practice of power, inasmuch as it affects *bodies*; *historicity* is seen not as the historicity of contradiction (whether this be viewed as an instance of the totalisation of different forms of struggle or as an instance of the interiorisation of their necessity) but in terms of the historicity of the *event*; the improbable outcome of various strategies of repression and of multiple and partially uncontrollable forms of subjugation.

Balibar's point that Foucault addresses the issue in a way that is "opposed" to Marx needs some qualification, however. Although Foucault does focus on power relations generally, rather than privilege productive economic relations specifically, his approach is still compatible with a *materiality of social relations* in this broader sense, as well as with a thesis of the "univocity of being" of material physical necessities of the world. In relation to *historicity*, moreover, while he does reject the notion of the dialectic, in preference for an ontology based on events and practices, his approach still implies the historicity and relativity of all established structures and orders, political, economic and theoretical, and of social systems, institutions and concepts.

His approach can be seen as representing, then, a complex relation to Marx. While Foucault clearly rejects the Feuerbachian humanist emphasis of the early Marx, which sees men as realising their essence in history, as they throw off the conditions of their repression and alienation, Foucault's anti-essentialism would signal a rejection of teleology, in that, for him, there is no essence to be liberated. For Foucault, development is not conceived as an unfolding, or unwinding, or recovery of one's true humanity, but as an act of individual and collective self-constitution.

Such a view is not, of course, necessarily in conflict with the more materialistic position of the later Marx, once he had recanted the Feuerbachian humanist emphasis of the earlier period. Indeed, in many respects, Foucault's theoretical anti-humanism accords with Althusser's (1969, 1970) interpretation of Marx's position, after the "epistemological break" of 1845. Certainly, in *The Holy Family*, written in Paris in the autumn of 1844, Marx reveals a new more materialist, less humanist, less idealist perspective, and repudiates the humanist metaphysical and contemplative materialism of his earlier *Thesis on Feuerbach*. It squares, too, with Engels's (1946, p. 36) description of *The Holy Family* when he wrote:

> The cult of abstract man, which formed the kernel of Feuerbach's new religion, had to be replaced by the science of real men and of their historical development. This fuller development of Feuerbach's standpoint beyond Feuerbach was inaugurated by Marx in 1845 in *The Holy Family*.

Such a perspective leads Foucault to represent history, as Althusser represents Marx's view, not as a teleology, but as "process without a subject" (see Althusser, 1969, 1970, 1982, p. 183). Yet, while the affinities are clearly there, unlike Althusser, Foucault seeks also to overcome the problems of structuralism, which posited a single founding structure as the basis of explaining the nature of experience.[23] Structuralism also fails to account for *agency* in history, or for any conception of the constitution of the identity of the self in history.[24] Foucault's more historical and more nominalist approach led him to express a fundamental optimism over the prospects for self-creation, emphasising the creative role of the human subject within the historical process. This gives a specifically critical role for the intellectual and educator. As he states (Martin et al., 1988, p. 10):

> My role ... is to show people that they are much freer than they feel, that people accept as truth, as evidence, some themes which have been built up at a certain moment during history, and that this so-called evidence

can be criticised and destroyed. To change something in the minds of people—that is the role of the intellectual.

This also gives a role to critique, and transcendence which, within the context of history and its contingencies seek to expose the historical transitory constraints of contemporary consciousness as realised in and through discursive practices. Such constraints impose limitations which have become so intimately a part of the way that people experience their lives that they no longer experience these systems as limitations but embrace them as the very structure of normal and natural human behaviour. Within these limits, seen as both the limits of reason and the limits of nature, freedom is subordinated to reason, which is subordinated to nature, and it is against such a reduction of reason to nature that Foucault struggles. His commitment is to a form of "permanent criticism" which must be seen as linked to his broader programme of freedom of thought. It is the freedom to think differently than what we already know.

Notwithstanding his opposition to Hegel, consensus politics, and utopian reasoning, with Foucault, as with Marx, the historical and social achieve an ontological status, which are to be understood more through individual and collective practices of trial and error, than through any appeal to the senses or the autonomy of reason. It is the practices of history and society that write the script on the body, and which constitute identity. This was an emphasis which made him depart from the linguistic turn in French thought.

Foucault sees Marx as writing squarely within an Enlightenment problematic, and as overemphasising the importance of rationality of the human subject, as well as human agency in both individual and collective terms. While reason is not impossible, it is not autonomous or independent of prevailing social and historical conditions, nor is it simply a pure expression of the prevailing socialised patterns of the class system, nor manifested solely in relation to the individual or the group. Reason is possible, but individuals' rational faculties are both clouded and impeded by prevailing ideologies, by oppressive social conditions, or by inadequate education of critical faculties and capabilities. Exercising rational capacity depends upon these prior resources and development; it depends on effective collective structures of education, deliberation, communication and dialogue. It depends too on the existence of democratic structures so that policies can be developed, discussed, framed and implemented.

As with Spinoza and Marx, for Foucault the fortunes of the individual are linked to those of the collective. It was in challenging domination, where the forces of power are unequal, not just in the economy, but as they echo throughout the entire social formation. If power operates everywhere, then it is in exposing the way it secretes itself in the fine textures of societies, and in how it manifests itself, unrecognised, in the operations of people's lives, that becomes of crucial concern. For Foucault, Nietzsche recovers Marx's original intention, in that while not neglecting economic power, he extends our understanding of it as something overdetermined and called forth in the processes, strategies and mechanisms by which reproduction and change are affected. As exemplified by what is rejected in deterministic and economistic versions of Marx, based on dialectical logics, the priorities of the economy, and historical teleologies, Foucault advances a conception of struggle, force and strategy; and rather than invariant ahistorical categories of class and economy, history is viewed as based on contingency and a conception of complex causality and chance. In this scenario, criticism is about identifying and removing constraints. As Foucault (1984c, p. 45) puts it in opposition to Kant:

> Criticism indeed consists of analysing and reflecting upon limits. But if the Kantian question was that of knowing what limits knowledge must abstain from transgressing it seems to me that the critical question today has to be turned back into a positive one: in what is given to us as universal, necessary or obligatory, what part is taken up by things which are actually singular, contingent, the product of arbitrary constraints? The point, in brief, is to transform critique conducted in the form of necessary limitations into a practical critique that takes the form of a possible transgression.

If for Foucault transcendence does not posit linear succession to a new tomorrow or posit solutions in a utopia of objectively ordered possibilities, this is because the utopian spirit, as I have argued elsewhere (Olssen, 2003), is embodied—"repressed"—within the present, in Foucault's work. This gives us a normative politics of the present based upon openness and struggle. Class struggles—yes, but not just class struggles. Also, race struggles, sex and gender struggles, developmental and lifestyle struggles, struggles to throw off domination and reclaim freedom through equalising power, challenging hegemonies, and resisting servitude. Like Marx, Foucault's reluctance to "posit solutions" left him without an articulated and developed conception of politics, which leaves an opening for future intellectual work as to how Nietzsche can supplement Marx, in the quest for a radical conception of democracy which overcomes the problems of totality and determination. In this sense, as McDonald (2002) notes perceptively, Marx's ideas represent an important "limit-experience" *within* Foucault's theory.[25] This is a Marx freed from the dogma of 19th-century categories, perhaps best illustrated in his Preface to *Anti-Oedipus*, which he titled "Introduction to the Nonfascist Life". Here Foucault (2001, pp. 108–109) lists the following principles:

- Free political action from all unitary and totalizing paranoia.
- Develop action, thought and desires by proliferation, juxtaposition, and disjunction, and not by subdivision and pyramidal hierarchization.
- Withdraw allegiance from the old categories of the Negative (law, limit, castration, lack, lacuna), which Western thought has long held sacred as a form of power and an access to reality. Prefer what is positive and multiple, difference over uniformity, flows over unities, mobile arrangements over systems. Believe that what is productive is not sedentary but nomadic.
- Do not think that one has to be sad in order to be militant, even though the thing one is fighting is abominable. It is the connection of desire to reality ... that possesses revolutionary force.
- Do not use thought to ground a political practice in Truth, nor political action to discredit, as mere speculation, a line of thought. Use political practice as an intensifier of thought, and analysis as a multiplier of the forms and domains for the intervention of political action.
- Do not demand of politics that it restore the "rights" of the individual, as philosophy has defined them. The individual is the product of power. What is needed is to "de-individualize" by means of multiplication and displacement, diverse combinations. The group must not be the organic bond uniting hierarchized individuals, but a constant generator of deindividualization.
- Do not become enamoured of power.

Given that Foucault's theories point logically in this direction, it is surprising that he at times underemphasised the importance of collective power and the state to the extent he did. Given the ever-present dangers thrown up by the unpredictable happenings of the global environment, the coordinative role of the state, and of global agencies, would seem to be of central importance as we enter the 21st century. What is in an individual's interests is inseparable from the collective interest of humankind, and from the security of the planet. In an age of terrorism and climate change, the possibilities of individuals existing in a quasi-anarchistic utopia, where the problems of individuals are not coordinated collectively, is unimaginable. Rather than accept a theory of the reduced or minimal state, as Hayek and liberals do, and as Foucault was at times inclined to do, as an answer to the significant problems posed by collective power today, one must, in a global era, adopt a different strategy and ask instead, how can state and collective power be harnessed and controlled, and how must institutional and international relations be reconfigured as a result. I have argued elsewhere for what can be called a *comprehensive theory of democracy* operating in the context of a global theory of institutional checks and balances, as well as within particular nation states. It is in this direction, supported by the norms of equalisation and democratisation, that a Foucauldian historical materialism of power must lead. If global society is a complex structure of conflicting powers, radical democracy would seem to be the best structure where conflict is best settled in a design for adaptive compromise in the interests of survival.

Acknowledgement

This chapter originally appeared as Olssen, M. (2004), Foucault and Marxism: Rewriting the theory of historical materialism, *Policy Futures in Education*, 2(3–4), 454–482, http://dx.doi.org/10.2304/pfie.2004.2.3.3. Reprinted here, with minor edits, with permission from the publisher.

Notes

1 I would like to thank Semiotext(e) for permission to publish this expanded quotation from Michel Foucault, *Remarks on Marx* (Foucault, 1991b).
2 In his review of Deleuze's books ("Theatrum philosophicum"), Foucault (1998, p. 366) reinforces the importance of chance: "The present as the recurrence of difference, as repetition giving voice to difference, affirms at once the totality of chance. The univocity of being in Duns Scotus led to the immobility of an abstraction, in Spinoza it led to the necessity and eternity of substance; but here it leads to the single throw of chance in the fissure of the present. If being always declares itself in the same way, it is not because being is one but because the totality of chance is affirmed in the single dice throw of the present".
3 As, for example, when they tried to test Copernicus's theories in astronomy by dropping stones from church spires to test to see whether the earth was rotating on its axis.
4 See, for instance, Foucault's essay "Truth and Juridical Forms", originally published in May 1973, where he summarises Spinoza in relation to Nietzsche (Foucault, 2001, pp. 11–12); again, Foucault refers to Spinoza in the debate with Chomsky (Foucault & Chomsky, 1997, p. 136); in "Theatrum philosophicum" (Foucault, 1998, pp. 359–360 and 366–367); and in "Afterword to *The Temptation of St Anthony*" (1998, p. 105), just to name a few. It is also noteworthy that Deleuze was influenced by Spinoza, as Deleuze had a strong influence on Foucault. See Paul Veyne (1997, pp. 63–64), "Foucault Revolutionizes History". Also see index entries to Deleuze & Guattari (1987), Deleuze (1990, 1994) and others. Like Deleuze, Foucault (1998, p. 364) "adapts" Spinozist concepts to express his views. For example: "The univocity of being, its singleness of expression, is paradoxically the principal condition that permits difference to escape the domination of identity, frees it from the law of the Same as a simple opposition within conceptual elements".

5 Foucault, like Nietzsche, wrote philosophically, and hence his use of terms like "chance", "unpredictability" possibly lacks technical translatability to the language of natural science. An account of classical definition of concepts such as "stability", "chance", etc. is given by Cilliers (1998). In complex systems, as Cilliers (1998, p. 109) says, "novel, unpredicted behaviour need not be a result of chance. It can be 'caused' by the complex interaction of a large number of factors. ... Complexity is not to be confused with randomness and chance but cannot be confused with first-order logical terms either". In this sense, we can speak of events which are theoretically unpredictable, which are not explainable in terms of "chance".

6 For other accounts of chaos theory, see Swinney (1983), Holder (1985), Gleick (1987), Sappington (1990) and Ayers (1997).

7 Chaos theory and complexity theories are distinct although chaos theory can be seen as one type of complexity theory, which emphasises the importance of sensitivity to initial conditions. This is not so important with complex systems in general, which stress the interaction of a large number of components (see Cilliers, 1998, p. IX).

8 Meaning is conferred not by one-to-one correspondence with the world but by relationships between structural components of the system. See Cilliers (1998, p. 81). His analysis of poststructural complexity is based on Saussure's well-known analysis in the *Course in General Linguistics* (1974). Having said this, it is interesting that Cilliers translates poststructural philosophy into Western analytic schemas rather than elaborate his thesis in relation to difference theory as elaborated by Foucault or Deleuze. I have done the same here simply to convey something of the tenor of the poststructural innovation.

9 Other forms of emergentist materialism in Western thought, see Bunge (1977), Haken (1977, 1990), or Skarda and Freeman (1990). Although such theories are broadly analogous to Foucault's materialism, the emphasis in poststructuralism on the open and incomplete character of the totality presents new insights into issues like determination and chance. Again, see Cilliers (1998)

10 For another view of complexity theory, see Kauffman (1991, 1993, 1995). Kauffman suggests that while events can be seen as having antecedent conditions which explain them, in open environments the possible combinations are unpredictable. Other characteristics of complex systems are that they do not operate near equilibrium; the relationships between components are non-linear and dynamic; elements do not have fixed positions; the relationships between elements are not stable; and there are always more possibilities than can be actualised.

11 The notion, for example, that carbon emissions can trigger climate change, which can have potentially unpredictable effects of unimaginable severity, is one illustration of how determination works in relation to complex causality.

12 For Derrida (1981, p. 26) the sign has no positive identity but comprises only the collection of traces of all the other signs that run through it.

13 If we think of someone like "Churchill", there is something trite in representing him as the outcome of the play of differences (Churchill is not Balfour, not Astor, not Baldwin, etc.), for agency in history established a substantial, yet non-essential sense. Yet this identity is still always precarious, incomplete, fragmented, inconsistent, and transitional. It represents at any particular time, a "settlement".

14 Liberals, especially Rawls (1971), bemoaned in *A Theory of Justice* that it was necessary to retreat to deontology (return to a rights discourse) because social approaches (including utilitarianism) could not account for the *distinctness* of identity.

15 Such theories of complex emergentist materialism can also account for the origins of mind as irrepressible (non-reducible) yet wholly material, or physical.

16 Such complex non-linear models are historically contingent in terms of their internal, substantive arrangements. In Althusser, the variability of the effectivity of the levels of practices of the social formation conforms to such a complex formula, albeit in structuralist and decid-

edly non-nominalistic terms. The ultimate necessity of the economic, however, does not conform, as it introduces a causal factor which is historically invariant across successive modes of production. In this sense, to use Deleuze and Guattari's (1987) language, Althusser's model of structural causality conforms to both *rhizonomic* and *arborescent* forms.

17 Damasio (2003, pp. 45–46) uses examples of social emotions, including sympathy, embarrassment, shame, etc., to exemplify the nesting principle. As he states (pp. 45–46), "a whole retinue of regulatory reactions along with elements present in primary emotions can be identified as subcomponents of social emotions in varied combinations. The nested incorporation of components from lower tiers is apparent. Think how the social emotion 'contempt' borrows from the facial expressions of 'disgust', a primary emotion that evolved in association with the autonomous and beneficial rejection of potentially toxic foods". The appropriate image for these reactions "is not that of a simple linear hierarchy" (p. 38).

18 Indeed, one might characterise the global community in such a way, but one could conceivably characterise various national communities in such a way as well.

19 For example, they may restrict the choices available to citizens. Many African states justified not having a British-styled higher education system based on the argument that they could not afford the luxury of a liberal education which was not vocationally oriented. Such societies may restrict choices without being totalitarian.

20 The Absolute for Hegel reconciled individual interests with the state, and ultimately, God, on the basis of a proscribed moral truth about how life should be conducted.

21 In the West, it is on the basis that the goals of survival and well-being are achieved that liberty is secured.

22 See Marx's "Critique of Hegel's Philosophy of the State", first published in 1843, reprinted in Marx (1967, p. 174). Here Marx says that "democracy, therefore, is the true unity of the general and the particular. ... In democracy there is *particular human existence*. ... This is the basic uniqueness of democracy".

23 Whether Marx did ever fully expunge all essentialist aspects from his anthropology is, of course, an issue of some debate, but not one that I wish to pursue here.

24 On Foucault and structuralism, see my article "Structuralism, Post-structuralism, Neo-liberalism" (Olssen, 2003).

25 The concept of "limit-experience" Foucault drew from George Bataille. For an early discussion, see his article "A Preface to Transgression" (Foucault, 1977a). Also see Foucault (1991b, pp. 31–32).

References

Althusser, L. (1969). *For Marx* (B. Brewster, Trans.). Penguin.

Althusser, L. (1970). *Reading capital*. New Left Books.

Althusser, L. (1982). *Montesquieu, Rousseau, Marx: Politics and history* (B. Brewster, Trans.). Verso.

Ayers, S. (1997). The application of chaos theory to psychology. *Theory and Psychology, 7*(3), 373–398.

Balibar, E. (1992). Foucault and Marx: The question of nominalism. In T. J. Armstrong (Ed. and Trans.), *Michel Foucault: Philosopher* (pp. 38–56). Harvester Wheatsheaf.

Barrett, M. (1988). *The politics of truth*. Polity.

Bateson, G. (1972). *Steps to an ecology of mind*. Ballantine.
Bunge, M. (1977). Emergence and the mind: Commentary. *Neuroscience, 2*, 501–509.
Cilliers, P. (1998). *Complexity and postmodernism: Understanding complex systems*. Routledge.
Currie, M. (2004). *Difference*. Routledge.
Damasio, A. (2003). *Looking for Spinoza*. Verso.
Davidson, A. I. (Ed.). (1997). *Foucault and his interlocutors*. University of Chicago Press.
Deleuze, G. (1985). Nomad thought. In D. B. Allison (Ed.), *The new Nietzsche* (pp. 142–149). MIT Press.
Deleuze, G. (1990). *The logic of sense* (M. Lester with C. Stiavale, Trans.; C. V. Bourdas, Ed.). Columbia University Press.
Deleuze, G. (1994). *Difference and repetition* (P. Patton, Trans.). Continuum.
Deleuze, G., & Guattari, F. (1987). *A thousand plateaus: Capitalism and schizophrenia* (B. Massumi, Trans. and foreword). Continuum.
Derrida, J. (1981). *Positions*. University of Chicago Press.
Dreyfus, H. (1992). On the ordering of things: Being and power in Heidegger and Foucault. In T. J. Armstrong (Ed. and Trans.), *Michel Foucault: Philosopher* (pp. 80–98). Harvester Wheatsheaf.
Engels, F. (1946). *Ludwig Feuerbach and the end of classical German philosophy* (with Appendix: K. Marx, *Thesis on Feuerbach*) (first published 1886 in Die Neue Zeit). Progress Publishers.
Engels, F. (1978). Letter to Joseph Bloch. In R. C. Tucker (Ed.), *The Marx–Engels reader* (2nd ed., pp. 760–765). W. W. Norton. (Original work published 1890)
Fisk, M. (1993). Poststructuralism, difference and Marxism. *Praxis International, 12*, 323–340.
Foucault, M. (1972). *The archaeology of knowledge* (A. Sheridan, Trans.). Tavistock.
Foucault, M. (1977a). A preface to transgression. In D. F. Bouchard (Ed.), *Language, counter-memory, practice: Selected essays and interviews* (D. F. Bouchard & S. Simon, Trans.; pp. 29–52). Cornell University Press.
Foucault, M. (1977b). *Discipline and punish* (A. Sheridan, Trans.). Pantheon.
Foucault, M. (1978). Politics and the study of discourse (C. Gordon, Trans.). *Ideology and Consciousness, 3*(Spring), 7–26.
Foucault, M. (1980a). Prison talk (C. Gordon, Trans.). In C. Gordon (Ed.), *Power/knowledge: Selected interviews and other writings 1972–1977* (pp. 37–54). Harvester Press.
Foucault, M. (1980b). Truth and power (C. Gordon, Trans.). In C. Gordon (Ed.), *Power/knowledge: Selected interviews and other writings 1972–1977* (pp. 109–133). Harvester Press.
Foucault, M. (1981). The order of discourse (I. McLeod, Trans.). In R. Young (Ed.), *Untying the text: A post-structuralist reader* (pp. 48–78). Routledge & Kegan Paul.
Foucault, M. (1984a). Politics and ethics: An interview (C. Porter, Trans.). In P. Rabinow (Ed.), *The Foucault reader* (pp. 373–380). Pantheon.

Foucault, M. (1984b). Preface to The history of sexuality, volume II (W. Smock, Trans.). In P. Rabinow (Ed.), *The Foucault reader* (pp. 333–339). Pantheon.

Foucault, M. (1984c). What is enlightenment? (C. Porter, Trans.). In P. Rabinow (Ed.), *The Foucault reader* (pp. 32–50). Pantheon.

Foucault, M. (1985). Final interview (T. Levin & I. Lorenz, Trans.). *Raritan, 5*(Summer), 1–13. (Interview conducted by G. Barbedette, published in *Les louvelles*, 28 June 1984)

Foucault, M. (1987). Questions of method. In K. Baynes, J. Bonman, & T. McCarthy (Eds.), *After philosophy: End or transformation?* (pp. 100–117). MIT Press.

Foucault, M. (1988). Critical theory/intellectual history (an interview with Michel Foucault by Gérard Raulet). In M. Foucault, *Politics, philosophy, culture: Interviews and other writings, 1977–1984* (A. Sheridan et al., Trans.; L. D. Kritzman, Ed.; pp. 17–46). Routledge.

Foucault, M. (1990). Maurice Blanchot: The thought from outside. In M. Foucault & M. Blanchot (Eds.), *Foucault/Blanchot* (J. Mehlman & B. Massumi, Trans.; pp. 7–60). Zone Books.

Foucault, M. (1991a). The ethic of care for the self as a practice of freedom: An interview (J. D. Gauthier, Trans.). In J. Bernauer & D. Rasmussen (Eds.), *The final Foucault* (pp. 1–20). MIT Press.

Foucault, M. (1991b). *Remarks on Marx: Conversations with Duccio Trombadori* (R. J. Goldstein & J. Cascaito, Trans.). Semiotext(e).

Foucault, M. (1994a). La philosophie analytique de la politique. In D. Defert & F. Ewald (Eds.) with J. Lagrange, *Dits et écrits, 1954–1988* (4 Vols., Vol. 3, No. 232, pp. 534–551). Éditions Gallimard.

Foucault, M. (1994b). Linguistique et sciences sociales. In D. Defert & F. Ewald (Eds.) with J. Lagrange, *Dits et écrits: 1954–1988* (4 Vols, Vol. 1, No. 70, pp. 821–842). Éditions Gallimard.

Foucault, M. (1994c). Interview avec Michel Foucault. In D. Defert & F. Ewald with J. Lagrange (Eds.), *Dits et écrits: 1954–1988* (4 Vols; Vol., 1, pp. 654–660). Éditions Gallimard.

Foucault, M. (1998). Theatrum philosophicum. In J. D. Faubion (Ed.), *Essential works of Foucault, 1954–1984, vol. 2: Aesthetics, method, epistemology* (pp. 343–368). Penguin.

Foucault, M. (2001). Interview with Michel Foucault. In J. D. Faubion (Ed.), *Essential works of Foucault, 1954–1984, vol. 3: Power* (R. Hurley et al., Trans.; pp. 239–297). Penguin.

Foucault, M., & Chomsky, N. (1997). Human nature: Justice versus power. In A. I. Davidson (Ed.), *Foucault and his interlocutors* (pp. 107–145). University of Chicago Press.

Frank, M. (1992). On Foucault's concept of discourse. In T. J. Armstrong (Ed. and Trans.), *Michel Foucault: Philosopher* (pp. 99–116). Harvester Wheatsheaf.

Gleick, J. (1987). *Chaos: Making a new science*. Abacus.

Grosz, E. (1989). *Sexual subversions*. Allen & Unwin.

Haken, H. (1977). *Synergetics: An introduction*. Springer.

Haken, H. (1990). Synergetics as a tool for the conceptualization and mathematization of cognition and behaviour: How far can we go? In H. Haken & M. Stadler (Eds.), *Synergetics of cognition* (pp. 2–31). Springer.

Holden, A. (1985). Chaos is no longer a dirty word. *New Scientist, 106*(1453), 12–15.

Jameson, F. (1984). Foreword. In J.-F. Lyotard (Ed.), *The postmodern condition: A report on knowledge* (G. Bennington & B. Massumi, Trans.; pp. vii–xxi). University of Minnesota Press.

Kauffman, S. A. (1991, August). Antichaos and adaptation. *Scientific American*, pp. 64–70.

Kauffman, S. A. (1993). *The origins of order: Self-organisation and selection in evolution.* Oxford University Press.

Kauffman, S. A. (1995). *At home in the universe: The search for laws of complexity.* Viking Press.

Margolis, J. (1993). *The flux of history and the flux of science.* University of California Press.

Martin, L. H., Gutman, H., & Hutton, P. H. (Eds.). (1988). *Technologies of the self: A seminar with Michel Foucault.* Tavistock.

Marx, K. (1904). *A contribution to the critique of political economy* (2nd ed.; N. I. Stone, Trans.). International Library.

Marx, K. (1967). Critique of Hegel's Philosophy of the state [1843]. In L. D. Easton & K. H. Guddat (Eds.), *Writings of the young Marx on philosophy and society* (pp. 151–190). Doubleday/Anchor.

Marx, K. (1973). *Grundrisse: Foundations of the critique of political economy* (M. Nicolaus, Trans.). Vintage.

Marx, K. (1977). Theses on Feuerbach. In D. McLellan (Ed.), *Karl Marx: Selected writings* (pp. ?–?). Oxford University Press.

May, T. (1994). Difference and unity in Gilles Deleuze. In C. V. Boundas & D. Olkowski (Eds.), *Gilles Deleuze and the theatre of philosophy* (pp. 33–50). Routledge.

McDonald, B. J. (2002). Marx, Foucault, genealogy. *Polity, 34*(13), 259–275.

Nietzsche, F. (1967). *On the genealogy of morals. Ecce homo* (W. Kaufmann, Trans.). Random House.

Olssen, M. (1999). *Michel Foucault: Materialism and education.* Bergin & Garvey.

Olssen, M. (2003). Totalitarianism and the "repressed" utopia of the present: Moving beyond Hayek, Popper and Foucault. *Policy Futures in Education, 1*(3), 526–552. https://doi.org/10.2304/pfie.2003.1.3.6

Pettit, P. (1997). *Republicanism: A theory of freedom and government.* Oxford University Press.

Poster, M. (1984). *Foucault, Marxism, History: Mode of production vs mode of information.* Polity.

Rabinow, P. (Ed.). (1984). *The Foucault reader.* Pantheon.

Rawls, J. (1971). *A theory of justice.* Oxford University Press.

Sappington, A. A. (1990). Recent psychological approaches to the free will versus determinism issue. *Psychological Bulletin, 108*, 19–29.

Sardar, Z., & Abrams, I. (1999). *Introducing chaos*. Icon Books.

Saussure, F. de. (1974). *Course in general linguistics*. Fontana.

Schrift, A. D. (1995). *Nietzsche's French legacy: A genealogy of poststructuralism*. Routledge.

Sheridan, A. (1980). *Michel Foucault: The will to truth*. Routledge.

Skarda, C. A., & Freeman, W. J. (1990). Chaos and the new science of the brain. *Concepts in Neuroscience, 1*, 275–285.

Swinney, H. L. (1983). Observations of order and chaos in nonlinear systems. *Physica, 7*, 3–15.

Thompson, K. (1986). *Beliefs and ideologies*. Ellis Harwood.

Veyne, P. (1997). Foucault revolutionizes history. In A. I. Davidson (Ed.), *Foucault and his interlocutors* (pp. 146–182). University of Chicago Press.

Williams, R. (1980). *Problems in materialism and culture*. Verso.

CHAPTER 4

Marx, Education and the Possibilities of a Fairer World

Reviving Radical Political Economy through Foucault

Mark Olssen and Michael A. Peters

Abstract

Although this paper constitutes a revision of a paper originally published in 2007 (see note 1), the editors are pleased to republish this paper due to its theoretical importance for the critique of Marxism as well the interest it creates for establishing the possibility of a new political economy based upon the work of Michel Foucault. The paper documents and interrogates the contradictions between postmodernism and poststructuralism with Marxism. Starting by documenting the crisis of the Left at the start of the 21st century, an attempt is made to radically critique and reappraise Marxism in a direction set out by Foucault. The paper is not so much an attempt to meld Marxism and poststructuralism but rather to generate a new poststructuralist historical materialism which still has equality and fairness as its central concerns, but which goes beyond the traditional problems of Marxism based on its adherence to outmoded methodologies and theoretical modes of analysis. Echoing well-known critiques of Marxist historical materialism, the paper focuses on forms of articulation drawn from the revolution in language influenced by postmodernism and by historically more recent post-quantum complexity theories.

1   Introduction[1]

> It is clear, even if one admits that Marx will disappear for now, that he will reappear one day. What I wish for is not so much the defalsification and restitution of a true Marx but the unburdening and liberation of Marx in relation to party dogma, which has constrained it, touted it, and brandished it for so long. (Foucault, 1998, p. 458)

Marxism, we are told by politicians and the popular press, is dead. The Left, as a historical movement tied to the labor movement, is frozen over, caught between the collapse of actually existing communism in Eastern Europe and the triumph of global market forces. Union membership in the traditional industrial economy in the United Kingdom is dwindling as multinationals relocate offshore; even insurance, information, banking and call center jobs of the "new economy" are increasingly outsourced to India and other emergent economies literate in information and computing technology and English. China has joined the World Trade Organization and committed itself to a post-socialist market economy. At a time of an intensification of inequalities between regions and, perhaps more significantly, between North and South—between the developed world and the developing world—the Left in Britain, the USA and most of Europe seems ideologically gutted by the "third way" preoccupation with the social market and with citizenship "responsibilities" rather than with traditional concerns of equality and advancing rights. The best offer on hand seems to be a *socialization* of the market and an acknowledgement of its moral limits. Neoliberalism, in the age of privatization, reduces the state's role more and more to one of regulation, rather than provision or funding of public services. The US–UK neoliberal model of globalization has dominated the world economy and world politics for the last 20 years, defining the present crisis of fundamentalisms and restyling imperialism as a new age of barbarism. In this age, American-style democracy is exported alongside the ideology of "free trade". Yet many Americans have shifted their view since the Vietnam War on whether the USA is a force for good in the world or an imperialist power, and this is so despite Bush's recent election victory. Even the philosophers of '68 have given way to a new breed of fashion-conscious savants, who now turn their attention to extolling the virtues of liberal individualism or sneer at the last great generation of Left-Nietzscheans, such as Foucault and Derrida.

The Left has certainly been marginalized and even in the home of European socialism it seems confused and crisis-ridden. Europe itself is fighting to establish a new identity, reshaping its territory through enlargement and integration, and desperately competing with the US juggernaut of global power and the rising stars of East Asia—not only China, but also Japan, Taiwan, Hong Kong, Singapore and Korea—which seem destined to develop a trading bloc at least as powerful as that of the USA and the European Union. The traditional Left, wedded to the rise of the industrial working class, some observers have remarked, is also tied to its demise. Is the Left history? Has it simply become an academic form of analysis or does it have the seeds to reconfigure itself as an organizing force once again?

In terms of emancipatory futures there are all sorts of oppressions to overcome; many of these oppressions have intensified in the neoliberal era. The question that Steve Brier asks is:

> How do we position ourselves as a movement in relation to all the particular forms of oppression experienced by specific communities and people, defined by race, gender, nationality, sexual orientation, etc., especially at a time when no unified working-class movement exists that encompasses these communities and fights to eradicate the special injustices they face? (Brier, 1999)

The question of unity becomes paramount. Against identity politics and certain forms of postmodernism we need to inquire: what is the unifying principle? Is it the concept of "class" or even an overlapping set of concepts? Brier was writing at a time that had not yet seen the neoconservative hegemony in the White House or its consolidation after the re-election of Bush for a second term. In this environment of voter fraud and corporate corruption it is difficult to see the flourishing of social democracy even though the White House wants to export American-style democracy to the world as part of its neoconservative agenda. In these circumstances is it really enough to talk of "beyond left and right" as the future of radical politics as Tony Giddens (1994) has done? Or does Alex Callinicos's *An Anti-Capitalist Manifesto* (2003) define a way forward?

These are weighty questions that do not admit easy answers. But it is clear that even in this environment of world politics there are new lines of struggle emerging that coalesce with the old articles of faith. There *are* expressions of new forms of socialism that revolve around the international labor movement and invoke new imperialism struggles based on the movements of indigenous and radicalized peoples. There are active social movements, perhaps less coherent but every bit as powerful as older class-based movements, such as the anti-capitalism, anti-globalization movements, women's and feminist movements, and environmental movements. These new expressions do require engagement and re-theorizing by the Left. One obvious challenge for Marxism and the Left more generally is its engagement with Islam and the enslavement of women.

There is also a host of struggles around the socialization of the market and a question of whether this can be pursued successfully at the level beyond the state. Indeed, as many theorists have asserted, the future of the Left is tied up with the future of world democracy and with the development of left media cultures and centers. Part of the success of the Right has been its ability to privatize thinking and media, moving beyond the academy to set up dozens of new think tanks, private consultancies, and media centers that propagate partisan "news" or lobby and influence government departments at the highest levels.

2   Marx's Radical Political Economy

This essay seeks to ask to what extent Foucault can provide a different vision of radical politics to that of Marx, and then to assess the implications of this for work in education, politics and ethics. Central to Marx's model of political economy was a particular materialist inversion of the Hegelian dialectic, giving rise in Western Marxism to a particular formulation of base and superstructure.

In his Preface to *A Contribution to the Critique of Political Economy* (Marx, 1971; hereafter CPE), written in 1859, Karl Marx, as he says, examines "the system of bourgeois economy" and he gives a biographical account of how he first came to realize the position he adopts on the issue of the relationship of the economy to the cultural, educational, legal and political domains of society—a fundamental and stunning insight whose force has not diminished even though the sophistication of structuralist and poststructuralist arguments against the rudiments of a base/superstructure model now have to be accepted. He indicates that he had started thinking about these issues in 1842 and returned to a fresh examination of Hegelian philosophy of law in order to rethink the origins of legal relations and political forms. As his massive bibliographical studies across several languages led him to conclude legal relations and political forms cannot be understood by themselves or as a product of the development of the human mind but only in "the material conditions of life", the totality of which Hegel called "civil society" and whose "anatomy" Marx argued must be sought in political economy.

In that remarkable work that took him over 17 years to bring to maturity, Marx addresses the question of the method of political economy and is clearly influenced in his construction not only by the history of political economy and especially the major figures of the 18th century (especially Smith and Ricardo) but also Charles Darwin from whom he takes a newly scientized view of historical evolution. Marx's view is tantamount to a form of *historical naturalism*, which assumes laws of historical development. Marx calls it a "materialist account of history" and Engels shortened it to "historical materialism". Thus, he argues:

> Bourgeois society is the most advanced and complex historical organization of production. The categories which express its relations, and an understanding of its structure, therefore, provide an insight into the structure and the relations of production of all formerly existing social formations the ruins and component elements of which were used in the creation of bourgeois society.[2]

Clearly his model here is Darwin as well as Hegel. This is confirmed when later in the text he argues: "The anatomy of man is a key to the anatomy of the ape".

Marx claimed that all history should be thought of as the history of class struggles over surplus value. Engels described "being determines consciousness" as the "law of evolution in human history" equating it with Darwin's "law of evolution in organic nature". The *Origin of Species*[3] was published in 1859 and Marx read it in 1860. Marx believed that Darwin's book "contains the basis in natural history for our views". In 1861 in a letter to Ferdinand Lassalle Marx wrote:

> Darwin's book is very important and serves me as a model for the class struggle in history. ... Despite all deficiencies, not only is the death-blow dealt for the first time here to "teleology" in the natural sciences, but its rational basis is empirically explained. (Marx & Engels, 1965, p. 123)

There is an oft quoted story that Marx sought permission to dedicate *Das Kapital* to Charles Darwin who declined the offer, but this now seems suspect.[4]

Naturalism is the tendency to look upon the material universe as the only reality and to reduce all laws to uniformities in nature. To this end it denies the dualism of spirit and matter regarding the social and cultural as manifestations of matter that are governed by its laws. Naturalism, as Quine has suggested, is the position that there is no higher tribunal for truth than natural science itself; scientific method alone must judge the claims of science and there is no room for metaphysics or first philosophy. Naturalism is in this sense derived from materialism or pragmatism. Historical materialism explains changes in human history through material factors, for Marx, economic and technological. Where Marx is both a historical materialist and naturalist, Foucault is the former (although as we shall see he places no particular priority on the economic) but also firmly anti-naturalist when it come to the market as we will see in more detail in later sections. Naturalism, like empiricism and older forms of materialism which seek to represent the real or nature outside of discourse and independent of historicity, fails to adequately recognize the contingent dimension of knowledge. For Foucault, knowledge, like the human subject, is always already social and attempts to establish a foundation in nature to anchor knowledge or the operations of institutions independently of history are not possible.

For Foucault, also, the Marxist conception of relations between economy and superstructures were problematic. In the Marxist conception of historical materialism, educational, legal, political institutions, as well as ideologies and discourses, are represented as part of the superstructure of society which is split from material practices of the economic foundation or base and are determined by it. In the same way, the mental operations of consciousness are represented as determined by the material base of society. As Marx (1971, pp. 20–21) expresses the point:

> In the social production which men carry on they enter into definite relations that are indispensable and independent of their will; these relations of production correspond to a definite stage of development of their material powers of production. The sum total of these relations of production constitutes the economic structure of society—the real foundation, on which rise legal and political superstructures and to which correspond definite forms of social consciousness. The mode of production in material life determines the general character of the social, political and spiritual processes of life. It is not the consciousness of men that determines their existence, but on the contrary, their social existence determines their consciousness.

In the 20th century one of the central issues addressed by Western Marxists has been an attempted resolution and reconceptualization of the nature of the relation between the economic base and the cultural superstructure of society. In the classical Marxist model both the character of a society's culture and institutions, as well as the direction set for its future development are determined by the nature of the economic base, which can be defined as the mode of production at a certain stage of development (Williams, 1980, p. 33). The simplest nature of this relation, as Williams (1980, p. 33) tells us, was one of "the reflection, the imitation, or the reproduction of the reality of the base in the superstructure in a more or less direct way"; that is, a relation in which the economic base and specifically the forces of production constituted the ultimate *cause* to which the social, legal and political framework of the society can be traced back.

In the attempt to reformulate Marxism in the 20th century the economic determinist conception is challenged by those who see Marxism as granting rather more "independence" or "autonomy" to the superstructures of society. Hence a "dialectical" notion of the relation was stressed suggesting a relation of reciprocal influence. It was argued that, although the base *conditions* and *affects* the superstructure, it is in turn *conditioned* and *affected* by it. In all cases, however, in order to remain as Marxists, the ultimate priority of the economic base as the causal determinant of the social character of a society was safeguarded by maintaining that the economic factor is "determining in the last instance". Hence, it was maintained that the superstructure had only a "relative autonomy", and the theory of "relative autonomy", as a shorthand designation of the base-superstructure relation, became a central concept of 20th-century Marxism.

All of the Marxist studies on different aspects of education reflected the problematic determinism of the relations between the economy and the various cultural and ideological aspects of the society. If we consider the application of a particular case of Marx's base-superstructure analysis to education one important theme has been an understanding of the schooling system as a production system related to capitalism. The best known contemporary form of this kind of application is Bowles and Gintis's (1976) correspondence theory that hypothesizes a set of correspondences between work and education at all levels: a subservient workforce, an acceptance of hierarchy, and motivated by external rewards.[5] In their later work they explain their original position as:

> schools prepare people for adult work rules, by socializing people to function well, and without complaint, in the hierarchical structure of the modern corporation. Schools accomplish this by what we called the *correspondence principle*, namely, by structuring social interactions and individual rewards to replicate the environment of the workplace. (Bowles & Gintis 2001, p. 1)

In this later work they endorse the correspondence principle as more or less correct although they also mention shortcomings of the original work. Criticisms of structural overdetermination of the lives of working-class kids has been explored by Paul Willis (1977) in *Learning to Labour* and by many others at the Centre for Contemporary Cultural Studies at the University of Birmingham who demonstrate that working-class kids choose to fail through the development of a counterculture.

3 Foucault's Radical Political Economy

Political economy has a much longer tradition than as used by Marx. The Greeks considered it as pertaining to the management of the household of the state, as did Jean-Jacques Rousseau and Adam Smith.[6]

Foucault's sense of the concept must be seen in relation to his way of conceptualizing social structure as well as his opposition to Marxism. In one sense, his own conception can be viewed as a form of "new political economy".[7] Foucault opposed both the determinism of the base-superstructure model as well as the Hegelian monistic conception of society and the Hegelian/Darwinian conception of progressive evolution of history through the unfolding of the dialectic to the communist utopia. Rather than seek to explain all phenomena in relation to a single center, Foucault is interested rather to advance a polymorphous conception of determination in order to reveal the play of dependencies in the social and historical process. Hence, in opposition to the themes of totalizing history as found in Hegel, Foucault (1978, p. 10) substitutes what he calls a "differentiated analysis":

> Nothing, you see, is more foreign to me than the quest for a sovereign, unique and constraining form. I do not seek to detect, starting from diverse signs, the unitary spirit of an epoch, the general form of its consciousness: something like a Weltanschauung. ... I have studied, one after another, ensembles of discourse; I have characterized them; I have defined the play of rules, of transformations, of thresholds, of remanences. I have established and I have described their clusters of relations. Whenever I have deemed it necessary I have allowed systems to proliferate.

In advocating pluralism in place of monism, Foucault believed Marxism to reflect theoretical rules inherited from its time of origins. As he says (2001a, p. 269):

> Marx's economic discourse comes under the rules of formation of the scientific discourses that were peculiar to the nineteenth century. ... Marxist economics—through its basic concepts and the general rules of its discourse—belongs to a type of discursive formation that was defined around the time of Ricardo.

A central element of Foucault's critique of Marxism relates to the notion of "totalization". Essentially, for Foucault, Marxism was not just a "deterministic" but a "deductivistic" approach. That is, it directs attention not just to the primacy of the economy but it seeks to explain the parts of a culture as explicable and decodable parts of the whole totality or system represented as a closed system. Marxism, claims Foucault, seeks to ascertain "the principle of cohesion or the code that unlocks the system explaining the elements by deduction" (Thompson, 1986, p. 106). This was the approach of Marx took from Hegel, which seeks to analyse history and society in terms of "totality", where the parts are an "expression" of the whole—hence the notion of an "expressive totality".

The dissociation between Marxism, and Foucault's own position became more apparent after Foucault's turn to genealogy and Nietzsche at the close of the 1960s. With his growing interest in genealogy, Foucault became more concerned with power and history, and the historical constitution of knowledge. In this process, there was, however, no integrative principle or essence, and history was not periodized according to economic stages. If the genealogist studies history "he finds that there is 'something altogether different' behind things: not a timeless and essential secret, but the secret that they have no essence or that their essence was fabricated in a piecemeal fashion from alien forms" (Foucault, 1977, p. 142).

Foucault's objection to elements of Marxism explicitly reflects his Nietzschean heritage and his belief that certain aspects of Marxism distorted the liberatory potential of the discourse.

> The interest in Nietzsche and Bataille was not a way of distancing ourselves from Marxism or communism—it was the only path towards what we expected from communism. (Foucault, 2001, p. 249)

It was in terms of the philosophy of difference and Nietzsche's conception of multiplicities through a rejection of Platonic hierarchies that Foucault enunciates a theory of discursive formations and rejects Marxist and Hegelian conceptions of history. The utilization of Nietzsche signaled a rupture from Marxism in relation to a series of interrelated conceptual, theoretical and methodological precepts, including power, knowledge and truth, the subject, and the nature of historical change and determination.

Nietzsche focused on power in an altogether different way to Marx. In "Prison Talk", Foucault (1980a, p. 53) states:

> It was Nietzsche who specified the power relation as the general focus, shall we say, of philosophical discourse—whereas for Marx it was the production relation. Nietzsche is the philosopher of power, a philosopher who managed to think of power without having to confine himself within a political theory in order to do so.

Power, for Nietzsche, was conceived as a relation of forces within an analytics of power/knowledge/truth, which became important for Foucault to understand in the later 1960s after the publication of *The Archaeology of Knowledge* and his growing friendship with the Parisian Nietzschean Gilles Deleuze. Foucault accredits Nietzsche as the source of his interest in the question of truth and its relation to power. As he states, in "Truth and Power" (Foucault, 1980b, p. 133), "The political question ... is not error, illusion, alienated consciousness or ideology; it is truth itself. Hence, the importance of Nietzsche". Nietzsche's importance to Foucault can be seen as "correcting" the Marxism developed after Marx, especially in relation to the linkage between power/knowledge/truth, and the functioning of knowledge as an instrument of power. As Alan Schrift (1995, p. 40) notes, Nietzsche's influence drew attention away from "substances, subjects and things, and focused attention instead on the *relations between* these substantives". In a related way, Foucault "draws our attention away from the substantive notion of power and directs our attention instead to the multifarious ways that power operates through the social order" (1995, p. 40). For Nietzsche, such relations were relations of forces. Foucault thus focused on new relations as the relations of forces that existed and interacted within social systems as social practices. These were forces of repression and production that characterized the disciplinary society; forces that enable and block; subjugate and realize, and normalize and resist. In this model, power is not a thing, but a process, a becoming.

Foucault rejects Marxist models of a determining economic base and a determined superstructure as well as refinements based on conceptions of totality by Marx's 20th-century successors. Foucault is not interested in accounting for the practices of the social structure solely in terms of a model of economic determination. Although, like Althusser, he utilizes a model of complex and multiple causation and determination within the social structure, the specific elements and mechanisms of such processes, as elaborated by Foucault, differ in important, indeed crucial, respects. In Foucault's conception of social structure, explaining the relations between discursive formations and non-discursive domains (institutions, political events, economic practices and processes) is recognized as the ultimate objective. As he formulates it in *The Archaeology of Knowledge* (1972), for archaeology, in comparison to Marxism:

> The *rapprochements* are not intended to uncover great cultural continuities, nor to isolate mechanisms of causality, ... nor does it seek to rediscover what is expressed in them. ... [I]t tries to determine how the rules of formation that govern it ... may be linked to non-discursive systems: it seeks to define specific forms of articulation. (Foucault, 1972, p. 162)

Unlike Marxists, he sees no one set of factors as necessarily directing human destiny. Rather, the forms of articulation and determination may differ in relation to the relative importance of different non-discursive (material) factors in terms of both place and time. In the shift from a purely archaeological to a genealogical mode of enquiry, Foucault's concern with the relation between discursive and non-discursive domains is given a more historical and dynamic formulation, although, the concern with synchronic analysis is not abandoned. Throughout, however, as Mark Poster (1984, pp. 39–40) explains, Foucault's central aim is to provide a version of critical theory in which the economic base is not the totalizing center of the social formation, whereby Hegel's evolutionary model of history is replaced by Nietzsche's concept of genealogy, and where causes and connections to an imputed center or foundation are rejected in favor of exposing the contingency and transitory nature of existing social practices. In Poster's (1984, pp. 39–40) view, this presents us with a crucial decision. In comparing Foucault and Althusser, he maintains that "the theoretical choice offered by these two theorists is dramatic and urgent. In my opinion Foucault's position in the present context is more valuable as an interpretative strategy. ... Foucault's position opens up critical theory more than Althusser's both to the changing social formation and to the social locations where contestation actually occurs". While having a generally historicized view of the nature and development of knowledge, Foucault rejects the possibility of any "absolute" or "transcendental" conception of truth "outside of history" as well as of any conception of "objective" or "necessary" interests which could provide a necessary "Archimedean point" to ground either knowledge, morality or politics. Read in this way, historical materialism does not prioritize the economy in any necessary or universal sense, but is about the systematic character of society and how it might change. It is about the processes of change internal to social systems. It holds that societies are to varying extents integrated systematically through their material practices and discursive coherences and break down and change as the component elements of the system change.[8]

4 Governmentality Studies

Based upon this general social ontology Foucault utilizes the notion of "governmentality" as the basis of his "new" conception of political economy. The working premise of governmentality studies is based on Foucault's insight and analysis of the modern regime of power in which power characteristically operates *internally* or subjectively in terms of a logic of "self-improvement" that demands the freedom of the individual. Governmentality is the key concept that links Foucault's genealogy of the subject with his interest in political rationalities, i.e., between the government of the state and the government of the self, and in so doing "solves" the problem of agency (liberal political economy) versus structure (Marxist political economy).

Foucault's overriding interest was not in "knowledge as ideology", as Marxists would have it, where bourgeois knowledge, say, modern liberal economics, was seen as false knowledge or bad science. Nor was he interested in "knowledge as theory" as classical liberalism has constructed disinterested knowledge, based on inherited distinctions from the Greeks, including Platonic epistemology and endorsed by the Kantian separation of schema/content that distinguishes the analytic enterprise. Rather, Foucault examined *practices* of knowledge produced through the relations of power.[9] He examined how these practices, then, were used to augment and refine the efficacy and instrumentality of power in its exercise over both individuals and populations, and also in large measure helped to shape the constitution of subjectivity. Fundamental to his governmentality studies was the understanding that Western society professed to be based on principles of liberty and the Rule of Law and was said to derive the legitimation of the state from political philosophies that elucidated these very principles. Yet, as a matter of historical fact, Western society employed technologies of power that operated on forms of disciplinary order or were based on biopolitical techniques that bypassed the law and its freedoms altogether. As Colin Gordon (2001, p. XXVI) puts it so starkly: Foucault embraced Nietzsche as the thinker "who transforms Western philosophy by rejecting its founding disjunction of power and knowledge as myth". By this he means that the rationalities of Western politics, from the time of the Greeks, had incorporated techniques of power specific to Western practices of government, first, in the expert knowledges of the Greek tyrant and, second, in the concept of pastoral power that characterized ecclesiastical government.

It is in this vein that Foucault examines government as a practice and problematic that first emerges in the 16th century and is characterized by the insertion of economy into political practice. Foucault (2001, p. 201) explores the problem of government as it "explodes in the sixteenth century" after the collapse of feudalism and the establishment of new territorial States. Government emerges at this time as a general problem dispersed across quite different questions: Foucault mentions specifically the Stoic revival that focused on the government of oneself; the government of souls elaborated in Catholic and Protestant pastoral doctrine; the government of children and the problematic of pedagogy; and, last but not least, the government of the state by the prince. Through the reception of Machiavelli's *The Prince* in the 16th century and its rediscovery in the 19th century, there emerges a literature that sought to replace the power of the prince with the art of government understood in terms of the government of the family, based on the central concept of "economy". The introduction of economy into political practice is for Foucault the essential issue in the establishment of the art of government. As he points out, the problem is still posed for Rousseau, in the mid-18th century, in the same terms—the government of the state is modeled on the management by the head of the family over his family, household and its assets.

It is in the late 16th century, then, that the art of government receives its first formulation as "reason of state" that emphasizes a specific rationality intrinsic to the nature of the state, based on principles no longer philosophical and transcendent, or theological and divine, but rather centered on the *problem of population*. This became a science of government conceived of outside the juridical framework of sovereignty characteristic of the feudal territory and firmly focused on the problem of population based on the modern concept which enabled "the creation of new orders of knowledge, new objects of intervention, new forms of subjectivity and ... new state forms" (Curtis, 2002, p. 2). It is this political-statistical concept of population that provided the means by which the government of the state came to involve individualization and totalization, and, thus, married Christian pastoral care with sovereign political authority. The new rationality of "reason of state" focused on the couplet *population–wealth* as an object of rule, providing conditions for the emergence of political economy as a form of analysis. Foucault investigated the techniques of police science and a new bio-politics:

> which tends to treat the "population" as a mass of living and co-existing beings, which evidence biological traits and particular kinds of pathologies and which, in consequence, give rise to specific knowledges and techniques. (Foucault, 1989, p. 106, cited in Curtis, 2002)

As Foucault (2001c) comments in "The Political Technology of Individuals", the "rise and development of our modern political rationality" as "reason of state", that is, as a specific rationality intrinsic to the state, is formulated through "a new relation between politics as a practice and as knowledge" (p. 407), involving specific political knowledge or "political arithmetic" (statistics); "new relationships between politics and history", such that political knowledge helped to strengthen the state and at the same time ushered in an era of politics based on "an irreducible multiplicity of states struggling and competing in a limited history" (p. 409); and, finally, a new relationship between the individual and the state, where "the individual becomes pertinent for the state insofar as he can do something for the strength of the state" (p. 409). In analysing the works of von Justi, Foucault infers that the true object of the police becomes, at the end of the 18th century, the population; or, in other words, the state has essentially to take care of men as a population. It wields its power over living beings, and its politics, therefore has to be a biopolitics (p. 416).

Foucault's lectures on governmentality were first delivered in a course he gave at the Collège de France, entitled *Sécurité, territoire, population*, during the 1977–1978 academic year. While the essays "Governmentality" and "Questions of Method" were published in 1978 and 1980, respectively, and translated into English in the collection *The Foucault Effect: Studies in Governmentality* (Burchell et al., 1991), it is only very recently that the course itself has been transcribed from original tapes and published for the first time (Foucault, 2004a), along with the sequel *Naissance de la biopolitique: Cours au Collège de France, 1978–1979* (Foucault, 2004b).[10] The governmentality literature in English, roughly speaking, dates from the 1991 collection and has now grown quite substantially (see, for example, Miller & Rose, 1990; Barry et al., 1996; Dean, 1999; Rose, 1999).[11] As a number of scholars have pointed out, Foucault relied on a group of researchers to help him in his endeavors: François Ewald, Pasquale Pasquino, Daniel Defert, Giovanna Procacci, Jacques Donzelot on governmentality; François Ewald, Catherine Mevel, Éliane Allo, Nathanie Coppinger and Pasquale Pasquino, François Delaporte and Anne-Marie Moulin on the birth of biopolitics. These researchers working with Foucault in the late 1970s constitute the first generation of governmentality studies scholars and many have gone on to publish significant works too numerous to list here. In the field of education as yet not a great deal has focused specifically on governmentality.[12]

Gordon (2001, p. XXIII) indicates three shifts that took place in Foucault's thinking: a shift from a focus on "specialized practices and knowledges of the individual person" "to the exercise of political sovereignty exercised by the state over an entire population"; the study of government as a *practice* informed and enabled by a specific rationality or succession of different rationalities; and the understanding that liberalism, by contrast with socialism, possessed a distinctive concept and rationale for the activity of governing. Liberalism and neoliberalism, then, for Foucault represented distinctive innovations in the history of governmental rationality. In his governmentality studies Foucault focused on the introduction of economy into the practice of politics and in a turn to the contemporary scene studied two examples: German liberalism during the period from 1948 to 1962, with an emphasis on the ordoliberalism of the Freiburg School, and American neoliberalism of the Chicago School. Foucault's critical reading of German neoliberalism and the emergence of the "social market" has significance not only for understanding the historical development of an economic constitution and formulation of "social policy" (and the role of education policy within it), but also the development of the European social model, more generally, and the continued relevance for "third way" politics of the "social market economy".

5   Neoliberalism and the Birth of Biopolitics

Naissance de la biopolitique (Foucault, 2004b) consists of 13 lectures delivered by Foucault at the Collège de France (10th January–4th April 1979). It is helpful to see this course in the series of 13 courses he gave from 1970 to 1984. The first five courses reflected his early work on knowledge in the human sciences, concerning punishment, penal and psychiatric institutions: "La volonté de savoir" (1970–1971), "Théories et institutions pénales" (1971–1972), "La société punitive" (1972–1973), "Le pouvoir psychiatrique" (1973–1974), "Les anormaux" (1974–1975). The remaining eight courses focused squarely on governmentality studies, with a clear emphasis also on the problematic (and hermeneutics) of the subject and the relation between subjectivity and truth: "It faut défender la société" (1975–1976), "Securité, territoire, population" (1977–1978), "Naissance de la biopolitique" (1978–1979), "Du gouvernement des vivants" (1979–1980), "Subjectivité et vérité" (1980–1981), "L'herméneutique du subjet" (1981–1982), "Le gouvernement de soi et des autres" (1982–1983), "Le gouvernement de soi et des autres: le courage de la vérité" (1983–1984). Even from this list of courses it becomes readily apparent that the question of government concerned Foucault for the last decade of his life and that for his governmentality studies, politics were inseparable in its modern forms both from biology—biopower and the government of the living—and truth and subjectivity. It is important to note that these same concerns in one form or another enter into Foucault's formulations in *Naissance de la biopolitique*.[13]

The *Ordoliberalen*[14] comprised a group of jurists and economists in the years 1928–1930 who published in the yearbook *Ordo*. Amongst their numbers were included William Röpke, Walter Eucken, Franz Böhm, Alexander Rüstow, Alfred Müller-Armack and others. Preaching the slogan that "inequality is equal for all" they devised a social market economy influencing the shaping of West German economic policy as it developed after the war. Foucault refers to these *Ordoliberalen* as the "Freiberg School" who had some affinities (of time and place) with the Frankfurt School but were of a very different political persuasion. While they held that Nazism was a consequence of the absence of liberalism, they did not see liberalism as a doctrine based upon the natural freedom of the individual that will develop by itself of its own volition. In fact, for the "Freiberg School" the market economy was not an autonomous, or naturally self-regulating, entity at all. As a consequence, their conception of the market and of the role of competition, says Foucault, is radically anti-naturalistic. Rather than the market being a natural arena which the state must refrain from interfering with, it is rather constituted and kept going by the state's political machine. Similarly, competition is not a natural fact which emerges spontaneously from human social intercourse, as a result of human nature, but must be engineered by the state.

As a consequence of this, the traditional distinction between a sphere of natural liberty and a sphere of government intervention no longer holds, for the market order and competition are engineered by the practices of government. Both the state and the market are on this conception artificial and both presuppose each other. In Foucault's view such a conception means that the principle of laissez-faire, which can be traced back to a distinction between culture (the artificial state) and nature (the self-regulating market), no longer holds. For the *Ordoliberalen*, the history of capitalism is an institutional, non-natural, history. Capitalism is a particular contingent apparatus by which economic processes and institutional frameworks are articulated. Not only is there no "logic of capital" in this model, but the *Ordoliberalen* held that the dysfunctions of capitalism could only be corrected by political–institutional interventions which they saw as contingent historical phenomena. What this means, says Foucault, is that the *Ordoliberalen* support the active creation of the social conditions for an effective competitive market order. Education thus becomes pivotal in this constructivism. Not only must government block and prevent anti-competitive practices, but it must fine-tune and actively promote competition in both the economy and in areas where the market mechanism is traditionally least prone to operate. One policy to this effect was to "universalize the entrepreneurial form" (Lemke, 2001, p. 195) through the promotion of an enterprise culture, premised, as Foucault put it in a lecture given on 14th February 1979, on "equal inequality for all" (Lemke, 2001, p. 195). The goal here was to increase competitive forms throughout society so that social and work relations in general assume the market form i.e., exhibit competition, obey laws of supply and demand. In the writings of Rüstow, this was called "vital policy" ("*Vitalpolitik*") which described policies geared to reconstructing the moral and cultural order to promote and reward entrepreneurial behavior, opposing bureaucratic initiatives which stifle the market mechanism. To achieve such goals, the *Ordoliberalen* also advocated the redefining of law and of juridical institutions so that they could function to correct the market mechanism and discipline non-entrepreneurial behavior within an institutional structure in accordance with, and supported by, the law. In this sense, the *Ordoliberalen* were not simply anti-naturalist, but constructivist.

In his analysis of neoliberalism, Foucault also directs his attention to the Chicago School of Human Capital theorists in America, focusing particularly on the works of Gary Becker. These neoliberals also opposed state interventionism when it was bureaucratic and supported it when it fostered and protected economic liberty. For Human Capital theorists the concern was the uncontrolled growth of the bureaucratic apparatus as a threat to the freedom of the individual. Foucault sees the major distinction between the German and US neoliberals existing in the fact that in the US neoliberalism was much less a political crusade as it was in Germany or France, for in the US the critique was centrally directed against state interventionism and aimed to challenge the growth of the state apparatus. In his lecture on 28th March, 1979, Foucault discusses Hayek and von Mises (whom he labels as the "intermediaries of US neoliberalism"), Simons, Schultz, Stigler and Becker, whom he says is the most radical exponent in the US. The US neoliberals saw the *Ordoliberalen* as representing the political as being above and outside the market but constantly intervening to correct its bureaucratic dislocations. From their viewpoint, they wanted to extend the market across into the social arena and political arenas, thus collapsing the distinction between the economic, social and political in what constitutes a marketization of the state.

As Foucault sees HCT, it is concerned with the problem of labor in economic theory. While classical political economy claimed that the production of goods depended upon real estate, capital, and labor, neoliberals held that only real estate and capital are treated appropriately by the classical theory, and that labor needs greater illumination as an active, rather than as a passive, factor in production. In this sense neoliberals concurred with Marx that classical political economy had forgotten labor and thereby they misrepresent the process of production. In order to correct this deficiency, neoliberals theorize the role and importance of labor in terms of a model of human capital. In essence their theory starts with the human individual in terms of a classification of skills, knowledge and ability. Although, unlike other forms of capital, it cannot be separated from the individual who owns these resources, they nevertheless constitute resources which can be sold in a market. Becker distinguishes two central aspects to such human capital: (1) inborn, physical and genetic dispositions, and (2) education, nutrition, training and emotional health. In this model, each person is now an autonomous entrepreneur responsible ontologically for their own selves and their own progress and position. Individuals have full responsibility over their investment decisions and must aim to produce a surplus value. As Foucault puts it in his 14th March, 1979, lecture, noting the educational implication, they are "entrepreneurs of themselves".

Graham Burchell (1996, pp. 23–24) has noted the core distinction between classical and neoliberalism. Whereas for liberalism the basis of government conduct is in terms of "natural, private-interest-motivated conduct of free, market exchanging individuals", for neoliberalism "the rational principle for regulating and limiting governmental activity must be determined by reference to artificially arranged or contrived forms of free, entrepreneurial and competitive conduct of economic-rational individuals". This means that for neoliberal perspectives, the end goals of freedom, choice, consumer sovereignty, competition and individual initiative, as well as those of compliance and obedience, must be constructions of the state acting now in its positive role through the development of the techniques of auditing, accounting and management. It is these techniques, as Barry, Osborne, and Rose (1996, p. 14) put it:

> [that] enable the marketplace for services to be established as "autonomous" from central control. Neo-liberalism, in these terms, involves less a

retreat from governmental "intervention" than a re-inscription of the techniques and forms of expertise required for the exercise of government.

Notwithstanding this rather crucial difference between the two forms of liberalism, the common element expresses a distinctive concern. For both classical liberalism as well as neoliberalism, what defines this concern is a common orientation concerning "the limits of government in relation to the market" (Burchell, 1996, p. 22).

In addition to a common priority concerning the scope of the market, both classical liberalism and neoliberalism share common views concerning the nature of the individual, as rational self-interested subjects. In this perspective the individual is presented as a rational optimizer and the best judge of his/her own interests and needs. Being rational was to follow a systematic program of action underpinned and structured according to rules. The rules were rendered coherent and permissible in relation to the "interests" of the individual.

In summary, then, central to neoliberals such as the *Ordoliberalen* and public choice theorists, the state actively constructs the market. Far from existing within a protected and limited space, market relations now extend to cover all forms of voluntary behavior amongst individuals. Rather than absenting itself from interfering in the private or market spheres of society, Foucauldian political economy points out that in the global economic era neoliberalism becomes a new authoritarian discourse of state management and control. Rather than being a form of political bureaucracy, which Weber (1921) saw as the supreme form of modernist rationality, neoliberalism constitutes a new and more advanced technology of control. It is both a substantive political doctrine of control and a self-driving technology of operations. It incorporates both more flexible and more devolved governmental steering mechanisms than does bureaucracy. If, for Weber, bureaucracy constituted large-scale organization comprising a hierarchy of offices and lines of control, enabling efficiency, predictability, calculability and technical control, then neoliberalism, while incorporating these factors, goes beyond them to enable an extension of control in more devolved forms and in more flexible systems. This enables the function of control to be differentiated from the function of operations, or to use Osborne and Gaebler's (1992) metaphor, "steering" from "rowing". It points to a more effective means of social engineering and control than classical bureaucracy, scientific management, or the Fordist assembly line. Its overall rationale is to measure the costs of, and place a monetary or market value on, all forms of human activity in order to render it controllable. It extends the market mechanism from the economic to the political to the social. Market exchanges now encapsulate all forms of voluntary behavior amongst individuals.[15]

6   Towards a Possible Foucauldian Politics

If Foucault is critical of neoliberalism as being a new form of superstructural sociology, in many ways highlighting a new operating model of capitalism in a global era, his model of political economy also supports, and has affinities to, a particular approach to economics and politics that can be represented to tie in closely with "regulation school" approaches developed by writers like Michel Aglietta, Hughes Bertrand, Robert Boyer, Alan Lipietz and Jacques Mistral. Aglietta has commented directly on Foucault's contribution in his conversations with François Dosse (1997, p. 291), where he describes Foucault's importance as being "because he raised questions about institutions and gave answers". Furthermore, as Dosse explains, Aglietta was especially influenced by Foucault's:

> concern for micropowers, his shift from the centre to the peripheral, his pluralization of a polymorphous power that corresponded to the regulationists' desire to reach intermediary institutional bodies. Moreover, Foucault had made it possible to take some distance from "the fundamental conception of Marxism" and to understand that this smooth growth curve depended on a system of conciliation and a concentration of interests. Until then, the antagonoism between capitalists and workers was considered irreconcilable. (Dosse, 1997, p. 291)

The "regulationists" rendered structuralism dynamic and bought microstructures and human beings back into the orbit of the analysis. As well as incorporating much from the tradition of Marxism, they were also influenced by Keynesian economics through the consideration of real demand, and by arguing for a consideration of money as an institution, and work as a relationship rather than a market. Robert Boyer (1986) and Alain Lipietz (1983, 1995) also accepted a "broad church" conception of the regulationist approach, distancing themselves from the more specific variations that also developed (see Dosse, 1997, pp. 290–294).

Central to the regulation school approach was its rejection of the market order as a self-regulating entity, and its "openness to social and historical elements" (Dosse, 1997, p. 292). This presents the future as an always existing constellation of dangers and has enormous implications for ethics and education. As with Foucault, there was an appropriation of some features of Marxism (especially Althusserianism), a conception of holism/particularism; an appreciation that the laws governing economic tendencies are historically contingent, and a concern for institutional forms of power as they arose from divergent conflicts or from market processes. The emphasis on historicity meant that there was no recognition of predetermined universal categories or systems such as forces of production, in preference for a recognition of the historical variability of other economic institutions, such as money or markets. What resulted was a reinterpretation of economic phenomena in terms of dynamic schemas as responding to dynamic mechanisms. Individual behaviors and identities were forged out of complex wholes, hence individual behaviors and subjects were viewed in ways that did not embody methodological individualism, enabling a reintroduction of individuals in relation to groups and social categories.

7 From Governmentality to the Hermeneutics of the Self as Education

The distinctiveness of Foucault's emerging problematic of governmentality, formulated in the years 1978–1979, also developed in a series of subsequent themes as "the government of the living", "subjectivity and truth", and "the government of self and others". These themes were also of relevance to education as a practice of struggle and engagement, and as such help us to understand the differences between a Foucauldian political economy of praxis, and that of Marxism. Of particular significance here are the themes on the problematic (and hermeneutics) of the subject and the relation between subjectivity and truth. These indeed signify a different relation between individual and collective in Foucault's work, compared to Marxism or Hegelianism. Although the individual subject is a product of social conditioning, they are always "free standing" in the sense they are never completely confined or defined by the determining structures from which they derive. Every convergence around culture or conditioning is also characterized by difference on the grounds that experience within space and time is itself both individuating and educative. Thus, while each individual is the product of class and culture each also has a situated and dated uniqueness. As Jane Bennett (1996, p. 660) states, citing Foucault:

> There is no *escaping* a regime of power, but this does not mean that subjectivation is simply subjection, for there is always the possibility of "practices of liberation, of freedom, as in Antiquity, starting of course from a certain number of rules, styles and conventions that are found in the culture". (Bennett is citing Foucault, 1989a, p. 313)

This theorization of the individual within the whole as something which both reflects and yet exceeds it, is distinctive of Foucault correction to Marxism, forcefully expressed in theoretical terms in works such as *The Archaeology of Knowledge* (1972).

Another difference from Marxism, springing from the rejection of Hegelian conceptions of a unilinear and progressive history is Foucault's distain for utopian ideas which aim for the realization of a perfected or harmonious future society. To aim for a specific ordered ideal written "only on paper" as something that could exist harbors dangers associated with both "radical and global" forms of theorizing. Foucault (1984a, p. 46) echoes liberal concerns with utopian engineering when he states that:

> we know from experience that the claims to escape from the system of contemporary reality so as to produce the overall programs of another society, of another way of thinking, another culture, another vision of the world, has led only to the return of the most dangerous traditions.

Foucault puts more emphasis on local struggle and resistance on the basis that existing historical discursive systems (such as those concerning liberty, rights, democracy, etc.) which can be seen *already*—in the present horizon—to harbor a "repressed" or "sedimented" utopian vision. Such existing discourses which always operate in local sites can be seen to constitute the complex outcome of struggles in history. And it is in this sense that local struggles can be seen as the basis of revolutionary activity. For Foucault, the revolution as Marxism conceived it as a single historical act of violence and transformation fails theoretically to be plausible in a global age because it can only be taken seriously within a unilinear and utopian frame of reference. What must be asked anew is how would such an idea of revolution can be conceived, planned for, and organized in an age which is both global and local. The notion of simultaneous and coordinated action across national contexts is no longer feasible in a global and "virtual" world. Indeed, to envisage a total sudden reconstruction or reordering of society given the dispersed digital character of financial and intelligence networks in advanced industrial nations boggles the mind. Hence, for Foucault, in a world which is both global and local the drive for change must take the form of resistance and struggle in specific sites, utilizing complex technologies and intellectual tools.

In addition to operating in specific sites, Foucault also emphasizes the tasks of the "specific intellectual" as "sapping power" rather than "proposing alternative visions" or "telling people what to do". A critical interrogation of power is thus central as the basis of a critical education. As Foucault (1977b, p. 208) explains to Gilles Deleuze:

> The intellectual's role is no longer to place himself "somewhat ahead and to the side" in order to express the stifled truth of the collectivity; rather, it is to struggle against the forms of power that transform him into its object and instrument in the sphere of "knowledge", "truth", "consciousness", and "discourse". In this sense theory does not express, translate, or serve to apply practice: it is practice. But it is local and regional ... and not totalizing. This is a struggle against power, a struggle aimed at revealing and undermining power where it is most invisible and insidious. It is not to "awaken consciousness" that we struggle ... but to sap power, to take power; it is an activity conducted alongside those who struggle for power, and not their illumination from a safe distance. A "theory" is the regional system of this struggle.

The impossibility of a discrete and total revolution also suggests the fact that on some issues and for some groups the revolution as Marxists conceived it might be considered in some senses as having already occurred. The theoretical task becomes in identifying those specific aspects or dimensions still not corrected such as climate change, the unjustified profits of many large multinationals, global inequality, the disadvantages of race, class, disability and gender both within societies and globally. The normative standards constitutive of a good for mankind are already present, in some cases manifest, in some repressed, within the existing horizon based upon what is necessary for both collective and individual survival. This is to say that complex historically generated discourses on such things as rights, equality, democracy and education for survival, already exist, and constitute the repositories of knowledge to become the curriculum for education for global citizenship in the future. Such a global polis is a thin, or de-centered community, rather than a unified mutuality in Hegel's sense. It is motivated not by a model of the truth, but more pragmatically, by a normative conception of survival characterized by a common integrity and flourishing but which may take many different forms. Foucault's fellow Nietzschean thinker, and lifelong inspiration, Georges Bataille, theorized the importance of survival as the pragmatic source and guide of ethics and education. For Bataille, like Nietzsche, the struggle for survival represents a specifically non-moral yearning once "God is dead", a goal that stretches out before one, as Bataille (2004, p. XVIII) puts it, "independently of moral goals or of serving God", and yet paradoxically itself becomes interpreted as a moral obligation, imposing an object "that surpasses all others in value" (p. XVII) and translating as a "demand for definite acts" (p. XVII). As in a complex global world people are interdependent, individual and collective goals are intertwined: the well-being of one is inseparable from the well-being of all. John Dewey's model of problem solving for survival resonates a similar approach.

It is well known that Marx never theorized the nature of existence in the communist utopia in any detail, and he may well have lacked the tools for such an analysis,[16] but there is reason to believe that he held intuitively to a similar conception to Foucault. Foucault sees difference as manifesting itself, necessarily, within unity, the latter which is always precarious, always changing and never completely predictable. Just for instance, as "Britishness" defines a common attribute between a group of people, so within the group, and simultaneous or identical with it, there are a myriad of differences, pertaining to appearance, gender, age, or what have you. In this sense commonness and difference are co-present features of any phenomena. Within the existing horizon of survival, there are many legitimate yet different ways to live. It is in this sense also that in place of unilinear conceptions of change and causality, Foucault's model of historical materialism is consistent with 20th-century conceptions of complexity theory. New realities, both physical and social, manifest themselves as emergent phenomena. While there is no necessary equilibrium which produces "happy endings" or "self-regulated markets", within limits we can understand the *affects* that particular combinations, alliances and choices entail. Understanding possible *affects* of combinations, and alliances, is indeed the task of education and of ethics. To understand education as concerned with a *theory of affects*, is of course to draw off Deleuze, as well as Spinoza and Nietzsche.[17] Yet it is an extension which we think (or hope) Foucault might approve.[18] Certainly it extends his thought in a way which brings out the important differences to Marxism, in a way related to how ethics and education would be conceived to have a role in the new era which is both global and national and which confronts a world that still awaits to be transformed.

The different way individual and collective are related in Foucault compared to Marxism indeed suggests a new order of ethics. In his later books, *The Use of Pleasure* and *The Care of the Self*, as Jane Bennett (1996, p. 655) explains, Foucault considers ethics as both a "code morality" and in relation to "subjectivation". As a "code morality", ethics relates to justified moral precepts and rules. Christianity comprised one set of these, yet today, the new demands of survival, centering on issues like climate change and the health of populations, presents a different set of precepts to guide action. In addition, however, such rules will not dictate or define conduct for each individual for every situation. While the tasks and requirements of survival will dictate some general, although historically specific, precepts and "rules", different contingent imperatives at different times and places will also operate, so the individuals' mode of ethical comportment will also reflect decisions, choices and commitments which only he/she can decide in particular situations. For Foucault, as for poststructuralism in general, every action, like every statement, has a novel aspect, a situated and dated uniqueness, whereby ethical decisions and actions assume great importance for society and for the groups and individuals that comprise it. In this sense, as Bennett (1996, p. 655) explains, "Foucault finds 'code morality' insufficient". She cites Foucault (1985, p. 28):

> In short, for an action to be "moral", it must not be reducible to an act or a series of acts conforming to a rule, or a value. There is no moral conduct that does not [also] call for forming of oneself as an ethical subject; and no forming of the ethical subject without "modes of subjectivation" and an "ascetics" or "practices of the self" that support them.

One dimension of Foucault's writings on ethics that assumes importance for education today relates to global activism. This is related to the propensity or preparedness of groups and individuals to speak out, take a stand, or to join together to protest. Foucault, in his own life, manifested a constant preparedness and concern with many causes including the rights of prisoners, of lawyers who defended radical groups, and of the poor. Hence, he voiced concern for the rights of those on the high seas, against piracy, where he speaks of "human rights" to "confront governments" which are beyond the limits of nationality.[19] As he puts it (Foucault, 2001b, p. 474):

> There exists an international citizenship that has its rights and its duties, and that obliges one to speak out against every abuse of power, whoever its author, whoever its victims. After all, we are all members of the community of the governed, and thereby obliged to show mutual solidarity. … It is the duty of this international citizenship to always bring the testimony of people's suffering to the eyes and ears of governments. … The suffering of men must never be the silent residue of policy. It grounds an absolute right to stand up and speak to those who hold power.

Foucault's approach, as extended through concepts such as *parrhēsia*, and contestation and resistance, also supports a model of global democracy and the role of grassroots critical social movements, which constitute a "bottom up" theory of the democratization of world order and suggests a conception of education as instilling radical global citizenship. Such global protest movements constitute a check on nation states and put them under an obligation to respect human rights, as well as to refrain from exploiting or persecuting individuals within their borders. It creates, also, the conditions where all nations' actions are monitored, and rendered accountable, at supra-national levels, and where each are encouraged to adjust their own regime to accord with international standards and principles that have been deemed important at this time. Although the Iraq war has set back the cause of constructive international relations by decades, undermining the role of the United Nations, and having a hugely detrimental affect on producing a viable global approach to humanitarian intervention, notwithstanding such setbacks, it is towards a stable and just international order that Foucauldian political economy strives.

Acknowledgements

This chapter originally appeared as Olssen, M., & Peters, M. A. (2015), Marx, education and the possibilities of a fairer world: Reviving radical political economy through Foucault, *Linguistic and Philosophical Investigations*, 14, 39–69, http://dx.doi.org/10.1057/9780230609679_9 (Original source: Olssen, M., & Peters, M. A. (2007), Marx, education, and the possibilities of a fairer world: Reviving radical political economy through Foucault, in A. Green, G. Rikowski, & H. Raduntz (Eds.), *Renewing dialogues in Marxism and education* (pp. 151–182), Palgrave Macmillan). Reprinted here, with minor edits, with permission from the publisher.

Notes

1 This introduction is based upon an editorial written for a special issue called "Marxist Futures" for the journal *Policy Futures in Education* (Peters, 2004a).
2 References here and below except where otherwise indicated are from web site: http://www.marxists.org/archive/marx/works/1859/critique-pol-economy/index/htm, transcribed by Tim Delaney.
3 The full title of Darwin's masterpiece is *On the Origin of Species by Means of Natural Selection, or the Preservation of Favoured Races in the Struggle for Life*, available at http://www.literature.org/authors/darwin-charles/the-origin-of-species/index.html.
4 While Marx did indeed send Darwin a copy of his famous work in second edition in 1873, it remained uncut on his shelves and there is no evidence that he read it. It also seems likely that the source of the myth is a confusion over a letter by Darwin published in a Soviet newspaper in 1931 which does not mention Marx but declines the offer of a dedication. The letter concerned Edward Aveling's (Marx's son-in-law) *The Students' Darwin* (Wheen, 1999); see also http://www.evowiki.org/index.php/Darwin_and_Marx.
5 See also Bowles and Gintis (2001), "*Schooling in Capitalist America* Revisited" at http://www.umass.edu/preferen/gintis/soced.pdf#search=%22Herbert%20Gintis%2C%20Schooling%20in%20Capitalist%20America%3A%20Educational%20Reform%20and%22.

6   Political economy originally in the Greek had three related meanings: *oikonomia* meant the management of a household or family, *politike* meant pertaining to the state; and, *ta oikonomika*, or economics, meant the art of household management. Thus, *political economy* originally meant the management of the household of the state. It was used in this sense both by Jean-Jacques Rousseau and Adam Smith. Rousseau in "A Discourse on Political Economy" in 1755 defines political economy as "the government of the State for the common good". Rousseau says, "The word Economy, or OEconomy, is derived from *oikos, a house*, and *nomos, law*, and meant originally only the wise and legitimate government of the house for the common good of the whole family. The meaning of the term was then extended to the government of that great family, the State. To distinguish these two senses of the word, the latter is called *general* or *political* economy, and the former domestic or particular economy" (http://www.constitution.org/jjr/polecon.htm).

7   New political economy seeks to combine "the breadth of vision of the classical political economy of the 19th century with the analytical advances of 20th-century social science"; to overcome old distinctions and divisions of the past (agency/structure; state/market) to provide an integrated analysis that draws on a range of concepts and methodologies without favoring adherence to one particular school, method or theoretical approach. New political economy might draw on a range of theory: institutional–organizational approaches in economics; comparative theories of institutional and economic change in economics and economic history; structuration theory and strategic-relational theory in sociology; critical theories in international relations. This is drawn from an editorial by Andrew Gamble, Anthony Payne, Michael Dietrich, Ankie Hoogvelt and Michael Kenny for the journal *New Political Economy* when it was established in 1996.

8   This paragraph is reformulated from the book by Mark Olssen (2006a), *Michel Foucault: Materialism and Education*.

9   In his *Résumé du cours* for 1979 (in Foucault, 2004b, p. 323) Foucault indicates that the method he will adopt is based on Paul Veyne's nominalist history and in this respect he writes:

> Et reprenant un certain nombre de choix de méthode déjà faits, j'ai essayé d'analyser le "libéralisme", non pas une théorie ni comme une idéologie, encore moins, bein entendu, comme une mannière pour la "société" de "se\ représenter"; mais comme une pratique, c'est-à-dire comme une "manière de faire" orientée vers objectifs et se régulant par une réflexion continue. Le libéralisme est à analyser alors comme principe et méthode de rationalisation de l'exercice de gouvernement–rationalisation qui obéit, et c'est là sa spécificité, à la règle interne de l'économie maximale.

10 The Foucault archives have been relocated from the IMEC (Institut Mémoires de l'Édition Contemporaine) Paris address (9, rue Bleue, F-75009 Paris) to Abbaye d'Ardenne (14280 Saint Germaine la Blanche-Herbe), email: bibliotheque@imec-archives.com. "Il faut défendre la société", a course Foucault delivered in 1975–1976, was translated by David Macey as *Society Must Be Defended* and was published in 2003 by Penguin (Foucault, 2003). While courses for 1977–1978, 1978–1979, as previously mentioned, and 1981–1982 ("l'herméneutique de sujet") have been recently published (in the Gallimand/Seuill series), courses for the years 1979–1980, 1980–1981, 1982–1983, 1983–1984 are still only available from the IMEC Foucault archive as recorded tapes. Some work has still to be translated.

11 The governmentality literature has grown up around the journal *Economy and Society*, and includes the work of Cruickshank, Hindess, Hunter, Larner, Minson, O'Malley, Owen, and others, as well as those referred to above, most of who have published in *Economy and Society* (for aims and scope, and table of contents, see http://www.tandf.co.uk/journals/titles/03085147.asp).

12 See Olssen, Codd, and O'Neill (2004, pp. 167–171); Olssen (2006, pp. 29–30, 108, chapter 10). Also see "Why Foucault?" (Peters, 2003c) where Peters discusses Foucault studies in the English-speaking world by reference to the work of Marshall, Olssen, Ball, Popkewitz and Brennan, Besley, Baker, Middleton and myself. My work on Foucault's governmentality dates from Peters (1994), with additional work in 1996 (with Marshall), Peters (1996), Peters (1997), and Peters (2001a, b, c). For additional work on Foucault, see Peters (2003a & b), Peters (2005a & b). A special issue of *Educational Philosophy and Theory* published a special issue in 2006 entitled "The Learning Society and Governmentality", edited by Masschelein, Bröckling, Simons, and Pongratz.
13 As he writes in his Résumé du cours (in Foucault, 2004b, p. 323):

> Le thème retenu était doc la "biopolitique": j'entendais par là la manière don't on a essayé, depuis le XVIII siècle, de rationaliser les problèmes posés à la pratique gouvenrement par les phénomènes propres à une ensemble de vivants constitutes en population: santé, hygiene, natalitié, longévité, races.

14 The remainder of this section is reformulated and drawn from Olssen, Codd, and O'Neill (2004).
15 This is the process which Ritzer (2000) describes as the "McDonaldization of Society".
16 The reason usually given, but which in any case would be consistent with our statement here, is that Marx considered theoretical speculation of this sort unscientific, indeed, utopian, because economic and social conditions would themselves change in ways that were unpredictable.
17 See Deleuze's (1988) book called *Spinoza: Practical Philosophy*, where he articulates the theory of affects.
18 Types of affects might include desire, sadness or joy, as they did for Spinoza. However, the reader should entertain the possibility that Foucault would quite possibly object to this form of theorizing on the ground he eschewed normative theorizing of this sort. In extending Foucault in this way, it is thus in the spirit of the types of educational possibility and the types of normative theory that we are observing might "fit" with his Nietzschean approach. This seems to be a worthwhile way to extend Foucault if the possibilities of a Foucauldian radical political economy are to be developed.
19 The occasion for the statement cited here, published in *Liberation* in June 1884, was the announcement in Geneva of the creation of an international committee against piracy.

References

Barry, A., Osborne, T., & Rose, N. (Eds.). (1996). *Foucault and political reason: Liberalism, neo-liberalism and rationalities of government*. UCL Press.

Bataille, G. (2004). *On Nietzsche*. Continuum.

Becker, G. (1964). *Human capital: A theoretical and empirical analysis, with special reference to education*. National Bureau of Economic Research/Columbia University Press.

Bennett, J. (1996). "How is it, then, that we still Remain Barbarians?" Foucault, Schiller, and the aestheticization of ethics. *Political Theory, 24*(4), 653–672.

Bowles, S., & Gintis, H. (1976). *Schooling in capitalist America: Educational reform and the contradictions of economic life.* Basic Books.

Boyer, R. (1986). *La théorie de la régulastion: une analyse critique.* La Découverte.

Brier, S. (1999). Contribution to a roundtable on the future of the Left. *Socialism & Democracy.*

Broyer, S. (1996). *The social market economy: Birth of an economic style.* Discussion Paper FS I 318, Social Science Research Center, Berlin.

Buchanan, J. (1991). *Constitutional economics.* Blackwell.

Burchell, G. (1991). Peculiar interests: Civil society and governing "the system of natural liberty". In G. Burchell, C. Gordon, & P. Miller (Eds.), *The Foucault effect: Studies in governmentality* (pp. 119–150). University of Chicago Press.

Burchell, G. (1996). Liberal government and techniques of the self. In A. Barry, T. Osborne, & N. Rose (Eds.), *Foucault and political reason* (pp. 19–36). University of Chicago Press.

Burchell, G., Gordon, C., & Miller, P. (Eds.). (1991). *The Foucault effect: Studies in governmentality.* University of Chicago Press and Harvester.

Callinicos, A. (2003). *An anti-capitalist manifesto.* Polity.

Carver, T. (1998). *The postmodern Marx.* Manchester University Press.

Curtis, B. (2002). Foucault on governmentality and population: The impossible discovery. *Canadian Journal of Sociology, 27*(4), 505–535.

Day, R. B. (2002). History, reason and hope: A comparative study of Kant, Hayek and Habermas. *Humanitas, 15*(2), 4–24.

Dean, M. (1999). *Governmentality: Power and rule in modern society.* Sage.

Deleuze, G. (1988). *Spinoza: Practical philosophy.* City Lights Books.

Derrida, J. (1994). *Specters of Marx: The state of the debt, the work of mourning, and the new international* (P. Kamuf, Trans.; Introduction by B. Magnus & S. Cullenberg). Routledge.

Desai, M. (2002). *Marx's revenge: The resurgence of capitalism and the death of statist socialism.* Verso.

Dosse, F. (1997). *History of structuralism, volume 2: The sign sets, 1967–present* (D. Glassman, Trans.). University of Minnesota Press.

Du Gay, P., Hall, S., Janes, L., Mackay, H., & Negus, K. (1997). *Doing cultural studies: The story of the Sony Walkman.* Sage.

Featherstone, M. (1991). *Consumer culture & postmodernism.* Sage.

Ferguson, A. (1996). *An essay on the history of civil society 1767* (D. Forbes, Ed.). Edinburgh University Press. (Original work published 1767)

Foucault, M. (1972). *The archaeology of knowledge* (A. Sheridan, Trans.). Tavistock.

Foucault, M. (1977). *Discipline and punish: The birth of the prison* (A. Sheridan, Trans.). Penguin.

Foucault, M. (1977a). Intellectuals and power. In D. F. Bouchard (Ed.), *Language, counter-memory, practice: Selected essays and interviews* (D. F. Bouchard & S. Simon, Trans.; *pp.* 205–217). Cornell University Press.

Foucault, M. (1977b). A preface to transgression. In D. F. Bouchard (Ed.), *Language, counter-memory, practice: Selected essays and interviews* (D. F. Bouchard & S. Simon, Trans.; pp. 29–52). Cornell University Press.

Foucault, M. (1978). Politics and the study of discourse (C. Gordon, Trans.). *Ideology and Consciousness, 3*(Spring), 7–26.

Foucault, M. (1980a). Prison talk (C. Gordon, Trans.). In C. Gordon (Ed.), *Power/knowledge: Selected interviews and other writings 1972–1977* (pp. 37–54). Harvester Press.

Foucault, M. (1980b). Truth and power (C. Gordon, Trans.). In C. Gordon (Ed.), *Power/knowledge: Selected interviews and other writings 1972–1977* (pp. 109–133). Harvester Press.

Foucault, M. (1982). The subject and power. In H. Dreyfus, & P. Rabinow (Eds.), *Michel Foucault: Beyond structuralism and hermeneutics*. University of Chicago Press.

Foucault, M. (1984a). Politics and ethics: An interview (C. Porter, Trans.). In P. Rabinow (Ed.), *The Foucault reader* (pp. 373–380). Pantheon.

Foucault, M. (1984). What is enlightenment? (C. Porter, Trans.). In P. Rabinow (Ed.), *The Foucault reader* (pp. 32–50). Pantheon.

Foucault, M. (1985). *The history of sexuality, volume 2: The use of pleasure.* (R. Hurley, Trans.). Pantheon.

Foucault, M. (1986). Kant on enlightenment and revolution (C. Gordon, Trans.). *Economy and Society, 15*(1), 88–96.

Foucault, M. (1989a). An aesthetics of existence. In S. Lotringer (Ed.), *Foucault Live* (pp. 450–454). Semiotext(e).

Foucault, M. (1989). *Résumé des cours: 1970–1982*. Julliard.

Foucault, M. (1997). The ethics of the concern of the self as a practice of freedom. In P. Rabinow (Ed.), *Essential works of Foucault, 1954–1984, vol. 1: Ethics* (pp. 281–301). Penguin.

Foucault, M. (1998). Structuralism and post-structuralism. In J. D. Faubion (Ed.), *Essential works of Foucault, 1954–1984, vol. 2: Aesthetics, method, epistemology* (pp. 433–458). The New Press.

Foucault, M. (2001). Governmentality. In J. D. Faubion (Ed.), *Essential works of Foucault, 1954–1984, vol. 3: Power* (R. Hurley et al., Trans.; pp. 201–222). Penguin.

Foucault, M. (2001a). Interview with Michel Foucault. In J. D. Faubion (Ed.), *Essential works of Foucault, 1954–1984, vol. 3: Power* (R. Hurley et al., Trans.; pp. 239–297). Penguin.

Foucault, M. (2001b). Confronting governments: Human rights. In J. D. Faubion (Ed.), *Essential works of Foucault, 1954–1984, vol. 3: Power* (R. Hurley et al., Trans.; pp. 474–476). Penguin.

Foucault, M. (2001c). The political technology of individuals. In J. D. Faubion (Ed.), *Essential works of Foucault. 1954–1984, vol. 3: Power* (R. Hurley et al., Trans., pp. 403–417). Penguin.

Foucault, M. (2004a). *Sécurité, territoire, population: Cours au Collège de France (1977–1978)* (F. Ewald, A. Fontana, & M. Senellart, Eds.). Gallimard and Seuil.

Foucault, M. (2004b). *Naissance de la biopolitique: Cours au Collège de France, 1978–1979* (F. Ewald, A. Fontana, & M. Senellart, Eds.). Gallimard and Seuil.

Giddens, A. (1994). *Beyond left and right: The future of radical politics.* Polity.

Gordon, C. (2001). Introduction. In J. D. Faubion (Ed.), *Essential works of Foucault, 1954–1984, vol. 3: Power* (R. Hurley et al., Trans.; pp. xi–xli). Allen Lane/Penguin.

Gray, J. N. (1982). F. A. Hayek and the rebirth of classical liberalism. *Literature of Liberty, 4*(Winter). http://www.econlib.org/library/Essays/LtrLbrty/gryHRC1.html

Hayek, F. A. (1960). *The constitution of liberty.* University of Chicago Press.

Jameson, F. (1991). *Postmodernism, or the cultural logic of late capitalism.* Verso.

Joerges, C., & Rödl, F. (2004). 'Social market economy" as Europe's social model? Working Paper LAW 8, European University Institute (Florence). https://ssrn.com/abstract=635362

Lemke, T. (2001). "The birth of biopolitics": Michel Foucault's lectures at the Collège de France on neo-liberal governmentality. *Economy and Society, 30*(2), 190–207.

Lipietz, A. (1983). *Le monde enchanté: De la valeur à l'envol inflationniste.* La Découverte.

Lipietz, A. (1995). *Green hopes: The future of political ecology.* Polity.

Marx, K. (1971). *A contribution to the critique of political economy* (Introduction by M. Dobb). Lawrence and Wishart.

Marx, K., & Engels, F. (1965). *Selected correspondence.* Foreign Languages Publishing House.

Miller, D. (1995). *Acknowledging consumption: A review of new studies.* Routledge.

Miller, D. (1997). Consumption and its consequences. In Makay, H. (Ed.), *Consumption and everyday life* (pp. 13–50). Sage.

Miller, P., & Rose, N. (1990). Governing economic life. *Economy and Society, 19*(1), 1–31, and *19*(3), 49–64.

Olssen, M. (2003). Structuralism, post-structuralism, neo-liberalism: Assessing Foucault's legacy. *Journal of Education Policy, 18*(2), 189–202. https://doi.org/10.1080/0268093022000043047

Olssen, M. (2004a). The school as the microscope of conduct: On doing Foucauldian research in education. In J. Marshall (Ed.), *Poststructuralism and education* (pp. 57–84). Kluwer Academic.

Olssen, M. (2004b). Foucault and Marxism: Rewriting the theory of historical materialism. *Policy Futures in Education, 2*(3–4), 454–482. http://dx.doi.org/10.2304/pfie.2004.2.3.3

Olssen, M. (2006a). *Michel Foucault: Materialism and education.* Paradigm.

Olssen, M. (2006b). Foucault and the imperatives of education: Critique and self-creation in a non-foundational world. *Studies in Philosophy and Education, 25,* 245–271. https://doi.org/10.1007/s11217-006-0013-0

Olssen, M. (2006c). Foucault, educational research and the issue of autonomy. In P. Smeyers & M. A. Peters (Eds.), *Postfoundationalist themes in the philosophy of education* (pp. 57–79). Blackwell.

Olssen, M. (2006d). Understanding the mechanisms of neoliberal control: Lifelong learning, flexibility and knowledge capitalism. *International Journal of Lifelong Education*, 25(3), 213–230. https://doi.org/10.1080/02601370600697045

Olssen, M. (2006e). Totalitarianism and the "repressed" utopia of the present: Moving beyond Hayek, Popper and Foucault. In M. Peters & J. Freeman-Moir (Eds.), *Edutopias: New utopian thinking in education* (pp. 99–123). Sense Publishers.

Olssen, M. (2007). Invoking democracy: Foucault's conception (with insights from Hobbes). In M. A. Peters & T. A. C. Besley (Eds.), *Why Foucault? New directions in educational research* (pp. 205–226). Peter Lang.

Olssen, M., Codd, J., & O'Neill, A.-M. (2004). *Education policy: Globalization, citizenship & democracy*. Sage.

Osborne, D., & Gaebler, T. (1992). *Reinventing government: How the entrepreneurial spirit is transforming the public sector, from schoolhouse to statehouse, city hall to the Pentagon*. Addison-Wesley.

Peters, M. A. (1994). Governmentalidade Neoliberal e Educação. In T. Tadeu da Silva (Ed.), *O Sujeito da Educação: Estudos foucaultianos* (pp. 211–224). Editora Vozes.

Peters, M. A. (1996). *Poststructuralism, politics and education*. Bergin & Garvey.

Peters, M. A. (1997). Neoliberalism, welfare dependency and the moral construction of poverty in New Zealand. *New Zealand Journal of Sociology*, 12(1), 1–34.

Peters, M. A. (2001a). Foucault, neoliberalism and the governance of welfare. In *Poststructuralism, Marxism, and neoliberalism: Between theory and politics* (pp. 73–96). Rowman & Littlefield.

Peters, M. A. (2001b). Education, enterprise culture and the entrepreneurial self: A Foucauldian perspective. *Journal of Educational Enquiry*, 2(2), 58–71.

Peters, M. A. (2001c). Foucault and governmentality: Understanding the neoliberal paradigm of education policy. *The School Field*, 12(5/6), 59–80.

Peters, M. A. (2003a). Truth-telling as an educational practice of the self: Foucault, parrhēsia and the ethics of subjectivity. *Oxford Review of Education*, 29(2), 207–223.

Peters, M. A. (2003b). *Educational research, "games of truth" and the ethics of subjectivity* [Paper presentation]. Symposium: Michael A. Peters, Tina Besley, and Clare Caddell, "Ethical Educational Research: Practices of The Self", BERA.

Peters, M. A. (2003c). *Why Foucault? New directions in Anglo-American educational research* [Keynote address]. The Conference "After Foucault: Perspectives of the Analysis of Discourse and Power in Education", 29–31 October, University of Dortmund. (Also in L. Pongratz et al. (Eds.), (2004), *Nach Foucault. Diskurs- und machtanalytische Perspektiven der Pädagogik* (pp. 185–219), VS Verlag für Sozialwissenschaften.)

Peters, M. A. (2004a). Marxist futures: Knowledge socialism and the academy. *Policy Futures in Education, 2*(3–4), 435–438.

Peters, M. A. (2004b). Citizen-consumers, social markets and the reform of public services. *Policy Futures in Education, 2*(3/4), 621–632.

Peters, M. A. (2005a). Foucault, counselling and the aesthetics of existence. *British Journal of Counselling and Guidance, 33*(3), 383–396.

Peters, M. A. (2005b). The new prudentialism in education: Actuarial rationality and the entrepreneurial self. *Educational Theory, 55*(2), 123–137.

Peters, M. A., & Marshall, J. (1996). *Individualism and community: Education and social policy in the postmodern condition.* Falmer Press.

Pignatelli, F. (1993). Dangers, possibilities: Ethico-political choices in the work of Michel Foucault. http://www.ed.uiuc.edu/EPS/PES-Yearbook/93_docs/PIGNATEL.HTM

Poster, M. (1984). *Foucault, Marxism, history: Mode of production vs mode of information.* Polity.

Ritzer, G. (2000). *The McDonaldization of society.* Pine Forge Press.

Rose, N. (1999). *Powers of liberty.* Cambridge University Press.

Schatzki, T., Knorr Cetiona, K., & Von Savigny, E. (Eds.). (2001). *The practice turn in contemporary theory.* Routledge.

Schrift, A. D. (1995). *Nietzsche's French legacy: A genealogy of poststructuralism.* Routledge.

Thompson, K. (1986). *Beliefs and ideologies.* Ellis Harwood.

Vanberg, V. (2004). *The Freiburg School: Walter Eucken and ordoliberalism.* Discussion Papers on Constitutional Economics, Freiburg. http://opus.zbw-kiel.de/volltexte/2004/2324/pdf/04_11bw.pdf

Weber, M. (1921). *Economy and society.* Bedminster.

Williams, R. (1980). *Problems in materialism and culture.* Verso.

Witt, U. (2002). Germany's "social market economy": Between social ethos and rent seeking. *The Independent Review, 4*(3), 365–375.

Willis, P. (1977). *Learning to labour: How working class kids get working class jobs.* Saxon House.

CHAPTER 5

In Conversation with Mark Olssen

On Foucault with Marx and Hegel

Rille Raaper and Mark Olssen

Abstract

It is challenging to define who Michel Foucault was, whether he was a theorist, a philosopher, a historian, or a critic. In many of his books, and essays, Foucault denied being a philosopher or a theorist, nor did he want to be called a writer or a prophet. He described himself as an experimenter by saying that his work simply consists of "philosophical fragments put to work in a historical field of problems". Like Ball (2013, p. 2), we believe that Foucault tried hard not to be "a something", opening up opportunities to develop and practise theory. Emeritus Professor Mark Olssen has written widely on Foucault's theoretical underpinnings and legacy. This conversation aims to revisit Olssen's work, as well as Foucault's own writings in order to engage with Foucault's philosophical background and the methods he developed. By exploring Foucault's theoretical and methodological approaches, the conversation situates his work within broader traditions of social theory, particularly within the works of Marx and Hegel. Our conversation starts by discussing Foucault's relationship with Marx and Hegel and moves towards his approach to history and his wider contribution to the poststructuralist school of thought.

Rille Raaper: *Foucault's transformative writing style is well known. Some Foucauldian scholars even differentiate between an early and late Foucault, pessimistic and optimistic Foucault among other similar contrasts. I have found these variations in his work fascinating. It seems that Foucault was also aware of his transformative style, if we can call it like that. He explained in one of his interviews that it was a desire to explore and understand the unknown that inspired his work: "I write a book only because I still don't know what to think about this thing I want so much to think about, so that the book transforms me and transforms what I think" (Foucault, 2002a, pp. 239–240). In other words, Foucault allowed himself to challenge and change his thinking over time. Perhaps one of the most important transformations in his work relates to his methodological shift from archaeology to genealogy. Foucault (1972, p. 154) explained archaeology as an approach that helps to resist the ideas of linear progression and* *continuous history, and it enables the abandonment of the "history of ideas … its postulates and procedures" to practise a "quite different history [to] what men have said". This means that archaeology focuses on processes as unique and discursive acts. Like archaeology, his genealogy was meant to function as a historical method but one that approached history from the perspective of discontinuity. It is not that society is just advancing and becoming a "better" place to live and work, but it repeats and disrupts itself. We will come back to his approach to history with one of my later questions. What interests me now, however, is Foucault's so called transformations. Foucault (1997b, p. 180) described his methodological shifts as "auto-critique". It was his "autocritique" that made it possible to shift from archaeology to genealogy. Furthermore, it was his "autocritique" that made him change his understanding of subjects as passively created by disciplinary power and normalisation—particularly evident in his writings on madness and penal systems—to individuals that have some agency over their own lives. His later work defined individuals as being controlled and constrained by someone else but also as being able to inform their own identity through conscience or self-knowledge (Foucault, 2002c). It looks to me that he managed to remain "true" to himself throughout his career. It was not just a fashion trend he followed, but it was something much bigger. How would you describe Foucault as a thinker and researcher?*

Mark Olssen: I think Foucault is a towering thinker. It is pointless to seek to rank or be precise as to exactly where he stands in a rather large list of 20th-century thinkers, but Foucault surely ranks as important, as does Deleuze, in reinterpreting Nietzsche, and Heidegger in a way that offered a new understanding of our most prized certainties, that incorporates them and underscores their importance for sociological and historical studies. It may seem strange to say this but he draws upon Nietzsche and Heidegger in a way that makes him more liberal than classical Western liberals at any rate. He finds teleology and vestiges of metaphysics not just in Hegel and Marx but in the standard Western liberal epistemologies and roads to truth, such as empiricism, and of course in that arch liberal, Kant, himself. In this, he agrees with and utilises Nietzsche, who finds in Kant too much metaphysics, especially concerning the foundational status of the subject, whose self-consciousness sits motionless and largely unaffected as history sweeps on past it. Such an anthropology of the subject underpins Kant's transcendentalism. It was this identification of a constant human subject, which depicts the subject as ahistorical, with an integral identity or "essence", that Foucault opposes under the umbrella of anthropological humanism.

Rille Raaper: *Can you explain a little further what Foucault means by humanism? It is obviously something that he perceives in relation to the Enlightenment episteme as we know from his essay "What Is Enlightenment?" (see Foucault, 1984). How does his perspective to humanism help us understand his work?*

Mark Olssen: The critique of humanism is consistent throughout his work, and must be seen as having a very specific and limited scope, in the sense just stated. As Foucault explains, it envelops the subject in multiple senses:

> By humanism I mean the totality of discourse through which western man is told: "Even though you don't exercise power, you can still be ruler. Better yet, the more you deny yourself the exercise of power, the more you submit to those in power, then the more this increases your sovereignty". Humanism invented a whole series of subjected sovereignties: the soul (ruling the body but subjected to God), consciousness (sovereign in a context of judgement, but subjected to the necessities of truth), the individual (a titular control of personal rights subjected to the laws of nature and society), basic freedom (sovereign within, but accepting the demands of an outside world and "aligned with destiny"). In short, humanism is everything in western civilisation that restricts the desire for power. ... [T]he theory of the subject is at the heart of humanism. (Foucault, 1980d, p. 221)

Unfortunately, many liberal critics of Foucault have extrapolated and embellished the argument in a way that is simply intended to debunk and mystify. Foucault was well aware that humanism as a concept can take various forms, and can be seen exemplified in Christianity, Marxism, Existentialism, Phenomenology, Liberalism, even Nazism and Stalinism. Further, he appreciated that:

> Humanism is ... a theme, or rather, a set of themes that have reappeared on several occasions over time, in European societies; these themes, always tied to value judgements, have obviously varied greatly in their content, as well as in the values they have preserved. ... From this we must not conclude that everything that has ever been linked with humanism is to be rejected, but that the humanistic thematic is itself too supple, too diverse, too inconsistent to serve as an axis for reflection. And it is a fact that, at least since the seventeenth century, what is called humanism has always been obliged to lean on certain conceptions of man

borrowed from religion, science or politics. Humanism serves to colour and to justify the conceptions of man to which it is, after all, obliged to take recourse. (Foucault, 1984, p. 44)

In this Foucault follows Nietzsche who sees no constant, ahistorical, essence or nature that characterises man. Influenced by Nietzsche, too, Foucault utilises and extends the focus on language and interpretation to a formalised system of discourse where prized certainties piled up over time by science operate as forms of power which function as instruments of power and control, inclusion and exclusion. Such scientific discourses operate as new forms of biopower which increasingly pervade the various spaces of reason, truth, authority, and legitimacy, making the viewpoints or expressions of marginalised groups difficult to be heard or gain traction. As Foucault (1981, p. 52) says in "The Order of Discourse": "in every society the production of discourse is at once controlled, selected, organised, and redistributed by a certain number of procedures whose role is to ward off its powers and dangers. ... [T]he procedures of exclusion are well known". Foucault manifests a concern with the oppressive consequences of reason and science, seeking to expose its irrational underside. Like Nietzsche, in this sense, Foucault subjects Kant to a historical and sociological critique. For Foucault, the unresolved tension of Kant's philosophical project is that he fails to appreciate the contingent and historically contextualised character of all truth claims, that is to advocate a notion of critique which claims to transcend specific historical conditions through the exercise of cognitive faculties (of understanding, reason, and judgement) deduced a priori as timeless structures. In this sense, Foucault rejects Kant's claims to have established the universal grounds for the conditions of possibility of human knowledge, and Kant's claims for transcendental reason are replaced for Foucault by a principle of permanent contingency. Importantly here, Foucault is within the Kantian theatre, and effects similar criticism to those made of Kant by Hegel. By extension, Foucault disputes Kant's claim to have established a secure foundation by which to differentiate various types of knowledge claims, relating to science, practical reason, or aesthetics. The objective is to switch from a conception of critique which is transcendentally grounded to a conception of critique—hence, *autocritique*—which conceives it as practical and as historically specific.

I have found Foucault's life and academic career also fascinating. He was lucky enough in the end to be appointed to a high-status position in the Collège de France, where he had relative freedom to develop his research programme. As with many leading French academics, Foucault was also passionately political. This link between academic life and the world outside the university is one thing that defines the distinctiveness of the French intellectual. Foucault commented upon and was involved with many causes, but his work with prison reform was pivotal. With Deleuze, Foucault was one of the founders of the Groupe d'information sur les prisons, an organisation established to enable prisoners to argue for improved conditions. It is here that Foucault's concept of the "specific intellectual" took much inspiration. This notion contrasts with the idea of the "traditional intellectual", who speaks as a general and detached observer on behalf of mankind, and provides important context for understanding his relationship and detachment from Marx and Hegel. In his famous interview with Deleuze, titled "Intellectuals and Power", Foucault (1980a, pp. 207–208) notes that "the intellectual's role is no longer to place himself 'somewhat ahead and to the side' in order to express the stifled truth of the collectivity; rather it is to struggle against the forms of power that transform him into its object and instrument in the sphere of 'knowledge', 'truth', 'consciousness', and 'discourse'". In working practically, Foucault observes in the same interview, that

> there exists a system of power which blocks, prohibits, and invalidates this discourse and this knowledge, a power not only to be found in the manifest authority of censorship, but one that profoundly and subtly penetrates an entire societal network. ... [I]ntellectuals are themselves agents of this system of power. (Foucault, 1980a, p. 207)

Rille Raaper: *I like your description of Foucault as an academic with a clear societal contribution, whether it was his contribution to prison reform in France, the Iranian Revolution or involvement in other political events. We also know that he we was a member of the French Communist Party during the Cold War years. This obviously is a factual detail in Foucault's autobiography rather than significant political engagement. There has been a lot of discussion around Foucault's relationship with Marxism. I know that you have explored Foucault's critique of Marxism in your writings. For example, in one of your earlier articles, you have argued that Foucault's archaeological method allowed him to "challenge Marxism, which is concerned with a narrow linear conception of causality and enables him to advance a non-reductive and holist analysis of social life" (Olssen, 2003, p. 192). It is obviously clear that Foucault did not speak the language of the "dominant left"; he did not perceive the world in terms of ideology or economic oppression. The social world from a Foucauldian perspective is much more complex—power is not necessarily negative but can be productive even if sometimes risky or dangerous (Foucault, 2002d). We could therefore say that Foucault promoted a shift from traditional understandings of power in which power only presses on the subject from the outside (characteristic of Marxist views of power and oppression) towards an understanding of power as something that forms the subject by "providing the very condition of its existence and the trajectory of its desire" (Butler, 1997, p. 2): power is what subjects depend on for their existence. From a Foucauldian* *perspective we could all be our own oppressors and liberators. So tell me, even if there is a fundamental difference in the ways in which Foucault understands power and inequality, did Marxist ideology have any impact at all on Foucault's career and early stage work? How would you describe his relationship with Marx?*

Mark Olssen: Foucault's thesis on the subjects of Marxism and totalitarianism were themselves relatively undeveloped, yet important. In my own work, I have sought to extrapolate Foucault's position on Marxism in relation to his express rejection of Hegel, his own more pluralist ontological position, as well as in relation to his scattered comments on Marx. I think also, his magazine articles, especially the one in *Le nouvel observateur* in 1977, were also insightful and effectively summarise his position. Foucault's endorsement of Glucksmann's "new philosophy"[1] reciprocated Glucksmann's positive endorsement of Foucault's thesis, and his earlier suggestion that political theory should take a "Foucauldian turn" (see Glucksmann, 1975). Foucault's endorsement of Glucksmann's book signalled a number of important political and philosophical dimensions, even if only developed in embryonic form: first, a consistent antitotalitarianism as an essential feature of Foucault's own philosophical pluralism; second, a disillusionment with 1968 and post-1968 revolutionary politics as potentially totalitarian; and third, a chance to crystallise his rejection of Marxism, Marxism–Leninism, Stalinism, and Maoism, as political movements. Glucksmann had in an earlier work analysed Alexandr Solzhenitsyn's *Gulag Archipelago* as representing the culmination of Marxist historical dialectical development, ending up in the residue of totalitarian politics as expressed in the camps of Siberia, genocide and, by extension, Nazism (Glucksmann, 1975). As Foucault wrote in his review of *Les maîtres penseurs*:

> Stalinism was the truth, "rather" naked, admittedly, of an entire political discourse which was that of Marx and of other thinkers before him. With the Gulag, one sees not the consequences of an unfortunate error but the effect of the most "true" theories in the order of politics. Those who hoped to save themselves by opposing Marx's real beard to Stalin's false nose are wasting their time. (Foucault, 1977a, p. 84)

Foucault, for his part, found sustenance in the anti-statist and pluralist discourses that characterised his own early works, focusing instead on the "micro powers" and "disciplines" that underpinned the state, and were prior to it. Marx is rejected, as is Hegel, as philosophers who totalise history and who represent the state as a legitimate organ of domination and truth. For Hegel it was philosophy that led to this totalisation through the reconciliation of opposites by which all contradictions were overcome. For Marx, it was the history of class struggles that achieved the same dialectical synthesis resulting in the communist utopia. These thinkers believe in "final solutions", "revolutionary goals and strategies", "the march of history", "dialectical progression", and identified power as emanating from a central agency in the state. Foucault agreed with Glucksmann's assessment that, influenced by thinkers such as Marx and Hegel, "[t]he Europe of states seeks to exclude the marginal" (Glucksmann, 1977, p. 119). Foucault's own alternative analysis denies any single location to power, representing it as a multiplicity of force relations across the entire social system in terms of which resistances are ubiquitous. By extension, class relations do not invariably determine power relations. This entails that there is no central agency of social change but rather a plurality of resistances and struggles against local fixations of power in specific sites.

Rille Raaper: *Can you be more specific about the concept of totality to which Foucault objects?*

Mark Olssen: The notion of totality is important here if one is to understand Foucault's relation to Hegel. Foucault's scepticism towards the idea of totality is developed forcefully in the "Introduction" to *The Archaeology of Knowledge*, where Foucault (1972, p. 10) distinguishes between "total history", which he opposes, and "general history" which characterises his own pluralist methodological approach, an approach which he says, "speaks of series, divisions, limits, differences of level, shifts, chronological specificities, particular forms of rehandling, possible types of relation". Although neither Marx nor Hegel is named in the text at this point, it is clear that Foucault is opposing a well-known trend in historical philosophy associated with their writings. As he says:

> The project of total history is one that seeks to reconstitute the overall form of a civilization, the principle—material or spiritual—of a society, the significance common to all the phenomena of a period, the law that accounts for their cohesion—what is called metaphysically the "face" of a period. ... [I]t is supposed that history itself may be articulated into great units—stages or phases—which contain within themselves their own principle of cohesion. (Foucault, 1972, p. 10)

The idea of society as an organic totality or whole had been an animating spiritual principle from ancient Greece through to the Middle Ages. The whole pertained to both the spiritual and physical order. Leibniz (1646–1716) had characterised society as a "pre-established harmony" in his *Monadology* based on the concept of the continuum; that the differences between things were differences of degree and were interconnected to the extent that "each simple substance has relations and express all the others, and consequently ... is a perpetual living mirror of the universe" (see Leibniz, 1898/1968, Section 78). At the start of the 19th century Hegel witnessed modernity as ravaged by crisis, division (*Entzweiung*), dirempion (*Trennung*), and social atomism, effected by the rising bourgeois order, and the question he sought to answer was: How is it possible to salvage the idea of unity given such a situation? The question was important for Hegel as he appreciated that man is in most respects a product of his environment and a fragmented society (*Bildung*) would mean a fragmented subject, pertaining both to the individual and to community. Hegel's answer, which is also important for understanding Marx, was to historicise the notion. He sought to preserve the idea of a closed totality against the fragmenting forces of modernism by historicising it and injecting it with an overarching spiritual significance in relation to progressive development.[2] Influenced by the experience of the French Revolution, as well as the philosophies of Jean-Jacques Rousseau[3] and Sir James Steuart,[4] Hegel claimed to detect a suprahistorical process of reason whereby such disintegrations were reconciled, preserving the unity of totality overall. Foucault (2005) comments in *The Hermeneutics of the Subject* that Hegel was characteristic of much of 19th-century thought (Schelling, Schopenhauer, Nietzsche, Husserl, and Heidegger) in linking knowledge to spirituality. John Grumley (1989) makes the point that this spiritual principle in important senses supersedes Kant and provides the major mechanism for preserving unity.[5] As Grumley (1989, p. 18) puts it, "Hegel's surprising shift from Kant to Jesus in 'The Spirit of Christianity' represents a final rejection of Kantian moral asceticism". Society could maintain itself and prosper notwithstanding fragmentary forces of division and diremption through processes of reconciliation and regeneration built into life itself. Just as the body repairs itself from disease and injury, achieving repair and integration over time, so, too, can economy and society. Instances of violence and division are represented as but "moments" in a larger dialectical process of reconciliation and adjustment whereby the totality reintegrates itself at a higher spiritual level of development. For Hegel, such a process was both sociological, historical, and metaphysical, and applied to the individual, community, and society. The ravages of the rising bourgeois world were transcendable preserving unity as a progressive developmental spiritual process, culminating in the Absolute, Perfect knowledge, or God. It is fundamentally this spiritual/teleological principle that Foucault finds objectionable and which is central to his own anti-totalising perspective. Closely linked to this is his rejection of dialectical method as a suprahistorical conception in terms of which historical change is schematically interpreted. As Foucault (1980c, pp. 114–115) told Alessandro Fontana and Pasquale Pasquino, dialectic constitutes "a way of evading the always open and hazardous reality of conflict by reducing it to a Hegelian skeleton".

Rille Raaper: *In his own pluralist approach, which shuns totality, we can note that power, particularly a location of power, is a key concept in understanding how Foucault differed from Marx and Hegel. You also argue in one of your articles that it was Foucault's methodological focus on discourse that makes his work distinctive and helps us understand the complex relationship between Foucault and thinkers like Marx and Hegel (see Olssen, 2010). I remember you explaining that Foucault used his archaeological and genealogical methods—which are discursive methods—to challenge Marxism and its linear conception of causality and power that operates between the oppressor and oppressed (Olssen, 2003). It is obviously clear that social world for Foucault is much more complex, and like you said, he promoted a shift from singular power towards an understanding of power that operates in multiplicity and also allows multiple resistances. Based on a similar logic, Foucault perceived discourse as something more complex than just written and oral language. Foucault (1981, p. 67) argued that discourses should be considered as "discontinuous practices" which can be juxtaposed with each other but may exclude each other. It seems to me that his understanding of plurality in both discourse and power allows him to develop his distinctive approach to history. He was able to shift away from linear approach to historic events and to rather investigate "series, divisions, limits, differences of level, shifts, chronological specificities, particular forms of rehandling and possible types of relation" (Foucault, 1972, p. 11). Can we explore Foucault's approach to history a little further, and how does Foucault's understanding of history make him differ from other influential theorists, say Hegel?*

Mark Olssen: The relation to Hegel and Marx, following Hegel, is of course central to understanding Foucault's methodology as well as his project as a whole. I have always emphasised this relation to Hegel by Foucault since my first book, *Michel Foucault: Materialism and Education* (see Olssen, 2006a). In a way, Foucault's entire approach reflects a conversation with Hegel. Another excellent more recent treatment appears by Gary Gutting, in his book, *Thinking the Impossible: French Philosophy since 1960* (see Gutting, 2011), where he points out the central role of Hegel as the figure to which French philosophy for much of the 20th century has responded.

Gutting (2011, p. 13) makes the point that "Foucault first came to full philosophical life when he encountered Jean Hyppolite". Hyppolite taught a course on Hegel's *Phenomenology of Spirit* at the Lycée Henri IV, where Foucault underwent his preparation for his entrance to the École Normale Supérieure

(ENS) (Gutting, 2011, p. 13). He later sided with Nietzsche in opposing Hegel. Those aspects of Hegel he rejects are of course the senses in which Hegel is a philosopher of the Absolute, his Absolute Idealism and of dialectical necessity whereby contradictions are reconciled at progressively higher planes, resulting logically in Perfection. This is the sense in which Hegel seeks to integrate all phenomenological experience, that experience of the "unhappy" and "partial consciousness", as but moments in a progressive realisation of spirit's development through the historical process of dialectical synthesis, ultimately to a full unity in God. Foucault cannot abide Hegel's teleology, where conflicts, wars, evil, and famines are all necessary "moments" of a purposeful dialectic, resolvable at each higher level where their necessity and rationality also become apparent. Although opposed to Hegel in this sense, Foucault was deeply influenced by Hyppolite's reading of Hegel. This includes Hegel's focus on history and time, as well as his focus on historicity, language, and interpretation, rather than on mind. Foucault shared Hyppolite's concern to move away from the anthropological reading of the existentialists who emphasised human consciousness, moving instead towards a position where all experience is necessarily mediated by conceptual structures or discourses. If consciousness and mind are socially and historically constituted, then consciousness and lived experience themselves become subordinate to language and discourse. Hyppolite showed the path, says Foucault (1981, p. 74), "by which one can get away from Hegel".

> For him the relation to Hegel was the site of an experiment, a confrontation from which he was never sure that philosophy would emerge victorious. He did not use the Hegelian system as a reassuring universe; he saw in it the extreme risk taken by philosophy. (Foucault, 1981, p. 74)

Foucault clearly credits Hyppolite, in the same way as Arkady Plotnitsky in his Foreword to Hyppolite's *Hegel's Philosophy of History*, as presenting a Nietzschean reading of Hegel (see Plotnitsky, 1996). Hyppolite concludes his thesis with the observation that:

> There exists in [Hegel's] thought an ambiguity. That ambiguity is that the reconciliation of subjective spirit and objective spirit, the supreme synthesis of this system, is perhaps not completely realizable. (Hyppolite, 1996, p. 72)

Hyppolite's reading of Hegel is represented by Foucault as being deeply sceptical and sets Foucault on a trajectory which takes him outside of the Hegelian system altogether, while retaining some aspects of it. Foucault certainly sees Hyppolite if not as modifying Hegel in the direction of Nietzsche, then certainly as allowing Foucault to do so. As he says, "Instead of conceiving philosophy as the totality at least capable of thinking itself and grasping itself in the movement of the concept, Jean Hyppolite made it into a task without end set against an infinite horizon" (Foucault, 1971, p. 75). It is, continues Foucault,

> [a] task without end and consequently as task forever recommenced. ... [T]he inaccessible thought of the totality was for Jean Hyppolite the most repeatable thing in the extreme irregularity of experience. ... He transformed the Hegelian theme of closure on to the consciousness of self into a theme of repetitive interrogation. (1971, p. 75)

For although the interest in obtaining absolute knowledge is rejected in Hegel, it is also the case that Foucault saw a similar concern as underpinning modernist thought in general, in that all major Western systems of knowledge saw truth as a slow upward pilgrimage towards greater and greater knowledge or truth. Notwithstanding all this, certain aspects of Hegel—the interest in historicity, mediation, language, culture, and history—are retained while being adapted. He was no doubt also aware of a certain non-foundationalism suggested by Hegel especially concerning notions such as truth, knowledge, ethics, culture and community could be retained while avoiding Hegel's overarching metaphysical system.[6] Rather than Hegel's system, then, it was the sense in which he conceptualises history teleologically and totalistically that is rejected. Foucault regarded Hegel's philosophy as a closed system. Having studied with Hyppolite then, Foucault is very aware of how and in what senses his own philosophy departs from Hegel's.

Rille Raaper: *So if Foucault rejected Hegel's Absolute Idealism and his way of doing philosophy, what was his influence on Foucault's approach to history?*

Mark Olssen: Foucault is concerned not just with Hegel, but with something much bigger. He wants to avoid totalising approaches because they are teleological and closed. He is concerned very directly in his early writings on literature and on history with a new way of writing history, a way that constitutes what has become very definitely a new paradigm or a word I like better, a new settlement for how we understand knowledge of the world, a settlement which is both beyond Aristotle, and also Newton and Descartes. At the same time, Foucault appreciates the many ways in which he is close to Hegel. One thing both thinkers agree upon is their rejection of representationalist or correspondence theories of truth, the view that truth resides in a more or less direct correspondence between mind and world. For Hegel the attempt to resolve or overcome this impasse is via phenomenology and idealism whereas Foucault approaches the matter through genealogy. Because for Hegel there is nothing outside consciousness, the true cannot be independent of mind but projected by it. So development in the world is through a reconciliation of mind to world through successive conflicts (or reversals) of consciousness at progressively higher levels. It is in this sense that phenomenology is idealist for it sees the object in the world as part of consciousness itself.

For Foucault, the empiricist claim to the immediacy of knowledge is simply error. This is an argument he shares with Hegel, who argues against the immediacy of knowledge in *The Phenomenology of Spirit* of 1807. Foucault signals an affirmation and continuation of the linguistic turn by noting the ineradicability of the discursive through which every translation much proceed. This gives us the possibility of knowledge which is not simply that of truth, although it may contain truths, but is also simultaneously that of error and illusion. We could say that discourse *exceeds* the empirical content it organises. Every translation offers the possibility of falsehood, of distortion, of deception. The ghosts of past ages are carried forward with us and inhabit the lens through which we view the present. Rather than immediate, or direct, knowledge is a process of becoming. Although we may strive to understand the world rationally, our methods do not vouchsafe certitude or truth but rather may combine a mix of practical wisdom, reasoned truths, as well as folklore, superstition and falsehoods. How to distinguish good sense from folklore is crucial to offsetting relativism. Knowledge thus proceeds through perception, language, discourse, and comprises idols, ghosts and verities of ages past, alas all mixed up together, which makes the irrationalities of our present world, with its conflicts, wars, violence and divisions, and misunderstandings, at least understandable.

Rille Raaper: *In other words, history as we know it is always biased and surrounded by falsehoods. We could even see the bias from the ways in which World War II is taught in different countries. It is the case of winners writing the history. So it is a very intriguing approach to history that Foucault was promoting, and I can see why he received and still receives quite a lot of opposition from historians. But if it diverges from Hegel and Marx, what else goes on here in Foucault's view of history? It cannot all come down to his opposition to empiricism and methodological focus on discourse?*

Mark Olssen: No, there is far more than simply an opposition to classical empiricism and phenomenology and his development of the concept of discourse.

Foucault is an empiricist, of sorts, too, of course, but not of the sort that Locke was. For Locke, the differences between things, although given as sensible qualities, are really differences in boundaries established by nature, and nature is presumed to be timeless and ahistorical, that is, a ground or foundation. Foucault would dispute such a naturalism, rejecting essential differences between things, asserting their interconnectedness, as well as their historical constitution. This view we might note is reminiscent of the early theorists of the continuum who dispute the "invincible solidity" of things or atoms.[7] For Foucault, too, there is a different sort of relation between part and whole; each element expresses the whole, but there is clearly no universal principle of such expression, for there is no single rule that determines it in all times and places, which is to say that it expresses the whole or aspects of larger structures contingently, itself being affected by a multiplicity of variables. Diversity can be maintained because the ideal conception of "unity" is effectively replaced by a notion of "concord". At the same time, Foucault's empiricism avoids the dualism of mind and matter as bequeathed by Descartes, which for him was the disastrous bequest of the Enlightenment on modernity. Hence, the model of an isolated cogito, of the Cartesian individual, and of the mechanical universe, and of unity in diversity, are all rejected in preference for a new form of holism which rejects a whole conceived additively as the sum of its parts, as with Descartes, or as a comprehensive all-embracing collectivity, as with Hegel, and emphasises instead the contingent connectedness and dynamic interplay between part and whole. For Foucault, it seems to me, the idea of the isolated, ultimate part is as difficult as that of the comprehensive whole. Foucault would see his role here as rejecting metaphysical demons not previously evacuated by the thinkers of the Enlightenment: ideas of substance, of essences, of mind–body dualisms, of unified spirits, of the immediacy of sensory experience, and so on. So, of course, he is not certainly an empiricist as we usually understand that term, but nevertheless, he has for all that a healthy respect for the empirical adequacy of claims and stands opposed to the top down theoreticism he associates with Hegel and Marx.

Rille Raaper: *What does this mean in terms of his methodological approach, genealogy in particular? I know he described genealogy as being "gray, meticulous, and patiently documentary", operating "on a field of entangled and confused parchments, on documents that have been scratched over and recopied many times" (Foucault, 1980b, p. 139). By working with a wide range of documentary evidence, he aimed to prove that humanity does not progress from "combat to combat" towards universal reciprocity but rather repeats its systems and mistakes (Foucault, 1980b, p. 151). I wonder if this is what you meant by interconnectedness* *and historical constitution in Foucault's approach to history. How would you explain Foucault's genealogy?*

Mark Olssen: Foucault's genealogical empiricism was an empiricism of history and conflict where Foucault sought to chart histories based upon detailed archival investigations where he sought to avoid a dialectical account of historical change or of subsuming facts to an already established teleological system of the sort that Hegel developed. Foucault wanted a lesson from history which did not state it in advance but emerged as the outcome of history. In addition to this, he opposed the phenomenological view of the subject and consciousness as a foundation for history, preferring instead to give an account of the manner in which concepts rules, structures, and practices developed and changed over time. In this, while avoiding Hegel's overall system, he invoked many of the elements with which he was concerned and he saw in Hegel many ideas from which he profited. Yet, Foucault was interested in describing the way fundamental ideas pertaining to a society changed and for this he invoked Nietzsche and Heidegger against Hegel.

Foucault's approach to history also introduces a new model of determination as it operates in the world and introduces complexity themes of non-linear determination, uncertainty, non-predictability, novelty, uniqueness, and chance (*aléa*) into the historical process. He also rejects the model of machine replacing it with that of power (*pouvoir, puissance, possibilitié, autorités, capacité, énergie, faculté, faire fonctionner, faire marcher, force*). This is not necessarily to replace the metaphor of machine in all cases, but to supplement the model of machine with another model, and to see power rather than mechanism as what is central and all pervasive. Foucault did not deny the existence of linear relations of causality but was also aware that in many instances they were inappropriate. This constitutes a view of power as ubiquitous, and as productive as well as constraining, making Foucault's conception quite different from the Marxist tradition. Although he did not use the language of the quantum or post-quantum complexity theorist, nevertheless, in articles such as "Nietzsche, Genealogy, History" (see Foucault, 1980b), in his major books (see Foucault, 1972, 1977b), and in some of the lectures in *Dits et écrits* (see Foucault, 1994a, 1994b), Foucault seeks to analyse different sorts of determination, characterised by non-linear relations, feedback loops, and chance. Notice that this approach to history is also holistic, both ontologically and methodologically. It is not holistic in Hegel's or Marx's sense, of course, in reducing everything to a single foundation, nor in the sense of the Romantics, in positing the whole to the exclusion of the parts, but it does assert an ontology of interdependence of part and whole, and is, centrally, non-reductionist as well. Foucault announces a view of history which seeks to account for elements of individuality, novelty, uniqueness and freedom from a platform of historical constitution. It is in fact a new model of order based upon contingent and non-contingent relations, and where everything affects and implicates everything else. He sought in other words to establish an alternative model of history which remains open to both present and future and incorporates differences and otherness rather than seeking to homogenise or reconcile them. In relation to developments in science, his approach has resonances with quantum and post-quantum developments, of Planck, Heisenberg, Schödinger, Bohr, and Prigogine. It also confronted the dominant modernist view of science and knowledge, premised on predictability and certainty, with ideas of non-predictability, chance (*aléa*), uncertainty, the unforeseen, and unforeseeable.

Rille Raaper: *You have written recently that Foucault developed much of this approach to history through his reading of literature. Can you say more on this?*

Mark Olssen: I wrote an extended review essay of Michel Foucault's *Language, Madness, and Desire: On Literature*. Gary Gutting from Notre Dame asked me if I would do it. I also published a shorter version of this article as a book review in the *Notre Dame Philosophical Reviews* (see Olssen, 2016). My central task was to illuminate Foucault's core ontological and epistemological themes that developed in these early commentaries on literature and that were to inform the philosophical orientation of his social science investigations, including madness, psychiatry, medicine, the prison, sexuality, and the care of the self. The article suggests that Foucault's early works on literature establish a thesis of philosophical materialism which articulates many of the themes of post-quantum complexity science as they affected the social and physical sciences in the late 20th and 21st centuries.

Rille Raaper: *This is very interesting. It also means that Foucault's relationship with literature was highly strategic, helping him to distinguish discursive practices from non-discursive practices. Can we then say that Foucault was searching for a non-Hegelian conception of history, something that would help to reject totality? Was this in your view central to Foucault?*

Mark Olssen: What emerged from his readings of literature was a view of history which sought to preserve the uniqueness, or if you like, the distinctiveness of the individual in their individuality, uniqueness, novelty, and freedom, which giving up on preformed, ahistorical essences and substances, and seeing individuals as socially and historically constituted. What he was looking for was an alternative model of history, which remains open to both the present and the future, and which incorporates, but does not "homogenise" or "unify" difference and otherness, and which preserves also ideas of non-predictability, chance events, uncertainty, the unforeseen, and the unforeseeable. Here we can see there is already an early resistance to Hegel interpretation of history, based upon a dialectical unfolding and progression towards the Absolute. It is not surprising in that Nietzsche maintains the same argument against Hegel consistently across his writing career.[8] We get the retention, of course, of the importance Hegel attributed to culture and the social, but the equation of the rational and the real, subject and object, and Hegel's notion of Geist, or Spirit, have completely gone. So has the dialectic both as an ontology and methodology. At the same time, he appreciated that Hegel is complex and difficult to escape, unless one goes completely the other way and accepts a classical atomism and individualism, where development is a result of internal essence or genetics, or soul, or whatever, and culture and the social are seen as purely derivative, secondary, non-efficacious and marginal. Post the development of quantum theory there is no possibility of going back in that direction. It is a dead end at any rate in a global interconnected world. What we need to do is confront those models of history that are presently on offer. And this means confronting Hegel. Hegel had a huge influence in Germany and on the Continent since the end of the 18th century and start of the 19th century, and a very large influence, too, from 1865 in Britain, when in political and social theory the British idealists became ascendant, until at least the turn of the century until they were knocked off their pedestal by Russell, Moore and the Logical Positivists. In France, too, the reception of Hegel has been variable and for most of the 20th century they have been trying to escape him. Foucault appreciates, however, that this is no easy matter. As he said in his inaugural lecture at the Collège de France:

> I know ... our age, whether through logic or epistemology, whether through Marx or through Nietzsche, is attempting to flee Hegel. ... But to truly escape Hegel involves an exact appreciation of the price we have to pay to detach ourselves from him. It assumes that we are aware of the extent to which Hegel, insidiously perhaps, is close to us; it implies a knowledge, in that which permits us to think against Hegel, of that which remains Hegelian. (Foucault, 1972, p. 235)[9]

This is a very interesting statement. In recent quantum and post-quantum complexity approaches to the social sciences, Hegel's representation of *Sittlichkeit*, or ethical life, as a general relational form of community, which stresses the social and historical constitution of individuals is clearly still present. It is not that the genetic is entirely discounted in such a view, but that it is seen as only one of many factors, in theory, of an infinite list of factors, that affect development. It is surprising how this view which gives a central role to nurture and to causal indeterminacy is now increasingly accepted in approaches such as epigenetics. [10] Also, now, Hegel's teleological dialectic is recast and translated into a protoperformativist view whereby the future must be consciously created in the light of the limited and fallible knowledge that we retain in the present. But what is gone is what was problematic in Hegel, such as the unity of reason and history, where Hegel would assert that whatever was real was rational. There is a passage in a paper by Suzanne Gearhart, which states:

> Whereas Hegel stresses that reason and history are one, Foucault seeks to write a history of madness; whereas Hegel seeks to guarantee historical continuity, through a dialectical process that links opposing and discontinuous terms, Foucault attempts to break with the various forms of historical continuity, and in particular the historical narrative. Whereas Hegel writes the history of the subject, Foucault focuses his "histories" on themes that reveal the precarious—or in any case the derivative—status of the subject. (1992, p. 58)

Rille Raaper: *Can we then say that Foucault's desire to find an alternative model of history is actually about finding a new way to explain social reality?*

Mark Olssen: Whereas Hegel unifies subject and object in the Absolute Spirit via successive reconciliations, Foucault rejects the dialectic in favour of an ontology of differences, and of the ultimate irreconcilability of discourse and practice. Foucault most emphatically objected to the idea of dialectical progression as well as the equation of the real and the rational. At one important level Foucault took this as to mean that there was an equivalence between perfected thought, and scientific observation, and reality itself. In their different ways, this was the dream of rationalism, positivism, empiricism, and phenomenology. Did not all of these advocates declare that there was no distinction between thought and reality, between ideas or words and things? Did they not all, like Hegel, declare there to be no such world of ideas separate from reality, which required relating to reality? Hegel, along with many others, thought that discourse, ideas, thought, what have you, was all of a piece. Russell criticised the British Hegelians for this, referring to it as *panlogicism*. For Foucault, similarly, reality always needed interpreting, not so much by thought, which is very idealist, and subjective, but by discourses, which are themselves historically constituted, and material. Unless we define it thus, we misunderstand the processes and nature of understanding as opposed to existence. To conflate them, or to dispense with discourse as not being an obstacle to true knowledge, is to make a serious error. Moreover, while established discourses permit some sort of correspondence with truth through careful triangulation in history, such truths are never easily maintained; they are never vouchsafe, and may often be paired with phantoms, idols, ideologies, and ghosts, which may distort them, or mislead.

Rille Raaper: *It clearly appears that it is the concept of discourse that reveals Foucault's understanding of reality and truth. In your very recent review paper, you described Foucault's work as constructivist (see Olssen, 2016). Correct me if I am wrong, but is not constructivism rooted in phenomenology and hermeneutics, shaped by the earlier works of Edmund Husserl on phenomenology as well as by German philosophers on hermeneutics. I suppose you understand why I am curious about your statement. Would you explain how does constructivism align with Foucault's work on discourse? Can you elaborate on that?*

Mark Olssen: A great deal of confusion has developed over the concept of constructivism. Many writers, especially feminists like Butler (1990), Haraway (1991), and Barad (2007), have all criticised use of the concept. Barad (2007, pp. 32, 90, 134–137) uses the concept of "proto-performativity" rather than constructivism and claims that the latter elevates the linguistic or the discursive over the material. I think the argument is trivial and pedantic in most respects in that words can mean anything you like, as Alice said, in Wonderland. It has been also rather confusing. Initially I stopped using the word "constructionism" because of its association with idealistic ontologies, that is, that discourse constitutes the things of which it speaks. I intended construct*ivism* to avoid such idealistic connotations by representing discourse as a way of organising or representing practices, by referring to its constructive aspect on the grounds that practices or world cannot be represented except through discourse. This is clearly more in the sense that Foucault intended it notwithstanding that some of his own phraseology contributed to the confusions in question.

Clearly the problems that Barad identifies as being associated with constructivism are indeed problems, if indeed one commits the sins she associates with the concept, and likewise that Butler (1990, pp. 109–114) and others associate with the concept, but my use of the term constructivism does not commit any of these fallacies. In my use of the concept, constructivism does a number of things: firstly, pertaining to an epistemological sense, it refers to the discursive construction of meaning and it challenges the representationalist claim that we have unmediated access to the real, or that language can faithfully and unproblematically represent the world as it really is independent of historically constituted discourse. In this sense, discourse is a way of organising practices. Although constructivism is social and historical, I also do not intend that discourse constructs the objects of which it speaks except in the sense that it always adds an interpretative context. This needs specifically pointing out as the phrase "discourse constructs the objects of which it speaks" is one Foucault used in one particular work to convey the constructive aspect of discourse. But as it becomes abundantly clear in *The Archaeology of Knowledge*, and the major works of the 1970s, although discourse maintains a constructive role, this does not deny that there is something there outside of discourse, a something Foucault refers to as the "non-discursive" that is independent of discourse (1972, p. 68). What it does suggest though is that discourse nevertheless adds something to representation. Any framing of reality will comprise multiple elements and may be more or less faithful to whatever is there independent of discourse. But it will also frame it in a particular way and comprise aspects of ideology from past ages. However reality is represented will reflect the paradigmatic assumptions of the age in terms of its ways of seeing and believing. It will include elements of good sense, based on truth, as well as elements of folklore and superstition. Hence, constructivism opposes crude representationism; it refers to the fact that our methods and representations are not simply unmediated representations of the world.

Secondly, pertaining to normativity, I am also referring to constructivism in an ethical sense as a task or challenge for humanity. In this sense, it is opposed to teleology and naturalism. This is the sense in which there is no pre-ordained telos, divine purposes, fate, or ends of man, or constant, ahistorical or timeless nature. Constructivism therefore stands opposed to Aristotle's essentialism which states that man seeks to fulfil his nature, as if the essence of being unravels through time. It stands opposed to all views of nature as timeless and ahistorical. Constructivism, therefore, signals that creating the future is an infinitely open endeavour on the basis of a past already provided, replete with uncertainty and danger, and can only be imposed by living beings. It will comprise numerous false starts, blind alleys, and wrong turnings. I always think it makes sense of Foucault's comment that "everything is dangerous".

So, despite a rather unnecessary fanfare over the issue, ultimately it does not matter which concept one uses so long as one does not commit the fallacies that Barad (2007, pp. 43, 133) detects. If those utilising the concept of construction have committed these, then they are in error. It is equally true that those using the concept of "proto-performativity", Barad's favoured term of expression, are equally in danger of accepting the "misconception that would equate performativity with a form of linguistic monism that takes language to be the stuff of reality", as Barad (2007, p. 133) herself notes. So we can all concur that a naïve form of anti-realism that sees the world of things as the product of language is not the thesis that is being advanced.

Rille Raaper: *Can we consider Foucault as being constructivist also in terms of science and scientific knowledge?*

Mark Olssen: Yes, Foucault is also a constructivist as regards scientific knowledge. Again, this does not entail that Foucault believes that the world is constructed through discourse, or that empirical adequacy is not important, or relevant, to knowledge. I think that methods of cross-referencing or triangulation can provide some basis for epistemological warrantability. At the same time, it is no use trying to insist that empirical adequacy contradicts or counters constructivism, or that it constitutes evidence of realism. The issues at stake are far more complex. Foucault is not, also, denying the existence of a mind or discourse or human independent world, nor is he denying that human independent facts are important constraints on the development of knowledge. What he is denying is that our perspectives of the world, generated through language and discourse, constitute in any sense, a "mirror of nature", in any simple or straightforward sense. Having said that, they are not straightforwardly either, mirrors of society or culture or power as wielded in history. Such views of constructivism are simply an oversimplification and generate simplistic confusions. As an epistemological issue, constructivism signals that discourse is not solely a vehicle for representing true knowledge, or reason, but contains also within the discursive framework of representation, various, let us say, non-epistemological factors—idols, ghosts, superstitions, ideologies, and distortions—that are carried along with it; that are generated within history, and which serve, in different ways, at different times, to distort, obfuscate, slant, warp, structure, or qualify, the epistemological returns of knowledge generation. In this sense, constructivism is a shaking free from Descartes dualist postulations about knowledge or science, mind and world. Science, of course, seeks to be systematic and objective, and sometimes it may be, but witness the many false starts, wrong turnings, reversals, setbacks, errors, and deceptive announcements.

Rille Raaper: *Isn't this an unacceptable scepticism? Is there any way to distinguish the idols or superstitions that inextricably accompany knowledge in order to gain reliable knowledge, in an epistemological sense, or are we forever with Foucault stuck deep in a quagmire of relativism?*

Mark Olsson: Foucault was well aware of this issue, of course, and Habermas and others levelled this charge at him. The very fact that power is always associated with knowledge raises the question as to warrantability for reliable knowledge. It raises serious problems such as how does one know if something is genuine knowledge or not, which cannot be fully gone into here. What can be said is two things: firstly, Foucault raises the matter of the *difficulty* of assessing reliable knowledge in the light of the fact that power is inextricably mixed up with it, and this is a difficulty which does indeed confront us in history, where the search for knowledge is full of errors, deceptions, false starts, wrong turnings, outright fraud, and other embarrassments. Secondly, Foucault's writings warn us as to our *arrogance*, or perhaps the arrogance of modernism, in believing naively in progress and infallibility, while failing to see the irrational underside of science and reason, with respect to nuclear power, climate change, environmental degradation, death, war, and destruction, that modernist science has unleashed. Given these issues, Foucault's insights invite circumspection, reflection, cautiousness, and humility—and these in themselves are not bad things. As to how relativism can be overcome, Foucault never really got round to addressing the problem. But given the difficulties of reliable knowledge, surely some tentative confidence can be gained through "cross-checking", "triangulation", "repetitions over time", within and between discourses and practices. The fact that science can achieve results, like putting a person on the moon, or curing a disease, would seem to inspire some confidence, tentative and cautious although we perhaps should be.

Rille Raaper: *If Foucault agreed with the existence of an independent reality, should not we say that he was a realist rather than a constructivist? For example, Al-Amoudi (2007) argues that while Foucault uses a vocabulary that is different from critical realist vocabulary, he still promotes a similar understanding of reality as the realist, Roy Baskhar, would do. Al-Amoudi (2007) explains that Foucault promotes a relational conception of society, while recognising that people's actions and social relations exist in two groups of mechanisms that are ontologically distinct: so-called strata of tactics/individuals and strategies/society. I wonder whether the two—critical realism and constructivism—are actually more alike than we usually think. What are your thoughts on it?*

Mark Olsson: Whereas the ontological fabric of reality is for the realist a matter of transparent discovery via a neutral method, for Foucault, discourse maintains an autonomous and constructive or dynamic relation to the world which means that it scars, it distorts, it conceals, and adds to or embellishes, simultaneous with any positive knowledge it generates. For Foucault, too, the being of the world is not discovered, but constructs in a further sense, in that it projects categories and frameworks; it sorts in historically variable ways. There is "instability of boundaries" by which objects are defined and which they can be defined as constituting some sort of a "natural kind". The problem for Foucault, I think, was not so much an issue with "nature", as an ontological existent, as such, but with the traditional postulations about nature which represented it as timeless and ahistorical, as some sort of "cosmological constant", to use Einstein's concept, as a benchmark which could ground objectivity and truth. Foucault utilises Barthes theory of semiotics to question any pre-established harmony between signifier and signified and focuses instead upon the role of language and discourse in establishing referentiality. I believe, though, that the sense in which Foucault was a constructivist was much more cautious than you read in Anglo-American philosophical critiques and the like, where constructivism is simply translated to refer to a fairly crass type of anti-realism. Foucault had the knack of creating the impression that he was much more extreme than he in fact was. I think for Foucault, that by accepting the cultural specificity and the role of extra-epistemological factors in discourse construction we do not have to completely give up on constructing theories that are adequate representations of an independent reality. Discourses of science put down stakes into the world; they "intervene" or "experiment". Ian Hacking's book, *Representing and Intervening* (see Hacking, 1982), marks a contribution here. Nietzsche's focus upon "experimentation" is perhaps also important. Hence, Foucault is saying that a theory, or discourse, may have access to the ontology of being of the world in the sense of being able to give a more or less adequate account of it, in terms of controlling it. What it cannot do, however, is claim to give an actual literal description of our world, or claim that representations "represent" an independent reality "without remainder", establishing objectivity and truth for all time. Foucault is, as I have pointed out before, a moderate constructivist in that he stands opposed to naïve traditional forms of representationalism. This has of course now been pointed out by many, including Butler, Haraway, Barad, and others, as already referred to. I like the point that Barad (2007, p. 48) makes, attributed to Joseph Rouse (1996) concerning the deep similarities between realists and constructivists, instead of always representing each other as maintaining "bizarre" and "far-fetched" antithetical positions. To summarise it, both groups see knowledge as mediating access to the material world which is there independently of humans, and other life forms. "Where they differ", says Barad (2007, p. 48), "is on the question of the 'referent'". Realists, however, see representations as being of things as they "really are" in a way that is both "timeless" and "ahistorical", whereas constructivists allow for a much greater role for culture, history, and language, and see representations as an admixture of both epistemological and extra-epistemological factors, the latter which may comprise various paradigmatic axioms concerning such matters as the conceptions of human agency, the role and existence of genetics, the respective weight put on nature or nurture, and so on. It is these factors which mean that representations are not likely to constitute an unproblematic, straightforward, or unmediated copy of a mind or human independent world.

Rille Raaper: *To conclude our conversation, let's explore Foucault's legacy a little further, particularly his contribution to poststructuralist school of thought as we understand it today. You have argued that you would align Foucault with poststructuralism, particularly of materialist tradition (see Olssen, 2010, 2006a; Olssen, Codd, & O'Neill, 2004). It is obviously clear that Foucault (1997a, p. 131) described his work as situated "at the intersection of different currents and different problems". He described those "currents" and "problems" as placed in phenomenology, Marxism and the history of sciences (1997a, p. 131). We also know that he tried to escape these dominant forces by studying Nietzsche, opposing Hegel and Marx, and aligning with thinkers such as Georges Bataille, Maurice Blanchot, Pierre Klossowski (Foucault, 2002a). Those scholars invited him to question "the category of the subject, its supremacy, its foundational function" (Foucault, 2002a, p. 247) and allowed him to develop the practice of desubjectivation: the process that Foucault described as "wrenching the subject from itself, of seeing to it that the subject is no longer itself, or that it is brought to its annihilation or its dissolution" (2002a, 241). This view of the subject, as well as his approach to history and reality as discussed earlier, is something we often associate with poststructuralism. To summarise our conversation, can you reflect on Foucault's role in poststructuralist school of thought? I mean, how did his readings shape his work and perhaps also his belonging to the new way of practising history, science and philosophy?*

Mark Olssen: It was through a very broad reading of literature in the library of the École Normale Supérieure that Foucault "deconstructed an order of discourse". The editors of Foucault's *Language, Madness, and Desire: On Literature* (see Artièries et al., 2015), cite Daniel Defert (2001) who fills in some of the detail of Foucault's engagement. We are told that Foucault read:

> Saint-John Perse in 1950, Kafka in 1951, Bataille and Blanchot in 1953, followed by the progress of the *nouveau roman* (including the work of Alain Robbe-Grillet), discovered Raymond Roussel in the summer of 1957, the authors associated with Tel Quel (Philippe Sollers, Claude Ollier) in 1963, reread Becket in January 1968. (Artièries et al., 2015, p. VIII)

During his travels, to Uppsala and Warsaw in the 1950s, Foucault both read literature and taught courses, from his favourite poet at the time, René Char, and from Sade to Genet.

The relationship with literature constitutes a testimony to understanding the way Foucault's philosophical mindset developed. Many of the literary gestures, insights and motifs from his early reading are incorporated within his great works in the sense that they generate philosophical axioms about general ontology and epistemology which remained central to his own philosophical project. Foucault utilises various forms of literature (narratives, epics, poetry, comedies, etc.) to demonstrate and inform his archaeological conception of discourse in relation to all number of philosophical concerns. Literature, in Foucault's hands, helps establish the manner and substance of his major arguments with respect to ontology and epistemology. On the one hand, it furthers the archaeological project in order to enquire into the distinctiveness of the literary discourse and position it in the field of discourses. On the other hand, Foucault is also saying that ideas float freely from one field or discourse to another and the thesis that such ontologies are purely a result of linear accretions of research in the domain of science are highly improbable. The ontological thesis that Foucault develops is one of radical linguistic or discursive indeterminacy by which any one translation can always be replaced by another, and which establishes the autonomy of discourse from the real is a thesis shaped by Foucault's early readings of literature. While he read, however, he was searching for the solution to deeper problems and topics. On its own, of course, he made clear in his book on Raymond Roussel,[11] literature has no specificity or strategic centrality. The thesis of the literary then turns out to be the thesis of discourse as autonomous, strategic, and constitutive which escapes empiricist formulations of representation as well as correspondence theories of the real which see the real as accurately and completely revealed through discourse. Literature is central to the development of his distinctive philosophical thesis although it sits somewhat uncomfortably with his shift to a more materialist position after 1968, I believe he retained this thesis. For Foucault the literary generates conceptions of indeterminateness, novelty, chance, unpredictability, and multiplicity of the meanings in relation to the real. His reading of literature thus solved puzzles and generated ideas, which he later on puts into play with his social science studies. Literature also opposes established and settled meanings; it deconstructs established hegemonies. It is this ontology of complex determination, developed initially by Foucault in the early 1960s, that he essentially counterpoises to Marx and Hegel.

Acknowledgement

This chapter originally appeared as Raaper, R., & Olssen, M. (2017), In conversation with Mark Olssen: On Foucault with Marx and Hegel, *Open Review of Educational Research*, 4(1), 96–117, http://dx.doi.org/10.1080/23265507.2017.1334575. Reprinted here, with minor edits, with permission from the publisher.

Notes

1. Translated by Michael Scott Christofferson, the article is reproduced under the title of "The Great Rage of Facts", in Zamora and Behrent (2016, pp. 170–175).
2. See, for instance, the "Preface" to the *Phenomenology of Spirit* (1807), where Hegel says: "The truth is the whole".
3. Hegel was impressed initially both by Rousseau's ideas of democracy as well as his thesis concerning the disintegration of society under the force of economic and social developments.
4. See Plant (1973). Plant argues that in his *An Enquiry into the Principles of Political Economy* (1767), Steuart develops a progressive, evolutionist approach to political economy. The thesis is included in Hegel's early essay "The Spirit of Christianity and Its Fate" (1798–1800); see Hegel (1948).
5. See Hegel (1948). I am indebted to John E. Grumley for his excellent discussion of the importance of religion in Hegel's early writings; see Grumley (1989).
6. The view that Hegel's philosophy can be interpreted to represent truth and knowledge in distinctively non-foundationalist and non-metaphysical terms has been suggested by many thinkers, for instance, in recent decades, Hartmann (1972), Rose (1981), Houlgate (1986), Maker (1994), Sallis (1995), Hutchings (2003) to name but some.
7. Such a view is found in Leibniz for instance, in both: Leibniz (1898/1968, Sections 8, 10, 16, 56–58, 61); and Leibniz (1898/2009, Sections 1, 2, 4). The phrase "invincible solidity" is from Leibniz, cited in Stark (1943).
8. See, for instance, the early essay, "On the Uses and Disadvantages of History for Life" (Nietzsche, 1997).
9. Foucault had earlier expressed this view in his eulogy to Hyppolite in French at the École Normale, published in 1969 in the *Revue de Métaphysique et de Morale*. See Canguilhem and Foucault (1969). The lecture was also presented at the Collège de France, 2 December 1970, and was appended, under the title "the discourse on language to the archaeology of knowledge".
10. Epigenetics asserts that environment is crucial in switching genetic predispositions on or off; see Carey (2012).
11. Published in English as *Death and the Labyrinth* in 1986; see Foucault (1986).

References

Al-Amoudi, I. (2007). Redrawing Foucault's social ontology. *Organization, 14*(4), 543–563. https://doi.org/10.1177/1350508407078052

Artières, P., Bert, J.-F., Potte-Bonneville, M., & Revel, J. (2015). Editors' introduction. In M. Foucault (Ed.), *Language, madness, and desire: On literature* (P. Artières, J.-F. Bert, M. Potte-Bonneville, & J. Revel, Eds.; R. Bononno, Trans.; pp. 7–16). University of Minnesota Press.

Ball, S. J. (2013). *Foucault, power, and education*. Routledge.

Barad, K. (2007). *Meeting the universe half way: Quantum physics and the entanglement of matter and meaning*. Duke University Press.

Butler, J. (1990). *Gender trouble: Feminism and the subversion of identity*. Routledge.

Butler, J. (1997). *The psychic life of power: Theories in subjection*. Stanford University Press.

Canguilhem, G., & Foucault, M. (1969). Jean Hyppolite (1907–1968). *Revue de Métaphysique et de Morale, 74*(2), 129–136.

Carey, N. (2012). *The epigenetics revolution*. Icon Books.

Defert, D. (2001). Chronologie. In D. Defert & F. Ewald (Eds.), *Dits et écrits, vol. 1, 1954–1975* (pp. 13–90). Quarto/Gallimard.

Foucault, M. (1971). *L'ordre du discours*. Gallimard.

Foucault, M. (1972). *The archaeology of knowledge* (A. Sheridan, Trans.). Tavistock.

Foucault, M. (1977a, May 9). La grande colere des faits. *Le nouvel observateur*.

Foucault, M. (1977b). *Discipline and punish: The birth of the prison* (A. Sheridan, Trans.). Pantheon.

Foucault, M. (1980a). Intellectuals and power. In D. F. Bouchard (Ed.), *Language, counter-memory, practice: Selected essays and interviews* (D. F. Bouchard & S. Simon, Trans.; pp. 205–217). Cornell University Press.

Foucault, M. (1980b). Nietzsche, genealogy, history. In D. F. Bouchard (Ed.), *Language, counter-memory, practice: Selected essays and interviews* (pp. 139–164). Cornell University Press.

Foucault, M. (1980c). Truth and power (C. Gordon, Trans.). In C. Gordon (Ed.), *Power/knowledge: Selected interviews and other writings 1972–1977* (pp. 109–133). Harvester Press.

Foucault, M. (1980d). Revolutionary action: "Until now". In D. F. Bouchard (Ed.), *Language, counter-memory, practice: Selected essays and interviews* (D. F. Bouchard & S. Simon, Trans.; pp. 218–233). Cornell University Press.

Foucault, M. (1981). The order of discourse (I. McLeod, Trans.). In R. Young (Ed.), *Untying the text: A post-structuralist reader* (pp. 48–78). Routledge & Kegan Paul.

Foucault, M. (1984). What is enlightenment? (C. Porter, Trans.). In P. Rabinow (Ed.), *The Foucault reader* (pp. 32–50). Pantheon.

Foucault, M. (1986). *Death and the labyrinth: The world of Raymond Roussel* (C. Ruas, Trans.). Introduction by J. Ashberry. Continuum.

Foucault, M. (1994a). Linguistique et sciences socials. In D. Defert & F. Ewald (Eds.), *Dits et écrits, 1954–1988* (4 Vols, Vol. 1, No. 70, pp. 821–842). Éditions Gallimard.

Foucault, M. (1994b). La philosophie analytique de la politique. In D. Defert & F. Ewald (Eds.) with J. Lagrange, *Dits et écrits, 1954–1988* (4 Vols., Vol. 3, No. 232, pp. 534–551). Éditions Gallimard.

Foucault, M. (1997a). What our present is. In S. Lotringer & L. Hochroth (Eds.), *The politics of truth* (pp. 147–168). Semiotext(e).

Foucault, M. (1997b). Subjectivity and truth. In S. Lotringer & L. Hochroth (Eds.), *The politics of truth* (pp. 171–198). Semiotext(e).

Foucault, M. (2002a). Interview with Michel Foucault. In J. D. Faubion (Ed.), *Essential works of Foucault, 1954–1984, vol. 3: Power* (R. Hurley et al., Trans.; pp. 239–297). Penguin.

Foucault, M. (2002b). Question of method. In J. D. Faubion (Ed.), *Essential works of Foucault, 1954–1984, vol. 3: Power* (R. Hurley et al., Trans.; pp. 223–238). Penguin.

Foucault, M. (2002c). The subject and power. In J. D. Faubion (Ed.), *Essential works of Foucault, 1954–1984, Vol. 3: Power* (R. Hurley et al., Trans.; pp. 326–348). Penguin.

Foucault, M. (2002d). The risks of security. In J. D. Faubion (Ed.), *Essential works of Foucault, 1954–1984, vol. 3: Power* (R. Hurley et al., Trans.; pp. 365–381). Penguin.

Foucault, M. (2005). *The hermeneutics of the subject: Lectures at the Collège de France 1981–1982* (G. Burchell, Trans.; F. Gross, Ed.). Palgrave Macmillan.

Gearhart, S. (1992). Irreconcilable differences: Kant, Hegel, and the "idea" of critical history. In M. Hays (Ed.), *Critical conditions: Regarding the historical moment* (pp. 56–81). University of Minnesota Press.

Glucksmann, A. (1975). De la violence: Entretien avec André Glucksmann. *Actuel, 17*, 54–76.

Glucksmann, A. (1977). *Les maîtres penseurs*. Grasset.

Grumley, J. E. (1989). *History and totality: Radical historicism from Hegel to Foucault*. Routledge.

Gutting, G. (2011). *Thinking the impossible: French philosophy since 1960*. Oxford University Press.

Hacking, I. (1982). *Representing and intervening: Introductory topics in the philosophy of natural science*. Cambridge University Press.

Haraway, D. (1991). *Simians, cyborgs, and women: The reinvention of nature*. Routledge.

Hartmann, K. (1972). Hegel: A non-metaphysical view. In A. MacIntyre (Ed.), *Hegel: A collection of critical essays* (pp. 104–124). Anchor.

Hegel, G. W. F. (1948). The spirit of Christianity and its fate. In *Early Theological Writings* (T. M. Know, Trans.; pp. 182–301). University of Pennsylvania Press.

Houlgate, S. (2004). *Hegel, Nietzsche and the criticism of metaphysics*. Cambridge University Press.

Hutchings, K. (2003). *International political theory: Rethinking ethics in a global era*. Sage.

Hyppolite, J. (1996). *Introduction to Hegel's philosophy of history* (B. Harris & J. Bouchard Spurlock, Trans.). University Press of Florida.

Leibniz, G. W. (1968). *The monadology* (R. Latta, Trans.). Forgotten Books. (Original work published 1898)

Leibniz, G. W. (2009). *Principles of nature and grace* (R. Latta, Trans.). Cornell University Library. (Original work published 1898)

Maker, W. (1994). *Philosophy without foundations: Rethinking Hegel*. SUNY Press.

Nietzsche, F. (1997). On the uses and disadvantages of history for life. In D. Breazeale (Ed.), *Untimely meditations* (R. J. Hollingdale, Trans,; pp. 104–108). Cambridge University Press.

Olssen, M. (2003). Structuralism, post-structuralism, neo-liberalism: Assessing Foucault's legacy. *Journal of Education Policy, 18*(2), 189–202. https://doi.org/10.1080/0268093022000043047

Olssen, M. (2006a). *Michel Foucault: Materialism and education*. Paradigm.

Olssen, M. (2006b). Foucault and the imperatives of education: Critique and self-creation in a non-foundational world. *Studies in Philosophy and Education, 25*, 245–271. https://doi.org/10.1007/s11217-006-0013-0

Olssen, M. (2006c). Foucault, educational research and the issue of autonomy. In P. Smeyers, & M. A. Peters (Eds.), *Postfoundationalist themes in the philosophy of education* (pp. 57–79). Blackwell.

Olssen, M. (2010). Discourse, complexity, life: Elaborating the possibilities of Foucault's materialist concept of discourse. In C. B. Grant (Ed.), *Beyond universal pragmatics: Studies in the philosophy of communication* (pp. 25–58). Peter Lang.

Olssen, M. (2016, March 28). Language, madness, and desire: On literature. *Notre Dame Philosophical Reviews*. https://ndpr.nd.edu/reviews/language-madness-and-desire-on-literature/

Olssen, M., Codd, J., & O'Neill, A.-M. (2004). *Education policy: Globalization, citizenship & democracy*. Sage.

Plant, R. (1973). *Hegel*. Allen & Unwin.

Plotnitsky, A. (1996). Foreword. In J. Hyppolite (Ed.), *Introduction to Hegel's philosophy of history* (B. Harris & J. Bouchard Spurlock, Trans.). University Press of Florida.

Rose, G. (1981). *Hegel contra sociology*. Athlone.

Rouse, J. (1996). *Engaging science: How to understand its practices philosophically*. Cornell University Press.

Sallis, J. (1995). *Delimitations: Phenomenology and the end of metaphysics* (2nd ed.). Indiana University Press.

Stark, W. (1943). *The ideal foundations of economic thought*. Kegan Paul.

Zamora, D., & Behrent, M. C. (2016). *Foucault and neoliberalism*. Polity.

PART 3

Social Democracy in the 21st Century

CHAPTER 6

From the Crick Report to the Parekh Report: Multiculturalism, Cultural Difference and Democracy

The Re-visioning of Citizenship Education

Abstract

This paper attempts to develop a more sophisticated notion of multiculturalism in Britain. It starts by examining the philosophical basis of the Crick Report on citizenship education to resolve the theoretical tension between liberal and multicultural approaches to the subject. To achieve this resolution, it compares the Crick Report to the Parekh Report on the Future of Multi-ethnic Britain, published on 11 October 2000. The Parekh Report is then used to critique the Crick Report and re-theorise the practical imperatives of multicultural citizenship education. I claim that the Crick Report, typical of liberal analyses, is suspicious of departure from the presumption of a unified social structure, and represents citizenship education as the imposition of a uniform standard applied to all groups and peoples. On this basis it is claimed that, although the Crick Report's conception of citizenship fails to adequately take account of cultural difference, it need not do so, as there is room within liberal approaches to citizenship education for a recognition of difference. The paper explains how such a resolution can be effected.

1 Introduction: The Crick Report

Citizenship, as conceived in the Crick Report (QCA, 1998) is not the neoliberal conception based on narrowly defined individual rights as has become familiar in certain quarters in recent years. The neoliberal conception, like the classical liberal parent, conceives citizenship as promoting a self-regarding individual who promotes their own interests in their own way without infringing (i.e., harming) the rights or interests of others. The conception advocated in the Crick Report has a much more communitarian resonance in that it refers to citizenship as entailing both "rights" and "duties", and as being concerned to promote the "common good". Crick's report seeks to educate young people in civic virtue, as well as autonomy and personal self-fulfillment. The upshot is a considerably stronger conception of citizenship than would be required for the development of citizens in a minimal liberal state which would be limited to protecting the individual from the intrusions of the state or from others. Centrally, in his own conception, Crick seeks to emphasise not simply rights and duties, and personal development, but civic participation as an important "end" or "good" in society. In this, he argues that these ends or goods coexist. Although, arguably, this could be represented as promulgating a substantive moral code, the *bête noir* of liberals everywhere, according to Pearce and Spencer (1999, p. 221), the Crick Report seeks "to place citizenship education within the context of a pluralist society which requires basic but robust civic and political foundations".

In developing and advocating this conception, the Crick Report refers explicitly to the conception of citizenship developed by T. H. Marshall (1997) in his now classic article, first published in 1950, "Citizenship and Social Class". Citizenship for Marshall is both a *right* and a *duty*. He defines citizenship (1997, p. 300) as an institution that developed from the latter part of the 17th century, its growth coinciding with the rise of capitalism. As its central feature it constituted "a status bestowed on all those who are full members of the community" (1997, p. 300). In the 19th century, this conception was to become one of the new "Rights of Man". Building on the philosophical preconceptions of John Stuart Mill, the "new Liberals"—T. H. Green, L. T. Hobhouse, and economists such as Alfred Marshall—advanced citizenship as a positive freedom, to supplement the negative rights of "life, liberty, and property" advanced since the 17th century by the classical liberals. As a right and duty for all, citizenship becomes a basic principle of equality. While earlier liberals saw such rights as limited, for the most part opposing even the public provision of education, under the period of the welfare state the entitlement to membership and participation also came to embody rights to work, to health, and to security. As such, citizenship expressed the new positive role of the state as the embodiment of social democracy.

Citizenship in this sense was an increase in the rights that could be enjoyed by all. In his essay, T. H. Marshall identifies three aspects of citizenship—civil, political and social. The civil element is composed of "rights necessary for individual freedom—liberty of the person, freedom of speech ... the right to own property and conclude valid contracts, and the right to justice" (1997, p. 294). The political element pertains to the extension of enfranchisement, according the "right to participate in the exercise of political power, as a member of a body invested with political authority or as an elector of the members of such a body" (1997, p. 294). By the social element Marshall means the "right to a modicum of economic welfare and security to the right to share in the full social heritage and to live the life of a civilised being according to the standards prevailing in the society" (1997, p. 294).

Following Marshall's tripartite distinction between civil, social and political citizenship, the Crick Report both draws upon, but modifies the stated citizenship model. Endorsing the views of the Commission on Citizenship's *Encouraging Citizenship* (1990), the report (QCA, 1998, p. 10) notes that with reference to the civil element, a greater stress than in Marshall should be placed upon the reciprocity between rights and duties, and also, to a greater extent than Marshall did, on welfare not just being provided by the state, but also concerning what people can do for each other through the voluntary groups and organisations of civil society, at the local or non-state level. The Crick Report (QCA, 1998, p. 10) then moves on to endorse social citizenship and political citizenship, also stressed by Marshall. Social citizenship, as the report maintains, concerns social and moral responsibility, which is an essential political and moral virtue, implying (a) care for others, (b) premeditation about the effect of actions on others, and (c) understanding and care for the consequences (QCA, 1998, p. 16). Political literacy concerns the acquisition of knowledge, skills, and attitudes necessary for effective participation. Taking all three, the Crick Report endorses the notion of "active" citizenship based upon modifying Marshall's first element, and endorsing his second and third elements.

2 Iris Marion Young and the Politics of Cultural Difference

One of the main objections to the welfare state, to T. H. Marshall's conception of citizenship, and by extension to the conception embodied in the Crick Report as well, resides in the fact that they embody the central axioms of liberalism in two distinct ways: firstly, of "universalism", whereby a uniform standard is applied to all no matter what the differences in their life circumstance; secondly, and relatedly, what could be referred to as "unitarism", or the "politics of consensus", by which I mean they are suspicious about recognising as legitimate the particular claims of different cultural groups. Criticisms of both these aspects have been mounted in various ways, and from various quarters, most notably, in recent years, from multiculturalists, and those arguing for the "politics of recognition" and the "politics of difference".

It is claimed in opposition to the liberal paradigm that the problem with the social democratic conception of citizenship is that injustice arises as much from treating different peoples as the same as it does from treating the same peoples as different. In relation to citizenship education, for instance, to make all peoples, irrespective of ethnicity, gender, sexuality, race, class, or culture, adhere to the same norms or standards of citizenship, is to fail to respect each particular group's own distinctive cultural values, attitudes and practices. Iris

Marion Young maintains such a thesis in a number of works over the last decade (see Young, 1986, 1989, 1990, 1995) where she argues against the liberal ideal of universal citizenship and for a concept of *"differentiated* citizenship as the best way of realising the inclusion and participation of everyone in full citizenship" (Young, 1989, p. 251).

According to Young, the ideal of universal citizenship embodied in the social democratic conception incorporates a sense of universality as (a) generality, and (b) equal treatment. In the first sense the ideal of citizenship that serves to "express or create a general will that transcends the particular differences of group affiliation, situation, and interest has in practice excluded groups judged not capable of adopting that general point of view" (1989, p. 251). In the second sense, universality functions "in the sense of laws or rules that stay the same for all and apply to all in the same way" (1989, p. 250). Her argument is that such a representation results in exclusions and/or homogeneity, and thus, the inclusion or participation of everyone on a fair basis is only possible if (a) there exist specific mechanisms for group representation, (b) the rule of equal treatment is departed from in specific cases so as to ensure fair and just treatment, and (c) where the articulation of special rights exists that attend to group differences so as to combat oppression and disadvantage.

This assumption of unity or generality that infected the ideal of citizenship also infected the social democratic ideal of the late 19th and 20th centuries. Young represents it as a metaphysical postulate that inhabits the Enlightenment urge to reduce differences to unity reinforced by the idea of a single truth in accord with universal reason, a single morality and a concern with normality. It embodies the ideal of a community that submits to the logic of identity, an ideal of a community that expresses a longing for harmony amongst persons. It is what Foucault calls the Rousseauist dream of a shared subjectivity or common consciousness where community is represented as a "copresence of subjects" (Young, 1990, p. 231), as a system of mutuality or reciprocity. Whether amongst the new bourgeoisie of the 17th or 18th centuries, or the new liberals of the 19th century, the striving for commonness threatened to suppress differences amongst citizens.

In place of a liberal universal citizenship, Young's model of a "differentiated citizenship" supports the model of a heterogeneous public where differences, which are irreducible, are publicly recognised and accepted, coexisting with supposedly common procedural commitments in a process of communication stretching across the differences involved. In Young's view this reconfiguration of political life does not require the creation of a unified public realm in which group differences are suppressed in preference of a common citizenship ideal, but preserves and facilitates minority group differences, based on the institutionalisation of mechanisms of minority group representation.

It is through the political and educational mechanisms of group representation that difference can operate. To install mechanisms for specific group representation is to increase political equality "providing institutionalized means for the explicit recognition and representation of oppressed groups" (1989, p. 259). It is failure to acknowledge the processes of group differentiation and oppression that becomes the key to understanding the weaknesses of the liberal model of citizenship. What such a model ignores is that there are differences of power between groups—that some are privileged and others are oppressed. Oppression constitutes the effects of imbalances of power to which the liberal model of citizenship is largely blind. It can take the form of systematic exploitation, marginalisation, powerlessness, cultural imperialism, or violence. Such differences in power undermine the axiom, inherent in the ideal of universal citizenship, of a level playing field where the structures of the system are somehow neutral or agnostic allowing all to participate on a fair and equal basis. It is because of such differences in power that different race or ethnic groups cannot hope to participate in education on the basis of a single set of rules and procedures.

3 The Crick Report and the Politics of Cultural Difference

That the Crick Report fails to respect the "politics of difference", and thus encourages an overly consensualist model of society, is argued for strongly by authors such as Audrey Osler (2000), Osler and Starkey (2001) as well as Pearce and Spencer (1999). Certainly their case seems at one level well founded. Clearly in the Crick Report there is the notion of a single national identity to which all is referred and to which citizenship education aspires. It is argued throughout the report that certain uniform conceptions of moral values and social development constitute an essential precondition for citizenship. As the Crick Report states:

> A main aim for the whole community should be to find or restore a sense of common citizenship, including a national identity that is secure enough to find a place for the plurality of nations, cultures, ethnic identities and religions long found in the United Kingdom. Citizenship education creates common ground between different ethnic and religious identities. (QCA, 1998, p. 17)

One criticism here is that there is unlikely to be agreement on substantive conceptions of the good life in a multi-ethnic society of diverse cultures, religions, beliefs and practices. Hence Osler and Starkey (2001) claim that the Crick Report makes very few references to cultural diversity and minorities, and almost no reference at all to racism. The issue of racism was eventually "tagged on" after the report, in response to criticism, and as a consequence of the Stephen Lawrence Inquiry Report (Macpherson, 1999). Hence, in the National Curriculum documents that were produced after the Crick Report had been reviewed (QCA/DfEE, 1999), the potential for citizenship education to contribute to the development of justice and equality by challenging racism and xenophobia was recognised. Yet, the Crick Report itself didn't emphasise this. According to Osler and Starkey (2001, p. 292), "the Report ... falls into the trap of presenting certain ethnicities as 'other' when it discusses 'cultural diversity'". Although the report claims to be "inclusive", this spirit of inclusion does not "extend to visible ethnic minorities" who are represented as not necessarily reliable in conforming to laws, standards, customs and conventions of a democratic society. Hence, there is a certain arrogant cultural paternalism here. To cite the report:

> Minorities must learn to respect the laws, codes and conventions as much as the majority—not merely because it is useful to do so, but because the process helps foster common citizenship. (QCA, 1998, pp. 17–18)

The report thus contains a latent racism, say Osler and Starkey (2001, p. 293). In that it assumes that visible ethnic minorities must change in order to participate in the common culture. This in turn implies a liberal model of assimilation or integration, and represents the white British as the majority who must learn to tolerate minorities, manifesting a "colonial approach to black British communities which runs throughout the Report" (2001, p. 293). Thus Osler and Starkey accuse the Crick Report of "institutional racism" (2001, p. 293). Although the report pays lip service to recognising minorities, overall its approach is monological, focusing on "national identity" and "common citizenship", and emphasising the need for cohesion and integration. It has, thus, a very limited approach to cultural diversity, advocating instead a "common citizenship" which parades as simply a set of procedural rules, but in reality constitutes a narrow liberal model of citizenship education. Often, too, this emphasis is veiled in terms of advocacy for promoting the processes of democracy, such as universal enfranchisement, which is seen as a linear upward progression from the earliest struggles in the 17th century, to the "enlightened" process we now have. When it does consider "exclusion" or "difference", it is represented in terms of interpersonal conflict, such as bullying (e.g., QCA, 1998, p. 19), rather than in terms of structural disadvantage (Osler & Starkey, 2001, p. 299).

4   The Parekh Report on the Future of Multi-Ethnic Britain: Multi-Ethnic Citizenship

The difference between the political themes of consensus and integration, and diversity and cultural difference, is manifest most clearly when the Crick Report on citizenship education is compared to the Parekh Report on the Future of Multi-ethnic Britain. The Parekh Report was the outcome of the Commission on the Future of Multi-Ethnic Britain (The Runnymede Trust, 2000), set up in January 1998 by the Runnymede Trust, an independent think tank devoted to the cause of promoting racial justice in Britain. The commission's remit was to analyse the current state of multi-ethnic Britain and propose ways of countering disadvantage and racial discrimination in order to make Britain a more vibrant multi-ethnic society.

In overall terms, the Parekh Report questioned the concept of "Britishness" as encapsulating a form of consensus that did not accurately capture, or assist, ethnic relations, and in a way that had definite implications for citizenship education. The Parekh Report advocated the use of "British" in a more multi-ethnic way, referring to different subgroups that make up the society—"black British", "Asian British", and so on (Davies, 2001, p. 301). Underpinning the report were several principles that placed it more on the difference end of the continuum rather than the consensus end, and it is on this basis that I claim that it represents an important and necessary counterweight to the Crick Report.

A first principle was that all people have equal worth irrespective of their colour, gender, ethnicity, religion, age or sexual orientation, and all should also have equal claims to the opportunities they need to realise their development and contribute to the collective well-being. A corollary of this point is that equal worth was held not to be possible in a society ravaged by deep economic or social inequalities.

A second principle located citizens as both individuals, as well as members of local and regional communities. As Parekh put it in his foreword to the report, "Britain is both a community of citizens and a community of communities, both a liberal and a multicultural society, and needs to reconcile their sometimes conflicting requirements" (The Runnymede Trust, 2000, Preface).

The third principle directly affirms the principle of difference:

> Since citizens have different needs, equal treatment requires full account to be taken of their differences. When equality ignores relevant differences and insists on uniformity of treatment, it leads to injustice and inequality; when differences ignore the demands of equality, they result in discrimination. Equality must be defined in a culturally sensitive way and applied in a discriminating but not discriminatory manner. (The Runnymede Trust, 2000, Preface)

But, just as diversity is important, so, a fourth principle asserts, every society needs to be cohesive, "and must find ways of nurturing diversity while fostering a common sense of belonging and a shared identity among its constituent members" (The Runnymede Trust, 2000, Preface).

A fifth principle continues this theme concerning the common basis underpinning difference. It asserts that while respect for deep moral differences is important, every society needs a broadly shared body of values, including human rights, ethical norms which respect human dignity, the equal worth of all, equal opportunity for self-development, and equal life chances, as well as procedural values such as tolerance, mutual respect, dialogue and the peaceful resolution of conflict. According to Parekh, "human rights principles provide a sound framework for handling differences, and a body of values around which society can unite" (The Runnymede Trust, 2000, Preface).

Finally, a sixth principle concerns racism which is understood:

> either as division of humankind into fixed, closed and unalterable groups or as systematic domination of some groups by others. ... Racism is a subtle and complex phenomenon. It may be based on colour and physical features, or on culture, nationality and way of life; it may affirm equality of human worth but implicitly deny this by insisting on the superiority of a particular culture; it may admit equality up to a point but impose a glass ceiling higher up. Whatever its subtle disguises and forms, it is deeply divisive, intolerant of differences, a source of much human suffering, and inimical to the common sense of belonging lying at the basis of every stable civilisation. It can have no place in a decent society. (The Runnymede Trust, 2000, Preface)

Based upon these principles, the Parekh Report assessed the current state of multi-ethnic Britain, examined the conceptual categories (for example, "majority", "minority", "ethnic group", "integration", and so on), the language systems employed, and conducted substantial empirical research, visiting many regions, consulting a wide range of organisations, conducting interviews, running seminars, and receiving written submissions. The report starts with a discussion of police and policing, for this is where, for many citizens and communities, the abstract concepts of equality, rights, difference and belonging are most clearly seen. The report moves on to examine the criminal justice system as a whole, and then goes on to examine immigration and asylum policy, the role and responsibility of government, religious motivations and affiliations, education, and other organisations in British society. Its overall theme is that of reducing inequalities in Britain today.

Inspired by the 1969 study *Colour and Citizenship* (Rose, 1969), its theoretical advance on the Crick Report is that it seeks to balance difference and diversity on the one hand, with commonality, universalism and consensus on the other. Far from seeking to legitimate any particular practices that are internal to a culture, no matter how "offensive", the Parekh Report seeks to both respect difference, but place it within the common bounds of a democratic community. Unlike some perspectives within multicultural education, and multiculturalism generally, where almost no attention is paid to the overarching political community that is fundamental to enable diversity to operate in a stable and secure manner, the Parekh Report seeks to balance the two poles. Unlike the Crick Report which, as Osler and others have argued, largely fits within an assimilationist political framework, paying little attention to the differences between cultural groups, as if diversity is something to be feared as a threat to unity, the Parekh Report bases its frame of reference on the interdependence of difference and unity, in a way similar to sophisticated poststructuralist writers like Todd May and Michel Foucault.

With reference to poststructuralism I have maintained that Foucault can be represented as having balanced these two poles, and hence warrants being labelled as a "thin" communitarian (Olssen, 2002). In the same way, Todd May has maintained such a synthesis is needed in relation to the philosophy of Gilles Deleuze. As May (1994) expresses the point:

> Thus Deleuze asks us to think difference as constitutive all the way, and of unity as a product of the play of difference. But if difference is to be thought of as constitutive, this is in order to rid philosophy not of unities, but of unifying forces or principles that either preclude difference or relegate it to a negative phenomenon.

Part of the point here is that difference must be seen as operating in the context of community. Thus, for Deleuze, neither difference nor unity can be seen as primary. As May (1994, pp. 46–47) puts the point expressed in relation to meaning and identity:

> If meaning were merely the product of difference, there would be no meaning, only noises unrelated to each other. In order for meaning to occur, identity must exist within difference, or better, each must exist within the other. To speak with Saussure, if language is a system of differences, it is not only differences but system as well; and system carries with it the thought of identity. ... [T]o posit a concept whose function is to be given primacy to difference is to violate the necessary chiasmic relationship between unity and difference.

To represent this argument in political terms, it can be said that pushing the principle of difference too far results in contradiction. While multiculturalists and those who advocate difference want to celebrate multiplicity and a decentred polis, the fundamental ambiguity results from the fact that respecting the autonomy of different groups—whether based on religion, race, gender, or ethnicity—is only possible within certain *common bounds*. Central to this perspective is that the notion of difference must presuppose a "minimal universalism" which in turn necessitates a certain conception of community. Hence, the New Zealand author, Andrew Sharp (1997, p. 36) argues in his book *Justice and the Māori*, that if difference is to operate on anything like a level playing field, whether national or global, then it requires, *at a minimum*, that the parties are "equally in subjection to the same normative system, the same rules distinguishing right from wrong". Such a presumption entails not just common normative-democratic standards, but that there is some basis of enforcing the rights and obligations of the agreed upon system—hence, a common system of justice. Certain common provisions, then, must underpin difference.

In that it recognises these common rules and provisions, the Parekh Report is superior to many models of multiculturalism which privilege difference outside of any unifying model of political community. It conforms, in this sense, to Young's ideal of "differentiated citizenship". It is superior, too, as a document, to the Crick Report, in that it recognises difference within unity, and seeks to advocate a model of citizenship on this basis. Having said this, it is not incompatible with the Crick Report, and by taking the two reports together a richer text on citizenship education is produced. Along with the Parekh Report's rich insights into diversity and difference, and into structural basis of inequality, its focused discussion and recommendations on the criminal justice system (including the police), it is possible to add the Crick Report's pedagogical and educational designs for teaching civic participation, social and moral responsibility, and political literacy, represented now as a system of norms constituting democratic culture, and based on deliberation, participation, and understanding the procedural basis of a democratic culture.

What sort of difference can be practiced in the context of this broader unified democratic community? Clearly cultural minorities whose practices are based on deeply illiberal oppressive relations based on gender, or sex, or any other basis of difference, cannot be tolerated, and neither can group practices that fail to respect the fundamentally important principles of democratic politics, such as respect for the other, a willingness to negotiate, tolerance, or the institutional basis of deliberation, or the rule of law. Thus, William Kymlicka (1999, pp. 31–32), in his more recent work, argues that what he calls "internal restrictions" must be disallowed. These types of rights, says Kymlicka, apply when an ethnocultural group claims rights against its own members, on the basis of cultural "tradition" or cultural "integrity", or on some other basis. Often these rights legitimate behaviours that are seen as deeply offensive to people in other cultures. The aim of these sorts of rights, says Kymlicka, is "to restrict the ability of individuals within the group ... to question, revise, or abandon traditional cultural roles or practices". For Kymlicka, "a liberal theory of minority group rights ... cannot accept such internal restrictions, since they violate the autonomy of individuals and create injustice within the group" (Kymlicka, 1999, p. 31).

Having dismissed the rights of any cultural group to do "anything they like", it is possible to accept, a second sort of group rights, which Kymlicka (1999, p. 31) calls "external protections", and take the form of "language rights, guaranteed political representation, funding of ethnic media, land claims, compensation for historical injustice, or the regional devolution of power" (1999, p. 31). According to Kymlicka (1999, p. 32), "all of these can help to promote justice between ethnocultural groups, by ensuring that members of the minority have the same effective capacity to promote their interests as the majority".

Susan Moller Okin (1999) argues that Kymlicka's account of "internal restrictions" is too narrow and doesn't effectively account for the types of restrictions and limitations on women within many ethnocultural groups. On this basis, Okin is deeply suspicious about the category of minority group rights, and that multicultural perspectives which argue for differences of different cultural groups to be respected represent a threat to the gains that feminists have made over the last several decades. Essentially, she argues that multiculturalists seek to legitimate many quite unacceptable practices (rape, clitoridectomy, *zij poj* (marriage by capture), polygamy, coerced marriages, the marriage of children) on the justifications of respecting cultural difference. As well as rejecting group rights, she holds that merely to give women individual rights on the same basis of men, will also be inadequate to women's equality. In addition, she argues against Kymlicka, that we must look at the structure of social institutions such as schools, media, and family, as these institutions frequently embody unacceptable practices and present distorted representations of gender, which systematically oppress women.

Okin's arguments represent a sound caution against the more extreme multiculturalists who seek to argue for group rights without considering the need for a common democratic norm as the basis on which the minority and majority group coexistence and survival depends. Her position is not incompatible with the more sophisticated multiculturalists, however, such as the group that wrote the Parekh Report, where it was also argued that the character and structure of institutions must be critically examined and reformed. In education, this is especially relevant to the practices of curriculum and behaviour, including language, timetabling, organisational rules, and so on, as these all have a tendency to take the majority culture as the "norm". This concern with "structures" has also united feminists, such as Okin, and multiculturalists in their opposition to liberalism, which focused only on individual rights, ignoring issues of structural disadvantage, power and oppression, notions such as "invisibility", and which tends to accept existing hierarchically structured social relations of gender (and other dimensions of difference) as natural and normal states of existence.

While it is true that the Crick Report tends to ignore racism, multiculturalism, and any sophisticated understanding of how the politics of difference might inform citizenship education, I am arguing here that it need not do so, at least on the grounds of theoretical coherence, and that the Parekh Report resolves the issues between difference and universality in a way that makes sense. This is to say, that to be a consistent multiculturalist one must be committed to democratic values at a minimum. This doesn't mean to say that such democratic principles are universally grounded, either in human nature, or in rationality, or in the way that Habermas has argued, and as at times, the Crick Report seems to imply. Rather, all one is committed to, logically, is that all groups and people adhere to a clustering of historically contingent mechanisms or techniques that enable or assist with the continuance of open dialogue, respect the integrity of all life forms, and which ensure their continued survival. What universal democratic justice promotes then, is the conditions for an effective multiculturalism, one that gives the members of minority groups equal rights to coexistence with majority culture. This promotes a conception of democracy that, while not neutral, permits public institutions to further particular cultural values on four conditions: (1) the basic rights of all citizens individually and as groups (freedom of speech, thought, religion, expression, association, lifestyle choice, etc); (2) no person or group is manipulated into accepting values represented by public institutions; (3) public officials and institutions are democratically accountable in principle and practice;

and (4) all members of minority groups have a right to exit the group freely if they choose.

In saying this, we have moved away from any conception of multiculturalism whereby cultural minorities can be completely unresponsive to the outside cultures, or where prohibitions against group members leaving the culture can be enforced. No minority, and no culture, can guarantee their own survival forever in any traditional or theoretically "pure" sense, as openness to others, and to the world outside, is one necessary principle of democracy. Hence, I suggest that certain presumptions of cosmopolitanism must necessarily infuse citizenship education post-9/11. The appropriation of the discourse of rights, by multiculturalists, also, shows the adoption by radicals of certain themes within liberal constitutionalism, which has occurred progressively over recent years. This explains the puzzling sense in which the language of human rights has become part of the language of emancipatory movements in education and society and will continue to do so as we move into the 21st century. As Boaventura de Sousa Santos (1999, p. 214) maintains, although rights emerged as part of the regulatory politics of the bourgeois state from the 17th century, they have in more recent times become part of the conceptual armoury of progressive multiculturalists, seeking to "reconstitute the language of emancipation".

This position is similar in some aspects to that of the American liberal educator, Amy Gutmann (1994), who also argues that multiculturalism is not incompatible with liberal universalism, at least in respect to difference/community. For Gutmann, the proposition need only be expressed in universalistic terms, i.e., that public institutions must recognise the particular cultural identities of all citizens. This means ceding basic rights to all people, recognising the essential pluralism of society, accepting political recognition and cultural particularity may require targeted specific policies, and accepting that institutions should acknowledge rather than ignore cultural distinctiveness. Gutmann, however, sounds more traditionally liberal when she "lapses" into recognising the "neutrality" of the public sphere, and accepting that depersonalised administration is the price we pay to be treated as equals. Putting these aside, she seems to see no difficulty of expressing the educational and political principles of multiculturalism in terms of the language of liberal universalism.

Charles Taylor (1994, pp. 51–60), too, argues for a synthesis of multicultural "recognition" with universal democratic norms. The demand to be recognised for one's particularity is *universal*, says Taylor, and further, it points in two directions: (1) protections of the basic rights of all citizens; and (2) acknowledgement of the particular needs of individuals as members of specific groups. Thus public recognition of difference requires two sorts of respect: (1) respect for the unique identities of individuals regardless of race or creed; and (2) respect for the distinctive practices, values and characteristics of people as members of groups. In this sense, to emphasise diversity is not an attempt to promote separatism for people or their children, or necessarily to try to preserve cultures over time. And to endorse multiculturalism should not lead us to endorse the hopelessly relativististic thesis of deconstructionism. Rather it is to both endorse the validity of multiculturalism, and to see certain values as universalistic. This was the impetus of Todd May's correction of Deleuze, and of Foucault, as I represented them above. This also accords with Dewey's endeavour to connect the democratic value of diversity and difference to the value of expanding cultural and intellectual horizons, as a way of increasing the possibilities for growth.

While the Crick Report can then in theory coalesce with, and accommodate, the major insights of the Parekh Report, if suitably reworked, it is nevertheless true that as Osler and others have argued, the Crick Report downplayed respect for cultural diversity and the need for recognition of minority cultures, as it was actually written. This is because, in the main, liberals like Crick have been suspicious of the demand to preserve subcultures, and of the "politics of recognition". My argument is that this is neither necessary nor wise, for if anything is truer of the world post-9/11 than before, it is, whether we like it or not, that we live in a multi-ethnic world. Democracy must expose individuals to a diverse set of cultural institutions, values and practices. This it can do while allowing for substantial cultural difference, as well as adhering to universal norms of inclusion based on the rights of all, and the rule of law. In this sense, there must be a commitment to a conception of democratic justice that both protects universal rights, and recognises the distinctiveness of particular subcultures as well, based not on the epistemological foundations of human nature, but on, simply, the equal inclusion of all, and the commitment to the continuation of open dialogue based on an interest in mutual universal survival. This is very Foucauldian in the sense that it constitutes a universalism of democracy as a contingent discourse of open protection and facilitation in a world of dangers.

5   Adding the Parekh Report to the Crick Report

Citizenship education, as the Crick and Parekh Reports together embody, emphasises the equal dignity of all citizens, an equalisation of rights and entitlements, equality of inclusion, an equalisation of the right to participation, and a principle of equal citizenship which is universally accepted. In addition, both reports can accept, in terms of these principles, that everyone should be recognised for his or her unique identity.

Having said this it must be stated that, in traditional liberal accounts, it is precisely the distinctiveness of cultures that has been glossed over and ignored, often by assimilation to the dominant majority identity, or through the sleight of hand of ignoring power, by representing the dominant viewpoint as "the standard view" or as "common sense". Hence as Charles Taylor (1994, p. 39) states:

> underpinning difference theory is a principle of universal equality, a demand that we give due acknowledgement ... to what is universally present—everyone has an identity—through recognising what is peculiar to each. ... It is a universal demand [which] powers an acknowledgment of specificity. Hence, the politics of difference grows organically out of the politics of universal dignity.

As such, both multiculturalism, and the politics of difference, with respect to students of colour, or of disability has, at its basis, the principle of universal human potential, a capacity that all humans share, and which underpins moral equality and equal dignity. As far as education is concerned, then, we must devise citizenship education strategies that: (1) treat all people the same to the extent that they are the same, yet, (2) recognise difference in its particularity. As Taylor (1994, p. 50) puts it, "the struggle for recognition can find only one satisfactory solution, and that is a regime of reciprocal recognition among equals".

On this conception, our model of society still cherishes liberty, and does not equate with the Rousseauian or Hegelian monological communities where all individual elements are subordinated to the general will, or to the totality. In addition, it maintains a certain commitment to liberal principles in that it holds that the schedule of individual democratic goods and rights must apply the same to all cultural groups, and be adapted to different collective goals only in ways that protect the essential bases of a group's right to exist, and yet in a way that does not inhibit *exit*. Yet, we must go beyond liberalism and not merely insist of the uniform application of rules without exception. In addition, we must not reject, *tout court*, collective goals.

Liberals must take special pains to ensure respect for diversity, especially to those that do not share its common goals, and this will undoubtedly involve adapting democratic procedures and mechanisms to specific values and practices of different cultural groups. In the sense that liberalism insists on both the uniform application of rules and principles, is suspicious of collective goals, and neglects the structural analysis of institutions, we must concur with Taylor (1994, p. 61) in seeing "liberalism as guilty as charged by the proponents of the politics of difference". Ultimately, then, difference and uniform treatment must be seen as a balance to be addressed contingently according to higher order principles of democratic justice.

Acknowledgements

I would like to thank Janet Soler for conducting an extensive literature research for this paper.

This chapter originally appeared as Olssen, M. (2004), From the Crick Report to the Parekh Report: Multiculturalism, cultural difference, and democracy—The re-visioning of citizenship education, *British Journal of the Sociology of Education*, 25(2), 179–192, https://doi.org/10.1080/0142569042000205127. Reprinted here, with minor edits, with permission from the publisher.

References

Arthur, J., & Davison, J. (2000). Social literacy and citizenship education in the school curriculum. *The Curriculum Journal*, 11(1), 9–23.

Davies, L. (2000). *Citizenship education and human rights education: An international overview*. The British Council.

De Sousa Santos, B. (1999). Towards a multicultural conception of human rights. In M. Featherstone & S. Lash (Eds.), *Spaces of culture: City–nation–world* (pp. 214–229). Sage.

Davies, L. (2001). Citizenship, education and contradiction: Review essay. *British Journal of Sociology of Education*, 22(2), 299–308.

Gutmann, A. (1994). Introduction: Part one. In C. Taylor (Ed.), *Multiculturalism: Examining the politics of recognition* (pp. 3–24). Princeton University Press.

Kymlicka, W. (1999). Liberal complacencies. In S. M. Okin (Ed.), *Is multiculturalism bad for women?* (pp. 31–34). Princeton University Press.

Macpherson, W. (1999). *The Stephen Lawrence inquiry*. Home Office.

Marshall, T. H. (1997). Citizenship and social class. In R. E. Goodin & P. Pettit (Eds.), *Contemporary political philosophy* (pp. 291–319). Blackwell.

May, T. (1994). Difference and unity in Gilles Deleuze. In C. V. Boundas & D. Olkowski (Eds.), *Gilles Deleuze and the theatre of philosophy* (pp. 33–50). Routledge.

Okin, S. M. (Ed.). (1999). *Is multiculturalism bad for women?* Princeton University Press.

Olssen, M. (2002). Michel Foucault as "thin" communitarian: Difference, community, democracy, *Cultural Studies/Critical Methodologies*, 2(4), 483–513. https://doi.org/10.1177/153270860200200403

Olssen, M. (2002). Terrorism, globalisation and democracy: On reading Michael Peters post 9/11. *Access: Critical Perspectives on Communication, Cultural & Policy Studies, 21*(1), 75–90.

Olssen, M. (2003). Totalitarianism and the "repressed" utopia of the present: Moving beyond Hayek, Popper and Foucault. *Policy Futures in Education, 1*(3), 526–552. https://doi.org/10.2304/pfie.2003.1.3.6

Olssen, M., Codd, J., & O'Neill, A.-M. (2004). *Education policy: Globalization, citizenship & democracy*. Sage.

Osler, A. (2000). The Crick report: Difference, equality and racial justice. *The Curriculum Journal, 11*(1), 25–38.

Osler, A., & Starkey, H. (2001). Citizenship education and national identities in France and England: Inclusive or exclusive? *Oxford Review of Education, 27*(2), 287–305.

Pearce, N., & Spencer, S. (1999). *Reports and surveys: Education for citizenship: The Crick report*. Blackwell.

QCA. (1998). *Education for citizenship and the teaching of democracy in schools (The Crick report)*. Qualifications and Curriculum Authority.

QCA/DfEE. (1999). *The national curriculum in England: citizenship*. Qualifications and Curriculum Authority and Department of Education and Employment.

Rose, J. (1969). *Colour and citizenship*. Oxford University Press.

Runnymede Trust. (2000). *The future of multi-ethnic Britain: The Parekh report*. Profile Books.

Scott, D. (2000). Editorial—Responses to Crick and citizenship education. *The Curriculum Journal, 11*(1), 1–7.

Sharp, A. (1997). *Justice and the Māori: The philosophy and practice of Māori claims in New Zealand since the 1970s* (2nd ed.). Oxford University Press.

Taylor, C. (1994). The politics of recognition. In C. Taylor (Ed.), *Multiculturalism: Examining the politics of recognition* (pp. 25–73). Princeton University Press.

Young, I. M. (1986). The ideal of community and the politics of difference. *Social Theory and Practice, 12*(1), 1–26.

Young, I. M. (1989). Polity and group difference: A critique of the ideal of universal citizenship. *Ethics, 99*(2), 250–274.

Young, I. M. (1990). *Justice and the politics of difference*. Princeton University Press.

Young, I. M. (1995). Together in difference: Transforming the logic of group political conflict. In W. Kymlicka (Ed.), *The rights of minority cultures* (pp. 155–178). Oxford University Press.

CHAPTER 7

In Defence of the Welfare State and Publicly Provided Education
A New Zealand Perspective

Abstract

This paper critically examines the crisis of welfare liberalism with specific reference to New Zealand education in order to speculatively reappraise the central principles upon which a revived welfare state could be constructed and in terms of which publicly provided education can be justified. Specifically, it will seek to achieve these goals through a number of interrelated tasks. Firstly, it will examine the claims of neoliberal theory and argue that contradictions within this theory make its demise likely. To do this it will focus on themes relating to the efficiency of markets, rationality and consumer choice, the state and central planning as well as the issue of liberty. Secondly, in a more positive analysis, it will examine prospects for a return to the welfare state in the near future. This will involve an examination of some important criticisms of the traditional welfare state and an assessment of possible models in terms of which a revived, non-bureaucratic welfare state could be constructed.

∙∙∙

There has been a crisis of welfare liberalism in the past decade in New Zealand. The crisis can be seen to originate with the election to office of the Fourth Labour Government in 1984, which saw the introduction of neoliberal policies in education and social welfare, forcing a reversal of Keynesian economic and social policy, and an assault on the structures and practices of the welfare state.

The crisis itself must be traced to a more deep-seated and global crisis occurring in socialist thought and practice since the Second World War. It has been a crisis of both practice and ideology. At one level the collapse of the communist regimes of Eastern Europe can be seen as both the effect of a general ideological crisis of left-wing thought and the cause of its more rapid demise. The collapse of communism has, by association, tainted the respectable left in Western countries. Added to this, the rise of neoliberalism and of postmodernism has served to undermine the legitimacy of left-wing thought. These developments must themselves be seen in relation to a general post-Fordist diversification of economic and social structure as well as the globalisation of economic, political and cultural life.

The resurgence of neoliberalism discredited any popular appeal that socialist politics in New Zealand might have had, although even without neoliberalism they were always only a numerically small proportion of the politically interested population. To a large extent, traditional socialist movements have always struggled for recognition in opposition to the politics of liberalism. What neoliberalism also effected, however, was to discredit the more moderate policy framework of Keynesianism—leading to a crisis of the welfare state (Joppke, 1987). Keynesianism sanctioned a mixed economy and interventionist monetary policy where the role of government and the scope of politics were expanded. As a consequence, during its "golden years" New Zealand experienced nearly full employment. While Keynesian demand management was the dominant policy framework for more than two decades, from the end of the 1960s it slid into crisis triggered by the general international economic recession of 1974–1975, the breakdown of regular exchange rates, the collapse of the profitability of business, and by its inability to maintain full employment. In more general terms, as Offe (1984), Habermas (1975) and O'Connor (1973) explain it, the crisis was a response to the increasing inability to reconcile the problems of capital accumulation with the political processes of democratic management and legitimation.

The neoliberalism that filled the gap was a revived form of classical liberalism. It critiqued both socialism and the welfare state in one stroke as plagued by the evils of "statism", "central planning", and bureaucratic, collective provision. It scolded statist options and posited non-statist alternatives emphasising a greater role for freedom and markets. Socialists and welfare state liberals were outflanked. Many conceded that the emphasis on a state provision had left a lot be desired, that it had been unresponsive to public needs, inefficient in providing for them, and at worst brutal and authoritarian (Martell, 1992, 1993; McLennan, 1993; Amin, 1994).

In the 20th century, neoliberal economic doctrines were elaborated by various "organic intellectuals" in economics, political science and in various business and management studies. Foremost amongst these were the "Chicago School" of pioneering economic researchers led by Friedrich A. von Hayek (1935, 1944) and Milton Friedman (1962, 1980), and the "Virginia School" of public choice theorists led by James Buchanan and his researchers at the Virginia Polytechnic's School of Political Science (Buchanan, 1960, 1969, 1975; Buchanan & Tullock, 1962).

Neoliberals supported the free market. The associated economic and social policies became central to the state's role in America under Ronald Reagan in the late 1970s, in England under Margaret Thatcher in the 1970s, and in New Zealand under the influence of Roger Douglas, the finance minister of the Fourth Labour Government, in the 1980s. The free-market line's appeal to business was obvious, and, although their ideas seemed extreme, they quickly gathered popular support. The doctrine of monetarism which entailed restraint of the money supply and the public sector replaced Keynesian demand management throughout OECD countries in the mid-1970s. In addition, and encouraged by international organisations such as the World Bank and the IMF, growth in government was halted in most Western advanced economies, the privatisation and commercialisation of the public sector began, and support for income redistribution and universal services became substantially weakened.

This paper will look critically at the crisis of welfare liberalism with specific reference to New Zealand in order to speculatively reappraise the central principles upon which a revived welfare state could be constructed and in terms of which publicly provided education can be justified. It will seek to do this through a number of interrelated tasks. Firstly, it will examine critically the claims of neoliberal theory, and argue that contradictions contained within these claims make the demise of the theory likely. Specifically, the issues which will be examined include those relating to the efficiency of markets, rationality and consumer choice, the state and central planning, as well as the important issue of liberty. Secondly, in a more positive analysis, I will examine the prospects for a return to the welfare state in the near future. This will involve a two-pronged approach including an examination of some important criticisms of the traditional welfare state and an assessment of alternative possible models in terms of which a revived, non-bureaucratic welfare state could be constructed. Prior to these tasks, and largely as a scene-setting exercise, this essay will briefly review the rise of neoliberal policy in New Zealand.

1   Neoliberalism and New Zealand Education

In the 1984 Treasury brief to the incoming Labour government, *Economic Management*, New Right theory and strategy in relation to the economy in general was established as necessary in relation to several Treasury arguments. In the 1987 brief, *Government Management* (Vols. 1 and 2), Treasury set forth its arguments in relation to more specific areas. Volume 2 was concerned specifically with education. In this they maintained that education could be analysed in a way similar to any other service (p. 2); that education shares the main characteristics of other commodities traded in the marketplace, and that it could not be analysed successfully as a "public good" (p. 33); that education should be more responsive to business interests and to the needs of the economy (p. 27); that the existing education system had performed badly despite increased expenditure on it (pp. 6, 16, 18, 140); that teachers and the educational establishment have pursued their own self-interest rather than those of pupils and parents, i.e., they had not been responsive enough to consumer interests and desires (pp. 37–38); that the educational system lacked a rigorous system of accountability, there being a lack of national monitoring procedures or of any satisfactory ways of comparing the effectiveness of schools in order to account for the public resources employed (p. 108); that educational management should be decentralised; that decisions could be more efficiently made at the local rather than at the central level; that under central planning mistakes are more likely, less easy to rectify and more costly (pp. 40–41); and that government intervention and control has interrupted the "natural" free-market contract between producer and consumer with all that entails for efficient and flexible producer responses to consumer demand (p. 41).

In short, Treasury argued that state-provided and state-controlled education had performed badly and would continue to do so unless radical changes were implemented. The Treasury buttressed its arguments for the necessity of change by reference to "falling standards", rising mediocrity, and "provider capture". They claimed that these threatened our future as a nation.

The second half of the 1980s saw the introduction of new policies[1] which caused a major revolution in education, resulting in changes in its operation and functioning at the early childhood, primary, secondary and tertiary levels. For the first time in New Zealand's history the conception of education as a commercial investment subject to market conditions has become a reality. The central issue of equality of opportunity which dominated the educational debate up until the end of the Muldoon era gave way to talk about "efficiency", "choice" and "competition". In 1990, a new Ministry of Education was established, replacing the old Department of Education and its regional offices and boards. A great deal of the administration of education was allocated to individual schools, now fitted out with "Charters" and "Boards of Trustees" (BOTS) which replaced the old "Boards of Governors" and "School Committees". The new structure increased the responsibilities of individual schools, although whether it increased actual effective control over key issues in education is more questionable and has been challenged (see Bates, 1990; Codd, 1990a, 1990b; Smith, 1991; Gordon, 1992; Kelsley, 1993). At a superficial level, the BOTS were given a whole series of new responsibilities, including staff employment, management of the institution's property, and the design and implementation of a charter (based on a contract). The Education Review Office (ERO) and the New Zealand Qualifications Authority (NZQA) were also established. These changes were instituted through the 1989 Education Act, the 1990 Education Amendment Act and the 1991 Education Amendment Act. These acts also laid the framework for bulk funding for both teachers' salaries and school operations, revoked compulsory registration for teachers, and abolished zoning for schools. In 1991, a "user pays" system of student fees in tertiary education was introduced which laid the basis for the latter modifications and changes introduced by the National government, resulting in the introduction of student loans.

The changes to education which resulted from the "insertion" of the New Right into policymaking in New Zealand were motivated by the adherence to the groups most centrally involved—the Fourth Labour Government, Treasury, the State Services Commission—to a particular strain of liberal thought referred to most often as "neoliberalism" (Codd, 1990a, 1990b; Marshall & Peters 1990; Peters & Marshall 1990; Peters et al., 1994). The central defining characteristic of this new brand of liberalism was that it was seen as a "revival" of the central tenets of classical liberalism, particularly classical economic liberalism. Notwithstanding a clear similarity between *neo* and *classical* liberal discourse, as Gordon (1991), Burchell (1993) and Marshall (1995) maintain, the two cannot be seen as identical, and an understanding of the difference between them provides an important key to understanding the distinctive nature of the restructuring of education in the 1990s.

Whereas classical liberalism represents a negative conception of state power in that the individual was taken as an object to be freed from the interventions of the state, neoliberalism has come to represent a positive conception of the state's role in creating the appropriate market by providing the conditions, laws and institutions necessary for its operation. In classical liberalism the individual is characterised as having an autonomous human nature and can practise freedom. In neoliberalism the state seeks to create an individual who is an enterprising and competitive entrepreneur. In the classical model the theoretical aim of the state was to limit and minimise its role based upon postulates which included universal egoism (the self-interested individual); invisible hand theory, which dictated that the interests of the individual were also the interests of the society as a whole; and the political maxim of laissez-faire. In the shift from classical liberalism to neoliberalism, then, there is a further element added, for such a shift involves a change in subject position from "Homo economicus", who naturally behaves out of self-interest, and is relatively detached from the state, to "manipulatable man", who is created by the state and who is continually encouraged to be "perpetually responsive". It is not that the conception of the self-interested subject is replaced or done away with by the new ideals of "neoliberalism", but that in an age of universal welfare, the perceived possibilities of slothful indolence create necessities for new forms of vigilance, surveillance, "performance appraisal" and of forms of control generally. In this new model the state has taken it upon itself to keep us all up to the mark. The state will see to it that each one of us makes a "continual enterprise of ourselves" (Gordon, 1991) in what seems to be a process of "governing without governing" (Rose, 1993).

The state seeks to assure then the conditions for perpetual human responsiveness and flexibility that are advanced most forcefully in modern "New Right" theories such as "human capital theory", "public choice theory", "agency theory", "cost transaction analysis" and the revival of various forms of "managerialism". these theories are variants of neoclassical liberal thought and share its major presuppositions that subjects are economically self-interested; that the economy is separate from the rest of society; that the uncoordinated self-interest of individuals correlates with the interests and the harmony of the whole; that individuals are rational optimisers and are the best judges of their own interests and needs; and that a "flexible"—that is, a deregulated—labour market provides the same opportunities for people to utilise their skills and therefore optimise their life goals. The fundamental aims of the reforms—to manage education to meet the demands of a more unequal society—is at the same time a spur to individuals to act rationally in the market in order to maximise their own production and profit. Individuals will work harder because they are working for themselves, and by such activity also ensure the optimum allocation of resources in society, maximising consumer satisfaction and total economic welfare.

2   The Failure of Market Theories

The fundamental untenability of the reform programme in relation to the provision of education and social services relates, I want to argue, to shortcomings in the theoretical underpinnings of free-market theory. Neoliberals seek to justify their policies in championing individual liberty against the excesses of the state in relation to central planning, regulation, and social ownership, as well as the inefficiency and lack of consideration for the rights of the consumer and the individual. Markets, they argue, have distinct advantages over state regulation. The laws of supply and demand operate as indicators of under- and over-supply as well as incentives for producers to produce high-quality, competitively priced goods for which there is an established demand. Markets, claim neoliberals, overcome the inefficiency and unresponsiveness of central state planning as they decentralise power downwards to enterprises, schools and individual consumers. It is in this way that power is shifted from the state into the hands of individuals or of individual schools.

While many on the left, including welfare liberals and older-style socialists, admit the obvious deficiencies of traditional socialism or of the overcentralisation of state ownership and planning, there are many problems with such a market perspective. Amongst the most important identified in recent research are:

1. Consumer demand cannot be seen as equivalent to social need, and in relation to the latter the market is a poor guide. Markets fail to ensure employment or to ensure, or be centrally concerned with, equality in the distribution of resources (Olssen & Morris Matthews, 1995).
2. Markets are cumulatively and inherently inegalitarian in relation to the distribution of resources in society (Martell, 1992). In relation to education, schools are also increasingly distinguishable in terms of resourcing. Rich schools grow richer while poor schools grow poorer (Gordon, 1993).
3. Markets fail to protect democratic rights, and the neoliberal advocacy of an unregulated market contradicts some established principles of democratic theory. According to Snook (1995, p. 64):

    It [neoliberalism] rejects majority rule because there is no "general will" but only the pressure of interest groups; and it opposes the equal involvement of all since only negative freedoms are to be protected and those with property have much more to be protected.

4. The market fosters competition at the expense of cooperation, and in fact a market orientation to social and economic policy establishes competition as a central structuring norm of a community. Relatedly, market policies underemphasise the requirement of cooperation and coordination in society in order for groups and individuals to work together (Martell, 1993).
5. Arguments for extending private schooling ignore the "social benefits" that publicly provided education provides. These benefits are related to issues such as citizenship, tolerance, literacy, and the democratic functioning of a community. As the "social benefits" of education, they cannot be reduced to individual self-interest, or rendered intelligible within a market perspective (Levin, 1987).
6. The consumer cannot be supposed to have perfect foresight or make rational decisions based on perfect knowledge or understanding of the situation as market theory implies. It is highly implausible, as Robert Lane (1993) points out, that all people can be represented as economic agents who can be relied on to make choices that are in all cases rational;

that they are infinitely clear-headed about how to go about realising their goals and obtaining their desires; that they are capable of foreseeing all of the consequences of their actions; that they can discover which is the best strategy to service their chosen ends; or that each can experience the necessary feedback to keep their expectations in balance with the objective possibilities. This applies to choices made in relation to education or any other social arena.

7. Individuals will clearly differ in their ability to act rationally in their own self-interests; some will be more successful than others. If this is so, then the welfare state liberal believes that there is no reason to structure society exclusively in the interests of those that can succeed. Indeed, as social democrats from John Stuart Mill to Lord Keynes have argued, there is every reason not to do so because, in the main, human beings are not self-sufficient and fiercely independent but are connected to other people and the structures of social support in various relations of dependence and need (relations which will vary depending upon their age, gender, financial means, race or other factors at a specific time and place). If this is so then the welfare liberals' demand for a state which is not exclusively geared to the self-interests of individuals but is generally committed to an overall conception of the good in the interests of all individuals is more likely to be acceptable to the vast majority of its citizens.

Central to predicting a return to the welfare state is the argument advanced by Polanyi (1969) that the state is the only agency that can correct the failings of the market. In Polanyi's view, the rise of the interventionist state in the late 19th and early 20th centuries was to check the excesses and failures of the market in its unregulated form. He argues that the increasing positive role of the state was not promoted by political arguments for socialism but by more pragmatic considerations related to weaknesses inherent in the market mechanism. As he puts it:

> The antiliberal conspiracy is pure invention. The great variety of forms in which the "collectivist" countermovement appeared was not due to any preference for socialism or nationalism on the part of concerted interests, but exclusively to the broader range of the vital social interests affected by the expanding market mechanism. This accounts for the all but universal reactions of predominantly practical character called forth by the expansion of that mechanism. Intellectual fashions played no role whatever in that process; there was accordingly no room for the prejudice which the liberal regards as the ideological force behind the antiliberal development. (1969, p. 16)

From the 1860s there was an expanding range of matters on which state action was taken, including legislation relating to employment (child labour), health and education. Polanyi argues, in fact, that the changes from liberal to collectivist solutions happened without any consciousness of deep-seated ideological and political changes on the part of those engaged in the process in countries as diverse as Prussia under Bismarck, Victorian England and France of the Third Republic. Each passed through a period of economic liberalism characterised by free trade and laissez-faire, followed by a period of antiliberal intervention in regard to public health, factory conditions, child labour, municipal trading, social insurance, public utilities and so on. Intervention in the markets, especially as it related to employment, social services and education, was increasingly designed to influence the quality as well as the quantity of its provision, because in fact the free market proved to be "a poor guide to the best means of satisfying the real wishes of consumers" (Shonfield, 1965, pp. 226–236). In relation to education, the operations of the market proved to be particularly pernicious for, without a reasonably planned approach, one is driven to reliance upon considerations of economic costs and benefits as criteria for the setting of educational goals with the consequent danger that the determination of educational goals and objectives is taken out of the education realm altogether. The weaknesses of such economic principles were set out by Keynes in his original arguments against free-market polities which he made in an article entitled "The End of Laissez-Faire" written in 1926.

> It is *not* true that individuals possess a prescriptive "natural liberty" in their economic activities. There is *no* "compact" conferring perpetual rights on those who Have or on those who Acquire. The world is *not* so governed from above that private and social interests always coincide. It is *not* so managed here below that in practice they coincide. It is *not* a correct deduction from the Principles of Economics that enlightened self-interest always operates in the public interest. Nor is it true that self-interest generally is enlightened, more often individuals acting separately to promote their own ends are too ignorant or too weak to attain even these. Experience does not show that individuals, when they make up a social unit, are always less clear sighted than when they act separately. (Keynes, 1926, cited in Rea & McLeod, 1969, p. 52; emphasis in original)

This statement illustrates the early rejection of market principles by many moderate liberals earlier this century who wanted to reform capitalism rather than abolish it. The real issue as Keynes saw clearly was in seeking to ascertain "what the state ought to take upon itself to direct by the public wisdom, and what it ought to leave with as little interference as possible to individual exertion" (Keynes, 1926, quoted in Rea & McLeod, 1969, p. 53). His arguments against the minimal state were based on the discovery that there is no tendency towards efficient equilibrium in capitalist markets. Keynes was not the first to recognise this, of course. It had concerned economists in both the liberal and radical traditions—Marx, Hobson, Kalecki and others—before Keynes's idea achieved orthodoxy. Specifically important in relation to the development of Western welfare states was his theory of consumption functions, and in particular his argument that the diminishing marginal propensity to consume creates a permanent tendency towards disequilibrium (or at least an inefficient equilibrium) as a result of the inefficient aggregate demand it generates.

2.1   The State and Central Planning

In the 20th century, at the very time welfare states were being constructed, a variety of counter-arguments against any extended role for the state were being developed by neoliberal writers. These arguments were both economic and political. Authors such as Hayek (1935, 1944, 1945, 1960), Friedman (1962, 1980), Buchanan (1960, 1969, 1975) and Nozick (1974) contended that all forms of state action beyond the minimal functions of the defence of the realm and the protection of basic rights to life and property are dangerous threats to liberty which are likely to lead down the "road to serfdom".[2]

For Hayek, the proper functioning of markets is incompatible with state planning of any sort, either full-scale socialism or the more limited conception of the welfare state. A full-scale rational socialism is impossible because it would have no markets to guide resource allocation (Mises, quoted in Hayek, 1935). In addition, central planning of any form, he claims, is not practical because of the scale of centralised calculation any effective attempt at allocation would require (Hayek, 1944). Hayek's main arguments against central planning are based on two claims: its inefficiency and the threat to freedom of the individual. It would be inefficient, in Hayek's view, because real knowledge is gained and true economic progress made as a consequence of locally generated knowledge derived from "particular circumstances of time and place" and the state is not privy to such knowledge (Hayek, 1945, p. 521). The market then is the mechanism which best allocates resources in society. Planning ignores this localistic character of knowledge and interferes with the market's self-regulating mechanism.

Socialist analyses of the role of markets and state planning in socialist societies depart radically from Hayek's view that planning and markets are incompatible with each other. Studies by Dickinson (1933), Lange (1939), Dobb (1955), Brus (1972), Nuti (1981) and Nove (1983) have argued for the central importance (although not priority) of markets moderated by the state. Nove, in his book

The Economics of Feasible Socialism (1983), argues against the case for generalised central planning as a desirable or workable alternative in Western Europe. He recommends an active market economy moderated by a strong state as well as extensive state social and cooperative property.

Hayek's arguments depend on a sharp dichotomy between markets and planning. For Hayek, mistakes and errors become "entrenched" in the process of planning. Yet why they should become "entrenched" rather than be "correctable", is not clear. The issue is important, for the idea that administrative lethargy and proneness to error are endemic to all forms of planning and are not "correctable" through internally applied quality controls is fundamental to the concept of "capture", which has become an important theoretical term used in policy reports throughout the Western world, including those introduced post-1984 in New Zealand. In addition, the extent to which Hayek's antipathy for planning is grounded in solid evidence or simply reflects his broader anticommunitarianism is problematic. Empirical studies of the history of planning in Britain, such as Wootton (1945), argue that there is little sign of any road to serfdom, or significant erosion of the liberty of the individual as a consequence of increases in state planning in the period between the two world wars.

Underpinning Hayek's views of markets and planning is the absolute priority he gives to a particular conception of freedom and liberty. As Tomlinson (1990, p. 40) observes, it is on the issue of liberty rather than inefficiency that Hayek's central objections to statism and communitarianism rest. Liberty is defined by Hayek as the basic feature of social organisation. It is "the state in which a man is not subject to coercion by the arbitrary will of another or others" (Hayek, 1960, quoted in Tomlinson, 1990, p. 40). All actions of the state are arbitrary except those that conform to the "rule of law". The rule of law embodies the legitimate limits of the state's proper functions and relates solely to the protection of personal property. It is a doctrine concerning the limits of the law aimed at restricting the coercive powers of the state. Freedom is threatened by state activity beyond these limits. For Hayek, as for Nozick (1974), or for that matter most neoliberals, this effectively excludes all welfare rights as well as rights to a minimum level of sustenance or recipience.

Keynes once commented upon Hayek's work that "it is an extraordinary example of how starting with a mistake a remorseless logician can end up in bedlam" (quoted in Tomlinson, 1940, p. 40). The alleged threat of the state rests upon a particular definition of freedom as "the absence of coercion by the state". It is a limited and unambitious concept of freedom and is enormously problematic.

First, it focuses on the coercion of the state power, but excludes economic threats to freedom, simply ignoring the fact that most of the significant obstacles to freedom are threatened by the impersonal forces of the labour market rather than the state. Why does not the unintended consequences of the behaviour of the market place count as an infringement of liberty? The answer is Hayek does not want to condemn but rather he wants to celebrate the unintended effects of the market on people's lives. It is only intentional, willed coercion by the state, or by individuals, that can diminish freedom. This theory conveniently has the effect of preserving existing property relations.

Second, although Hayek sees a positive role for the state in constructing the human subject, his concept of freedom as it pertains to the individual is a purely negative one; it allows no notion of freedom *to act*. The concept of negative liberty relates only to the *absence* of coercion. As Isaiah Berlin (1969, p. 122) puts it:

> Coercion implies the deliberate interference of other human beings within the area in which I could otherwise act. You lack political liberty or freedom only if you are prevented from attaining a goal by human beings. Mere incapacity to attain a goal is not lack of political freedom.

The central characteristics of negative liberty can thus be formally stated: (1) liberty is defined in terms of an absence rather than in terms of any positive capacity of individuals to achieve their objectives, and (2) poverty, illiteracy or unemployment may severely restrict what individuals are able to do but none of these affect one's "negative liberty".

Negative liberty can be contrasted with positive liberty. While one offers *freedom from*, the other *offers freedom to*. While individuals are given freedom from state coercion, it does not offer "equal access to the means of life and the means of labour" (Macpherson, 1973, p. 96). To discuss freedom merely in terms of what it prevents being done to the individual ignores the public significance of many freedoms. By ignoring any conception of positive freedom, it ignores the sense in which people's freedom to act depends on, and presupposes a certain degree of equality in the distribution of societal resources.

Although neoliberals maintain a sharp distinction between negative and positive liberty, and emphasise only the former, writers such as MacCallum (1967) and Martell (1993) question whether such a separation is viable at all. To be concerned with negative freedom from coercion is also to be concerned with positive freedom from coercion to do whatever one wants to do. If state coercion is removed, but I still lack the opportunity, then freedom is pointless. As Martell (1993, p. 110) states:

> This makes the idea of liberty a nonsense because a person is just as unfree to pursue a path of action because of the lack of resources they have been left with as a result of their position in the market as they are

because the state has deliberately deprived them of a right to do so. One coercion may be more acceptable than another.

Negative liberty is achievable in a strictly inegalitarian society, and means that some have greater capacities to act freely than others. To believe in positive liberty is to maintain that all people should have the resources and capacities to express and realise their freedom in their actions. This would entail a broadly egalitarian society, at least in the sense of offering equality of access, a minimum acceptable standard of living, as well as access to forms of cultural capital such as literacy and numeracy.

A third problem with Hayek's concept of liberty is that it constitutes a purely abstract and formal claim that tells us nothing about what life is like for most people in society most of the time. What people tend to do depends upon the character of the society in which they live and on the conditions they find themselves occupying within it.

A fourth problem with Hayek's concept of liberty is the absolute priority claimed for the freedom of the individual. For socialists and welfare liberals, liberty is one of the desirable attributes of social organisation, and individual self-interest is not necessarily an appropriate basis for collective decisions (Wootton, 1945, p. 11; Tomlinson, 1990, p. 40). In exalting the liberty of the individual, not only does it deny that the state can have purposes and duties other than those arising from the purposes and interests of specific individuals or groups of individuals, but if followed logically as a principle it would prevent the state undertaking projects for or on behalf of communities (e.g., education and health). It is not necessary to deny that there are many specific freedoms whose social value consists in allowing individuals to pursue their own ends nor that the market is not the best means of allocation for many resources. The central issue is how far the liberty of the individual and the market can be extended before choices in certain areas need to be limited because of the undesirable consequences of unrestricted individual liberty on society generally. This might occur, for instance, in relation to allowing such things as unrestricted access to fishing reserves, or in relation to being prepared to tolerate enormous levels of poverty in the society. It may be that under certain conditions a government that refuses to act with regard to the distribution of income and wealth may well be more coercive than a government that attempts redistribution (Hindess, 1990). A more communitarian approach has attractions for all those who think of society as a community independent of individuals and who think of the well-being and liberty of individuals as in some way dependent upon the good or well-being of society. One argument for recognising the importance of society independently of the individuals which constitute it relates to the fact that there are general interests, social benefits and public goods which cannot be identified with the interests of individuals. As a result, then, the protection and promotion of these interests must be the responsibility of the state. That is, in order to protect the liberties of all individuals, the state must act to restrain those forms of actions which would necessarily damage or curtail the liberties of any members of the community through either the intended or unintended actions of the labour market, the state, or any other person(s) or group(s) within society. The state should also act "positively" to enhance the opportunities of all members of society. State action in relation to the environment (e.g., clean air) or education have been advocated on this ground.

2.2 Freedom vs Control

Arguments against central planning may be persuasive against the idea of completely centralised decision-making for the entire economy or in situations where the personal political and civil liberties of individuals are not protected in law. Beyond this Hayek's account of planning is simply a caricature. One strategy he uses is to posit a single polarity between the individual and centralised decision making, representing the issue as "freedom vs control".[3] The implication is that a market orientation does not advocate a particular form of society but simply indicates a preference for individuals to "freely" plan their own futures, leaving the constitution of society to take care of itself. Such a view is hardly sustainable. In the first place, society necessarily always takes a substantive form, and the argument by neoliberals that within its policy formulations it is not implying a particular preferred shape to society, or that it does not advocate the establishment of a "social good" over and above what individuals desire, does not rule out substantive commitments about what society should be like. In effect, in a theoretical sense the substantive commitments of neoliberals are as much a holistic blueprint for society as are those of Keynesians or even traditional socialists. As Martell (1992) states, to claim that they are not making a choice about what form society should take must be seen, in fact, as a choice. If decisions are not made about the desirable shape of society publicly by social interests as a whole but left to emerge from the competitive interactions of individuals then the shape of society will be moulded by a combination of laissez-faire and the influence of powerful interests. In short, the neoliberals claim that their own social "plans" are not really "plans" must be viewed critically. In Martell's own words:

> [It] all sounds very nice until you realise that what it does, in effect, is to let in just another particular substantive vision of society as consisting

of the sum total of individuals' preferences over which individuals have no overall control. In this sense [neoliberalism] is in fact a highly substantive doctrine—one which posits a competitive individualist society immune to overall democratic direction. (Martell, 1992, p. 156)

Neoliberals might counter that any alternative to a market society is a monolithic community in which all individuals deny their own individuality for the good of the community. Defenders of market liberal societies like Hayek (1935, 1944) or Popper (1961) represent all alternatives to such an order as forms of monist communitarianism. For Hayek, state planning was a slippery slope leading to full-scale totalitarianism (Hayek, 1935, p. 24; 1944, chapter 3). As Tomlinson points out, he typically dismisses any midway point between centralised and decentralised planning except "the delegation of planning to organised industries" (Hayek, 1945, quoted in Tomlinson, 1990, p. 49). For Popper, although concerned more generally with the opposition between liberal individualism and Marxism rather than the technical specifications of the market model, all alternatives to a society based on individual values and exchanges were also represented as forms of authoritarian control or as tending to such control. Methodologically, and in terms of policy analysis and implementation they are "holists". In his classic discussion of the principles which underlie an "open society", Popper argues against "utopian" or "holistic" engineering in favour of piecemeal social engineering. Whereas piecemeal engineering favours a pragmatic and limited approach to change based on an awareness of the limits of human knowledge and allowing adequate room for the correction of errors, holistic engineering pursues large-scale social experiments. Popper further suggests that the persecutions in Communist countries were the result of a holist conception of society. The holist, says Popper, believes that society is more than the sum of the individuals who comprise it, which gives a licence to those who wish to curtail the rights and freedoms of the individual in the name of society's greater good (Popper, 1961, pp. 76–93).

While Popper's arguments were directed against the Marxist–Leninist regimes of Eastern Europe, it is through such forms of reasoning (aided, abetted and extended by neoliberals such as Hayek, Friedman and Nozick) that milder forms of democratic socialism and welfare statism have been also discredited. Such arguments must be seen as caricatures. Those who criticise neoliberal restructuring need not deny the importance of individuality or the regard for liberty or plurality in order to advocate some form of social planning in the interests of the public good. It is perfectly conceivable for individuals to make concessions in the interests of a public good of society as a whole and still maintain a commitment to liberty. In fact, it might be said that it is hardly possible to maintain otherwise. In addition, as I will argue shortly, the "social good" need not be imposed in any dictatorial sense but can itself be the outcome of a democratically negotiated process. This, one might add, is how it should be.

The anti-statism of the neoliberal needs careful examination. Is it not possible for individual rights and public goods to exist together and be held in balance? Is there no "middle-ground" position which excludes the view that any degree of state planning throws us onto the slippery slope to serfdom? Can we not hold that societies exist independently of human beings without thereby committing ourselves to the beliefs about one being more important than another? It would also seem that individuals are socially constructed to a large extent in that they depend for all manner of things on society's opportunity structure. Yet it is possible to hold to this view without denying that liberty and choice are important. We can also hold that all that happens and is important to human beings is not to be explained entirely in terms of individual motivations and actions, and hold nevertheless that its *importance* is to be explained by appeal to the desires and interests of individuals.

2.3 *Individualism*

The individualism of neoliberalism attests to the extreme nature of its doctrine. In a tradition extending from Hobbes to Locke and onwards, classical liberals gave a moral priority to members of society as individuals, and marked the priority by according them non-legal and natural rights, which means that there are things the state cannot do to them even in the interests of society as a whole, and further that their obligations to the state as individuals are limited. In the Lockean conception, both the state and society were viewed as "artifices", i.e., there is nothing necessary or natural about them. They came into being only by the consent of freely contracting individuals.

The individualism of neoliberalism can be broken down into three different types: ontological, methodological and political individualism. Ontological individualism holds that only individuals are real and that the individual is "prior" to society. Methodological individualism is the doctrine that collective phenomena (the state, class, education) can for the purposes of explanation be reduced to statements about individual actions and events, and political individualism holds that social policies and state actions are to be judged good or bad only insofar as they serve the desires and purposes of individual members of society. One problem for neoliberals is that one can be politically individualist without being committed to ontological or methodological individualism.

At a theoretical level, the neoliberals' individualism is flawed on the grounds that it relies on a view of the individual which is ontologically suspect and psychologically unrealistic, an ideal which C. B. Macpherson (1962) has called the "possessive individual". In this model the individual is held to be proprietor of his or her own capacities and person, owing nothing to society for them. Not only does the individual own his or her own capacities, but each is morally and legally responsible for herself or himself. The individual is held to be asocial and ahistorical. Such a conception also implies a model of society. Freedom from dependence upon others means freedom from relations with others except those relations entered into voluntarily out of self-interest. Human society for the neoliberal, as for their classical precursors, is simply a series of market relations between self-interested subjects.

What individualist theories overlook in this regard is the significant sense in which people are socially constructed (Gergen, 1985; Hindess, 1990; Hacking, 1995). Individuals are not the constitutive subjects of social life, and their concerns and objectives depend on a variety of social conditions that are independent of and external to them as individuals. In addition, the concepts, language and forms of thought on which individuals depend, also exist in advance of and separate to them. Hence, as Hindess (1990, p. 19) points out, there is no particular inherent plausibility to the view that policy decisions by the state should be grounded in the choices of its individuals. In that the concerns and interests of individuals will depend on conditions prevailing in the society, some of which could be defined as "public goods", there is no reason why the overall interests of individuals could not be addressed by focusing on those *conditions* and in seeking to establish the *structures* necessary for individuals to go about their lives. While the overall ends of state policy would in this case still be for the individuals that constitute the society, the means of fulfilling those ends is not therefore relegated to the decisions of the individuals themselves.

Another point that individualist theories overlook is that there are significant actors other than individuals (Hindess, 1990). There are, for instance, significant corporate actors which are influential members of the economic community. What neoliberals do is dispute the ontological status of such corporate groups. While they recognise that they exist, they claim that for the purposes of explanation and analysis they can be treated as individuals. As a result, powerful institutional actors such as capitalist enterprises, churches or political parties have no effective, theoretical standing in terms of neoliberal political theory. Yet such reductionism is unsatisfactory. As Hindess has put it:

> Reductionism (of methodological individualism) in principle offers no practical guidance. It does not tell us how the actions of say, IBM or the Roman Catholic Church should in practice be reduced to the actions of the relevant individuals. Even if there were a clear sense in which the

actions of corporate actors could in principle be reduced to the actions of human individuals we should still have to reckon with the concerns and objectives of corporate actors and what they do in their pursuit. (1990, pp. 26–27)

3 Alternatives

3.1 *Towards a Reappraisal of Socialist Principles*

If neoliberal arguments against a positive role for the state are deficient, and if it can be argued, as Polanyi does, that the state's role is necessary in order to remedy the contradictions of the unregulated market, then what remains to be discussed is problems in the theory and practice of socialism and of welfare states.

There is more than just a theoretical interest in the reappraisal of socialist principles. First, socialist principles and themes have been historically important in the formation of the welfare state. Secondly, various forms of social (state and community) ownership have existed within welfare state societies, and to this extent democratic socialism is not necessarily incompatible with welfare liberalism. As it is by no means vouchsafed that neoliberal hegemony will survive as the dominant discourse structuring state education policy, a renewal of the discussion on the possibility of a revived welfare state is of considerable importance. Although my interest here is speculative, i.e., relevant to the practical possibilities for New Zealand politics in the year 2000, the theoretical reconsideration of models of socialism emerging now in Britain is a suitable place to start in the attempt to reconstruct the welfare state, and to the central role of public education in such a structure.

3.2 *Models of Socialism*

New models of the welfare state which permit the coexistence of social ownership together with a private market sector are premised on anti-statist agendas and draw off both the liberal and socialist traditions, acknowledging both the rich conceptions of rights to be found in liberalism and the commitments to equality and justice in the socialist and welfare state traditions. In this sense it is also acknowledged that forms of social (state and community) ownership are compatible with the welfare state.

Individualist socialism: The notion of "individualist socialism" is referred to by Martell (1992) to characterise the work of British writers like Roy Hattersley (1987) and Raymond Plant (1988). Essentially, Hattersley and Plant offer a socialist conception of liberty supplementing negative with positive liberty, and maintain that all people should have the resources and capacities to express and realise their freedom and actions. According to both Hattersley and Plant, an inegalitarian distribution means that some people have a greater capacity to act freely than others and hence a precondition for positive liberty is that resources should be distributed evenly. Such a theory is not sufficient, however. While it is a good socialist theory of liberty, it is not a good theory of the welfare state.

Market socialism and socialism with markets: Welfare state liberals have never disputed an important role that markets play within the economy. By and large, democratic socialists have not manifested any blanket hostility to markets either. Work by Dickinson (1933), Lange (1939), Dobb (1955) and Nove (1983) all supported both a strong state and a strong market. While the socialists preferred social, state and community ownership, the welfare statists opted for a private/public mix.

Views about the role of the market in the welfare state must be distinguished from more recent conceptions about "market socialism" (Gould, 1985; Forbes, 1986; Le Grand & Estrin, 1989). Market socialism constitutes a mix of neoliberal principles and traditional welfare concerns. Their vision of socialism is constituted by a commitment to "equity" or "starting-gate equality" (Martell, 1992) but has no concern to redress structural imbalances through distributional resources. In Hayekian fashion, it exhibits two key characteristics: the essentialisation of the market, and the priority it gives to individual liberty. In doing this it tends to place the market at the centre of concern, subverting traditional welfare ideals. Not only do they short-change important values other than liberty, they also (mis)represent the market as the ideal arena of individual choice and liberty. As a consequence, "consumer demand" is represented as "choice" which is confused with "social need". Mistakenly believing that markets conform to a model of "equality of opportunity", they overlook their inherent power inequalities. In short, "consumer demand" must be kept analytically and theoretically distinct from "social need". Consumer demand is skewed by people's ability to pay, and, because it is shaped by unequally distributed purchasing power, market forces are a poor indicator of social need (Martell, 1992). Producers will not respond to needs of groups who cannot pay or which translate as weak demands due to differences in purchasing power. Markets breed inequality in relation to prosperity/neglect, high earners/low earners, wealth/poverty, and success/failure (Martell, 1992). The extent to which this is so needs to be monitored on an ongoing basis through research by the state.

The traditional welfare state: A return to the "golden days" of the welfare state once the "blue wave" is over is seen by many as a likely scenario. This position maintains and hopes that when the New Right finally recedes things will return to social democracy as usual (McLennan, 1993, p. 111). There are pluses and minuses to this prospect As McLennan puts it, the pluses are that "looking back on it, corporatism *did* generally raise the status and standards of labour in the state and the welfare state *did* 'provide' for people on a universalist basis" (ibid.; emphasis in original).

The minuses are not insignificant, however. The distributional failures of the old welfare state are well documented. Julien Le Grand's (1982, 1987) studies of the British welfare state claims on the basis of a study of empirical data that the welfare state is not redistributive across class lines but that most redistribution is intra-class and over the course of an individual's lifetime. In addition, the middle and upper classes secured a disproportionate amount in terms of per capita share of the total available equity of state-provided resources and services.

Le Grand's and other similar studies influenced the New Zealand Treasury in preparing their brief to the incoming Labour government in 1984. As the brief reported:

> A variety of studies (in countries with welfare systems broadly similar to New Zealand's) have concluded that most public expenditure on social services is actually distributed in a manner that favours the middle and higher social (income or occupation) groups, despite its notational targeting at low income groups. (New Zealand Treasury, 1984, p. 259)

This especially applies to education, and it is claimed that the middle classes consume more publicly funded education per capita than the poor.

The New Zealand Treasury uses the theoretical concept of "capture" to ground their critique of the welfare state. This concept is used both to account for the inefficiencies of existing welfare policies in terms of egalitarian objectives and to advocate a shift to neoliberal solutions based on the minimal state and individual choice.

Bertram (1988) summarises the Treasury's use of the three forms of capture which they claim have been central in criticisms of the welfare state. These are:

Consumer capture: which occurs when a group of users of state services secures preferential treatment against the interests of other users;

Provider capture: which refers to the situation where those who supply state services pursue their own interests at the expense of the interests of consumers;

Administrative capture: which refers to a situation where government departments not directly involved in the production of state-provided services act to advance their own interests at the expense of the quality of those services.

Bertram then argues that the concept of "capture" presupposes the neoliberal's individualist assumptions about society; that it presupposes that the welfare state is a zero-sum game; and that it initiates a critique which discounts externalities, public goods, and economies of scale. In overall terms, the concept is inherently biased and fails "to distinguish the different particular problems while conveying the unsubstantiated impression that there is some overarching meta problem with the welfare state" (Bertram, 1988, p. 115).

A further problem with critiques of the traditional welfare state relates to controversy over the interpretation of distributional data. In 1985, O'Higgins disputed Le Grand's analysis, arguing that while social welfare spending in Britain has not brought about greater overall equality, between 1975 and 1982 it has *combated and significantly modified the effects of pressures towards increased inequality*. On this point, Peters and Marshall note that:

> this is an extremely important point, ... a crucial matter calling for careful research. It may be that the existing provision for state education in New Zealand has not reduced inequalities of race, class and gender to any significant degree: the salient point for educational researchers is whether the proposed restructuring of educational administration indicated by the Picot Taskforce will diminish or exacerbate existing inequalities. (1988e, p. 88)

The point is important, not just as regards education but to all social services. Clearly, as Bertram (1988, p. 163) notes, there were problems with the traditional welfare state. The main three he lists are the distribution or "targeting" of benefits or resources, the exercise of monopoly power by suppliers of services, and administrative distortions. These problems, I will argue, far from being insolvable can be overcome through the implementation of ongoing quality controls and research as well as a commitment by the state to certain fundamental principles. A commitment by the state to established welfare principles of full employment and a living minimum wage would establish a context for the achievement of essential welfare goals without the need for a cumbersome bureaucracy. A commitment to these principles, in fact, solves most of the problems associated with the administration of the welfare, and, it might be added, with many other problems of the society generally (e.g., crime).

3.3 *The Changing Social Structure*

There have been other, more recent challenges to the notion of the traditional, bureaucratic welfare state from both left and right. While time and space do not enable me to do more than briefly outline their main features, as challenges to the possibility or desirability of a welfare state they can be considered under the following headings:

Fordism–post-Fordism: This thesis maintains the view that society has remorselessly "moved on" from the 1960s and 1970s and that the revival of neoliberal policy reflects the different technological, economic and political developments in the material structure of advanced capitalism. The post-Fordist thesis maintains that the character of work itself is changing away from mass production models towards individualised, flexible specialisation. This will result in short-term and frequently changing employment patterns. It involves a complex and interrelated series of changes in the labour process and the overall dynamic of macroeconomic change (Hall, 1988; Jessop, 1994). The Fordism–post-Fordism thesis is both an economic and cultural thesis. In the cultural orbit it is associated with greater fragmentation and pluralism, the weakening of older, collective solidarities and block identities, and the emergence of new identities associated with greater work flexibility, and the maximisation of individual choices through individual consumption (Hall, 1988, p. 251). It essentially involves theorisation of the process of change over the passing age, the origins of the crisis, and the shape of things to come.

Globalisation: This refers to the internationalisation of both capital and culture which will diminish the significance and power of national politics, as politics and identity at once become "both more local and more global" (McLennan, 1993, p. 110). As Stuart Hall (1988) notes, it refers to an economy increasingly dominated by multinationals, and to the rise of computer-based information technologies which diminish the importance of national boundaries, undermine the autonomy of the nation state, and involve a reorganisation of the state's activities along supra-national lines.

Enterprise culture: This challenge to the welfare state comes from neoliberalism and involves the charge that the traditional welfare state constitutes a culture of dependency and laziness where the individual regards others and not him/herself as primarily responsible for their own well-being. The essential idea of an "enterprise culture" emerged first in Britain during the 1980s (Morris, 1991) and, according to Keat (1991, p. 1), functions to represent classic liberal arguments in cultural terms. The concept of "enterprise culture" typically conveys a number of different meanings. On the one hand, it is a culture that encourages the acquisition of enterprising qualities such as self-help, self-reliance, initiative, energy, independence, boldness, a willingness to take risks, and to accept responsibility for one's actions and so on (Keat, 1991, p. 3). On the other hand, it elevates the model of the business enterprise as the preferred model for economic and social reconstruction. It also involves a sustained attempt to neutralise those qualities which are inimical to business values. This charge that the welfare state "kills off enterprise" is one of the most popular and widespread arguments levelled against it (Keat, 1991; Peters, 1992).

Modernism–postmodernism: The postmodernist argument advances yet another version of the thesis that "things have moved on since the days of the welfare state". The shift from modernism to postmodernism parallels in many ways the shift from Fordism to post-Fordism, and from the Keynesian welfare state to neoliberalism. The postmodernist argues against the very idea of a central state on the grounds that such an institution is "centrist" and "totalistic" and cannot possibly claim to represent, let alone interpret, the needs and interests of the complex and multiple realities that constitute the social domain. In this the postmodernist opposes all integrating and unifying narratives displaying a preference for the values of "difference", "dispersion", "localism", and "plurality" (Yeatman, 1990; Young, 1990).

The postmodernists' opposition to centrism can be illustrated with reference to Foucault's distinction between "total" and "general" history (Sheridan, 1980, p. 92). Whereas total history explains all phenomena in relation to a single centre, "general history employs the space of dispersion", and operates in terms of the principle of difference. For the postmodernist, then, the modernist conception of history and society imposes a false unity on the cultural formation by searching for its central organising principle—whether "the state", or "the economy" or "social classes". The ultimate effect, says the postmodernist, is to underemphasise the essential plurality of the social order. The upshot of this form of theorising has been to usher in a new form of anti-statism.

3.4 Towards a Revised, Non-Bureaucratic Model of the Welfare State

Neither the post-Fordist nor the postmodernist arguments seriously undermine the possibility of a new welfare state. The post-Fordist thesis has in fact been accused by Gregor McLennan of being misleading pop sociology:

> The solidaristic effects of being a wage-earner, even today, remain in my view full of political potential in the face of extraordinary predatoriness of international capital; work itself (and its absence) still dominates the lives and potentials of people like *nothing else*. (McLennan, 1993, p. 110; emphasis in original)

In addition to this, in spite of the fact that it constitutes a form of analysis stemming from the left, it tends almost by implication to suggest that the ascendency of neoliberalism is in some sense "inevitable" and "could not have been otherwise". It also suggests that it has emerged as a direct consequence of deeper changes in society and thus ends up by suggesting that neoliberal options are an inevitable and necessary development. Notwithstanding such inferences, it can be argued that the developments that the post-Fordist identifies constitute an argument for rather than against the construction of a new welfare state. If work is to be of a more "temporary" and "varied" nature, and characterised by constant changes and a need for "perpetual retraining", this would seem to me to create an indispensable case for the existence of some agency which can mediate the growing unpredictability of the relationship between individual human beings and the demands of capital accumulation.

The difficulties with the argument that the welfare state encourages dependency rather than enterprise are numerous. One is the abstractness of the claim. While it may conceivably have some validity in some situations with regard to some forms of state policy, it is difficult to understand as a blanket claim how all forms of welfare policy erode enterprise values. How, for instance, does universal health provision relate to enterprise? Should we all be self-reliant with respect to health care or medical treatment? The absurdity of such a possibility also highlights the fact overlooked by neoliberals that all human beings are reliant on the structures of state support at one time or another. It is easy to overlook the profundity of this fact. Let me state it as a general principle. *All individuals depend at some stage in their lives on the structures of social support and on resources that they have not personally owned or created.*

Related to this, a second issue is concerned with the fact that people vary in respect to the extent in which they need support and assistance from the state. A person with multiple disabilities who is confined to a wheelchair may require greater assistance than the daughter of a multi-millionaire who has just won a scholarship to Harvard. A single mother with three small children may require forms of assistance that her ex-partner who owns a successful business does not. There are both *subgroups* of people as well as *critical periods* in all people's lives where welfare rights may be required. The existence of welfare rights in relation to health or education, or for people when they are sick or have special needs, does not signal "dependence" as opposed to "self-reliance" but rather indicates specific forms of dependence in a world where all people are dependent at some stage upon the structures of social support. The illusion of self-reliance simply indicates a privileged position in relation to the opportunity and reward structures of our society. As a consequence, it can be seen that the representation of the issue as being one of either "dependency" or "enterprise" is a false polarity. People do differ in the extent to which they rely on their own resources, but the neoliberal needs to acknowledge that such resources are often achieved with social and institutional support. And just as every one of us has at some stage been dependent upon the resources of society, so too every one of us is potentially in need of assistance again.

Thirdly, a welfare state need not discourage enterprise, and hence a welfare state can also be an "enterprise culture". Unlike the neoliberal conception of enterprise, however, the welfare liberal's view of enterprise is not limited to forms of "busnocratic rationality" (Marshall, 1995). Rather, "enterprise" is defined more broadly to include both business and nonbusiness forms of initiative and creativity. It may include financially unrewarding activities such as art, scholarship, or child-rearing. In this sense, the concept of "enterprise" may coexist and be consistent with a need for various forms of assistance.

Fourthly, in that the welfare state allows a significant private-sector market, there is plenty of scope for individual business enterprise of the sort the neoliberal likes.

Fifthly, the "dependence/enterprise" dualism of neoliberalism fails to recognise that some people, or groups of people, can experience bad luck, and that groups within society can be disadvantaged, just as it fails to recognise that the apparent self-reliance of some individuals and groups within society is based upon resources that were socially given.

The globalisation argument has some implications for the prospects for a new welfare state in as much as the increasing internationalisation of capital may well affect the ability of the nation state to act unilaterally. To this extent the contradiction between capital accumulation and democratic legitimation (Offe, 1984) will increasingly weight the power imbalances in favour of capital. Yet this in itself must not mean that a legally independent sovereign nation state should give up in despair. Politics, after all, is the "art of the impossible".

The concern with the issue of central planning may have some validity. It may well be, as the postmodernist argues, that the traditional welfare state has been unduly insensitive to local minorities and oppressed groups. It may also have been overly centrist and monolithic. Much of the tenure of postmodernism, like post-Fordism, and like neoliberalism, has been against the forms of monist communitarianism where an overarching central state exerts its hegemony over the entire society.

There is no reason why a revised welfare state should be statist or overly centralised, however. Many of the left in recent years have acknowledged problems with statism and many have searched for non-statist formulae which force a democratisation of the public good rather than via neoliberal private instrumentalism and market anarchy. The development of forms of "associational socialism" (Martell, 1992; Hirst, 1990) or of decentralised democratic socialism (Bobbio, 1987) have called for radical, democratic, socialist alternatives based on citizenship, parliamentary democracy, the rule of law, the strengthening of the institutions of civil society and liberal democracy, as well as decentralisation. This model of democratic socialism has much to teach welfare liberals who have traditionally supported the institutions of liberal democracy. Essentially, the future for a revived welfare state lies in its commitment to democratisation through new forms of decentralisation, citizenship and participation. Such commitments can also, under certain circumstances, imply the extension of democracy from the polity to the economy and to civil society. As Bowles and Gintis (1986) point out, it is one of the glaring contradictions which neoliberals don't like to talk about too much, that they support democratic control and decision-making in relation to the political system but not in relation to the economic system. The welfare state liberal, then, can support the strengthening of the institutions of civil society, from parent involvement in boards of school trustees to consumer representatives on the boards of large business enterprises, through to new radical, pluralist, decentralised and participatory forms of democracy.

The welfare state liberal thus has a different response to the crisis of the state than does the neoliberal. Rather than abandon ideas of the common good and of collectivism, the welfare state liberal's response to statism is not to abandon the state in preference for the abstract individual or to abandon public goods in favour of privatisation and markets but rather to bring them under greater democratic control. As Hirst (1990) has observed, democracy is the best answer the left has to the right. This might conceivably mean decentralising state powers into civil society; strengthening controls and checks on central government and on employers and all corporate actors; promoting a more active role for citizenry; and promoting a commitment to "positive" as well as "negative" liberty. Controls on government can be extended through legal and constitutional safeguards, through extending the separation and devolution of state powers, through promoting a vibrant civil society, increasing the number and strength of counteracting centres of power to the state, and promoting a strong role for independent associations. Activities of specific individuals or groups of individuals will only be restrained to the extent they conflict with the rights of other individuals or with certain democratically negotiated public goods.

In Britain, Luke Martell is one recent author who has advocated a theory of associational democracy (Martell, 1992, 1993). While his own thesis is developed in relation to a broader examination of new models of socialism, the general idea of strengthening the associations of civil society, of devolving state powers and of increasing checks and controls on the state power can contribute towards a model of a revived welfare state. In Martell's theory, associations (such as teachers' unions, for instance) can provide the institutions appropriate to participatory democracy. First, associations can provide forums for the active popular participation of individuals at accessible decentralised levels. Second, an inclusive corporatist polity comprised of associations representing the plurality of interests is capable of negotiating agreed social priorities. Third, the state can decentralise functionally, bringing democracy down to small-scale, local levels. Fourth, associations, being corporate entities, can check the power of other corporate entities, including the state. Such a solution, says Martell, is neither statist nor laissez-faire.

3.5   *Education*

The provision of public education is based on a number of historically important rights and claims. The "positive" rights associated with social democratic liberalism entailed that a universal and free education was the indispensable prerequisite to the freedom of the individual. Such education was to be compulsory because children needed to be protected against the individual self-interest of their parents. Such rights underpinned the goals of a democratic society to ensure its reproduction through a common set of skills and values. Public education thus served the community by addressing social needs. Schools provided students with a common set of values and knowledge, thus creating the basis for citizenship and the democratic functioning of society. Schooling also contributed to scientific and cultural progress and played an important role in economic and social growth, ensuring the conditions for full employment.

The public benefits of education cannot simply be seen as the sum of individual private benefits. Norms such as political or civic tolerance, literacy, or the values required for democratic functioning adhere to the quality of a community and are not reducible to the psychological characteristics of individuals. In short, essential to producing the public benefits of schooling, all children must experience certain common benefits which are not safeguarded for by a privatised education without the regulation and monitoring of the state. In a private system some parents will not be able to obtain schooling for their children at all; others might seek schooling that reinforces sectarian religious, political, ethnic or cultural ends. As a consequence, certain social benefits are not safeguarded and important issues to do with the regulation and control over such things as the "quality of teacher training" or "the nature of the curriculum" are not protected. Universal and compulsory education established common uniform features in order to guarantee skills such as universal literacy and numeracy as the universal common basis necessary for active citizenship and democratic participation.

By the intrinsic nature of their social organisation, private schools, argues Levin (1987), are also likely to neglect areas concerned with specific aspects of schooling, such as the curriculum, which are necessary to public benefits such as tolerance or citizenship. This is so, he argues, because private schooling is less likely to introduce students to, and encourage in them, a tolerance of diverse cultures and values. In a related sense, reflecting the specific social attributes on which they are based, they are likely to undermine the level of social and cultural integration, thus exacerbating differences in relation to class, race and religion within the community.

In that private schooling cannot provide for important social benefits, a suitably public-provided education can account for individual "choice" through the provision of a greater variety of options and offerings within the public system. To this extent a publicly provided education can adapt itself flexibly to individual preferences, thus reconciling the twin goals of preserving the "public goods" of education and protecting individual rights (which have historically given to parents the ability to decide exactly how and where their children will be educated, and to withdraw them from the state system if they so wish). For the welfare liberal, the ideals of public education depend on a conception of schooling as a shared experience rather than based on "choice". Hence I would argue that while a public system can produce private benefits (such as individual qualifications and skills), a private system cannot provide for the social benefits which are necessary to the functioning of a democratic society and which education under the welfare state has historically provided. In fact, extensive privatisation is likely to undermine the public basis of a democratic, literate society itself.

3.6 *Community*

The model of a decentralised welfare society advanced here is compatible with the notion of "community", which has been advocated as the basis of a revived welfare state since the 1970s (Le Grand, 1982; Joppke, 1987). The model is compatible, too, with Peters and Marshall's notion of an "empowerment community" which they argue is consistent with a genuine state of participatory democracy (1988a, 1988b, 1988c, 1988d, 1988e, 1989). Such a notion of community embodies the strengthening of the institutions of civil society and an increase in the possibilities for democratic participation. In relation to education, Robinson (1988) has argued in this respect that the Picot Report presented possibilities for democratic participation that had not previously existed in schooling practices.

There is nothing inherently wrong with arguments for devolution of authority to schools or other community agencies. Such a devolution must be accompanied, however, as Marshall (1981) has argued, by theories of participatory structures that are genuinely democratic. This would entail moves towards a more responsive, community-based, service delivery welfare state which might involve power-sharing and devolution, as well as forms of community-based public ownership of business enterprises (along the lines of the Trustee Savings Banks in New Zealand, for example). Such a conception is consistent with those that advocate a conceptual shift from the notion of a "welfare state" to that of a "welfare society" in which family, voluntary societies, local bodies, trade unions and employers play a greater role (Davey & Dwyer, 1984). It is a welfare state which is sensitive to institutional abuses of power, which is committed to the twin goals of full employment and equality of opportunity as well as to universal welfare entitlements and Keynesian demand management. It is a welfare state which constitutes a viable alternative to the bureaucratic welfare state. In Joppke's words (1987, p. 250), "it pursues the egalitarian project of a non-bureaucratic decentralized and self-reliant welfare society". Consistent with Peters and Marshall's "empowerment community", it is based on the values which encourage and promote cooperative rather than competitive behaviour and which make for a sense of cohesion and community. As Peters and Marshall put it:

> This is tantamount to arguing simply that a welfare state ought to be concerned with developing a sense of *communal* rather than *self* interest, that values of the private and the individual ought not to be privileged or aggrandized over those of the public and the community; and that collective provision based on communal interest is potentially more egalitarian, socially responsible and democratic than similar services provided by the free market. (1990, p. 81; emphasis in original)

This is a far cry from the neoliberal's conception. It rejects the notion of the market as a superior mechanism for allocating resources in society or as the instrument of a self-regulating or spontaneously ordered social system. It supports the notion that the real purposes of central planning are the creation of a genuinely free society, and that collective powers of the state are used only to protect individual rights and to enable individuals to "pursue their own goals in their own way" (Hindess, 1990, p. 10).

It supports the idea, too, that such a welfare society is committed to the principle of equality, although it acknowledges that the concept of equality, and its relationship to liberty, needs careful theorising. I am not so convinced that the traditional concern with equality needs ditching, as Gregor McLennan (1993, p. 109) has suggested, although if it could be shown that the concept generated undesirable features then these could be acknowledged and the welfare state's concern with equality could be modified accordingly. For McLennan, any merits in the concept can be recast in more precise terms which include a focus on "access", "needs fulfilment", "social justice", and "self-realisation". In addition, the term sometimes conflates concerns such as equality of opportunity with universal provision and with equality of outcomes.

Equality itself has not been the failing of socialist or welfare states. The failing has been identified as having more to do with means rather than ends (Martell, 1992), and in this sense tends to focus on the failings of the state (such as central planning and the encroachment of liberty). I have already questioned whether this association is not itself ideologically in support of a certain conception of property relations and class interests. Yet to abandon a concern for equality is, in my view, to abandon a concern for the welfare state, and in a world of dangerous arms stocks, starvation, huge extremes of wealth and poverty, it would seem to me that nothing could be more needed than a doctrine that stresses equality, community and the public good. In short, the concept of equality performs an important political function. Equality in all of its different senses is a precondition for freedom. Equality is a basis for an increase in the sum of liberty as well as in its equal distribution. Ultimately, as far as most people are concerned, a state that ignores the issue of equality is more coercive than a state that takes no action. In addition, the cumulative and compounding nature of the inequalities that the market generates relates to all of the different senses that McLennan mentions and yet it still means that such inequalities need to be rectified by distributional political decisions. Such a commitment need not entail a subordination of individual liberties in preference for extreme forms of communitarianism. Indeed, such egalitarianism is not, in my view, the same thing as "uniformity", and in fact is fully compatible with pluralist politics and liberal democracy. What is important for liberal democracy is not to abolish the state in preference for market anarchy, nor to abolish liberty in preference for an all-powerful state, but to "rescue the middle ground" (Martell, 1993). In the final analysis, it is the inability to adopt a balanced perspective that stamps neoliberal restructuring as an extreme doctrine.

4   Conclusion

The welfare state, then, can assure a degree of both equality and community in a number of politically important respects. More specifically, it assures a number of important functions. As Bertram (1988, p. 135) suggests:

> [It] improves resource allocation, minimises qualitative differentiation of service, is politically sustainable because of the wide spread of

beneficiaries, and performs an important socially integrative function by underpinning rights of citizenship.

In addition, it is suggested that problems of administrative inertia or of various forms of "capture" can be overcome by the institutionalisation of quality checks and controls, through ongoing research, by the decentralisation of services, by the establishment of countervailing associational networks of power which can mediate and represent the diverse interests of individuals, and through publicly provided education.

Acknowledgement

This chapter originally appeared as Olssen, M. (1996), In defence of the welfare state and publicly provided education: A New Zealand perspective, *Journal of Education Policy*, *11*(3), 337–362, https://doi.org/10.1080/0268093960110305. Reprinted here, with minor edits, with permission from the publisher.

Notes

1 The most important of these policies were the Picot Report (1988); the Meade Report (1988); Tomorrow's Schools (1988); the Lough Report (1988); the National Curriculum of New Zealand (1991); the New Zealand Curriculum Framework (1993); the Hawke Report (1988).
2 In bracketing various neoliberal writers together, I am not wishing to deny that there are important differences between their theories. This is especially so in respect to the libertarian political philosophy of Nozick. Yet it is claimed that the common features that their works stress (anti-statism, individualism, priority on liberty, priority on the market) have generally contributed to the ascendency of a neoliberal hegemony, and in this respect their common features become germane to understanding the decline of the welfare state. Having said this, specific analysis will focus principally on Hayek's formulations.
3 In this respect (again) the arguments of writers like Friedman (1962, 1980), Buchanan (1975) and Nozick (1974) are similar.

References

Amin, A. (1994). Models, fantasies and phantoms of transition. In A. Amin (Ed.), *Post-Fordism: A reader* (pp. 1–40). Blackwell.

Bates, R. (1990). Educational policy and the new cult of efficiency. In S. Middleton, J. Codd, & A. Jones (Eds.), *New Zealand education policy today: Cultural perspectives* (pp. 40–52). Allen & Unwin.

Berlin, I. (1969). *Four essays on liberty*. Oxford University Press.

Bertram, G. (1988, April). Middle class capture: A brief survey. In *Future directions, vol. 3, part 2: Report of the Royal Commission on Social Policy* (pp. 109–170). Government Printer.

Bobbio, N. (1987). *The future of democracy*. Polity.

Bowles, S., & Gintis, H. (1986). *Democracy and capitalism*. Routledge.

Brus, W. (1972). *The market in a socialist economy*. Routledge & Kegan Paul.

Buchanan, J. (1960). *Fiscal theory and political economy*. University of North Carolina Press.

Buchanan, J. (1969). *Cost and choice*. Markham.

Buchanan, J. (1975). *The limits of liberty: Between anarchy and leviathan*. University of Chicago Press.

Buchanan, J., & Tullock, G. (1972). *The calculus of consent: Logical foundations of the constitution of democracy*. University of Michigan Press.

Burchell, G. (1993). Liberal government and techniques of the self, *Economy and Society, 22*(2), 267–281.

Codd, J. (1990a). Policy documents and the official discourses of the state. In J. Codd, R. Harker, & R. Nash (Eds.), *Political issues in New Zealand education* (pp. 133–149). Dunmore Press.

Codd, J. (1990b). Educational policy and the crisis of the New Zealand state. In S. Middleton, J. Codd, & A. Jones (Eds.), *New Zealand Educational Policy Today* (pp. 191–205). Allen & Unwin.

Davey, J., & Dwyer, M. (1984). *Meeting needs in the community: A discussion paper on school service*. New Zealand Planning Council.

Dickinson, H. (1933). Economics of socialism. *Economic Journal, 11*(3), 237–250.

Dobb, M. (1955). *On economic theory and socialism*. Routledge & Kegan Paul.

Forbes, I. (Ed.). (1986). *Market socialism: Whose choice?* Fabian Tract 516. London Fabian Society.

Friedman, M. (1962). *Capitalism and freedom*. University of Chicago Press.

Friedman, M. (1980). *Free to choose*. Penguin.

Gergen, K. (1985). The social constructionist movement in modern psychology. *American Psychologist, 40*, 266–275.

Gordon, C. (1991). Government rationality: An introduction. In G. Burchell, C. Gordon, & P. Miller (Eds.), *The Foucault effect* (pp. 1–51). Harvester Wheatsheaf.

Gordon, L. (1992). The state, devolution and educational reform in New Zealand. *Journal of Education Policy, 7*(2), 187–203.

Gordon, L. (1993). *"Rich" and "poor" schools in Aotearoa* [Paper presentation]. Annual Conference of the New Zealand Association for Research in Education, Hamilton, December.

Gould, B. (1985). *Socialism and freedom*. Macmillan.

Habermas, J. (1975). *Legitimation crisis* (T. McCarthy, Trans.). Beacon Press.

Hacking, I. (1995). *Rewriting the soul: Multiple personality and the sciences of memory.* Princeton University Press.

Hall, S. (1988, October 24–29). Brave new world. *Marxism Today.*

Hattersley, R. (1987). *Choose freedom: The future for democratic socialism.* Penguin.

Hayek, F. A. (Ed.). (1935). *Collectivist economic planning.* Routledge & Kegan Paul.

Hayek, F. A. (1944). *The road to serfdom.* Routledge & Kegan Paul.

Hayek, F. A. (1945). The use of knowledge in society. *American Economic Review, 35*(4), 519–530.

Hayek, F. A. (1960). *The constitution of liberty.* Routledge & Kegan Paul.

Hindess, B. (1990). Liberty and equality. In B. Hindess (Ed.), *Reactions to the right* (pp. 7–31). Routledge.

Hirst, P. (1990). Democracy: Socialism's best answer to the right. In B. Hindess (Ed.), *Reactions to the right* (pp. 148–176). Routledge.

Jessop, B. (1994). Post-Fordism and the state. In A. Amin (Ed.), *Post-Fordism: A reader* (pp. 251–279). Blackwell.

Joppke, C. (1977). The crisis of the welfare state: Collective consumption and the rise of new social actors. *Berkeley Journal of Sociology, 32,* 237–260.

Keat, R. (1991). Introductions: Starship Britain or universal enterprise? In R. Keat & N. Abercrombie (Eds.), *Enterprise culture* (pp. 7–17). Routledge.

Kelsey, J. (1993). *Rolling back the state: Privatization of power in Aotearoa.* Bridget Williams Books.

Lane, R. (1993). *The market experience.* Cambridge University Press.

Lange, O. (1939). *On the economic theory of socialism* (B. Lippincott, Ed.). University of Minnesota Press.

Le Grand, J. (1982). *The strategy of equality.* Allen & Unwin.

Le Grand, J. (1987). The middle class and the use of British social services. In R. Goodin & H. Le Grand (Eds.), *Not only the poor: The middle classes and the welfare state* (pp. 91–108). Allen & Unwin.

Le Grand, J., & Estrin, P. (1989). *Market socialism.* Clarendon.

Le Grand, J., & Robinson, R. (1984). Privatisation and the welfare state: An introduction. In J. Le Grand & R. Robinson (Eds.), *Privatisation and the welfare state* (pp. 1–14). Allen & Unwin.

Levin, H. (1987). Education as a public and private good. *Journal of Policy Analysis and Management, 6*(4), 628–641.

MacCallum, G. G. (1967). Negative and positive liberty. *Philosophical Review, 76,* 312–334.

McLennan, G. (1993). The concept, history, situation and prospects of social democracy: A modest overview. *Sites, 26*(Autumn), 103–114.

Macpherson, C. B. (1962). *The political theory of possessive individualism.* Clarendon Press.

Macpherson, C. B. (1973). *Democratic theory: Essays in retrieval.* Oxford University Press.

Marshall, J. (1981). *What is education?* Dunmore Press.

Marshall, J. (1995). Skills, information and quality for the autonomous chooser. In M. Olssen & K. Morris Matthews (Eds.), *Education, democracy and reform* (pp. 44–59). New Zealand Association for Research in Education (NZARE)/Research Unit for Maori Education (RUME), University of Auckland.

Marshall, J., & Peters, M. (1990). The insertion of "New Right" thinking into education: An example from New Zealand. *Journal of Educational Policy, 5*(2), 143–156. https://doi.org/10.1080/0268093900050204

Martell, L. (1992). New ideas of socialism. *Economy and Society, 21*(2), 152–172.

Martell, L. (1993). Rescuing the middle ground: Neo-liberalism and associational socialism. *Economy and Society, 22*(1), 100–113.

Morris, P. (1991). Freeing the spirit of enterprise: The genesis and development of the concept of enterprise culture. In R. Keat & N. Abercrombie (Eds.), *Enterprise culture* (pp. 21–37). Routledge.

New Zealand Treasury. (1984). *Economic management: Brief to the incoming government.* Government Printer.

Nove, A. (1983). *The economics of feasible socialism.* Allen & Unwin.

Nozick, R. (1974). *Anarchy, state, and utopia.* Basic Books.

Nuti, D. (1981). Socialism on earth. *Cambridge Journal of Economics, 4,* 391–403.

O'Connor, J. (1973). *The fiscal crisis of the state.* St. Martin's Press.

Offe, C. (1984). Some contradictions in the modern welfare state. In G. Offe (Ed.), *Contradictions of the Welfare State* (pp. ?–?). MIT Press.

Olssen, M., & Morris Matthews, K. (1995). Education, democracy and reform: An introduction. In M. Olssen & K. Morris Matthews (Eds.), *Education, democracy and reform* (pp. 1–13). New Zealand Association for Research in Education (NZARE)/Research Unit for Maori Education (RUME), University of Auckland.

Peters, M. (1992). Starship education: Enterprise culture in New Zealand. *Access: Critical Perspectives on Education Policy, 11*(1), 1–12.

Peters, M., & Marshall, J. (1988a). Social policy and the move to "community". In *Report of the (NZ) Royal Commission on Social Policy, vol. 3, part 1* (pp. 655–676.). Government Printer.

Peters, M., & Marshall, J. (1988b). Social policy and the move to "community": Practical implications for service delivery. In *Report of the Royal Commission on Social Policy, vol. 3, part 1* (pp. 677–702). Government Printer.

Peters, M., & Marshall, J. (1988c). *Te reo o te Tai Tokerau*: Community evaluation, empowerment and opportunities for oral Maori language reproduction. In *Report of the Royal Commission on Social Policy, vol. 3, part 1* (pp. 703–743). Government Printer.

Peters, M., & Marshall, J. (1988d). Empowerment and the ideal learning community: Theory and practice in Tai Tokerau. In G. Wylie (Ed.), *Proceedings of the first*

Research into Educational Policy conference, NZCER, 17–19 August. New Zealand Council for Educational Research.

Peters, M., & Marshall, J. (1988e). The politics of "choice" and "community". *Access, 7,* 84–109.

Peters, M., & Marshall, J. (1989). *Education and empowerment: Postmodernism, humanism and critiques of individualism* [Paper presentation]. New Zealand Association for Research in Education Annual Conference, "Educational Research: Can It Make a Difference in the Classroom?", 30 November–3 December, Wellington.

Peters, M., & Marshall, J. (1990). Education, the New Right and the crisis of the welfare state in New Zealand. *Discourse, 11*(1), 77–90.

Peters, M., Marshall, J., & Massey, L. (1994). Recent educational reforms in Aotearoa. In E. Coxon, K. Jenkins, J. Marshall, & L. Massey (Eds.), *The politics of learning and teaching in Aotearoa–New Zealand* (pp. ?–?). Dunmore Press.

Plant, R. (1988). *Citizenship rights and socialism.* Fabian Society.

Polanyi, K. (1969). The birth of the liberal creed. In K. J. Rea & J. T. McLeod (Eds.), *Business and government in Canada* (pp. ?–?). Methuen.

Popper, K. R. (1961). *The poverty of historicism.* Routledge.

Rea, K. J., & McLeod, J. T. (Eds.). (1969). *Business and government in Canada.* Methuen.

Robinson, V. (1988). An opportunity for participatory democracy. *Access, 7,* 16–26.

Rose, N. (1993). Government, authority and expertise in advanced liberalism. *Economy and Society, 22*(3), 283–299.

Sheridan, A. (1980). *Michel Foucault: The will to truth.* Routledge.

Shonfield, A. (1965). *Modern capitalism: The changing balance of public and private power.* Oxford University Press.

Smith, G. (1991). *Reform and Maori educational crisis: A grand illusion* [Keynote address]. PPTA Conference, Otautahi.

Snook, L (1995). Democracy and education in a monetarist society. *Educational Philosophy and Theory, 27*(1), 55–67.

Tomlinson, J. (1990). Market socialism: A basis for socialist renewal? In B. Hindess (Ed.), *Reactions to the Right* (pp. 32–49). Croom Helm.

Wootton, B. (1945). *Freedom under planning.* Allen & Unwin.

Yeatman, A. (1990). A feminist theory of social differentiation. In L. J. Nicholson (Ed.), *Feminism/postmodernism* (pp. 281–299). Routledge.

Young, I. (1990). The ideal of community and the politics of difference. In L. J. Nicholson (Ed.), *Feminism/postmodernism* (pp. 300–323). Routledge.

CHAPTER 8

Education Policy, the Cold War and the "Liberal–Communitarian" Debate

Abstract

This paper examines different philosophical frameworks by which policy decisions concerning education are made and over which issues concerning the distribution of resources in society can be determined. These frameworks include classical liberalism, which constitutes the philosophical basis of choice theories regarding education, and which includes both rights-based as well as utilitarian approaches; Rawlsianism, which constitutes a 20th-century form of social democratic liberalism, frequently invoked by those seeking to philosophically justify some minimal form of welfare state; and communitarian frameworks, represented in the 20th century by writers such as Charles Taylor, Michael Sandel, Michael Walzer, and Alistair MacIntyre, which stands opposed to the basic postulates and axioms of liberalism. The paper also examines liberal criticisms of communitarianism and argues that communitarianism can be defended against such criticisms. As such, communitarianism constitutes a viable philosophical and political orientation in terms of which social democratic principles, incorporating a respect for freedom of thought and expression, personal autonomy, individual rights and democratic practice can be based, and which avoids the fundamental problems of liberalism. In the final section, current neoliberal policies of education based on choice are examined, in relation to the New Zealand context, in terms of communitarian criticisms.

1 Introduction

John Codd (1993b) suggests that an ethical framework based on the work of John Rawls is superior to those based on "choice" for the analysis, development and implementation of policy analysis. Inspired by Codd's argument this paper outlines three possible philosophical frameworks that could guide policy determination and argues that while Rawls's "social justice as fairness" ethic marks an advance over "choice" theories, the limitations and weaknesses of Rawls's work, related to its deep affinities with the classical liberal tradition of which it is a part, make some form of philosophical communitarianism a more adequate basis for policy determination. In terms of structure, this article will first discuss the philosophical traditions underpinning "choice", second it will discuss Rawls's work, and third it will outline the main ideas and problems with communitarianism relating each to education as it proceeds.

Consistent with international trends in America and Britain and many others parts of the developed Western world, "choice" has been a central plank in educational reforms that have taken place in New Zealand since 1987. In the Picot Report, as Codd (1993a) tells us, where these reforms were initially proposed, "choice" is declared to be one of the core values on which the new system is based. The Picot Report, says Codd (1993a, p. 31), begins by critiquing the present administrative structure as one which is "over-centralised" and as having "too many decision points" (see, for instance, Taskforce to Review Education Administration, 1988, p. XI). The report expresses such a commitment when it states that:

> Consumers need to be able to directly influence their learning institution by having a say in the running of it or by being able to turn to acceptable alternatives. Only if people are free to choose can a true cooperative partnership develop between the community and learning institutions. Choice will involve providing a wider range of options both for consumers and learning institutions. (Taskforce to Review Education Administration, 1988, p. 11)

According to Codd (1993a, p. 32), such a conception of choice reflects a

> deeply individualist approach to social policy. All state intervention, in this view, is especially bad, and all social goods are reduced to private goods that can be achieved only by individuals exercising rational choice within a free market. ... "[S]ociety" or the "public" has no definable features and therefore no existence beyond the cumulative actions of individuals.

As Marshall (1995) maintains, assumed in such a notion of "choice" is that the quality of educational choices made by the consumer is superior to those offered to consumers by providers with expert knowledge. Educators' knowledge in this model is considered as being of secondary importance. It is held that the choices of individual consumers are more rational and better both for the individual and for the community.

2   Classical Liberalism

In that "choice" proposals entail policies based on the freedom of individuals in a legacy deriving from both classical political and economic liberalism, they contain as a consequence the following presuppositions:
1. that economic subjects are self-interested and act individually (i.e., as "Homo economicus"). In this sense the individual is a rational optimizer and the best judge of his/her own interests and needs;
2. that the state is limited within its "negative" role and acts neutrally between different individuals' interests and desires;
3. that the uncoordinated self-interest of individuals correlates with the interests and harmony of the whole society;
4. that a "free market", i.e., an unregulated market, provides the best opportunities for people to utilize their skills and therefore optimize their life goals.

In its earliest development liberalism can be traced to the 17th-century efforts to establish a secular state in which religious differences would be tolerated and where the interests of the emerging propertied classes would be safeguarded. As the most coherent expression of early liberal theory, Locke articulated a view which shared much of Hobbes's vision of the need for the collective (i.e., state) protection of property and which, also like Hobbes, was greatly concerned with the political problems surrounding the growth of religious diversity. Locke supposed that the most convenient way to organize society was on weakly democratic principles concerned to safeguard the freedom of the individual against the arbitrary power of the sovereign, including (1) government by consent, (2) natural rights of citizens to private property protected against infraction by arbitrary acts of government, (3) periodic popular elections, and (4) citizen right of revolt against governments that violate natural rights.

It was Locke who most clearly expressed the individualist conception of classical liberalism as it developed from the 17th century. The Lockean tradition was individualist both politically and economically, and can be distinguished from the continental liberal tradition represented by Rousseau, who gave a greater emphasis to "equality" as against "individual rights", placed a greater emphasis on public life as opposed to the individual, saw society as having a moral or metaphysical status over and above that *of* individuals, and extended individualism from the intellectual sphere to that of the passions, foreshadowing writers like Nietzsche (Russell, 1961, p. 580).

In the interaction of economic and political liberalism, Robert Green McCloskey makes the point that in the initial development of the doctrine in the 16th and early 17th centuries, liberalism represented "personal experience" and was concerned to champion the liberty of the individual against the arbitrary power of the state. The privileged position it gave to capital, and to the market as the desirable allocator of resources, represented:

> a degeneration of the liberal democratic tradition. ... When he used the term "liberty", the early democrat meant, first of all, freedom of experience—moral liberty—rather than freedom of business enterprise. His chief interest, in short, was in the right of the individual to realize his moral personality, and not the right to buy and sell and prosper economically. (McCloskey, 1951, pp. 2–3)

A more explicit and formal legitimization of capital and private property was to come later in the century. According to McCloskey, the exalted position given to capital and private property derived principally from two sources:

> The first from radical Christian democrats ... [and] the second from the sober-sided English middle class bent on shaping a doctrine congenial to men of property. ... Locke fastened onto democracy the idea that the right of private property is fundamental; he set in train a materialisation of democratic ideals that led ultimately to their perversion. (McCloskey, 1951, pp. 5–6)

While radical democrats in the 17th century supported equal and limited rights to property as part of their campaign to extend the franchise, it was Locke who, through his theorization of the role of money, introduced into liberal discourse an inalienable right to *unlimited* property (Macpherson, 1962, p. 203). For Locke, rights to unlimited property were justified as natural rights, and one of the central functions of the state was to protect such property.

During the 17th century, liberalism came increasingly to develop policies and attitudes which harmonized with the class interests of the bourgeoisie. England during this period was a transitional society between feudalism and capitalism, characterized by the emergence of early modern notions of contract, a growing wage labour force, and emerging national markets in a variety of commodities (Shapiro, 1986, p. 77).

3   Classical Economic Liberalism

Classical liberalism can be bifurcated in yet another way: between the predominantly political/philosophical orientation of the 17th century, and the predominantly economic/scientific orientation of the 18th century. In the 18th century, science replaced philosophy as the principal means of uncovering the natural laws of society. It was able to do this because it no longer sought to criticize the political order from the viewpoint of abstract human nature but from the standpoint of economic social progress. There was a shift from the philosophical investigation of human nature to the scientific investigation of the laws that governed the economic progress of society. Different forms of property were considered not solely according to natural rights but increasingly also according to the contribution to progress. The change of focus signalled a growing concern with economic questions, and political philosophy gave way to political economy as the basis of a theory of science and society.

From the 18th to the mid-19th century, classical economic liberalism developed within the tradition of political economy represented in the writing of Bernard de Mandeville, David Hume, Adam Smith, Thomas Malthus, David Ricardo, James Mill and John Stuart Mill. Many of their economic and social ideas were developed from the writings of the Physiocrats, whose theories came to dominate French views of society in the mid-18th century. Society was no longer viewed as an expression of human nature but as a self-regulating and spontaneously ordering system; that is, a system regulated by its own laws rather than as a result of human design. If such laws were respected and not interfered with, the harmony of the entire society would prevail.

4   Utilitarianism

The utilitarian moment within liberalism is best expressed in the writings of Jeremy Bentham at the start of the 19th century. Prioritizing "utility" over "natural rights", Bentham claims that:

> it is the greatest happiness of the greatest number that is the measure of right and wrong. (Bentham, 1775/1969, p. 45)

Building on the work of de Mandeville, Hume, Smith and others, Bentham was to articulate a moral and political philosophy that has shaped policy analysis within a liberal political agenda for over a century. With Bentham, although the liberal cornerstone of natural rights as a justification of liberal principles gave way to the principle of utility as the calculus of moral evaluation, the central conceptions of individual self-interest and laissez-faire remained at the basis of liberalism.

In rejecting conceptions of "natural rights", as Ernest Barker (1928, p. 205) tells us, Bentham paradoxically paved the way for an increasingly interventionist role of the state in the second half of the 19th century. Bentham advocated two principles which stood in a not altogether consistent relationship to each other. On the one hand, he advocated the principle which belongs chiefly to the economic field of the right of each individual to pursue his/her own interest; on the other hand, he had urged, in the political sphere, the right and duty of the state to secure the greatest happiness of the greatest number. Time, says Barker, was to emphasize the second of these principles.

John Stuart Mill's writing also assisted in undermining the principles of laissez-faire and extended the utilitarian cause preparing the way for the developments in English thought that were to occur after 1880. It is Mill more than any other writer in the 19th century who serves as the bridge from laissez-faire to the idea of social readjustment by the state. In this sense, Mill represents a transitional force between individualism of which he remained ultimately a prophet, to the more collectivist solutions and concerns with social effectiveness and "efficiency" introduced at the end of the 19th century. In his hands, utilitarianism begins to be less individualistic, and assumes more and more of a social democratic quality. In short, after the 1860s, Mill became progressively uneasy with classical liberalism's inability to resolve the social chaos wrought by unregulated capitalism and the growth of collectivist politics. A double emphasis now existed within liberalism: the stress on "rights" was counterbalanced, and surpassed, by the utilitarian stress on social effectiveness.

5   The Moment of Equality in Liberal Theory: John Rawls

What is neglected by advocates of choice, whether in terms of "rights" or "utility", is a consideration of the actual political and social context which negates the possibility of "choice" within a stratified and complex social structure. Less-well-off families have fewer options. Poor people must accept their neighbourhood schools regardless of the quality. Highly regarded wealthy schools are likely to be "over-chosen" with the practical outcome that the school will effectively "choose" its customers rather than the other way round. General equity issues tend to be neglected, meaning that an emphasis on choice will result in a corresponding increase in inequality, increasing social divisions between rich and poor schools and rich and poor areas in the community. As a consequence, there will be little incentive for schools in wealthy areas to admit the children from the disadvantaged sectors of the community, or of race minorities.

Critics of "choice" argue, therefore, that "choice" proposals jeopardize the ability of public schooling to promote equal outcomes and equality of opportunity. In addition, running schools of choice will structure admissions processes so as to avoid undesirable students, giving the schools rather than the consumers the ultimate choice. Studies show that under "choice" schemes funds are directed to schools that represent predominantly middle-class (wealthy, white and well-behaved) students while less desirable students are excluded from entry (Moore & Davenport, 1990).

For both "rights" theorists and utilitarians, education does not differ substantially from other exchangeable commodities. Education for both is defined essentially as the sum total of individuals' preferences. While the "greatest happiness" principle introduced a more instrumentalist societal procedure of calculation, in practice it dovetailed neatly with the interests of an expanding capitalist class—one of the main reasons why Marx parodied Bentham's efforts.

From the 1880s, liberalism was restructured by what Stuart Hall (1986, p. 64) calls a "series of *ad hoc* revisions spanning five decades", ushering in what was frequently referred to as "social democratic" liberalism or "welfare state" liberalism. The major advocates of this more collectivist model included the neo-Kantian philosopher T. H. Green, the Oxford "democratic collectivist" L. T. Hobhouse, the "liberal-socialist" economist J. A. Hobson, the social theorist/economist Alfred Marshall, and his student John Maynard Keynes.

Social democratic liberalism supplemented "negative" liberty with a new form of "positive" liberty. As the 19th century progressed many liberal writers, increasingly perturbed by the social chaos wrought by the industrial revolution, placed a greater emphasis on "positive liberty" and "welfare rights". Drawing off Kant, Aristotle and Rousseau, this once again raised the issue of "equality" within liberal theory, eclipsing the importance of the "deontological" tradition as represented by Locke.

The stress on "equality", which came to underscore the welfare tradition, put an emphasis on "justice" as well as "rights", and what the precursors of the welfare state all subscribed to in common was a "social justice ethic". In the 20th century, the major exponent of a "social justice ethic" is John Rawls. Rawls abandoned the ruling theory of utilitarianism and created a version of contract theory and Kantian liberalism bypassing the issues of political obligation and the state in preference for a consideration of distributive justice. Although not endorsing a positive role for the state as in the tradition of late-19th-century social democratic liberalism, Rawls's work constitutes a possible alternative philosophical framework within the broad tradition of liberalism which could be utilized to justify policy development. In what follows I will assess its suitability.[1]

Rawls's position contrasts sharply with market liberal positions which stress individual "choice" over equality. In the Lockean conception of distributive justice, for instance, individual choice is prioritized in that individuals have a right to whatever they have, i.e., whatever they mix their labour with. In the utilitarian conception aggregate social effectiveness is given priority. For Rawls, on the other hand, equity is given priority over choice as a primary policy objective, as expressed in the phrase "social justice as fairness". Equity for Rawls presupposes a certain form of "equality". It is embodied in two principles of social justice.

The first is that:

1. Each person is to have an equal right to the most extensive total system of equal basic liberties compatible with a similar system of liberty for all. (Rawls, 1971, p. 302)

The second principle is called "the difference principle" and states that:

2. Social and economic inequalities are to be arranged so that they are both (a) to the greatest benefit of the least advantaged and (b) attached to offices and positions open to all under conditions of fair equality of opportunity. (Ibid.)

In addition, third, Rawls posits a "General Conception":

3. All social primary goods—liberty and opportunity, income and wealth, and the bases of self-respect—are to be distributed equally unless an unequal distribution of any or all of these goods is to the advantage of the least favoured. (Ibid., p. 303)

Rawls argues that these principles have a rational basis and thus constitute an Archimedean point for judging the basic social structures of a society. His theory of justice is an attempt to identify the deep structures which shape our common-sense judgements about what is right and proper. Rather than the utilitarian view which seeks to maximize aggregate happiness, Rawls provides a modern contract theory extending the traditional theory of social contract as set down by Locke, Rousseau and Kant, and which he summarizes in shorthand form in the phrase "justice as fairness".

The rationale for implementing "justice as fairness" is relatively straightforward. Rawls posits a modern "thought experiment" which involves ascertaining the principles by which rational people would distribute resources in society uninfluenced by knowledge of their own social situation, their own wealth, or their own future life plans or prospects. He imagines such people making such decisions behind this "veil of ignorance" about their own position or prospects in such a society in order to "nullify the effects of specific contingencies which put men at odds and tempt them to exploit social and natural circumstances to their own advantage" (Rawls, 1971, p. 136). Rawls conceptualizes such people in the position of erecting a new social contract and charges them as rational beings with establishing the social arrangements according to principles which reason dictates, which in turn will enable basic political and economic policies to be derived in the interests of the least well off, as well as the basic rights and duties of its members.

John Codd (1993b) advocates a Rawlsian "social justice" ethnic against the market-liberal ethic of "choice", which he claims is compatible with the organization of education under the welfare state in New Zealand, and which has constituted a dominant structuring principle for most of the 20th century. According to Codd (1993b, p. 82), the application of these principles to education would mean that resources were to be allocated "so as to improve the long-term expectation of the least favoured ... rather than simply evening out existing inequalities or improving the economic efficiency of the system". This differs fundamentally from the distributive conception entailed by choice theories. One point of central difference is that for Rawls, because education is necessary to the formation of people's desires and preferences, it constitutes what he calls a *primary good*. As Codd explains it:

> Primary social goods are things that all reasonable people would want because without them they cannot even choose the kind of life they would want. For example, reasonable people would want to be able to participate in decisions that affect their welfare, and to be able to develop skills and acquire knowledge necessary to participate in the political and economic institutions of society. Education, in these terms, becomes defined as a basic human right. It is not something we can simply choose to have from a position of not having it. Education is not something we simply acquire: it changes who we are. (Codd, 1993b, p. 83)

In Rawls's view, the notion of justice entails that material goods and educational resources must be distributed fairly, according to a criterion of "need", rather than according to individual "rights" or in terms of "economic efficiency". The principles that Rawls lists (as stated above) are prioritized, which means that policymakers should first attend to basic liberties; second, to issues concerned with equality of opportunity; and third—"the difference principle"—concerns matters related to the welfare of the least well-off members of the society.

For Rawls (1971, p. 3), then, "justice is the first principle of social institutions, as truth is of systems of thought". As such it offers an alternative to utilitarianism, libertarianism and meritocratic theories. As Kahne puts it:

> He faults utilitarians for violating individual rights when they attempt to maximize aggregate utility, libertarians for permitting distribution of positions and rewards to be influenced "by … factors [both native abilities and social and economic status] so arbitrary from a moral point of view", … and those who support meritocratic systems because he feels the distribution of natural assets is every bit as arbitrary as that of social assets. "Equality of opportunity", he writes "means an equal chance to leave the less fortunate behind in the personal quest for influence and social position". (Kahne, 1996, p. 21)

In relation to education, Rawls's commitment to the disadvantaged under the difference principle would not necessarily mean that the relatively more successful or "gifted" students would be neglected at the expense of the worst off. Yet, the educational emphasis on meritocracy would be modified, and although incentives could still be linked to performance, they would be structured so as to benefit the worst off first.

According to Kahne (1996, p. 22), Rawls's proposals are similar in many respects to those of James Coleman, who wanted to shape policy within liberal agendas to compensate those "born into less favourable social positions" (see Coleman et al., 1982; Coleman & Hoffer, 1987). Yet, unlike Coleman, Rawls wants to compensate "those with fewer native talents" as well. As Rawls puts it:

> [I]n order to treat all persons equally, to provide genuine equality of opportunity, society must give more attention to those with fewer native talents and to those born into less favourable social positions. The idea is to redress the bias of contingencies in the direction of equality. In pursuit of this principle greater resources might be spent on the education of the less rather than the more intelligent. (Rawls, 1971, pp. 100–101, cited in Kahne, 1996, p. 23)

6 The Unsatisfactory Basis of Rawls's Theory

Rawls's social justice as fairness ethic is one alternative to conceptualizing the organization of schooling according to "choice" and has appeal to all those who think of the well-being and liberty of individuals as in some way mutually related to the well-being and good of society. Yet while Rawls's theory constitutes a definite advance over "choice" theories in this sense, it is ultimately unsatisfactory. The reasons for this are as follows.

Rawls's principles of justice, as embodied in the "original position" do not lead to a single rational outcome as Rawls intends. While the structural conditions of the "original position" may have consequences for decision-making within a broadly specifiable limit, there is a high degree of vagueness and indeterminacy. Rawls assumes, for instance, that behind the "veil of ignorance" the original contractors will proceed *cautiously*, allocating resources in the interests of the worst off and that, on balance, this is the most rational thing to do. But is it? What is irrational, asks Alan Brown (1960, p. 61), about risk-taking? That is, about allowing enormous extremes of inequality to occur, based on the "gamble" that if they are lucky they will win all and if they are unlucky they will lose all, or lose nearly all. In short, the caution Rawls builds into his contractors is unconvincing. There is nothing irrational in risking life and limb for the chance of higher gains and the fact that the stakes are high does not mean, as Rawls falsely supposes, that people will refrain from such high-risk strategies.

In addition, the original contractors might consider varied strategies based on various degrees of "caution" and "risk", all of which could be considered rational, and yet all of which have different outcomes. The most conservative strategy would be to accept that resources distributed in the interests of the worst off results over time in absolute equality in that the successive and cumulative implementation of such a policy would progressively redistribute resources according to a mathematical formula from "best off to worst off" in a series of successive approximations to the equal (although this might conflict with Rawls's prioritizing of liberty over welfare). Yet a different strategy based on a different mix of "caution" and "risk" by the original contractors might produce a completely different outcome. It might be prepared to tolerate huge extremes of wealth so long as no one is allowed to fall below a certain minimum level (the "safety net" argument). Along the same lines it might be further argued that the contractors could accept a "trickle down" theory of resource distribution, allowing for even greater levels of wealth and greater levels of inequality, so long as the overall position of the worst off also continued to improve. In short, it is very doubtful in my view that the original contractors will be "convinced by the same arguments", as Rawls (1971, p. 139) claims.

Following from the above point, Rawls's theory says nothing about how his principles of justice affect policy implementation. All of the traditional political arguments between left and right over welfare provision, service delivery, targeting, bureaucracy, self-reliance, etc., are left "up in the air". Because his theory specifies such a general rule it is of very little value in terms of being able to influence practical policy implementation.

Rawls's theory is in all respects consistent with the deontological liberal tradition and he embodies in his theory a classical liberal conception of the self-expressing a broadly negative conception of freedom. For Rawls, the rational individual is exclusively concerned with finding the solution, i.e., those principles of justice, that most clearly advance his own interests. He is the classical "Homo economicus":

> A rational person is thought to have a coherent set of preferences between the options open to him. He ranks these options according to how well they further his purposes; he follows the plan which will satisfy more of his desires rather than less, and which have greater chance of being successfully executed. (Rawls, 1971, p. 43)

What Rawls does not do, but needs to do, is justify political liberalism by offering arguments for moral scepticism and the autonomy of individual choice in matters moral and political. If my argument is valid, this would be an extremely difficult thing to do.

Finally, Rawls's theory constitutes a "thin" conception of the good, based as it is on a single and very general principle. Many "goods" such as friendship, civic participation and the structures necessary for personal development are not effectively catered for, or theorized. As a consequence, says Michael Sandel (1982), a certain range of conceptions of the good will be unable to flourish in Rawlsian society. The underlying reason for this is again traceable to the individualist and asocial metaphysical foundations of liberal principles, which generate an inability to acknowledge or even perceive the types of goals that communities inevitably must strive for and the social objectives they must fulfil. For Rawls, society is still essentially the aggregation of self-interested egoists of classical liberalism who generalize their own self-interest. In this context his principles of justice constitute limiting ethical boundaries within which market exchanges can take place.

7 The Communitarian Response to Liberal Frameworks

Communitarianism is the name commonly used to refer to a philosophical viewpoint that can be distinguished from liberal schools of thought (rights, theories, utilitarianism, Rawlsianism) on a number of dimensions.[2] The most important of these are: (1) social ontology: the priority of the good over individual rights or utilities; (2) a recognition of the social nature of the self.

7.1   The Priority of the Good

In contrast with Rawls, and with other liberal thinkers, communitarians place a greater emphasis on the "common good", i.e., on collective goods, including the shared values and practices of a community. While collective goods are institutional and include such things as buildings used for sports and intangible goods such as education, community values include the shared norms and beliefs that constitute a society's cultural belief systems. In essence, communitarians argue that individual values are derived from community values and not from human nature. Hence, the weakness of the liberal position.

In talking about "community", contemporary communitarians are not talking about hastily gathered collectivities of friendly people. In addition, communitarianism is not primarily a moral claim about how societies ought to operate. Rather, what it constitutes is an ontological claim which prescribes a social ontology and theory of human development, and, *on this basis*, makes both descriptive and normative claims which tell policymakers how they ought to orientate themselves to question of how distribution should be decided as well as to the more practical aspects of their role (see Taylor, 1989).

Communitarians would argue that Rawls's deontological conception constitutes a rights-based morality which decentralizes any notion of the "common good" and does not allow for a conception of public goods over and above the sum of individual private desires and preferences. As Seung-Hwan Lee puts it:

> A rights-based morality does not give central place to the common good and a shared life. Rather it emphasises the notion of what each member of the community is entitled to claim from other members. The moral bonds of the community are founded on mutual respect, demonstrated by recognising the rights of each individual, rights such as those of freedom, property, and well-being. (Lee, 1992, p. 241, cited in Gasson & Rich, 1995, pp. 7–8)

Communitarians argue that as the common good is not simply the sum of individual rights-based actions, it cannot be reduced to them. On the one hand, a conception based on rights will ensure many community ends (housing for elderly, clean air, etc.). On the other hand, the community good is a structural precondition for human development and selfhood (as will be discussed further below) and because it denies this to be the case, "liberal theory", says Walzer (1990, p. 9), "radically misrepresents real life". Yet another factor is that by denying the priority of the good over the right the liberal is being inconsistent, for any theory of human rights must necessarily imply and rely upon a complex and sophisticated conception of the good and, in this sense, what the liberal fails to do is clearly work out the substantive presuppositions which necessarily underpin a theory of rights. The communitarian view thus differs fundamentally from liberal conceptions which see the state as neutral or, in the case of Rawls or Bentham, as governed by a "thin" conception of the good. In contrasting his conception with Bentham's, Philip Selznick states:

> The alternative [to Bentham's view] is to think of the common good as more profoundly systemic, not reducible to individual interests or attributes, yet testable by its contribution to personal well-being. The common good is served, for example, by institutions that provide collective goods, such as education or public safety. The strength or weakness of these institutions is a communal attribute, not an individual one. (Selznick, 1992, p. 537)

In short, without an adequate theory of the good it is not possible, argue communitarians, to provide answers to the questions as to what kind of society best provides for the good of its members.

7.2 The Social Nature of the Self

Another closely related feature common to all forms of communitarianism is their rejection of the liberal conception of a pre-social (i.e., natural) self. In contrast, they maintain that the nature of the self is social in the sense of being "embedded in", "constituted by" and "dependent upon" the community. As Charles Taylor puts it:

> What has been argued in the different theories of the social nature (of human beings) is not just that they cannot physically survive alone, but much more that they only develop their characteristically human capacities in society. The claim is that living in a society is a necessary condition of the development of rationality, in some sense of this property, or of becoming a moral *agent* in the full sense of the term, or of becoming a fully responsible autonomous being. (Taylor, 1985, pp. 190–191)

Rawls's view, like Locke's and like Kant's view, posits a conception of the self which is "atomistic", says Taylor:

> We can describe as atomist views of the human good for which it is conceivable for man to attain it alone. ... The basic error of atomism in all of its forms is that it fails to take account of the degree to which the free

individual with his own goals and aspirations is himself only possible within a certain kind of civilisations; that it took a long development of certain institutions and practices, of the rule of law, of rules of equal respect, of habits of common deliberation, of common association, of cultural self-development, and so on, to produce the modern individual, and without these the very sense of oneself as an individual in the modern meaning *of* the term would atrophy. (Taylor, 1985, pp. 292, 309)

For Taylor the community constitutes a common culture which is a precondition for individual moral autonomy. In a slightly different sense, MacIntyre (1992) limits the notion of community to particular subgroups such as the family, the neighbourhood or the region, arguing that the culture or nation as a whole lacks a sufficient basis for shared understandings or common values. In this view, the derivation of the self is still social, however, according to MacIntyre, one's life can only be understood by looking at one's actions within a story or "narrative". As any understanding of one's own narrative converges with the narratives of others, the attempt to understand anything can only be obtained in the context of a community, which is responsible for determining the form and shape of all narratives (Avineri & de-Shalit, 1992, p. 3).

Irrespective of the differences amongst them, all communitarians claim that liberals overemphasize the autonomy of individuals, as in Kantian ethics, for instance; that they perpetuate a myth of a pre-social and ahistorical individual; that they adhere to an arrogant universalism; and that they neglect the central role of community in providing necessary structures of learning, of language and of opportunity. As Mary Ann Glendon (1991, p. 109) puts it:

> Neglect of the social dimension of personhood has made it extremely difficult for us to develop an adequate conceptual apparatus for taking into account the sorts of groups within which human character, competence, and capacity for citizenship are formed. In a society where the seedbeds of civic virtue—families, neighbourhoods, religious associations, and other communities—can no longer be taken for granted, this is no trifling matter.

Dewey (1927/1954, p. 158) also criticized the liberal conception of "the self":

> At the basis of the scheme lies what Lippman has well called the idea of the "omnicompetent" individual: competent to frame policies, to judge their results, competent to know in all situations demanding political action what is for his own good. [It] held that ideas and knowledge were

functions of a mind or consciousness which originated in individuals by means of isolated contact with objects. But, in fact, knowledge is a function of association and communication, it depends upon tradition, upon tools and methods socially transmitted, developed and sanctioned.

While the factors related to social ontology and the nature of the self constitute the major points of difference between liberals and communitarians, other factors related to politics, philosophy and ethics arise from these. Amongst communitarians, too, there are considerable variations, representing various shades of political opinion.

One form of traditional, conservative communitarianism is that advanced by Plato in *The Republic*. This is a form of communitarianism which sees individuals as directly subservient to community-defined roles and positions, which, in turn, are conceptualized as hierarchical, narrow and unchanging. As John Dewey writes, for instance:

> No one could better express than [Plato] the fact that a society is stably organised when each individual is doing that for which he has aptitude by nature in such a way as to be useful to others (or to contribute to the whole to which he belongs); and that it is the business of education to discover these aptitudes and progressively to train them for social use. (Dewey, 1916, p. 102)

For Aristotle, on the other hand, the form of communitarianism is different, in that there is an attempt to balance individual goals and purposes with community ends and values. One of Aristotle's objections to Plato was that for Plato collective ends were treated as ultimate and represented as having "interests". For Aristotle it makes no sense to talk of the well-being of a community apart from the well-being of its members. While the individual is seen as a member of a community, and as developing within a community, less importance is given to the "majesty" of the state, or to the view that the individual exists in order to perform an allotted function in the life of the community. Rather the emphasis is the other way round: the community exists for the sake of the development of its individual members, but at the same time is essential to that development.

In Aristotle's view the theory of the "good" is tied up with a view about the nature of man and his relation to the rest of the universe. The nature of the good life and its priority is established by the nature of human beings as a species group. Aristotle sought to "ground" the good naturalistically. In his *Ethics* he argues the essentialist thesis that by identifying man's nature as a species being, we can discover the nature of man's "good" or well-being. Following from this, by virtue of the kind of beings that people are, there are certain modes of living and kinds of activity that are characteristic of them, i.e., that are constitutive of the good life.

Aristotle, like Marx, Hegel and Dewey, saw the good of society as being to promote good lives on the part of its members. The state exists for the sake of the good life. The good life, hence, is the essence of happiness and well-being and is much broader than the utilitarian or any other of the liberal conceptions. It allows for physical and mental well-being, material sustenance, the exercise and realization of human capacities and potentialities, for individual development in accordance with choice and reason, for action in accord with virtue, for friendship (*philia*) and interpersonal relations, and for pleasure.

As Richard Miller (1989) points out, Marx's view was very much in accord with Aristotle's in that societies are judged in relation to the kinds of human lives they permit. Alienated labour on this view entails a view of deprivation which in Aristotle's view would deny people realization of the good life. For Marx, the extremes of inequality of the type generated by unregulated capitalism deprive workers and their families of the basis of the good life, inhibiting non-alienated relationships and depriving people of the ability to exercise their capacities.

In the 20th century John Dewey has developed a communitarian philosophy based on a conception of individuals who work collectively to overcome common obstacles in their environment through "problem solving", thus ensuring "growth" in both individual and community terms. Dewey's emphasis shows similarities to Marx in the sense that he is especially interested in the mechanisms by which communities change. In addition, Dewey shows a careful respect for the fundamental liberal values of freedom and democracy. In commenting upon Dewey's work, Amy Gutmann (1992, p. 133) claims that "communitarianism has the potential for helping us discover a politics that combines community with a commitment to basic liberal values".

Gutmann's suggestion that communitarianism may be compatible with certain aspects of liberalism can be taken as valid, and it can be noted that nearly all present-day communitarians acknowledge the importance of such things as "rights", "personal autonomy" and "democratic practices". Lee (1992) points out, for instance, that there is an emphasis on individual rights in many communitarian societies, although as such they are defined in relation to the "good" and not prior to it. In his own analysis, Lee documents the emphasis on "rights" in the "virtue-based" society of Confucian China.

In this sense, too, the "welfare state" liberals of the late 19th century—T. H. Green and L. T. Hobhouse—were as much "communitarian" as they were "liberal". As well as seeking to preserve the liberal emphasis on "rights", and recognizing limits to the state, they advocated a positive role for the state, and rejected the classical liberal conception of a "self-interested chooser" in favour of a more "ethical" conception.

In that communitarianism and liberalism are based on fundamentally different and mutually exclusive axioms it is not possible to provide a "synthesis" by simply mixing the two philosophical perspectives together. What is possible, though, is to incorporate certain elements of liberalism into the communitarian perspective or conversely to incorporate certain communitarian ideas into liberalism. While in recent years this latter option has become increasingly popular, in its own right, communitarianism designates those writers who acknowledge the central importance of the "good" over individual preferences and desires, ontologically represent the social as "prior" to the individual in the sense that the existence of the former is the condition for the development of the latter, are ontological and epistemological holists rather than individualists, and see issues of "distributive justice" in historical and community terms.

The last named factor does not necessarily make all communitarians epistemological or moral relativists. Although writers like Pierce have tended to equate scientific rationality with whatever views happen to prevail in the scientific community, and writers like Walzer (1983) seem to hold that morality cannot be conceived in universal terms since the values people hold derive from their communities, many communitarians have been committed to objectivist conceptions which transcend particular communities and hence are not relative to a particular community or to a particular time. The 19th-century idealist philosopher T. H. Green posits a notion of overlapping communities culminating in a "universal brotherhood" in order to avoid moral relativism.

In the 20th century Jürgen Habermas (1984, 1987b) posits a transhistorical and cross-cultural conception of rationality which locates it neither in the rational Cartesian subject, nor the objective data, but rather in the nature of *unconstrained communication*, as resolved through *argumentation* and *deliberation*. For Habermas, rational decision making is inherently inter-subjective. Presupposed in every speech act, says Habermas, is the possibility of separating the "strategic" from the "communicative" uses of language, a circumstance that makes it possible to assess the validity of perspectives based on the "force of the better argument" alone.

In this sense Habermas's "ideal speech community" bears an uncanny similarity to Rawls's "original position", for both arguments presuppose the possibility of an innocent authoritative language whereby it is possible to argue in purely rational terms. Although both are influenced by Kant, whereas Rawls posits asocial Kantian subjects, for Habermas rational decision making is dialogical and resides not in the human subject but rather in the nature of communication. Rawls's individualism resides in the fact that he sees those having to make decisions in society as possessing an "already formed will" (Manin, 1994, p. 193), whose already know exactly what they want, and only need to apply their criteria of evaluation to the proposed solutions. There is an important sense, in fact, in which Rawls's "original position" does not constitute agreement between individuals at all, for the individuals present are stripped of everything that makes them individuals. Rawls's view of political decision making merely consists in hypothetical agreement between disembodied subjects, and on this ground it is not *genuinely* a "contractarian" position at all. What Habermas recognizes is that the process of deliberation is itself social and political, not metaphysical, and is worked out in a process of confrontation and argumentation. What is rational in this process is not the performed wills of individuals, but rather the process of communication itself.

In that Habermas's approach has similarities to Rawls's approach it also suffers from some of the same problems. It is far from clear, as Steven Lukes (1982, p. 142) argues, for instance, that unconstrained discourse between conflicting subjects will yield consensual action-guiding principles. In addition, there is a distinctively Hegelian dimension to Habermas's proposal in that he postulates the development of increasingly transparent structures of communication and self-reflection through successive stages of evolution which many would find unacceptable. While it is not possible to resolve, or even do justice to, the difficult issues involved in the context of an article like this, my own view is that while Habermas's conception of "undistorted communication" offers a worthy ideal, and obviously should be strived for in our sort of society, it would need to be supplemented by more adequate theoretical accounts. In my view, the best possible basis for such a "supplementation" exists in relation to the sort of approaches taken to this issue by writers such as Aristotle, Marx and Dewey. For Marx, the criterion of rationality in terms of which ethical decisions concerning distribution are to be made is in terms of a normative conception of community, i.e., each according to his/her needs, grounded in a theory of the *species characteristics* of human beings. Aristotle's approach was based on his view that each class of thing has its own "mode of flourishing", i.e., its own goal, end or purpose from which its *ergon* or *telos* can be discerned. If the good for man can within broad limits be discerned then the structures of society can be organized to allow for that. Similarly, Dewey's approach is grounded in his conception of individuals as social beings actively engaged in "problem-solving" behaviour.

In terms of implications for "distributive justice", Brown (1990, pp. 143–151) distinguishes "externalist" and "internalist" approaches to justification. Externalist approaches have attempted to justify various types of distribution according to such things as the "will of God", "self-evident axioms", "moral intuition", "human nature", "formalist language constraints", "contract theories" or "state of nature" theories, or "ideal observer" or "fundamental human rights" theories. In relation to these types of approach, Brown agrees with Rawls (1971, p. 578) that "there are no set of first principles ... especially suited to carry the burden of justification". In his own approach he favours "internalist theories" of justification deriving principles to guide policy formation with respect to redistribution directly from the common good itself. Hence the idea that there are certain "ends", "goals", or "modes of flourishing" for human beings has implications for the sorts of political policies that should be developed with respect to both education and the polity in general.

There are of course problems and objections to this way of proceeding. The liberal writer Bernard Williams (1972, p. 76) argues that there is "no direct route from a consideration of human nature to a unique morality and a unique moral ideal". In addition, as has often been argued before, the problem with accounts based on the species characteristics of human beings is that they ignore issues of war and cruelty which also are characteristic features of human behaviour. Another objection relates to the difficulty in establishing what human nature *is* for human nature is frequently represented in different ways. (It might be remembered, for instance, that Aristotle's views were sexist, racist and elitist!) Yet while these issues here are not straightforward, such objections, says Brown, do not entail a rejection of the *essence* of this type of approach. While there may be no necessary or logical entailment, one approach might be to seek to *construct* a theory of the good based on an *abstraction* from human species nature. In arguing for an approach similar to this, Brown contends that while there may be problems, they are fewer and easier to overcome (or at least to live with) than those in the liberal tradition. He argues that a theory of the common good, and its corollary, an objectivist theory of morality, is badly needed in political theory. This sort of approach is also broadly compatible with Habermas's theory of "communicative rationality".

While it is hoped that these comments of "distributive justice" and the issue of relativism might assist us to start reasoning on this complex issue, many questions remain in response to which only a few broad suggestions can be given here. One issue concerns the actual types of principles that might serve as guides to issues of distribution in Western societies, while there is no easy path in this respect, Charles Taylor attempts to make some headway while appreciating the difficulties involved. Deriving his insights from Aristotle, he maintains:

> [While] we have to abandon the search for a single set of principles of distributive justice, ... [t]his need not reduce us to silence, but it means that there are no mathematical proofs about distributive justice. Rather the judgement of what is just in a particular society involves combining mutually irreducible principles in a weighting that is appropriate for the particular society, given its history, economy, degree of integration. It is hard to set out knock-down proofs of such judgements. But some things can be said in general about western societies. All or most aspire to be republican societies sustaining the sense of individual liberty and common deliberation; and at the same time most are also experienced by their members as collaborative enterprises for the furtherance of individual prosperity. The first aspect is the basis for a principle of equal sharing, the second for what I call the contribution principle. ... [W]e depend on society to be fully human agents, and also to be capable of the contribution we are making. Taking account of these would require that the contribution principle be combined with other more egalitarian considerations. (Taylor, 1985, pp. 312–314)

Taylor is referring here to principles or agreed rules internal to Western-type societies of which New Zealand is also one. What it also suggests is what can be "claimed" as true about a society is important to establishing further claims about distribution. Hence, *if* a society is committed to meritocratic recruitment procedures, this will have implications for policies of recruitment and how jobs are distributed. *If* we accept the right of all—irrespective of race or gender—to partake of the good, certain things *follow*. In addition, says Taylor, we need not confine our claims to our own society or abandon our claim to universalize either cross-culturally or trans-historically, for certain rights, or "modes of flourishing" or "needs" may be "trans-societal" (1985, p. 302). In general on this matter philosophers have been insufficiently sensitive to the ever present possibilities of colonialism and imperialism, as poststructuralist writers of various sorts have pointed out (see, for instance, Spivak, 1987, 1988, 1989). Notwithstanding the difficulties, however, and without intending to defend them here, let me state cautiously, and with due rights of "appeal" to anyone who cares to complain, that there are some claims we can make that extend across other societies and cultures both cross-culturally and trans-historically, and that this provides *some* basis on which to start. Thus, putting my head gently "on the block", I will agree with Finnis (1983, p. 76):

> Proper attention to the historical and anthropological data shows that the basic forms of human good ... are recognised, by human beings, both in thought and action, with virtual universality in all times and places.

8 Communitarianism and the Philosophers of the Cold War

While it is not possible to adequately recount the complexity of the issues at stake between liberals and communitarians, it is possible to briefly summarize the main points of contention and to indicate the main approaches taken by communitarians in defence.

One line of argument, advanced by writers like Isaiah Berlin, focuses on the diversity of opinion concerning the nature of the good, such diversity rendering any final solution or resolution in the sense of identification of a "good" as impossible. The outcome of this belief in an "irreducible pluralism of conflicting values" (Brown, 1990, p. 157) is, of course, another way of justifying political pluralism, where freedom as an end in itself is all that remains given the necessary incompatibility between versions of the good.

Following on from this line of reasoning, writers like Berlin and Popper maintained that communitarianism leads to a mindlessness and fanaticism of the "total" community. This criticism maintains that an emphasis on community results in totalitarianism or some form of police state.

For the most part, this criticism relates to the liberal view of the state. Liberals from the 17th century, and in the 20th century, including such writers as Hayek (1935, 1944), Arendt (1958), Popper (1945, 1961), Talmon (1955), and Berlin (1969), have represented any form of state planning based on a "positive" conception of the state's role as inherently dangerous and likely to lead to totalitarianism.[1] For Hayek (1944), it was what took society down "the road to serfdom".

The positive view of freedom as active self-determination implies, says Isaiah Berlin (1969), a distinction between two selves—a higher self that determines, and a lower self that is subject to determination. Berlin argues that in the history of political thought, it is all too easy for the higher self to become identified with the state or society, or with a particular political group's conception of what is "rational". Freedom then tends to become defined as obedience to what is rational, or obedience to the will of the state, or conformity to a predetermined pattern of thought or life. As a consequence, claims Berlin, positive freedom is transposed into the opposite of freedom: totalitarianism or tyranny.

In its extreme form, argues Nel Noddings (1996), it is claimed that the positive conception of liberty which is a feature of communitarianism often leads to the promulgation of a single ideal—a description of "man" as a spiritual being whose ultimate rationality and reality are grounded in a unified spirit. In its fascist form, in fact, says Noddings, every individual is depicted as a representative of a universal spirit. Noddings quotes the prominent Italian fascist Giovanni Gentile:

> The Ego cannot think or feel or realize itself in any way that is not universal. It thinks of everything in and along with itself: in its feeling the feeling of the whole universe is gathered up and concentrated; nor can it separate itself in any way from the rest of the world and consider itself as a part only. Every time that man achieves a further awareness of the Whole, what he feels "no mortal tongue can utter", for his voice echoes within him as the voice of all men, of the whole, the voice of eternal and the infinite. (Gentile [Genesis and Structure: 80], cited in Noddings, 1996, p. 253)

The total community = fascism = the nation state. If the state is right, then there is no room for dissent, and liberty is equated with full immersion in the community. Liberals claim that individuality is wiped out by "normcentricity". In this way, Eric Hoffer maintained that communities foster "unity" and "self-sacrifice" along with conformity to established norms. In Hoffer's words:

> Unity and self-sacrifice, of themselves, even when fostered by the most noble means, produce a facility for hating. Even when men league themselves mightily together to promote tolerance and peace on earth, they are likely to be violently intolerant towards those not of like mind. (Hoffer, 1951, p. 92)

Steven Heyman (1992) claims that the most striking thing about Berlin's analysis of Liberty is the way it is distorted by the political circumstances in which the essay was written, and as such his comments also apply to Hoffer and other liberals who believe that there are dangers of community. As Heyman puts it:

> Berlin was writing in the late 1950s, at the height of the Cold War. He casts the debate between negative and positive liberty as a crucial battle in "the open war that is being fought between two systems of ideas", and between the political systems allegedly based on them—Western liberal democracy and totalitarian regimes of the left and right. ... With the passing of the Cold War, it may be easier to understand the relationship between positive and negative liberty in our political tradition. (Heyman, 1992, pp. 81–82)

With the passing of the Cold War, it can be more easily seen, I think, that the liberals' criticisms of communitarianism largely miss their mark. To the extent that there are dangers inherent in human societies, such dangers inhere in all sorts of society, and it is difficult to identify such dangers as belonging specifically to a form of societal organization distinguishable as communitarian. While it is not possible to consider in detail the complex arguments in the debates between liberals and communitarians here, it is possible to briefly consider some of the more pertinent issues as they affect this debate.

Communitarianism can be politically individualist and yet collectivist in relation to ontology and epistemology. Political individualism holds that social policies and state actions are to be judged good or bad only in so far as they serve the desires and purposes of individual members of society. Ontological individualism subscribes to the untenable thesis that the individual exists as independent from any community context and that there is no good over and above individuals that links them to social relations. Epistemological individualism claims that it is possible to know something separate from its relations to other things.

MacCallum (1967) has convincingly argued that negative and positive liberty cannot logically or conceptually be separated and that, as a consequence, any attempt to construe the Cold War, or political differences such as totalitarianism/democracy, in terms of "negative" or "positive" conceptions of the role of the state are misguided. What provides a safeguard against the state is not whether it is structured "negatively" or "positively" but the extent to which discourses of democratic practice are institutionalized.[2] (For a discussion of democratic processes, see Olssen [1996].)

Arguments that communitarianism manifests a theoretical tendency to "totalization", obliterating "individuality" and "identity", swallowed up as if by some Hegelian "Geist", overlook arguments within broadly communitarian or social constructionist frames of thought which argue against "totalization". Both the realist philosopher of science Roy Bhaskar and the French poststructuralist Michael Foucault argue that novelty, creativity, idiosyncrasy, unpredictability and chance are ensured owing to causal complexity, and what realists call "emergence", which operate in "open systems" and militate against the possibility of "closure", or reductionism. For Bhaskar (1978), "open systems" are inevitably characterized by a multiplicity of generative causal mechanisms, and as a result, the achievement of scientific closure, in the sense of "deduction" or "predictability", is impossible. Foucault also argues against the forms of closure dictated by Hegelian conceptions of "totality". For Foucault (1981), the totality always eludes understanding in terms of "necessity", and hence the ability to predict the future course of events, or eradicate or submerge the identity of an individual person or thing is impossible. Rather, the social whole is characterized by incompleteness, indeterminacy, complexity and chance.[3]

Accounts by liberals concerning the origins of totalitarianism, and possible dangers in communitarianism, are also linked to the claim that liberalism is not a substantive political doctrine but rather a neutral discourse which arbitrates impartially between competing versions of the good. According to liberals, doctrines or states that make substantive commitments (to principles such as equality) can only carry such commitments out through the "positive" arm of the state apparatus. This in turn requires "state planning", and arguments by writers like Hayek (1935, p. 24) and Popper (1961, pp. 76–93) oppose any form of state planning on the grounds that it leads inevitably to full-scale totalitarianism.[4] Such arguments must be seen as caricatures. While they correctly recognize communitarianism (including as it does in this context, forms of "ethical liberalism" [Jonathon, 1997] and "perfectionism" [Raz, 1986]) as a substantive political theory which stipulates the preconditions of a social ontology, the implication that liberalism itself does not advocate a particular substantive form of society, but rather simply indicates a preference for individuals to freely plan their own futures, leaving the constitution of society to take care of itself, cannot be sustained as a legitimate mode of reasoning. As Jonathon (1997, p. 184) states, "social arrangements can always be otherwise—but they can never be nowise". The communitarian maintains in other words that society always takes a substantive form, and that the argument by liberals that within its policy formulations it is not implying a particular preferred shape to society, or that it does not advocate the establishment of a "social good" over and above what individuals desire, is quite frankly unacceptable: it cannot rule out substantive commitments about what society should be like. As Martell states:

> [It] all sounds very nice until you realise that what it does, in effect, is to let in just another particular substantive vision of society as consisting of the sum total of individuals' preferences over which individuals have no overall control. In this sense [liberalism] is in fact a highly substantive doctrine—one which posits a competitive individualist society immune to overall democratic direction. (Martell, 1992, p. 156)

The communitarian response to the liberal on this issue, then, is that the liberal cannot be agnostic over the good and its claim to do so is more apparent than real. In other words, liberalism "implicitly" assumes, or relies upon, a hegemonically embodied conception of the good which it then refuses to acknowledge as a real entity, but seeks to reduce it to an aggregate conception of "subjectivist" or "emotivist" states.

A further argument against the liberal's claim of the "irreducibility of conflicting values" is that the theory of the good exists at a sufficiently abstract level to accommodate diversity, and that divergencies and differences, even if incompatible, rest upon factors *exogenous* to such a theory. Important in this regard are arguments that such a conception of the good is compatible with political pluralism, which is to say that it operates within limits broad enough for political differences to be accommodated and for "neutrality" to be guaranteed (Raz, 1986; Brown, 1990).[5]

Another criticism maintains that the communitarian "community" manifests *functionalist* tendencies to reproduce and consolidate whatever the existing practices and values of a community happen to be. While functionalism is certainly a problem amongst conservative forms of communitarianism, it is a problem that Habermas has sought to address head on. It also marks a further important difference between Habermas and Rawls. Whereas Rawls and the "conservative" communitarians see the processes of communication and deliberation as consolidating existing practices and values of a community, in Kymlicka's phrase, of "promoting people's embeddedness in existing practices" (Kymlicka, 1992, p. 176), Habermas recognizes the "emancipatory" interest people have in escaping from ideological conceptions and oppressive structures. For Habermas, political deliberation is required "precisely because in its absence people will tend to accept existing practices and givens and thereby promote the false needs and false consciousness which accompany these historical practices" (ibid.; also see Habermas, 1979, pp. 198–199)

Finally, as I have noted above, communitarianism does not entail abandoning commitments to individual rights, democratic practice or personal autonomy. What it disavows is the "thin" conception of (market) freedom entailed in the negatively construed conception of Lockean rights which has dominated liberal thought since the 17th century. Conceptions of rights as advocated, for instance, by Steven Heyman (1992) based on what he argues is a correct reading of the "classical conception", incorporating both negative and positive moments, and which locate rights and autonomy in relation to a social and legal context, constitute conceptions that most communitarians could agree to.[6]

Thus, as well as arguing for a view of the "embodied self", and of the necessity of substantive theory, democratic communitarians maintain that human beings can only make meaningful choices (and therefore exercise freedom) against a background context of alternatives constituted in a community. Individual autonomy to choose as well as individual rights presuppose in this sense the existence of structures that are institutionally embodied. As a consequence communitarians stress protecting the rights of individuals in relation to institutionally embodied democratic practices which mediate relations to the community good. It is such democratic practices that most effectively put controls upon the state.

On this basis contemporary communitarians are as much concerned with liberty and autonomy as are liberals. The crucial difference is in what liberty really involves and how it can best be provided for. The communitarian would argue that if freedom is an ultimate value then it must be safeguarded by collective action to provide necessary goods for *all* members of a community. As Raz (1986, p. 207) states, for instance "the provision of many collective goods is constitutive of the very possibility of autonomy. ... [I]f autonomy is an ultimate value, then it affects wide-ranging aspects of social practices and institutions". This is to say, in effect, that communitarians recognize that many private goods such as freedom depend for their effective realization upon state provision and institutional support. The communitarian would not believe that worthwhile social opportunities would emerge simply as a result of market exchanges, or that free market exchanges, by themselves, will produce a liberty worthy of the name for *all* of the citizens of a society.

9 Communitarianism and School Choice

In relation to education, democratic communitarians hold that the extent to which systems of choice operate must ensure the provision of resources and opportunities are equally available to, and are of equal value for, *all* citizens. "Choice" of the sort that the market liberal advocates tends to exacerbate inequality, undermine community integration and promote sectarian divisions in terms of class (wealth), race and creed. Not only does it promote some private interests at the expense of others, but given the competitive context within which it operates, it insulates community subgroups from communicating with those who hold alternative perspectives. Hence on this basis democratic communitarians would argue against the interest group politics of choice advocates like Chubb and Moe. Rather, they are oriented to schooling as a mechanism for promoting shared goals for their children and more generally their community. In this context, they emphasize the need for public debate, inclusive community forums, and a more expansive relationship between the school and the community. Michael Walzer (1983), for instance, places emphasis on these issues and argues that children need protecting by the state against their parents. On this basis, choice plans, if pushed very far, undermine the process of democratic deliberation by permitting the wealthy to ignore the less-well-off members of the community, thereby inadequately representing the diverse populations which make it up.

In Dewey's communitarian view, the two central traits of a democratic community are (1) the existence of shared interests between members of groups in

common and (2) interaction with other groups (Dewey, 1916, p. 100). These two criteria generate two questions:
1. How numerous and varied are the interests which are consciously shared?
2. How full and free is the interplay with other forms of association? (Dewey, 1916, p. 100, cited in Kahne, 1996, pp. 105–106)

In relation to Dewey's questions, Joseph Kahne asks two further questions concerning their implication for educational policy:
1. Will school choice proposals constrain or promote interaction among students of varied communities?
2. Will school choice proposals increase or decrease the number of interests students consciously share? (Kahne, 1996, p. 106)

From Dewey's point of view, says Kahne (ibid.), choice proposals would be seen to *constrain* interaction among different groups and *decrease* the number of interests students consciously share. Hence the development of private interests exacerbates conflict and undermines the democratic functioning of the community. As Dewey puts it:

> The isolation and exclusiveness of a gang or clique brings its anti-social spirit into relief. But this same spirit is found wherever one group has interests "of its own" which shut it out from full interaction with other groups, so that its prevailing purpose is the protection of what it has got, instead of reorganisation and progress through wider relationships. It marks nations in their isolation from one another, families which seclude their domestic concerns as if they had no connection with larger life; schools when separated from the interests of home and community; the division of rich and poor; learned and unlearned. (Dewey, 1916, p. 99)

Similarly, Dewey argues that families cannot be seen as isolated from the community. Rather, says Dewey:

> [Families enter] intimately into relationships with business groups, with the schools, with all the agencies of culture, as well as with other similar groups, and that it plays a due part in the political organisation and in return receives support from it. In short, there are many interests consciously communicated and shared; and there are varied and free points of contact with other modes of association. (Dewey, 1916, pp. 96–97)

From the perspective of either welfare state liberals or democratic communitarians like Dewey, unregulated choice proposals have several undesirable effects: they protect privilege; they deny all students equal access to education; they deny all students exposure to alternative perspectives; they limit the community's progress as a democratic community, and they undermine the basis of its integration socially and politically. Such views seem supported by Moore and Davenport's research on schools in America where they conclude that "school choice schemes have become a new form of segregation ... based on race, income level and previous school experience" (1990, p. 189). Similarly, Michael Walzer has stated:

> For most children, parental choice almost certainly means less diversity, less tension, less opportunity for personal change than they would find in schools to which they were politically assigned. (Walzer, 1983, p. 219)

In New Zealand research also attests to the negative effects of market policies on issues of community. Wylie (1994) has documented the broad effects of increasing competition under schemes of choice, citing changes in ethnic and socioeconomic composition of schools as well as deterioration in the relations between schools. In her interviews with school principals, Wylie notes:

> Deterioration in the school's relationship with other local schools since the start of *Tomorrow's schools* reforms was more likely to be reported by principals at those schools whose socio-economic composition had altered, and whose own school promotion had been affected by other local schools' actions. (Wylie, 1994, p. 106)

The Smithfield study (Lauder, 1994) also documents the negative social effects of choice proposals. In the first report, it is reported that the abolition of zoning had markedly increased competition and had significantly affected the rolls and composition of the schools. The overall effects of "choice" were to magnify existing trends.

Hence a school at the "bottom of the heap" had almost halved its third-form intake since 1990, while a successful school which served able middle-class students was increasing its roll rapidly. Ultimately, it adopted an enrolment scheme to cap its roll (Lauder, 1994, pp. 50–51).

In an analysis of the Smithfield data, Waslander and Thrupp (1995) concluded that social class factors had impacted directly on school choice, noting the tendency for schools to be chosen for reasons relating directly to the social and ethnic climate of the school.

> In general terms our study has found that the concerns of market critics are justified. The choice to travel out of what was defined as the local

zone prior to 1991 *is* more likely to be made by those from the upper end of each social stratum, irrespective of the ethnic background of the parents. Socio-economic segregation between schools *has* been exacerbated more than would be predicted simply on the basis of residential segregation. (Waslander & Thrupp, 1995, p. 22; emphasis in original)

Liz Gordon's research also documents the effects of class on school choice. It concluded that the status of a neighbourhood was a powerful factor influencing school choice. While poorer parents do not have the same option to shift their children from one school to another more affluent parents do. An implication of this trend, says Gordon, "is that within schools, there will be increasingly homogeneous class groupings, while between schools differences will be enhanced" (1994, p. 15). Similar patterns of segregation operate in respect of ethnicity. The class exclusivity of a school's population is enforced through the adoption of "enrolment schemes" which place limits on numbers, and effectively enable schools to determine which type of pupils they will accept. Hence "because patterns of residence are themselves linked closely to ethnicity, Maori and Pacific Island students tend to be maintained in schools at the lower end of the market hierarchy" (Gordon, 1994, p. 15). The net consequence of this process is that "schools at the bottom of the local market tend to lose pupils to neighbouring schools" (ibid.). The process, in turn, promotes a "spiral of decline" (ibid.):

> As a result of the loss of students, funding is reduced, although the cost of running the schools barely changes. ... Teaching positions are lost, and the number of classes taught and the diversity of subjects declines as a result. ... As social disadvantage becomes concentrated in schools it becomes increasingly more difficult to raise funds through school fees and community fund-raising, while the costs of social disadvantage are increased. ... As Boards of Trustees in poorer schools tend to have fewer qualifications than those in wealthy schools, the decline in roll numbers and associated effects may easily be blamed on poor governance. ... Further, the process of decline causes enormous insecurity among poor schools as the threat of decreasing resources prevents planning for the future. (Ibid., pp. 15–16)

10   Conclusion

The neoliberalism motivating the restructuring of education and social policy over the last 20 years is a "more pure strain" of classical liberalism whose contradictory basis was concealed to some extent due to the partial substantive concessions it made to equality as part and parcel of Keynesian economic management of the economy. This "more pure strain" is justified by neoliberalism on the basis of freedom and "consumer sovereignty". Yet as Jonathon (1997) says, the freedom is "illusory" as the promises it makes cannot be provided for *all*. In fact, within the zero-sum context within which competitive market choice is structured, the "freedom" of few is premised on the "non-freedom" of many. With the ascendancy of neoliberalism the contradictions of the original doctrine became apparent, exposing its hollow claims to neutrality as well as its thin conception of freedom, and its pretence to function free from a conception of the good simply as an overseer of individual preferences and satisfactions. The attempt to reframe educational policy is thus an attempt to expose liberalism as an incoherent and contradictory doctrine feigning neutrality between competing conceptions of the good, while actively tolerating and perpetuating increased inequality. In the last 30 or so years, under the theoretical guidance of the neoliberal theorists, liberalism's horse has bolted, displacing the few substantive commitments it ever made, exposing its own substantive principles for what they really are, and revealing its professors and experts as demagogues of a selfish morality after all.

What the future holds is hard to gauge. Charles Taylor (1991, p. 96) has noted "the hardening of the atomistic outlook". In addition, he says (1985, p. 305), there is a vicious circle of reinforcement between neoliberal policies of privatization as they have been implemented in the Western world in the last quarter of the 20th century, which ensures the unfavourability of communitarian views and at the same time promotes the continued survival of liberal individualism. It is hoped that this article has contributed in some small way to break this circle.

Acknowledgement

This chapter originally appeared as Olssen, M. (1998), Education policy, the cold war and the "liberal–communitarian" debate, *Journal of Education Policy*, *13*(1), 63–89, https://doi.org/10.1080/0268093980130105. Reprinted here, with minor edits, with permission from the publisher.

Notes

1 This is not a complete list. Amongst other might be included Bernard Williams (1985) and John Plamenatz (1954, 1963).
2 Gerald MacCallum, one of Isaiah Berlin's most well-known critics, maintains that liberty is always a triadic relation, under which subject X is free *from* constraint Y *to* do action Z. On this view liberty is always both positive and negative.

3   See Foucault (1981, p. 69). Much of the importance of the poststructuralist concept of "difference" is as a correction to Hegel's emphasis on "totality" and "unity". In sociological terms it reintroduces a pluralist orientation to the polity and avoids the possibility of reductionism while retaining an ontological and epistemological holism and a social constructionist view of the self. If this is acceptable then the communitarian "community" need not manifest tendencies to "unity" or "integration" beyond a minimum level necessary for citizenship and democratic functioning. There is no desired level of integration of human relations beyond this.

4   Defenders of market liberal societies like Hayek (1935, 1944) or Popper (1961) represent all alternatives to such an order as forms of monist communitarianism. For Hayek, state planning was a slippery slope leading to full-scale totalitarianism (Hayek, 1935, p. 24; 1994, chapter 3). As Tomlinson points out, he typically dismisses any midway point between centralized and decentralized planning except "the delegation of planning to organised industries" (Hayek, 1945, cited in Tomlinson, 1990, p. 49). For Popper (1961, pp. 76–93), although concerned more generally with the opposition between liberal individualism and Marxism rather than the technical specifications of the market model, all alternatives to a society based on individual values and exchanges were also represented as forms of authoritarian control or as tending to such control. In terms of policy analysis Popper distinguishes between piecemeal engineers and holists. He also suggests that the persecutions in communist countries were the result of a holist conception of society. This viewpoint is also indicative of how the liberal–communitarian debate featured as part of the "Cold War". While Popper's and Hayek's arguments were directed against socialism or Marxism, it can also be noted that it is through such forms of reasoning that milder forms of democratic socialism and welfare statism have been discredited.

5   First, related closely to the argument that liberalism is inconsistent for denying its own existence as a substantive theory, it also is inconsistent in relation to the role of the state, for if the liberal turned around and looked behind, he/she could in fact "work out" the theory of the "good" that the liberal state promotes. In other words, to say that the state is neutral as regards different conceptions of the good is incoherent! And while the liberal state does endeavour to respect "pluralism" (democratic practices) and "autonomy" (within boundaries) it is also "coercive", for even the liberal state allows autonomy only "within boundaries" (i.e., it excludes crime, paedophilia, certain marriage codes, etc. and imposes "taxation"). Second, Raz's work (1986) has made a substantial contribution here to the communitarian critique of liberalism (in spite of Raz's [peculiar] tendency to call himself a "perfectionist liberal"). Raz argues that the state's commitment to an ideal of the "good life" does not mean it has to coerce people; nor does it mean that amongst the values of the good to which it is committed are not included democratic principles as having "pride of place"; nor does it mean that the state does not respect individual or subgroup autonomy "within boundaries". For Raz (1986, p. 161) the state can be "encouraging" or "facilitating" without being "directive" or "coercive". As he says (ibid.): "Not all perfectionist action is a coercive imposition of a style of life. Much of it could be encouraging and facilitating action of the desired kind, or discouraging undesired modes of behaviour". If this is so, then extending the same line of argument, the state's actions *may* simply be "enabling", and in this sense, may therefore seek neither to encourage nor discourage an individual's behaviour. It may, for instance, "enable" artistic pursuits by assisting with the provision of institutional structures without directing people to take advantage of them. The argument might be clarified and extended to some extent by distinguishing *nondirective* from *directive* state action. "Non-directive" state action is action in support of certain activities without "specifying" or "directing" people to take advantage of them. For example, the state may encourage artistic pursuits, yet nobody is forced to go to

the theatre. Similarly the state may realize that people's need to eat is essential to the good and take action to provide for it, "non-directively", without specifying substantively what and when people actually do eat. The state may, of course, "set boundaries" and encourage certain eating habits (in the interests of good nutrition) as well. The point here, however, is that the failure of the liberal to be precise about *modes of state action*, as well as realizing that a theory of the good is *necessary* to state action, has too readily resulted in the identification of state action in the interests of the good as "coercion", or as "tending towards coercion", or by extension, as "tending towards totalitarianism". Such a theory of totalitarianism is inadequate, however, for all that will protect the state from being "illegitimately" coercive is its commitment to democratic practices and constitutional principles. In other words, the perfectionist state must be committed to democratic principles as essential to the good life, and if it is, then the values Raz likes (which are the values we all like)—"autonomy" and "pluralism"—will be protected. Because for communitarians the ability of individuals to live their lives in accord with different ideals is essential to the good life, then communitarianism is compatible with moral pluralism. This is another way of saying that recognition of the good does not mean the state is restricted to one morally approved style of life and the suppression of all others (as is frequently represented by liberals). State action in terms of the good allows, then, that "there are many morally valuable forms of life which are incompatible with each other" (Raz, 1986, p. 161). The state acts "directively" when it directs or coerces people through sanctions or penalties attached to various forms of behaviour (refusing to pay taxes, paedophilia, etc.) and it is important to see that all states, even the liberal state, act coercively in this sense. For a similar argument that the communitarian theory of the objective good which exists over and above individual desires and preferences is compatible with political pluralism; see Brown (1990).

6   Steven Heyman (1992, p. 83) argues that the classical conception of liberty from the time of Locke through to the middle of the 19th century was "far richer and more complex" than the critics of positive freedom like Isaiah Berlin maintain or than is often represented as being by either its critics or defenders today. Heyman reviews texts such as Blackstone's *Commentaries on the Laws of England*, which defines liberty as "a power of acting as one thinks fit, without any restraint or control unless by the law of nature" and argues convincingly that such a definition contains both a positive and a negative element, and further that such a view reflects a long tradition which can be traced back to classical Roman Law and shared by many in the scholastic tradition whose works influenced modern natural rights theory. Heyman also claims that Locke's definitions of liberty, in *Two Treatises of Government II* (where Locke defines the natural liberty of men as the "*perfect Freedom* to order their Actions, and dispose of their Possessions, and Persons as they think fit, within the bounds of the Law of Nature, without asking leave, or depending upon the Will of any other Man") also contains both a positive and negative element. Similarly with Locke's account of liberty in terms of power given in *An Essay Concerning Human Understanding* (1975), Book II, Chapter XXI; and variously in nearly all conceptions of personal, civil and political liberty in the classical period.

References

Arendt, H. (1958). *The origins of totalitarianism*. Allen & Unwin.
Avineri, S., & de-Shalit, A. (1992). *Communitarianism and individualism*. Oxford University Press.

Barker, E. (1928). *Political thought in England 1848 to 1914* (2nd ed.). Thornton Butterworth.

Bentham, J. (1969). A fragment on government. In M. Mack (Ed.), *A Bentham reader* (pp. 45–72). Pegasus. (Original work published 1776)

Berlin, I. (1969). *Four essays on liberty*. Oxford University Press.

Bhaskar, R. (1978). *A realist theory of science* (2nd ed.). Harvester Press.

Brown, A. (1990). *Modern political philosophy: Theories of the just society*. Penguin.

Chubb, J., & Moe, T. (1990). *Politics, markets and America's schools*. Brookings Institute.

Codd, J. (1993a). Neo-liberal education policy and the ideology of choice. *Educational Philosophy and Theory, 24*(2), 31–48.

Codd, J. (1993b). Equity and choice: The paradox of New Zealand educational reform. *Curriculum Studies, 1*(1), 7590.

Coleman, J., & Hoffer, T. (1987). *Public and private schools: The impact of communities*. Basic Books.

Coleman, J., Hoffer, T., & Kilgore, S. (1982). *High school achievement*. Basic Books.

Coons, J., & Sugarman, S. (1978). *Education by choice: The case for family control*. University of California Press.

Dewey, J. (1916). *Democracy and education*. Macmillan.

Dewey, J. (1954). *The public and its problem*. Swallow Press. (Original work published 1927)

Finnis, J. (1983). *Fundamentals of ethics*. Oxford University Press.

Foucault, M. (1980). Truth and power (C. Gordon, Trans.). In C. Gordon (Ed.), *Power/knowledge: Selected interviews and other writings 1972–1977* (pp. 109–133). Harvester Press.

Foucault, M. (1981). The order of discourse (I. McLeod, Trans.). In R. Young (Ed.), *Untying the text: A post-structuralist reader* (pp. 48–78). Routledge & Kegan Paul.

Frazer, E., & Lacey, N. (1993). *The politics of community: A feminist critique of the liberal–communitarian debate*. Harvester Wheatsheaf.

Friedman, M. (1955). The role of government in education. In R. A. Solo (Ed.), *Economics and public interest* (pp. 123–144). Rutgers University Press.

Friedman, M., & Friedman, R. (1979). *Free to choose*. Avon.

Gasson, N. R., & Rich, P. (1995). *Are ethical disputes between different communities rationally resolvable?* [Paper presentation]. NZARE Conference, Palmerston North, 7–10 December.

Glendon, M. A. (1991). *Rights talk: The impoverishment of political discourse*. Free Press.

Gordon, L. (1994). Is school choice a sustainable policy for New Zealand? A review of recent research findings and a look to the future. In H. Manson (Ed.), *New Zealand Annual Review of Education, Te Arotake a Tau o te Ao o te Matauranga i Aotearoa, 4*, 9–24.

Gutmann, A. (1992). Communitarian critics of liberalism. In S. Avineri & A. de-Shalit (Eds.), *Communitarianism and individualism* (pp. 120–136). Oxford University Press.

Habermas, J. (1971a). *Knowledge and human interests* (J. Shapiro, Trans.). Beacon Press.

Habermas, J. (1971b). *Towards a rational society: Student protest, science and politics* (J. Shapiro, Trans.). Heinemann Educational Books.

Habermas, J. (1979). *Communication and the evolution of society* (T. McCarthy, Trans., and introduction). Beacon Press.

Habermas, J. (1984). *Theory of communicative action, vol. 1: Reason and the rationalisation of society* (T. McCarthy, Trans.). Beacon Press.

Habermas, J. (1987a). *The philosophical discourse of modernity* (F. Lawrence, Trans.). MIT Press.

Habermas, J. (1987b). *Theory of communicative action, vol. 2: System and lifeword: A critique of functionalist reason* (T. McCarthy, Trans.). Beacon Press.

Habermas, J. (1989). *The structural transformation of the public sphere: An enquiry into a category of bourgeois society* (T. Burger, Trans., with the assistance of F. Lawrence). Polity.

Hall, S. (1986). Variants of liberalism. In D. James & S. Hall (Eds.), *Politics and ideology* (pp. 34–69). Open University Press.

Hayek, F. A. (Ed.). (1935). *Collectivist economic planning*. Routledge & Kegan Paul.

Hayek, F. A. (1944). *The road to serfdom*. Routledge & Kegan Paul.

Heyman, S. (1992). Positive and negative liberty. *Chicago-Kent Law Review, 68*(1), 81–98.

Hoffer, E. (1951). *The true believer*. Harper & Row.

Jonathon, R. (1997). *Illusory freedoms: Liberalism, education and the market*. Wiley.

Kahne, J. (1996). *Reframing educational policy: Democracy, community and the individual*. Teachers College Press, Columbia University.

King, D. S. (1987). *The New Right: Politics, markets and citizenship*. Macmillan.

Kymlicka, W. (1992). Liberal individualism and liberal neutrality. In S. Avineri & A. de-Shalit (Eds.), *Communitarianism and individualism* (pp. 165–185). Oxford University Press.

Lauder, H. (1994). *The creation of market connections for education in New Zealand: An empirical analysis of a New Zealand secondary school market 1990–1993*. Ministry of Education.

Lee, S. H. (1992). Was there a concept of rights in Confucian virtue-based morality? *Journal of Chinese Philosophy, 19*, 241–250.

Levin, H. (1987). Education as a public and private good. *Journal of Policy Analysis and Management, 6*(4), 628–641.

Locke, J. (1976). *An essay concerning human understanding* (4th ed.; Peter H. Nidditch, Ed.). Clarendon. (Original work published 1700)

Lukes, S. (1977). *Essays in social theory*. Columbia University Press.

Lukes, S. (1982). Of gods and demons: Habermas and practical reason. In J. B. Thompson & D. Held (Eds.), *Habermas: Critical debates* (pp. 213–232). Macmillan.

MacCallum, G. G. (1967). Negative and positive liberty. *Philosophical Review, 70*, 312–334.

MacIntyre, A. (1992). Justice as a virtue: Changing conceptions. In S. Avineri & A. de-Shalit (Eds.), *Communitarianism and individualism* (pp. 51–64). Oxford University Press.

Macpherson, C. B. (1962). *The political theory of possessive individualism.* Clarendon Press.

Manin, B. (1994). On legitimacy and political deliberation. In M. Lilla (Ed.), *New French thought: Political philosophy* (pp. 186–200). Princeton University Press.

Marshall, J. (1995). Skills, information and quality for the autonomous chooser. In M. Olssen & K. Morris Matthews (Eds.), *Education, democracy and reform* (pp. 44–59). New Zealand Association for Research in Education (NZARE)/Research Unit for Maori Education (RUME), University of Auckland.

Martell, L. (1992). New ideas of socialism. *Economy and Society, 21*(2), 151–172.

McCloskey, R. G. (1951). *American conservatism in the age of enterprise.* Harper & Row.

Miller, R. (1989). Marx and Aristotle: A kind of consequentialism. In A. Callinicos (Ed.), *Marxist theory* (pp. 323–352). Oxford University Press.

Moore, D., & Davenport, S. (1990). Choice: The new improved sorting machine. In W. L. Boyd & H. J. Walberg (Eds.), *Choice in education: Potential and problems* (pp. 187–223). McCutchan.

Mulhall, S., & Swift, A. (1992). *Liberals and communitarians.* Blackwell.

Noddings, N. (1996). On community. *Educational Theory, 46*(3), 245–267.

Nozick, R. (1975). *Anarchy, state, and utopia.* Blackwell.

Olssen, M. (1996). In defence of the welfare state and publicly provided education: A New Zealand perspective. *Journal of Education Policy, 11*(3), 337–362. https://doi.org/10.1080/0268093960110305

Peters, M., & Marshall, J. (1990). Education, the New Right and the crisis of the welfare state in New Zealand. *Discourse, 11*(1), 77–90.

Plamenatz, J. (1954). *Marxism and Russian communism.* Longmans.

Plamenatz, J. (1963). *Man and society: A critical examination of some important social and political theories from Machiavelli to Marx* (2 Vols.). Longmans.

Popper, K. R. (1945). *The open society and its enemies.* Routledge.

Popper, K. R. (1961). *The poverty of historicism.* Routledge.

Purkey, S., & Smith, M. (1983). Effective schools: A review. *Elementary School Journal, 83*(4), 427–452.

Rawls, J. (1971). *A theory of justice.* Harvard University Press.

Rawls, J. (1975). Fairness to goodness. *Philosophical Review, 84,* 536–554.

Rawls, J. (1980). Kantian constructivism in moral theory. *Journal of Philosophy, 77*(9), 515–572.

Rawls, J. (1985). Justice as fairness: Political not metaphysical. *Philosophy and Public Affairs, 14*(3), 223–251.

Rawls, J. (1987). The idea of an overlapping consensus. *Oxford Journal of Legal Studies, 7*(1), 1–25.

Rawls, J. (1988). The priority of the right and ideas of the good. *Philosophy and Public Affairs, 17*(4), 251–276.

Raz, J. (1986). *The morality of freedom*. Clarendon Press.

Russell, B. (1961). *A history of Western philosophy*. Allen & Unwin.

Sandel, M. (1982). *Liberalism and the limits of justice*. Cambridge University Press.

Selznick, P. (1992). *The moral commonwealth*. University of California Press.

Shapiro, I. (1986). *The evolution of rights in liberal theory*. Cambridge University Press.

Spivak, G. C. (1987). *In other worlds: Essays in cultural politics*. Methuen.

Spivak, G. C. (1988). Can the subaltern speak? In C. Nelson & L. Grossberg (Eds.), *Marxism and the Interpretation of Culture* (pp. 271–313). University of Illinois Press.

Spivak, G. C. (1989). Three women's texts and a critique of imperialism. In C. Moore & J. Moore (Eds.), *The feminist reader: Essays in gender and the politics of literary criticism* (pp. 175–195). Macmillan.

Talmon, J. L. (1955). *The origins of totalitarian democracy*. Secker & Warburg.

Taskforce to Review Education Administration. (1988). *Picot report: Administering for excellence*. Government Printer.

Taylor, C. (1985). *Philosophy and the human sciences: Philosophical papers 2*. Cambridge University Press.

Taylor, C. (1989). Cross-purposes: The liberal–communitarian debate. In N. Rosenblum (Ed.), *Liberalism and the moral life* (pp. 159–182). Harvard University Press.

Taylor, C. (1990). *Sources of the self*. Cambridge University Press.

Taylor, C. (1991). *The malaise of modernity*. Anansi Press.

Tomlinson, J. (1990). Market socialism: A basis for socialist renewal? In B. Hindess (Ed.), *Reactions to the Right* (pp. 32–49). Croom Helm.

Treasury, The. (1987). *Government management* (Vol. 2). Government Printer.

Waslander, S., & Thrupp, M. (1995). Choice competition and segregation: An empirical analysis of secondary school markets 1990–1993. *Journal of Education Policy, 10*(1), 1–26.

Waldron, J. (1992). Minority cultures and the cosmopolitan alternative. *University of Michigan Journal of Law Reform, 25*(3 & 4), 751–795.

Walzer, M. (1981). Philosophy and democracy. *Political Theory, 9*(3), 379–399.

Walzer, M. (1983). *Spheres of justice*. Basic Books.

Walzer, M. (1990). The communitarian critique of liberalism. *Political theory, 18*(1), 6–23.

Williams, B. (1972). *Morality*. Cambridge University Press.

Williams, B. (1985). *Ethics and the limits of philosophy*. Fontana.

Wylie, C. (1994). *Self-managing schools in New Zealand: The fifth year*. New Zealand Council for Educational Research.

CHAPTER 9

Social Democracy, Complexity and Education

Perspectives from the Writings of John Atkinson Hobson and John Maynard Keynes

Abstract

In the second half of the 19th century, in the period after John Stuart Mill, and into and including the first third of the 20th century, a group of philosophers, sociologists, economists and journalists systematically adapted classical liberal arguments to make them relevant to the appalling social conditions generated by the development of capitalism in the 18th and 19th centuries. Their writings contained distinctive models of society, of human nature, and of change that are relevant to sociologists studying education in the 21st century. My aim throughout this paper will be to work through the arguments of the new liberals accepting those that meet the tests of a critical interrogation as being relevant to 21st-century global capitalism and adapting or rejecting them as is appropriate. Although some of their arguments will be found wanting, I will argue that their original ideas in defence of social democracy can be restated in terms of developments in science and philosophy over a century since they wrote. Developments in post-quantum complexity theory, within both the physical and social sciences, will enable us to re-ground social democratic arguments and state them in a more plausible way for the 21st century.

1   The Philosophy of John Atkinson Hobson

In the last decades of the 19th and the first decade of the 20th century the economist John Atkinson Hobson advanced a justification for the welfare state complementing the contributions of T. H. Green and L. T. Hobhouse. In a way similar to Hobhouse's "harmonic principle", Hobson's analysis of individual and society was facilitated methodologically by the organic model of social structure. The organic model was analogical in that it likened society to a "social organism". In utilising such an analogy Hobson invoked comparisons with Hegel and German idealism which created alarm amongst classical liberals. In developing his conception of the organic view, Hobson was influenced by John S. Mackenzie, whose book *An Introduction to Social Philosophy* (2006), originally published in 1890, developed a coherent conception of the organic to challenge both the monadistic view (of classical liberalism and Leibniz) and the monistic view, which asserted the priority of the whole over the parts (idealism). The organic view sees the individual as determined by social conditions. In this sense, the relation of individual to society is an "intrinsic one" (p. 150). Society is not a mere aggregate of separate individuals, nor is it a mechanist (dualist) or chemical combination of them. The evidence that it is not a monistic system is that if that were the case, as society changed, so the parts would change almost simultaneously. This is not to say that there is not an aspect of the monadic, and an aspect of the monistic, which operate at different times and places, in different contexts, for there are mixed modes; just as complexity does not completely displace mechanism, but rather should be seen as supplementing or extending it. Further, although we are all penetrated and constituted by our surroundings this does not mean that we are all the same. As Mackenzie put it, there is no contradiction between social determinism and the independence of the individual:

> That there is no contradiction between the independence which is now claimed for the individual and the fact of his social determination, becomes evident when we consider the nature of that determination and of that independence. That the individual is determined by his society, means merely that his life is an expression of the general spirit of the social atmosphere in which he lives. And that the individual is independent, means merely that the spirit which finds expression in him is a living force that may develop by degrees into something different. (1890/2006, p. 158)

Hobson's use of the organic metaphor is compatible with Mackenzie's and like Mackenzie's it has received stringent criticism. As R. N. Berki (1981, pp. 193–194) notes, Hobson was frequently characterised as an idealist and his idealism was "born of the endeavour to comprehend political reality in *unitary* terms". Although Hobson claimed to reject the monistic doctrine of idealism, in that he rejected prioritising the force of the whole over the parts, he was idealist in the weaker sense that he still saw society as a unified whole. Such a whole in his sense was merely a system of interactions and unity was represented as not incompatible with difference. Besides, Hobson did not see unity itself of value, but recognised specific normative criteria drawing on Ruskin's concept of *life* as determining the conditions for inclusion and exclusion from the whole. The common good is thus represented by Hobson as a unified development of the whole society which contrasts from those aspects which are dysfunctional, evil, or represent what he termed, following Ruskin, *illth*. This is the sense that David Long detects idealism in Hobson's approach for he "idealistically condemned present arrangements for failing to come up to the standards of his rational ideal" (1996, p. 16).

Although not problem-free, Long concludes that "the organic analogy remains a useful start for a holistic analysis of society and Hobson's use of the analogy was certainly progressive for his time" (1996, p. 16). One must not expect too much from an analogical method, of course. It must be seen, as is true for all analogies, as comprising both likenesses and unlikenesses. Human societies are in some ways like living things but in others not. For classical liberals, the analogy does not do justice to the issue of the claimed independence of individual consciousness. One can also criticise the analogical weighting given to uneven influence of the central organs over other parts of the body. Yet, in that it differentiates a particular form of unity from those types characteristic of monism, monadism, chemical integration, or mechanical solidarity, it presents a certain viability even given its analogical limitations.

One possible sense that the organic model can be criticised was its implications for conservativism. Although Hobson wrote against the politics of conservativism, John Allett (1990, p. 74) argues that "there is a significant conservative aspect to Hobson's thought". In Allett's view, "Hobson's conservativism is centred in his sociology" (p. 76). As he puts it:

> Hobson's interest in conservativism is limited primarily to its usefulness as a corrective (not an alternative) to liberal individualism. There are occasions, however, when he engages in a kind of high moralizing about supra-individual forces of restraint that threatens to propel him beyond liberalism and its ultimate commitment to the self-directing personality.

The entailment of conservatism cannot simply derive from the axiom of interdependence, or from the recognition of society as structure separate from its parts but must reside in privileging unity or harmony above what is normatively required by life. While Hobson would have disputed any such charge, appealing to the independent normativity of his notions of *life* and *illth*, it may be that the model of organicism exerts, as Allett sees it, an independent pressure for unity and the status quo at the expense of justice or equality implied by a model of democratic socialism.

2 Complexity Theories

To the extent that the organic analogy coerces undue support for unity, I want to suggest that complexity theory can offer a more nuanced model in order to theorise the relations between individuals and social structures, as well as to theorise conception of causality, change, or evolution, creativity, originality, agency, and much else besides. Indeed, I will claim, it provides a revised model for social science, and especially for educational research. Although Hobson recognised certain complexity formulations, in most senses the organic analogy still conforms to the prevailing notions of Enlightenment science in its focus on closed, deterministic and integrable systems. In contrast, complexity theory represents a shift from matter-based to an energy-based physics, and offers a non-reductionist conception of the relationship between parts and whole which stresses the open nature of systems and where difference and unity are paired in a new and novel manner.

Complexity theories thus provide better models which enable an avoidance of conservative priority on unity or the status quo, do not prioritise the whole over the parts, or the spiritual over the material, and are compatible with recent post-quantum traditions in science as they have developed in the 20th century. Although having roots in ancient Chinese and Greek thought, versions of complexity theory are a relatively new field of scientific enquiry, and are perhaps one of the most notable new developments since the advent of quantum theory in the early 1900s. Such theories are not only compatible with materialism, but are systemic, or holist, in that they account for diversity and unity in the context of a systemic field of complex interactional changes.

In his book *Complexity and Postmodernism*, Paul Cilliers (1998, p. VIII) defines complexity in the following way:

> In a complex system ... the interaction constituents of the system, and the interaction between the system and its environment, are of such a nature that the system as a whole cannot be fully understood simply by analysing its components. Moreover, these relationships are not fixed, but shift and change, often as a result of self-organisation. This can result in novel features, usually referred to in terms of emergent properties. The brain, natural language and social systems are complex.

Cilliers presents a useful contemporary summary and update of complexity research. Complex systems interact dynamically in a non-linear and asymmetrical manner. Interactions take place in open systems through "self-organisation" by adapting dynamically to changes in both the environment and the system. Self-organisation is an *emergent* property of the system as a whole. An emergent property is a property that is constituted due to the combination of elements in the system as a whole. As such it is a property possessed by the system but not by its components.[1] Cilliers (1998, p. 90) defines "self-organisation" as "the capacity of complex systems which enables them to develop or change internal structure spontaneously and adaptively in order to cope with or manipulate the environment". Such systems are not in equilibrium because they are constantly changing as a consequence of interaction between system and environment, and as well as being influenced by external factors are influenced by the history of the system (1998, p. 66). Cilliers identifies social systems, the economy, the human brain, and language as complex systems.[2]

In the recent history of science, the work of Ilya Prigogine (1980, 1984, 1989, 1994, 1997, 2003) has advanced the field of post-quantum complexity analysis at the macroscopic and microscopic levels, based in non-equilibrium physics, linked to the significant work of the Solvay Institutes for Physics and Chemistry. Prigogine received a Nobel Prize in 1977. Like Nietzsche and others before him, he translated the effects of a theory of becoming, based on an Heraclitean idea of ceaseless change, providing a post-quantum understanding of the universe in terms of dimensions of chance, self-organisation, unpredictability, uncertainty, chaos, non-equilibrium systems, bifurcation and change. Prigogine's central contribution was to non-equilibrium statistical mechanics and thermodynamics and the probabilistic analysis of dissipative structures (2003, pp. 45, 82). His main ideas (expressed non-mathematically) were that "nature leads to unexpected complexity" (2003, p. 8); that "self-organization appears in nature far from equilibrium" (p. VII); that "the universe is evolving" (p. 9); that the messages of Parmenides (that nothing changes) must be replaced by those of Heraclitus (that everything always changes) (pp. 9, 56); that "time is our existential dimension" (p. 9); that "the direction of time is the most fundamental property of the universe" (p. 64); that nothing is predetermined (p. 9); that non-equilibrium, time-irreversibility, feedback, non-integration, and bifurcation are features of all systems, including evolution, which is to say that our universe is full of non-linear, irreversible non-determined processes (p. 59); that life creates evolution (pp. 61, 65), and that everything is historical (p. 64).[3] Writing over the same period as Michel Foucault,[4] he was concerned to analyse *irreversible processes* that generate successively higher levels of organisational complexity, where the complex phenomena are not reducible to the initial states from which they emerged. His work has been especially important for understanding changes within open systems,[5] for theorising time as a real dimension,[6] and for theorising interconnectedness as a "characteristic feature of nature" (2003, p. 54).[7] Of especial relevance, his work theorises the possibilities of chance as the outcome of system contingencies.[8]

Prigogine speaks highly about Henri Bergson. Although in his famous debate with Einstein, Bergson clearly misunderstood relativity theory, he was right about the issue of time, says Prigogine (2003, p. 61). For Bergson, time was a real dimension, and contrary to classical views, saw it as irreversible: "We do not *think* real time. But we *live* it, because *life* transcends intellect" (p. 46). The irreversibility of time dictates the impossibility of turning back, as well as the irreversibility of decisions and actions. The broader view is one of life and the universe as changing where time means creation and elaboration of novel and original patterns. It enables an understanding of how each individual is shaped by her society and yet unique. In such a conception where duration represents the real dimension of time:

> consciousness cannot go through the same state twice. The circumstances may still be the same, but they will act no longer on the same person, since they find him at a new moment in his history. Our personality, which is being built up each instant with its accumulated experience, changes without ceasing. By changing, it prevents any state, although superficially identical with another, from ever repeating it in its very depth. That is why our duration is irreversible. (1998, pp. 5–6)

New actions will take place at new times. Life changes constantly and new states are never precisely repeated in identical form. In drawing from Bergson, Prigogine (2003, p. 20) notes how such a thermodynamic vision once again makes individual agency pivotal. Independence develops not apart from the system, but in and through the system.

Such a complex analysis which retains a conception of individual agency within system parameters was also centrally important for Hobson. In order to give his theory normative anchorage, though, Hobson utilises a philosophy of life. It was certainly Hobson's normative vision to promote enhanced well-being and human welfare as central. In accord with life philosophy, it was Ruskin who gave Hobson his concept of social welfare. This involved redefining the concept of wealth a way from a concern with exchange, to a concern with its intrinsic worth, or as Allett (1981, p. 18) puts it, for its "life sustaining properties". In representing individuals as social beings, Hobson echoed the insights of Mackenzie, who had written that "[i]t is only through the development of the whole human race that any one man can develop" (Mackenzie, 1890/2006, p. 180). This is a crucial theoretical axiom from the standpoint of educational analysis for it formulates the social democratic idea that it is the way we organise the society at large and its institutional structures that is so crucial for the development of each and every person. In such a view, the entire social democratic structure of society is a prerequisite for the application of liberal principles, for uneven development and social inequality negate the significance of liberal ideals such as freedom.

It was the inadequacy of representing individuals as solitary atoms that Hobson derived the central importance of social and institutional organisation. What frequently went unacknowledged was the assistance which individuals utilised in achieving their plans. To embark on a business initiative, for instance, presupposes sufficient acumen, skills, knowledge, resources, capital, and infrastructures, which presuppose their availability in institutional form. Production thus has a "social element" underpinning it. So, too, does individual development, for each human being could only develop with various familial, educational, and community assistance. Once one acknowledges this, one sees that the development of adequate social structures is a *prerequisite* for individual development.

Progress for Hobson was concerned with enhancing well-being, which exalted human welfare as the end or good to be sought after. For Hobson, welfare was a necessary social good. It is through his focus on welfare that he develops his economic philosophy concerned to develop the well-being of all of the international community and all humanity. Work was the medium through which individuals and societies would invest creative energy for production and progress. It was work that generated "the power to sustain life".[9]

Hobson recognised that society was more than the separate individuals who comprised it and that classical liberalism could not adequately theorise the organic relations of individuals within society. It was based on such a view that he advanced his theory of surplus.[10] He theorised surplus as arising through organised cooperation which was essential to social and economic production. It is through cooperation that individuals produce more than is possible simply as a function of each individual contribution.[11] Cooperation is thus a productive power in Hobson's theory, both productivity and well-being being increased by it.

3   Hobson and Keynes

It was from his theory of cooperation that Hobson developed his theory of underconsumption which has been his chief contribution to economic theory and was to have a major influence on Keynes. In his classic book co-authored with A. F. Mummery, *The Industrial System*, underconsumption is represented as the manifestation of dysfunctional economic development which distorts the system of the distribution of wealth and income by creating waste and inequality. Capitalism inherently supports a system of distorted development. The very process by which unproductive surplus was obtained, by business cunning and other strategies of deception, meant that the overall distribution and investment lacked any correlation with what the future of humanity required. Hobson proposed that a rational law of distribution would be in accord with human needs and capacities, thus affirming an affinity with democratic socialism of a distinctively social democratic variety.

Underconsumption was a surplus of production and too little consumption. It was an economy with not enough spending. In Hobson's view, underconsumption results from three principal causes: overproduction, over-saving, and unequal distribution of surplus. It was the over-savings aspect that Keynes responded to. For Keynes, Hobson failed to distinguish *savings* from *investment*. In Keynes's theory, it was the distinction between savings and investment that became central to his break from neoclassical economics. Too much saving in his view resulted in too little investment, and hence the classical adage concerning the virtues of thrift were incorrect from the point of view of benefit to the community. It was for this reason the Keynes favoured public spending and government direction of investment to restore demand in aggregate spending, whereas Hobson advocated a more moral and political argument against unregulated capitalism.

Keynes can, in this sense, be seen as part of a tradition of social democratic thinking which developed from the 1870s to the 1930s. In his later life he acknowledged great respect for Hobson's influence. His great contribution to social democracy was his appreciation of complexity dynamics as effecting outcomes which rendered traditional neoclassical conceptions of equilibrium effectively redundant. In this sense, he took Hobson's organic analogy and rendered it more fittingly as a complexity model.

His conception of uncertainty was not seen as something which could be overcome, or which only operated in certain situations, but arose as a consequence of the complexity created by real time. Because individuals' actions in time created unique patterns it was theoretically impossible to predict or foretell future events. As he states:

> We have, as a rule, only the vaguest idea of any but the most direct consequences of our acts. ... Thus the fact that our knowledge of the future is fluctuating, vague and uncertain, renders wealth a peculiarly unsuitable topic for the methods of classical economic theory. ... [A]bout these matters there is no scientific basis on which to form any calculable probability whatsoever. We simply do not know. (Keynes, 1937, pp. 213–214)

Keynes proposed in *The General Theory* (1953, p. 152) that in such a situation the only recourse is reliance on rules or conventions as to how the economy ought to work in order to produce stability through institutional coordination.

He thus incorporates post-quantum complexity themes *avant la lettre*. This is especially important in relation to his conception of real time, which underpins his views on ignorance, uncertainty, and human agency. His conception of real time replaces the traditional Newtonian conception, which characterised neoclassical economics as well as standard models of science. As O'Driscoll and Rizzo (1985) explain it, Newtonian time is spatialised, represented as a succession of points (continuous time), or line segments (discrete time) (p. 53), and is characterised by homogeneity, mathematical continuity and causal inertness (p. 54). For Bergson (1998, p. 338), change, or succession, is not real in the Newtonian theory. When it is conceived as a real additive dimension, no matter how much action reproduces the patterns of the past, any future actions will be unique for the context of repetition will always vary.

It is this reconfiguration of time through the recognition of complexity that results in the emphasis on uncertainty in Keynes's work. Uncertainty also incorporates novelty, non-repeatability, and unpredictability, and also entails indeterminism in decisions. It thus asserts a thesis of creative human agency and imperfect foresight and knowledge. While creative decision-making is possible, it is in relation to a world that is not only unknown but unknowable. Hence the importance of ignorance means: "[t]he (perceived) unlistability of all possible outcomes" (O'Driscoll & Rizzo, 1985, p. 62). For Keynes, institutions while not eliminating uncertainty, attempt to control it. To see Keynes as a complexity management theorist broadens the scope and relevance of his insights from economics to politics, and from politics to education. For all institutions play a crucial role in sustaining life and achieving equilibrium of forces.

4   Complexity and Education

Keynes arguments for the economy regarding uncertainty, risk, and ignorance, as the outcome of complex determinations are applicable outside of the economy narrowly defined, and can be seen to apply to other areas: welfare, various forms of assistance for disability and critical need; matters of urgency or crisis (floods, tornados, tsunamis, hurricanes, etc.); health, or education or training.

In this quest for complexity reduction education is a central institution, as was recognised by John Dewey, who explored the role and function of education in adapting to and coping with uncertainty in the environment. For Dewey, education was conceptualised not as a discipline-based mode of instruction in "the basics" but according to an interdisciplinary, discovery-based curricula defined according to problems in the existing environment. As Dewey says in *Experience and Nature*, "The world must actually be such as to generate ignorance and inquiry: doubt and hypothesis, trial and temporal conclusions" (1929, p. 41). The rules of living and habits of mind represent a "quest for certainty" in an unpredictable, uncertain and dangerous world (p. 41). For Dewey, the ability to organise experience proceeded functionally in terms of problems encountered, which needed to be overcome in order to construct and navigate a future. In terms of learning theory, Dewey used the concept of "continuity" in order to theorise the link between existing experience and the future based upon the "interdependence of all organic structures and processes with one another" (1929, p. 295). Learning for Dewey thus represented a cooperative and collaborative activity centred upon experiential, creative responses to contingent sets of relations to cope with uncertainty. As such, Dewey's approach conceptualises part and whole in a dynamic interaction, posits the learner as interdependent with the environment, as always in a state of becoming, giving rise to a dynamic and forward-looking notion of agency as experiential and collaborative. In such a model learning is situational in the sense of always being concerned with contingent and unique events in time.

Central to such a complexity approach, in that learning must deal with the uncertainty of contingently assembled actions and states of affairs, and by so doing it transforms itself from an undertaking by discrete individuals into one that is shared and collective activity. In terms of navigating a future in relation to economics, politics, or social decisions, it places the educational emphasis upon the arts of coordination. It is through plan or pattern coordination that institutions function and that a future is embarked upon. Because in planning one must assume incomplete information due to the dispersal of knowledge across social systems, such coordination can be more or less exact or loosely stochastic and probabilistic in terms of overcoming uncertainty. Because learning is time-dependent, and individuals and communities are always experiencing unique features of their worlds, uncertainty cannot be eliminated. Hence, all that is possible is pattern coordination in open-ended systems, where planning is formed around "typical" rather than "actual" features. Such plan or pattern coordination can only be a constructed order. Constructing plans becomes the agenda for education for life in Dewey's sense. Dewey ultimately held to the faith, as Keynes did, that despite unpredictability and uncertainty, the macro-societal (or macro-economic) coordination of core social problems was possible.

Such a complexity approach is also pertinent for new research in the sociology of education for such approaches can contribute to the study of non-linear dynamics in order to better understand schooling. Rather than view the social system in the image of traditional social science, inspired by Newtonian mechanics, as a linear system of predictable interactions, the approach of both

Hobson and Keynes highlights the emergent character of social systems as self-organising non-linear and evolving systems characterised by uncertainty and unpredictability and emphasising both determinism and chance in the nature of events. What characterises an emergent phenomena is that it cannot be characterised reductively solely in terms of an aggregative product of the entities or parts of a system, understood through linear mechanistic causal analysis, in terms of the already known behaviours and natures of the parts, which are themselves ontologically represented as constants, but must be seen non-reductively in relation to their contingent self-organisation in terms of non-linear dynamics as well as a theory of real time and of emergent phenomena. Schooling in such a view is characterised as a dynamic system whose states change with time through iteration, non-linearity and self-organisation. Such an approach does not displace traditional mechanistic linear analyses such as those that assert correlations between social class and educational attainment but supplement them. It enables a more nuanced consideration of their variabilities. For the sociology of education this has the advantage of forging a new reconciliation of the micro–macro issues, enabling a theory of social life where levels of analysis between individual and group, as well as determinism and human agency, can be more accurately assessed. Its mission becomes that of describing and explaining the complexity of systems and their changes, starting from a conception of the whole, while avoiding an exclusive emphasis on atoms or sensations which characterised the old Newtonian paradigm. It offers the scope of supplementing linear mathematical analyses with non-linear mathematical or qualitative analyses for addressing issues of future concern. Theoretically, too, it enables a new approach to the modelling of social systems where the parts of a system interact, combine and modify or change in novel and unpredictable ways, and where the parts themselves may change in the process. In this, it enables us to better understand the role of individuals and of human agency in relation to systems, institutions, and cultural patterns; how decisions of the will may introduce into the course of events a new, unexpected and changeable force; how the moral qualities of individuals can alter the course of history; and why, as some older sociological and philosophical approaches tended to maintain, such phenomena as the qualities of individuals, or actions in life, cannot be explained solely by general sociological laws of development, social class attributes, or cultural patterns. Although individuals are constituted by external social forces, given that time and space individuate those forces, the products of social evolution are inevitably unique and, in addition, through the exercise of imagination, choice operates to forge a conception of freedom quite compatible with the social production of selves. Such an account thus makes possible more historical forms of method where contingency (both dependent causality, mutability, and uncertainty), as well as novelty, free choice, creativity, and unpredictability become integral elements of the research approach and where top-down forms of deductive reasoning must be balanced by bottom-up analyses of individual or group agency and social interaction.

Finally, to conclude, we can also note that contemporary sociological approaches, such as that of Michel Foucault, contain complexity accounts of change of relevance for extending work in the sociology of education. Foucault's notion of *dispositif*, or *apparatus*, as a "strategic assemblage" enables a conceptualisation of the school within a new pluralist reconciliation of part and whole simultaneously balancing the poles, as he calls them, of "individualisation" and "totalisation". For Foucault, the *dispositif* is defined as "a resolutely heterogeneous grouping comprising discourses, institutions, architectural arrangements, policy decisions, laws, administrative measures, scientific statements, philosophic, moral and philanthropic propositions, in sum, the 'said' and the 'not-said', these are elements of apparatus. The apparatus is itself the network that can be established between these elements" (Foucault, 1980, p. 194). In this conception, Foucault makes it clear that the apparatus permits a duality of articulation between discourse and material forms which varies contingently and operates in non-linear ways resisting linear, mechanical, causal explanations of the traditional Newtonian sort. It is in this sense that every form is a contingently expressed compound of relations between forces. Such multiple articulations are indeed essential to his idea of how an entity or construct constitutes its being in time, as well as to his conception of historical change, as well as to his conception of *strategy* as a non-subjective intentionality; that is, as an order that cannot be reduced to a single strategist, or underlying cause or actor, but which nevertheless has intelligibility at the level of the society or institutions that emerges from an assemblage of heterogeneous elements, operating contingently and unpredictably within time and space. For Foucault, phenomena like sexuality, security and normalisation constitute such strategic assemblages. In such a model, as for Dewey, the school functions as a stabilising mechanism which reduces or manages complexity, constituting it as a variably and contingently constituted disciplinary strategy within life itself. Issues such as "early school leaving", "employability", or "the curricula" define the school as such a stabilising institution concerned to adapt education to labour market requirements and citizens to society. In such a model the school is an institution that enables the navigation of an uncertain future.

Acknowledgement

This chapter originally appeared as Olssen, M. (2010), Social democracy, complexity and education: Sociological perspectives from welfare liberalism, in M. W. Apple, S. J. Ball, & L. A. Gandin (Eds.), *The Routledge international handbook of the sociology of education* (pp. 79–89), Routledge. Reprinted here, with minor edits, with permission from the publisher.

Notes

1. Other forms of emergentist materialism in Western thought, see Bunge (1977), Haken (1977, 1990), Eve, Horsfall, and Lee (1997).
2. For another view of complexity theory, see Kauffman (1993, and 1995). Kauffman suggests that while events can be seen as having antecedent conditions which explain them, in open environments the possible combinations are unpredictable. Other characteristics of complex systems are that they do not operate near equilibrium; the relationships between components are non-linear and dynamic; elements do not have fixed positions; the relationships between elements are not stable; and there are always more possibilities than can be actualized.
3. Prigogine mostly applies these ideas to physical systems but does sometimes demonstrate their applicability to the social and human world. Discussing his theories of time and irreversibility, he notes how all events (e.g., "a marriage is an irreversible event" (2003, p. 67). The consequence of irreversibility is that "it leads to probabilistic descriptions, which cannot be reduced to individual trajectories or wave functions corresponding to Newtonian or Quantum mechanics" (p. 75).
4. Prigogine's publications date from 1964 until shortly before his death in 2003.
5. This involves a different description at the level of physics of elementary processes and a reversal of classical physics which saw systems as integrable, leading to determinism, and premised on time reversibility and equilibrium (as from Newton to Poincaré). Prigogine's approach replaces classical and Quantum mechanics in a concern for thermodynamics and probability and emphasizes variables such as noise, stochasticity, irreversibility. Such an approach suggests distinct limits to reductionism.
6. In this, he differs from Einstein who saw time as an illusion, as well as from classical mechanics. He acknowledges debts to Bergson (Prigogine, 2003, pp. 19–20); to Heidegger (2003, p. 9), and to Heraclitus (2003, pp. 9, 10).
7. Interconnectedness means that "individualities emerge from the global" and counters the idea that "evolution is independent of environment" (2003, p. 54).
8. Pomian (1990) discusses issues such as determinism and chance in relation to Prigogine's work. Also see Prigogine (1997).
9. Hobson adopted a number of Ruskin's phrases, and this is one of them. (I cite from Long, 1996, p. 18.)
10. Surplus was either productive, through labour and cooperation, or unproductive, through rents, interests, or profit.

11 Hobson gives the example of three persons building a boat to illustrate how through cooperation, each can contribute to something that individually they could not have produced (see Hobson, 1996, pp. 146–147).

References

Allett, J. (1990). The conservative aspect of Hobson's new liberalism. In M. Freeden (Ed.), *Reapraissing J. A. Hobson: Humanism and welfare* (pp. 74–99). Unwin Hyman.

Baier, A. C. (1991). *A progress of sentiments: Reflections on Hume's Treatise*. Harvard University Press.

Bergson, H. (1998). *Creative evolution* (A. Mitchell, Trans.). Dover. (Original work published 1911)

Berki, R. N. (1981). *On political realism*. Dent.

Bunge, M. (1977). Emergence and the mind: Commentary. *Neuroscience, 2*, 501–509.

Cilliers, P. (1998). *Complexity and postmodernism: Understanding complex systems*. Routledge.

Dewey, J. (1929). *Experience and nature*. Dover.

Eve, R. A., Horsfall, S., & Lee, M. E. (1997). *Chaos, complexity and sociology: Myths, models and theories*. Sage.

Foucault, M. (1980). The confession of the flesh (C. Gordon, Trans.). In C. Gordon (Ed.), *Power/knowledge: Selected interviews and other writings 1972–1977* (pp. 194–228). Harvester Press.

Haken, H. (1977). *Synergetics: An introduction*. Springer.

Haken, H. (1990). Synergetics as a tool for the conceptualization and mathematization of cognition and behaviour: How far can we go? In H. Haken & M. Stadler (Eds.), *Synergetics of Cognition* (pp. 2–31). Springer.

Hobson, J. A. (1904). *International trade: An application of economic theory*. Methuen.

Hobson, J. A. (1996). *The social problem*. Thoemmes Press. (Reprint of the 1902 edition)

Hume, D. (1978). *A Treatise on Human Nature* (2nd ed., P. H. Nidditch, Ed.). Clarendon Press.

Kauffman, S. A. (1993). *The origins of order: Self-organisation and selection in evolution*. Oxford University Press.

Kauffman, S. A. (1995). *At home in the universe; The search for laws of complexity*. Viking Press.

Keynes, J. M. (1937). The general theory of employment. *Quarterly Journal of Economics, 51*(2).

Keynes, J. M. (1953). *The general theory of employment, interest and money*. Harcourt, Brace, Jovanovich. (Original work published 1936)

Long, D. (1996). *Towards a new liberal internationalism: The international theory of J. A. Hobson*. Cambridge University Press.

Mackenzie, J. S. (2006). *An introduction to social philosophy*. Elibron Classics. (Original work published 1890)

O'Driscoll, G. P., & Rizzo, M. J. (1985). *The economics of time and ignorance*. Basil Blackwell.

Pomian, K. (Ed.). (1990). *La querelle du determinisme. Philosophie de la science aujourd'hui*. Gallimard/Le Debat.

Prigogine, I. (1980). *From being to becoming*. W. H. Freeman and Co.

Prigogine, I. (1994). *Time, chaos and the laws of chaos*. Ed. Progress.

Prigogine, I. (1997). *The end of certainty: Time, chaos and the new laws of nature*. The Free Press.

Prigogine, I. (2003). *Is future given?* World Scientific.

Prigogine, I., & Nicolis, G. (1989). *Exploring complexity*. W. H. Freeman and Co.

Prigogine, I., & Stengers, I. (1984). *Order out of chaos*. Bantam.

Swinney, H. L. (1983). Observations of order and chaos in nonlinear systems. *Physica, 7*, 3–15.

PART 4

Neoliberal Governmentality

CHAPTER 10

Neoliberalism and Laissez-Faire
The Retreat from Naturalism

Abstract

This article starts by restating the core theoretical differences between liberalism and neoliberalism, most essentially concerning the principle of the active or positive state that I have claimed characterizes neoliberal governmentality, premised upon a distinction between naturalistic and anti-naturalistic views of state functioning and entailing the abandonment or severe qualification of laissez-faire. Of the differences between liberal and neoliberal government, I will recommit to my original thesis of the distinction between the positive state and the erosion of laissez-faire, as well as to the distinction between naturalism and anti-naturalism as being important to understanding the two variants of liberalism and to understanding as well the anti-democratic tendencies of the neoliberal variant. Here I will maintain that the key neoliberals in a theoretical sense are the European ordoliberals, such as Walter Eucken and Wilhelm Röpke, as well as US writers such as James Buchanan (public choice theory) and Henry Simons, while others such as Friedrich Hayek, although politically mobilizing for and actively supporting the advent and ascendency of neoliberalism, as witnessed by his formative role in establishing the Mont Pelerin Society, were, I will argue, much more cautious about jettisoning laissez-faire and of adopting an anti-naturalistic perspective. After setting out the distinctive features that characterize neoliberalism, the consequences for education will be briefly investigated.

1   The Problem of Laissez-Faire in Neoliberal Thought[1]

Foucault's (2008) analysis of the ordoliberals in Germany focused on the discrepancy between their advocacy of laissez-faire and the polarity between their views on the role of government. On the one hand, the German ordoliberals distrusted large concentrations of power and opposed action to "interfere" in markets, through wages and price fixing, or administrative or bureaucratic involvement, but on the other hand, they favoured and supported the actions of government to reinforce and strengthen the institutional infrastructures, to arrange and enable the "conditions" necessary for the market to operate. This was supported, for instance, by ordoliberals such as Walter Eucken, who took the view that the economy required an "economic constitution", which must be created and protected by the state. The possible conflict with free market principles is evident in the following statement:

> A solution of this task of which much depends (not only men's economic existence), requires the elaboration of a practicable economic constitution which satisfies certain basic principles. The problem will not solve itself simply by our letting economic systems grow up spontaneously. The history of the last century has shown this plainly enough. The economic system has to be consciously shaped. (Eucken, 1940/1992, p. 314)

Eucken sought to chart the basic principles of "economic politics" (*Wirtschaftspolitik*) in order to establish the "conditions" for a competitive market order to arise and continue. Establishing competition as the cornerstone of the economy became the key principle of a neoliberal order. It was concerned not with "interfering" with the day-to-day processes of the economy, but seeking to establish and protect the "conditions" that were favourable to an effective and efficient economic system. As Eucken put it, "[t]he answer is that the state should influence the *forms* of economy, but not itself direct the economic process" (1940/1992, p. 95).

It was also supported amongst the US free market advocates, such as Henry Calvert Simons. As "father" of the Chicago School of free market economics, Simons was expected to champion a consistently traditional approach accepting the classical postulates of laissez-faire. This was as a natural equilibrium between supply and demand which ensured the "self-regulation" of the economy, as if directed, in Adam Smith's phrase, by an "invisible hand", i.e., laws of nature. Yet, in his pamphlet, *A Positive Program for Laissez-faire,* first published in 1934, Simons seems ambivalent over laissez-faire:

> The representation of laissez-faire as a merely do nothing policy is unfortunate and misleading. It is an obvious responsibility of the state under this policy to maintain the kind of legal and institutional framework within which competition can function effectively as an agency of control. The policy should therefore be defined positively, as one under which the state seeks to establish and maintain such conditions that it may avoid the necessity of regulating "the heart of the contract"—that is to say, the necessity of regulating relative prices. Thus, the state is charged, under this "division of labor", with heavy responsibilities and large "control" functions: the maintenance of competitive conditions in industry, the control of the currency, ... the definition of the institution of property, ... not to mention the many social welfare functions. (Simons, 1948, p. 42)

Indeed, Ronald Coase was so shocked at Simons's pamphlet that he questioned Simons's credentials as a classical liberal and free market advocate:

> I would like to raise a question about Henry Simons. ... [His] *Positive Program for Laissez-faire* ... strikes me as highly interventionist pamphlet. ... [I]n antitust, [Simons] wanted to ... restructure American industry. ... In regulation ... he proposed to reform things by nationalization. ... I would be interested if someone could explain. (Cited in Kitch, 1983, pp. 178–179)

Coase maintains that Simons's *Positive Program* constitutes a blueprint for intrusive state interventions in the market of the sort advocated by social democrats and socialists who Simons most vehemently opposed and who advocated forms of state regulation of economic processes because they distrusted unregulated marketplace interactions. According to J. Bradford De Long of Harvard University, who also cites the quotation above (1990, p. 601), Coase's question (above) raised some interesting responses:

> Simons' former Chicago pupils, his successors as upholders of classical liberalism in economics, did not rise to his defense. Instead, they responded as follows: First, they acknowledged that Simons was not a pure liberal, but at best a mixed breed. "You can paint him with different colors ... ", said Harold Demsetz. "It's quite a mixed picture", said George Stigler. Second, they admitted that Simons *was* an "interventionist", that he did not believe that, in general, economic activity should be organized through free markets. "[H]e was the man who said that the Federal Trade Commission should be the most important agency in government, a phrase that surely should be on no one's tombstone", joked Stigler; "Everything Ronald [Coase] says is right". And Milton Friedman joined in: "I've gone back and reread the *Positive Program* and been astounded. ... To think that I thought at the time that it was strongly pro-free market in orientation!" (Cited in De Long, 1990, pp. 601–602)

Not only did Simons advocate regulation, but he even advocated nationalization. As Simons states in his pamphlet:

> Political control of utility charges is imperative ... for competition simply cannot function effectively as an agency of control. ... In general ... the state should face the necessity of actually taking over, owning, and managing directly, both railroads and utilities, and all other industries to which it is impossible to maintain effectively competitive conditions. (Simons, 1948, p. 57)

De Long defends Simons as a classical liberal on the grounds that "[Simons] thought that a primary function of government in a free society is to manage competition" (De Long, 1990, p. 610). Simons represented a strain of thinking in liberal economics that had been prominent in Europe in the work of the German ordoliberals, foremost amongst them economists such as Eucken and Röpke, who distinguished the "conditions" necessary to sustain a free market economy from the intervention of the government in the processes or actual functioning of the economy itself.

State intervention is necessary for the ordoliberals in order to establish the conditions under which laissez-faire can effectively operate. Indeed, Eucken appears to be quite dismissive of what is central to laissez-faire:

> The solution to the problem of control was seen by [the advocates of laissez-faire] to be in the "natural" order, in which competitive prices automatically control the whole process. They thought that this natural order would materialise spontaneously and that society did not need to be fed a "specific diet", that is, have an economic system imposed on it, in order to thrive. Hence, they arrived at a policy of laissez-faire; this form of economic control left much to be desired. Confidence in the spontaneous emergence of the natural order was too great. (Eucken, 1989, p. 38)

This interventionist current in liberal thought was alive and well in America amongst other liberals than Henry Simons. James Buchanan, the founder of public choice theory, shares with the ordoliberals this more directive orientation to state action. Although the classical liberal tradition had stressed the role of markets as "self-regulating", representing a strong commitment to liberalism as a naturalistic doctrine, and as supported by arguments based on the freedom of the individual from the state, Buchanan so distrusted that the required efficiency gains would emerge through automatic mechanisms of the market that, in a way similar to writers like Röpke and Eucken, he supported efficiency achievements through a the deliberate tightening of state control. As he says in his criticism of Hayek:

> My basic criticism of F. A. Hayek's profound interpretation of modern history and his diagnosis for improvement is directed at his apparent belief or faith that social evolution will, in fact, ensure the survival of efficient institutional forms. Hayek is so distrustful of man's explicit attempts of reforming institutions that he accepts uncritically the evolutionary alternative. (1975, p. 194n)

It was on this ground that he opposed Hayek's naturalist faith in markets as spontaneous self-ordering systems which had been the hallmark of the classical liberal view since its inception. In Buchanan's view, the state should actively construct the competitive market economy and utilise supply-side monitoring in the interests of promoting efficiency in market terms.

2   Foucault, Röpke and Neoliberalism

Michel Foucault studied neoliberalism in his 1978 course at the Collège de France, *The Birth of Biopolitics*. For Foucault, neoliberalism signals "a shift from exchange to competition in the principle of the market" (2008, p. 118). Competition assumes the role of a fundamental principle that subtends democracy, which is to say, that the basic ordering of society as an enterprise culture structured by competition is to be enforced by government across all domains of the society. It becomes, as it were, the organising framework guaranteed by the state rather than as a function of the market. Foucault marshals evidence by citing Eucken who tells us that the government must be "perpetually vigilant and active" (p. 138), and must intervene to establish this context through both regulatory actions (*actions régulatrices*) and organizing actions (*actions ordonnatrices*) (p. 138).

Although during the first half of the 20th century Western welfare states were constituted through democratic determination, the accomplishment of neoliberalism, for the ordoliberals at least, was to attempt to establish the principle of competition as prior to and outside of democratic decision-making; as determining the "framework" through which the market would rule. The framework must attend to both the population, the order of justice and opportunity, as well as the techniques, such as the availability of implements concerning such things as population, technology, training and education, the legal system, the availability of land, the climate, all seen by Eucken as the "conditions" for the market. Foucault refers to this active, top-down, positive role of the state as constituting a "sociological liberalism" (p. 146, footnote 51), or a "policy of society" (p. 146) which permits a new "art of government" which differs radically from Keynesian-type systems. What is crucial is that for neoliberalism the object of government action becomes "the social environment" (p. 146) acting on behalf of capital, or those the create wealth. The aim is to engineer competition:

> It is the mechanisms [of competition] that should have the greatest possible surface and depth and should also occupy the greatest possible

volume in society. This means that what is sought is not a society subject to the commodity effect, but a society subject to the dynamic of competition. (p. 147)

Competition becomes the new "*eidos*" (p. 147), the new dynamic of this new form of society:

> Not a supermarket society, but an enterprise society. The *homo oeconomicus* sought after is not the man of exchange, or man the consumer; he is the man of enterprise and production. (p. 147)

Wilhelm Röpke fundamentally sets out the neoliberal social policy in his text "The Orientation of German Economic Policy", where he says that social policy must aim at:

> the multiplication of the enterprise form within the social body. ... It is a matter of making the market, competition, and so the enterprise, into what could be called the formative power of society. (Cited by Foucault, p. 148)

In his book A *Humane Economy: The Social Framework of the Free Market* (1958/1971), Röpke's new form of liberalism becomes even more readily apparent. The book aims to establish the appropriate foundations of the market economy by outlining the conditions necessary for the free market beyond the previously accepted context of supply and demand. For such a market order cannot function, he says, "in a social system which is the exact opposite in all respects" (p. 94). The cultural context of the social structure is part of this and must support this:

> We start from competition. ... Competition may have two meanings: it may be an institution for stimulating effort, or it may be a device for regulating and ordering the economic process. In the market economy competition ... constitutes therefore an unrivalled solution of the two cardinal problems of any economic system: the problem of the continual inducement to maximum performance and the problem of continuous harmonious ordering and guidance of the economic process. (p. 95)

The foundation for this is not laissez-faire; Röpke, like Eucken, and like Simons, is not describing a naturalistic but has succumbed to advocating a historical thesis. Laissez-faire was the naïve thesis of early liberalism. For Röpke it was a fiction:

> In all honesty, we have to admit that the market economy has a bourgeois foundation. ... The market economy, and with it social and political freedom, can thrive only as a part and under the protection of a bourgeois system. This implies the existence of a society in which certain fundamentals are respected and color the whole network of social relationships. (p. 98)

Röpke's conception of liberalism is clearly more authoritarian in the sense that it seems to represent an imposed order. Such a view seems reinforced when he acknowledges that:

> In a sound society, leadership, responsibility, and exemplary defense of society's guiding norms and values must be the exalted duty and unchallengeable right of a minority that forms and is willingly and respectfully recognized as the apex of the social pyramid hierarchically structured by performance. ... What we need is true *nobilitas naturalis*. ... We need a natural nobility whose authority is, fortunately, readily accepted by all men, an elite deriving its title solely from supreme performance and peerless moral example and invested with the moral dignity of such a life. ... No free society ... which threatens to degenerate into mass society, can subsist without such a class of censors. (p. 131)

Röpke adds that "the task of leadership falls to the natural aristocracy by virtue of an unwritten but therefore no less valid right which is indistinguishable from duty" (p. 133). Only such persons can save us from the "slowly spreading cancers of our western economy and society" (p. 151), which include the "irresistible advance of the welfare state" (p. 151).

3   Hayek and Neoliberalism

Did Friedrich Hayek also accept this new view of "economic politics"? My answer is not in the same sort of way, although he shared the pro-free market values that they supported. Hayek was too steeped in the classical liberal tradition to easily give up its naturalistic assumptions concerning laissez-faire and the conception of the subject who should be trusted as a rational, autonomous citizen and who should remain unconditioned or uncoerced by the state. Yet the theoretical difficulties that afflicted Simons, Buchanan, Eucken, and Röpke, also weighed heavily on Hayek. He not only struggled with the notion of laissez-faire, but also appreciated that over time the democratic will of citizens tends to favour restrictions on the free market economics and supports an expanded role for government as respects to both welfare and redistribution.[2]

Although I have written several articles and chapters on Hayek, one is always learning new things. In a PhD doctoral *viva voce* examination on Foucault and neoliberalism that I had the honour to examine at the University of Brighton in 2018, Lars Cornelissen, the disputant, alerted me to several works of Hayek that I had been unaware of. One was an article by Hayek, titled "Marktwirtschaft und Wirtschaftspolitik",[3] published in the journal ORDO in 1954 where Hayek laments the fact that classical economists had not adequately defined "intervention" because, as Cornelissen summarizes Hayek's view, "many of them held 'economic politics', of the sort advocated by Eucken and Röpke, to be antithetical to 'the fundamental principles of liberalism'" (Cornelissen, 2017, p. 206; citing Hayek, 1954, p. 4).

Being aware of the controversy between classical liberalism and the "economic politics" of Eucken and Röpke, Hayek is more careful to limit the active role of the state to establishing the juridical structure of society. For Hayek, the creation and maintenance of a competitive order is primarily a *legal* affair. The only type of intervention for an "economic politics" is in the "permanent juridical framework" as opposed to "constant intervention of state force [*Staatsgewalt*]" (Cornelissen, p. 206; Hayek, p. 5). Hayek thus restricts intervention of the state to the legal order and thus has a much narrower view of active state intervention to establish the "conditions" of economic activity than does either Röpke or Eucken.

4   Planning and the Rule of Law

Throughout his career Hayek remained steadfastly committed to the idea that markets best guaranteed the freedom of citizens, and on this ground remained staunchly opposed to all forms of state planning and control. What essentially undermines state planning in Hayek's view is that real knowledge is gained and true economic progress made as a consequence of locally generated knowledge derived from "particular circumstances of time and place" and the state is not privy to such knowledge (Hayek, 1949b, p. 79). Planning ignores this localistic character of knowledge and thus interferes with the self-regulating mechanism of the market.

It is on these grounds that Hayek argues that the state should only be concerned with the protection of individuals by "general rules", such as the "rule of law", but not with what he refers to as "central planning". If we look to Hayek, both to *The Road to Serfdom* (1944) and *The Constitution of Liberty* (1960), where

Hayek discusses planning and the rule of law, in contrast to the rule of law's *formal*, and a priori character, the plan's approach to decision-making is *ad hoc* and *arbitrary*. A plan also embodies, says Hayek (1944, p. 91) "substantive" commitments on ends and values, whereas the rules constitutive of the rule of law are "general", "formal", "impartial" and "systematic" (pp. 90–92). Formal rules operate "without reference to time and place or particular people" (p. 92). They refer to "typical situations. ... Formal rules are thus merely instrumental in the sense they are expected to be useful to yet unknown people" (p. 92). On the other hand, planning involves "a conscious direction towards a single aim" (1944, p. 72), and "refuses to recognize various autonomous spheres in which the ends of individuals are supreme" (p. 72) As such the plan embodies general substantive goals linked to the "'the general welfare', or the 'common good', or the 'general interest'" (p. 72). Yet, it is Hayek's view that the welfare of people "cannot be adequately expressed as a single end" (p. 73) for to have such a conception of the general welfare requires a "complete ethical code", which would require knowledge of everything. The difference between the two kinds of approach, says Hayek, is like the difference between the "'Rules of the Road', as in the Highway Code, and ordering people where to go" (1944, p. 91).

5   A Critique of Hayek's Concept of Planning

Hayek acknowledges that while his distinction between formal rules, and planning "is very important ... at the same time [it is] most difficult to draw precisely in practice" (1944, p. 91). This, it seems to me, understates what is problematic about his argument. While his points about the need for general rules that are formal, and apply to all, are highly important, his characterization of planning is largely a caricature, and his arguments against it do not stand serious scrutiny. Indeed, it would seem, as many economists in his own Department at the LSE believed, that any serious analysis of Hayek's arguments leads us straight to Keynesian conclusions.[4]

Hayek's arguments against central planning have been seriously challenged.[5] What is conflated in his treatment is a failure to distinguish "central planning", as exemplified by the model of the Soviet Union, and aspects of planning in general, as adopted routinely in Western democracies.[6] While his arguments may be persuasive against the idea of highly centralized decision-making for the entire economy, beyond this the assessment of his legitimate empirical arguments are difficult to untangle from what is the deeply ingrained ideological nature of his opposition to social democracy or socialism. Certainly the emergence of highly centralized economies of Eastern Europe from the 1920s could be seen to inhibit the emergence of Schumpeter-styled entrepreneurs, and to erode possibilities for enterprise and initiative. As developed in the Soviet Union after the Revolution of 1917, the model of state capitalism (*capitalisme de parti*) which was based on the attempts by a single political party to manage the operations of the economy through the direct transmission of orders from the centre, including the establishment of centralized socialist trusts, involving the direct control of recruitment, production schedules and wages met with severe problems of the sort Hayek describes. Beyond this, however, it can be claimed that the problem is not so much with planning, but with the broader political model in operation.

That Hayek extends his objections from a concern with Soviet-styled central planning to forms of state planning in Western societies, and specifically against those forms of general planning being developed in countries like Britain at the onset of the welfare state, constitutes a major problem. For what can be claimed is that there is no objection to planning as such, nor even to central planning, but only against types of planning that are ad hoc and arbitrary, and not subject to democratic controls of auditing, accountability, contestation, debate and revision. Planning, in fact, is amenable to the same types of assessment as Hayek maintains for the rule of law, and like the rule of law, it should comprise codified procedures which are formal, systematic, a priori (written in advance) and general or impartial. Planning also must be democratically accountable. Planning, in this sense is compatible with open economies, individual initiative, local autonomy in decision-making, and decentralization.[7]

One important issue that Hayek never considers is whether markets and planning could (or should) coexist. That is, whether there is not some middle ground position between the "serfdom" associated with state planning, and the "freedom" associated with markets. As Jim Tomlinson (1990, p. 49, note 3) notes:

> [I]n his 1945 article ["The Use of Knowledge in Society"], Hayek typically dismisses any mid-way point between centralised and decentralised planning except "the delegation of planning to organised industries, or, in other words, monopoly" (p. 521). Plainly this does not exhaust the possibilities of levels of planning, nor does it provide a helpful starting point for discussing mechanisms of planning.[8]

6 Knowledge and Planning

Markets are also preferred to planning on grounds of efficiency and because of the local nature of knowledge. When planning takes the place of markets, mistakes and errors become "entrenched" because only the price mechanism can coordinate the diverse activities of individuals, says Hayek. Partly, this is due to the absence of local or contextual knowledge which actors in the marketplace have and state bureaucrats don't have. But, although Hayek distinguishes important characteristics of local knowledge, he fails to consider whether other sorts of knowledge might not be important; or perhaps whether or not knowledge might not work differently at the macro, meso, and micro orders of society. To use Hayek's language, from "The Use of Knowledge in Society", while he celebrates knowledge of "time and place" which is not accessible to planners, he gives no value to the benefits of "aggregated" or "statistical-type" knowledge, which enables perspective, and which could be held to constitute an equally important type of knowledge which "planners" *do* have, and which is *denied* to agents in local contexts. This latter type of knowledge might be claimed to be concerned with general guidelines, limits, or contexts, and coordination, rather than specifically with day-to-day operations. It therefore maintains a different relation to time and place, and hence, the practical problem which Hayek notes about transmitting information about events which are situationally local need not arise.[9] Certainly, if planning sought to replace or override market mechanisms, or disregard, interfere with, or override local knowledge, one could see that would constitute a serious problem, but this does not mean that markets and planning cannot compliment and assist each other in turn.[10]

Various distinctions could be made which Hayek also does not make, between "normal" versus "exceptional" operations of markets, between the "macro", "meso", or "micro" levels of the economy, or the distinction made above, concerning the context effectively regulated by supply and demand and the price mechanism (where a rough equilibrium may persist for a certain time) versus the context of coordination (requiring macro-management, planning, agenda setting, and steering). While it may well be so that local knowledge and the fragility of the price mechanism means that normal day-to-day operations of markets should be relatively autonomous from the arbitrary interference of the state, there will be exceptional circumstances where "communicating knowledge to a board" for urgent or non-urgent action is highly appropriate. Within normal markets, behaviour which signals exceptional development ("a run on the pound"); or behaviour which signals unusual development ("a contaminated product"; "a suspicious behavior") are cases in point. Just as the doctor–patient relation for the most part is a private contract, evidence of certain types of symptoms must be immediately reported. In addition, there will be routine situations where guiding the economy within established limits require specific actions in line with established policies. Introducing policies to counter economic inequalities in capital accumulation, or to assist in creating fair opportunities, also constitute legitimate activities that can be planned for. Hence, there are different sorts of functions which require different types of coordination, and different types of knowledge.

"In a democratic society", wrote Karl Mannheim, "state sovereignty can be boundlessly strengthened by plenary [planning] powers without renouncing democratic control" (1940, p. 340). Yet, Hayek maintains that democratic assemblies have problems producing a plan. Either they cannot manage the whole view, or obtain adequate knowledge, or, if delegated, they cannot integrate it (Hayek, 1944, pp. 82–84). Such a claim is highly dubious, especially given the sophisticated planning instruments and communication technologies available today. But regardless of that, government has responsibility to oversee and steer the whole. The delegation of particular powers to separate boards and authorities is a part of that responsibility. Yet the parliamentary system renders the state as democratically accountable and is as necessary to the formal legitimacy of the rule of law as it is to the formal legitimacy of planning.

Amongst existing democratic mechanisms, parliament is one mechanism of accountability; the official opposition are charged with discussion and debate, and with highlighting abuses, identifying shortcomings, as well as criticizing delegated or contracted groups whose performance is not up to the mark. In addition, the free mass media, as well as institutions of judicial review, make existing democratic assemblies and procedures crucial underwriters to both the formality and generality of policy, whether through law, or planning, and they legitimate *both* law *and* planning. It is the democratic assemblies which both enable and legitimate the formality of the rule of law and are accountable for good as opposed to bad legislation.[11] What Hayek doesn't seem to realize is that they are similarly able to perform this function in relation to planning. Through various codified and formal rules of procedure and process, planning can be legitimate or illegitimate. Hence, I would reject Hayek's thesis that "planning leads to dictatorship" (p. 88) or that "dictatorship is essential if planning on a large scale is to be possible" (p. 88), just as I would reject the thesis that planning is necessarily arbitrary.

Another factor makes planning important here. At the start of the 21st century, collective action and sophisticated planning operations have become increasingly necessary on all manner of issues ranging from matters relating to general security and the response to crisis and urgency, to arranging social insurance, and the provision of opportunities, structures, and capabilities on a fair and equitable basis. Increased pressures associated with global population growth, climate change, ecological degradation, nuclear proliferation, terrorism, viral pandemics, or economic or political collapse create a situation in which *not* planning is simply *not an option*. Believing that laissez-faire will deliver security and stability for all on a global basis simply constitutes the naïve faith of classical economic liberalism.

While Hayek's opposition to all forms of state planning might be seen as viable if he can argue that the economic system is naturally self-regulating, should this later thesis founder, so the former will also be in difficult straights. Yet, just as we found for Simons, Buchanan, Eucken and Röpke, Hayek's views on the self-regulating capacity of the system, implying laissez-faire, do not inspire confidence. Although he had substituted his "empirical conception" (of laissez-faire) for what he considered to be the inadequate neoclassical conception, his "knowledge papers" of the 1930s and 1940s revealed increasing doubts about both its theoretical and practical viability. In his paper "Economics and Knowledge", first presented in 1937, he notes that although traditional experience has more or less confirmed equilibrium theory "since the empirical observation that prices do tend to correspond to costs was the beginning of our science" (1949a, p. 51), his own confidence in the idea was waning. The following statement is not exactly brimming with confidence:

> I am afraid that I am now getting to a stage where it becomes exceedingly difficult to say what exactly are the assumptions on the basis of which we assert that there will be a tendency toward equilibrium and to claim that our analysis has an application to the real world. I cannot pretend that I have as yet got much further on this point. Consequently all I can do is to ask a number of questions to which we will have to find an answer if we want to be clear about the significance of our argument. (1949a, p. 48)

In the same article, Hayek observes that both Smith and Ricardo had noted that the stability of community structures were essential preconditions for any equilibrium to operate (1949a, p. 48, note 13).[12] By 1945, in "The Use of Knowledge in Society", he recognizes that the concept of equilibrium was irrelevant for practical purposes, had "mislead ... leading thinkers" in economics, and he represents it as "no more than a useful preliminary to the study of the main problem" (1949b, p. 91). In "The Meaning of Competition" of 1946, also, he notes how "the modern theory of competitive equilibrium assumes the situation to exist" (1949c, p. 94). In his doubts, expressed across all of these papers, Hayek's was also to observe that even if it can be recast as an empirical proposition, subject to verification, equilibrium theory then becomes only a possibility rather than an actuality. More to the point, Hayek was by no means certain what sorts of empirical tests could validate it, and he very much doubted "whether [any] such investigations would tell us anything new" (1949a, p. 55). He also notes how simply to assume equilibrium overlooks the negative externalities and global disparities associated with markets, including increasing inequalities of wealth and resources, and increasingly monopolistic behaviour of large companies and multinationals. His confidence did not improve in later years.

It was related to these doubts that many economists from Hayek's own department—Hicks, Kaldor, Lerner, Scitovsky and Shackle—retreated to Keynesianism under the influence of the Cambridge model in the 1930s. Shackle reasoned that given Hayek's conception of history, emphasizing as it did the limits to reason, uncertainty, spontaneous unpredictable choices, as well as the unpredictability of unintended effects at any single point in time we can have little faith in the logical coherence of market equilibrium over time to "self-regulate" unless we believe in a metaphysic of nature as functionally optimal at the economic and social levels, or as tending towards the functionally optimal. If the market cannot be relied upon, then what mechanism can guarantee socially optimal consequences for distribution and for the continuance of the market mechanism as a predictable framework in terms of which economic interactions between humans can be guided? Further, what mechanism can guarantee that the effects of the market are not dysfunctional in relation to the social and physical environment? In Shackle's view, these ideas suggest a coordinative mechanism is required, not to substitute for the rational decisions for individuals, but to ensure distribution, security and liberty and to undertake collective action in areas where individuals are unable to address. For Shackle, and his fellow Keynesians at least, planning was clearly back on the agenda.

Keynes had argued something similar to this in his theoretical justifications for the welfare state. In Keynes's view, as a general consequence of our ignorance of the future, planning was an essential feature of the welfare state. In a letter he wrote to Hayek while on an ocean liner en route to the Bretton Woods Conference in June 1944, after reading Hayek's book *The Road to Serfdom*, in what could possibly be seen as a case of classic understatement, Keynes (1980, pp. 385–388) raises the issue that he regards Hayek as not addressing or resolving:

> I come finally to what is really my only serious criticism of the book. You admit here and there that it is a question of knowing where to draw the line. You agree that the line has to be drawn somewhere [between free markets and planning], but that the logical extreme is not possible. But you give us no guidance whatever as to where to draw it. In a sense this is shirking the practical issue. It is true that you and I would probably draw it in different places. I should guess that according to my ideas you greatly under-estimate the practicality of the middle course. But as soon as you

admit that the extreme is not possible, and that a line has to be drawn, you are, on your own argument, done for since you are trying to persuade us that as soon as one moves an inch in the planned direction you are necessarily launched on the slippery path which will lead you in due course over the precipice. I should therefore conclude your theme rather differently. I should say that what we want is not no planning, or even less planning, indeed I should say that we almost certainly want more.

7 Lars Cornelissen on Hayek and Democracy

One question that remains for Hayek is how, if the state can intervene only in the legal structures of society through formal processes, is Hayek able to protect free market economics from the possibility of democratic rejection. This is, after all, why Eucken and Röpke wanted state intervention to establish the "conditions" of an enterprise culture in a much broader sense; not only legal, but political, cultural, and educational as well. This is an important question for Hayek especially given his own doubts about the efficacy of laissez-faire. The answer is, as Cornelissen argues, Hayek has a vastly attenuated conception of democracy which:

> must give way to a form of constitutionalism that explicitly seeks to eliminate popular sovereignty. This … does not entail a principled rejection of democracy. Rather, it comprises a far reaching restriction of the democratic mechanism, such that democratic citizens may exert an influence on the governmental apparatus but are simultaneously prevented from changing the overarching legal framework. (2017, p. 222)

Hence, Cornelissen argues that "the primary aim of Hayek's democratic theory is to banish popular sovereignty from political thought" (p. 223).

Noting that Hayek's democratic theory constitutes the "privileged object of analysis for a critical account of the place occupied by democracy in neoliberal thought" (p. 226), Cornelissen starts by noting Hayek's "ambivalence towards democracy" (p. 244), and his decision to limit it to "describe a method of government—namely majority rule" (p. 244). Democracy then constitutes a "method of deciding but emphatically not 'an authority for what the decision ought to be'" (p. 244). In general terms, Hayek claims to support democracy as the best method of change; as the best mechanism compatible with liberty, and as the best method for educating the majority, because it has better results overall. At the same time, Hayek makes frequent negative comments about democracy, or aspects of democracy. Cornelissen notes Hayek's antipathy to what he refers to as "the doctrinaire democrat" (cited from Cornelissen, p. 245). In a previous article of my own (Olssen, 2010, chapter 2), I also noted Hayek's disparaging reference to forms of "plebiscitarian dictatorship" (1944, p. 86), which may suggest a rather disrespectful slur on citizens in general. Various negative comments can be found, such as in *The Constitution of Liberty* (1960), where Hayek says: "[t]hose who profess that democracy is all-competent and support all that the majority wants at any given moment are working for its fall" (1960, p. 183). Cornelissen concedes, however, that as he aged, Hayek "became inclined to mount a principled defense of democratic government" (p. 245). Where he falters, in Cornelissen's view, is in the model democratic constitution he develops in the third volume of *Law, Legislation and Liberty*. Here, Hayek favours the establishment of both a representative government as well as an upper house legislature, the latter which would "completely be insulated from popular control" (p. 253). As Cornelissen continues:

> In Hayek's model constitution, then, the average citizen can exert some influence on the direction of government, thus modestly guiding the allocation of public resources, but has virtually no control over the law, which is articulated by a council, consisting of "wise and fair" legislators, that can neither be recalled nor corrected by the people. In Hayekian democracy, concisely put, each individual citizen is equal before the law over which they can exert no significant control. (pp. 253–254)

It is perhaps unfair to suggest that Hayek's model constitution invokes "echoes" of Plato's Guardians.[13] Yet, Cornelissen notes that Pierre Rosanvallon also observes that Hayek has "'abandoned' the 'democratic idea,' ... [in] 'radically severing the concept of democracy from legislation' and thereby in insulating legislation from popular sovereignty" (Cornelissen, p. 254, citing Rosanvallon, 2011, p. 153).[14]

8   Education

For Foucault, the fear of power does not in his case give rise to an unbridled love of markets. Foucault makes it clear in "The Risks of Security" that he is no supporter of those who denigrate the state:

> In fact, the idea of an opposition between civil society and the state was formulated in a given context in response to a precise intention: some

liberal economists proposed it at the end of the eighteenth century to limit the sphere of action of the state, civil society being conceived of as the locus of an autonomous economic process. This was a quasi-polemical concept, opposed to administrative options of states of that era, so that a certain liberalism could flourish. (2000, p. 372)

Foucault's writings on neoliberalism represent it as a dis-equalizing and anti-democratic force.[15] What is more important, however, is that while liberalism represented man as free and uncoerced, who obeyed market laws because they were natural laws, as if ruled by an "invisible hand", in Smith's words, neoliberalism is authoritarian in important respects. This is in the sense that the faltering confidence in laissez-faire and naturalism by liberals led those we can dub as neoliberals to advocate the necessity of the state constructing the "framework" and the "conditions" by which the free market could be assured. What we have seen is that for the German ordoliberals, their distrust in laissez-faire has meant that rather than see the market as natural they see it as historical and in need of conditioning by the state. There is the danger, of course, that this function will be progressively "immunized" from genuine democratic contestation or control.

Amongst the public sector institutions which constitute part of the "conditions" for a competitive market economy, are the various educational institutions, from preschool to higher education, including universities. In higher education, for instance, neoliberal governmentality has subverted what I have called elsewhere a "collegial–democratic" model and replaced it with a new model based upon external audits and performance appraisals, premised upon performance incentive targets and increased monitoring and managerialism.[16] You can see the top-down, authoritarian aspect of neoliberalism in the new forms of governmentality implemented from the 1980s in universities. It gives a new significance to the notion of "rule by managers" when one understands that the neoliberal theorists advocated the interpellation of a new strata of managers to counter the classical liberal conception of professionalism, based as it was upon an autonomy of spheres, and to counter it as a form of what Buchanan refers to as "rent-seeking" behaviour. In Britain, four years after Margaret Thatcher was elected, for instance, the Griffith Report of 1983 proposed reforms for the health sector, which included the creation of new senior management roles in the NHS, in order to replace the traditional management functions in health as carried out by professional medical staff. This emergence of a stratum of dedicated professional managers quickly became embedded in legislation and transferred laterally from health to higher education and then across the entire public sector. Ideas of "internal markets" were also current in relation to health in the 1980s, and received expression in the 1989 white paper "Working for Patients". New models of "student-led" funding and new corporate managerial models of governance and line management were also implemented at this time, feeding off theoretical ideas developed in supply-side economics, public choice theory, agency theory, and transaction-cost economics. Ideas of line management, based upon "principal–agent" hierarchies of command and compliance replaced "collegial–democratic" patterns of governance based upon classical liberal models of professionalism premised upon autonomy and self-governance, exercised through senates. Suggestions that universities should increase the appointments of lay and business personnel on councils and boards of governors, as advocated in the US by McCormick and Meiners (1988), was intended to reduce academic internal influence and increase the responsiveness of universities to the outside business community. Further governance ideas and techniques saw the downgrading of the influence of senates, as well as the rise of closed "executive boards" to augment the implementation of line-management systems. In Britain, the major responsibility for all of these developments emanates directly from the state through the funding councils. The major levers are all imposed by the state, which itself responds to global interests. The revolution in the way universities were run was worldwide. Collegial models of self-governance premised upon autonomous institutional spheres are replaced by "top-down" managerial models, directed from the centre—the state and global capital.

This also undermines universities semi-autonomous power within civil society, which is itself historically important in terms of understanding liberalism as a natural autonomous system of the different spheres of society and of the free expression of rational individuals. Universities, as once upon a time, a fifth estate, a critical bulwark for the safeguarding of democracy, are now, in this new age of neoliberalism, compromised in relation to the powers of business, superbly administered by the state. The neoliberals' analysis seems particularly apt as a form of market rationality. The abolition of tenure and the enforcement of new norms with regards to research, research funding, and teaching means that most academics are too intent on watching their backs to speak of opposition or serious critique. The assessment of "impact" in Britain escalates this process and seeks now to control and monitor the "content" of what universities produce, to render knowledge production as "useful" for society. In this sense, it constitutes a very worrying "sign", especially given the epistemic difficulties with the way impact is capable of being assessed. The implications for democracy here are in a number of senses: in relation to the end of self-governance through collegial models of academic participation, as well as externally through the erosion of the independent critical authority of universities, relatively free of dependence on finance, in relation to business and the state.

In higher education, state conditioning or engineering has substantially undercut the university as a traditional liberal institution. For the difference between liberal and neoliberal is important here. The liberal university was premised upon the freedom of the subject and the dispersal of power across different domains. The parallel at the institutional level was what I have called elsewhere the "collegial–democratic" model administered and managed by academics themselves institutionally provided for by the democratic forum of the senate.[17] The neoliberal university is top-down, run from the centre. While neoliberals typically heralded their policies with catchcries of freedom and liberty, neoliberalism is in fact a highly centrist, authoritarian, form of liberalism. Distrusting laissez-faire naturalism, they came to share the same perspective on the economy as writers like Karl Mannheim[18] and Karl Polanyi,[19] who saw the market order as a historical rather than a natural construct. Whereas Mannheim and Polanyi argued that the government should control and condition the market in order to redistribute wealth in the interests of greater equality and protect freedom, the neoliberals argued that it should work in the interests of capital by creating the conditions for the market to operate as efficiently as possible. The state conditions the market in order that subjects conform.

Perhaps we could conclude this article by asking a number of questions designed to highlight the possible problems with neoliberal governance: Why did the neoliberals feel uneasy with naturalistic explanations of the market and start seeing it as a historical phenomenon that must be conditioned? Is there a problem with naturalistic explanations? Does intervention by the state to establish and maintain the conditions for the market run the risk of frustrating the democratic aspirations and rights of citizens? Could such action by the state be seen to contradict the core principles upon which classical liberalism was founded upon? In whose interests ought the government to act in legislating laws for society? In creating the conditions for competitive market behaviour, is the state reflecting the interests of the whole society or of particular groups in the society? Is it appropriate to subject higher education institutions, such as universities, to market norms of competition as a general strategy of administration and governance? In what ways is education not like other consumer commodities? What are the costs and benefits of such policies in relation to education? The neoliberals said that academics, teachers and educators were not subject to reliable standards of accountability, but could accountability be organized that didn't involve the competitive restructuring of the entire system of education? Do competitive norms conflict with those norms that are deemed to be important in education? What is the difference between treating education as a market commodity, as opposed to treating it as a public good? Do supply-side funding policies, such as student fees, exercise conservative pressures on curriculum planners? If so, in what ways? What other effects might they have? Given the relatively modest salaries that are paid to academics and educators, to what extent are academic change-management strategies, such as restructuring, which were initially introduced for those in management on very high incomes, acceptable to use in education institutions? To what extent are managers any less biased or subject to "provider capture" than academics? Have managers or educators and academics become more or less professionalized over the last thirty years? Is there a conflict of interest between professional managers on the one hand and educators on the other?

Acknowledgement

This chapter originally appeared as Olssen, M. (2018), Neoliberalism and laissez-faire: The retreat from naturalism, *Šolsko Polje*, 29(1–2), 33–56. Reprinted here, with minor edits, with permission from the publisher.

Notes

1. In the preparation of the paper, some paragraphs draw from my previous writings on neoliberalism, specifically Olssen (2010, 2016, 2018) and Olssen, Codd, and O'Neill (2004). The publishers of those articles and books are thanked for any replication in this paper.
2. Hayek blames this on the fact that the prevailing conception of democracy is, as Cornelissen puts it, "rooted in the collectivist tradition" and, that as a result, "the particular set of institutions which today prevails in all Western democracies" is inherently inclined towards unlimited government" (2017a, p. 246). Cornelissen cites Hayek, *Law, Legislation and Liberty* (2013, p. 345); *New Studies* (1978, pp. 92, 107, 155).
3. "Market Economy and Economic Politics" (translation).
4. Hicks, Kaldor, Lerner, Scitovsky, and Shackle all deserted Hayek, and became Keynesians in the 1930s.
5. See, for instance, Gray (1984), Hindess (1990), Tomlinson (1990), and Gamble (1996).
6. It can be claimed as a bold conjecture at the outset that empirical research has not revealed any significant erosion of democracy in a country like Britain during the period after the inception of the welfare state. Leaders like Asquith claimed that the state was in fact necessary to safeguard freedom.
7. There is no evidence that the development of the welfare state, either in Britain from 1945, or New Zealand from 1933, resulted in an erosion of democracy, or human rights under the law, which, if corroborated, would offer an empirical refutation of Hayek's thesis in *The Road to Serfdom* (1944).

8   Hayek, F. A. (1945), "The use of knowledge in society", *American Economic Review*, 35(4), 519–530.

9   Hayek makes this point repeatedly in "The Use of Knowledge in Society" (1945:, pp. 525, 526). My point is that a different type of knowledge, concerned with guidelines, or limits, or "steering", may not be so sensitive to issues of time and place, but may have a longer term frame of reference. An additional point might be that advances in communications technology may make the transmission of what knowledge is relevant to the centre, easier and faster to transmit.

10 Hayek's argument against early communist regimes which sought to replace markets with state planning are indeed valid, but these were based on the idea that markets were not important, and sought amongst other things, to override the price mechanism as a routine matter of policy. I am accepting Hayek's argument that markets convey an important form of knowledge through the price mechanism which determines that the context of operations should be semi-autonomous from the state. This also applies, I would argue, to the family, the educational system, the health system, and personal life, although clearly, there is no such thing as the price mechanism as an indicator of quality. But I am suggesting that the knowledge generated by markets, or in other local contexts, is not the only form of knowledge necessary to a healthy social structure, and that planning can (and must) compliment markets in this quest.

11 Hayek of course sees legislation as emerging in the spontaneous order of society and formed solely out of natural rights. His faltering commitment to laissez-faire and naturalism would make this assumption problematic even on his own terms. But that negative and positive liberty, or state action on such a ground, could be used to justify law *vis-à-vis* planning is disingenuous. The law even it is claimed only to codify natural rights needs *interpreting* and *being acted upon*, and these functions imply a positive dimension to all state action, whether law or planning.

12 He quotes Smith (*The Wealth of Nations*, Bk. I, 116): "In order, however, that this equality [of wages] may take place in the whole of their advantages or disadvantages, three things are required even when there is perfect freedom. First, the employment must be well known and long established in the neighbourhood"; and David Ricardo (Letters to Malthus, October 22nd, 1811, p. 18): "It would be no answer to me to say that men were ignorant of the best and cheapest mode of conducting their business and paying their debts, because that is a question of fact, not of science, and might be argued against almost every proposition in Political Economy".

13 Unfair, of course, in that Plato was not a democrat, and opposed democracy. Yet, many of the details of Hayek's constitution seem to be excessively protective of the legislators with respect to immunizing them from economic hardship once they have served their time. He specifies, for instance, elaborate conditions and "safeguards" such as that members of the legislature should be elected for reasonably long periods, of 15 years so that they would not be subject to insecurity. Only people "who have proved themselves in the ordinary business of life" should be eligible for election; they should only be removable for "gross misconduct"; after serving their term "they should not be re-eligible nor forced to return to earning a living in the market but be assured of continual public employment". See *Law, Legislation and Liberty*, Vol. 3, pp. 95–96, 448–450.

14 Cornelissen argues that the separation of legislation from democracy became increasingly pronounced in Hayek's thought over time, reaching its ultimate status as part of the spontaneous order of society in Volume 3 of *Law, Legislation and Liberty*. There is, it seems, more scope for further study of Hayek's conception of democracy.

15 But see Zamora and Behrent (2016) who maintain a contrary thesis.

16 See Raaper and Olssen (2016).
17 Ibid.
18 See Mannheim (1940, 1951/1977).
19 See Polanyi (1944/2001).

References

Buchanan, J. (1975). *The limits of liberty: between anarchy and leviathan.* University of Chicago Press.

Cornelissen, L. S. (2017). *The market and the people: On the incompatibility of neoliberalism and democracy* [Unpublished doctoral dissertation]. University of Brighton.

De Long, J. B. (1990). In defense of Henry Simon's standing as a classical liberal. *Cato Journal, 9*(3), 601–618.

Eucken, W. (1951). *The unsuccessful age, or, the pains of economic progress.* William Hodge and Co.

Eucken, W. (1989). What kind of economic and social system? In A. Peacock & H. Willgerodt (Eds.), *Germany's social market economy: Origins and evolution* (pp. 27–45). Palgrave Macmillan.

Eucken, W. (1992). *Foundations of economics: History and theory in the analysis of economic reality* (T. W. Hutchinson, Trans.). Springer Verlag. (Original work published 1940)

Foucault, M. (2000). The risks of security. In J. D. Faubion (Ed.), *Essential works of Foucault, 1954–1984, vol. 3: Power* (R. Hurley et al., Trans.; pp. 365–381). Penguin.

Foucault, M. (2008). *The birth of biopolitics: Lectures at the Collège de France, 1978–79* (G. Burchell, Trans.; M. Senellart, Ed.). Palgrave Macmillan.

Gamble, A. (1996). *Hayek: The iron cage of liberty.* Avalon.

Gray, J. (1984). *Hayek on liberty.* Blackwell.

Hayek, F. A. (1944). *The road to serfdom.* Routledge & Kegan Paul.

Hayek, F. A. (1945). The use of knowledge in society. *American Economic Review, 35*(4), 519–530.

Hayek, F. A. (1949a). Economics and knowledge. In F. A. Hayek, *Individualism and economic order* (pp. 33–56). Routledge & Kegan Paul.

Hayek, F. A. (1949b). The use of knowledge in society. In F. A. Hayek (Ed.), *Individualism and economic order* (pp. 77–91). Routledge & Kegan Paul.

Hayek, F. A. (1949c). The meaning of competition. In F. A. Hayek (Ed.), *Individualism and economic order* (pp. 92–106). Routledge & Kegan Paul.

Hayek, F. A. (1949d). Socialist calculation I: The nature and history of the problem. In F. A. Hayek (Ed.), *Individualism and economic order* (pp. 119–147). Routledge & Kegan Paul.

Hayek, F. A. (1949e). Socialist calculation II: The state of the debate. In F. A. Hayek (Ed.), *Individualism and economic order* (pp. 148–180). Routledge & Kegan Paul.

Hayek, F. A. (1949f). Socialist calculation III: The "competitive" solution. In F. A. Hayek (Ed.), *Individualism and economic order* (pp. 181–219). Routledge & Kegan Paul.

Hayek, F. A. (1954). Marktwirtschaft und Wirtschaftspolitik. *ORDO: Jahrbuch für die Ordnung von Wirtschaft und Gesellschaft, 6*(4), 3–17.

Hayek, F. A. (1960). *The constitution of liberty*. Routledge & Kegan Paul.

Hayek, F. A. (1978). *New studies in philosophy, politics, economics and the history of ideas*. Routledge.

Hayek, F. A. (2013). *Law, legislation and liberty: A new statement of liberal principles of justice and political economy* (3 Vols.). Routledge Classics.

Hindess, B. (1990). Liberty and equality. In B. Hindess (Ed.), *Reactions to the Right* (pp. 7–31). Routledge.

Keynes, J. M. (1980). Keynes letter to Hayek, 28th June 1944. In D. Moggridge (Ed.), *Collected writings of John Maynard Keynes, vol. 27: Activities 1940–1946* (pp. 385–388). Macmillan/Cambridge University Press.

Kitch, E. W. (1983). The fire of truth: A remembrance of law and economics at Chicago, 1932–1970. *The Journal of Law and Economics, 26*(1), 163–234.

Mannheim, K. (1940). *Man and society in an age of reconstruction* (E. Shils, Trans.). Kegan Paul, Trench, Trubner & Co.

Mannheim, K. (1977). *Freedom, power and democratic planning*. Routledge. (Original work published 1951)

McCormack, R. E., & Meiners, R. E. (1988). University governance: A property rights perspective. *The Journal of Law and Economics, 31*(2), 423–442.

Olssen, M. (2010). *Liberalism, neoliberalism, social democracy: Thin communitarian perspectives on political philosophy and education*. Routledge.

Olssen, M. (2016). Neoliberal competition in higher education today: Research, accountability and impact. *British Journal of Sociology of Education, 37*(1), 129–148. https://doi.org/10.1080/01425692.2015.1100530

Olssen, M. (2018). Neoliberalism & democracy: A Foucauldian perspective on public choice theory, ordo liberalism and the concept of the public good. In D. Cahill, M. Konings, M. Cooper, & D. Primrose (Eds.), *Sage handbook on neoliberalism* (pp. 384–396). Sage.

Olssen, M., Codd, J., & O'Neill, A.-M. (2004). *Education policy: Globalization, citizenship & democracy*. Sage.

Polanyi, K. (2001). *The great transformation: The political and economic origins of our time* (2nd ed.). Beacon Press. (Original work published 1944)

Raaper, R., & Olssen, M. (2016). Mark Olssen on the neoliberalisation of higher education and academic lives: An interview. *Policy Futures in Education, 14*(2), 147–163. https://doi.org/10.1177/1478210315610992

Röpke, W. (1971). *A Humane Economy: The Social Framework of the Free Market*. Liberty Fund, Inc. (Original work published 1958)

Rosanvallon, P. (2011). *Democratic legitimacy: Impartiality, reflexivity, proximity* (A. Goldhammer, Trans.). Princeton University Press.

Simons, H. C. (1934). *A positive program for laissez-faire: Some proposals for a liberal economic policy*. University of Chicago Press.

Simons, H. C. (1948). *Economic policy for a free society*. University of Chicago Press.

Tomlinson, J. (1990). Market socialism: A basis for socialist renewal? In B. Hindess (Ed.), *Reactions to the Right* (pp. 32–49). Routledge.

Zamora, D., & Behrent, M. C. (Eds.). (2016). *Foucault and neoliberalism*. Polity.

CHAPTER 11

Neoliberal Competition in Higher Education Today

Research, Accountability and Impact

Abstract

Drawing on Foucault's elaboration of neoliberalism as a positive form of state power, the ascendancy of neoliberalism in higher education in Britain is examined in terms of the displacement of public good models of governance, and their replacement with individualised incentives and performance targets, heralding new and more stringent conceptions of accountability and monitoring across the higher education sector. After surveying the defeat of the public good models, the article seeks to better understand the deployment of neoliberal strategies of accountability and then assess the role that these changes entail for the university sector in general. Impact assessment, I claim, represents a new, more sinister phase of neoliberal control. In the concluding section it is suggested that such accountability models are not incompatible with the idea of the public good and, as a consequence, a meaningful notion of accountability can be accepted and yet prized apart from its neoliberal rationale.

1 Introduction

The changes to higher education inaugurated in Britain in the 1980s, as a result of the election of Thatcher's Conservative government, ushered in a sea change of how the public sector was to be managed, and of the role of government in relation to public spending. The broad faith in Keynesian demand management was replaced by a range of new economic, financial and administrative perspectives whose central common assumptions can be seen as constituted by a particular strain of liberal thought referred to most often as "neoliberalism". The central defining characteristic of this new liberalism was based on an application of the logic and rules of market competition to the public sector.

Understanding the differences between neoliberal and classical liberal discourse provides an important key to understanding the distinctive nature of the neoliberal revolution as it impacted throughout much of the Western world in the last three decades. Michel Foucault's (2008) lectures at the Collège de France of 1978–1979 provide an important text for understanding the nature of these differences.[1] Whereas classical liberalism represents a negative conception of state power in that the individual was taken as an object to be freed from the interventions of the state, neoliberalism has come to represent a positive conception of the state's role in creating the appropriate market by providing the conditions, laws and institutions necessary for its operation. Whereas in classical liberalism the individual is characterised as having an autonomous human nature and can practice freedom, in neoliberalism the state seeks to create an individual who is an enterprising and competitive entrepreneur. Foucault (2008, pp. 176–179) recounts how the ordoliberal programme in Germany embodied this positive state role. It is not that the conception of the self-interested subject is replaced or done away with by the new ideals of "neoliberalism", but that in an age of universal welfare the perceived possibilities of slothful indolence create necessities for new forms of surveillance, performance appraisal and accountability, and ever more vigilant forms of monitoring and control.

Also central to neoliberalism is an attack on the idea of the public good. It is indeed the displacement of public good models of governance, and their replacement with individualised incentives and performance targets, heralding a new, more stringent conception of accountability and monitoring, with which this article is primarily concerned. The initial criticism of the public good can be seen as developing in American social sciences in the first half of the 20th century, in the work of Schumpeter (1943/1976), who linked the concept of the good to the classical doctrine of democracy. Schumpeter identified the pre-Enlightenment philosophy of democracy as "that institutional arrangement for arriving at political decisions which realize the common good by making the people decide issues through the election of individuals who are to assemble in order to carry out its will" (1943/1976, p. 250). As such, the common good functioned as "the obvious beacon light of policy which is always simple to define and which every normal person can be made to see by means of rational argument" (1943/1976, p. 250). As is well known, Schumpeter opposed the idea. First, he denied any notion of "a uniquely determined common good that all people could agree on or be made to agree on through the force of rational argument" (1943/1976, p. 250). Second, he appealed to the fact that "some people may want things other than the common good" as well as "to the much more fundamental fact that to different individuals and groups the common good is bound to mean different things" (1943/1976, p. 251). Third, he stated that even if a general good, such as the utilitarian good of maximising pleasure, could be agreed upon, essential conflicts (such as whether "socialism" or "capitalism" should prevail, or over the limits and nature of "health") would be left unresolved (1943/1976, pp. 251–252).

Schumpeter set the scene in the second half of the century for economic theorists such as Henry Calvert Simons, father of the Chicago School of economics,[2] and Kenneth Arrow, originator of social choice theory, and later influenced James Buchanan and the "New Right".[3] While the Chicago School initiated a major resurgence of free market economics, the major effect of Arrow's work was to challenge all conceptions of collective politics. As Amartya Sen (2002, p. 330) reports, Arrow had been asked by Olaf Helmer, a logician at the Rand Corporation who was interested in applying game theory to international relations: "In what sense could collectivities be said to have utility functions?" Arrow determined that no satisfactory method for aggregating a multiplicity of orderings into one single ordering existed. Hence, there was "a difficulty in the concept of social welfare" (1950, p. 328). The outcome was a PhD that formulated the General Possibility Theorem, which was a modification of the old paradox of voting. As Sen (2002, p. 262) notes, this theorem was "an oddly optimistic name for what is more commonly—and more revealingly—called Arrow's 'impossibility theorem'", in that it describes "that it is impossible to devise an integrated social preference for diverse individual preferences". Arrow's claim was that a unified coherent social welfare function, expressing a single value, such as a public good, could not be expressed from the disaggregated preferences of individuals, without dictatorially discounting some at the expense of others. As Arrow (1951, p. 24) states:

> If we exclude the possibility of interpersonal comparisons of utility, then the only method of passing from individual tastes to social preferences which will be satisfactory and which will be defined for a wide range of sets of individual orderings are either imposed or dictatorial.

For Sen (2002, p. 343), such work has relevance "in the context of political thought in which aggregative notions are used, such as the 'general will' or the 'common good' or the 'social imperative'". What became apparent to Buchanan was that "these political ideas require[d] re-examination in the light of Arrow's results" (1954b, p. 343). Two of Buchanan's articles published in 1954 reveal the major influence of Arrow's work in his conception of and attack upon the notion of public interest.[4] Under conditions of optimal social choice, which included all, individual rankings of states of affairs or preferences could not be calculated in terms of a single value, like stability, or be Pareto optimal, unless conditions of dictatorship were presumed to operate.

The attack on the notion of the public good went hand in hand with new theories of institutional and organisational behaviour, and new models of public service. As founder of the school of public choice, Buchanan advocated the application of economic theories to public-sector institutions in the interest of making public organisations subject to the similar costs and benefits that operate in the private sector.[5] Collective entities such as the "public good" were held not to exist because they were reducible to individual experiences. This "methodological individualism" was fundamental. As Buchanan acknowledged in *The Calculus of Consent*, "the whole calculus has meaning only if methodological individualism is accepted" (Buchanan & Tullock, 1962, p. 265).

It is on this basis that public choice theory (PCT) attacks as "myth" the idea that public services are able to function in terms of the public good. PCT asserts the view that the notion of the public good is a fiction which cloaks the opportunistic behaviour of bureaucrats as they seek to expand their bureaus, increase their expenditures and maximise their own personal advantages. Buchanan maintains that a coincidence of interests between the civil servant's private interests and their conception of the public interest ensues, such that "within the constraints that he faces the bureaucrat tends to maximise his own utility" (1975, p. 161). If preferences are inherently subjective they cannot be known and transferred into a collective value judgement, such as a public good, because such a notion neglects the rights of consumers whose interests the public service and politicians are meant to serve, but do not. In arguing such a view, as Brian Barry (1990, p. 256) notes, Buchanan and Tullock "aim to destroy a whole tradition of political theorizing". Essentially, "the public has no place in their world". This is the tradition that recognises the existence and "promotion of widely shared common interests—public interests—the most important reason for the existence of public authorities" (1990, p. 256).

Despite the rejection of the notion of the public good, what is centrally important here in terms of understanding the advent of neoliberal accountability and monitoring mechanisms is that Buchanan does not abolish the idea of an active or positive state. He stood opposed to Hayek's naturalist faith in markets as spontaneous self-regulating systems on this ground. As he says:

> My basic criticism of F. A. Hayek's profound interpretation of modern history and his diagnosis for improvement is directed at his apparent belief or faith that social evolution will … ensure the survival of efficient institutional forms. Hayek is so distrustful of man's explicit attempts of reforming institutions that he accepts uncritically the evolutionary alternative. (Buchanan 1975, p. 194n)

In this, Buchanan introduced a major shift from liberal to neoliberal governmentality—from a naturalist faith in self-regulating markets to an anti-naturalistic thesis that expresses a much greater faith in conscious political action to legitimate the "long over-due task of institutional over-haul" (see Reisman, 1990, p. 74). For Buchanan, rather than trust individuals to act autonomously, as in classical liberalism, under his neoliberal variant the state should engineer and monitor the accountability of individuals and institutions to promote efficiency in market terms.

2   Research and Accountability

In disputing that civil servants served the public interest, PCT advocated such a "positive" state to develop quasi-market procedures in order to render institutions efficient based on the classical economic model of individuals as "self-interested appropriators", At the operational level it suggests redesigning public institutions to reflect more accurately the preferences of individuals, thus counteracting possible forms of "capture", which deflect public officials from the public's real needs, and advocating a variety of quasi-market strategies. These include the following:
– contracting out services to the private sector;
– increasing competition between units within the public sector;
– placing all potentially conflicting responsibilities into separate institutions;
– separating the commercial and non-commercial functions of the state;
– separating the advisory, regulatory and delivery functions into different agencies;
– introducing an assortment of accountability and monitoring techniques and strategies aimed to overcome all possible sources of inequity, inefficiency, corruption and "capture", particularly those arising from the pursuit of self-interest; and
– ensuring international competitiveness, efficiency and excellence.

It is on this basis that public-sector reforms relating to health, security or education have sought to restructure the basis of accountability through notions tied to individually attached incentives and targets, and through monitoring and assessment through audits.

PCT and other neoliberal theories were adopted in Britain soon after the election of the Thatcher government in 1979. In higher education the first major external mechanism introduced was to assess accountability in research. The British government asked the UK funding councils to devise a means to assess research output and quality. One of the primary reasons given was to inform funding council allocations of the grant for research. The idea that some form of individualised accountability was necessary had been debated for some considerable time. When Margaret Thatcher invited James Buchanan to London, he talked frankly about public servants as exploiting the conditions of their offices whilst hiding behind notions of "public duty" or "professionalism", and as indulging repeatedly in "rent-seeking behaviour". Anecdotal "evidence" of shirking, free-riding, slothfulness or corruption led many to agree that an increased level of accountability was warranted (Curtis, 2007).[6]

The Research Assessment Exercise (RAE) in Britain was first implemented in 1986 and then in 1989, 1992, 1996, 2001 and 2008. Its main purpose was to survey the quantity and scope of research in order to provide data for the distribution of funding through the funding councils. When introduced, the stated purposes related to accountability and efficiency, to gauge resource allocation and improve decision-making, and to assist with governance. Later RAEs maintained essentially similar aims and rationales. Each Unit of Assessment (UoA) supported a panel comprising expert peer-reviewers from across the disciplinary areas. Academics were "returnable" based on four pieces of research published over the six years preceding the RAE assessment. The criteria used by the panels included originality, significance and rigour. In later RAEs work was also codified in terms of "quality", "excellence", "international status" and "robustness".

Notwithstanding a general consensus as to the need for accountability, criticisms of the particular approach employed by the RAE and of the way such processes are carried out have become increasingly clear over time. As Brian Findsen notes, in a commentary on the 2008 RAE, the peer reviewers that constitute the expert panels mean essentially a system of:

> subjective judgements and this subjectivity can change depending on who is making the judgement. Hence, who gets to read the actual individual pieces and make recommendations to the next level above can heavily influence the outcome. (2008, p. 65)

That the expertise combined in UoA panels could not possibly represent the diversity of disciplinary frameworks represented within each UoA underscores the significance of this criticism. That subjective valuations or interdisciplinary politics could make particular individual rankings unreliable also became evident during the "dummy runs" that individual universities organised as a practice before the final submission. It became evident that many academics were unhappy about the role played by internal departmental politics in favouring some paradigms over others, prioritising some sorts of academic research over others, prioritising approaches which fitted with a department or schools core offerings, or represented personal or paradigm animosities or factionalism.

Another criticism related to the effect of national assessment monitoring on the internal work life of higher education institutions. Both the former 2008 RAE and the 2014 Research Excellence Framework (REF) have sought to impose a single set of narrowly defined norms constructing a single unitary model that should define all academic research success. There is very little room in this model for the view that academia is an enterprise which supports a variety of different approaches or undertakings. That such an external accountability system substantially increases stress and anxiety has been well documented (Barnett, 2000; Bates, 2003; Coryn et al., 2007; Currie, 2008; Sharp, 2004). The full emotional costs of such processes on individual academics' lives and careers have yet to adequately studied. The competitive nature of the process, together with the complexity of compliance, at the university, faculty, department and individual levels, will not only affect anxiety and stress but also research productivity itself. Not only does it place too much emphasis on research productivity and performativity, it militates against "blue skies" research, encourages dubious research tactics and strategies for maximising publications, citations and team-based research, and from the individual researcher's viewpoint over-encourages conformity to the system of external expectations concerning research.

These consequences of the audit process constitute some of the ways in which the academic career is being "deprofessionalised" or, stated differently, by which professionalisation is being redefined. A change in the system of accountability impacts strongly on the academic career. For Alis Oancea (2008, p. 157), "the RAE model contributes to the routinization of formal, bureaucratic accountability, and hinders democratic dialogue among the research, practice and policy communities concerned". She cites Stewart Ranson (2003, p. 460), who describes it as a "revolution in accountability" to "preserve public trust". Ranson (2003, pp. 463–464) distinguishes five types or modes of accountability:

- professional, based on professional judgement and expert knowledge;
- consumer, based on market competition and market choice;
- contract, based on tendering and efficiency;
- performative, based on public inspection and standards; and
- corporate, based on business plan and profit.

While "professional" constitutes a pre-neoliberal method of accountability, the remaining types all constitute forms of "neoliberal" accountability. In previous work (Olssen, 2002a, 2002b), I distinguished between "bureaucratic–professional" and "consumer–managerial" models based on a model initially put forward in New Zealand by the State Services Commission (New Zealand State Services Commission, 1992). Under the consumer–managerial forms of accountability:

> the assumption is that academics must demonstrate their utility to society by placing themselves in an open market and accordingly compete

for students who provide the bulk of core funding through tuition fees. If academic research has value, it can stand up to the rigours of competition for limited funds. (New Zealand State Services Commission, 1992, p. 15)

From the neoliberal perspective, however, old forms of professionalism are distrusted in that they generate conditions for opportunism, free-riding, shirking and "rent-seeking behaviour".

3 From Bad to Worse: The REF and the Impact of Research

There are many other criticisms of the old RAE. What became clear is that the process benefited some universities over others. As Sharp (2004, p. 202) notes: "The RAE is essentially an 'old' universities exercise designed to give more to the already well-off and to deny opportunities for newer institutions".[7] It became apparent that the RAE caused a shift in what was to count as research, demoting the importance of the "book", or "monograph", traditionally important in the social sciences and humanities, in preference for the "journal article" (Lingard 2008, p. 180). What also occurred is that such accountability and monitoring processes downgraded the professional work of many departments and schools, especially in disciplines like education, nursing or social work where there was a practice and policy focus (Lingard, 2008, p. 180).

Due to cumulative criticisms of the RAE, the government announced in March 2006 that the 2008 RAE round would be the last one, and that it would be replaced by the REF. Notwithstanding the shift in nomenclature, the REF was similar to the RAE. As with the RAE, the Higher Education Funding Council for England (HEFCE, 2010) states that "through the REF, the UK funding bodies aim to develop and sustain a dynamic and internationally competitive research sector that makes a major contribution to economic prosperity, national wellbeing and the expansion and dissemination of knowledge". As with the previous RAE, the REF was also a process of expert review. Submissions were made to each UoA. Although the use of metric-based indicators and especially citation information to inform the reviews of outputs was originally envisaged to be considerably greater, the process of putting it into operation saw a retreat from this position.[8] Other aspects were also much the same.[9]

It was in relation to the nature of these submissions, and the assessment of non-academic impact, that the major difference was manifest. Although "user-assessors" had been included on the 2008 RAE panels, there was no formal requirement to assess research in terms of its socio-economic impact, which meant that the non-academic "user-assessors" included on the panels would be crowded out by academic assessment. While quality of research outputs would continue to be the primary factor in the assessment, it was required in the REF that research was also to be formally assessed in relation to its "wider impact" on "the economy, society, culture, public policy or services, health, the environment or quality of life, beyond academia" (HEFCE, 2011, p. 26). Impact case studies represented a particular unit or subgroup within a UoA (representing a department or school) rather than being submitted by individuals. The REF required institutions to each submit one impact template (statement), as well as (essentially) one impact case study for every 10 academics returned, per UoA.[10] While this means, importantly, that nine out of 10 academics were not being judged on impact, the narratives prepared needed to show that all academic staff were supporting impact. This means that there could be one or several impact case studies for each UoA assessed by expert panels comprising discipline specialists as well as industry and/or wider policy "user-assessors".[11] The relative weightings in the overall assessment were 65% quality of research, 20% impact and 15% environment.

The effects of assessing impact signal a new emphasis in neoliberal technologies: no longer concerned solely with demonstrating productivity and the quality of research, but with a new concern to assess and authorise the relevance of research being undertaken in terms of the contribution and significance for the wider society. Stefan Collini (2009) has documented some of the possible consequences of this approach to academia in an article, "Impact on Humanities", in the November 2009 issue of the *Times Literary Supplement* and also in his book (Collini, 2012). One important problem he identifies relates to the effect of such an approach on the humanities, where he believes it will have a seriously distorting effect on research. He conjectures the difficulty of classifying a book on Victorian poetry in such a way, and envisages a situation where, despite being viewed by peers as "one of the best books in the field", it scores "zero impact" for research.

Putting aside the issue as to whether having a high impact makes one's research better, it is likely to "marketise" research in a chillingly new way, for it will constitute a "structural selectivity" or "pressure" forcing every academic into hustling and hawking their wares to the media, and into fervent "networking" to "end-users" in society. As Collini (2009) says:

> Not only do a variety of uncontrollable factors determine the chances of such translation into another medium, but there is also no reason to think that the success of such translation bears any relation to the quality of the original work. If anything, meretricious and vulgarizing treatments (which concentrate on, say, the poet's sex life) will stand a greater chance of success than do nuanced critical readings.

Departments, Collini predicted, would become "marketing agents". Substantial administrative reorganisation at every level of the university and beyond would be required.

Having been through the recent REF has not diminished or clarified these difficulties. Rather, it has revealed deep structural fissures at the core of the impact system—concerning what is impact, as well as how to assess it. As those disciplines (UoAs) that did not score well have discovered, obtaining reliable feedback on the basis for impact assessment has proved well-nigh impossible. Feedback so far given reveals that the recent impact evaluation in the REF is clouded in obscurity and a lack of transparency as regards both the context of feedback as well as of the sense as to how impact determinations were made.[12] What would seem evident is that assignment of impact scores has been a socially engineered activity massively influenced by who the various panel members are as well as the ability and willingness of panels to enact consensual agreements on behalf of the discipline.[13] What also appears valid is that user-group assessors played only a minimal role but were (as in 2008) "crowded out" by the academic panel members acting as a group. Although formally included as members of the UoAs, the anecdotal evidence to hand would appear to suggest that the "industry user-assessors" did not participate in the impact-evaluation process independently of other members of the panels. Although at this stage these conjectures must remain hypotheses in need of corroboration, it will be interesting whether the opacity of the process here suggested can, in time, be challenged.

If, so far, impact assessment conveys images of the "emperor's new clothes", constituting, as one is inclined to conjecture, a "nod, nod, wink, wink strategy" for UK higher education, the basis for such accusations and doubts were amply highlighted in discussions prior to the REF by Collini, who referred to the sheer "epistemic difficulty" in assessing impact. To assess impact, audit panel members will need to become "implausibly penetrating and comprehensive cultural historians". Collini wonders:

> Has anyone really thought about what this could involve where ideas are concerned? An experienced cultural or social historian, working on the topic for years, might—just might—be able to identify the part played by a particular piece of academic research in long-term changes in certain social practices and attitudes, but it would require a highly detailed study and could probably only be completed long after the event and with full access to a wide range of sources of different kinds. Yet every department in the land is going to have to attempt something like this if they are to get credit for the "impact" of their "excellent" research. (Collini, 2009)

While discussing the epistemic difficulties concerning impact, it can be observed that in a strictly methodological sense its assessment suffers from similar difficulties to the types of proclamations and judgements made in the past by "old boy networks", "class-based elites", "the landed nobility", "statesmen of the era of empire" or "colonial power cabals"—namely that there is no epistemological basis independent of the privileged power such groups hold by which to warrant the legitimacy of the assessments made. The assessments of impact are, we could say, inextricably "entangled" with the privileged positions of the REF panel who establish them. Reliability in this sense is difficult to establish on a genuinely independent basis.

A somewhat related criticism could be addressed toward the RAE/REF system of assessment in general. While the RAE/REF is a neoliberal imposition, because it maintains the continued dominance of peer review it fails completely to remove the downsides of "professional capture" that neoliberalism sought to address. Just as "managers" have proved vulnerable to being "captured" by "managerialism", and thereby failing to understand the vulnerabilities and "special needs" of the academy, or the public good, so academics who are appointed to these audit panels become the willing functionaries, themselves cherishing the esteem conferred, and supporting the neoliberal "gaming" by which universities, in the context of the plethora of outcome measures available, can "cherry pick" their way to improved rankings.

While no one disputes that academics should seek to explain the significance of what they do to the wider public, to policymakers, and specialist groups who may be interested, the demand to quantify impact to industry and societal end-users within a specific set time period simply beggars belief.[14] Yet, in that it represents a new dimension of audit evaluation and constitutes a substantial percentage of the overall assessment, impact constitutes a new "structural selectivity", or "lever", contributing to the major transformation of academia. Impact, indeed, I argue, constitutes an extension of the neoliberal project from accountability for how academics have met their responsibilities to control over the content of research itself. What is being proposed by impact is "the uptake of research by external users" (i.e., industry and societal policy groups). In doing so, it constitutes a new definition of research and of what is allowed, and perhaps more importantly not allowed, which is dangerously open to interpretation by the hegemony of dominant and powerful groups.

We can all agree today that some form of accountability is important. Yet the impact agenda goes well beyond the initial reasons provided for introducing accountability of research and extends into dangerous areas of monitoring and control. In that it does so, the accountability comes perilously close to contradicting traditional understandings of academic freedom. Although it could be said that researchers are still free to research what they like, with no interference, the fact that some academics or department's work might be graded as having "no impact" constitutes at least indirect pressure on what should be researched. Will a university be prepared to continue to employ a researcher whose work is judged by panels of their peers as not contributing to the impact agenda? Could this be seen as pressure directed at academics, departments, schools, faculties and universities as to what topics, discipline subjects and areas they should be researching? If this is the upshot of the impact agenda, then accountability takes on a more positive force which functions as a form of political control.

4 Neoliberalism and Democracy

The erosion of individual researcher autonomy and control and the increased constraints exerted over professionalism are not the only serious issue here. The REF, like the RAE, erodes the autonomy of universities as independent agents within the larger political society. In this sense, supply-side funding is being increasingly used to exert political control over universities and their functioning. Whereas until the REF these have tied universities into control through financial accountability in order to justify expenditure and inform decision-making, now, with the REF, there is an increasing concern with control over the substance and content of what is being researched.

The consequence of this increasing central control is to erode the two central roles of the liberal university. First, as a consequence of the increased pressure over what is researched, researcher creativity is diminished, and the nature of knowledge production in universities is altered. By insisting that research must be evaluated according to its impact on "end-users" (industry, policy, society), the traditional separation of universities and higher education from the market and from politics is undermined. It inserts an additional commercial driver which undermines traditional academic principles based on disinterested academic research, open enquiry, intellectual curiosity and discovery. It is what John Ziman (2000), the physicist, terms "post-academic research" (pp. 172, 327) based on a model of "instrumental research" (pp. 15–17) driven by "market forces" (p. 173).

The rise of neoliberalism thus signals a significant modification to the liberal values of individual rights and freedom concerning research. Not only will this militate against individually driven "blue skies" research in preference for short-run collectively imposed research objectives which can demonstrate impact, but it also neglects that most research of value is contributed after many years of activity, comprising modest returns, false starts and blind alleys. Research of real benefit to society proceeds from trial and error and is "curiosity-driven" from the "bottom-up"; that is, by researchers themselves, largely unencumbered by directives from on high. Increasingly, however, the RAE/REF is dictating and controlling what researchers must do: if a department or school is submitting to a particular UoA, research by individuals which does not "fit" the scope of expertise considered will be rendered invalid and discouraged or disallowed. Such researchers may well, quite legitimately, fear for their futures.

A second consequence is equally insidious. Real quality, it can be argued, does not necessarily correlate with what sort of journal one publishes in, or whether one publishes journal articles, monographs, books, textbooks or edited collections. Yet as we now know, the REF demands only certain outputs, and it is highly likely that such a process will undermine what is important for research. Whether in science, social science or humanities, serendipity, luck, long-term perseverance and commitment have been central to outcomes and these cannot always be predicted from the standpoint of the present. There is a danger that in trying to second-guess good research in advance by assessing and funding it in terms of "impact", the very preconditions of discovery and innovation that are central to our futures and our conceptions of ourselves as free liberal beings are being undermined. Good research is not only unpredictable in advance but it can also take an inordinately long time. John Rawls (1971) reputedly took seven years to write *A Theory of Justice*, and one may be excused for wondering whether the REF will be able to accommodate such an endeavour today. Of course, many writers whose work has had impact have produced very little in quantitative terms during their lives. Ludwig Wittgenstein, one of the great philosophers of the 20th century, published only one book during his lifetime, and that numbering only 70 pages.[15]

Third, what is also eroded through neoliberal reforms is the political autonomy of the university, which constitutes a traditional foundation of the democratic polity, and which was central to its role of offering objective, detached and informed policy advice, as well as critical insights to the government of the day. This was a role that was central to the very first universities, emerging in Bologna in the 9th century, Paris in the 12th century, and at Oxford and Cambridge in the 13th century. As Max Weber (1921) argued, the independence of universities from the state served an important political function as it ensured the separation of knowledge and its production from those who exercised political rule. In this sense, the separation of universities was similar to the separation of powers as formulated by John Locke and Baron de Montesquieu in the 17th and 18th centuries. The autonomy, professionalism, security of tenure and academic freedom of individual academics is derived from this.

In Britain it has been long understood that the liberal university performed such a role. Its critical independence from the state was jealously guarded. Such was presumed in the institution of the "university constituency", for instance.[16] Although Labour politicians criticised such a system as being elitist,[17] the system did assist with the disbursement of power and in a peculiar way exemplified the model of the liberal university as being semi-autonomous from the state.

It is this system which has lost its independence with the onset of supply-side funding from the 1980s and the calls for greater accountability. From being an autonomous centre of power—the fifth estate, as it were—which could both inform and criticise government, universities have had that autonomy curtailed. Increasingly, they have become *neoliberalised*, thus comprising the "willing lackeys" of the state's positive higher education agenda. The RAE/REF constitutes a specific technology in this process. Added to this technology are many others—the new tendency to recruit to university councils from business expertise outside the university, which has in some cases displaced academics from effective control and governance; the erosion of the powers of the senate and the establishment of executive boards; statutory deregulation, through application to the Privy Council; the abolition of tenure and the importation of systems of line management, and the frequent and widespread use of restructuring—that seriously threaten academic professionalism, institutional autonomy and academic freedom today. The control of financial resources through research funding (via Research Councils UK or other providers, and by the funding councils), as well as through periodic external audits (RAE/REF), and the external assessment of teaching (National Student Survey [NSS]) further increase the pressures and contribute to the *deprofessionalisation* of academic staff at the same time as the traditional autonomy of the university is undermined by subjecting it to market forces.

A final consequence of neoliberal reforms discussed in this article is the erosion of academic professionalism as a group of highly trained individuals who exercise control over their own institutions and conditions of work. Deprofessionalisation operates at several levels: firstly, through the external imposition on universities of models of assessment by the state. Secondly, a parallel process operates internal to universities. Universities have inaugurated line-management systems which have excluded academics from meaningful and effective participation in running the institutions. Through techniques such as "restructuring", widely employed over the last two decades, academics have been rendered effectively docile, in many cases unwilling to resist. Such a managerialism, it must be concluded, has been deliberately engendered, and has seen higher education increasingly managed and governed according to the dictates of the market. As a result, the influence of academics over the governance and management of universities has waned and there has been a significant increase of non-academic managers from outside. As Kolsaker (2014) has found, while academic autonomy and participation in governance have been eroded, resulting in deprofessionalisation, non-academics and those in management positions have experienced greater professionalisation. The conflict reflects a division between the authoritarian, top-down nature of line-management systems, based upon "principal–agent" relations, as formulated in terms of agency theory, and the more collegial, deliberative, models of democratic governance associated with traditional models of academia. Although we acknowledge that non-academic expertise can certainly lend important skills and knowledge to university governance and management, it is important that academics are not themselves displaced from effective decision-making and participation in the governance and management of their institutions.

It was of course the idea of universities as separate from state control and from public scrutiny that led to criticisms of them as "ivory towers" where both the university and those employed inside them were unaccountable in terms of standards understood and maintained in the "real world". It is in this sense that the neoliberal criticisms of "professionalism" as a form of "rent-seeking behaviour" were widely perceived as valid. In that I am supporting a certain form of accountability as important, there is no objection to individual employee assessments to ensure "a fair day's work for a fair day's pay" being operated by universities themselves. To achieve this, the concept of the public good, introduced at the start of this article, can serve as a more neutral and fairer category than market competition to operate accountability in higher education. Importantly, if structured this way, it would dispense with the market mechanism which maintains inbuilt biases towards the business and the wealthy, propels cumulative and compounding inequality, is insensitive to job security and employee aspirations, increases stress, and confounds consumer wants and desires with genuine need. Although both Schumpeter and Buchanan rejected the concept of the public good in its preference for individualised performance targets *in toto*, there is actually nothing necessarily incompatible between the two. The public good is normative in that it represents genuinely shared interests, is positive rather than zero-sum, has an inbuilt sense of fairness, and would not be motivated solely by university league tables as the motor by which assessment is driven. That individual performance should be rendered accountable to ensure basic honesty and fairness in relation to acceptable public standards is acceptable, albeit not in a neoliberal way. Indeed, it should not require that academia is dominated by an Orwellian bureaucracy which pressures every day of an academic's life, impacting massively on staff time over six-year cycles.

This would acknowledge that some of the initial arguments from neoliberals concerning accountability can be accepted. While Foucault is often represented as a critic of neoliberalism, recent work by Zamora (2015) claims that Foucault remains agnostic on neoliberalism as to political solutions generally but seems to suggest that "supply-side" models offer some insurance against the "bads" associated with old socialistic models of the state or with "ivory tower" elitism that has been seen to characterise the university in times past where regimes of accountability and transparency were seen as lacking. While we can thus accede to the neoliberals' call for accountability as important, it should be related to consensual standards of the public good, rather than reflecting the vagaries of endless market competition in an economic model of higher education. Although Foucault might therefore give a limited endorsement to some of the concerns raised by the neoliberals, he also thought that such governance models would need regulatory guidance and control by the state in order to obviate tendencies to inequality and constrain the antisocial consequences associated with purely market models.

Accountability and transparency must be incorporated at various levels, of course. In addition to individualised performances by academics, management itself must be subject to such monitoring. Over the last four decades or so it would seem that managerialism has gone too far and there is a need to restore a balance. To this end, one important development that can help check, or offset the new managerialism, is the development within higher education of staff associations (academic assemblies), which are independent of trade unions, and which can "square the circle" of accountability and transparency, by assuring academic representation on all governance committees and management bodies within the institution, and where they have statutory protection to declare whatever opinions on management they see fit to make.[18] This would seem to be appropriate for higher education in a country where most universities are "exempt charities" and serve important public functions. As well as academics and/or staff associations, the other key stakeholder of universities—students—should similarly be represented, through their associations. What must occur, to use the language of Kofi Annan, is that "we, the academics", must recapture the governance and management to restore the autonomy of the estate. One cannot do better than to cite an extract from the 1997 UNESCO Recommendation on the Status of Higher Education Teaching Personnel as a place for my article to end, and for the process of the reprofessionalisation of academia in Britain and across the world to start:

> Section B, Clauses 31 and 32. Self-governance and collegiality
> 31. Higher-education teaching personnel should have the right and opportunity, without discrimination of any kind, according to their abilities, to

take part in the governing bodies and to criticise the functioning of higher education institutions, including their own, while respecting the right of other sections of the academic community to participate, and they should also have the right to elect a majority of representatives to academic bodies within the higher education institution.

32. The principles of collegiality include academic freedom, shared responsibility, the policy of participation of all concerned in internal decision-making structures and practices, and the development of consultative mechanisms. Collegial decision-making should encompass decisions regarding the administration and determination of policies of higher education, curricula, research, extension work, the allocation of resources and other related activities, in order to improve academic excellence and quality for the benefit of society at large. (UNESCO, 1997)

Acknowledgement

This chapter originally appeared as Olssen, M. (2016), Neoliberal competition in higher education today: Research, accountability and impact, *British Journal of Sociology of Education*, 37(1), 129–148, https://doi.org/10.1080/01425692.2015.1100530. Reprinted here, with minor edits, with permission from the publisher.

Notes

1 Although Foucault's (2008) lectures on biopolitics provide an important influence on how neoliberalism is conceptualised in this article, his own contribution will not be directly discussed in detail.
2 See Simons (1948).
3 In my account of neoliberalism here, I have deliberately accorded several US institutionalists, such as Joseph Schumpeter and Kenneth Arrow (elsewhere also, John Nash and others), a central role, although I am aware that many standard accounts of neoliberalism (Simon Marginson, David Harvey, and others) do not even mention them.
4 See Buchanan (1954a, 1954b).
5 Buchanan visited Margaret Thatcher in London in the early 1980s and in this sense was a direct influence on neoliberalism in higher education.
6 The television programmes *Yes Minister* and *Yes, Prime Minister* were, as Adam Curtis (2007) documents, inspired by PCT and contributed to the general perception of the public sector as characterised by wastage and incompetency. Another who

adopted a satirical approach specifically was Laurie Taylor, whose columns in the *Times Higher Education* made Poppleton University, founded in 1979, appear a fit institution for reform.

7   Ball (1997) also argues that the RAE separates the "old" from the "new" universities. Hence, the first 59 are almost all "old" universities, while 60 to 111 are predominantly "new".

8   Because citations were dropped as a means to assess the quality of research, the differences between the REF and the RAE were greatly reduced, as predicted by Zoë Corbyn (2010).

9   Other changes, all of a more minor nature, are documented in HEFCE (2011, p. 10).

10 See HEFCE (2011, p. 28).

11 Industry user-assessors were appointed to all UoA panels in the 2014 REF. This parallels the Warry Report recommendation to Research Councils UK (RCUK) on the efficiency and effectiveness of peer review that an individual competent on the economic impact of research should be accommodated on each panel, when deliberating on research grant bids. The incorporation of impact statements for research grant bids can in an important sense be seen as a precursor for their incorporation into the REF. In a submission by the Russell Group on the Warry Report to RCUK, it was stated that "[t]here is no evidence to date of any rigorous way of measuring economic impact other than in the very broadest of terms and outputs. It is therefore extremely difficult to see how such panel members could be identified or the basis upon which they could be expected to make their observations" (see Russell Group, 2007).

12 One head of school, after admitting that no reliable feedback was obtainable, indicated that another UoA had sought to obtain information by taking the chair of a UoA panel out to dinner.

13 Although research on the issue would need to be conducted carefully, it would be interesting to see in this regard whether UoA panel members' universities scored higher on impact than those not so represented.

14 Case studies must describe impacts that occurred between 1 January 2008 and 31 July 2013 although these "effects, changes or benefits" may have started earlier than the designated period. The impacts must have been underpinned by research produced by the submitting unit, during the period 1 January 1993–31 December 2013.

15 This was the *Tractatus Logico-Philosophicus* (Wittgenstein, 1922/2007). In addition, it can be noted that he had considerable help with it. Russell wrote the foreword, Ogden wrote the translation, and Keynes helped find the publisher (see Peters & Olssen, 2005).

16 University constituencies can be traced in their origins to Scotland, where the earliest universities held representation in the unicameral Estates of Parliament. England adopted the same system in 1603 as the basis of its Parliament, with the

accession of James VI to the throne. In the 18th century the system was continued in the Parliament of Great Britain, and in the UK Parliament until the mid-20th century, as well as in Ireland (see Pugh, 1978).

17 It was held by socialists and others on the political left that possession of a degree should not confer greater electoral rights.

18 Presently, such associations still exist at a small number of universities.

References

Arrow, K. J. (1950). A difficulty in the concept of social welfare. *The Journal of Political Economy, 58*(4), 328–346.

Arrow, K. J. (1951). *Social choice and individual values.* Wiley.

Ball, D. F. (1997). Quality measurement as a basis for resource allocation: Research assessment exercises in United Kingdom universities. *R&D Management, 27*(3), 281–289.

Barnett, R. (2000). *Realising the university in an age of supercomplexity.* Open University Press.

Barry, B. (1990). *Political argument.* Harvester Wheatsheaf.

Bates, R. (2003). Phelan's bibliometric analysis of the impact of Australian educational research. *The Australian Educational Researcher, 30*(2), 57–64.

Buchanan, J. (1954a). Social choice, democracy, and free markets. *Journal of Political Economy, 62*(2), 114–123.

Buchanan, J. (1954b). Individual choice in voting and the market. *Journal of Political Economy, 62*(4), 334–344.

Buchanan, J. (1975). *The limits of liberty: Between anarchy and leviathan.* University of Chicago Press.

Buchanan, J., & Tullock, G. (1962). *The calculus of consent: Logical foundations of constitutional democracy.* University of Michigan Press.

Collini, S. (2009, November 13). Impact on humanities. *Times Literary Supplement.* http://entertainment.co.uk/tol/arts_and_entertainment/the_tls/article6915986.ece

Collini, S. (2012). *What are universities for?* Penguin.

Corbyn, Z. (2010, April 1). Nervous HEFCE "edging out" of REF citations. *Times Higher Education.*

Coryn, C., Hattie, J., Scriven, M., & Hartman, D. (2007). Models and mechanisms for evaluating government-funded research: An international comparison. *American Journal of Evaluation, 28,* 437–457.

Currie, J. (2008). Research assessment exercises and some negative consequences of journal rankings and citation indices. *Access: Critical Perspectives on Communication, Cultural & Policy Studies, 27*(1–2), 27–36.

Curtis, A. (2007). *The Trap* [Television documentary in three parts: Part 1: *Fuck you, buddy* (March 11); Part II: *The Lonely Robot* (March 18); Part III: *We will force you to be free* (March 25)]. BBC Television.

Findsen, B. (2008). The RAE in Scotland: A Kiwi participant–observer in an ancient university. *Access: Critical Perspectives on Communication, Cultural & Policy Studies, 27*(1–2), 61–72.

Foucault, M. (2008). *The birth of biopolitics: Lectures at the Collège de France, 1978–79* (G. Burchell, Trans.; M. Senellart, Ed.). Palgrave Macmillan.

HEFCE. (2010). *Research excellence framework*. Higher Education Funding Council for England. http://www.hefce.ac.uk/research/ref/

HEFCE. (2011, July; updated January 2012). *Assessment framework and guidance on submissions: REF 2014*. REF team, Higher Education Funding Council for England.

Kolsaker, A. (2014). Relocating professionalism in an English university. *Journal of Higher Education Policy and Management, 36*(2), 129–142.

Lingard, B. (2008). Globalising research accountabilities. *Access: Critical Perspectives on Communication, Cultural & Policy Studies, 27*(1–2), 175–188.

New Zealand State Services Commission. (1992). *Governance of tertiary institutions*. Paper submitted to the Taskforce on Capital Charging of Tertiary Institutions. Government Printer.

Oancea, A. (2008). Performative accountability and the UK Research Assessment Exercise. *Access: Critical Perspectives on Communication, Cultural & Policy Studies, 27*(1–2), 153–173.

Olssen, M. (2002a). *The neo-liberal appropriation of tertiary education policy in New Zealand: Accountability, research and academic freedom*. "State of the Art" monograph no. 8. New Zealand Association for Research in Education.

Olssen, M. (2002b). The restructuring of tertiary education in New Zealand: Governmentality, neoliberalism, democracy. *McGill Journal of Education, 37*(2), 57–88.

Olssen, M., & Peters, M. A. (2005). Neoliberalism, higher education and the knowledge economy: From the free market to knowledge capitalism. *Journal of Education Policy, 20*(3), 313–345. https://doi.org/10.1080/02680930500108718

Peters, M. A., & Olssen, M. (2005). "Useful knowledge": Redefining research and teaching in the learning economy. In R. Barnett (Ed.), *Reshaping the university: New relationships between research, scholarship and teaching* (pp. 37–48). Society for Research in Higher Education & Open University Press.

Pugh, M. (1978). *Electoral reform in war and peace 1906–1818*. Routledge & Kegan Paul.

Ranson, S. (2003). Public accountability in the age of neoliberal governance. *Journal of Education Policy, 18*(5), 459–480.

Rawls, J. (1971). *A theory of justice*. Oxford University Press.

Reisman, D. (1990). *The political economy of James Buchanan*. Texas A & M University Press.

Russell Group. (2007). *RCUK consultation on the efficiency and effectiveness of peer review*. http://www.csc.liv.ac.uk/cmsweb/down loads/rcuk/research/peer/russell.pdf

Schumpeter, J. (1976). *Capitalism, socialism and democracy*. Routledge. (Original work published 1943)

Sen, A. (2002). *Rationality and freedom*. The Belknap Press of Harvard University Press.

Sharp, S. (2004). The Research Assessment Exercises 1992–2001: Patterns across time and subjects. *Studies in Higher Education, 29*(2), 201–218.

Simons, H. C. (1948). *Economic policy for a free society*. University of Chicago Press.

UNESCO. (1997). *Recommendation of the status of higher education teaching personnel*. UNESCO.

Weber, M. (1921). *Economy and society*. Bedminster.

Wittgenstein, L. (2007). *Tractatus logico-philosophicus*. Cosimo. (Original work published 1922)

Zamora, D. (Ed.). (2015). *Critiquer Foucault: Les années 1980 et la tentation néolibérale* (with J.-L. Amselle, M. C. Behrent, M. S. Christofferson, & J. Rehmann). MCM.

Ziman, J. (2000). *Real science*. Cambridge University Press.

CHAPTER 12

Foucault and Neoliberalism

A Response to Recent Critics and a New Resolution

Abstract

While Foucault has traditionally been represented as a critic of neoliberalism, recent work by Zamora (2016), Zamora and Behrent (2016), as well as François Ewald, and others (see Becker et al., 2012), claims that Foucault's later writings demonstrate a degree of support for neoliberalism and that "supply-side" models offers some insurance against the "bads" associated with old socialistic models of the state. This paper critically re-examines Foucault's perspectives on neoliberalism in order to ascertain the extent to which he can be seen as offering support or opposition to the neoliberal revolution. After briefly summarizing the recent literature on the topic, I will seek a more nuanced reconsideration whereby I aim to dampen the exuberance of these critics who have called Foucault's criticisms of neoliberalism into question. While Foucault saw neoliberal technologies as manifesting some positive effects, in overall terms he sees it as a new form of biopower which replaces liberalism's protections of naturalistic rights and freedoms in order to extend forms of control from the arena of the economy to apply to all spheres of society and all forms of voluntary behaviour. In the final section of the paper, I claim that far from supporting neoliberalism, Foucault can be seen to advocate a form of republican social democracy, based upon the final lecture (April 4th) in *The Birth of Biopolitics*, where he identifies Adam Ferguson as effectively resolving the conundrums of laissez-faire, Homo economicus and positive state power, in a distinctively 18th-century conception of "civil society".

1 Introduction

In this article I start with a critique of the book *Foucault and Neoliberalism*, edited by Daniel Zamora and Michael Behrent (2016), and question the way in which they, and some of the contributors therein, notably, Michael Scott Christofferson and Mitchell Dean, seek to represent Foucault's orientation toward neoliberalism. The paper begins with a brief survey of these writers' perspectives, and then seeks to rescue Foucault from the perspectives they suggest, representing Foucault's approach as constituting simultaneously as both a critique of neoliberal governmentality and defence of a type of social democracy, one based upon the writings on civil society of Adam Ferguson, a thesis maintained by Foucault, but ignored by those who see him as an apologist for neoliberalism. Having rescued Foucault from these critics, I will focus upon the one essential theoretical argument he maintains which is also ignored by the contributors to *Foucault and Neoliberalism*. This concerns Foucault's thesis on "biopolitics" or "biopower", which presupposes a conception of an active, or in the language of liberalism, a "positive" state apparatus which systematically constructs the competitive and enterprising dispositions of its subject-citizens in a way that has scant regard to the liberal virtue of freedom or liberty.

Some commentators might question whether such a minority reading of Foucault warrants such focused attention. A search of the literature, however, reveals that it is not only the seven contributors to the *Foucault and Neoliberalism* volume, but a variety of others (to be discussed below) who have questioned Foucault's own normative stance on the matter. This has produced a conflict of interpretations, with many prominent interpreters of Foucault, such as Audier (2015), Brown (2015), Gane (2014), Gordon (cited in Provenzano, 2016), Harcourt (cited in Becker et al., 2012), Lebaron (2001), Nealon (2008), Provenzano (2016), Revel (2005), to name but some, challenging the overhasty incorporation of Foucault as offering support for the narratives of liberalism or neoliberalism. While summarizing these counter-views below, I will advance a resolution of the controversy by arguing that Foucault's own approach is not only resistant to and critical of neoliberalism, but that taking the lectures of *The Birth of Biopolitics* as a whole, Foucault can be seen to resurrect a form of social democracy of a distinctly communitarian sort. This I will argue is supported from his final lecture of *The Birth of Biopolitics*, on Adam Ferguson, which I will claim can be viewed from a peculiar perspective as simultaneously genealogical and normative, where Foucault documents the 18th-century concern to constrain and limit economy on behalf of society, a constraint which he also suggests neoliberalism does away with, rendering subjects-citizens as endlessly manipulable in that it applies economic logic to all forms of voluntary behaviour across the entire domain of the social. My argument here will be congruent with, and offer further support to, the thesis initially put forward in the US in my article "Michel Foucault as 'Thin' Communitarian" (Olssen, 2002).

2   Criticisms of Foucault

In the book, *Foucault and Neoliberalism*, edited by Daniel Zamora and Michael C. Behrent,[1] Daniel Zamora, a Belgium PhD student, notes at the outset the range of contradictory views relating to Foucault's position on neoliberalism, views documented in various chapters within the book. He references in passing several not included in the book, such as Moreno Pestaña (2011), who represents Foucault as "enamoured of neoliberalism" (Zamora & Behrent, 2016, p. 4) to those that saw Foucault as more critical of it, to those who saw Foucault as indirectly and paradoxically creating the ground to "legitimate a neoliberal common sense" (p. 4). As he says in an article in the French Magazine *Ballast*, "Foucault was very attracted by economic liberalism: he saw in it the possibility of a form of governmentality much less prescriptive and authoritarian than the socialist and communist left".[2] In this context, Zamora sets his book's aim as being "to examine Michel Foucault's work and commitments during his final years" (p. 5).

Michael Scott Christofferson starts off (Chapter 1) analysing Foucault's endorsement of Andre Glucksmann's book *Les maîtres penseurs* (1977).[3] Foucault's endorsement of Glucksmann's "new philosophy" in the 9 May–15 May 1977 issue of *Le nouvel observateur*[4] reciprocated Glucksmann's positive endorsement of Foucault's thesis, and his earlier suggestion that political theory should take a Foucauldian turn.[5] Christofferson notes that given the lack of subtlety and sophistication which many commentators, including Deleuze, accorded Glucksmann's analysis, Foucault's support can perhaps be explained by the fact that in the mid-1970s, his own thesis on the subjects of Marxism and totalitarianism were themselves relatively undeveloped. Yet, Foucault's reciprocal endorsement of Glucksmann's book signalled a number of important political and philosophical dimensions, even if only developed in embryonic form: first, a consistent anti-totalitarianism as an essential feature of Foucault's own philosophical pluralism; second, a disillusionment with 1968 and post-1968 revolutionary politics as potentially totalitarian; and third, a chance to crystalize his rejection of Marxism, Marxism–Leninism, Stalinism, and Maoism as political movements. Glucksmann had in an earlier work analysed Alexandr Solzhenitsyn's *Gulag Archipelago* as representing the culmination of Marxist historical dialectical development, ending up in the residue of totalitarian politics as expressed in the camps of Siberia, genocide and, by extension, Nazism.[6] As Foucault wrote in his review of *Les maîtres penseurs*:

> Stalinism was the truth, "rather" naked, admittedly, of an entire political discourse which was that of Marx and of other thinkers before him. With the Gulag, one sees not the consequences of an unfortunate error but the effect of the most "true" theories in the order of politics. Those who hoped to save themselves by opposing Marx's real beard to Stalin's false nose are wasting their time. (Foucault, 1977, p. 84)

Foucault, for his part, found sustenance in the anti-statist and pluralist discourses that characterized his own early works, focusing instead on the "micro powers" and "disciplines" that underpinned the state, and were prior to it. Marx is rejected, as is Hegel, as philosophers who totalize history and who represent the state as a legitimate organ of domination and truth. These thinkers believe in "final solutions", "revolutionary goals and strategies", "the march of history", "dialectical progression", and identified power as emanating from a central agency in the state. Foucault agreed with Glucksmann's assessment that, influenced by thinkers such as Marx and Hegel, "[t]he Europe of states seeks to exclude the marginal" (Glucksmann, 1977, p. 119). "Science and the texts of the master thinkers are simply strategies of domination", says Christofferson (2016, p. 9), summarizing Glucksmann's thesis. Foucault's own alternative analysis denies any single location to power, representing it as a multiplicity of force relations across the entire social system in terms of which resistances are ubiquitous. By extension, class relations do not invariably determine power relations. This entails that there is no central agency of social change but rather a plurality of resistances and struggles against local fixations of power in specific sites.

The upshot of Christofferson's portrayal sets the scene for later chapters in the book to problematize Foucault's analysis of neoliberalism where Foucault is represented as being not entirely opposed to the doctrine. The rejection of Marx and Hegel are seen as offering indirect support at least for what some authors portray as a sympathetic assessment, one which can be seen to dovetail with the anti-statism and decentralized pluralism which characterize Foucault's assessment of micro powers circulating in the blood stream of the body politic and outside the orbit of the state. There is a suggestion that neoliberal governmentality constitutes a parallel structure of indirect, non-centralized mechanisms or governmental techniques which, consistent with the anti-totalitarian politics of Glucksmann, as well as Foucault's decentralized pluralism, stand opposed to centralized, demand-led, "statism" which, it is implied, characterize both old models of socialism and welfare state reformism.

The rest of the chapters in the book offer variable assessments of the issue, some being more nuanced, than others. Michael C. Behrent, in "'Liberalism without Humanism'", while defending Foucault as a "man of the Left" (2016b, p. 25), notes the criticisms directed against him as a "young conservative" and recalls the accusations of Jean-Paul Sartre, who once called Foucault "the last barrier that the bourgeoisie can still raise against Marx" (Sartre, 1966, p. 88, cited in Behrent, 2016b, p. 25). While such comments do not disqualify Foucault as "of the Left", they do signal, says Behrent, a highly original note, one which he suggests, is neither Marxist nor social democratic. Indeed, says Behrent:

> In the late 1970s, the same Foucault who academic radicals have lionized flirted with an outlook anchored on the political Right: the free-market creed known as neoliberalism. For his defenders, the notion that Foucault

might have taken seriously a school of thought embraced by Ronald Reagan, Margaret Thatcher, and Alan Greenspan defies credibility. Yet Foucault's attraction to neoliberalism was real, and the logic of his interest understandable—provided that we grasp precisely what attracted him to it. (2016b, p. 26)

For Behrent, this "crucial episode in Foucault's thought has been neglected in part because these lectures [on neoliberalism] have only recently appeared in print" and "an equally important factor is the unwillingness of many of his readers to hear what he is saying" (p. 27). Behrent proceeds to identify "a deep affinity between Foucault's thought and neoliberalism" based upon "a shared suspicion of the state" (p. 29). As he puts it:

> Foucault found economic liberalism to be intellectually appealing for two crucial reasons. First, at a juncture when he, like a number of his contemporaries, was attempting to free French intellectual life from the headlock of revolutionary Leftism, ... economic liberalism proved to be a potent theoretical weapon for bludgeoning the Left's authoritarian proclivities. Second, Foucault could endorse economic liberalism because unlike its political counterpart, it did not require him to embrace philosophical humanism—the outlook that Foucault had, from the outset of his career, contested with all the energy that his intellectual skills could muster. The theoretical condition of possibility of Foucault's neoliberal moment was his insight that economic liberalism is, essentially, a liberalism without humanism. ... [T]his is precisely why Foucault found economic liberalism so appealing: it offered a compelling terrain upon which his practical aspiration for freedom might merge with his theoretical conviction that power is constitutive of all human relationships. (2016b, pp. 30–31)

Behrent sees Foucault's interest in the Second Left as indicative of this new interest. The Second Left had emerged in the mid-1970s as a counter to French socialism's statist conception of politics under François Mitterrand. In *The Birth of Biopolitics*, Foucault speaks highly of a new book by its principal theorist, Pierre Rosanvallon (1979), who advocated a form of social market democracy with a reduced state and active market sector.[7] In Foucault's view, Rosanvallon's book was important in that it advocated a form of social democracy where the market functioned as a "test" in order to "pinpoint the effects of excessive governmentality" (p. 320).

In the book's "Conclusion", Behrent identifies his other collaborators ("Zamora, Christofferson", "more loosely, Dean and Amselle", as well as "Waquant and Rehmann") as all subscribing to the main thrust of the thesis outlined within. "Taken together", he says, these authors provide "a series of warnings" regarding "attempts to use Foucault's thought for understanding neoliberalism" (2016a, p. 180). These contributors are not alone in identifying Foucault's "neoliberal moment" (Behrent, 2016b, p. 26). Mark Kelly (2015) informs us that an American History PhD student, Eric Paras, had stated a similar thesis concerning Foucault's support for neoliberalism in a seminar in London in 2004, later to present his own particular reading of Foucault in a book titled *Foucault 2.0* (Paras, 2006).[8] David Newheiser (2016, p. 4), notes various others, including Mirowski (2013, p. 97), Deuber-Mankowsky (2008, p. 157), Dilts (2011, p. 132), de Lagasnerie (2013), Maxwell (2014, p. 161), and Miller (1993, p. 315), who see Foucault as "attracted to neoliberalism" (p. 4). This is, he says, "because Foucault's normative attitude in *The Birth of Biopolitics* is difficult to detect" (p. 4).

It is not merely the secondary commentators cited above, but also one of the most senior associates of Foucault that can be counted amongst their ranks. In the seminar at the University of Chicago, on 12 May 2012, Foucault's former student and editor of his lectures, François Ewald, characterises Foucault, at the end of the 1970s, in a lecture at the Collège de France, as being the location "where he would make the apology of neoliberalism—especially the apology of Gary Becker, who is referred to in the book, *The Birth of Biopolitics*, as the most radical representative of neoliberalism" (Becker, Ewald, & Harcourt, 2012, p. 4). For Ewald, Foucault is representing neoliberalism positively as a late-liberal discourse which enables and fosters a new type of liberty (pp. 4, 6).

3 Rescuing Foucault

The perspective offered by Ewald at the Chicago seminar is challenged by Harcourt, who suggests that Foucault's view of human capital theory, rather than an "apology" should be seen as a "critique" (p. 7). Neoliberalism as Becker develops it, in Foucault's view, says Harcourt, invokes a new insidious governmental technology of power, one without direct or apparent state coercion, and yet which still relies on ethical and political "distinctions and discriminations as to which parts of the population you invest in and which parts you don't invest in" (p. 9). This in turn presupposes biopolitical decisions which enable the construction of a new kind of subject and a new "art of governing".[9] It is for this reason that Foucault sees the problem of the improvement of human capital as not only linked to education, but also potentially linked to the re-emergence of eugenics, for "it is inevitable that the problem of control, screening and improvement of the human capital of individuals ... [is] called for" (Foucault, 2008, p. 228; cited by Harcourt in Becker, Ewald, & Harcourt, 2012, p. 8). As Harcourt says, "once we have *all* bought into the notion of human capital, once it is part of our collective imagination, it then produces these policies of growth that involve investing in some populations and not in others" (p. 9). That such technologies can become amenable to political manipulation is a point made forcefully by Foucault in the 28th March Lecture where he refers to B. F. Skinner, noting that neoliberal technologies of the sort Becker advocates are potentially repressive and open to behavioural manipulation (Foucault, 2008, p. 270). It is this that increases what Foucault calls "the coefficient of threat" for a society or population (Foucault, 2008, p. 233; cited by Harcourt in Becker, Ewald, & Harcourt, 2012, p. 10). For Harcourt, therefore, neoliberalism constitutes a set of indirect, non-centralized mechanisms or governmental techniques with potentially repressive effects.[10]

To the extent that Foucault's anti-statism translates as a defence or support for neoliberalism, as Christofferson, Behrent and others suggest, my argument is that the analysis is flawed. In this sense, I argue that anti-Hegel and anti-Marx do not translate straightforwardly as "anti-statism". In seeing Foucault as having a "neoliberal moment" (2016b, p. 30), therefore, Behrent is choosing to see the analysis of neoliberalism as a part and parcel of "[Foucault's] theoretical objection to state-based conceptions of power" (p. 31), and as part and parcel of his "anti-totalitarianism or the so-called 'death of Marx'" (p. 31).

For his part, Ewald's comment must also be treated with caution. As Mitchell Dean notes, "[Ewald] is something of a problematic figure for the Left: a 'right Foucauldian'",[11] who would utilize Foucault's research "for reconstructing society according to neoliberal principles" (2016, p. 87).[12] Although in his youth a militant Maoist, Ewald worked in senior positions in the insurance industry in France, and notably, in the context of the seminar where he made the comment on Foucault as the "apologist of neoliberalism", is in the company of Gary Becker, one of America's foremost neoliberal theorists, and Bernard Harcourt, professor of law at the University of Chicago, and a former co-editor of a volume of Foucault lectures, *Mal faire, dire vrai*.[13] Ewald's view may appear to be endorsed for, as Dean also notes, "Foucault's lectures on neoliberalism have now been positively received by the two most important schools they discuss: Freiburg and Chicago" (Dean, 2015, p. 390). Yet, whatever Ewald meant by such a comment at the time, he was later to deny that he saw Foucault as a neoliberal. As he said in an interview for the *Los Angeles Review of Books* in 2017 "in terms of actual evidence, the claim that Michel Foucault held neoliberal views is just so far-fetched. … [I]t doesn't make sense to me that Foucault was a closet neoliberal, either".[14] If this later view constitutes a reflective correction to his earlier comment, then that is certainly to be welcomed. For, as I will demonstrate, Ewald's initial comment cannot be unambiguously supported in terms of textual evidence from either Foucault's texts or speeches generally, or from *The Birth of Biopolitics* lectures themselves. While Ewald may see Foucault as making "an apology of neoliberalism", it is apparent from Harcourt's more grounded empirical assessment of Foucault's text that the "apology" is more fittingly described as a "critique". This at least is the view I shall defend.

Although Foucault supported the "new philosophers" in their attacks on Marxism, it is a mistake to see his appraisal of economic liberalism as representing an endorsement of the doctrine of neoliberalism *as a doctrine*. Although Foucault may well have manifested conditional support for certain supply-side technologies, and perhaps even foresaw their relevance within a new non-statist conception of social democracy, his admiration, if that what it should be called, is for the use of such technologies as *means* rather than as *ends*, or as employed on an ad hoc basis in highly specific contexts. "Only their purpose is mad" was the title of a book by the New Zealand writer, Bruce Jesson (1999), in referring to the profit-making interests of big capital, and affirming simultaneously that the techniques of neoliberalism were in themselves neither good nor bad. Foucault did take the view that some neoliberal technologies allow for "an optimization of systems of difference' and propel a system "in which the field is left open to fluctuating processes, in which minority individual practices are tolerated, in which action is brought to bear on the rules of the game rather than on the players, and finally in which there is an environmental type of intervention instead of an internal subjugation of individuals" (pp. 259–260). Foucault thus believed potentially that 'what appears on the horizon of this kind of analysis is not at all the ideal or project of an exhaustively disciplinary society in which the legal network hemming in individuals is taken over and extended externally by ... the normative mechanisms" (p. 259). He believed that American-styled neoliberalism of the sort Becker developed manifested an agnosticism to deviance and minority group traits.[15]

At the same time, Foucault was critical of such technologies on other grounds, namely that they constituted a potentially manipulable biopolitics that subjected the amorphous yet unequally prepared populations of subjects-citizens to the equal impositions of competitive market norms. Furthermore, across the lectures as a whole, Foucault is also clearly sensitive to the changes wrought as neoliberalism supplants classical liberalism, i.e., as it cuts across and disorganizes the autonomous spaces of liberty which defined the raison d'être of the classical liberal doctrine. In all of these observations, there is an acute if unstated awareness that neoliberalism is more efficient from the perspective of business and government in that it is compatible with and productive of lower spending on welfare and social benefits. This is to say also that it blunts the potential possibilities of resistance that the earlier model of liberalism, with its stringently naturalistic conception of rights and freedoms, permitted.

4   Neoliberal "Biopower" as a Form of "Positive" State Power[16]

If the thesis of Zamora, Behrent, Ewald and others is mistaken, how should Foucault's approach to neoliberalism be understood? Far from being an apologist for neoliberalism, Foucault's thesis is that the state actively constitutes neoliberal rationality to the detriment of civil society from the early 20th century as a way of reconciling economic efficiency in relation to population and security. In this process one major thing it does is to eclipse the space of liberty as an autonomously protected preserve of individual rights that defined classical liberalism as it developed from the 17th century. The theory of "positive" and "negative" state power, as encapsulated within liberal theory, is thus central to Foucault's thesis.[17] The thesis of the "positive", or "active" state is writ large throughout *The Birth of Biopolitics* and constitutes Foucault's distinctive thesis distinguishing liberal from neoliberal governmentality.

In the 14th February Lecture, Foucault notes the term "positive liberalism" was used by one neoliberal as an alternative to neoliberalism.[18] Foucault says that "[p]ositive liberalism, then, is an intervening liberalism" (2008, p. 133), and he also cites Röpke who says that "[t]he free market requires an active and extremely vigilant policy" (2008, p. 133). Foucault further says, that "in all the texts of the neo-liberals you find the theme that government is active, vigilant, and intervening in a liberal regime, and formulae that … the classical liberalism of the nineteenth century … could [not] accept" (p. 133). He also cites Walter Eucken who says that the "state is responsible for the result of economic activity" (p. 133). Whereas "liberalism of the 18th century … was to distinguish between actions that must be taken and actions that must not be taken, between domains in which one can intervene and domains in which one cannot intervene" (p. 133), for neoliberals this was a "naive position. … [T]he problem is not whether there are things that you cannot touch and others that you are entitled to touch. The problem is how you touch them" (p. 133). Hence for neoliberals it is a matter of "governmental style" (p. 133).

It is left to the reader to synthesize how these "mutations"[19] of liberal discourse relate to the central concept of "biopolitics", which figures in the title of the published lecture series, as well as to the closely related concepts of "biopower" and, after 1978, of "governmentality".[20] As Vernon W. Cisney and Nicolae Morar (2016, p. 7) tell us, the "biopolitics" concept was first introduced by Foucault in 1974 in a lecture given in Rio de Janeiro, and the concept of biopower in the spring of 1976 in the March 17th Lecture at the Collège de France. Both concepts were employed in Section 5 of *The History of Sexuality* (1976), and in the 1975–1976 lecture series published as *Society Must Be Defended* (Foucault, 2003). In addition, Foucault opens his first lecture (January 11th) in his lecture course of 1977–1978 (published as *Security, Territory, Population* in 2007), with the sentence: "This year I would like to begin by studying something that I have called, somewhat vaguely, bio-power" (p. 1).

In that "biopolitics" and "biopower" refer to the constructive aspect of historical discourses, and governmentality to the particular arts and techniques of governing, all three are implicitly important as to how historical discourses are sustained or transformed.[21] Foucault says in the first lecture of the 11th January that an analysis of biopolitics can get underway only when the general regime of governmental reason "and the question of truth, [and] economic truth in the first place, within governmental reason" (pp. 21–22) have been attended to. For "only when we know what this governmental regime called liberalism [is] … will we be able to grasp what biopolitics is" (p. 22). Foucault asks to be "forgiven if for some weeks—I cannot say how many—I will talk about liberalism", rather than biopolitics. In terms of understanding his thesis as critique, as opposed to "apology", however, some exploration of the nature of these concepts is warranted.

Biopower, we are told, constitutes "a new mechanism of power, absolutely incompatible with relations of sovereignty" (Foucault, 2003, p. 35). Whereas sovereign power is concerned with "the right to *take* life or *let* live", biopower aims to "*foster* life or *disallow* it to the point of death" (Foucault, 1976, p. 138). Thus, it is concerned with the "expansion and efficiency of life" (Cisney & Morar, 2016, p. 4). As such, it has two poles: one disciplinary, which develops in the 17th century, concerned with individual subjects and what Foucault refers to as "*an anatomo-politics of the human body*" (1976, p. 139). The second pole develops in the 18th century and while often incorporating disciplinary techniques, is concerned with shaping and regulating populations. Both sorts constitute mechanisms of power that actively limit or shape. The biopolitics of populations is harnessed in the interests of security or the health of society made possible via statistics and the emerging arts of regulation. The apparatus (*dispositif*) of security considers elements "within a series of probable events", in terms of "a calculation of cost", and "instead of a binary division between the permitted and the prohibited, one establishes an average considered as optimal on the one hand, and on the other, a bandwidth of the acceptable that must not be exceeded" (2007, p. 6).

Neoliberalism can be conceived here then as a biopolitical technology of biopower. Foucault is aware that neoliberalism constitutes a threat to liberalism in that it potentially displaces the naturalistic value of freedom and autonomy of subjects in the context of a natural realm of laissez-faire, carefully constructed and protected in the classical doctrine, with a form of political authority that is state driven and enforced, and which actively disintegrates civil society by subjecting it to the competitive rules of the market. As a form of positive governmental power, it is always thus potentially totalitarian, unless appropriately guided and controlled. It has its origins in the changing material needs of capitalism, in seeking to render power more efficient. As Foucault says in *The History of Sexuality*, "biopower was without question an indispensable element in the development of capitalism" (1976, pp. 140–141). It is necessary for "the insertion of bodies into the machinery of production and the adjustment of the phenomena of population to economic processes" (p. 141). This explains Foucault's interest in both German ordoliberalism and US neoliberalism. This is especially so with regards to Becker's human capital theory, which provides for a framework for the behaviourist manipulation of Homo economicus, and which can be conceived as constituting "an entire series of interventions and *regulatory controls: a biopolitics of the population*" (1976, p. 139).[22] While fascinated with neoliberal technologies as a mix of direct, indirect, obvious and non-obvious forms of power, Foucault clearly sees them as a series of "techniques of power present at every level of the social body" (p. 141), "factors of segregation and social hierachization" (p. 141), "the adjustment of the accumulation of men to that of capital" (p. 141), which comprises "measures relative to man's life and survival" (p. 142).

While there is some reference to Foucault's thesis of "biopower" as a technology of power in the Zamora and Behrent reader, the treatment of neoliberalism as a positive form of state biopower fails to link it to a positive state or anti-naturalistic thesis and thus fails to see the true meaning and significance of Foucault's intended critique.[23] Indeed, Behrent comes to a view which I would maintain is fundamentally incorrect. As he says: "What biopower in the form of economic liberalism demonstrates is that liberty is powers necessary correlate—its very condition of possibility" (2016b, p. 44). Although there is a possible metaphysical sense in which such a statement can be correct, as stated it is so general as to mystify. It is also unfortunate that Behrent speaks of "economic liberalism" as it confuses the distinction between classical liberalism and neoliberalism as distinct modes of governmentality. For important to Foucault's thesis, I would suggest, is that the biopower of the latter (i.e., neoliberalism) undoes or contradicts the biopolitical constructions of the former (liberalism), a point that seems to be missed by Behrent.

In my reading, Foucault's (2008) lectures at the Collège de France of 1978–1979 provide an important text for understanding the nature of these differences between liberal and neoliberal governmentality. Whereas classical liberalism was constructed to represent a "negative", or naturalistic conception of state power, viewing the individual as an object to be freed from the interventions of the state, neoliberalism represents a positive, non-naturalistic conception, viewing the state as actively creating the appropriate market by providing the conditions, laws, and institutions necessary for its operation (see Foucault, 2008, 7th and 14th February Lectures, especially).

In this theorization, neoliberal biopolitics therefore contradicts laissez-faire. It constrains subjects by establishing the conditions of existence of the market in terms of which subjects must live their existences. As such, it operates through mechanisms of power that are frequently masked and which are primarily concerned with security, or the continuance of life in society. It constitutes, as Foucault says, "an essentially normalizing power ... whose functions are for the most part regulatory" (1976, p. 144).[24]

The textual evidence for these claims are presented throughout *The Birth of Biopolitics*, especially the lectures of 21st and 31st January, and 7th and 14th February, where Foucault discusses the transition in governmentality from a naturalistic conception, which defined classical liberalism, to an anti-naturalistic conception, which characterizes neoliberalism. As a naturalistic doctrine, liberalism emerges as a doctrine of the internal limitations of governmental reason in the middle of the 18th century with the Physiocrats, Smith, and Kant and the 18th-century jurists. Political economy "discovers a certain naturalness specific to the practice of government itself" (2008, 10th January, p. 15), and "governmental practice can only do what it has to do by respecting nature" (p. 16). While in the Middle Ages, the market was essentially seen as a site of justice, limited by strict regulations, from the middle of the 18th century the market is characterized by spontaneous (i.e., natural) mechanisms, which pertained to such things as prices, exchange, and distribution. So, the market of the 18th century was premised upon the ground of an "unlimited nature" (24th January, p. 56) which guaranteed both the "wealth of nations" and "perpetual peace" (p. 57). Foucault characterizes this as a "governmental naturalism" which legitimises both the practices and outcomes of markets (p. 57) and also guarantees liberty by virtue of a contract.

With the neoliberals of the 20th century there are a number of rather crucial changes. To start with, says Foucault, there is "a shift from exchange to competition in the principle of the market" (7th February, p. 118). For the neoliberals, the concept of exchange is not important, but rather a fiction of the 18th-century economists. It is competition that is essential. Whereas for the classical liberal economists' exchange required laissez-faire, for the neoliberals, says Foucault, "neoliberalism should not ... be identified with laissez-faire, but rather with permanent vigilance, activity, and intervention" (p. 132). For to see laissez-faire as the conclusion drawn from the principle of competition constitutes a "naive naturalism" (p. 120). For "pure competition is not a primitive given" (p. 120). As Foucault elaborates:

> For what in fact is competition? It is absolutely not a given of nature. ... Pure competition must and can only be an objective, an objective presupposing an indefinitely active policy. Competition is therefore an historical objective of governmental art and not a natural given that must be respected. (p. 120)

Foucault (2008, pp. 76–79) recounts how the ordoliberal programme in Germany embodied this positive, active view of the state's role, resulting often in exclusionary and repressive effects. As he puts it: "neoliberalism is no more than a cover for a globalised administrative intervention by the state which is all the more profound for being insidious and hidden" (p. 130). Rather than trying "to cut out or contrive a free space of the market within an already given political society, ... the problem of neoliberalism is rather how the overall exercise of political power can be modelled on the principles of the market economy" (p. 131). Neoliberalism in this sense constitutes a general form of political rationality rather than a specifically economic doctrine.[25] Similarly, for the US neoliberals, like Becker, who formulate political targets through behavioural techniques to render all spaces governable. Significantly, for Foucault, it dismantles the space of freedom cut out and protected in the classical model through a reformulation of the theory. As such, it constitutes a general guiding discourse which is infinitely adjustable in different contexts to affect psychological and behavioural adaptations. It seeks changes in all of life and applied to all forms of voluntary behaviour.[26]

5 A Possible Resolution: Adam Ferguson and the Concept of Civil Society as a Category in Governmentality

My argument so far, contra a major core premise of Behrent's arguments, that Foucault's support for Rosanvallon and the Second Left, who advocated a form of non-statist social democracy, as well as his antipathy to Marx and Hegel, cannot in any way be represented as an endorsement of unbridled neoliberalism.

In my view, Foucault's assessment of neoliberalism constitutes the broad outlines of a genealogy of liberalism which signals a new phase of post-liberal governmentality premised upon the transition from liberalism as a naturalistic doctrine of autonomous freedom and a "do-nothing" state, to an anti-naturalistic thesis of the state as an active, or positive form of biopolitical power exercised by the state on behalf of economic policy elites. While Foucault sees certain neoliberal technologies as of potential political use, in that they achieve their purposes efficiently, and even, perhaps, that they might function as a counterweight to overly statist-centrist techniques of politics, on their own, if unregulated, they displace necessary forms of civil society and government that could function to assure order and stability and even justice in the context of economic development.

The main evidence for this is stated by Foucault in the last two lectures of *The Birth of Biopolitics*. These are the lectures of 28th March and 4th April. These two lectures are central to understanding Foucault's genealogy of neoliberalism, for it is in these two lectures that Foucault articulates the necessary "conjunction" developed by the modellers of civil society between economic rationality on the one hand and governmentality on the other.

It is here that Foucault announces that in the history of economics, the economic was never seen as a single domain with its own laws, models, rationality, and method, standing alone, but as existing always within a political context of society. In the final lecture, Foucault selects the model of the Scottish Enlightenment as expounded by Adam Ferguson (1723–1816) in his 1767 book *An Essay on the History of Civil Society* (1995) and subjects it to an analysis as a form of governmentality. One major question to be asked here is *why*? Why Ferguson?

In the edited volume by Zamora and Behrent it is significant that there is very little reference to the 28th March Lecture and no references at all by anyone in the volume to the 4th April Lecture.[27] Although the 4th April Lecture is overlooked completely by Zamora and the other contributors, Behrent does mention Ferguson's name once. By placing him in a list of names, he incorrectly categorizes him as a neoliberal. As he puts it, whilst referring to Foucault, "when considering neoliberalism, almost exclusively on texts (by Walter Eucken, Wilhelm Röpke, Friedrich Hayek, Gary Becker, and Adam Ferguson, to name a few)" (Behrent, 2016a, p. 178), we see a startling truth revealed: Behrent does not actually know who Adam Ferguson really is! For if he did know who Ferguson was, he would never have included him in a list of otherwise "dyed-in-the wool" neoliberals. Foucault, however, did know who Ferguson was, and of his impeccable communitarian–liberal principles, and as a theorist of civil society that gave a markedly different analysis to those given by Hobbes, Locke, Rousseau, or Hegel, whom Foucault explicitly considers, and rejects.

Although Foucault's approach to civil society in the final lecture is genealogical, what I am suggesting is that there is more than a hint of normativity suggested by the exclusions, partitions and preferences which Foucault alludes to, and by the very manner in which Ferguson is discussed. Firstly, to answer the question, why focus on Ferguson? Ferguson reinstates the necessary elevation of the political over the economic displaced previously in the 17th century when man was represented as a predominantly economic subject. Hence, Ferguson's history of civil society constituted an open question or retort concerning societal stability to the development of economic theories in earlier times. Could it not also be Foucault's open question to neoliberalism in the 20th century? Is neoliberalism not the doctrine which represents the arrogance of economists in applying economic models of competitive behaviour to every sphere of society?

No doubt Zamora and colleagues would claim the 4th April Lecture to be insignificant, as representing merely a continuation of the genealogy of forms of governmentality in relation to the market as they arose and developed in the 18th century. Yet why focus on Ferguson, specifically? And why do so as the last of 12 lectures on liberalism and neoliberalism? Foucault's interest seems at least in part normative, I will argue, in that Ferguson is represented in passing as endorsing Foucault's own preferred axioms, concerning the social nature of the subject, the fallacy of the theory of the social contract, and so on. In addition, alternative models of civil society developed by Locke, Hobbes, Rousseau, Montesquieu, and Hegel, are all briefly entertained and rejected (2008, pp. 308–309). Ferguson's model might be being recounted genealogically, but it also represented as the *best* model of civil society on offer! There is a sense, also, that this final lecture serves as something of a "conclusion" in that Foucault is embarking on an assessment of the Scottish Enlightenment as a way of tying up loose ends, or of reaching some sort of resolution of the conundrums around liberalism and neoliberalism identified in the earlier eleven lectures. He tells us, for instance, in the "Course Summary" that "[t]his year's course ended up being devoted entirely to what should have been only its introduction" (p. 317).[28]

Then again, the thesis on Ferguson is significant for Foucault because it reintroduces *Homo politicus* in a way in which Foucault clearly approves. With certain modifications with respect to naturalism and essentialism, Ferguson reintroduces Aristotle's conception of man as "by nature intended to live in a polis" (Aristotle, 1946, Section 1.7.9). Ferguson reinstates, for Foucault, the elevation of the political over the economic, which was displaced in the 17th century as economic self-interest became ascendant and man became seen as a predominantly economic subject. Such a displacement of the political continued throughout the 18th century under the dominance of economic liberalism. With Ferguson there is a rearticulation of the human subject as a fundamentally political being who must live first of all in a social community and manage the economic motives in the confines of that community. Many argue that the same sort of thesis is evident in Smith, especially relating to his earlier work, *The Theory of Moral Sentiments,* first published in 1859. In this sense, Ferguson reintroduces what in the Middle Ages was the control of the market in the interests of continued political stability. As Karl Polanyi (1944) argues in *The Great Transformation,* markets played little role in many pre-modern societies in the way that Smith described in *The Wealth of Nations*. Indeed, during the Middle Ages markets were regarded with suspicion and kept under firm political and community control so as to minimize their dysfunctional consequences. Broader anthropological research of other non-Western societies supports a similar conclusion. In order that markets can function properly in an industrial–capitalist economy, says Polanyi, various objects that were not initially commodities (land, money, labour, implements) had to be constructed and conceptualized *as commodities*, that is, as objects tradeable on a market. Polanyi introduces the concept of "commodity fiction", defined as a "vital organizing principle in regard to the whole of society", which was circulated as a consequence of industrialization (quote from Davis, 2009, p. 235).

Foucault utilizes Ferguson as a counterbalance to Smith to conceptualize how the economic must always sit within civil society. But, importantly, we learn something else, of great interest to Foucault. We learn that "[c]ivil society is ... a concept of governmental technology, or rather it is the correlate of a technology of government, the rational measure of which must be juridically paired to an economy understood as a process of production and exchange" (Foucault, 2008, p. 296). It is not for nothing, then, that the last lecture of *The Birth of Biopolitics* is on civil society. This, in a sense, reintroduces some of the core propositions of the Physiocrats as a supplement to Smith. Homo economicus regulates in the domain of economy on the principle of interest. Yet, the imperatives of good government require knowledge as to how civil society is managed, according to the dictates of knowledge of the whole, utilizing the exercise of "oversight", on the basis of "*évidence*", and more. The Scottish Enlightenment carefully balanced economy and governmentality in a way that reintroduced elements advocated by the Physiocrats. Governmental regulation would be according to the "Economic Table" which generated for the Physiocrats knowledge of the whole, of distributions, and probabilities, as they affected stability, growth and security in terms of the continual likelihood of growth for the future. It is in these dual conjunctions of the economic and the political through which governmental reason regulates the economic and the political along different lines, but simultaneously. As Foucault says:

> It is here, and only here that we can find the idea that economic agents must be allowed their function and that political sovereignty will cover the totality of the economic process with a gaze in the uniform light, as it were, of evidence. (Foucault, 2008, 28th March, p. 286)

This is compatible with Ferguson, but the exact opposite of Adam Smith's "invisible hand": to conduct matters in accord with "evidence". Smith criticized the

Physiocratic theory of evidence as "oversight", i.e., as interrupting the arena of economic freedom. The Physiocrats introduced Smith's idea as a partial zone applying only to the economy and only a part of a governmental rationality. As Foucault summarizes the common thread between the Physiocrats and Ferguson:

> Political economy is indeed a science, a type of knowledge (*savoir*), a mode of knowledge (*connaissance*) which those who govern must take into account. But economic science cannot be the science of government and economics cannot be the internal principle, law, rule of conduct, or rationality of government. Economics is a science lateral to the art of governing. One must govern with economics, one must govern alongside economists, one must govern by listening to the economists, but economics must not be and there is no question that it can be the governmental rationality itself. (28th March, p. 286)

Foucault utilizes Ferguson to expound the notion of civil society that will bed down economy and governmentality in a single regulatory pact. As Alexander Broadie summarizes in his seminal work, *The Scottish Enlightenment* (2001), Ferguson's central thesis is that "[i]t would be fatal to civil liberties if the citizens dedicated themselves to commercial activities to the exclusion of political activity" (p. 90). Politics was central to Ferguson's thesis as a corrective to the "psychopathology of the commercial society" (p. 97). Homo economicus was only a partial and incomplete view, which failed to achieve the detachment of Smith's "impartial spectator" (pp. 100–101). Commercial relations, also, can if uncontrolled, impede or disrupt family and social accord, which is why during the Middle Ages the market was tightly controlled and subservient to the community. Freedom is itself ensured and underwritten by culture and government. The law is the vehicle "[that] ensures our liberty to live civilized, cultured lives" (p. 86). All this was derivative from Ferguson's thesis that we are naturally social animals and that the principles of union and freedom are themselves social and historical. Only in society are we complete.

For Ferguson, too, says Foucault, government replaces the state (p. 310). Further, Ferguson, like Paine, does not confuse "society" and "government" (p. 310). Governmentality operates across civil society, in diverse sites, through a balance of powers, via institutional autonomy, as powers which have earned, or are awarded privileged status, can resist the centralizing powers of a unified state.[29] The distributions of powers provide for checks and balances in the society overall. In such a way, governmentality provides an opening for social democracy; and for the death of the state. Not "anarchism", as Christofferson (2016, p. 20) incorrectly claims, but "republican pluralism", within a socially and historically constituted civil society. In Ferguson's seminal arguments against corruption, he argued strenuously for a system of checks and balances across the body politic in order to avoid corruption posing a threat to the system. This argument was central to his arguments against the passivity and for the political participation of citizens, says Broadie (pp. 88–90). As Broadie concludes, "Ferguson is ... arguing for a form of republicanism: citizens should see themselves as the guardians of civic virtues and civic liberties" (p. 90).

Such an analysis of Ferguson causes us to ask the extent to which there has been an overhasty incorporation of Foucault to an insufficiently elaborated thesis of anti-statism? There is no "phobia of the state" (*phobie d'état*); simply a re-theorization and de-transcendentalization of the state.[30] Given, as Foucault famously said, that "what socialism lacks is not so much a theory of the state but of governmental reason" (2008, p. 91), it may be, as Colin Gordon asks, whether it was necessary for Foucault to invent a new form of governmentality for a new type of socialism that is non-statist ("il faut l'inventer").[31] If this is so then possibly Ferguson was not just a response to the past, but to the future as well. Ferguson, I suggest, was important for Foucault in this quest, for Foucault makes it clear that the models of civil society proposed by Hobbes, Rousseau, Montesquieu, or Hegel, lack the appropriate strengths of Ferguson's model.

Ferguson first provides a model of how the economic and the political, interest and right, are related and managed in terms of a governmental rather than a state-centric theory. As Foucault states, for Ferguson:

> Economic rationality is not only surrounded by, but founded on the unknowability of the totality of the process. ... Thus the economic world is naturally opaque and naturally non-totalizable. ... Economics is an atheistic discipline; economics is a discipline without God; economics is a discipline without totality; economics is a discipline that begins to demonstrate not only the pointlessness, but also the impossibility of a sovereign point of view over the totality of the state that he is to govern. ... [L]iberalism acquired its modern shape precisely with the formulation of this essential incompatibility between the non-totalizable multiplicity of economic subjects of interest and the totalizing unity of the juridical sovereign. (28th March, p. 282)

What Ferguson introduced in his *Essay on the History of Civil Society* of 1767, was a new reference point for governmentality, one which superseded the economic:

> [T]he art of governing must be given a reference, a domain or field of reference, a new reality on which it will be exercised, and I think this new field of reference is civil society. (4th April, p. 295)

Foucault asks: "What is civil society?" And the answer is that it is a governmental technology that involves:

> how to govern, according to the rules of right, a space of sovereignty which for good or ill is inhabited by economic subjects? ... Civil society is not a philosophical idea therefore. Civil society is, I believe, a concept of governmental society. (4th April, pp. 295–296)

Civil society, which came to be called simply "society", or "nation", is what enables government on the basis of "self-limitation" "which infringes neither economic laws nor principles of right" (p. 297). As Foucault continues to develop inspiration from Ferguson:

> Civil society, therefore, is an element of transactional reality in the history of governmental technologies, a transactional technology which seems to me to be absolutely correlative to the form of governmental technology we call liberalism, that is to say, a technology of government whose objective is its own self-limitation insofar as it is pegged to the specificity of economic processes. (4th April, p. 297)

Such is Ferguson's concept of civil society. Such a concept "may indeed resolve the problems that I have just tried to indicate", he says (p. 297). "We have here the political correlate ... of what Smith studied in economic terms" (p. 298). Ferguson adds something for the entire debate, then. He adds a question directed at the economists of earlier times in its narrowest or literal sense. But, is this not a question that applies to, or could apply to, neoliberalism also?

The significance theoretically is that Foucault conceptualizes governmentality as extending across the society in the context of checks and balances, and it would also appear plausible that he chose Ferguson on the grounds that the model of civil society represented, first, governmentalizes the state and, second, protects liberal and market freedoms within limits. Such a model would be capable of incorporating supply-side technologies also, on an ad hoc basis, as part of a broader programme of social democracy. These limits or checks, however, are exactly what neoliberalism advanced by Becker does away with. The logic of the market for neoliberalism "break[s] with the tradition of eighteenth and nineteenth century liberalism" (Foucault, 2008, p. 119). Rather, the market now constitutes a "general index ... for defining all governmental action. ... [T]he relationship defined by eighteenth century liberalism is completely reversed" (p. 121). Neoliberalism offers, then, "the analysis of non-economic behavior through a grid of economic intelligibility" (p. 248). There is "a generalization of the grid of *homo oeconomicus* to domains that are not immediately and directly economic" (p. 268), "the economization of the entire social field" (p. 242). This is precisely what Ferguson says is not possible, although which can with dire consequences represent itself to be so, from time to time.

Within the body of the April 4th Lecture, Foucault identifies four elements of civil society, which permit us to see in more detail why he is so interested in Ferguson. These buttress the case for considering Foucault's treatment of Ferguson as "normative" (as opposed to merely genealogical) on the grounds that each of the postulates identified can be seen to be ones that Foucault would approve of as constituting the *best* 18th-century account of how governmentality could manage the contradictions of the economy.

The argument would be that Ferguson's approach recognized governmentality as opposed to the centralized state, differentiated government from society, was compatible concerning a pluralism of the micro-powers, and yet permitted the economy to operate in terms of its own laws. Such an argument might appear strengthened further by his naming and rejection of other possible candidates for consideration—Hobbes, Rousseau, Montesquieu (p. 308), Locke (p. 297), Hegel (p. 309). In considering Ferguson's strengths, Foucault, in effect, shifts from simply presenting a descriptive genealogy to overlaying a consideration of the normative question, i.e., what makes Ferguson's the most appropriate response to the economics of earlier times? He presents four reasons why Ferguson's views are the most plausible.

First, Ferguson's concept of civil society constitutes a "historical–natural constant" (p. 298). By this he means that for Ferguson "the social bond has no prehistory ... [and] however far back we go in the history of humanity, we will find not only society, but nature", which is to say that "[civil society] is as old as the individual" (p. 299). For Foucault to draw out this point is of great interest, for it is to say, in effect, that many of those who have developed exaggerated economic analyses, including the economic rationalists of the 17th century (and the neoliberals of the 20th century), have abstracted the economy from the domain of society in which it inevitably must reside.

Second, says Foucault, civil society in Ferguson "assures the spontaneous synthesis of individuals", which is to say essentially that economy and society constitute a *necessary couple*:

> there is no explicit contract, no voluntary union, no renunciation of rights, and no delegation of natural rights to someone else. ... In other words, there is reciprocity between the whole and its components. Basically, we cannot say, we cannot imagine or conceive an individual to be happy if the whole to which he belongs is not happy. ... Every element of

civil society is assessed by the good it will produce or bring about for the whole. (p. 300)

This is why, says Foucault, for Ferguson, "civil society can be both the support of the economic process and economic bonds, while overflowing them and being irreducible to them" (p. 301). What Ferguson recognizes is that civil society is the necessary container which, via governance, constrains and regulates economy in the interests of security.

What holds civil society together for Ferguson is not self-interest, but sympathy and sentiment, which attests to the impulses of benevolence that individuals feel for each other. For Ferguson, as well as the bonds that bring economic subjects together, "there is a distinct set of non-egoist interests, a distinct interplay of non-egoist, disinterested interests which is much wider than egoism itself" (4th April, p. 301). "Civil society, Ferguson says, leads the individuals to enlist 'on the side of one tribe or community'. Civil society is not humanitarian but communitarian" (p. 302).

The bonds of civil society, then, are diametrically opposed to those of economic self-interest, and yet are necessarily simultaneous with them. This is always necessarily so, although at one time or another in history one pole can always dominate. The economic bond serves as a principle of dissociation in relation to what Foucault calls "communitarian bonds" (2008, p. 302, footnote) "of compassion and benevolence, love for one's fellow and sense of community", in that the former seeks to constantly undo the latter.[32]

The third characteristic of Ferguson's civil society, says Foucault, is that it is a "permanent matrix of political power" (p. 303). This formation of power is "brought about ... by a de facto bond which links different concrete individuals to each other" (p. 304). "So, it cannot be said", says Foucault, "that men were isolated, that they decided to constitute a power, and then here they are living in a state of society" (p. 304). For Ferguson rejects the very idea of the social contract as propounded by Hobbes, Locke and Rousseau.

The fourth characteristic of Ferguson's civil society is that it constitutes the "motor of history" (p. 305). In this sense, says Foucault, it integrates and manages conflicting tendencies, and establishes a "stable equilibrium" of the whole. It is both a historical–natural constant and principle of transformation. Civil society thus "harbors" the economic game "within itself" (p. 306).

It is in this context that the issue of the relationship and role of the state to civil society arises. The state, for Ferguson, emerges as "one of the dimensions and forms of civil society" (p. 309) along with the "family" and the "the household or estate" (p. 309). But Ferguson stops well short of Hegel, who sees the state as the "self-consciousness and ethical realization of civil society" (p.

309) and the interpreter and enforcer of all forms of right. Foucault subtly appreciates Ferguson's "downsizing" of the state in comparison to Hegel, and in particular, as in England, "where the analysis of civil society is developed in terms of government rather than in terms of the state" (p. 310). Hence, Ferguson's model of civil society constitutes a post-Hegelian model of how to govern rationally according to the dictates of "the rational behavior of those who are governed" (p. 312).

Even at the end of the 4th April Lecture, Foucault may be thought to be attempting to provide a genealogy of forms of governmentality, and of liberal governmentality, in particular. Yet, it seems to me that he is providing at the same time what he considers to be the *best* model of civil society and governmental regulation on offer, the best response to the economic rationalists of the century before, the *only* response than can be made, in fact, the response that must necessarily be made, to those that seek to assert the dominance of the economic over the social. The 18th and 19th centuries saw the theorization of civil society; and civil society is represented as constituting an integral and always present counterbalance to the dissociative norms of economy which constitute an ever-present threat to society as such. As Foucault would have it, Ferguson, like him, believes that, against all theories of economization, "society must be defended" (Foucault, 2003).

6 Conclusion

In my view, Foucault's focus on Adam Ferguson in the last lecture (April 4th) of *The Birth of Biopolitics*, a lecture not focused upon, or even mentioned, by any of the contributors to the Zamora and Behrent volume, constitutes a much more impressive case for his normative position than that he supported neoliberalism.

It is at least a possible resolution and would support the proposition that Foucault advocated implicitly for a version of social democracy. For Foucault appears to be saying that, outside of a plausible political model, that is, conception of governmentality, neoliberalism as the active policy of state, could easily give rise to either forms of totalitarian rule through the political manipulation of neoliberal technologies, or to complete chaos via a lack of governmental regulation. The thesis in short is that neoliberalism reformulates liberalism, making it easier to manage subjects and render them docile from the perspectives of capital. As Becker's human capital theory makes clear, neoliberalism redirects and reconstitutes human subjects' behaviours to infinity with the consequence of making them more productive and docile. And as such political ends are embedded within the designs of its technologies, they cannot involve any aprioristic disqualification of state direction or intervention, as entailed by concepts such as Homo economicus or laissez-faire.

As well as ignoring the thesis concerning the *active*, or *positive* character of biopower, Zamora et al., also ignore Foucault's April 4th Lecture on Adam Ferguson. Given the ontological thesis that Foucault detects in Ferguson that the economic and the political necessarily constitute a "historical–natural constant", and are in this sense, two sides of the same coin, and given neoliberalism's potential for exorcising all governmental power, the Scottish Enlightenment is at least a plausible contender for a re-governmentalization of the economy. If this is so then it can also be noted that such a pluralistic, social democratic model, complete with checks and balances throughout civil society, would also "harmonize" with Foucault's concerns for the over-centralization of state power, his anti-totalitarianism, and his general cynicism towards Marxism as well.

Finally, Zamora, Behrent and others, in my view, project intentions to Foucault's writing that are arguably not present. Behrent's argument maintains throughout an elision between Foucault's critique of statism, his support for the Second Left, and writers like Rosanvallon, and his (therefore) *likely* sympathy for the types of economic analysis suggested by neoliberals. My own assessment supports no such identity, despite apparent "harmonisation" (Behrent, 2016a, p. 181),[33] but rather positions Foucault as a social democrat, rehabilitating the political as ultimately ascendant over the economic, in the interests of community stability and continuance. In saying this, I agree with Wendy Brown that Foucault is not "offering a neo-Marxist critique of neoliberal rationality" (2015, p. 55). For me, ultimately, Foucault is still a type of social democrat, a thesis that I first argued more than a decade ago (Olssen, 2002). In my view, the final lecture of *The Birth of Biopolitics* (2008) offer further support for that view.

Acknowledgement

This chapter originally appeared as Olssen, M. (2018), Foucault and neoliberalism: A response to recent critics and a new resolution, *materiali foucaultiani*, 7(13–14), 28–55, http://www.materialifoucaultiani.org/images/02olssen.pdf. Reprinted here, with minor edits, with permission from the publisher.

Notes

1   First published in French as *Critiquer Foucault: Les années 1880 et la tentation néoliberale*, Les Éditions Aden, 2014, but with some changes which are listed in the English translation.

2 Published 3 December 2014. Translated by Seth Akerman and republished in *Jacobin*, 12 October 2014.
3 The chapter is an expanded version of Christofferson (2004).
4 Translated by Michael Scott Christofferson, the article is reproduced under the title of "The Great Rage of Facts", in Zamora and Behrent (2016, pp. 170–175).
5 "De la violence: entretien avec André Glucksmann", *Actuel* 54, May 1975, p. 17.
6 See Glucksmann (1975).
7 See Foucault (2008, p. 320).
8 According to Kelly, Paras's book "cherry-pick[s] the most extreme moments in Foucault's output and assemble[s] them to make him a figure of wild contradictions" (2015, p. 1).
9 Harcourt amplifies these points at the March 2016 Paris conference on Foucault and neoliberalism, noting that human capital theory contradicts the theory of Homo economicus and permits political manipulation of the population, especially through behavioural governmental techniques.
10 Harcourt also expounded many of the dangers (*menace*) of human capital theory at the conference on Michel Foucault and Neoliberalism, held at the American University of Paris, 25 and 26 March 2016.
11 The phrase, "right Foucauldian" is Antonio Negri's, cited in Dean (2016, p. 87). Kelly calls Ewald "a Foucauldian neoliberal apparatchik of French capitalism" (2015, p. 2).
12 Dean is here citing Maurizio Lazzarato (2009, p. 110).
13 "Doing bad, speaking truth".
14 *Los Angeles Review of Books*, 3 November 2017.
15 See Audier (2015), who maintains that American neoliberalism involves shifts in governmentality that Foucault thought displayed greater agnosticism towards minority groups and deviance.
16 This section repeats the positive state thesis that I have argued has been maintained by Foucault in relation to his concepts of "biopolitics", "biopower" and 'governmentality" that has been central to my scholarship over the last two decades. As such, there is some overlap in terms of ideas, sentences, and language expression with Olssen, Codd, and O'Neill (2004), Olssen and Peters (2005), Olssen (2016), and Olssen (2017).
17 The positive/negative axis of state power and liberty is a central concept of liberal theory. A "positive" state is a state, such as a socialist or the welfare state, that actively provides for goods and services for society based upon a general conception of the best sort of life for all. A "negative" state is a state that is a "minimalist" state, which leaves provision to the market, and provides only goods and services that a market cannot provide, based upon the idea, broadly speaking, that individuals should be free to decide their own lives. Both terms are derived from the concepts of "positive" and negative" liberty, where "negative liberty" refers to the "absence of external constraint", and "positive liberty" to "the pursuit of some favoured course (see Berlin, 1969, for an extended analysis).
18 The editors note that L. Rougier was the neoliberal Foucault had in mind and that Rougier used the term first at the Walter Lippmann Colloquium in 1939.
19 In the English translation of *The Birth of Biopolitics*, neoliberalism is represented as a "mutation with regard to traditional liberal projects, those that were born in the eighteenth century" (2008, p. 117).
20 Governmentality, for Foucault, refers to a particular "art of government" comprising "the techniques and practices of governing populations … over an entire society" (Gordon, 1991, p. 4). See also Foucault (1991, 2007, pp. 108–109, 115–116).
21 Both terms are taken here as complementary and mutually supportive. In this sense, biopolitics is the political process which builds upon biopower, which embodies the way in which

life entails power, or the way in which power makes and sustains life. Although Paul Patton (2016, p. 102) argues that both concepts are "confused and confusing terms which never achieved the status of determinate concepts", I maintain that they are definitionally distinct and mutually supporting. They are also distinct from, but support, the concept of governmentality, which Foucault is centrally concerned with after 1976/1977.

22 While this is written in *The History of Sexuality*, where Foucault discusses the concept of biopower in depth, it is noteworthy also that the material was written only a few years before *The Birth of Biopolitics*.
23 No reference under "state", "active", "positive", "naturalism", or "antinaturalism" appears in index. Although "bio-power" is discussed, the idea of neoliberalism as a form of state-engendered bio-power is not discussed. Christofferson discusses formal definitions on pp. 19–20; Behrent gives a history and definition of bio-power on pp. 40–45 and does consider Foucault's view that economic liberalism constituted a form of biopower (2016b, p. 42).
24 For earlier analysis of Foucault's perspective on the "active" state, see Olssen, Codd, and O'Neill (2004); Olssen and Peters (2005); and Peters (2011).
25 Although, since Foucault wrote, it has developed considerably in its general configuration, and been supplemented by corporatist strategies aimed at security and surveillance, neoliberalization processes have been entrenched across the global economy since the 1980s.
26 The sense in which neoliberalism is being reformulated to render it more useful to capital, less awkward and costly (in relation to rights, etc.), although not explicitly pointed out by Foucault would seem nevertheless implied.
27 Only Dean references any pages in the 28th March Lecture. One is to Gary Becker, as "the most radical of the US neoliberals", on p. 269, of the 28th March Lecture. and the other is to a reference to B. F. Skinner, on p. 270, in the same lecture.
28 It can be noted given the widespread perplexity as to why the concept of biopolitics is absent from the main body of the text that this observation is quite consistent with Foucault's note in the first lecture on pp. 21–22 that he would need to postpone such discussion until he has dealt with the matter of liberalism.
29 In this sense, Foucault's thesis of the omnipresence of power as a descriptive ontology *becomes* normative as some powers become *guiding* and *safeguarding* of the political process.
30 See Dean and Villadsen (2016), who seek to go beyond Foucault, yet in my view, they do not exhaust the possibilities for state theorisation present in Foucault's work.
31 Gordon's view as summarised by Provenzano (2016).
32 The possible interest in communitarian solutions has been neglected in Foucault scholarship, but see Olssen (2002).
33 Behrent actually uses the word "harmonized".

References

Amselle, J. L. (2016). Michel Foucault and the spiritualization of philosophy. In D. Zamora & M. C. Behrent (Eds.), *Foucault and neoliberalism* (pp. 159–169). Polity.

Aristotle. (1946). *The politics* (E. Barker, Trans.). Clarendon.

Audier, S. (2015). *Penser le "néolibéralisme": Le moment neoliberal Foucault et la crises*. Le Bord de l'eau.

Becker, G. (1976). *The economic approach to human behaviour*. University of Chicago Press.

Becker, G., Ewald, F., & Harcourt, B. (2012, October). *"Becker on Ewald on Foucault on Becker": American neoliberalism and Michel Foucault's 1979 Birth of biopolitics lectures: A conversation with Gary Becker, François Ewald, and Bernard Harcourt*. The University of Chicago—May 9, 2012. Chicago Institute for Law and Economics Working Paper no. 614 (2nd series), Public Law and Legal Theory Working Paper no. 401. http://dx.doi.org/10.2139/ssrn.2142163

Behrent, M. C. (2016a). Conclusion: The strange failure and peculiar success of Foucault's project. In D. Zamora & M. C. Behrent (Eds.), *Foucault and neoliberalism* (pp. 176–186). Polity.

Behrent, M. C. (2016b). "Liberalism without humanism": Michael Foucault and the free market creed, 1976–1979. In D. Zamora & M. C. Behrent (Eds.), *Foucault and neoliberalism* (pp. 24–62). Polity. (Reprinted from *Modern Intellectual History, 6*(5), 539–568).

Berlin, I. (1969). *Four essays on liberty*. Oxford University Press.

Broadie, A. (2001). *The Scottish Enlightenment: The historical age of the historical nation*. Birlinn Ltd.

Brown, W. (2015). *Undoing the demos: Neoliberalism's stealth revolution*. Zone Books.

Christofferson, M. S. (2004). *French intellectuals against the Left: The antitotalitarian moment of the 1970s*. Berghahn Books.

Christofferson, M. S. (2016). Foucault and new philosophy. In D. Zamora & M. C. Behrent (Eds.), *Foucault and neoliberalism* (pp. 6–23). Polity.

Cisney, V., & Morar, N. (2016). Introduction: Why biopower? Why now? In V. W. Cisney & N. Morar (Eds.), *Biopower: Foucault and beyond* (pp. 1–28). University of Chicago Press.

Davis, G. F. (2009). *Managed by the markets: How finance reshaped America*. Oxford University Press.

Dean, M. (2015). Foucault must not be defended. *History and Theory, 54*(October), 389–403.

Dean, M. (2016). Foucault, Ewald and neoliberalism. In D. Zamora & M. C. Behrent (Eds.), *Foucault and neoliberalism* (pp. 85–113). Polity.

Dean, M., & Villadsen, K. (2016). *State phobia and civil society*. Stanford University Press.

de Lagasnerie, G. (2013). Néolibéralisme, théorie politique et pensée critique. *Raisons politiques, 52*(4), 63–76.

Deuber-Mankowsky, A. (2008). Nothing is political, everything can be politicized: On the concept of the political in Michel Foucault and Carl Schmitt. *Telos, 142*, 135–161.

Dilts, A. (2008). Michel Foucault meets Gary Becker: Criminality beyond *Discipline and punish*. *Carceral Notebooks, 4*, 77–100.

Ferguson, A. (1995). *An essay on the history of civil society* (F. Oz-Salzberger, Ed.). Cambridge University Press. (Original work published 1767)

Foucault, M. (1976). *Histoire de la sexualité, I. La volonté de savoir*. Gallimard.

Foucault, M. (1977, May 9). La grande colere des faits. *Le nouvel observateur*, p. 84.

Foucault, M. (1991). Governmentality. In G. Burchell, C. Gordon, & P. Miller (Eds.), *The Foucault effect: Studies in governmentality* (pp. 87–104). University of Chicago Press.

Foucault, M. (2003). *Society must be defended: Lectures at the Collège de France, 1975–76* (D. Macey, Trans.; M. Bertani & A. Fontana, Eds.). Allen Lane/Penguin.

Foucault, M. (2004). *Naissance de la biopolitique: Cours au Collège de France, 1978–1979* (F. Ewald, Ed.). Seuil.

Foucault, M. (2007). *Security, territory, population: Lectures at the Collège de France, 1977–1978* (G. Burchell, Trans.; M. Senellart, Ed.). Palgrave Macmillan.

Foucault, M. (2008). *The birth of biopolitics: Lectures at the Collège de France, 1978–79* (G. Burchell, Trans.; M. Senellart, Ed.). Palgrave Macmillan.

Gane, N. (2014). The emergence of neoliberalism: Thinking through and beyond Michel Foucault's lectures on biopolitics. *Theory, Culture & Society, 31*(4), 3–27.

Glucksmann, A. (1975). *La cuisinière et le manageur d'hommes: Essai sur les rapports entre l'État, le marxisme et les camps de concentration.* Seuil.

Glucksmann, A. (1977). *Les maîtres penseurs.* Grasset.

Gordon, C. (1991). Governmental rationality: An introduction. In G. Burchell, C. Gordon, & P. Miller (Eds.), *The Foucault effect: Studies in governmentality* (pp. 1–52). University of Chicago Press.

Jesson, B. (1999). *Only their purpose is mad: The money men take over New Zealand.* Dunmore Press.

Kelly, M. G. E. (2015, March 9). Foucault and neoliberalism today. *Contriver's Review.* http://www.contrivers.org/articles/12/

Lazzarato, M. (2009). Neoliberalism in action: Inequality, insecurity and the reconstitution of the social. *Theory, Culture & Society, 25*(6), 109–133. https://doi.org/10.1177/0263276409350283

Lebaron, F. (2001). De la critique de l'économie à l'action syndicale. In D. Eribon (Ed.), *L'infrequentable Michel Foucault. Renouveaux de la pensee critique. Actes du colloque Centre Georges-Pompidou, 21–22 juin 2000* (pp. 157–167). EPEL.

Maxwell, J. (2014). Killing yourself to live: Foucault, neoliberalism and the auto-immunity problem. *Cultural Critique, 88,* 160–186.

McCormick, R. E., & Meiners, R. E. (1988). University governance: A property rights perspective. *The Journal of Law and Economics, 31*(2), 423–442.

Miller, J. (1993). *The passion of Michel Foucault.* Simon & Schuster.

Mirowski, P. (2013). *Never let a serious crisis go to waste: How neoliberalism survived the financial meltdown.* Verso.

Moreno Pestaña, J. L. (2011). *Foucault, la gauche et la politique.* Textuel.

Nealon, J. T. (2008). *Foucault beyond Foucault: Power and its intensifications since 1984.* Stanford University Press.

Newheiser, D. (2016). Foucault, Gary Becker and the critique of neoliberalism. *Theory, Culture, Society, 33*(5), 3–21.

Olssen, M. (2002). Michel Foucault as "thin" communitarian: Difference, community, democracy. *Cultural Studies/Critical Methodologies, 2*(4), 483–513. https://doi.org/10.1177/153270860200200403

Olssen, M. (2016). Neoliberalism and higher education today: Research, accountability and impact. *British Journal of Sociology of Education, 37*(1), 129–148. https://doi.org/10.1080/01425692.2015.1100530

Olssen, M. (2017). Neoliberalism and beyond: The possibilities of a social justice agenda. In S. Parker, K. N. Gulson, & T. Gale (Eds.), *Policy and inequality in education* (pp. 41–72). Springer.

Olssen, M., Codd, J., & O'Neill, A.-M. (2004). *Education policy: Globalization, citizenship & democracy*. Sage.

Olssen, M., & Peters, M. A. (2005). Neoliberalism, higher education and the knowledge economy: From the free market to knowledge capitalism. *Journal of Education Policy, 20*(3), 313–345. https://doi.org/10.1080/02680930500108718

Patton, P. (2016). Power and biopower in Foucault. In V. W. Cisney & N. Morar (Eds.), *Biopower: Foucault and beyond* (pp. 102–117). University of Chicago Press.

Paras, E. (2006). *Foucault 2.0: Beyond power and knowledge*. Other Press.

Peters, M. (2011). *Neoliberalism and after: Education, social policy and the crisis of Western capitalism*. Peter Lang.

Polanyi, K. (1944). *The great transformation*. Beacon.

Provenzano, L. (2016, March 28). *Foucault and neoliberalism: A report from American University of Paris* [Blog post]. http://blogs.law.columbia.edu/foucault1313/2016/03/28/foucault-813-epilogue-foucault-and-neoliberalism-conference-report/

Raaper, R., & Olssen, M. (2016). Mark Olssen on the neoliberalisation of higher education and academic lives: An interview. *Policy Futures in Education, 14*(2), 147–163. https://doi.org/10.1177/1478210315610992

Revel, J. (2005). *Expériences de la pensée: Michel Foucault*. Bordas.

Rosanvallon, P. (1979). *Le capitalisme utopique: Critique de l'idéologie économique*. Le Seuil.

Sartre, J.-P. (1966). Jean-Paul Sartre répond. *L'arc, 30*(October).

Walzer, M. (1983). The politics of Michael Foucault. *Dissent, 30*(Fall).

Zamora, D. (2016). Foucault, the excluded, and the neoliberal erosion of the state. In D. Zamora & M. C. Behrent (Eds.), *Foucault and neoliberalism* (pp. 63–84). Polity.

Zamora, D., & Behrent, M. C. (Eds.). (2016). *Foucault and neoliberalism*. Polity.

PART 5

Complexity, Democracy, Ethics

∴

CHAPTER 13

Foucault as Complexity Theorist

Overcoming the Problems of Classical Philosophical Analysis

Abstract

This article explores the affinities and parallels between Foucault's Nietzschean view of history and models of complexity developed in the physical sciences in the 20th century. It claims that Foucault's rejection of structuralism and Marxism can be explained as a consequence of his own approach which posits a radical ontology whereby the conception of the totality or whole is reconfigured as an always open, relatively borderless system of infinite interconnections, possibilities and developments. His rejection of Hegelianism, as well as of other Enlightenment philosophies, can be understood at one level as a direct response to his rejection of the mechanical atomist, and organicist epistemological world views, based upon a Newtonian conception of a closed universe operating upon the basis of a small number of invariable and universal laws, by which all could be predicted and explained. The idea of a fully determined, closed universe is replaced; and in a way parallel to complexity theories, Foucault's own approach emphasises notions such as self-organisation and dissipative structures; time as an irreversible, existential dimension; a world of finite resources but with infinite possibilities for articulation, or reinvestment; and characterised by the principles of openness, indeterminism, unpredictability, and uncertainty. The implications of Foucault's type of approach are then explored in relation to identity, creativity, and the uniqueness of the person. The article suggests that within a complexity theory approach many of the old conundrums concerning determinism and creativity, social constructionism and uniqueness, can be overcome.

1 Introduction

In my book *Michel Foucault: Materialism and Education* (original Bergin & Garvey, 1999, chapter 11; paperback edition, Paradigm, 2006, chapter 12), I consider Foucault as a complexity theorist and relate him to contemporary conceptions of complexity as they are being utilised in the physical and social sciences. In order to set the background to a discussion of Foucault as complexity theorist it is necessary to consider briefly both his appropriation of Nietzsche and his rejection of Marx in relation to the themes of chance and pluralism within his work.

Foucault's rejection of structuralism and Marxism, and his turn to genealogy and Nietzsche as the basis of his pluralistic conception, became clearer at the close of the 1960s. With his growing interest in genealogy, Foucault became more concerned with power and history, and with the historical constitution of knowledge. Although history was a process, it was a process that recognised no integrative principle or essence. If the genealogist studies history, "he finds that there is 'something altogether different' behind things: not a timeless and essential secret, but the secret that they have no essence or that their essence was fabricated in a piecemeal fashion from alien forms" (Foucault, 1977a, p. 142).

Foucault's conception of history explicitly reflects his Nietzschean heritage and his belief that certain aspects of Marxism and structuralism distorted the liberatory potential of the discourse.

> The interest in Nietzsche and Bataille was not a way of distancing ourselves from Marxism or communism—it was the only path towards what we expected from communism. (Foucault, 2001, p. 249)

It was in terms of the philosophy of difference and Nietzsche's conception of multiplicities through a rejection of Platonic hierachies that Foucault enunciates a theory of discursive formations, rejects Marxist and Hegelian conceptions of history and establishes an approach which broadly parallels contemporary complexity theories. The utilisation of Nietzsche signalled a rupture from Marxism in relation to a series of interrelated conceptual, theoretical and methodological precepts, including power, knowledge and truth, the subject, and the nature of historical change and determination.

Nietzsche focused on power in an altogether different way to Marx. In "Prison Talk", Foucault (1980a, p. 53) states:

> It was Nietzsche who specified the power relation as the general focus, shall we say, of philosophical discourse—whereas for Marx it was the production relation. Nietzsche is the philosopher of power, a philosopher who managed to think of power without having to confine himself within a political theory in order to do so.

Power, for Nietzsche, was conceived as a relation of forces within an analytics of power/knowledge/truth, which became important for Foucault to understand in the later 1960s after the publication of *The Archaeology of Knowledge* and his growing friendship with the French Nietzschean, Gilles Deleuze. Foucault accredits Nietzsche as the source of his interest in the question of truth and its relation to power. As he states in "Truth and Power" (Foucault, 1980b,

p. 133), "The political question ... is not error, illusion, alienated consciousness or ideology; it is truth itself. Hence, the importance of Nietzsche". Nietzsche's importance to Foucault can be seen as "correcting Marx", especially in relation to the linkage between power/knowledge/truth, and the functioning of knowledge as an instrument of power. As Alan Schrift (1995, p. 40) notes, Nietzsche's influence drew attention away from "substances, subjects and things, and focused attention instead on the *relations between* these substantives". In a related way, Foucault "draws our attention away from the substantive notion of power and directs our attention instead to the multifarious ways that power operates through the social order" (ibid.). For Nietzsche, such relations were relations of forces. Foucault thus focused on new relations as the relations of forces that existed and interacted within social systems as social practices. These were forces of repression and production that characterised the disciplinary society: forces that enable and block, subjugate and realise, and normalise and resist. In this model, power is not a thing, but a process, a relation of forces.

Beyond these concerns with power–truth–knowledge, and language and discourse, Foucault acknowledges the influence of Nietzsche in reference to the decentring of the subject, and the constitutive ethics of self-creation.

In the *Genealogy of Morals* Nietzsche (1967) traces the processes of descent or provenance (*Herkunft*) and emergence (*Entstehung*), but distinguishes these from a concern with origins (*Ursprung*) or essences. Nietzsche's thesis is that the subject is historically constituted and does not exist as something given metaphysically in advance. This is what Nietzsche (1967, pp. 1, 13) means when he says "there is no "being" behind doing, effecting, becoming; "the doer" is merely the fiction added to the deed—the deed is everything". For Foucault, accepting this view, the subject is an ideological product, an effect of power, whose identity is defined in relation to the practicalities of power and discourse.

Nietzsche constitutes important background to understanding Foucault as a complexity theorist in relation to his critique of mechanical philosophy and his writings on causation, determinism and free will. In his book *The Will to Power*, which had a central influence on both Heidegger and Foucault, Nietzsche (1968, p. 339) attacks the mechanical physicalistic world view:

> Physicists believe in a "true world" in their own fashion: a firm systematization of atoms in necessary motion, the same for all beings—so for them the "apparent world" is reduced to the side of universal and universally necessary being which is accessible to every being in its own way. But they are in error. The atom they posit is inferred according to the logic of perspectivism of consciousness—and is therefore itself a subjective fiction.

One way of interpreting the significance of such a statement from Foucault's perspective is to indicate the measure of his constructivism, or non-realism, over concepts and categories of science. While Foucault subscribed to the view that sciences like physics clearly maintain parallels to the extractive powers of the universe, judged purely by the fruits of its efforts, such a science does not imply the actual existence of atoms or the workings of a mechanical system or a particular individualist representation of the world.

For Nietzsche, the Will to Power operates as a general metaphysic of which "life is merely one special case" (Nietzsche, 1968, p. 369). In Nietzsche's view, all being is *becoming*. As a method of critique it aims to expose illusion and falsehood. And on this basis Nietzsche criticises the concepts of necessity and law, determinism and freedom. As he states (1968, p. 337):

> Let us here dismiss the two popular concepts "necessity" and "law": the former introduces a false constraint into the world, the latter a false freedom. "Things" do not behave regularly, according to a *rule*; there are no things (—they are fictions invented by us); they behave just as little under the constraint of necessity. There is no obedience here: for that something is as it is, as strong or as weak, is not the consequence of an obedience or a rule or a compulsion—

Or, in even starker terms (1968, p. 297):

> From the fact that something ensues regularly and ensues calculably, it does not follow that it ensues *necessarily*. That a quantum of force determines and conducts itself in every particular case in one way and manner does not make it into an "unfree will". "Mechanical necessity" is not a fact.

In his rejection of mechanical philosophy and organicism Nietzsche asserts a radical ontology whereby the conception of the totality or whole is reconfigured as an always open, relatively borderless system of infinite interconnections, possibilities and developments. Nietzsche's "fundamental metaphysical position", as Heidegger (1984, Vol., 2, chapter 12) reminds us, posits a philosophical ontology that, while it comprises a semiotic system of *finite* particulars, is nevertheless a system which is open-ended and contains *infinite* possibilities for reinvestment. The conception of an infinite relational order liberates conceptions of the whole from the traditional finitude associated with Hegel. This can be seen as an opening towards a non-linear system of dynamics and change. In relation to a politics of space, the conception of the community becomes reconfigured as an open borderless arena where changes are instrumented both internally and externally as elements within and without themselves undergo change. This applies to any system, including language, and can be represented in relation to the economy of the metaphor. In the words of David B. Allison (1977, p. XVI):

> [M]etaphorical signification amounts to a chain of substitutions. ... While the number of possible substitutions ... is finite, i.e., is bounded by resources of a given language—the process of substituting one for another is open-ended. The constitution of the metaphor is thus a process that is at least temporarily open to infinity. The metaphor, then, enjoys a "finite" but "open" economy.

This finite but open economy of signification also works, says Nietzsche, in relation to the will to power. While the field of forces is finite, it can be continually expended and recombined. Allison (p. XVII) cites Nietzsche from S. 639 of *The Will to Power*:

> Regarded mechanistically, the energy of the totality of becoming remains constant; regarded economically; it rises to a high point and sinks down again in an eternal circle. This "Will to Power" expresses itself in the interpretation, in the manner in which force is used up.

In his own representation, Heidegger (1991, Vol. 2, chapter 12) summarises the "Presentation and grounding" of Nietzsche's doctrine with regards to "Being as a whole as Life and Force", and "the World as Chaos". Heidegger lists several core theses which are central to Nietzsche's world view:

> Force is the pervasive character of the world. Force, for Nietzsche, is the will to power. (ibid., Vol. 2, p. 86)

> Force is limited, because it is finite. "In itself" force is "determinate" and "inherently limited" (ibid., Vol. 2, p. 87). "Because force, which is essentially finite, is the essence of the world, the totality of the world itself remains finite" (ibid., Vol. 2, p. 88). Hence there is a "firm confinement within boundaries". (ibid., Vol. 2, p. 88)

> "The lack of diminuation and accretion in universal force signifies not a 'standstill' ... but a perpetual 'Becoming'". There is no equilibrium of force. Heidegger continues, "We must grasp 'Becoming' here quite generally in the sense of transformation or—still more cautiously—change". (ibid., Vol. 2, p. 88)

"Precisely because the world is perpetual Becoming, and because as a totality of force it is nonetheless inherently finite, it produces 'infinite' effects". Nietzsche uses the phrase "infinitely waxing" to describe force in relation to its potentials. (ibid., Vol. 2, p. 87)

"In contrast to the imaginary character of space, *time* is *actual*" (ibid., Vol. 2, p. 90). Furthermore, "It is also—in contrast to the bounded character of space—unbounded, infinite". He quotes Nietzsche from *The Gay Science* (S. 341), where he speaks of "the eternal hourglass of existence". For Heidegger (1991, Vol. 2, p. 90), "Such actual, infinite time, Nietzsche grasps as *eternity*".

Heidegger (1991, Vol. 2, p. 91) cites Nietzsche from *The Gay Science* (S. 109): "The collective character of the world is ... to all eternity—chaos"—and this is "the fundamental representation of being as a whole" (Heidegger, 1991, Vol. 2, p. 91). In this representation, as Nietzsche notes (S. 109), chaos applies not in the sense of a "lack of necessity, but a lack of order" (Heidegger, 1991, Vol. 2, p. 90). Hence, the world lacks order or lawfulness, as well as predictability.

The idea that beings proceed according to "laws" is a "humanization", or "moralistic-juridical mode of thought", says Heidegger (1991, Vol. 2, p. 92). It is "anthropomorphic". He continues: "Nor are there in beings any 'goals' or 'purposes' or 'intentions'; and if there are no purposes, then 'purposelessness' and 'accident' as well are excluded" (ibid., Vol. 2, p. 92). Just as mechanics is wanting, so too is the idea of the universe as an "organism". Such a notion is for Nietzsche just a further "humanization", says Heidegger. (1991, Vol. 2, p. 93)

Heidegger draws his summary of Nietzsche's position largely from *The Gay Science* and *The Will to Power*. But most of Nietzsche's texts from the 1880s until his death could be drawn upon for support. With Nietzsche, then, we have an ontological position which stresses "force, finitude, perpetual Becoming, the innumerability of appearances, the bounded character of space, and the infinity of time" (1991, Vol. 2, pp. 90–91). And these relate back to the collective character of the world. While, as Heidegger (1991, Vol. 2, pp. 91–92) notes, "although Nietzsche distinguishes the concept of the world from the notion of fortuitous and arbitrary jumble, a sort of universal cosmic porridge, he nevertheless fails to liberate himself from the transmitted sense of chaos as something that lacks order and lawfulness". Such are the labyrinths of Nietzsche's thought.

That Foucault's agreement with the broad philosophical ontology of Nietzsche's approach has influenced his own epistemological constructivism, social constructionism, as well as the theory of social forces and power, is now well known. In general terms, Nietzsche's constructivism and his belief in chance were to become hallmarks of Foucault's own approach. The view of history as pluralist and not accounted for within a context of causal, linear determinism was thus important in Foucault's debt to Nietzsche, and also contributes background to understanding the affinities with complexity theory. Whereas Marxists like Althusser adopted a totalistic programme of seeking to explain the whole by understanding the interrelations between its component parts, for Foucault the totality always eluded analysis or understanding in terms of structure, but rather was characterised by *incompleteness, indeterminacy, complexity* and *chance*. This was the core of his pluralism. As Foucault says, "though it is true that these discontinuous discursive series each have, within certain limits, their regularity, it is undoubtedly no longer possible to establish links of mechanical causality or of ideal necessity between the elements which constitute them. We must accept the introduction of the *aléa* [chance] as a category in the production of events" (1981, p. 69).[1]

In seeking to characterise the nature of his "pluralism" and how it effects the analytics of discourse as operating through complex laws, Foucault (1978, p. 11) explains how he "substitutes the analysis of different types of transformation for the abstract, general, and monotonous form of "change" in which one so willingly thinks in terms of succession". In this, he seeks to define with the greatest care the transformations which have constituted the change, replacing the general theme of *becoming* ("general form, abstract element, primary cause, and universal effect") by the analysis of the transformations in their specificity, an examination of "the diversity of *systems* and the play of discontinuities into the history of *discourse*" (1978, p. 15). This involves, says Foucault (1978, pp. 11–12), within a given discursive formation, (1) detecting the changes which effect the operations, objects, theoretical choices, etc.; (2) detecting the changes which effect the discursive formations themselves (e.g., changes in the boundaries that define the field); and (3) detecting the changes which effect simultaneously several discursive formations (e.g., reversal of the hierarchy of importance, as happened, for instance, in the Classical period when the analysis of language lost the "directing role" that it had in the first years of the 19th century to biology, which in turn led to the development of new concepts such as "organism", "function", "organisation", etc., which in turn effected other sciences). All of these types of changes, says Foucault, characterise changes to both individual discourses and effect modifications in the episteme itself: its "redistributions", i.e., "the different transformations which it is possible to describe concerning ... states of a discourse".

In opposition to totalising models, Foucault sees his own analysis as more limited: to searching for the empirical historical grounds for discursive consistency or coherence; to recognising in discourse its empirical worldly features—"the work of the author. And why not?—His juvenilia or mature work, the patterns of a linguistic or rhetorical model (an idea, a theme)"; and acknowledging that the transformatory operations are all carried out "prior to discourse and outside of it" (1978, p. 17).

In his later reflections on method, in response to interviews on the subject of *Discipline and Punish*, Foucault (1977) asserts the "pluralist" nature of his project through his use of concepts like "eventalization"; that "specific events" ("*événements signuliers*") cannot be integrated or decoded simply as an application of a uniform and universal regularity. In this non-unified sense, the analysis of discourse effects a non-unified method. As Foucault (1972, p. 8) explains it:

> It has led to the individualisation of different series, which are juxtaposed to one another, follow one another, overlap and intersect, without one being able to reduce them to a linear schema. Thus, in place of the continuous chronology of reason, which was invariably traced back to some inaccessible origin, there have appeared scales that are sometimes very brief, distinct from one another, irreducible to a single law, scales that bear a type of history peculiar to each one, and which cannot be reduced to the general model of a consciousness that acquires, progresses, and remembers.

The notion of "eventalization" itself contains a number of elements. First, it treats all objects of knowledge as historical *events*. Second, it refers to a "pluralisation of causes" (Foucault, 1987, pp. 104–105):

> Causal multiplication consists in analysing an event according to the multiple processes that constitute it. ... "[E]ventalization" thus works by constructing around the singular event analysed as process a "polygon" or rather a "polyhedron" of intelligibility, the number of whose faces is not given in advance and can never properly be taken as finite. One has to proceed by progressive, necessarily incomplete saturation. And one has to bear in mind that the further one decomposes the processes under analysis, the more one is enabled, and indeed obliged to construct their external relations of intelligibility.

In addition, says Foucault (1987, p. 104) eventalization refers to the rediscovery of the "connections, encounters, blockages, plays of forces, strategies, etc.

that at a given moment establish what consequently comes to count as being self-evident, universal and necessary". In this sense, it constitutes a "breach of self-evidence", i.e.:

> It means making visible a *singularity* at places where there is a temptation to invoke historical constants, an immediate anthropological trait, or an obviousness that imposes itself uniformly on all. To show that things "weren't as necessary as all that; that it wasn't a matter of course that mad people came to be regarded as mentally ill; it wasn't self-evident that the only things to be done to a criminal were to lock him up, it wasn't self-evident that the causes of illness were to be sought through the individual examination of bodies; and so on".

In this sense, *eventalization* opposes the evidences upon which knowledge sequences and practices rest. Its theoretical quest is endlessly open. It operates in Foucault's (1987, p. 105) view, "as a procedure for lightening the weight of causality".

Alongside the concept of *eventalization* are those of *exteriority/interiority*, which Foucault (1972, pp. 120–122, 125, 140) discusses in *The Archaeology of Knowledge*, as well as in his inaugural lecture at the Collège de France (see Foucault, 1981), and also in his essay on Blanchot (Foucault, 1990). What Foucault means by "exteriority" is that the being of discourse resides in the "pure dispersion" of the socio-historical processes of reproduction and change; in the "particular events, regularities, relationships, modifications and systematic transformations", which constitute an "autonomous (although dependent)" domain, and "which can be described at its own level" (1972, pp. 121–122). As expressed in his essay on Blanchot (1990, p. 15), it is "the breakthrough to a language from which the subject is excluded ... : the being of language only appears for itself with the disappearance of the subject". This places the emphasis on "speech" rather than on the Cartesian *Cogito*. As he states (1990, p. 13):

> "I speak" runs counter to "I think". "I think" led to the indubitable certainty of the "I" and its existence; "I speak", on the other hand, distances, disperses, effaces that existence and lets only its empty emplacement appear. Thought about thought, an entire tradition wider than philosophy, has taught us that thought leads us to the deepest interiority. Speech about speech leads us, by way of literature as well as perhaps by other paths, to the outside in which the speaking subject disappears. No doubt that is why Western thought took so long to think the being of language:

as if it had a premonition of the danger that the naked experience of language poses for the self-evidence of the "I think".

Manfred Frank emphasises the ontological and methodological functions of exteriority. What Foucault means by exteriority, he says (1992, p. 108), is that each individual element in discourse is irreducible "to the unified discursive principle, or to an internal core of meaning to be found in the discourse". As he continues:

> What the rule of exteriority of discourse means then, is: "not moving from the discourse towards its internal, hidden core, towards the heart of the thought or the meaning, which is manifest in it". So the procedure of the analytic of discourse is external because it wishes to leave the series (*série*) of single events, mutually irreducible (in terms of a deductive or teleological principle), just as they are "external" to any totalizing general concept.

In a methodological sense, in that events and instances are individualised, "individualised" means here, as Frank (1992, p. 110) states it, "not predictable from the point of view of their structure, and contingent with respect to the way they happen to be". What is important in terms of the analytics of discourse is not seeking such a reduction: hence the analytics of discourse is *external* to the process of analysis. What is important to Foucault (1990, pp. 15–16) is that:

> thought stands outside subjectivity, setting its limits as though from without, articulating its end, making its dispersion shine forth, taking only its invincible absence; and that at the same time stands at the threshold of all positivity, not in order to grasp its foundation or justification but in order to regain the space of its unfolding, the void serving as its site, the distance in which it is constituted and into which its immediate certainties slip the moment they are glimpsed—a thought that, in relation to the interiority of our philosophical reflection and the positivity of our knowledge, constitutes what in a word we might call "the thought from the outside".

As well as referring to consciousness, interiority thus refers also to any foundation or centre to the social formation which the events or parts echo or reflect. Hence, again, this can also be seen as consistent with, and expressing, his opposition to the notion of a determined causality embodied in the Hegelian conception of an "expressive totality" and, by derivation, also embodied in the notion of "a primary causal necessity" (*"un causalisme primaire"*), which he sees as central to Marxism. In this sense, the analytics of discourse must resist interiorisation, "forsaking the wordy interiority of consciousness", as well the appeal to a centre or foundation, and become, as in Bataille, the "discourse of the limit" (1990, p. 18).

What Foucault, following Nietzsche, Blanchot and Bataille, also elaborates as a theme, is the "uniqueness" and "unpredictability" of the singular historical instance, and it is this that I will claim below enables us to forge links between Foucault and complexity theory. What he seeks to do is introduce conceptions of *indeterminacy, irregularity, openness, complexity*, and *uniqueness* as integral to his conception of the historical process. This means that any event contains an element of uniqueness. In *The Archaeology of Knowledge* (Foucault, 1972, p. 101) examples abound: it takes the form of establishing the spatio-temporal co-ordinates that ensure the novel aspect of the "statement" (*"énoncé"*): "The enunciation is an unrepeatable event; it has situated and dated uniqueness that is irreducible. Yet this uniqueness allows of a number of constants—grammatical, semantic, logical—by which we can, by neutralising the moment of enunciation and the co-ordinates that individuate it, recognise the general form". Or again (ibid., pp. 146–147): "every statement belongs to a certain regularity—that consequently none can be regarded as pure creation, as the marvellous disorder of genius. But we have also seen that no statement can be regarded as inactive, and be valid as the scarcely real shadow or transfer of the initial statement. The whole enunciative field is both regular and alerted: it never sleeps". This fact that the future never simply reproduces the past, but adds always elements of novelty, means that the self is never simply the reproduced habitus of its socialisation, but due to its necessarily distinct location in time and space and culture, as well as its progressively growing capacity for agency, is characterised by elements of difference and uniqueness. Yet this difference and uniqueness is not an artefact of language but a real phenomenon. In addition, it means that ethical values can never simply be expressed merely as *repeatable* rules of conduct—which increases, rather than decreases, our sense of ethical responsibility in action.

Such a conception also expresses an "internalist" view of history, which is central to how Foucault understands change and how issues like freedom and determinism are resolved. Such a view of history means that there is no guiding principle underlying structures or their emergence. Difference then is historical, and resists both the univocity of being, as well as transcendence in all its forms, whether God, *Cogito*, Forms, Economy. There is nothing outside of history. Although such a conception does not adopt a uniform ahistorical model of temporalisation, or prioritise one element (economy) over others, neither does it deny that invariant necessities may exist which can express themselves through the different discursive lenses of particular historical periods. In this sense, as Joseph Margolis (1993, p. 204) notes, Foucault does not deny a world of "things", for he:

> does not dismiss *de re* necessities of this or that episteme; they are rightly recognised there as the necessities they are. But they are also not enshrined as universal, changeless structures of any kind (regarding world or reason). [Rather,] [w]e are always invited to "test" for the "limits" that we may go beyond. That's to say: the invariances of any proposed transcendental limits of reason may be tested by exploring whether we can alter such a model of coherence convincingly, in a way that rests on historical change.

Similarly, such a conception can be claimed to resist the charge of epistemological relativism. As Foucault (1984a, p. 335) puts it in the "Preface to the *History of Sexuality*, Volume II", he says that he is not denying the possibility of universal structures:

> Singular forms of experience may perfectly very well harbor universal structures; they may well not be independent from the concrete determinations of social existence. ... [T]his thought has a historicity which is proper to it. That it should have this historicity does not mean it is deprived of all universal form, but instead that the putting into play of these universal forms is itself historical.

Like Heidegger, in *Being and Time*, Foucault manifests a pragmatic anti-foundationalism. Such an approach bares a similarity to parallel developments in Western Anglo-American philosophy in writers like Dewey, Quine, Davidson, Putnam, Kuhn, and Goodman, and in the continental tradition to writers like Habermas, Bourdieu and Apel. While all developed versions of historicism, all denied any total pernicious form of relativism and all claimed a measure of objectivity. For Foucault, the maxim that "everything is historical" means that while we remain forever imprisoned by contingency, non-correspondence, relativity and ideological prejudice, there are some "footholds", even if they do not lead easily to a uniform consensus. Foucault's anti-essentialism places him alongside a possible (pragmatic) reading of Popper, who also rejected essentialist ontologies, in that there is nothing that prevents testing and attempted falsifications in order to "take a bearing", or "check the situation out". While this will give a certain form of confidence on some issues, on others, the conditions of what constitutes falsifiability will not be so easy to foresee.[2] Foucault's realism holds to the view that correspondence or synchronisation of discourse and reality is not required. Rather than correspondence, we must speak of isomorphism. There is no assurance, pace Kant, either, of transcendentally valid and universally reliable cognitive schemata, for such a conception relies on a conception of a subject posited prior to history. What justified Kant's cognitive schemata depends on various historically contingent conditions within what Heidegger would call the "horizon" within which they appear. This doesn't mean there are no historical justifications (survival), and nor does it mean there are no footholds of any sort. But with Heidegger, Foucault's thesis of the historicity of existence would deny that there is any eternal "point of view".

Although Foucault acknowledges a debt to Nietzsche, it would be an error to represent his approach as simply Nietzschean, and this would misrepresent his relation to Marx and to radical politics. As well as Nietzsche, Foucault has debts to Heidegger: Herbert Dreyfus (1992, pp. 80–81) claims that "it was through Heidegger that Foucault came to appreciate Nietzsche". As Foucault (1985, p. 9) says: "it is possible that if I had not read Heidegger, I would not have read Nietzsche. I had tried to read Nietzsche in the fifties but Nietzsche alone did not appeal to me—whereas Nietzsche and Heidegger, that was a philosophical shock". Ultimately, Foucault "nevertheless recognised that Nietzsche outweighed [Heidegger]". But both exacted an influence. One of the central themes which Foucault shared with Heidegger and Nietzsche, as well as with Althusser, was their challenge to the Cartesian and Kantian conceptions of the subject. He was also influenced by Heidegger in terms of the understanding of Being as indicating the presuppositions, things, tools, language, institutions, shared understandings, and other people which determine what is deemed possible or impossible, or what counts as important or unimportant, or meaningful or unmeaningful. Like Heidegger, Foucault came to reject the view of a constant, ahistorical, universal truth, which came to influence his rejection of essentialism and other forms of foundationalism, thereby influencing the precise nature of his materialism. Yet another writer that Foucault has course to refer to is Spinoza, whom he refers to and summarises in several of his papers over the course of his writing career.[3] While Spinoza cannot be represented as a direct influence, and one must be cautious about attribution of themes or concepts, Foucault's detailed understanding of Spinoza is suggestive in that Spinoza's concepts of power, politics, of collective and individual praxis, and of republican constitutionalism, and general theme of complexity can, if suitably modified according to the dictates of difference, be rendered broadly compatible with Foucault's approach.[4]

2 Complexity and Openness

In that Foucault talks of "chance" and "unpredictability", such a conception of historical openness is not technically incompatible with deterministic Newtonian physics, in the sense that events and outcomes are still the result of antecedent conditions. Foucault, however, follows Nietzsche who introduced indeterminacy into the Newtonian theory. Rather than postulate a closed universe with a small number of invariable, universal laws which could explain everything, and predict the future, the universe is theorised as an infinitely open, complex whole, characterised by unpredictability, uncertainty and change. Causation in Foucault's view is conceived of *systemically*, in terms of a model of holism–particularism, or complex causation, which makes events, which are the outcomes of interactions in open systems, effectively unpredictable, in that the full range of possible combinations or effects cannot be specified in advance. Complex systems, moreover, are contingent and dynamic—the structure of the system is continuously transformed through the interaction of the elements—and are not explainable by reference to any external principle, origin, or foundation. In this process, says Cilliers (1998, pp. 107–108), "no complex system, whether biological or social, can be understood without considering its history. ... To be more precise, the history of a system ... co-determines the structure of a system". In this theory, while change is understood as the outcome of contingent complex activity, human agency is understood as an emergent property of the historical and social system.[5]

In insisting on the open nature of the historical system, Foucault's approach to understanding history parallels Derrida's critique and revision of Saussure in stressing the open and incomplete character of the totality of social relations. In Foucault, however, the analysis proceeds beyond the textual to an analysis of the historical relations between the discursive and pre-discursive, whereas for Derrida and Saussure the analysis is synchronic and confined to language. Throughout his career, in fact, it can be said that Foucault maintains a distinction between the discursive and the pre-discursive. In his early period, prior to *The Archaeology of Knowledge*, published in 1968, Foucault sees discourses formed on the basis of *epistemes* that provide a unified view of intellectual life during a particular period or age. After his turn to genealogy, he developed such an approach more directly in relation to how the practices discursive and pre-discursive were related. As a consequence, in retaining the poststructuralist emphasis on the open and incomplete nature of the totality, but applied to history and social relations, rather than language, Foucault's more materialist approach has radical implications for our understanding of concepts like determinism, predictability, and the future.

In this context, it is worth noting the parallel between Foucault's systemic conception of change, linked closely to a system of open possibilities or variations, and what is now known as complexity theory. Although having roots in ancient Chinese and Greek thought, versions of complexity theory are a relatively new field of scientific enquiry and are perhaps one of the most notable new developments since the advent of quantum theory in the early 1900s. Such theories are not only compatible with materialism, but are systemic, or holist, in that they account for diversity and unity in the context of a systemic field of complex interactional changes. Chaos theory is one version of complexity. Partly with origins in computing technology, and partly in the development of new non-Euclidean structures of fractal geometrical mathematics, chaos theory became concerned with explaining "the qualitative study of unstable aperiodic behaviour in deterministic non-linear dynamical systems" (Sardar & Abrams, 1999, p. 9).[6] It is complexity theory more broadly, however, that has drawn off poststructuralist methods, and establishes them as a form of critical realism.[7]

In the recent history of science, the work of Ilya Prigogine (1980, 1984, 1989, 1994, 1997, 2003) has advanced the field of post-quantum complexity analysis at the macroscopic and microscopic levels, based in non-equilibrium physics, linked to the significant work of the Solvay Institutes for Physics and Chemistry. Prigogine received a Nobel Prize in 1977. Like Nietzsche and others before him, he translated the effects of a theory of becoming, based on an Heraclitean idea of ceaseless change, and providing a post-quantum understanding of the universe in terms of dimensions of chance, unpredictability, uncertainty, chaos, non-equilibrium systems, and change. Prigogine's central contribution was to non-equilibrium statistical mechanics, thermodynamics and the probabilistic analysis of complex systems (Prigogine, 2003, pp. 45, 82). His main ideas (expressed non-mathematically) were that "nature leads to unexpected complexity" (ibid., 2003, p. 8); that "self-organization appears in nature far from equilibrium" (ibid., p. VII); that "the universe is evolving" (ibid., p. 9); that the messages of Parmenides (that nothing changes) must be replaced by those of Heraclitus (that everything always changes) (ibid., pp. 9, 56); that "time is our existential dimension" (ibid., p. 9); that "time is an invention" (ibid., p. 10); that "the direction of time is the most fundamental property of the universe" (ibid., p. 64); that nothing is predetermined (ibid., p. 9); that non-equilibrium, time-irreversibility, and non-integration, are features of all systems, including evolution, which is to say that our universe is full of non-linear, irreversible processes (ibid., p. 59); that life creates evolution (ibid., pp. 61, 65), and that everything is historical (ibid., p. 64).[8]

In his book *Complexity and Postmodernism*, Paul Cilliers (1998, p. VIII) defines complexity in the following way:

> In a complex system ... the interaction of constituents of the system, and the interaction between the system and its environment, are of such a nature that the system as a whole cannot be fully understood simply by analysing its components. Moreover, these relationships are not fixed, but shift and change, often as a result of self-organisation. This can result in novel features, usually referred to in terms of emergent properties. The brain, natural language and social systems are complex.

Poststructuralism, says Cilliers, has introduced a new conception of complexity based on "distributed" or "relational" representation, following Saussure.[9] Such a system is complex in relation to the fact that it has a large number of elements which interact dynamically in a non-linear and asymmetrical manner. Interactions take place in open systems through "self-organisation" by adapting dynamically to changes in both the environment and the system. Self-organisation is an *emergent* property of the system as a whole. An emergent property is a property that is constituted due to the combination of elements in the system as a whole. As such it is a property possessed by the system but not by its components.[10] Cilliers (1998, p. 90) defines "self-organisation" as "the capacity of complex systems which enables them to develop or change internal structure spontaneously and adaptively in order to cope with or manipulate the environment". Such systems are not in equilibrium because they are constantly changing as a consequence of interaction between system and environment, and, as well as being influenced by external factors, are influenced by the history of the system (1998, p. 66). Cilliers identifies social systems, the economy, the human brain, and language as complex systems.[11]

Hence one could characterise Foucault's conception of societies as "non-equilibrium systems", where no general laws can predict the detailed behaviour of such systems. As much that develops does so as a consequence of emergence, life is created as a consequence of the collective interactions of parts. This entails not only the limitless possibility of combinations that can occur in open environments, but also that as the collectivity possesses properties and energies not possessed by the parts, but through which change can take place, new forms and patterns can develop. Relatively small changes in initial conditions can trigger major changes throughout the system, in part or whole. Such a perspective gives a new insight to the "contradictions of capitalism".[12] Although for Foucault the economy cannot be represented as a transhistorical foundation permitting an understanding of change in history, it can be analysed internally, i.e., a genealogy of capitalism in terms of the history of economic structures, and the effects they engender throughout the social structure. Although I realise that this brief account cannot possibly do justice to the topics of complexity theory, emergence, chance or critical realism, it is broadly in this direction that Foucault's historical materialism leads.

3 The Nature of Identity

Such a notion of Foucault as complexity theorist also enables us to understand his views about identity, as well as many other philosophical conundrums. Let me start with identity. Given that structural linguistics seeks to define identity relationally, Saussure (1974, p. 120) argued that it cannot posit a theory of identity as a substantive entity, or as a concrete "positive" unique particularity. This was retained by Derrida in his revision of Saussure's view, seeing identities as constituted by the series of *traces* of the differences in the system.[13] But if one conceives of identity in purely relational terms, as Mark Currie (2004, p. 13) notes, "it could be said that the concept of difference is no respecter of difference". As he continues, in explaining Saussure's view:

> A theory of subjectivity, or personhood, for example, might locate identity not in the body of the individual but in the relations between that person and others. In other words a person might not be defined by inherent characteristics, but like Saussure's train or chess piece, be understood as an identity only because of the relationships that person has with other people, in a system of family, friendship and social relations. This would be referred to as a relational view of personal identity. The same might be said of collective identities. It might be argued for example, that a national identity is not one that is made up of inherent qualities (of "positive terms" in Saussure's language) but of relational ones concerned with how a nation distinguishes itself from other nations.

For Nietzsche, Deleuze and Foucault, difference operates historically and has a dynamic quality that the theories of Saussure and Derrida lack. On this basis there is no reason why the traces that infuse identity could not be seen as leaving a residue or mark, developing into a positive conception of self constituted through complex interactions in the push and pull of the historical process. The stress on historical praxis creates a more enduring sense of identity in this sense. While this still leaves identity as relational in terms of its constitution, an identity which can be represented as positive and substantial (in the sense of its being irrepressible or non-reducible) is the outcome of self-creation or constitutive praxis in history.[14]

Such a view has the advantage over Saussure's and Derrida's view in that it can account for a substantial conception of the self and can explain, in the context of historical and social constructionist views of the self, how identities can emerge that are both *distinct* and *unique*,[15] which are non-reversible, and irreducible to the social whole.[16] For Nietzsche and Deleuze, following Duns Scotus, Spinoza and Hume, identities are constituted in experience, which is defined in terms of complex effects and relations, as practices (or, for Deleuze, *haecceities*) whose complex modes of operation are individuating (but not personalising or privatising). For Deleuze (1985, 1987, chapter 1), such patterns show parallels to nomadology or rhizomatic (rather than arborescent) development. For Foucault (1990), it is "outside thought"; for Nietzsche, "gay science". In 20th-century Marxist thought, Althusser's conception of structural causality, as outlined at the start of this paper, partly fits such a model.[17] Similar models of organisation and development are also evident in Spinoza's "ethics", as what Spinozian interpreters like Damasio (2003, p. 37) call "nesting" theories of development, where the "parts of simple reactions [are] incorporated as components of more elaborate ones, a nesting of the simple within the complex".[18] Yet other approaches utilizing complex models, although in somewhat variable ways, are cybernetics, or the early theories of Gregory Bateson (see Bateson, 1972).

4 Holism–Particularism, Uniqueness and Creativity

We can see how Foucault's general method enables uniqueness to emerge from antecedent conditions. I have described his method elsewhere as one of "holism–particularism" (Olssen, 1999, chapter 11). Foucault (1994b, pp. 824–825) himself talks about his own method in *Dits et écrits* as a "logical analysis of reality", and distinguishes it from "the determinist ascription of causality" in Marx, as well as from "logic of the Hegelian type". Arnold Davidson (1997, p. 11) in a review of *Dits et écrits* to which my own analysis is indebted, characterises Foucault's methodological strategy in terms of a "non-reductive" and "holistic" analysis of social life. As he puts it (Davidson, 1997, p. 11):

> This kind of analysis is characterized, first, by anti-atomism, by the idea that we should not analyze single or individual elements in isolation but that one must look at the systematic relations amongst elements; second. it is characterized by the idea that the relations between elements are coherent and transformable, that is, that the elements form a structure.

Thus, in his dissertation on the knowledge of heredity as a system of thought, submitted as part of his application for his position at the Collège de France,

Foucault seeks to describe the changes, transformations, and conditions of possibility that made genetics possible, that constituted it as a science based on a series of discourses concerning breeding, just as in *The Order of Things* (1970) he had done for natural history and biology. What factors led to the emergence of these fields as sciences? What elements changed to make such developments possible? What made them possible as systems of thought? Thus Foucault seeks to describe the relations among elements as structures which change as the component elements change, in an always open system where unexpected outcomes and novel features are contingent inevitabilities of the process of history.

Such an approach makes it possible to explain how individuals are, on the one hand, the outcome of social and historical processes and yet how, on the other, novelty, uniqueness and creativity are possible. By interpreting Foucault in such a light, we can begin to make sense of his comments and general sense of incredulity in response to questions that were put to him on the general dimension of "social construction/individuation". As he says in *The Archaeology of Knowledge* (1972, p. 200):

> If I suspended all reference to the speaking subject, it was not to discover laws of construction or forms that could be applied in the same way by all speaking subjects, nor was it to give voice to the great universal discourse that is common to all men at a particular period. On the contrary, my aim was to show what the differences consisted of, how it was possible for men, within the same discursive practice, to speak of different objects, to have contrary opinions. ... [I]n short I want not to exclude the problem of the subject but to define positions and functions that the subject could occupy in the diversity of discourse.

It is not unrelated to his general conception of complexity that Foucault also seems to suggest the genuine possibility of free agency and creativity. With reference to thought, for instance, he describes it as an original and creative response in relation to social determinants. As he (1984b, pp. 388–389) puts it:

> For a domain of action, a behaviour, to enter the field of thought, it is necessary to have made it lose its familiarity, or to have provoked a certain number of difficulties around it. These elements result from social, economic, or political processes. But here their only role is that of castigation. They can exist and perform their action for a very long time, before there is effective problematization by thought. And when thought intervenes, it doesn't assume a unique form that is the direct result or the necessary expression of these difficulties; it is an original or specific

response—often taking many forms, sometimes even contradictory in its different aspects—to these difficulties, which are defined for it by a situation or a context and which hold true as a possible question.

Thought, then, arises as a unique event from a context of rules. Hence it is always the case, says Foucault (1984b, p. 389), that:

> to a single set of difficulties, several responses can be made. ... But what has to be understood is what makes them simultaneously possible: it is the point in which their simultaneity is rooted; it is the soil that can flourish them all in their diversity and sometimes in spite of their contradictions.

A similar line of reasoning, dissecting the general from the particular, and the social from the individual, is evident in his debate with Chomsky (Foucault & Chomsky, 1997, pp. 119–120) where he refers to "free creation within a system of rules":

> One can only, in terms of language or of knowledge, produce something new by putting into play a certain number of rules. ... Thus we can roughly say that linguists before Mr Chomsky mainly insisted on the rules of construction of statements and less on the innovation represented by every new statement. ... And in the history of science or in the history of thought, we place more emphasis on individual creation, and we had kept aside and left in the shadows these communal general rules, which obscurely manifest themselves through every scientific discovery, every scientific invention, and even every philosophical innovation.

In this sense, Foucault explains the originality and uniqueness of the subject in the same way, and using the same arguments as he explains the originality of statements (*énoncés*). In the interview with Chomsky, Foucault agrees that "rules and freedom are not opposed to each other". In fact, the point he is at pains to stress in the interview with Chomsky is that within any system of rules, in the long run "what is striking is the proliferation of possibilities by divergences" (p. 122). As he says (p. 123):

> [C]reativity is possible in putting into play a system of rules; it is not a mixture of order and freedom. ... [W]here I don't completely agree with Mr Chomsky is when he places the principle of these regularities, in a way, in the interior of the mind or of human nature. ... If it is a matter of whether these rules are effectively put to work by the human mind, all right; all right, too, if it is a question of whether the historian and the

> linguist can think it in their turn; it is all right also to say that these rules should allow us to realise what is said or thought by these individuals. But to say that these regularities are connected, as conditions of existence, to the human mind or its nature, is difficult for me to accept; it seems to me that one must, before reaching that point, ... replace it in the field of other human practices, such as economics, technology, politics, sociology, which can serve them as conditions of formation, of models, of place, or apparition, etc. I would like to know whether one cannot discover the system of regularity, of constraint, which makes science possible, somewhere else, even outside the human mind, in social forms, in the relations of production, in the class struggle, etc.

While Chomsky is interested in the "intrinsic capabilities of mind", Foucault is interested in explaining how infinite possibilities of application arise from a limited number of rules which constitute the social conditions of existence.

In insisting on the open nature of the historical system, Foucault's approach to understanding history parallels Derrida's critique and revision of Saussure's in stressing the open and incomplete character of the totality of social relations. In Foucault, however, the analysis proceeds beyond the textual to an analysis of the historical relations between the discursive and pre-discursive, whereas for Derrida and Saussure the analysis is synchronic and confined to language. For Foucault, what is analysed is social practices—both discursive and non-discursive. Although this establishes a sociological holism and social objectivism which is anterior to the individual human subject, it is not a "spirit" or "mind" in the Hegelian (*Geist*) or Durkheimian (collective representations or consciousness) sense, but, influenced by the linguistic turn, a series of practices—habits, actions, mores, customs, languages—which function like a language, and from which individuals derive and alter meanings. In this sense, Foucault's sociological objectivism is akin to Wittgenstein's (*forms of life*), or Lévi-Strauss's (*symbolic systems*), in that objective social reality, while having ontological status, is not posited as a superior mind or intelligence which presides over other (mere ordinary) individual actors in history.

Acknowledgement

This chapter originally appeared as Olssen, M. (2008), Foucault as complexity theorist: Overcoming the problems of classical philosophical analysis, *Educational Philosophy and Theory*, 40(1), 96–117, https://doi.org/10.1111/j.1469-5812.2007.00406.x. Reprinted here, with minor edits, with permission from the publisher.

Notes

1. In his review of Deleuze's books ("Theatrum philosophicum"). Foucault (1998, p. 366) reinforces the importance of chance: "The present as the recurrence of difference, as repetition giving voice to difference, affirms at once the totality of chance. The univocity of being in Duns Scotus led to the immobility of an abstraction, in Spinoza it led to the necessity and eternity of substance; but here it leads to the single throw of chance in the fissure of the present. If being always declares itself in the same way, it is not because being is one but because the totality of chance is affirmed in the single dice throw of the present".
2. As, for example, when they tried to test Copernicus's theories in astronomy by dropping stones from church spires to test to see whether the earth was rotating on its axis.
3. See, for instance, Foucault's essay "Truth and Juridical Forms", originally published in May 1973, where he summarises Spinoza in relation to Nietzsche (Foucault, 2001, pp. 11–12); again, Foucault refers to Spinoza in the debate with Chomsky (Foucault, 1997, p. 136); in "Theatrum Philosophicum" (Foucault, 1998, pp. 359–360 and 366–367); and in "Afterword to *The Temptation of St Anthony*" (1998, p. 105), just to name a few. It is also noteworthy that Deleuze was influenced by Spinoza, as Deleuze had a strong influence on Foucault. See Paul Veyne (1997, pp. 63–64), "Foucault Revolutionizes History". Also see index entries to Deleuze and Guattari (1987), Deleuze (1990, 1994) and others. Like Deleuze, Foucault (1998, p. 364) "adapts" Spinozist concepts to express his views. For example: "The univocity of being, its singleness of expression, is paradoxically the principal condition that permits difference to escape the domination of identity, frees it from the law of the Same as a simple opposition within conceptual elements".
4. Michael Hardt has already noted the importance of Spinoza's conception of power on Foucault. See "Translator's Foreword: The Anatomy of Power", in Antonio Negri's *The Savage Anomaly: The power of Spinoza's metaphysics and politics* (1991). On the theme of complexity, see Damasio (2003).
5. Foucault, like Nietzsche, wrote philosophically, and hence his use of terms like "chance" and "unpredictability" possibly lack technical translatability to the language of natural science. An account of the classical definition of concepts such as "stability", "chance", etc. is given by Cilliers (1998). One way to define "chance" might be to see it as not incompatible with a Newtonian universe. In complex systems, as Cilliers (1998, p. 109) says, "novel, unpredicted behaviour need not be a result of chance. It can be 'caused' by the complex interaction of a large number of factors. ... Complexity is not to be confused with randomness and chance, but cannot be confused with first-order logical terms either". In this sense, we can speak of events which are theoretically unpredictable, which are not explainable in terms of "chance".
6. For other accounts of chaos theory, see Swinney (1983), Holden (1985), Gleick (1987), Sappington (1990) and Ayers (1997).
7. Chaos theory and complexity theories are distinct, although chaos theory can be seen as one type of complexity theory, which emphasises the importance of sensitivity to initial conditions. This is not so important with complex systems in general, which stresses the interaction of a large number of components (see Cilliers, 1998, p. ix).
8. Prigogine mostly applies these ideas to physical systems, but does sometimes demonstrate their applicability to the social and human world. Discussing his theories of time and irreversibility, he notes how all events are irreversible events. The consequence of irreversibility is that "it leads to probabilistic descriptions, which cannot be reduced to individual trajectories or wave functions corresponding to Newtonian or Quantum mechanics" (Prigogine, 2003, p. 75).

9 Meaning is conferred not by one-to-one correspondence with the world but by relationships between structural components of the system. See Cilliers (1998, p. 81). His analysis of poststructuralist complexity is based on Saussure's well-known analysis in the *Course in General Linguistics* (1974). Having said this, it is interesting that Cilliers translates poststructuralist philosophy into Western analytic schemas rather than elaborate his thesis in relation to difference theory as elaborated by Foucault or Deleuze. I have done the same here simply to convey something of the tenor of the poststructuralist innovation.

10 For other forms of emergentist materialism in Western thought, see Bunge (1977), Haken (1977, 1990), Rapp et al. (1986) or Skarda and Freeman (1990). Although such theories are broadly analogous to Foucault's materialism, the emphasis in poststructuralism on the open and incomplete character of the totality presents new insights into issues like determination and chance. Again, see Cilliers (1998).

11 For another view of complexity theory, see Kauffman (1991, 1993, 1995). Kauffman suggests that while events can be seen as having antecedent conditions which explain them, in open environments the possible combinations are unpredictable. Other characteristics of complex systems are that they do not operate near equilibrium; the relationships between components are non-linear and dynamic; elements do not have fixed positions; the relationships between elements are not stable; and there are always more possibilities than can be actualised.

12 The form of complexity may itself change, as is happening with globalisation. The notion, for example, that carbon emissions can trigger climate change, which can have potentially unpredictable effects of unimaginable severity, is one illustration of how determination works in relation to complex causality.

13 For Derrida (1981, p. 26) the sign has no positive identity but comprises only the collection of traces of all the other signs that run through it.

14 If we think of someone like Winston Churchill, there is something trite in representing him as the outcome of the play of differences (Churchill is not Balfour, not Astor, not Baldwin, etc.), for agency in history established a substantial, yet non-essential sense. Yet this identity is still always precarious, incomplete, fragmented, inconsistent, and transitional. It represents at any particular time, a "settlement".

15 Liberals, especially Rawls (1971), bemoaned in *A Theory of Justice* that it was necessary to retreat to deontology (return to a rights discourse) because social approaches (including utilitarianism) could not account for the *distinctness* of identity.

16 Such theories of complex emergentist materialism can also account for the origins of mind as irrepressible (non-reducible) yet wholly material, or physical.

17 Such complex non-linear models are historically contingent in terms of their internal, substantive arrangements. In Althusser, the variability of the effectivity of the levels of practices of the social formation conforms to such a complex formula, albeit in structuralist and decidedly non-nominalistic terms. The ultimate necessity of the economic, however, does not conform, as it introduces a causal factor which is historically invariant across successive modes of production. In this sense, to use Deleuze and Guattari's (1987) language, Althusser's model of structural causality conforms to both *rhizonomic* and *arborescent* forms.

18 Damasio (2003) uses examples of social emotions, including sympathy, embarrassment, shame, etc., to exemplify the nesting principle. As he states (pp. 45–46): "a whole retinue of regulatory reactions along with elements present in primary emotions can be identified as subcomponents of social emotions in varied combinations. The nested incorporation of components from lower tiers is apparent. Think how the social emotion "contempt" borrows from the facial expressions of 'disgust', a primary emotion that evolved in association with the autonomous and beneficial rejection of potentially toxic foods". The appropriate image for these reactions "is not that of a simple linear hierarchy" (p. 38).

References

Allison, D. B. (Ed.). (1977). *The new Nietzsche: Contemporary styles of interpretation.* Dell.

Ayers, S. (1997). The application of chaos theory to psychology. *Theory and Psychology, 7*(3), 373–398.

Bateson, G. (1972). *Steps to an ecology of mind.* Ballantine.

Bunge, M. (1977). Emergence and the mind: Commentary. *Neuroscience, 2,* 501–509.

Cilliers, P. (1998). *Complexity and postmodernism: Understanding complex systems.* Routledge.

Currie, M. (2004). *Difference.* Routledge.

Damasio, A. (2003). *Looking for Spinoza.* Verso.

Davidson, A. I. (Ed.). (1997). *Foucault and his interlocutors.* University of Chicago Press.

Deleuze, G. (1985). Nomad thought. In D. B. Allison (Ed.), *The new Nietzsche* (pp. 142–149). MIT Press.

Deleuze, G. (1990). *The logic of sense* (M. Lester with C. Stiavale, Trans.; C. V. Bourdas, Ed.). Columbia University Press.

Deleuze, G. (1994). *Difference and repetition* (P. Patton, Trans.). Continuum.

Deleuze, G., & Guattari, F. (1987). *A thousand plateaus: Capitalism and schizophrenia* (B. Massumi, Trans. and foreword). Continuum.

Derrida, J. (1981). *Positions.* University of Chicago Press.

Dreyfus, H. (1992). On the ordering of things: Being and power in Heidegger and Foucault. In T. J. Armstrong (Ed. and Trans.), *Michel Foucault: Philosopher* (pp. 80–98). Harvester Wheatsheaf.

Foucault, M. (1970). *The order of things.* Random House.

Foucault, M. (1972). *The archaeology of knowledge* (A. Sheridan, Trans.). Tavistock.

Foucault, M. (1977a). Nietzsche, genealogy, history. In D. F. Bouchard (Ed.), *Language, counter-memory, practice: Selected essays and interviews* (D. F. Bouchard & S. Simon, Trans.; pp. 139–164). Cornell University Press.

Foucault, M. (1977b). *Discipline and punish: The birth of the prison* (A. Sheridan, Trans.). Pantheon.

Foucault, M. (1978). Politics and the study of discourse (C. Gordon, Trans.). *Ideology and Consciousness, 3*(Spring), 7–26.

Foucault, M. (1980a). Prison talk (C. Gordon, Trans.). In C. Gordon (Ed.), *Power/knowledge: Selected interviews and other writings 1972–1977* (pp. 37–54). Harvester Press.

Foucault, M. (1980b). Truth and power (C. Gordon, Trans.). In C. Gordon (Ed.), *Power/knowledge: Selected interviews and other writings 1972–1977* (pp. 109–133). Harvester Press.

Foucault, M. (1981). The order of discourse (I. McLeod, Trans.). In R. Young (Ed.), *Untying the text: A post-structuralist reader* (pp. 48–78). Routledge & Kegan Paul.

Foucault, M. (1984a). Preface to The history of sexuality, volume II (W. Smock, Trans.). In P. Rabinow (Ed.), *The Foucault reader* (pp. 333–339). Pantheon.

Foucault, M. (1984b). Polemics, politics, problematizations (L. Davis, Trans.). In P. Rabinow (Ed.), *The Foucault reader* (pp. 381–389). Pantheon,

Foucault, M. (1985). Final interview (T. Levin & I. Lorenz, Trans.). *Raritan, 5*(Summer), 1–13. (Interview conducted by G. Barbedette, published in *Les louvelles*, 28 June 1984)

Foucault, M. (1987). Questions of method. In K. Baynes, J. Bonman, & T. McCarthy (Eds.), *After philosophy: End or transformation?* (pp. 100–117). MIT Press.

Foucault, M. (1990). Maurice Blanchot: The thought from outside. In M. Foucault & M. Blanchot (Eds.), *Foucault/Blanchot* (J. Mehlman & B. Massumi, Trans.; pp. 7–60). Zone Books.

Foucault, M. (1994a). La philosophie analytique de la politique. In D. Defert & F. Ewald (Eds.) with J. Lagrange, *Dits et écrits, 1954–1988* (4 Vols., Vol. 3, No. 232, pp. 534–551). Éditions Gallimard.

Foucault, M. (1994b). Linguistique et sciences sociales. In D. Defert & F. Ewald (Eds.) with J. Lagrange, *Dits et écrits: 1954–1988* (4 Vols, Vol. 1, No. 70, pp. 821–842). Éditions Gallimard.

Foucault, M. (1998a). Afterword to *The temptation of Saint Anthony*. In J. D. Faubion (Ed.), *Essential works of Foucault, 1954–1984, vol. 2: Aesthetics, method, epistemology* (pp. 103–122). Penguin.

Foucault, M. (1998). Theatrum philosophicum. In J. D. Faubion (Ed.), *Essential works of Foucault, 1954–1984, vol. 2: Aesthetics, method, epistemology* (pp. 343–368). Penguin.

Foucault, M. (2001). Interview with Michel Foucault. In J. D. Faubion (Ed.), *Essential works of Foucault, 1954–1984, vol. 3: Power* (R. Hurley et al., Trans.; pp. 239–297). Penguin.

Foucault, M., & Chomsky, N. (1997). Human nature: Justice vs. power. In A. I. Davidson (Ed.), *Foucault and his interlocutors* (pp. 107–145). University of Chicago Press.

Frank, M. (1992). On Foucault's concept of discourse. In T. J. Armstrong (Ed. and Trans.), *Michel Foucault: Philosopher* (pp. 99–116). Harvester Wheatsheaf.

Gleick, J. (1987). *Chaos: Making a new science*. Abacus.

Haken, H. (1977). *Synergetics: An Introduction*. Springer.

Haken, H. (1990). Synergetics as a tool for the conceptualization and mathematization of cognition and behaviour: How far can we go? In H. Haken & M. Stadler (Eds.), *Synergetics of cognition* (pp. 2–31), Springer.

Heidegger, M. (1991). *Nietzsche* (2 Vols.; D. Farrel Krell, Trans.). Harper Collins.

Holden, A. (1985). Chaos is no longer a dirty word. *New Scientist, 106*(1453), 12–15.

Kauffman, S. A. (1991, August). Antichaos and adaptation. *Scientific American*, pp. 64–70.

Kauffman, S. A. (1993). *The origins of order: Self-organisation and selection in evolution*. Oxford University Press.

Kauffman, S. A. (1995). *At home in the universe: The search for laws of complexity*. Viking Press.

Margolis, J. (1993). *The flux of history and the flux of science*. University of California Press.

Negri, A. (1991). *The savage anomaly: The power of Spinoza's metaphysics and politics* (M. Hardt, Trans.). University of Minnesota Press.

Nietzsche, F. (1967). *On the genealogy of morals. Ecce homo* (W. Kaufmann, Trans.). Random House.

Nietzsche, F. (1968). *The will to power* (W. Kaufmann & R. J. Hollingdale, Trans.; W. Kaufmann, Ed.). Vintage.

Olssen, M. (1999). *Michel Foucault: Materialism and education*. Bergin & Garvey.

Olssen, M. (2006). *Michel Foucault: Materialism and education*. Paradigm.

Prigogine, I. (1980). *From being to becoming*. W. H. Freeman and Co.

Prigogine, I. (1994). *Time, chaos and the laws of chaos*. Ed. Progress.

Prigogine, I. (2003). *Is future given?* World Scientific.

Prigogine, I., & Nicolis, G. (1989). *Exploring complexity*. W. H. Freeman and Co.

Prigogine, I., & Stengers, I. (1984). *Order out of chaos*. Bantam.

Prigogine, I., & Stengers, I. (1997). *The end of certainty: Time's flow and the laws of nature*. The Free Press.

Rapp, P. E., Zimmerman, I. D., Albano, A. M., deGuzman, G. C., Greenbaun, N. N., & Bashore, T. R. (1986). Experimental studies of chaotic neural behaviour: Cellular activity and electroencephalographic signals. In H. G. Othmer (Ed.), *Nonlinear oscillations in biology and chemistry* (pp. 175–205). Springer.

Rawls, J. (1971). *A theory of justice*. Oxford University Press.

Sappington, A. A. (1990). Recent psychological approaches to the free will versus determinism issue. *Psychological Bulletin, 108*, 19–29.

Sardar, Z., & Abrams, I. (1999). *Introducing chaos*. Icon Books.

Saussure, F. de. (1974). *Course in general linguistics*. Fontana.

Schrift, A. D. (1995). *Nietzsche's French legacy: A genealogy of poststructuralism*. Routledge.

Skarda, C. A., & Freeman, W. J. (1990). Chaos and the new science of the brain. *Concepts in Neuroscience, 1*, 275–285.

Swinney, H. L. (1983). Observations of order and chaos in nonlinear systems. *Physica, 7*, 3–15.

Veyne, P. (1997). Foucault revolutionizes history. In A. I. Davidson (Ed.), *Foucault and his interlocutors* (pp. 146–182). University of Chicago Press.

CHAPTER 14

Exploring Complexity through Literature
Reframing Foucault's Research Project with Hindsight

Abstract

This article constitutes an extended review essay of Michael Foucault's *Language, Madness, and Desire: On Literature*, Robert Bononno (trans.), Philippe Artières, Jean-François Bert, Mathieu Potte-Bonneville, and Judith Revel (eds.), University of Minnesota Press, 2015. A shorter version of this article was published as a book review in the *Notre Dame Philosophical Reviews*, March 2016, Unique Identification Number 2016.03.28. In performing this review the article seeks to illuminate Foucault's core ontological and epistemological themes that developed in these early commentaries on literature and that were to inform the philosophical orientation of his social science investigations, including madness, psychiatry, medicine, the prison, sexuality and the care of the self. The article suggests that Foucault's early works on literature establish a thesis of philosophical materialism which articulates many of the themes of post-quantum complexity science as they affected the social and physical sciences in the late 20th and 21st centuries.

• • •

Language, Madness, and Desire: On Literature, originally published in French as *La grande étrangère: À propos de literature* in 2013, comprising Foucault's comments on literature, constitutes a welcome if late addition to the Foucault archive of accessible books. It presents Foucault's views on literature presented in different contexts and formats over the period from 1960 to 1971. It is based upon typed transcripts of oral presentations given by Foucault in the form of radio broadcasts and lectures. The editors have rendered these presentations as literal as possible, correcting errors and punctuation for the purposes improving readability but being careful to comply with Foucault's original intentions. The book also includes a valuable assemblage of notes and biographic information about the editors. The first section, "Language and Madness", comprises two radio broadcasts presented by Foucault in 1963. They were originally part of a series of five talks for a program titled as "The Use of Speech", broadcast by RTF France III, produced by Jean Doat, a television and theatre actor and writer. The five broadcasts, titled "Celebratory Madness", were initially presented on a weekly basis. The last two, titled "The Silence of the Mad" and "Mad Language", are reproduced in this book "because of the mirror structure they employ and their focus on literature" (p. 6). The other three focus more directly on madness, or at least the language of the mad, and were left out on this basis. The second section, titled "Literature and Language", reproduces a lecture Foucault presented to the Facultés universitaires Saint-Louis in Brussels by the same title. Here Foucault re-examines the major themes that appeared in his writing on literature from the early 1960s, referring to writers such as Bataille, Blanchot, Sade, Cervantes, Joyce, Jakobson, and others. It is here that Foucault locates the historical emergence of literature in its modern form in the period from the end of the 18th to the early 19th century. Foucault's interest here is in the way that language is encoded within the literary form of discourse and what function literature plays in relation to discourse in general. In this lecture, Foucault's early concern with archaeological investigations concerned as they were with identifying literatures core discursive features becomes apparent as he asks the question, firstly, "What is literature?" and, secondly, "What is the language of literature?" His excursus proceeds from Gutenberg's invention of printing to the emergence of the book, where, finally, "literature finds and founds its being" (p. 64):

> Although the book existed, and with a very dense reality, for several centuries prior to the invention of literature, it was not, in fact, the site of literature: it was merely a material opportunity for transmitting language. ... But in fact if literature fulfils its being in the book, it doesn't placidly welcome the essence of the book (besides, the book, in reality, has no essence, has no essence other than what it contains); that is why literature will always be the simulacrum of the book. It behaves as though it were the book, it pretends to be a series of books. (p. 64)

What distinguishes literature is its transgressive language, "a mortal, repetitive, redoubled language, the language of the book itself" (p. 65). In literature, says Foucault, it is the book that speaks. The third section, titled "Lectures on Sade", comprises two lectures given in 1970 at the State University of New York at Buffalo which illustrates and adds depth to Foucault's views on literature and which also signal many of the themes that were to emerge in his later book-length studies. The first lecture was on Flaubert's *Bouvard and Pécuchet*, the second on Sade's *La nouvelle Justine*, which, as the editors note, Foucault says was written "entirely with an eye to the truth" (p. 95). Foucault's interest in Sade had developed before and after *The History of Madness*. Sade, as the editors note, represented "countermodernity" as that author concerned with "politics and truth", as "the transgressor subject to defamatory judgments and censorship", who "condemned the justice of the ancient regime" (p. 95). In addition, in the 53-page manuscript, as the editors continue, for Foucault, Sade represented a "'sergeant of sex', the promoter of a disciplinary eroticism accompanying the implementation of an instrumental rationality" (p. 96). What is important about this book, and these lectures and radio broadcasts, is the indication they present at an early stage of Foucault's scholarly career, of the way his analysis of literature informs and is informed by the central themes to emerge later on in his major works.

As the editors point out in their excellent and very detailed introduction, it was in his unrestricted reading in the library of the École Normale Supérieure that Foucault "deconstructed an order of discourse" through his close reading of literature. They elicit the support of Daniel Defert in his chronology in *Dits et écrits* to flesh out the detail of Foucault's engagement. We are told that Foucault "read Saint-John Perse in 1950, Kafka in 1951, Bataille and Blanchot in 1953, followed by the progress of the *nouveau roman* (including the work of Alain Robbe-Grillet), discovered Raymond Roussel in the summer of 1957, the authors associated with Tel Quel (Philippe Sollers, Claude Ollier) in 1963, reread Becket in January 1968" (p. VIII, summary). During his travels to Uppsala and Warsaw in the 1950s, Foucault both read literature and taught courses, from his favorite poet at the time, René Char, and from Sade to Genet.

The relationship with literature, which this book explores, constitutes a magnificent testimony, claim the editors, to understanding the way Foucault's philosophical mindset developed, as simultaneously "critical, complex and strategic". They point out how many of these literary gestures, insights and motifs are incorporated within Foucault's great works, thus rendering "fiction and poetry as touchstones of the philosophical act" (p. x). While this is by no means original or untypical amongst French philosophers (witness Bachelard, Sartre, Merleau-Ponty), Foucault, they argue, utilizes such literatures (narratives, epics, poetry, comedies, etc.) to demonstrate and inform his archaeological conception of discourse in relation to "both the order of the world and its representations at a given moment" (p. x) in order to reveal "just how much our way of organizing discourse about the world owe[s] to a series of historically determined divisions" (p. x). Literature, they point out, in Foucault's hands, becomes "strategic" (p. XI). To start with, it furthers the archaeological project in order to enquire into the distinctiveness of the literary discourse, and position it in the field of discourses. But, more than that, Foucault seeks to assess the form and function of a literary discourse to reveal the "concerted incertitude of morphology" in the sense of "a rigorous and uncontrollable polyvalence of forms" (Foucault, 1999, p. 27). This ontological thesis of radical linguistic or discursive indeterminacy by which any one translation can always be replaced by another, and which establishes the autonomy of discourse from the real is a thesis shaped by Foucault's early readings of literature. On its own, of course, as Foucault (1963) made clear in his book on Raymond Roussel,[1] literature has no specificity or strategic centrality. The thesis of the literary then turns out to be the thesis of discourse as autonomous, strategic, and constitutive which, as the editors say, "escapes the dynasty of representation … which, depending on the situation, can be: inaudible, scandalous, unclassifiable, untranslatable, undecidable, fragmentary, aleatory, inconstant, vertiginous" (p. XII). Finally, literature functions as strategy in that it opposes established and settled meanings "destroying the economy of narrative, which involves the construction of a battlefield against the hegemony of meaning" (p. XII). Literature thus constitutes "the establishment of another mode of being of discourse" (p. XII).

The editors note that by the end of the 1960s this "strange relationship to literature seemed to dissipate" (p. XII). They accept here the conventional understanding of Foucault's oeuvre as passing between distinct modalities each characterized by a different onto-epistemic figure or grounding. The early period is characterized by the priority of the discursive over non-discursive practices. The order of discourse constitutes a historically determined order through which actions and relationships and practices are organized. I doubt myself whether Foucault ever really jettisoned this heuristic although he did seek to reassert the priority of the extra-discursive material practices, or rather he endeavored perhaps to reassert the centrality of non-discursive practices whilst not abandoning the thesis as to the autonomy of the discursive, albeit, an autonomy that was contingently and variously enabled and restricted. Both of these orders—the discursive and the non-discursive—would be needed in order for Foucault to articulate a new model of determination about the world. This displacement of literature is a matter of record, however. As the editors put it: "the gradual abandonment of the field of literature as a 'duplication' of Foucault's own research can be attributed to the desire to extend his enquiry to broader themes—this time presented in terms of power and resistance" (pp. XII–XIII).

This displacement of an obvious concern with the literary at the end of the 1960s and a greater concern with power and resistance, and by extension, the political, which eventually leads to "the transition to a collective dimension" where it becomes apparent that "the muffled roar of battle is anything but a *literary* metaphor" (p. XIII). Finally, they note that at the end of the 1960s, Foucault also abandoned the figure of the "outside", and committed himself to a model of difference inside history, i.e., an "internal history", giving rise to the question "of how we might, from within a certain epistemic and historical configuration, from within the 'network of the real' deployed by a certain economy of discourse and practice at a given moment—in short, from within the grammar of the world as historically determined—unearth and reverse connections, shift lines, move points, hallow out meaning, and reinvent equilibria" (p. XIV). It is this problem they state, "very clearly revealed in his work on literature, that will continue to haunt Foucault: the possible overcoming of historical determination of what we are must be conceived not in terms of a contradiction, but in terms of compossibility" (p. XIV). The extent to which we can from within history "free ourselves of those determinations [that constitute us] and paradoxically establish a space [always internal] of a different speech or a way of life" (p. XIV).

It is this last suggestion that what was central to Foucault's philosophical project as a whole, including the possible overcoming of determination in terms of compossible futures that suggest to me that Foucault's engagement with literature saw the preparatory development and fine-tuning of what is central to his oeuvre as a whole. If so, there is an important sense in which Foucault's early engagement with literature continues to haunt even given its visible presence appears displaced by the end of the 1960s. Not just parallels between the literary and madness as signifying phenomena whose infinitely flexible sign systems create spaces for secret, marginalized and chaotic discourses, but literature itself attests to the creative power of language to both traverse and transcend the social field. A space of compossibility for divergent or heterogeneous things; the accidental nature of chance occurrences, or "branchings"; these core insights that inhabit the discursive in Foucault, and were developed later in more philosophical terms by Deleuze in his books on Leibniz, Hume, Spinoza, and Bergson, can be clearly seen here in these early lectures and talks on Foucault's engagement with the literary.[2] In his radio talk, "Mad Language" of 1963, Foucault's constructivist ontology of language is already clear. "Words, their arbitrary encounter, their confusion, all their protoplasmic transformations are sufficient in themselves to bring into being a world that is both true and fantastic" (p. 28).

The importance of language is highlighted here in these lectures. He has said in his interview with Claude Bonnefoy that "language is what we use to construct an absolutely infinite number of sentences and utterances" (Foucault & Bonnefoy, 2011, pp. 65–66). Moreover, says Foucault, "the body itself ... is like a language node" (p. 26). In "Mad Language", Foucault invokes Freud, who understood well that "our mind was a wit" (p. 26), "a kind of master craftsman of metaphors" which "[takes] advantage of all resources, all the richness, all the poverty of our language" (p. 26). Reason therefore can be infinitely transcended for speaking is a form of freedom which allows for madness, and madness is that medium which "permits the unrestricted seepage of language outside itself" (p. XII). In this sense, literature represents both a "crystallization" and "transgression" of language.

In "Why Did Sade Write?", the first part of Foucault's lectures given at the University of Buffalo in March 1970, Foucault "uses" Sade to analyse amongst other things, the role and function of writing. I will focus on this here because of the role it plays in enunciating Foucault's developing onto-epistemic orientation that resists and escapes previous models of determination and which influences his project overall. For Foucault, writing constitutes a material force that "enables us to push the reality principle as far from the borders of the imagination as possible" (p. 108). The first function of writing, therefore, is to abolish the barrier between reality and imagination" (p. 108). Therefore, says Foucault:

> writing is the principle of repeated enjoyment, writing is what delights or enables us to repeat, … writing will serve to erase the limitation of time, it will enable the limits of exhaustion, fatigue, old age, and death to be wiped away. Through writing everything will be able to begin again perpetually, indefinitely, fatigue, exhaustion, death will never appear in this world of writing. … The second function of writing, therefore, is to erase the limitations of time and free repetition for itself. … [I]t is precisely in this world of writing that temporal limits vanish. (p. 109)

Here is a new relational holism which is not the classical Hegelian holism of old, but one where subject and object, ideal and actual, discourse and real, are prized apart in a conception of discourse and extra-discourse, where difference is retained within a historical variable and contingent model of unity which now only occurs at the limits of the material, i.e., at the limits necessary for life to sustain itself. Within unity, difference proliferates. Although Foucault does not utilize the concept, "holism", as such, he does invoke Sade's concept of "system". As such this relational holism is articulated with reference to a concept of "system" and a principle of interconnectivity. Writing plays a central role alongside a similar importance for language and speech. For one role of writing "is not simply to introduce indefinite repetition … it is also to exceed" (p. 109). Foucault's predilection for a correct onto-epistemic orientation causes him to classify himself in *Speech Begins after Death* as a "diagnostician" (Foucault & Bonnefoy, 2011, p. 45). In this, he claims to follow Nietzsche for whom "philosophy was above all else a diagnosis … for the disease of culture" (p. 46). Foucault "uses" Sade to elucidate these points. But his interest was no more in the author than it was in mental illness. As he argued in "What Is an Author?", the author is a "function" of discourse, a conception which by the end of the decade would witness the author's demise and "death". Foucault's own article on the author was originally couched in the context of Roland Barthes essay "La mort de l'auteur", written in 1967. Barthes asked:

> Who is speaking thus? Is it the hero of the story ... ? Is it the individual Balzac ...? Is it Balzac the author ... ? Is it universal wisdom? Romantic psychology? We shall never know, for the good reason that writing [*écriture*] is the destruction of every voice, of every origin. Writing is that neutral, that composite, that oblique space where our subject slips away, the [photographic] negative where every identity is lost, starting with the identity of the very body which writes. (Barthes, p. 142)

Foucault's answer was that "the author's name serves to characterize a certain mode of being of discourse. ... The author's name manifests the appearance of a certain discursive set and indicates the status of the discourse within a society and a culture" (p. 211). In this, the author is a subordinate figure: "the author does not precede the works; he is a certain functional principle by which, in our culture, one limits, excludes, and chooses; in short, by which one impedes the free circulation, the free manipulation, the free composition, decomposition, and recomposition of fiction" (Foucault, p. 221). In everyday parlance, says Foucault, we represent the author as a "genius", an "inventor"; but this is the opposite of what he really is. In this sense, the author as we know him/her is "an ideological product, since we represent him as the opposite of his historically real function" (pp. 221–222). In reality, "the author is ... the ideological figure by which one marks the manner in which we fear the proliferation of meaning" (p. 222). "Perhaps", says Foucault, "it is time to study discourse not in terms of their expressive value or formal transformations but according to their modes of existence. The modes of circulation, valorization, attribution, and appropriation of discourses vary with each culture and are modified within each" (p. 220).

The discourse of literature is both transgressive and singular. Through literature, Foucault establishes a new onto-epistemic orientation to space and time as real resulting in perpetual novelty and creativity. With literary figures like Sade, Roussel or Artaud, Foucault argues that their mode of literature emerges from "deep within them", from their "uniqueness, their particularity, their symptom, their anxiety, and finally their illness" (p. 58).

So, writing constitutes a technology of repetition and multiplication, as that which "exacerbates", "augments", and "multiplies without end" (p. 110). It pushes thought and imagination ever outwards: "every time we write we prepare to exceed new limits. Writing exposes and is witness to the opening up of infinite space before it in which images, pleasures, and excess are multiplied without limit" (p. 110).

It not only opens up space; it constitutes agency and freedom: "It expresses the unlimitedness of pleasure with respect to reality, the unlimitedness of repetition with respect to time, is at the same time the unlimitedness of the image itself; it is the unlimitedness of the limit itself because all limits, one by one, are exceeded. No image is stabilized once and for all" (p. 110).

So, paradoxically, the "author function" of writing individuates as socially and historically constituted individuals and discourses become differentiated within the culture structured as an open series of possibilities within a network of constraints. Writing, for Foucault, is that material activity which spatializes, individuates and alters, thus is a mechanism for creativity, novelty and uniqueness. It opens up "an infinite space before it in which images, pleasures and excess are multiplied without limit" (p. 110).

Finally, says Foucault, anticipating a complexity science which was still embryonic at the time, writing renders reversibility impossible. Through writing, the subject "can no longer turn back". Writing, like action in general, establishes the agent as absolutely unique. As the post-quantum theorist might say, action within curved space/time differentiates the agent from their social and historical origins of their constitution. While Foucault came, at the end of the 1960s and after, to apply these insights with reference to the social sciences, in this book they are extracted from his analyses of literature and especially from his essay on Sade. It is Sade, we are told, who eliminates limits and introduces irregularity in an uncertain world. It is Sade who "erases the limits between the licit and the illicit, the permitted and the not permitted, of the moral and the immoral" (p. 112). It is through Sade that "writing introduces desire into the space of the indefinitely possible and always unlimited possible" (p. 112). It is Sadean discourse that "unique individuality" is conceptualized. Writing establishes "the illimitability of desire and expression". Sadean literature establishes its materiality through signs that can be read, corrected and revised indefinitely, says Foucault. Finally, Sade defines four elements (God, Nature, Soul, Law) which form a "network" or what Sade terms a "system" (p. 139) where the elements are "infinitely recombinable", adaptable "like crystals", to construct discourse "absolutely specific to a situation or an individual" (p. 139), a process Sade refers to as "the irregularity of individuals" (p. 140): "Every individual is irregular and his own irregularity is manifested, is symbolized, in his system" (p. 140).

The consequential novelty and uniqueness mean that Sade's characters "cannot be substituted for one another, cannot replace one another, and remain isolated from one another" (p. 140). It is this revised onto-epistemology that overcomes all past determinations that Foucault will project outward in his social science studies, of madness, of medicine, of psychiatry, of sexuality, of epistemology and of discipline. What Foucault effectively manages to elicit from Sade is how in the context of a social and historical constructionist theory of knowledge, both uniqueness and separateness of identity is assured, and further, how in the determined order of the past, novel elements and actions that could not be predicted in advance manage to proliferate. The great contribution of this little book is that, through Sade, Foucault thus makes clear a revolutionary reconfiguration of the prevailing order of chance and constraint, or at least in the way it needs to be addressed. He even compares Sade's logic to that of Russell and Descartes. Constituted within history, individuals—now—no longer are the straightforward echoes or reflections of their cultural group or class. As Sade teaches us, systems of "infinitely recombinable" elements can generate "perpetual novelty.... This consists in distinguishing ... individuals who cannot be reduced to one another, individuals who are characterized by their system, because the systems differ from individual to individual" (p. 139).

Like Leibniz's monads, in each system, the whole is refracted differently, like prisms, ensuring, as Foucault writes: "that Sade's libertines cannot be substituted for one another, cannot replace one another, and remain isolated from one another" (p. 140).

Finally, Foucault ponders as always the issue of madness and its meaning. Although not in this book, he told Claude Bonnefoy at the end of the 1960s: "What astonishes me, what I keep wondering about, is how is it that a work like this, which comes from an individual that society has classified—and consequently excluded—as ill, can function, and function in a way that's absolutely positive, within a culture? ... It's this positive function of the negative that has never ceased to interest me" (Foucault & Bonnefoy, 2011, pp. 58–59).

Foucault's *Folie et déraison: histoire de la folie à l'âge classique* had occupied his research in the years prior to these lectures and radio broadcasts, and Sade's madness is broached indirectly and a possible meaning of madness alluded to when Sade rejects all authority—God, Nature, Law, Soul—and has no reason to deny death.

> Isn't this the greatest offence against nature—to give up, to accept death? For nature has created us, but no sooner have we been created that it abandons us, leaving us with nothing more than the need to survive, the only trace, in a way of the gesture it made in creating us. From that moment on, when we renounce the need to survive and turn the need to survive into the need to die, we turn against nature, we scorn nature, we commit against ourselves the greatest crime imaginable, and at that moment, it is obvious that it is also the greatest pleasure. (p. 142)

Is this what madness is, then? Is madness the abandonment of a commitment to life? A derailment from what seems immanent to life? Is this what is being expressed in this lecture on Sade? I wish I had read these little gems years ago. It is as though they, belatedly, that is, here and now, answer a nagging question and fill in a piece of the puzzle regarding the Foucault I have been searching for all these years. Here, in literature of all things, written in the early part of Foucault's career, Foucault finds an ontology of physics and the world that he could not find easily in the theory of physics or chemistry or the philosophy of science at the time he was writing. It is "mad" Sade that blazes forth full of insight to explain how things are, and how the world works. It is odd that these small radio talks, and a couple of lectures, one in Brussels and one in New York, fill so many gaps and articulate so much of his oeuvre, and that they have also waited so long to be released in the readily accessible form of the book, making us "work out" the coherence of his program before having these little "summaries" to guide us, as it were, after the event.

Acknowledgements

I would like to thank Dr. Janet Soler of the Open University for research assistance and discussions regarding the initial planning and writing of this paper.

This chapter originally appeared as Olssen, M. (2017), Exploring complexity through literature: Reframing Foucault's research project with hindsight, *Linguistic and Philosophical Investigations*, 16, 80–89, https://doi.org/10.22381/LPI1620174. Reprinted here, with minor edits, with permission from the publisher.

Notes

1 Published in English as *Death and the Labyrinth* (1986).
2 An affinity can be noted in relation to historical determination and compossibility between this position of Foucault as noted by the editors, and Deleuze's notes in *Cinema II*, drawing on Jorge Luis Borges, that as Leibniz postulated, contradictions that can coexist and that "several mutually incompatible worlds do in fact exist" (p. XIV).

References

Barthes, R. (1977). The death of the author. In *Barthes, image, music, text* (S. Heath, Trans.). Fontana/Collins.

Foucault, M. (1963). *Raymond Roussel*. Gallimard.

Foucault, M. (1986). *Death and the labyrinth: The world of Raymond Roussel* (C. Ruas, Trans.). Introduction by J. Ashberry. Continuum.

Foucault, M. (1998). What is an author? (J. V. Harari, Trans.). In J. D. Faubion (Ed.), *Essential works of Foucault, 1954–1984, vol. 2: Aesthetics, method, epistemology* (pp. 205–222). Allen Lane/Penguin.

Foucault, M. (1999). Speaking and seeing in Raymond Roussel. In J. D. Faubion (Ed.), *Essential works of Foucault, 1954–1984, vol. 2: Aesthetics, method, epistemology* (pp. 21–32). New Press.

Foucault, M. (2015). *Language, madness, and desire: On literature* (P. Artières, J.-F. Bert, M. Potte-Bonneville, & J. Revel, Eds.; R. Bononno, Trans.). University of Minnesota Press.

Foucault, M., & Bonnefoy, C. (2011). *Speech begins after death* (R. Bononno, Trans.; P. Artières, Ed.). University of Minnesota Press.

CHAPTER 15

Complexity and Learning

Implications for Teacher Education

Abstract

This article traces the development of complexity research which underwent its formative development in the physical sciences from the start of the 20th century, and later exerted an effect on the social sciences as well. Over the last 50 years, in fact, the complexity paradigm has generated a quiet revolution in both the physical and social sciences. The appeal of the approach is that it liberates philosophy and social science from the prison house of a constraining scientific past based on linear determinism, reductionism, and methodological individualism. In addition, it presents a view of science that supports the social sciences claims that history and culture are important. One consequence of these developments is that it permits a reformulation the traditional dilemmas around the individual and the collective, around nature and nurture, around the one and the many. In this paper my purpose is to elaborate the normative possibilities of complexity theory for learning theory and teacher education.

1   An Introduction to the Science of Complexity

Although complexity research takes its origins from its applications in physics, chemistry and mathematics and the "hard" sciences, undergoing its formative development in the early and mid-20th century, during the second half of the 20th century it has exerted an effect on the social sciences as well. Today while there exists a multitude of different approaches and research centres across the globe, complexity research is generating a quiet revolution in both the physical and social sciences. One interest in the approach is that it liberates philosophy and social science from the prison house of a constraining scientific past based on linear determinism, reductionism and methodological individualism. Another is that it presents a view of science that supports the social sciences claims that history and culture are important. Arguably, it permits an approach in the social sciences and philosophy that heralds the rise of a "third way" between the stark individualism of liberal philosophy, and what many consider to be the (equally) oppressive sociologicism of "thick" communitarianism.[1] As an offshoot of this, complexivists also claim their new approach reinstates, and possibly elevates, a previously marginalised cadre of scholars within the Western intellectual tradition.[2] In this paper my purpose is to elaborate the normative possibilities of complexity theory for learning theory and teacher education.

The core distinctiveness of complexity approaches can be seen most easily in relation to traditional mechanical models of science in relation to the particular ontology they presuppose. In Newton's science, the world is represented deterministically as a mechanical system, with parts comprised of particles subject to the unchanging influence of universal laws, and reducible to mathematical codification. Newtonian mechanics posited closed systems where time was "reversible", which meant it was irrelevant to the laws, which were represented as capable of moving forwards or backwards, i.e., independently of time. Because Newton's model presumed a static, atemporal view of the universe, systems were assumed to be simple, i.e., not to be affected by outside events. Laws (for example, on temperature or the movement of the planets) were held to operate given constant conditions and not subject to interference. Hence, because the axioms of such systems were reducible to physics, once ascertained, the laws constituted a basis for prediction. Causation was represented in linear terms, much as Hume described the process, which requires that a trajectory is identified where a cause can be shown to precede the effect, where "contiguity" operates in time, where a "necessary connection" can be established.[3]

In a range of publications from the 1980s to 2004 Ilya Prigogine developed a complexity formulation relevant to both the physical and social sciences. In works such as *Order Out of Chaos* (1984), written with Irene Stengers, and *Exploring Complexity* (1989), written with Grégoire Nicolis, it is claimed that complexity theory offers a bold new and more accurate conception of science and the universe. They claim that complexity theory offers a more advanced formulation of science and is superseding standard traditional models, including quantum mechanics and relativity, which came to prominence at the beginning of the 20th century as "corrections to classical mechanics" (Nicolis & Prigogine, 1989, p. 5). Newtonian mechanics and quantum theory represented time as reversible, meaning that it was irrelevant to the adequacy of laws.[4] Complexity theory builds on and intensifies the "'temporal' turn" introduced by this "correction". Prigogine places central importance on time as real and irreversible. With Newton, say Prigogine and Stengers (1984), the universe is represented as closed and predictable. Its fundamental laws are deterministic and reversible.

Prigogine's revolution in response to the classical and quantum paradigms stated in formal terms was to challenge the *principle of ergodicity* which resulted in Poincaré recurrence. This was the principle which, in conformity with the law of the conservation of energy, that system interactions in physics would eventually reproduce a state or states almost identical to earlier initial states of the system at some point in the future.[5] It was based on such an approach that time reversibility had been defined as real, and time irreversibility an illusion. Prigogine challenged the applicability of these assumptions as relevant to classical or quantum measurement. If systems are never isolated or independent from their surroundings, then in theory even small perturbations or changes in the surroundings could influence the system functioning or trajectory. Even *very* small perturbations could cause *major* changes.[6] "The consequences of this way of thinking are profound", says Alastair Rae (2009, p. 113), for they replace assumptions of reversibility with irreversibility (p. 114), introduce notions of indeterminism into physics (p. 113), and project future states of affairs in terms of multiple "consistent histories" (p. 122).[7] Although quantum theory had introduced notions of indeterminacy, through the interaction with measurement, for Prigogine, such an indeterminism is more centrally associated with "strong mixing" in initial system interactions.[8]

What non-ergodicity means in less technical terms, as Stuart Kaufmann states, is that "at the level of the evolution of the species, of human economy, of human history, and human culture ... the universe is vastly non-repeating, hence vastly nonergodic" (2008, p. 123). Such a message was popularised recently by Nassim Taleb (2007) in his book *The Black Swan* in order to underscore the centrality of uncertainty and non-predictability in both science and human affairs. Although Taleb claims that traditional predictive models can be applied when predicting variables such as human weight, or height, and thus demonstrates the continued relevance of closed mechanical models, in relation to such phenomena as economies, the immune system, or the human brain, and life itself, where a system of specific parts can generate complex outcomes, traditional models and outcomes cannot be held to apply. One of Taleb's key points in his book is that algorithms cannot be utilised as the basis for predicting the future due to contingent contextual conditions which are ceaselessly changing and cannot be predicted in advance. Invisible causal generators comprising the system produce different outcomes at different locations in space and time. This raises the issue of unobservable generators which, as Mark Blyth (2009, p. 450) puts it, "might produce different outcomes in the future than they did in the past". This means, says Blyth (p. 457), that:

> causes are inconstant; they change over time, and they are emergent. New elements combine to create causes of future events that were impossible before—not just impossible to foresee, since they did not exist in the prior period. In short, "the new" is not necessarily an informational problem.

Although regularity operates predictably for many purposes, it is thus never assured. The whole constitutes a context which is always changing, and where new and unique actions and events constantly *emerge*. For Taleb, this means that the world of the future is not simply *unknown*, but *unknowable*, and there is no basis for predictability of events, as either visible or invisible contingent factors may derail mechanical outcomes. In mathematical terms, a somewhat similar thesis was formulated by writers like Alan Turing and Kurt Gödel.[9] Such a thesis will, as we shall see, have major implications for education.

Prigogine introduces the concept of *bifurcation* to explain the central importance of non-predictability and indeterminacy in science. When a system enters far-from-equilibrium conditions, its structure may be threatened, and a "critical condition", or what Prigogine and Stengers call a "bifurcation point" is entered. At the bifurcation point, system contingencies may operate to determine outcomes in a way not causally linked to previous linear path trajectories. The trajectory is not therefore seen as determined in *one* particular pathway. Although this is *not* to claim an absence of antecedent causes, it is to say, says Prigogine (1997, p. 5), that "nothing in the macroscopic equations justifies the preferences for any one solution". Or, again, from *Exploring Complexity*, "[n]othing in the description of the experimental set up permits the observer to assign beforehand the state that will be chosen; only chance will decide, through the dynamics of fluctuations" (Nicolis & Prigogine, 1989, p. 72). Once the system "chooses", "[it] becomes an historical object in the sense that its subsequent evolution depends on its critical choice" (p. 72). In this description, they say, "we have succeeded in formulating, in abstract terms, the remarkable interplay of chance and constraint" (p. 73).

A schematic diagram of *bifurcation* appears in Figure 15.1, reproduced from Nicolis and Prigogine (1989, p. 73). Highlighting their thesis of indeterminacy, Nicolis and Prigogine make the following comment upon the model:

> A ball moves in a valley, which at a particular point λ_c becomes branched and leads to either of two valleys, branches b1 and b2 separated by a hill. Although it is too early for apologies and extrapolations, ... it is thought provoking to imagine for a moment that instead of the ball in Figure [1] we could have a dinosaur sitting there prior to the end of the Mesozoic era, or a group of our ancestors about to settle on either the ideographic or the symbolic mode of writing. (p. 73)

It is due to the perturbation (λc in Figure 15.1) that causation operates contingently to effect an outcome at a particular time in a way that cannot be predicted in advance. Although, due to system perturbations and fluctuations, it is

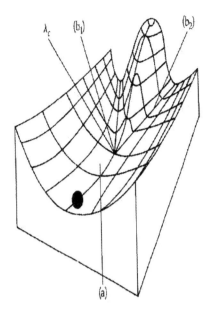

FIGURE 15.1
Mechanical illustration of the phenomenon of bifurcation (from Nicolis and Prigogine, 1989, p. 73, reprinted with permission of Henry Holt and Company, LLC)

impossible to precisely ascertain causes in advance, retrospectively, of course, we find the "cause" there in the events that lead up to an event, in the sense that we look backwards and point to plausible antecedent factors that contributed to its occurrence. While therefore not undetermined by prior causes, the dislocation of linear deterministic trajectories and the opening-up of alternative possible pathways that cannot be *pre-ascertained* in open environments, is what Prigogine means by "chance".[10]

In thermodynamics, Nicolis and Prigogine give the examples of thermal convection, the evolution of the universe itself, as well as climate and all physical processes. They were also aware that their conclusions extended to the social and human sciences, embracing life, biological organisms, and to social, economic and political processes, as an illustration of non-equilibrium developments in human development, learning and education. Central to such a model is the ability for new and novel developments to take place within systems through the emergence of new patterns and features. The model of explanation in complexity science places a greater importance on system affects and interactions, action from a distance, the unintended consequences of actions, the impossibility of predicting linear trajectories or the future, a restricted capacity of individual agents to understand system developments, and conveys new understanding of ignorance, restricted cognition, novelty, uniqueness, and creativity of action in open environments.

Two key ideas of complexity theory include *self-organisation* and *emergence*. The idea of self-organisation entails that systems are not organised by anything external to themselves, in the sense of a foundation or essential principle, and it also explains how systems generate new patterns of activity through dynamic interactions over time.

Complexity theorists also typically represent the world as stratified, characterised by levels of systems or subsystems, interconnected by interactions. Within complex systems, the interconnectedness of part and whole means that interactions of various sorts will define relations at various levels. Interactions also characterise relations within the world as we live it, both at the microscopic (organisms, cellular life) and macroscopic levels. In this sense, interactions can be of qualitatively different orders and types, both linear and non-linear, and "multi-referential" in Edgar Morin's (1977/1992, p. 47) sense. For Morin:

> Interactions (1) suppose elements, beings or material objects capable of encountering each other; (2) suppose conditions of encounter, that is to say agitation, turbulence, contrary fluxes, etc.; (3) obey determinations/constraints inherent to the nature of elements, objects or beings in encounter; (4) become in certain conditions interrelations (associations, linkages, combinations communications, etc.) that is to say give birth to phenomena of organization. (1977/1992, p. 47)

It is through interactions at different levels that ontological emergence[11] takes place, and it is this that defeats the possibilities of reductionism.[12] At its most basic sense, emergence describes the constitution of entities through their synthetic combination in time and space. As a consequence, as Kauffmann (2008, p. 34) explains it, "[o]ntological emergence has to do with what constitutes a real entity in the universe: is a tiger a real entity or nothing but particles in motion, as the reductionists would claim?" Complexity theorists maintain, in opposition to classical physics, that many phenomena, including consciousness and life itself, must be considered as emergent, in the sense of being historically or cosmologically constituted as well as ontologically independent (in relation to its necessary genesis) from its physical basis.[13]

2   The Normative Consequences of Complexity for Learning and Teacher Education

Central to the complexity perspective on learning theory is its opposition to traditional empiricist and rationalist models which assume that learning is an individual matter which is linear and non-generative. The tradition of empiricism, associated with Bacon, Locke, Berkeley and Hume challenged Aristotle for being too unconcerned with the world and with sensory experience and too concerned with reasoning according to established and fixed principles. In Hume's *associationist* psychology, simple ideas (*hard, soft, round, square*) are formed through basic sense impressions, which through associations form the basis of composite ideas. Central to all empiricist approaches, whether Hume, or Locke, or John Stuart Mill, is the priority on experience as the basis of ideas, that complex ideas can be reduced to simple ideas, that basic sensations lie at the foundation of all ideas, and that the rules of getting from simple to complex ideas and upon which predictions are made are additive. Rationalistic approaches, as sponsored by Descartes, Spinoza and Leibniz, rejected the strong emphasis on sensory experience made by empiricism, and suggested instead that our knowledge of the world came from innate ideas, which made reliable reasoning possible. The differences between these two approaches were not as great as the similarities: both were reductionist. Complexity theories, while not denying a role for experience, including sensation, differ from both empiricist and rationalist approaches in that they are non-reductionist or holist. They emphasise that the system is more than the sum of its parts, and recognise system effects through "downward causation" and non-linear feedback loops, as well as contingent assemblages of time and place, as being central.

Learning must be seen, in this sense, as a goal-directed activity, related to the evolution and survival of life. It involves a qualitatively different type of thinking, one that recognises uncertainty, unpredictability, novelty, openness, a balance between order and disorder, and which represents discursive elements, such as concepts and words, as conventional and historical. Due to human fallibility and limitations, the type of knowledge that complex learning results in is bereft of the arrogance of the Enlightenment claim to know (*aude sapere*) according to the newfound faith in reason. Rather, it is more modest, humble, less self-assured, recognising "partial knowledge", "human error", and limited cognition. At the same time, it also encompasses processes of creativity and of possibilities of unexpected developments within situations. Complex education implies, say Trueit and Doll (2010, p. 138), a view of "education as a journey into the land of the unknown taken by ourselves but with others". Yet, within this paradigm, many questions are unanswerable and remain an impenetrable barrier of the human condition. Matters of determinism-free will, the existence of God, and issues of a metaphysical nature unlinked to human concerns must remain beyond the limits of positive knowledge, and limits beyond which learning cannot form a bridge. Complexity's emphasis upon the non-linearity, unpredictability and recursivity of educational processes, while not denying order, state that that the policy response to uncertainty and chance should be one of coordination through institutions. This entails managing elements within a system as well as recognising the practical context in terms of which learning is situated.

How we characterise the processes of learning and teaching is thus important. In recent times, some educational literature has focused upon what is termed "complexity reduction", which potentially creates the view that the task of education is to attempt to contain, reduce and even "tame" the complex uncertainties of the world. The conservative politics of Burke comes to mind in such a situation. Burke endorses a conception of community as the taming of chaos, the ordering of life, and the constraint of danger.

In his article "Five Theses on Complexity Reduction and Its Politics", Gert Biesta (2010) utilises the concept of "complexity reduction" which to my mind may place too much emphasis on control. Whether Biesta would agree that he intends such a description to entail normative and political senses as I suggest above is perhaps problematic. For Biesta complexity reduction is inescapable. For him, as he states it in one place, it is a claim about *language use*. As he puts it:

> Learning is neither a noun nor a verb. To use the word "learning" rather means that one makes a value judgment about change and identifies some changes as valuable. Such judgments can only be made retrospectively, which means that using the word "learning" is itself a form of retrospective complexity reduction. (2010, p. 11)

Earlier in the same article, however, he seems to assert a different claim as a strict thesis about the use of words, and specifies it as a claim about how *systems function*. As he states:

> Complexity reduction has to do with reducing the number of available options-for-action for "elements" within a system. Fast food restaurants are a good example of a system with reduced complexity, as the number of available option for action—both for customers and staff—are significantly reduced to make a quick and smooth operation of the system possible. ... Education, particularly in the form of organised schooling, is another prominent example of a system operating under conditions of complexity reduction. (p. 7)

Although Biesta may intend use of the term "reduction" only in the sense of a Deleuzean *mot d'ordre*, to suggest that any attempt to codify reality entails a particular organisation, there is a strong risk that it may begin to function as an inserted metaphysic. To my mind the concepts of "organisation" and "management" better characterise the process by which discourses organise the world. I think of words, concepts and discourses as *organising* complexity, and of actions (which are normative and end-orientated) as *managing* or (even) as *controlling* or *channelling* complexity. To speak of "reduction" risks imposing an unnecessary direction or character to the ordering of diversity.

In this quest for "thinking complexly", Trueit and Doll (2010, p. 138), see education as a central institution in a way recognised by Dewey, who explored the role and function of education in adapting to and coping with uncertainties of the environment. For Dewey (1958, 1997), education was conceptualised, not as a discipline-based mode of instruction in "the basics", but according to an interdisciplinary, discovery-based curricula, defined according to obstacles in the existing environment. As Dewey says in *Experience and Nature*, "The world must actually be such as to generate ignorance and inquiry: doubt and hypothesis, trial and temporal conclusions" (1958, p. 41). The rules of living and habits of mind represent a "quest for certainty" in an unpredictable, uncertain and dangerous world (p. 41). For Dewey, the ability to organise experience proceeded functionally in terms of problems encountered, which needed to be overcome in order to construct and navigate a future. This was the basis of his "problem-centred" pedagogy of learning. While it could be seen to concentrate on transferable skills from a complexity perspective of coping with an environment, Dewey can be criticised for an overly functionalist concern with system adaptation, in the same way that structural–functionalist sociologists, like Talcott Parsons, or contemporary systems theorists, such as Niklas Luhmann can be. By focusing on a "problem-centred" approach runs the risk, in other words, of neglecting the critical tasks of ideological reflexivity and criticism which are so important to the educative tasks of myth demystification and cleansing the discursive template of history from its distorted and ideological elements. There is little in Dewey, for instance, that suggests any parallel with Gramsci's distinction between "good sense" and "folklore" as the basis of a critical pedagogy and common sense. Dewey's functionalism is further reinforced through his utilisation of terms such as "interaction" and "growth", which run the risk of contributing to a naive Enlightenment conception of "progress", leading inevitably to the successful resolution of both individual and societal problems and leading, onward and upward, to ever higher levels of experience. Yet, while Dewey runs a risk, like Hegel, of being identified with a progressive evolutionary theory of history and development, unlike Hegel, Dewey posited no end point, or resting place; for the end of growth was more growth; and the end of learning was further learning. In terms of learning theory, Dewey used the concept of "continuity" in order to theorise the link between existing experience and the future based upon the "interdependence of all organic structures and processes with one another" (1958, p. 295). Learning for Dewey thus represented a cooperative and collaborative activity centred upon experiential, creative responses to contingent sets of relations to cope with uncertainty in a never-ending quest. It is in this sense that the processes of iteration are central for Dewey. As such, Dewey's approach conceptualises part and whole in a dynamic interaction, posits the learner as interdependent with the environment, as always in a state of becoming, giving rise to a dynamic and forward-looking notion of agency as experiential and collaborative. In such a model learning is situational in the sense of always being concerned with contingent and unique events in time.

It is through plan or pattern coordination that institutions function and that the learning experiences of future generations are embarked upon. Because in planning one must assume incomplete information due to the dispersal of knowledge across social systems, such coordination can be more or less exact or loosely stochastic and probabilistic in terms of overcoming uncertainty. Learning will be invariably situational and involve experiences that are always unique. It will involve what Aristotle called *phronēsis,* that is, practical judgement within a context. Such practical judgement is holistic and goal-orientated action sensitive to the exigencies of time and place. In elucidating the tasks of *phronēsis,* Aristotle emphasises the integrity of the speaker, their skills as a communicator, the context of the message, as well as the interests and dispositions of the audience. Because learning is time-dependent, and individuals and communities are always experiencing unique features of their worlds, uncertainty cannot be eliminated. Hence, all that is possible is skills of coping, problem-solving, and pattern coordination in open-ended systems, where planning is formed around "typical" rather than "actual" features. Such plan or pattern coordination can only be a constructed and probabilistic order. Constructing plans becomes the agenda for teacher education both individuals and societies in Dewey's sense. Dewey ultimately held to the faith that despite unpredictability and uncertainty, the macro-societal (or macro-economic) coordination of core social problems was possible.

3   A Possible Ethical Theory for a Complex Global Society

Finally, what are necessary for a theory of learning in a complex world is a normative theory and a global ethic. As Paul Cilliers (2010, p. VIII) notes, "complexity leads to the acknowledgement of the inevitable role played by values". If the world is complex and uncertain, the educational consequence suggests that education is ethical and political.

More than ever, today, individual aspirations can only be realised through the coordinated action of the local and the global. The good then, must recognise *survival*, but also *well-being*, of all life forms. Such a good need not be seen as in the classical era, as emanating from a teleology of nature, but rather as a shared or collective end as they expand or contract in different historical times.[14]

In addition to a new global ethics, complexity posits a model of the global citizen who has knowledge of global processes, procedures, and forces, well-developed *agentic* skills and abilities, as well as a multidimensional global identity which is both local and global. By *agentic* skills, I mean to refer to such things as the capacity to understand and access global knowledge systems; the awareness of multi-perspective orientations to self and culture, based upon an understanding of diverse human experiences, as well as the ability to construct new ideas. Cognitively and intellectually, such an education must develop a knowledge and sensitivity to global concerns and issues; an awareness of emerging conflicts and disputes, issues and problems, as well as the capabilities for critical deconstruction and judgement in relation to historical documents, identities and systems.

Although for complexity uniqueness and uncertainty constitute core ontological postulates, we can still posit some educationally relevant universal postulates concerned with the ubiquity of certain types of experience that will need to be confronted, certain dispositions that will be important, and certain virtues and values that students will profit from. Such dispositions and virtues that constitute the ethics of life continuance might include a will to learn, to critically engage and inquire, to be receptive, to be open, and to actively negotiate the future. Virtues might include criticality, creativity, carefulness, care toward others and the environment, courage, self-discipline, equity, equality, integrity, caution, respect, flexibility and openness.

In previous work on an ethics of life continuance, I represent it as both deontological and consequentialist, and as simultaneously both objectivist and subjectivist. It is objectivist in terms of ethics in that some things are clearly better or worse, right or wrong in terms of the values of what best continues life irrespective of time or place and for all life forms. It is also subjectivist in that in a world of infinite options and choices, each individual is also faced with innumerable personal ethical choices, conflicts and conundrums which they much resolve within the contingent circumstances of the present. Although Anglo-American philosophy has traditionally represented the objectivist and subjectivist approaches in ethics as two mutually incompatible approaches, my suggestion here is that within a complexivist understanding certain senses of both approaches can potentially cohere.

To reconcile deontology and consequentialism is far more difficult and must necessarily await some later study. Indeed, despite its importance for teachers, it can only be alluded to here in the most general of senses. We would start with the proposition that life in a complex world is both gratuitous and contingent; that it has no essential raison d'être, a fact which a priori gives no moral justification for privilege or hierarchy of value or precedence. We might acknowledge also that complexity provides a cruel mathematics of existence and yet despite this life has value to all beings that live, at least as judged by virtue of the fact that all forms of life strive to survive and continue. This then can constitute a foundation for both an individual and collective ethic of humanity. According to Doubrovsky (1962, p. 75), this deontological view is essentially the message of Camus, in *L'étranger*, where "[t]hreatened with annihilation, life gathers and concentrates its force, becomes conscious of itself and proclaims that it is the only value". This immanent value that life affirms is the source of moral sentiment. It motivates for Camus the ethics of rebellion. As Camus states, "il ... fait intervener un judgement de valeur, si peu gratuity, qu'il le maintient au milieu des périls" (Camus, 1951, p. 28).[15] Bataille makes a similar argument in arguing that moral sense arises from the self-consciousness of life in a system of parts and whole where the "sovereignty of each individual" needs protection in order to survive. Morality is the protest of fairness in a limited and dangerous world. It therefore constitutes as it were a sentiment common to all men, which constitutes their humanity, a view also admirably stated by David Hume. There is therefore a deontological dimension of value adhering to life itself that propels ethics, establishes right, resists perfectibility and rational becoming should they conflict with right, and yet acts for and simultaneously with the actions of life to survive in a view of becoming as the continuance of life itself. Life therefore has value which it constructs and interpolates in the course of it monitoring and critically evaluating the future horizon that both enables it and threatens it. In a complex world human history can have no overall "inner logic" or "overall design" or "direction" in Hegel's sense which morally justifies them (i.e., the end cannot justify the means), yet, nevertheless, the value of life requires a context, a system, and a goal for life operates in time. Consequences and goals are thus important although do not override the rights of life itself. These two domains are independent in the sense that conflicts can only be resolved through democratic deliberation in a public forum. While the moral value of life is determined by sentiment, it is reason, albeit now with a small "r", and within a complex and uncertain world of risks, gambits and calculations, that guides life on its way.

Acknowledgements

This paper is a revision of a paper that first appeared as Olssen, M. (2011), Learning in a complex world, *Access: Critical Perspectives on Communication, Cultural & Policy Studies, 30*(1), 11–24. The publisher of the journal is thanked for its reproduction in this context.

This chapter originally appeared as Olssen, M. (2017), Complexity and learning: Implications for teacher education, in M. A. Peters, B. Cowie, & I. Menter (Eds.), *A companion to research in teacher education* (pp. 507–519), Springer, http://dx.doi.org/10.1007/978-981-10-4075-7_34. Reprinted here, with minor edits, with permission from the publisher.

Notes

1 My own work has promoted writers like Nietzsche and Foucault as representing a "third way" between Kant and Hegel in philosophy.
2 Including John Stuart Mill, Alexander Bain, C. D. Broad, Samuel Alexander, Friedrich A. Hayek, Friedrich Nietzsche, Charles Babbage, George Herbert Mead, Charles Sanders Pierce, Martin Heidegger, Michel Foucault, Jacques Derrida and John Maynard Keynes.
3 Always providing that Humean scepticism can be offset by the specification of the appropriate operational force—which enlightenment science was quick to do!
4 If a film can represent motion running backwards in the same way as running forwards, then it is said in physics that time is reversible. The rotation of the hands of a clock is reversible, whereas tearing a piece of paper is irreversible. Prigogine does not deny that time reversibility has relevance but wishes to add that in many areas including life itself time is irreversible.
5 The amount of time taken for repeatability is known as "Poincaré cycle time".
6 This is the phenomenon of "strong mixing" (see note 9 for a definition).
7 The main idea of the "consistent histories" approach in Prigoginian physics is that new knowledge must connect with already consistent histories of possibilities to be taken as valid. It therefore is not just the results of "measurements" as it was for the quantum theorists. Rae (p. 123) says that it thus "has the advantage of being more general as well as more objective". "The consistent-histories approach claims that we have reached the point where a purely mathematical map is unable to give a unique description of the physical universe. It can, however, provide a map book containing all possible histories and their probabilities. Perhaps this is the best we can expect to achieve" (p. 127). Prigogine, says Rae (p. 126), is also more materialist in that he is not simply concerned with how the world can be observed, but how it can be.
8 "Strong mixing" refers to the effect of influences or instabilities on a system, which is frequently chaotic, small and arbitrary.
9 In 1931, Kurt Gödel, a 25-year-old mathematician, presented his "incompleteness" theorem which demonstrated the mathematical inability to predict future events. Alan Turing's basic claim was that decisions regarding methodology in mathematics were always in excess of the programme or algorithm that generated them, and hence could not be determined axiomatically from such an algorithm. Turing also reiterated a point made by Heisenberg that "when we are dealing with atoms and electrons we are quite unable to know the exact state of them;

our instruments being made of atoms and electrons themselves" (Turing, cited in Hodges, 2000, p. 497). This means that there are limitations to what it is possible to compute and to know (Hodges, 2000, pp. 493–545).
10 At times Prigogine appears to suggest that the limitation is fundamentally epistemological, and concerned with measurement, as it was for Heisenberg. But, at other times, he notes that as fluctuations and perturbations occur in open environments are theoretically without limit in terms of their reinvestment within a system, the indeterminism is also ontological, not in the sense of there being no antecedent conditions, but in terms of there being alternative options available which can be determined by contingent variables. In this "ontological" view, he seems to follow Neils Bohr.
11 Kauffman (2008, p. 34) also refers to "epistemological emergence", which he defines as "an inability to deduce or infer the emergent higher-level phenomenon from underlying physics".
12 In physics, the reductionist programme maintained that all social, biological, chemical and physical reality could be explained by physics, ultimately reducing to particles and laws.
13 Kauffman (2008, Chapters 3–5) cites a "quiet rebellion" within existing physics, and science more generally, as to adherence to reductionism. He notes various Nobel Laureates, such as Philip W. Anderson, Robert Laughlan, and Leonard Susskind, who all argue for versions of emergentism and against reduction to physical laws in order to explain life processes, biology, or forms of social organisation.
14 In *Capitalism, Socialism and Democracy*, Joseph Schumpeter says that while we must reject the classical conception of good, of old, there is nothing to "debar us from trying to build up another and more realistic one" (p. 252–253). Despite his antagonism towards the classical doctrine of good, Schumpeter sees nothing amiss with representing aggregate human interests in history as common collective interests, by which he means "not a genuine, but a manufactured will. And often this artifact is all that in reality corresponds to the *volonté génerale* of the classical doctrine" (p. 263).
15 "He ... brings in a moral judgement, so un-gratuitous, that he maintains throughout his perils".

References

Biesta, G. (2010). Five theses on complexity reduction and its politics. In D. Osberg & G. Biesta (Eds.), *Complexity theory and the politics of education* (pp. 5–14). Sense Publishers.
Blyth, M. (2009). Coping with *The black swan*: The unsettling world of Nassim Taleb. *Critical Review: A Journal of Politics and Society, 21*(4), 447–465.
Camus, A. (1951). *L'homme revolté*. Gallimard.
Cilliers, P. (2010). Foreword. In D. Osberg & G. Biesta (Eds.), *Complexity theory and the politics of education* (pp. VII–VIII). Sense Publishers.
Dewey, J. (1958). *Experience and nature*. Dover. (Original work published 1925)
Doubrovsky, S. (1962). The ethics of Albert Camus. In G. Brée (Ed.), *Camus: A collection of critical essays* (pp. 71–84). Prentice-Hall.
Hodges, A. (2000). Turing: A natural philosopher. In R. Monk & F. Raphel (Eds.), *The great philosophers: From Socrates to Turing* (pp. 493–554). Phoenix/Orion Books.

Kauffman, S. A. (2008). *Reinventing the sacred: A new view of science, reason and religion*. Basic Books.

Morin, E. (1992). *Method: Towards a study of humankind, vol. 1: The nature of nature*. Peter Lang. (Original work published 1977)

Nicolis, G., & Prigogine, I. (1989). *Exploring complexity*. Freeman.

Prigogine, I. (1997). *The end of certainty: Time, chaos and the new laws of nature*. The Free Press.

Prigogine, I., & Stengers, I. (1984). *Order out of chaos*. Bantam.

Rae, A. (2009). *Quantum physics: Illusion or reality?* (2nd updated ed.). Cambridge University Press.

Taleb, N. (2007). *The black swan: The impact of the highly improbable*. Random House.

Trueit, D., & Doll, W. E. (2010). Thinking complexly. In D. Osberg & G. Biesta (Eds.), *Complexity theory and the politics of education* (pp. 135–152). Sense Publishers.

PART 6

Political Theory in the 21st Century

CHAPTER 16

Globalisation, the Third Way and Education Post-9/11

Building Democratic Citizenship

Abstract

This paper examines the prospects for social democracy and individual citizenship in an age of terrorism and rapid material changes of the sort unleashed by climate change, overpopulation, viral pandemics, and other threats in the environment. It is argued that such changes are profoundly altering the social and political landscape forging new relations between the individual and the collective, and between the state and the citizen. It is claimed further that such changes will impact drastically upon the prevailing economic and social framework of neoliberalism, and eventually undermine it. Taken together, such changes paired with the hegemony of neoliberal governmentality, run the risk of resulting in a new post-liberal political authoritarianism where traditional liberal freedoms associated with citizenship are undermined and the social democratic state is "hollowed out" and rendered ineffective. The only alternative to this, an alternative likely coerced by such developments, is an increasingly active, positive state which operates both nationally and globally, and which can check the dangers that classical liberals saw of totalitarianism through a deeper global commitment and enforcement of democracy, as both global and multicultural.

1 Introduction

The possibility of acts of terror, whether committed by rogue states, or transnational groups, forces a new consideration of the themes of democracy, community and individual rights. And there must also, I believe, be a new understanding of what citizenship entails, and what the role of education is in relation to creating citizens. The new realisation that the world is full of dangers is leading to a reappraisal of the relations between the state and the individual and between collective interests and individual rights. What confronts us now, more than at any time since the 17th century, is the prospect of a new political settlement that involves a radical revision and restriction of traditional rights and liberties given to individuals. At the same time as states are encouraged to adhere to the "steer but not row" philosophy of neoliberalism in economic affairs, in the political sphere the state's need to know, involving increased surveillance and data gathering for the purposes of fighting crime, fraud and preventing acts of terror, has now become an *explicit agenda of states*. What is being ushered in, indeed, is a new post-liberal political settlement. Within this scenario there are possibilities, openings and dangers. In this paper I will seek to reassess the significance of globalisation, neoliberalism, human rights, community, democracy and the role of education, taking the events of 9/11 into account.

2 Neoliberalism, Globalisation and the Move to the "Third Way"

Neoliberalism is that form of economic reason encapsulated in the notion of Homo economicus which represents individuals as rational self-interested choosers, which was based on a revitalisation of neoclassical economic liberalism and which, as Peters (2001, p. 9) says "has been remarkably successful in advancing a foundationalist and universalist reason as a basis for a radical global reconstruction of all aspects of society and economy". During the last several years neoliberalism has been adapted, rescued one might say, under the mantle of the "third way" which aims to retain the neoliberal concern with efficiency in the economic sphere while avoiding traditional policies of redistribution, still defining freedom in terms of autonomy of action, but now mixed in with a concern for the values of social justice and democracy and increased involvement and participation in the local community.

Critics suggest that the "third way" is an amorphous linking of disparate elements, lacking any distinctive economic policy, based upon an attempt to find a middle way. Giddens (2000, p. 163) suggests that the "third way" is not an attempt to occupy the middle ground but rather is "concerned with restructuring social democratic doctrines to respond to the twin revolutions of globalization and the knowledge economy". What the "third way" tries to do, in my view unsuccessfully, is theorise the need for a more active state intra-nationally in order to deal with the crucial national issues concerning social democracy, while retaining economic commitment to neoliberalism as its central orientation to both domestic and global relations. In this sense, the "third way" politics of New Labour in Britain maintains that it constitutes a melding of traditional concerns of social democracy while retaining the central neoliberal insights over economic policy, the role of the state, and the need for accountability. This is the political discourse that presently dominates New Labour's policies towards education, health, crime, and the role of social services. Dubbed the "new localism", it is based on the state philosophy of "steer but not row", and signals the end of the centrally planned welfare state as established in Britain in 1945. It entails the death of what British Prime Minister Tony Blair called a "one size fits all" model of public service provision, whereby spending and direction was determined from the centre, moving towards a model whereby spending and direction is determined at the local level via the people directly affected and involved. As such, the "third way" affects fundamentally a shift in the role of the state. As Tony Blair stated at the recently held Labour Party Conference at Bournemouth: "Just as mass production has departed from industry, so the monolithic provision of services has to depart from the public sector. Out goes the big state. In comes the enabling state" (Wintour, 2002).

This idea of an enabling state is central to "third way" politics of New Labour, and to new policy initiatives on education and health. In education, it has involved the expansion and development of specialist schools as part of the "post-comprehensive era". This has resulted in new legislation to encourage successful specialist schools to operate autonomously, to expand, and to encourage school takeovers. Choice policies which enable parents to secure the school of their preference are being encouraged, and privatisation initiatives are also being encouraged in order to extend private sector involvement in public services through a proliferation of public–private partnerships (PPPs), and private finance initiatives (PFIs) and public interest companies (PICs). As such, the enabling state constitutes a model of semi-autonomous public services supposedly free of Whitehall control. Both schools and hospitals are being granted autonomy where they can establish new directions of travel. Controls on local councils are being released and voluntary organisations are being allowed to run public services. New Labour theorists, such as the New Economics Foundation, the New Local Government Network, and the Institute of Public Policy Research represent this agenda as moving beyond old distinctions between the state and the market. The idea is that services funded by the state need not be run by the state. Such a model thus entails an increased role for the private sector and increased choice.

Whether this "third way" model really does manage to reconcile neoliberal and social democratic agendas is a much-contested issue. Whether state control is any less, or any different, than it was in the pre-Thatcher years is indeed a meaningful question. Supposedly, according to Rhodes (2000), the new governance narrative which is espoused by New Labour is based on networking, partnerships, autonomy of providers, interdependence between organisations, and trust. The state's role is to facilitate and coordinate without treading on the autonomy of foundation hospitals, schools, or higher education institutions. In reality the state under-emphasises its control, for although it may not actively be delivering services, it can still be seen to be effecting control, and at least some studies claim that this control, rather than decreasing, is simply taking a different form (Rhodes 1997a, 1997b, 2000; Cloke et al., 2000, p. 130). In addition, in that the power of the state is being reorganised rather than reduced, in its relationship to local groups, the organisation of governance in networks and partnerships is producing new obstacles as far as traditional democratic forms of accountability are concerned. A governance model which delegates power to local agencies is producing problems relating to representation, accountability, openness to criticism, as well as to the rights of consumers or users. The ability of local agencies to work together, or coordinate service provision is offset by the differences in power and influence between them; by the adherence to traditional norms of exclusivity and non-cooperation; by the inequalities between the different partners or actors providing services in the state, voluntary and private spheres; and by the fragmentation of services across different sectors.

Thus, whether new models of governance based on networks and partnerships can constitute a solution to traditional forms of state bureaucracy or markets or overcome the limitations inherent in forms of state bureaucracy or markets, is unlikely. Research by Rhodes (2000), Cochrane (2000), Cloke et al. (2000), Glendinning et al. (2002) and others cast doubt on whether patterns of state control have significantly altered, and whether ad hoc adjustments and interference are not constantly required to overcome inequities, unfairness, inequalities that arise when localistic solutions and policy operates. As Karl Polanyi (1944) observed with reference to the rise of the welfare state, the growth of central state involvement in economic and social policy arose not because of any pre-determined political plan or conspiracy, but because of the shear complexity of government. This complexity is likely to increase apace given the inherently individualist and self-serving nature of neoliberal reason. In the end, the resources and manpower invested in "steering" becomes as great if not greater than in "rowing" until it is not clear what the differences between them are.

Indeed, we might be tempted to say that the bride is too beautiful, for any marriage of private investment with state "steering" will likely result in a greater and greater role for the state as it attempts to level out the bumps and potholes in the playing field, provide reasonable mechanisms of representation and accountability, and ensure some measure of rights and fair treatment for the unsuspecting and often unenlightened public whose education and welfare is at stake. This seems to be what is indeed happening in "third way" policy delivery. In Britain, Railtrack which was privatised under Thatcher, has recently returned to public ownership due to the shear operational chaos that private ownership produced. More recently, British Energy has had to be bailed out by the state. The government had to underwrite its risks due to the sensitive place it occupies in the economy, which of course was one of the reasons for nationalising it in the first place. Under private ownership it has become obvious that neither managerial efficiency nor public safety are guaranteed. The history of the past year in Britain is littered with examples of the failings of privately run prisons, schools and hospitals. It is a situation, as Roy Hattersley (2002, p. 18) has quipped, of "taxpayers servicing the debt, and shareholders receiving the dividends".

If the "third way" attempt to marry social democracy and neoliberalism in terms of governance is problematic, the rise of the "third way" does suggest a more positive message in that it speaks to a more active state than was entailed under traditional laissez-faire models. Indeed, even if the state under the "third way" seeks to change the form of its operation, from traditional bureaucracy to governance through networks, the model still speaks to the idea of a strong state. The idea of an enabling state is indeed quite compatible with a conception of the state that sets up the rules of the game, that passes legislation to enforce minimum conditions of acceptable treatment for all of the various groups in society (children, the aged, women, ethnic minorities, etc.), and that seeks to ensure adequate protection and rights for all through the framing and introduction legislation. The notion of "enabling", like that of "steering" does not of itself speak to the size of the state, and conceivably, a state that "steers" might be just as big as a state that "rows". At the same time, so long as the state can assure the important platforms of universal entitlement, equality of opportunity, and equality before the law, then the attempt to actively co-opt the citizenry in running their own lives can only be seen as positive and a major backdown from the discourse of a reduced state which became the catchcry of neoliberal reason during the Thatcher years.

3 What Is Globalisation?

What is thus most positive about the third way's conception of the enabling state is the very recognition of a *role for the state* in an age of globalisation. The central thesis of the doctrine seems to suggest that the state can act as a powerful force to regulate and supervise and to initiate and direct policy within national contexts. This recognition of the power of the state would seem to contradict the thesis of a "powerless state", as writers like Manuel Castells (1997) (who used this phrase as the title to a chapter), or Naomi Klein (2000), or Kenichi Ohmae (1990, 1995) have depicted, and which has been generally the dissertation of so many globalisation theorists of recent years.

In my view, globalisation does not spell the end, or even, necessarily, the demise, of the nation-state as an autonomous force. Writers who suggest that it does are failing to differentiate the different theses entailed in the notion of globalisation. In order to make this thesis clear it is important to distinguish the senses of globalisation. For a start we can note how this concept has functioned to displace other related concepts and theories to do with cultural, economic and political "colonialism", "neo-colonialism" or "imperialism". It is as if suddenly these more specific theories, which were more politically charged, and made explicit the relations of power and knowledge entailed in state actions in international affairs, were replaced by a more general concept where the relations of power are not so obvious or were seen to be manifested in a different way. Yet, the concept is clearly important, and it has become more so post-9/11 in that it gives recognition to the undeniable fact that our lives are becoming more intertwined. This, it may be argued, has always been the case, and there is a certain sense in which that is true, as David Held (1995) has argued, but a number of 20th-century developments in technology, science, communication and travel, and the economy have arguably increased or at least changed the sense in which it is so. From developments in communications technology, the mass media, the internet, the increasing availability and possibility of travel, the growth in multinational trade and international marketability of goods and services, the general growth in the circulation of money and goods, through to developments in science, and to the spread of knowledge and its democratisation, which make weapons of mass destruction and acts of terror as possible acts within the sphere of capability of private citizens, transnational groups and rogue nations, all serve to reinforce the "intertwined" nature of our existence. The events of 9/11 and the 2002 Bali bombings have brought home dramatically the sense in which what happens in one part of the world effects what happens everywhere. Cultures mix through migration, education, the General Agreement on Trade in Services, news and information, ideas and fashions, brands and marketing. Terrorism increases, at the political level, the degree of interdependence in terms of political governance and regulatory arrangements between nation states and amongst transnational political and economic agencies and organisations such as the EU, WB, IMF, OECD, NAFTA, APEC and WTO.

The fact that globalisation is promoting greater integration between countries and regions is not of itself of concern. One must take each issue and each effect separately in order to assess its positive or negative consequences, and one must do this one issue at a time. That one can discern many issues of exploitation and oppression is clearly evident. At the cultural level, for instance, it can be observed that the spread of information technology and the communications revolution tends to operate as forms of imperialism, in that the ideas, images, and even language of communication is provided by the more powerful Western states, led by the USA and Britain. If globalisation increases the speed and intensity of the circulation of ideas across the globe, then the effect on small relatively powerless states will be the same as has always been the case: the cultural and intellectual sovereignty of their customs, beliefs, and ways of life, will be undermined. At the same time, one must be open to the fact that there are some possible positive effects of globalisation. Recent moves to internationalise in higher education have resulted in the large-scale international movement of students and staff across national borders. PhD students at Surrey, to give one very local example, are now selected from many countries. Similarly, as with most universities, and many other institutions, higher education staff are recruited internationally. Growing internationalisation leads to increasingly innovative attempts to standardise procedures such as criteria of admission and recruitment, resulting in new forms of global communication and regulation. These trends, which are merely small examples of how global cooperation and exchange can have positive effects, are not without elements of injustice and oppression, of course, and this is especially so in that they are structured within neoliberal economic frameworks. They are also not really new, but as with international travel and migration, the scale and scope have both increased. We can, in this sense, I believe, agree, at least in part, with Held (1995) in the relevance of a new concept of *cosmopolitanism*. This is so in a number of senses. Firstly, with changes to the material basis of culture in the West since the scientific revolution, but especially in the 20th century, it has become increasingly true that there are a great number of events and developments (Chernobyl, acid rain, oil slicks) which have impacts across national borders. Secondly, relatedly, in relation to international trade and 20th-century economic developments, there have been huge increases in the global circulation of goods, ideas and information, and money, all of which are more global in terms of both the speed and scale of distribution than at any previous time in history. If these speak to a new sense of cosmopolitanism, which I see as an extension of the idea of republicanism, it is only partly in the sense elaborated by Held, however. For while both these developments clearly entail a growth in the importance of international agencies and regulatory bodies, as Hirst and Thompson (1996) argue, any mandate for the democratic functioning of these agencies still resides within individual nation states. It is at the national level, ultimately, that accountability resides.[1]

4 A New Political Settlement?

At the political level, globalisation can also be represented as a dynamic process. In that the scale and scope of communication and travel have increased, so we can say that since 9/11 the potential risks and dangers have also increased. It is at this level that 9/11 serves to denote a major epistemological–political break with previous discursive systems. Since 9/11 we can say indeed that there has been a keener interest by Western states in the uniform global imposition of standard systems of security and surveillance which is altering the traditional nature of the relations between individuals and the state. What private individuals do in Baghdad, Afghanistan, Cairo, Naples, London, or Auckland, or what they carry through airports, is now of vital concern to policymakers and ruling elites and some might argue, ordinary citizens, in America and Britain, and many other countries. In a way it has taken the prospect of terror to make us painfully aware of our interrelatedness. The effects of this show the signs of crystallizing a new political settlement that has been perhaps embryonic as an emergent discourse for some time, but after 9/11 has been given a new impetus. Whether it represents a "permanent settlement", or just a "temporary tendency", is as yet uncertain, and while I will refer to the former, I leave open the possibility, and the hope, that it is only the latter. At least some early signs are appearing as emergent forms within the existing political milieu.

The emergent new tendency/settlement has two elements: economic and political. At an economic level, it is based on neoliberal freedom, which is now more obviously confined to the "freedom of commerce", or to "free trade". In this sense, neoliberalism must clearly be seen as a particular element of globalisation in that it constitutes the form through which domestic and global economic relations are structured. Yet, neoliberalism is only one form of globalisation, and only pertains to economic globalisation. It is not something that has evolved naturally as a consequence of changes in technology or science. And it must not be confused with globalisation as such. Rather it must be seen as a specific economic discourse or philosophy which has become dominant and effective in world economic relations as a consequence of superpower sponsorship. Neoliberalism is a politically imposed discourse, which is to say that it constitutes the hegemonic discourse of Western nation states. As such it is quite independent of the forms of globalisation that we have spoken of above, based as they are on changes in technology and science, nor can it be seen as part of their effects, although this is not to say that there is no relationship at all. Its major characteristics emerged in the USA in the 1970s as a forced response to stagflation and the collapse of the Bretton Woods system of international trade and exchange, leading to the abolition of capital controls in 1974 in the USA and 1979 in Britain (Mishra, 1999; Stiglitz, 2002). This made it extremely difficult to sustain Keynesian demand management. Financial globalisation made giant strides. Exchange rates were floated and capital controls abolished, giving money and capital the freedom to move across national boundaries. The changes in technology did certainly facilitate these changes, for developments in microelectronics and computers made it possible to shift financial reserves within seconds. To the extent that neoliberalism was effective it certainly compromised the autonomy of national governments in the sphere of managing their economies. This depended upon political alliances to support such policies, however. By this I mean that there was nothing necessary about this decentring of the nation state. The very emergence of the "third way", and of New Leftist traditional Labour adaptations within the "third way", some of which are now claiming "limits to privatisation",[2] make the latent power of the state in an age of globalisation eminently visible. The equation is not globalisation *or* the nation state but globalisation *and* the nation state.

At a political level the signs of what could be seen as a new post-liberal settlement is premised on greater control, increased surveillance, and an eclipse of liberal rights that have prevailed since the 17th and 18th centuries. Terrorism, as Charles Townsend (2002, p. 137) has noted, constitutes "a calculated assault on the culture of reasonableness", which is central to democratic civic culture. Such a culture is epitomised by norms such as "toleration", "moderation", "the principle of proportionality", and "non-violence", which form the conditions for the exercise of civil liberties. Townsend (2002, p. 134) reports the conclusions of the Dutch political scientist Alex Schmid (1993) who has concluded that democracies experience weaknesses when faced with terrorism related to (a) freedom of movement, (b) freedom of association, (c) an abundance of targets, and (d) the constraints of the legal system.

While the liberal rights of free association and free speech make democracies slow to respond, some significant changes have come in a number of respects. Firstly, as concerns rights within the law, in respect to being imprisoned without being charged, and to being detained for an indefinite period. A relaxation of traditional judicial cautiousness has been introduced as the condition upon which the safety of each person can be assured. In Britain, the legislative basis was introduced in December 2001 in the Anti-Terrorism Crime and Security Act, which introduced internment without trial or the necessity of levelling charges. October 2002 saw this act being used to effect the imprisonment of the radical Muslim cleric Abu Qatada in London, who was suspected to be an Al-Qaeda agent. This legislation and other legislation also enables state surveillance and control over banking and information resources.

A second sense in which traditional political settlement has altered relates to the doctrine of "pre-emptive strike" (and the associated notion of "regime change"), which supersedes the doctrine of deterrence or containment and which has been the bedrock of stability, and the traditional Westphalia model of international relations which established the principle of state sovereignty by a treaty signed in 1648. Under deterrence, a country could retaliate if its national borders were violated. Under the doctrine of pre-emptive strike, a country may anticipate aggression, and "retaliate in advance". This enables states to attack who they like, based solely on the perception of a threat. This represents a move beyond what Henry Kissinger called "realpolitik" and castes aside traditional tenets of international law as well as UN and NATO charters. The new doctrine makes no qualification as to its use, so pre-emption becomes a new universal principle available to every nation. In addition, the new doctrine is not required to conform to international law, but can be justified as self-defence for individual countries to take action unilaterally. Except in these new circumstances, self-defence is redefined from meaning "actual attack by another country" to "perceived imminent attack".[3]

In addition to these changes post-9/11 there has been a sharp increase in surveillance and data sharing which have effected changes in the conception of citizenship. As part of this there has been an increase in the demands for information in the name of the public interest which is affecting the boundaries between the private and public spheres. A recent *Guardian* feature on privacy (Guardian, 2002) documented a whole range of forms of surveillance across both the private and public spheres, including data trawling, data sharing, visual surveillance (CCTV), DNA testing, fingerprinting, communication interception, and identity cards. In Britain, where liberal protections of the individual privacy and autonomy have a strong tradition, a recent report has been published on privacy and data sharing which aims to balance the dual concerns of protecting the rights of the individual and the state's interest in collecting and sharing data more efficiently across various public and private agencies for the purposes of creating "joined-up" government. Although critics are representing the report as a "snooper's charter" enabling the state to know everything about you, and are doubtful, to use Charles Raab's (2002, p. 16) words, that "the circle of privacy and data sharing can be squared", certain measures have been taken to protect the individual as well as minority groups within this legislation. These measures range from the establishment of a public services "trust charter" and other devices which oblige all public services to state how data can be shared, how individual privacy can be protected, and how individuals can assert their rights. Also proposed are the appointment of chief knowledge officers in state bodies with responsibility for managing data and overseeing an organisation's privacy commitments. In addition, in Britain, there have been several pieces of legislation which help to protect the rights and interests of individuals. These range from the Human Rights Act, which aims to balance the needs of the state and the rights of the citizen, and is arguably one of the Blair governments most significant achievements to date; the Data Protection Act of 1998, which gives to all citizens the right to know who holds information about them (subject access), as well as rights to object and remedy errors; the Freedom of Information Act 1999, and the Regulation of Investigatory Powers Act 2000, both of which seek to ensure that the use of communication data are properly controlled with independent oversight and proper complaints procedures, and which introduce new and supposedly improved regulatory machinery which didn't previously exist. In addition, the Anti-Terrorism, Crime and Security Act of 2001, although it requires communications companies to retain basic details of internet activity longer than was the case previously, and to report suspicious and irregular activity, also forbids data "fishing" and "trawling" expeditions, confining access to information strictly in relation to specific inquiries about crime or terrorism.

A key question here relates to the issue that in tackling a minority or criminals or terrorists in our midst, are we not trampling on the rights of the vast majority of citizens? The answer to this is of course complex, but we must not see the issue in terms of privacy as a natural right of individuals pitted against the common good. The classical liberal conception of privacy is linked integrally to the conception of the self as the private, self-interested chooser who exists prior to society and is endowed with natural rights. What such a conception ignores is that such a conception is, as Foucault and others have identified, a fiction. Such rights are indeed internal, not antecedent to, community, and as such are not absolute. Moreover, as the framers of the recent Human Rights Act, as well as the European Convention of Human Rights, which was its inspiration, knew only too well, different rights and interests need to be kept in balance. Privacy, like autonomy and freedom, is rooted in human dignity and speaks to the demands for safety and respect. It is not, however, an absolute right, but must be balanced by the right to safety and security by all, including children, women, and employees.[4] In this balance of forces, the state must be seen as both a negative as well as a positive force. It is a negative force in that it protects the safety of all, and it is a positive force in that it empowers and enables people to shape their lives, constituting, as it were, a collective vehicle to achieve progressive change. This notion of positive freedom, which starts with the Greek polis, and can be seen evident in writers like John Dewey, sees the full development of human beings as only possible through active participation in the affairs of the community.

5   Totalitarianism

This form of positive government was seen by liberals like Isaiah Berlin, Friedrich Hayek and Karl Popper as likely to lead towards totalitarianism.[5] The classic liberal theory of totalitarianism sees it as a form of government that develops out of the structures of the positive state. For liberals a positive conception of liberty leads the state to promote a single substantive ideal of the good—a description of man as a spiritual being whose ultimate rationality and reality are grounded in a unified spirit. This leads to a nation state which imposes a substantive conception of the good life, eradicating individuality by a concern with "normcentricity".[6]

Positive freedom worries liberals. The positive view of freedom as active self-determination implies, says Berlin (1969), a distinction between two selves—a higher self that determines, and a lower self that is subject to determination. Berlin argues that in the history of political thought, it is all too easy for the higher self to become identified with the state or society, or with a particular political groups conception of what is "rational". Freedom then tends to become defined as obedience to what is rational, or obedience to the will of the state, or conformity to a predetermined pattern of thought or life. As a consequence, claims Berlin, positive freedom is transposed into the opposite of freedom: totalitarianism or tyranny.

In its extreme form, argues Nel Noddings (1996), it is claimed that the positive conception of liberty often leads to the promulgation of a single ideal—a description of "man" as a spiritual being whose ultimate rationality and reality are grounded in a unified spirit. In this model, the state is seen as the expression of collective will (positive freedom), rather than the (mere) protector of individual liberties (negative freedom).

The total community equals fascism which equals the nation state. If the state is right, then there is no room for dissent, and liberty is equated with full immersion in the community. Liberals claim that individuality is wiped out by "normcentricity". In this way, Eric Hoffer maintained that communities foster "unity" and "self-sacrifice" along with conformity to established norms. In Hoffer's words:

> Unity and self-sacrifice, of themselves, even when fostered by the most noble means, produce a facility for hating. Even when men league themselves mightily together to promote tolerance and peace on earth, they are likely to be violently intolerant towards those not of like mind. (Hoffer, 1951, p. 92)

While writers like Berlin, Popper and Hayek believe that any state, over and above a concern with negative liberties, constitutes a threat to the freedom of the individual, as if inherently unable to respect a diversity of lifestyles, their argument falters on a number of grounds which I have summarised more fully elsewhere,[7] and can only outline briefly in this context: Firstly, their arguments technically rule out even a welfare state, for welfare rights are "positive" rights, and for Hayek, the welfare state is the start of the "slippery slope", leading down "the road to serfdom".

Secondly, it is neither logically or empirically entailed that a state that acts positively in terms of a specific substantive conception of the good, must ignore a respect for diversity and difference, or fail to respect the plurality of groups and subgroups in the wider society. As postmodernists and others have suggested, the good can accommodate difference. To suggest, therefore, that any state that does not confine itself to the minimum protection of individual liberties, but acts in terms of a general substantive vision, even if conceived in sophisticated terms, will unleash a pressure towards "unity" or "normcentricity", is a flawed argument, for it assumes that a theory of the good cannot exist at an abstract enough level to accommodate diversity or pluralism. Further, it attributes a failure of democracy to the particular way the state acts, *as a general orientation*, rather than to a specific analysis of *particular* societies in *particular* historical circumstances.

Thirdly, the liberal theory of totalitarianism depends on presumptions that liberalism constitutes a neutral agenda where freedom is defined as the natural property of individuals outside of society. Based on this argument, writers like Berlin (1969) maintain that liberalism advocates no substantive conception of the good. The identification of a good is impossible, in Berlin's view, as individuals manifest such diversity of opinion over the nature of the good. Because of this irreducible pluralism over values and preferences, and consequent incompatibility over versions of the good, individual freedom is all that remains. It is only as a consequence of this axiom that the state can be represented as *the enemy*, rather than the *precondition*, of freedom.

Notwithstanding Berlin's view, it can be claimed that liberalism itself implies a substantive conception of the good. The argument by liberals that within its policy prescriptions liberalism does not invoke a particular preferred shape to society, or that it does not advocate the establishment of a social good over and above what individuals desire, cannot rule out substantive commitments about what society should be like. As Luke Martell (1992, p. 156) states:

> It all sounds very nice until you realise that what it does, in effect, is to let in just another particular substantive vision of society as consisting of the sum total of individuals' preferences over which individuals have no overall control. In this sense, liberalism is in fact a highly substantive doctrine—one which posits a competitive individualist society immune to overall democratic direction.[8]

Fourthly, as Steven Heyman (1992, pp. 81–82) claims with respect to Berlin's (1969) analysis of liberty, what is striking about it is the way it is distorted by the political circumstances in which the essay was written:

> Berlin was writing in the late 1950s, at the height of the Cold War. He casts the debate between negative and positive liberty as a crucial battle in "the open war that is being fought between two systems of ideas", and between the political systems allegedly based on them—Western liberal democracy and totalitarian regimes of the left and right. ... With the passing of the Cold War, it may be easier to understand the relationship between positive and negative liberty in our political tradition.

Although we must applaud classical and neoliberals for being against totalitarianism, their specific theoretical analysis as to *what causes* totalitarianism became mixed in with both "left–right" politics and analysis of the role of the state in general, and "Cold War" politics in particular. Although Heyman discusses this contention with specific regards to Berlin, I would claim the thesis is generally applicable to many others, *to varying extents*, including Hayek, Popper, and Plamenatz, to name but a few.[9]

With the passing of the Cold War, it can be more easily seen that liberal explanations as to the origins of totalitarianism are woefully inadequate. To the extent that there are dangers inherent in human societies, such dangers inhere in all sorts of society, and it is difficult to identify such dangers as belonging specifically to a particular form and organisation of the state, in promoting the conditions for positive or negative freedom. Although it is not possible to do justice to such a complex topic in the short space available here, any adequate explanation for the origins of totalitarianism must take adequate account of the *historical, political, cultural and economic specificity of particular states at particular locations in history*. What produces totalitarianism is not a particular gearing of state power (such as "positive" or "negative", or even "holist", or "piecemeal" engineering, to use Popper's terms), but quite simply, the *absence of democracy*, or of the *conditions* which enable democracy to flourish. On this criteria, the Marxist–Leninist regimes of Eastern Europe failed in that they lacked a strong or deep conception of democracy, as well as the range of specific *mechanisms* by which democracy operates. As democracy is a structural arrangement, with specific techniques and mechanisms and processes that can be analysed, the best way to safeguard against totalitarianism is by ensuring that the state is a *democratic* state, and by seeking to *deepen* the specific senses in terms of which democracy operates.

To the extent that the state is solely concerned with the negative goals supporting the protection of individual liberties, and does not focus on the expression of a public will, it will be poorly equipped to deal with terrorist attacks. To the extent that terrorism forces the liberal state to reveal its "dormant will", liberals, who always thought that no such thing existed, will, of course, be perturbed.

Many, including myself, who support a "positive" role for the state, while acknowledging that there are dangers in relation to this, as there are in relation to any form of social and political organisation, believe that the answer is best sought in the strengthening or deepening of democracy.[10]

6 Rights Talk

The changes to traditional liberal safeguards and forms of governmentality, indicative of a new political tendency or settlement, outlined above, signal the sense in which certain liberal discursive patternings of power have constituted the taken-for-granted basis of Western political and educational arguments over the last century. There was a time, not too far back, when the left saw "rights talk" as having little relevance to their discourses of emancipation or to educational programmes, seeing issues to do with "rights" as either part of the regulatory politics of the bourgeois state, focusing too specifically on individual as opposed to collective concerns, or as part and parcel of Cold War politics. The events of 9/11 may hopefully reintroduce a concern for rights, and maybe other themes within liberal constitutionalism, in both educational and political research, as fundamental to emancipatory and progressive concerns. Indeed, it can be said that within what I am calling (following Held, 1995) *the new cosmopolitanism*, human rights and democratic justice must be called upon to fill the void of traditional concerns with socialist politics. In this sense, for educators, 9/11 has introduced much more pressing concerns, for one of the more important functions of education is in citizenship for democratic participation. This unfortunately is something that universal education in the Western world has almost single-mindedly avoided during the 20th century. While it has been recognised that the concerns with literacy and numeracy and social studies have positive externalities for democratic citizenship, the emphasis has been on "teaching" citizenship in the curriculum, rather than through involvement of students in the active decision-making processes of the school where it could be argued that democracy is learnt. As Walter Parker (2001, p. 9) has observed, citizenship education has largely been concerned with *learning about democracy* rather than *involvement in democracy*. What must be implemented is a form of citizenship education which is *extra-curricular*, focusing not only on what is taught in the classroom, but on *indirect* learning through participation in the governance of the school (the processes through which both school and classroom policies are made), in school-community forums, and in inter-school forums for broader educational-community relations.

7   A New Multicultural Cosmopolitanism

In this sense, the new cosmopolitanism must embody an educational conception of democracy which is truly *multicultural*. As well as aiming to promote the skills of sharing and deliberation through active participation in democratic processes of the school, what is brought home with the events of 9/11 is the need to involve students in democracy in a genuinely multicultural sense. For what is crucial in the world post-9/11 is that it is a global world which urges us to recognise those people and cultures who inhabit the world in addition to us, as those others who are inhabiting the cities, libraries, and schools that we think of as ours, a world which is increasingly cosmopolitan, if not in the sense that we all travel more, or at all, then certainly in the sense that what happens in one part of the globe now affects us all. Multicultural citizenship is now a matter of vital concern.

As democracy must respect multiculturalism, so multiculturalism must respect democracy. Democratic norms must necessarily cross-cut multicultural groups to protect three conditions: (1) the basic rights of all citizens individually and as groups (freedom of speech, thought, assembly, expression, lifestyle choice, etc); (2) that no person or group is manipulated into accepting values represented by public institutions; and (3) that public officials and institutions are democratically accountable in principle and practice.

Democracy in this sense must constitute a new universal. In this sense, it is a more basic set of procedural norms and rules than are the rights of any minority to do what they like. We must move away from any conception of multiculturalism whereby cultural minorities can be completely unresponsive to outside cultures, or where prohibitions against group members leaving the culture can be enforced. No minority and no culture can guarantee their own survival forever, as openness to the world outside is a necessary principle of democracy. This openness is indeed a core principle of cosmopolitanism, which must infuse citizenship education post-9/11. The point here is that a democratic rights culture must underpin any conception of multiculturalism, so defined.

By making a "rights culture" fundamental, in this sense, limits are placed upon the "discourse of diversity" that multiculturalism entails. This does not mean that the recognition of distinct identities and differences, as argued for by multiculturalists, are not important. Liberalism has clearly failed to sufficiently acknowledge such insights from "the politics of recognition", tending to represent justice as the *imposition of a single standard or rule* to all of the diverse groups within the social structure. Yet, while we can accept that multiculturalists have contributed something important in arguing for the recognition of distinct cultural identities, based on ethnicity, race, religion, gender or class, as Kymlicka (1999) has argued, such arguments cannot be used to legitimate "internal restrictions" (e.g., prohibiting group exit) which violate or contradict democratic principles, or interfere with the rights of others individuals or groups. By the same token, multicultural advocacy may result in "external protections" to counter group disadvantage or marginalisation. Such claims may themselves vary from one historical period to another, and should thus be deliberated and enacted through the democratic process itself.

Although multiculturalism advances a "discourse of diversity", it is different from, and largely unrelated to, the "discourse of diversity and devolution" advanced by neoliberalism. In that the multicultural stress on diversity has been influenced by postmodernist theorising, neoliberal diversity is sponsored by the market mechanism, which results in compounding and cumulative inequalities. With multiculturalism, diversity may also be dysfunctional to the extent that it undermines the degree of societal cohesion necessary for different groups to work and live together. The extent to which multicultural diversity reinforces norms of intolerance and conflict also takes on a new and altered significance post-9/11. Clearly the balance of contending forces between the common interests of society and the subgroupings within it, and the overall extent to which diversity is *recognised* and permitted is itself a question of democratic deliberation and adjudication, which may alter in different places and times.[11]

8 Democracy

The principle of democracy that I am talking about is *non-foundational* but *universal*. By this I mean that it is not based upon any fixed conception of human nature, or of a premise, as with Habermas, of universal rationality whereby conflicts can be redeemed dialogically through communicative action in the ideal speech community. Rather, the principle of democracy which we favour insists on the protection of human rights, recognises the distinctiveness of subcultures, ensures the principles of inclusion and openness, and ensures the universal application of the rule of law, and of open dialogue, not based upon any faith in rationality, but based purely on a principle of a *mutual interest in universal survival*. Thus, while such a conception of democracy is "deliberative", it is pragmatically rather than epistemologically based.[12] This is to say that the safety of all is guaranteed *in the final analysis* on the basis of an interest in survival, and it is the same grounds which justify the culture of reasonableness, as well as liberal values such as freedom of association, expression, and the like. *In an age of terrorism, democracy is the condition upon which survival can best be assured.* Such a conception is universal to the extent that it is *willed*. The inspiration is Nietzschean rather than Kantian. It is also very Foucauldian in the sense that it constitutes *a universalism of democracy as a contingent discourse of open protection and facilitation in a world of dangers.*[13]

Although survival may justify democracy, as an end or goal it is too thin to be fully adequate, of course, for mere survival cannot possibly satisfy a complete account of life's ends and aims. And it may not be universally agreed to, if we mean by universal "agreed to by all", for there are no doubt some, including "suicide bombers", for whom it holds no sway at all. Ultimately, that is the choice of course, and certainly it focuses the concentration. For if democracy is the *precondition* of survival, then it requires a democratic mandate to be effective, even so.

Beyond this, it is possible to build a much richer conception of democracy on this basis. If survival is a final justification and focuses our attention as to why democracy is important, survival with dignity resonates of a more traditional concern with *ends*. This, of course, is the classic conception of democracy as a doctrine based on the ultimate worth and dignity of the human being, as espoused in the republican tradition. Thus, it is not the narrow "realist" theory of democracy that has been articulated and advocated by post-war American political science, commonly associated with the writings of Joseph Schumpeter's (1976) *Capitalism, Socialism and Democracy*, which refers to a narrow system of representative government and a means of changing governments through a system of elections (Hindess, 2000). Rather, if safety, dignity, and survival are to be possible, it must be deepened, once again, to refer to a substantive end which is something more than mere utility but which also encompasses the well-being and safety "of each and all" (Shapiro, 1999). Such a conception must once again entail a certain idea of participation and equality as well. While some philosophers and political theorists will sense a resonance here with Rousseau's general will, this would be mistaken, for the model suggested here is not a totalising one, which presupposes unity between individual and collective, but a *detotalising* one that is based on the notion of general well-being, while recognising the diversity and differences between cultures and people. This is what I have referred to elsewhere as "thin communitarianism". The formulation owes its general inspiration to Foucault, whose conception of the "equalisation of power relations" and "non-domination", can be used to support, I argue, a general conception of democratic justice (see Olssen, 2002). In terms of social ontology such a conception can be thought of as similar to Martha Nussbaum's (1995, p. 456) "thick vague conception of the good". Nussbaum advances "a soft version of Aristotelian essentialism" (p. 450) which incorporates a "determinate account of the human being, human functioning and human flourishing" (p. 450). While in formal terms it recognises that all individuals and cultures have certain developmental and lifestyle needs, this "internal essentialism" (p. 451) is "an historically grounded empirical essentialism" (p. 451). As such, it is purely formal, for within this broad end, and subject to the limits necessary for its realisation and continuance, it permits and recognises a multitude of identities and projects and ways of life.

Attempts to reconcile diversity with social unity are not new. John Rawls seeks to account for a "reasonable pluralism" within the context of the "overlapping consensus", as the basis of "justice as fairness" (Rawls, 1996, Lecture IV).[14] Arguments from postmodernists have also sought to throw new light on how difference and unity can be reconciled. For Foucault (1981, p. 69), the social whole is never a "sealed" unity, or resistant to change, but is characterised rather by incompleteness, indeterminacy, complexity and chance (*aléa*). Such theorising by Foucault, and others, utilising models of non-linear complex causality,[15] has led to fresh interest in how freedom, creativity and difference can exist and be safeguarded in a community. Similar initiatives, relating to Foucault and other postmodernist thinkers, are summarised by William Corlett (1989) in his book *Community without Unity: A Politics of Derridian Extravagance*.

9   Deepening Democracy through Education

If post-9/11 makes democracy of more pressing concern; our conception has moved a long way from a narrow theory of universal enfranchisement. To the extent that counterterrorist action now constitutes an important item, it must itself be subject to the democratic norms of public visibility and critical scrutiny, together with open processes of deliberation and debate, as well as traditional rights of contestation in terms of the rule of law. If our substantive conception posits certain general ends, which allow for a degree of diversity and pluralism, our procedural view of democracy is as a multifaceted array of mechanisms and processes instituted to ensure the *inclusion*, *security* or *safety* (including sexual safety) as well as *development* and *opportunities* of all individuals and groups. In this respect research needs to focus on the means of *deepening* democracy to satisfy these goals. As a way of concluding this chapter, one might consider the development of research on all or any of the following themes:

- *The concern with equality*: The development of any conception of democratic justice must seek to deal with rather than avoid issues to do with distribution of resources and life chances. Given a rejection of the classical liberal fiction regarding entitlement to property based on a model of pre-social, possessive individuals who "owe nothing to society", it is important to theorise the implications of a social ontological framework of community for considerations of democratic justice as it pertains to distributional ethics. Community in this sense is definable as an all-encompassing arena without fixed borders or unity, which comprises an assortment of values, norms and institutions that enable life to be lived. Such a conception of community recognises social ties and shared values, as well as practices of voluntary action and public institutions like education which constitute the conditions for stability and reproduction of society. Although neoliberal philosophers like Nozick have shifted political philosophy away from a concern with issues of distributive justice in recent years, my own view is similar to the 19th-century social democrat L. T. Hobhouse, who held that a person's entitlement to rewards and gain must be balanced by one's obligation to society. What liberal conceptions of democracy obscured, in Hobhouse's view, was the interdependence between individuals and the social structure, or for the social and moral obligation of the society (acting through the vehicle of the state) to assist in arranging the social futures of each rising generation. As he argued in his book *Liberalism* (1911, pp. 189–190), in his justification for redistributive policies of progressive taxation, the state has an obligation to enforce reasonable conditions of equality on the basis that while a society should provide the conditions for enterprise, all individuals are correspondingly indebted to society for the conditions and structures provided, and on this basis, individuals should contribute in direct proportion to the luck or good fortune they experience.
- *The role of the state*: The role of the state should be concerned with guaranteeing both negative freedom and positive freedom. *Negative freedom* involves the state's responsibility for ensuring the universal entitlements to safety and reasonable autonomy for all. The trade-off in respect to privacy will be necessitated to the extent that these obligations are threatened. To the extent that greater surveillance is deemed necessary, the proposals must be themselves subject to democratic processes that ensure visibility, openness, deliberation and debate. The state's obligations as regards *positive freedom* involve it in developing opportunities based on people's rights to inclusion and the development of their capacities. This obligation gives the state a role in the provision of social services, health care, and education. In brief, the role for the positively geared state lies in relation to socially

directed investment decisions, to provide for the general conditions for all species needs and development, including education and training, and to create and maintain quality infrastructure such as schools, hospitals, parks and public spaces.

– *The development of civil society*: A vibrant civil society can constitute a check on the powers of government. Civil society refers to that sector of private associations relatively autonomous from the state and economy, which spring from the everyday lives and activities of communities of interest. Clearly, one principle of democracy is the idea of multiple centres of power, and of their separation, as suggested by writers like Montesquieu and de Tocqueville. Another principle of democracy is the right to contest, challenge or oppose. Institutions of civil society, as writers like Paul Hirst have maintained, can be seen to constitute an important powerful network of quasi-independent associations, which can strengthen democratic rule through checking the power of the state. If democracy is rule by the people, the ability, and opportunity to "speak the truth to power", as Michel Foucault (2001) has put it, is itself one of democracy's crucial rights, indeed its very condition. According to Cohen and Arato (1992) civil society strengthens democracy in both a defensive and offensive sense. The defensive aspect refers to the way that associations and social movements develop forms of communicative interaction that support the development of people's identities, expand participatory possibilities and create networks of solidarity. The offensive aspect refers to how associational networks and institutions come to exert influence on, and constitute checks to, the state, and to each other.

– *The role of education*: the role of education is crucial for democracy, as educational institutions, whether compulsory or post-compulsory, intersect with, and therefore mediate between, institutions like the family and those of the state and the economy. Although formal institutions of education have been in the main public institutions, there is an important sense in which they are semi-autonomous from the state. This is not the neoliberal sense where management and administration are devolved to the local school, but the sense in which the schools are located in, and represent local community groups. In this sense, schools are important as democratic organisations, through the particular way that they are connected to communities, through their ability to empower families, and involve minority groups in participatory projects. Education is also crucial as the central agency responsible for the production of democratic norms such as trust and political decision-making. This is to say, as Mill recognised in *Representative Government*, educational institutions are important as sites where democracy and self-government are learnt. Deliberative democracy is especially complex, for it involves not just norms and procedures of debate but norms and procedures of contestation, inclusiveness, tolerance, compromise, solidarity with others, generosity, care, the operations of forums, and of checks and balances, the use of sanctions and screens, and the separation of powers. In the republican tradition, schools are instrumental in the development of civic virtue and habits of good citizenship. This is what signals the real importance of the "knowledge economy". For education is essentially important in its role of constructing democratic civic norms, and this must become one of the central aims of government policy in this regard. It is not a case of "brainwashing" or "socialisation" but of teaching skills and establishing models of civic conduct based on tolerance, deliberation, conflict resolution, give and take, and trust. While educational processes depend upon fairness of political processes, and in the distribution of economic resources, education is necessary to construct the network of norms that permit both the market and democracy to function. As Philip Pettit (1999, p. 255) puts it, education represents a "stark choice between the invisible hand and the iron hand: between a strategy of marketing and a strategy of management". It is for this reason of course that education should ideally be *public, universal compulsory* and *free*. For if education is vital in constructing norms that nurture the market, it cannot be itself subject to the market's disorganising effects.

Acknowledgement

This chapter originally appeared as Olssen, M. (2005). Globalization, the third way and education post 9/11: Building democratic citizenship. In M. A. Peters (Ed.), *Education, globalization, and the state in the age of terrorism* (pp. 145–177). Routledge. Reprinted here, with minor edits, with permission from the publisher.

Notes

1. For a more nuanced discussion of cosmopolitanism, see Olssen, Codd, and O'Neill (2003, chapter 11).
2. *The* Guardian, 4 November 2002. A headline on page 1 reads "Brown Camp Seeks Sell-off Limit", revealing a faction in the government with a more cautious view towards privatisation. This reinforces a widely held view amongst journalists that within New Labour there are different factions on privatisation.

3   Yet a third sign of a change in the political settlement is the ignoring of the Geneva Convention by the US in its imprisonment of suspected Al-Qaeda terrorists at Guantanamo Bay, Cuba. Other possible signs include proposals in Britain in 2002 to do away with the "double jeopardy" rule, which has traditionally prevented people from being tried twice, as well as proposals to restrict trial by jury, and to reveal a person's previous convictions.
4   In legal terms, this idea of balance is covered by the "principle of proportionality".
5   See Berlin (1969), Hayek (1935, 1944) and Popper (1945, 1961).
6   See also Arendt (1958) and Talmon (1955).
7   See Olssen (1996, 1998).
8   This objection, which has been formulated many times by many writers, concerns the difficulty of distinguishing "procedural" from "substantive" goals (see Dahl, 1999, pp. 25–26; Honohan, 2002, p. 9; Sandel, 1982; Walzer, 1985; MacIntyre, 1984). Given that even "autonomy", or "democratic citizenship" can be construed as "substantive goals", on this basis, all states can be seen as having *some* substantive concerns.
9   See Hayek (1944), Popper (1945, 1961), Plamenatz (1954, 1963). For a brief argument to this effect, see Olssen (1996, 1998). A more substantial critique of the liberal theory of totalitarianism has yet to be made.
10 Social democrats traditionally have supported a positive view of freedom. For a recent expression, see David Blunkett (2002), the current British Home Secretary, who writes: "I prefer a positive view of freedom, drawing on another tradition of political thinking that goes back to the ancient Greek polis. According to this tradition, we only become fully free when we share, as active citizens, in the government of the affairs of the community. Our identity as members of a collective political community is a positive thing. Democracy is not just an association of individuals determined to protect the private sphere, but a realm of active freedom in which citizens come together to shape the world around them. We contribute and we become entitled".
11 Sharon Gewirtz (2002) suggests that official government support towards state funding of "faith-based" schools in England has altered post-9/11, suggesting that forms of religious separatism over education are being seen as socially dysfunctional for the production of democratic values, such as tolerance.
12 It thus has the character of a "settlement", rather than a "consensus", or a "reflexive equilibrium", although the latter concept (which is Rawls's) may, in this view, form part of a broader conception of citizenship which the state seeks to democratically promote.
13 My view is that "survival" is a better basis to justify democracy than "social contract". However, it is not possible to explore the differences in this paper.
14 While we can accept much of Rawls's argument in practice, it is Rawls's commitments to liberal contract theory that we find problematic and which prevents him from, amongst other things, developing a viable notion of community (see Rawls, 1996).
15 For Foucault's model of holism/particularism, or system/originality, see my brief summaries (Olssen, 1998, pp. 79–80; 2002, pp. 490–491). For a general account of theories of complex determination that are being used to explain how infinite possibilities, and unpredictable occurrences are derivable from a set of determined rules or structure, see Cilliers (1998).

References

Arendt, H. (1958). *The origins of totalitarianism*. Allen & Unwin.
Berlin, I. (1969). *Four essays on liberty*. Oxford University Press.

Blunkett, D. (2002, September 14). Civic rights. *The Guardian.* https://www.theguardian.com/uk/2002/sep/14/privacy.freedomofinformation

Castells, M. (1997). Globalization, identification and the state: A powerless state or a network state? In *The information age: Economy, society and culture, volume II: The power of identity* (pp. 303–364). Blackwell.

Cilliers, P. (1998). *Complexity and postmodernism: Understanding complex systems.* Routledge.

Cloke, P., Milbourne, P., & Widdowfield, R. (2000). Partnership and policy networks in rural local governance: Homelessness in Taunton. *Public Administration, 78*(1), 111–113.

Cochrane, A. (2000). New Labour, new urban policy. *Social Policy Review, 12*, 184–204.

Cohen, J. L., & Arato, A. (1992). *Civil society and political theory.* MIT Press.

Corlett, W. (1989). *Community without unity: A politics of Derridian extravagance.* Duke University Press.

Dahl, R. (1999). Can international organisations be democratic? A skeptic's view. In I. Shapiro & C. Hacker-Cordón (Eds.), *Democracy's edges* (pp. 19–36). Cambridge University Press.

Falk, R. (1995). *On humane governance.* Polity.

Foucault, M. (1981). The order of discourse (I. McLeod, Trans.). In R. Young (Ed.), *Untying the text: A post-structuralist reader* (pp. 48–78). Routledge & Kegan Paul.

Foucault, M. (2001). *Fearless speech* (J. Pearson, Ed.). Semiotext(e).

Glendinning, C., Powell, M., & Rummery, K. (2002). *Partnerships, New Labour and the governance of welfare.* Policy Press.

Giddens, A. (2000). *The third way and its critics.* Polity.

Gewirtz, S. (2002). Faith-based schooling and the invisible effects of September 11th: The view from England [Unpublished paper].

Guardian, The. (2002, September 14). Special report: Big Brother: Part two: State surveillance. https://www.theguardian.com/bigbrother/privacy/statesurveillance/0,,783342,00.html

Hattersley, R. (2002, 30 August). The silly season. *The Guardian*, p. 18.

Hayek, F. A. (Ed.). (1935). *Collectivist economic planning.* Routledge & Kegan Paul.

Hayek, F. A. (1944). *The road to serfdom.* Routledge & Kegan Paul.

Held, D. (1995). *Democracy and the global order.* Polity.

Hindess, B. (2000). Representative government and participatory democracy. In A. Vandenberg (Ed.), *Citizenship and democracy in the global era* (pp. 33–55). Macmillan Press.

Hirst, P., & Thompson, K. (1996). *Globalization in question.* Polity.

Honohan, I. (2002). *Civic republicanism.* Routledge.

Hoffer, E. (1951). *The true believer.* Harper & Row.

Kymlicka, W. (1999). Liberal complacencies. In S. M. Okin (Ed.), *Is multiculturalism bad for women?* (pp. 31–34). Princeton University Press.

Klein, N. (2000). *No logo*. Flamingo.

MacIntyre, A. (1984). *After virtue* (2nd ed.). University of Notre Dame Press.

Martell, L. (1992). New ideas of socialism. *Economy and Society, 21*(2), 151–172.

Mishra, R. (1999). *Globalization and the welfare state*. Edward Elgar.

Noddings, N. (1996). On community. *Educational Theory, 46*(3), 245–267.

Nussbaum, M. (1995). Human functioning and social justice: In defence of Aristotelian essentialism. In D. Tallack (Ed.), *Critical theory: A reader* (pp. 449–472). Harvester Wheatsheaf.

Ohmae, K. (1990). *The borderless world*. Harper Business.

Ohmae, K. (1995). *The end of the nation state: The rise of regional economics*. The Free Press.

Olssen, M. (1996). In defence of the welfare state and publicly provided education: A New Zealand perspective. *Journal of Education Policy, 11*(3), 337–362. https://doi.org/10.1080/0268093960110305

Olssen, M. (1998). Education policy, the cold war and the "liberal–communitarian" debate. *Journal of Education Policy, 13*(1), 63–89, https://doi.org/10.1080/0268093980130105

Olssen, M. (2002). Michel Foucault as "thin" communitarian: Difference, community, democracy. *Cultural Studies/Critical Methodologies, 2*(4), 483–513. https://doi.org/10.1177/153270860200200403

Olssen, M., Codd, J., & O'Neill, A.-M. (2003). *Education policy: Globalization, citizenship & democracy*. Sage.

Peters, M. (2001). Education and culture in postmodernity: The challenges for Aoteroa/New Zealand [Unpublished paper]. The Macmillan Brown Lectures.

Pettit, P. (1999). *Republicanism: A theory of freedom and government*. Oxford University Press.

Plamenatz, J. (1954). *Marxism and Russian communism*. Longmans.

Plamenatz, J. (1963). *Man and society: A critical examination of some important social and political theories from Machiavelli to Marx* (2 Vols.). Longmans.

Polanyi, K. (1944). *The great transformation*. Beacon Press.

Popper, K. (1945). *The open society and its enemies*. Routledge.

Popper, K. (1961). *The poverty of historicism*. Routledge.

Raab, C. D. (2002, September 21). Privacy in the public interest. *The Guardian*. https://www.theguardian.com/uk/2002/sep/21/privacy.freedomofinformation3

Rawls, J. (1996). *Political liberalism*. Columbia University Press.

Rhodes, R. W. (1997a). *Understanding governance: Policy networks, governance, reflexivity and accountability*. Open University Press.

Rhodes, R. W. (1997b). From marketization to diplomacy: It's the mix that matters. *Public Policy and Administration, 12*(2), 31–50.

Rhodes, R. W. (2000). Governance and public administration. In J. Pierre (Ed.), *Debating governance* (pp. 54–90). Oxford University Press.

Sandel, M. (1982). *Liberalism and the limits of justice.* Cambridge University Press.

Schumpeter, J. (1976). *Capitalism, socialism and democracy* (5th ed.). Allen & Unwin.

Schmid, A. (1993). Terrorism and democracy. In A. Schmid & R. Crelinsten (Eds.), *Western responses to terrorism* (pp. 14–25). Frank Cass.

Shapiro, I. (1999). *Democratic justice.* Yale University Press.

Stiglitz, J. (2002). *Globalization and its discontents.* Allen Lane/Penguin.

Talmon, J. L. (1955). *The origins of totalitarian democracy.* Secker & Warburg.

Townshend, C. (2002). *Terrorism: A very short introduction.* Oxford University Press.

Walzer, M. (1985). *Spheres of justice.* Basil Blackwell.

Wintour, P. (2002, October 12). Parties consign welfare state to history. *The Guardian*, p. 13.

CHAPTER 17

Totalitarianism and the "Repressed" Utopia of the Present

Moving beyond Hayek and Popper with Foucault

Abstract

This article starts by reviewing the negative account of utopian thinking in dominant liberal Western political theory, through the positing of a link between utopianism and totalitarianism, as present in the writings of liberal writers like Hayek, Popper, Berlin and others. As such, this article constitutes a critique of the liberal theories of utopianism and totalitarianism as well as positing alternative conceptions. It uses Michel Foucault's views to advance beyond the liberal mindset in order to rehabilitate the concept of utopia as both a substantive and methodological conception for both democratic and educational theory. By redefining what utopia means, it argues for a revival of a new form of utopian thinking as necessary for extending and deepening democracy in the world post-9/11.

1   Introduction

A utopia, from one point of view, implies a distinction between things as they are and things as they should be. In this sense, a utopia implies an ideal society created by deliberate human endeavour. Such a definition typically includes a vision of an ideal existence for a collectivity. The utopias of the Renaissance, for instance, described ideal imaginary societies characterised as if they operated in the present. They were fictional characterisations expressed so as to represent an ideal blueprint of how human groups could or should coexist. As blueprints they combined both substantive and methodological concerns. That is, they spelt out the substance of how human society should be structured, and they constituted a method to enable comparison with actually existing societies. As often as not, because they were structured systemically, representing the individual in relation to complex institutional and social processes, they would address and resolve complex issues relating to structure and agency, freedom and determinism, morality and law, and social justice as well. The utopias of the Renaissance, for instance, represented a possible future, recapturing the authority and stability of the ancients. Most stressed stability at the expense of change, and repressed expressions of difference and diversity. Thomas More,[1] writing in the early 16th century, for instance, imposed restrictions on travel, public gatherings, and the expression of political ideas, especially as influenced by the rise of the recently invented printing machines. More's conception of utopia, like those of von Gunzburg,[2] Doni,[3] Campanella,[4] Andreae,[5] Burton,[6] and Bacon,[7] emphasised social justice, the moral life, the relations of the individual to the polis and the absence of exploitation. Miriam Eliav-Feldon (1982, p. 85) characterises Renaissance utopias as resting on four motives: social justice, a religiously moral life, the eradication of individualism, and simplicity.

It may be this Renaissance characterisation of utopia, with its emphasis upon stability, consensus, and holistic construction, that accounts for the bad image of utopian thinking in Western political culture. Such a negative view is expressed by Ralph Dahrendorf (1967, p. 139), for instance:

> One of the basic assumptions of all utopian constructions is that conditions may be created under which conflicts become superfluous. Indeed, the resulting state of harmony is the theoretical basis of the persistence of the social structure of utopia. But in reality these conditions do not exist. In fact, with the terrible dialectics of the non-rational, it happens that utopia first requires and then glorifies suppression.

What Friedrich Hayek termed, as Erik Olin Wright (1995, p. x) reminds us, the "fatal conceit"—"the belief that through rational calculation and political will, society can be designed in ways that will significantly improve the human condition" (Wright, 1995, p. x)—symbolises the negative view of utopian theorising that has characterised liberal analyses. This type of anti-utopian thought, expressed forcefully in Hayek's *The Road to Serfdom*, was to be taken up by political philosophers like Karl Popper, in *The Open Society and Its Enemies* and *The Poverty of Historicism,* and, in more recent times, such an anti-utopian conception has been echoed by Michel Foucault in an assortment of comments and interviews. In this short essay I want first to spell out the anti-utopian argument as represented by Hayek and Popper representing it as embodying a distinctively liberal viewpoint. I then want to consider Foucault's viewpoints on utopias in order to gain some insight into how the liberal objections can be overcome. Finally, I will argue that a utopia is best represented as embodying an ideal of social organisation that is not only representable in models of an ideal form of society in the future, but also always necessarily inheres in any present form of social organisation. That is, within actually existing societies, as depicted by liberals, there is I will argue a "latent" or "repressed" utopian ideal.

My argument is that Hayek, Popper and other "Cold War" liberals attack a partial representation of what is called utopian thinking which should not and does not exhaust the meaningful and useful senses in which utopian thought is possible and desirable. In this sense, I argue that the idea of utopia has useful purposes and needs rehabilitation in Western political thought. I argue further that much anti-utopian thought from liberal quarters is incoherent on the subject of utopia, and reflects the particular vision of society, connected through free trade and the unfettered development of capital, of classical liberalism.

2 Hayek and Popper: Utopianism, Planning and Holistic Engineering

As the leading intellectual of the Austrian School, Hayek is a writer of enormous importance in influencing the negative view of utopian thinking in Western political culture. His major books, including *The Road to Serfdom* (1944), *The Constitution of Liberty* (1960) and the three volumes of *Law, Legislation and Liberty* (1973, 1976, 1979), represent the most complete and coherent statement of the liberal principles of individualism, of a limited, constitutionally specified role for the state, of a faith in the market, and of the evils of all utopian conceptions and forms of planning. Hayek's intellectual project was to develop the economic theory of liberalism as well as to delegitimate the post-war theory of interventionism and oppose the extension of welfare rights throughout society.

Hayek maintains that the proper functioning of markets is incompatible with state planning or utopian conceptions of any sort, either full-scale socialism or the more limited conception of the welfare state. A full-scale rational socialism is impossible because it would have no markets to guide resource allocation. In addition, central planning of any form, he claims, is not practical because of the scale of centralised calculation any effective attempt at allocation would require. On this basis, Hayek (1944) contends that all forms of state action beyond the minimal functions of the defence of the realm and the protection of basic rights to life and property are dangerous threats to liberty which are likely to lead down the "road to serfdom".

His main arguments against central planning in relation to utopian blueprints are based on two claims: (1) on its inefficiency, and (2) on the threat to freedom of the individual. It would be inefficient, in Hayek's view, because real knowledge is gained and true economic progress made as a consequence of locally generated knowledge derived from "particular circumstances of time and place" and the state is not privy to such knowledge (Hayek, 1944, p. 521). The market then is the mechanism which best allocates resources in society.

Planning ignores this localistic character of knowledge and interferes with the self-regulating mechanism of the market.

Also derived from von Mises, Hayek's work was characterised by a strong anti-socialism, most vehemently expressed in his opposition to Marxism, which he held did not constitute a rational means of organising an economy. For Hayek, economies are the outcome of spontaneous evolution and demonstrate the superiority of unregulated markets for creativity and progress as against all utopian conceptions or models of centralised planning. A spontaneous societal order such as a market order can utilise practical fragmented knowledge in a way in which a holistically planned order cannot. A spontaneous order emerges as a natural process. It can be observed in population biology of animal species, in the formation of crystals, and even in galaxies (Hayek, 1952, p. 180; 1967, p. 76; 1973, p. 39; 1976, pp. 39–40). It is this idea that self-organising and self-replicating structures emerge without design, and that knowledge about some parts of the structure permits the formation of correct understanding about the behaviour of the structure as a whole, that Hayek is most keen to emphasise. It underpins his rejection of Cartesian rationalism, his anti-historicism, his anti-foundationalism, his strictures against state planning, and his anti-utopianism. In that the market is a spontaneous order, it displays a tendency to equilibrium, although an actual perfect equilibrium is never achieved but must be viewed as a constantly changing process of tending towards orderliness. This is not only with reference to economic life and the spontaneous emergence of markets, but also in social life in relation to the growth of language where we find the spontaneous formation of self-regulating structures, as well as in relation to the development of moral norms. Hence, as Gray points out, the emergence of spontaneous systems is "somewhat akin to the generalisations of Darwinian evolution" (Gray, 1984, p. 31) in that Hayek maintains that "selective evolution is the source of all order" (Gray, 1984, p. 32). Thus, in a market economy there is a real analogy to Darwinian natural selection in that the "profit–loss system provides a mechanism for the elimination of unfit systems" (Gray, 1984, p. 32) with the proviso that, in contradistinction to Herbert Spencer or W. G. Sumner, natural selection is not solely about individuals but is also about groups and populations. Such a thesis incorporates Hayek's arguments that social institutions arise as a result of human action but not human design (the "invisible hand" thesis); that knowledge embodied in practices and skills that is practical, tacit and local, is primary in terms of its epistemological status; and that there is a natural selection of competitive traditions whereby rules and practices that confer success come to replace those unsuited to the human environment. Following closely in the footsteps of von Mises, Hayek argues that any attempt to supplant market relations by public planning cannot avoid calculational calamities and is therefore doomed to failure.

Hayek's arguments against central planning have been seriously challenged.[8] While they may be persuasive against the idea of highly centralised decision making for the entire economy, beyond this his account of planning is simply a caricature, and the assessment of his legitimate empirical arguments is difficult to untangle from what is the deeply ingrained ideological nature of his anti-communitarianism. Hayek never considers whether markets and planning could (or should) coexist. That is, whether there is not some middle-ground position between the "serfdom" associated with state planning, and the "freedom" associated with markets. As Jim Tomlinson (1990, p. 49, note 3) notes:

> [I]n his 1945 article ["The Use of Knowledge in Society"], Hayek typically dismisses any mid-way point between centralised and decentralised planning except "the delegation of planning to organised industries, or, in other words, monopoly" (p. 521). Plainly this does not exhaust the possibilities of levels of planning, nor does it provide a helpful starting point for discussing mechanisms of planning.

Hence, as Tomlinson argues, it is not clear what scale of knowledge is deemed necessary by Hayek, for central planning to be effective. Apart from a persuasive argument against the idea of a single planning command centre for the whole economy, Hayek does not discuss *levels* of economic planning. As Tomlinson (1990, p. 41) continues:

> His argument works with a simple polarity between individual (or decentralised) and centralised decision-making—but the degree of centralisation is never discussed, so it is unclear as to whether the argument applies to the one-person business as to the multinational corporation.

The reader is also frequently left unaware of what freedom for Hayek involves. It is simply the state of not being coerced by governments or other people. It does not exclude huge inequalities of wealth and it does not prevent poverty and destitution. Why do the unintended consequences of the behaviour of the marketplace not count as an infringement of liberty? The answer is Hayek does not want to condemn but rather he wants to celebrate the unintended effects of the market on people's lives. What it does, in fact, is give an absolute priority to freedom as though this was the only value to be taken into account in society. Yet, for welfare liberals, liberty is only one of several desirable attributes of social organisation, others being equality, inclusion, participation, and justice.

In exalting the liberty of the individual as his sole concern, not only does he deny that the state can have purposes and duties other than those arising from the purposes and interests of individuals, or of groups of individuals in market contexts, but if followed logically as a principle it would prevent forms of sensible state planning to constrain the excesses of the market, or to enable projects on behalf of communities (e.g., education and health). This is not to deny that there are many specific freedoms whose social value consists in allowing individuals to pursue their own ends, nor need we deny that the market is the best means of allocation for many resources. The central issue, not considered by Hayek, is how far the liberty of the individual and the market can be extended before choices in certain areas need to be limited because of the undesirable consequences of unrestricted individual liberty on society generally. That there could be general purposes, social benefits and public goods which are not provided for by markets, and which cannot be directly identified with individual interests, and which therefore must reside with the state, or the community, as the collective expression of people's interests, is simply not seriously considered by Hayek. His own arguments depend on a sharp dichotomy between markets and planning where mistakes and errors become "entrenched" in the process of planning. Partly, this is due to the absence of local or contextual knowledge which actors in the marketplace have and state bureaucrats don't have, but why they should become "entrenched" rather than "correctable" is not clear. To use Hayek's (1945) language, while he celebrates knowledge of "time and place" which is not accessible to planners, he gives no value to the benefits of "aggregated" or "statistical" knowledge, which enables perspective, which constitutes the *equally important* knowledge which "planners" *do* have, and which is *denied* to agents in local contexts. Certainly, if planning sought to replace or override market mechanisms, one could see that would constitute a serious problem,[9] but this does not mean that markets and planning cannot complement and assist each other in turn, as Keynes argued in his theoretical justifications for the welfare state. Certainly, in Western countries, although state planning became central to the Keynesian welfare state settlements from the 1930s to the 1970s, one would be hard pressed to point to any significant erosion of liberty or "road to serfdom" (i.e., totalitarian tendencies) that developed as a result.

3   Karl Popper: "Utopian" and "Piecemeal" Engineering

Karl Popper argues against what he terms "utopian social engineering" in favour of a "piecemeal" approach in both *The Open Society and Its Enemies*

TOTALITARIANISM AND THE "REPRESSED" UTOPIA OF THE PRESENT   445

(1945) and more systematically in *The Poverty of Historicism* (1961). The distinction between "utopian" or "holist" engineering and "piecemeal engineering" is the distinction between two philosophical systems. As Popper represents it, the utopian approach says that the action is directed to an ultimate goal, end or aim, and agents act rationally when their actions accord with such an aim or goal. As Notturno (2003, p. 80) explains:

> The utopian engineer must first identify his ultimate end. He must next choose the means most appropriate for attaining it, bearing in mind that they are merely means to the end and not the ultimate end itself. And he must then consciously and consistently pursue his ultimate end. Applied to practical political reform, the utopian approach says that we must identify our ideal state or society—the achievement of which is presumably the ultimate goal of our political action—before we can do anything to reform our institutions or improve our situation.

In contrast to this large-scale social experimentation, piecemeal engineering favours a more limited, more pragmatic, "trial and error" approach based upon an awareness of the limits of human knowledge and allowing adequate room for the correction of errors. As Notturno (2003, p. 80) states:

> The piecemeal engineer ... searches for and fights against the greatest and most urgent evils of society, instead of searching and fighting for its ideal ultimate good. Instead of formulating an idea of his ultimate ideal state, he tries to identify the most pressing social problems in the state that actually exists. And instead of using his vision of the ideal state to bring them about, he tries to design and redesign social institutions that will alleviate actual suffering. The rationality of his action consists not in his consciously and consistently trying to bring about his ideal state, but in an experimental approach that acknowledges his own fallibility and the possibility that his actions may have consequences that are very different from what he intends. He thus proposes tentative solutions to problems, tests them, and tries to eliminate their errors.

In Popper's view the utopian approach is dangerous, and piecemeal engineering is the only viable way for policy design and change. Popper further suggests that the persecutions and undemocratic practices in totalitarian societies are the result of a holist conception of society and a holist approach to policy design and implementation. The holist, says Popper, believes that society is more than the sum of the individuals who comprise it, which gives a license to those who wish to curtail the rights and freedoms of the individual in the name of society's greater good (see Popper, 1961, pp. 76–93).

Popper's distinction between "utopian" and "piecemeal" is problematic on several grounds and can be critiqued in terms of the general arguments I will make below. While policy formulations that lack democratic mandate, or aim to implement poor designs without consultation, or in huge sweeps, are clearly suspect, my problem is rather with Popper claiming that utopian engineering is unacceptable because it is executed in terms of an *ideal pattern or state*. In my view, this is unavoidable and must necessarily apply also to piecemeal engineering. It is not possible to frame policy except in relation to some ideal. By the same token, it seems somewhat far-fetched to imagine how any "utopian strategy" could be executed "all at once". Even with policy in support of a revolutionary programme, planks of the programme must be implemented piece by piece. In terms of policy implementation at the level of day-to-day politics, then, the utopian and piecemeal policy plans will have much the same appearance. Popper would still claim that an inherent difference exists in that the piecemeal planner lacks any tie to a programmatic idea that influences the utopian planner. Yet my argument here is that liberals simply fail to see the programmatic ideal that lies "repressed" within their own conception. With sectional policy reforms in Western countries, to do with say housing or health, the *ideal* of Western democratic communities constitutes a programmatic constraint, albeit sometimes at the level of the political unconscious. Or when, for instance, George Bush and Tony Blair illegally commence a war on Iraq, their policy initiative reflects the ideals of the Western world, as frequently stated by both men, with their frequent use of words like "freedom", "democracy" and the like. Such a world is both a world of the future and of the present. It is both an actually existing society and an ideal which guides and constrains. What the piecemeal planner does differently, in that he does anything differently at all, is proceed along lines that are more cautious, more circumspect, more in terms of trial and error, and with democratic legitimacy. Popper's real intended distinction, then, should be between policy planning that has this democratic, i.e., tentative, character, and that which hasn't, which is to say, between planning that is *democratically mandated and executed, and that which is not*. In a strictly epistemological sense, however, what should be noted is that both forms of policy are *utopian*.

One further aspect of Popper's thought relevant to liberal views concerning utopianism and totalitarianism concerns his privileging of the binary dualism of "open/closed" as in his two-volume *The Open Society and Its Enemies* (1945). Although this is an important dimension for consideration, its relevance will have to await further analysis.[10] Again, however, I am confident that the argument

I am maintaining would hold valid: to the extent that Popper makes valid points, they relate to differences between the two systems as regards democracy (or its absence). Popper's (1992, p. 70) points on democracy are indeed insightful, especially his observation that as well as constituting "rule by the people", democracy must also be represented as a process by which individuals are protected against their leaders, and a mechanism by which their leaders can be replaced.[11] Yet it is *only* the presence or absence of democracy that makes a society "open" "closed" in a political sense. Beyond this, Popper's attempt to tie differences over democracy to fundamental philosophical and political outlooks simply reflects the Cold War politics of the time, as well as Popper's personal commitments to liberal politics and philosophy, and the resulting conflation of epistemological and ideological arguments entailed as a result.

4 Utopianism and the Totalitarian State

Utopianism, as liberals represent it, implies a positive conception of freedom and of the state's role in relation to freedom. This form of positive government was seen by liberals like Isaiah Berlin, as well as Hayek and Popper, as what essentially led towards totalitarianism. The classic liberal theory of totalitarianism sees it as a form of government that develops out of the structures of the positive state—that is, a state that decides to actively do things for its people, rather than maintain a laissez-faire stance. For liberals a positive conception of liberty leads the state to promote a single substantive ideal of the good—a description of man as a spiritual being whose ultimate rationality and reality are grounded in a unified spirit. This leads to a nation state which imposes a substantive conception of the good life, eradicating individuality by a concern with "normcentricity".

Positive freedom worries liberals. The positive view of freedom as active self-determination implies, says Berlin (1969), a distinction between two selves—a higher self that determines, and a lower self that is subject to determination. Berlin argues that in the history of political thought, it is all too easy for the higher self to become identified with the state or society, or with a particular political group's conception of what is "rational". Freedom then tends to become defined as obedience to what is rational, or obedience to the will of the state, or conformity to a predetermined pattern of thought or life. As a consequence, claims Berlin, positive freedom is transposed into the opposite of freedom: totalitarianism or tyranny.

In its extreme form, argues Nel Noddings (1996), it is claimed that the positive conception of liberty often leads to the promulgation of a single ideal—a description of "man" as a spiritual being whose ultimate rationality and reality are grounded in a unified spirit. In this model, the state is seen as the expression of collective will (positive freedom), rather than the (mere) protector of individual liberties (negative freedom).

The total community = fascism = the nation state. If the state is right, then there is no room for dissent, and liberty is equated with full immersion in the community. Liberals claim that individuality is wiped out by "normcentricity". In this way, Eric Hoffer maintained that communities foster "unity" and "self-sacrifice" along with conformity to established norms. In Hoffer's words:

> Unity and self-sacrifice, of themselves, even when fostered by the most noble means, produce a facility for hating. Even when men league themselves mightily together to promote tolerance and peace on earth, they are likely to be violently intolerant towards those not of like mind. (Hoffer, 1951, p. 92)

If one examines other major authoritative studies on totalitarianism from a liberal perspective, one is also struck by their ideological and polemical nature. J. L. Talmon's *The Origins of Totalitarian Democracy* is a case in point. Talmon argues that totalitarian forms based on messianism and utopianism emerged in the 18th century.

> Men were gripped by the idea that the conditions, a product of faith, time and custom, in which they and their forefathers had been living, were unnatural and had all to be replaced by deliberately planned uniform pattern, which would be natural and rational.

Essentially, Talmon's (1952) argument is that almost all philosophical systems that are not based on classical liberalism have political implications that lead towards totalitarianism. These were based on the idea that a sole exclusive truth in politics postulated a preordained, harmonious and perfect scheme of things, recognised the political as the only plane of existence, saw human beings as social and political constructions, saw freedom as the realisation or attainment of a collective purpose, conceived of an enlarged state which actively constructed the conditions for human development. Further, "empiricism is the ally of freedom, and the doctrinaire spirit is the friend of totalitarianism" (1952, p. 4). Centrally important is the idea "of a homogeneous society, in which men live upon one exclusive plane of existence" (1952, p. 4), a unitary principle of social existence which Talmon traces to Hegel, Rousseau, Hellvetius, Holbach, Morelly, Mably, Sieyes, the Jacobins, Babeuf, and Buonarroti. While liberals fell back upon the trial-and-error philosophy, totalitarian messianism hardened into an exclusive doctrine represented by a vanguard of the enlightened, who justified themselves in the use of coercion against those who refused to be free and virtuous (1952, p. 5).

William Montgomery McGovern (1946), in *From Luther to Hitler: The History of Fascist-Nazi Political Philosophy*, also identifies specifically non-liberal forms of thought as leading to *authoritarianism* and *etatism*. Amongst such thinkers or groups were Rousseau, the absolute idealists, Schlegel, Shelling, Hölderlin, and Hegel, the "subjective" idealists, Fichte and Kant, and Kant's idealistic British disciples, who were the "advance guard of the Fascist forces" (p. 133). Kant is seen "as the forerunner of the neo-absolutist tradition" as although he was a liberal in his own times, his views could be "twisted in such a way as to make them the foundation stone of *etatism* and authoritarianism". Specifically here, Kant's maxim concerning the supremacy of reason, and that for laws to be valid they must accord with rational principles, bolstered the authoritarian tradition for it countenanced the disregard of the concrete wishes and desires of every section of the community (p. 141). Similarly, Kant's argument concerning the supremacy of universal moral law, where all human conduct should be regulated by the categorical imperative, reinforced the political importance of the views of the "wise few" as being in a better position to judge over the wishes of the individual (p. 142). Following Rousseau, Kant argued that the state is a positive good and should represent the "general good" of the whole society, and his views thus break with the individualism of the old order.

Ralf Dahrendorf maintains what is philosophically a similar thesis in his book *Society and Democracy in Germany* (1967). In asking, "How was National Socialism possible?", he looks to the contrast between "Germany and the West", as reflected in the different intellectual value systems. By the West, Dahrendorf (1967, p. 11) means "a set of values ... certain valued attitudes and patterns of social life". Western values emphasise tolerance, imperfection, trial and error, neutrality, openness, plurality, an experimental and empirical approach to research, and that certain philosophical principles have a propensity to absoluteness. Amongst these latter are "utopian constructions" (p. 139) which "use techniques designed to suppress conflict" (p. 140) and as "conflict is liberty" this amounts to a "suppression of liberty". In addition, the German idea of truth postulates a "non-experimental conception of science", which while it stresses "inner freedom" does not require "political freedom". Rather than deal with propositions individualistically, it consistently reaches for what amounts to an elite theory of truth:

> [F]or the imaginary whole ... James B. Conant has a point when he remarks that in Germany people refer "with enthusiasm to the 'total image', the 'great order', the 'great overview', to what is 'universally valid',

and they feel a certain disquiet about the confusing and somewhat disorderly diversity and ambiguity of things and events". (1967, p. 151; citing Conant, 1957, p. 8)

In addition, the German people glorified the state as a unified and substantial will which suppressed all opposition. This was essentially Hegel's conception in *The Philosophy of Right* of 1821, where morality trumps liberty in Hegel's scheme. As Hegel writes (1942, p. 257):

> The State is the reality of the moral idea—the moral spirit as the revealed will, apparent to itself, substantial, which thinks and knows itself and accomplishes that which it knows and in so far as it knows it.

This view of the state was the logical derivation from "absolute idealism" which Hegel and the absolute idealists drew from the monism of Spinoza, the rationalism of Plato, and the vital materialism of Leibniz. In such a conception the universe was conceptualised as a single reality, as an organic whole, where the whole determines the identity of its parts, and each part also determines the identity of the whole (Beiser, 2002, pp. 355–357).

5 The Poverty of the Liberal Critique of Totalitarianism

Certainly we can agree with liberals that an overly unified state or too great an emphasis on consensus would pose a threat to the freedom of individuals, if such principles became effective at the level of actual politics. Beyond this, however, I believe their account of totalitarianism is weak and their arguments falter on a number of grounds.

Firstly, it is neither logically nor empirically entailed that a state that acts positively in terms of a specific substantive conception of the good, must ignore a respect for diversity and difference, or fail to respect the plurality of groups and subgroups in the wider society, or not be accountable in the last instance to the individuals who constitute it. To claim that the ideal of community is inextricably tied to an inexorable quest for unity or totality is a deeply mistaken premise. As postmodernists and pragmatists like John Dewey, and more recently Michael Sandel, have suggested, the good can accommodate difference. To suggest, therefore, that any state that does not confine itself to the minimum protection of individual liberties, but acts in terms of a general substantive vision, even if conceived in sophisticated terms, will unleash a pressure towards "unity" or "normcentricity" is a flawed argument, for it assumes that a theory of the good cannot exist at an abstract enough level to accommodate diversity or pluralism.

Secondly, the liberal theory of totalitarianism depends on presumptions that liberalism constitutes a neutral agenda where freedom is defined as the natural property of individuals outside of society. Based on this argument, writers like Berlin (1969) maintain that liberalism advocates no substantive conception of the good. The identification of a good is impossible, in Berlin's view, as individuals manifest such diversity of opinion over the nature of the good. Because of this irreducible pluralism over values and preferences, and consequent incompatibility over versions of the good, individual freedom is all that remains. It is only as a consequence of this axiom that that the state can be represented as the *enemy*, rather than the *precondition*, of freedom.

Notwithstanding Berlin's view, it can be claimed that liberalism itself implies a substantive conception of the good, and, in this sense, utopian conceptions of the ideal society are also embedded in liberal social relations. This is something which Hayek and Popper, operating within the epistemology of empiricism, believing that they operate from a neutral world where facts are neatly differentiated from values, never contemplated. The argument by liberals that within its policy prescriptions liberalism does not invoke a particular preferred shape to society, or that it does not advocate the establishment of a social good over and above what individuals desire cannot rule out substantive commitments about what society should be like. The point is made in one way by Luke Martell (1992, p. 156), who states:

> It all sounds very nice until you realise that what it does, in effect, is to let in just another particular substantive vision of society as consisting of the sum total of individuals' preferences over which individuals have no overall control. In this sense, liberalism is in fact a highly substantive doctrine—one which posits a competitive individualist society immune to overall democratic direction.

Developing this line of thinking further, the neoliberal organisation of society implies an *ideal* about the form of a best possible future which is nestled in the present relations of actually existing societies. Such an ideal can be discerned in the statements and visions of powerful world leaders and dominant global institutions such as the World Trade Organization, the World Bank, or the International Monetary Fund in support of a model of international structural adjustment and policies of free trade.

Thirdly, the liberals' arguments technically rule out even more moderate forms of state regulation. For Hayek, as welfare rights are "positive" rights, the welfare state is the start of the "slippery slope", leading down "the road to serfdom". In his account Montgomery McGovern (1946) identifies moderate liberals such as Kant, and the "British idealists" (Green, Hobhouse and Bosanquet) as contributing to totalitarianism. What is argued, in fact, is the proposition that almost any philosophical system other than pure classical liberalism results in *etatism* and *authoritarianism*. Hence, Green harbours "germs of authoritarianism" (in spite of his strong support throughout his life for democratic control and the parliamentary system of government). Kant also supports authoritarian politics (in spite of his standing as one of the founders of liberal philosophy). In addition, Talmon identifies Mably with arguments for state regulation in defence of the poor and of "state control and interference with trade" (1952, p. 61) (especially in control of corn trade) as contributing to *causing* totalitarianism. Instead of the "postulate of liberty [suggesting] the release of spontaneity, ... we are faced with the idea of the State acting as the chief regulator ... with the purpose of enforcing ascetic austerity" (p. 62). There is a preoccupation with the general interest and the general good. It seems that for Talmon anything outside of pure classical liberal orthodoxy produces totalitarianism, including moderate forms of social democracy.

A further important point looms here as regards to the context and period in terms of which these liberals wrote, and which perhaps helps us understand liberal writers' views. As Steven Heyman (1992, pp. 81–82) claims with respect to Berlin's (1969) analysis of liberty, what is striking about it is the way it is distorted by the political circumstances in which the essay was written:

> Berlin was writing in the late 1950s, at the height of the Cold War. He casts the debate between negative and positive liberty as a crucial battle in "the open war that is being fought between two systems of ideas", and between the political systems allegedly based on them—Western liberal democracy and totalitarian regimes of the left and right. ... With the passing of the Cold War, it may be easier to understand the relationship between positive and negative liberty in our political tradition.

Although we must applaud classical and neoliberals for being against totalitarianism, their specific theoretical analysis as to *what causes* totalitarianism became mixed in with both "left–right" politics and analysis of the role of the state in general, and "Cold War" politics, in particular. Although Heyman discusses this contention with specific regards to Berlin, I would claim the thesis is generally applicable to many others, *to varying extents*, including Hayek, Popper, Plamenatz, Talmon, Dahrendorf, and Montgomery McGovern, to name but a few. What liberals fail to notice is the way it manifests its own form of unitarism centring on reason, truth and liberal ideas. The way Popper,

Hayek, Talmon, Montgomery McGovern and Dahrendorf reject *all philosophical alternatives* to classical liberalism, as leading to totalitarianism, reveals its own peculiar unitarist mantle.

With the passing of the Cold War, it can be more easily seen that liberal explanations as to the origins of totalitarianism are misleading. To the extent that there are dangers inherent in human societies, such dangers inhere in all sorts of society, and it is difficult to identify such dangers as belonging specifically to a particular form and organisation of the state, in promoting the conditions for positive or negative freedom. While we can readily agree that too great an emphasis on normcentricity constitutes a potential threat to democracy, such dangers are present in both Western and Eastern societies. Any adequate explanation for the origins of totalitarianism must take adequate account of the *historical, political, cultural and economic specificity of particular states at particular locations in history*. What produces totalitarianism is not a particular gearing of state power (such as "positive" or "negative", or even "holist", or "piecemeal" engineering, in Popper's sense), but quite simply, the *absence of democracy*, or of the *conditions* which enable democracy to flourish. On this criteria, the Marxist–Leninist regimes of Eastern Europe failed in that they lacked a strong or deep conception of democracy, as well as the range of specific *mechanisms* by which democracy operates. As democracy is a structural arrangement, with specific techniques and mechanisms and processes that can be analysed, the best way to safeguard against totalitarianism is by ensuring that the state is a *democratic* state, and by seeking to *deepen* the specific senses in terms of which democracy operates.

This, I believe, is a far better explanation of totalitarianism than that which is provided in liberal criticisms which fail to sufficiently stress the processes through which mechanisms of democracy are institutionalised, in preference for explanations which stress the importance of philosophical and intellectual ideas as causative factors. While a neglect of democratic ideas and theory may of course impact upon the culture, the actual extent to which particular philosophers' views can be held to be *causative forces* is problematic. An overemphasis on "normcentricity" or "consensus" may certainly unleash dangerous political forces, but whether they do so in a specific country where such philosophical views are developed, or whether at times they have not operated in liberal cultures, is a moot point, and one that could prompt serious debate. For Talmon, however, it is taken for granted that such philosophical systems will *cause* totalitarianism. In his view (1952, p. 11), political messianism and totalitarianism constitute a:

> state of mind, a way of feeling, a pattern of mental, emotional and behaviouristic elements, best compared to a set of attitudes engendered by a

religion. Whatever may be said about the significance of the economic or other factors in the shaping of beliefs, it can hardly be denied that the all-embracing attitudes of this kind, once crystallized, are the real substance of history.

This, needless to say, advances a highly contentious view, and places an overemphasis on intellectual ideas as influencing the culture, which in turn influence the politics. Such factors as institutional mechanisms, the existence of checks and balances, and the actual way that power is distributed in societies, would seem to me to be somewhat neglected in these accounts. This introduces yet a further weakness of liberal explanations for totalitarianism. In that their explanations attribute a failure of democracy to the way the state acts, the arguments are couched in terms of *a general timeless theoretical argument*, rather than as a specific empirical analysis of *particular* societies in *particular* historical circumstances. In this sense, the identification of particular non-liberal philosophical viewpoints is meant to *explain* totalitarianism in *all countries and at all times*, no matter how different in terms of history and tradition. It is also not asked whether such political philosophies are compatible with democracy, or whether in fact better models of democracy could not be constructed in their light.[12] Such general philosophical broadsides are no substitute for a detailed historical analysis as to why discourses of democracy did not take root, or prevent abuses of power, in a number of different countries, in the first half of the 20th century.[13]

6   Foucault and Totality

The idea of a uniform and totalistic society, consistently challenged by liberals, was also opposed by Foucault. In opposition to totalising approaches, Foucault draws a methodological distinction between total and general history giving his allegiance to the latter. The central differences between the approaches are:

> The project of total history is one that seeks to reconstitute the overall form of a civilization, the principle—material or spiritual—of a society, the significance common to all the phenomenon of a period, the law that accounts for their cohesion ... [G]eneral history on the contrary, would deploy the space of dispersion. ... [I]t speaks of series, divisions, limits, differences of level, shifts, chronological specificities, particular forms of rehandling, possible types of relation. ... The problem which defines the task of general history is to determine what form of relation may be

legitimately described between these different series. (Foucault, 1972, pp. 9–10)

In terms of political relations and utopian theorising, Foucault's (1991, p. 18) opposition to "totality" can be seen expressed in his opposition to Habermas's modernist and liberal conception of truth and reason. As Foucault states:

> [In Habermas's work] there is always something which causes me a problem. It is when he assigns a very important place to relations of communication and also to functions that I would call *"utopian"*. The thought that there could be a state of communication which would be such that the games of truth could circulate freely, without obstacles, without constraint, and without coercive effects, seems to me to be Utopia. It is being blind to the fact that relations of power are not something bad in themselves, from which one must free oneself. I don't believe there can be a society without relations of power. ... The problem is not of trying to dissolve them in the utopia of a perfectly transparent communication, but to give oneself the rules of law, the techniques of management, and also the ethics, the ethos, the practice of self, which would allow these games of power to be played with a minimum of domination. (Emphasis added)

For Foucault, such a modernist view of reason is itself utopian. In his view, the political is not equated with the rational as a unified consensual form, for such a form ignores power, conflict and diversity. Essentially, Habermas's view ignores the reality of diversity and conflict in preference for what is a new rationalist conception of utopia. As with Plato or Hegel, Habermas, in asserting the intersubjective and procedurally pure nature of rationality, fails to acknowledge the realities of power and conflict. Whereas for Habermas, consistent with liberalism generally, the 'strategic' and 'communicative' dimensions of language-use can be kept separate, thus assuring the veracity of reason and truth, for Foucault, truth and power are practically inseparable, and circulate together. Hence, in Foucault's view, any consensus reached is not necessarily the outcome of a purely rational process, but rather represents a functionally expedient and provisional political settlement.

Apart from charging liberalism with adhering to a conception of reason that is itself utopian, many of Foucault's other arguments have a surface similarity to the liberals. For Foucault, the opposition to Marxism and Hegelianism is in terms of the closed and unitary notion of "totality", which seeks to explain the individual instances of a culture as decodable parts of the whole totality or system. This was the approach of Hegel, as well as Marx, which seeks to analyse history and society as totalities, where the parts are an expression of the whole—hence the notion of an expressive totality. For both Hegel and Marx, also, the political project was one that sought to restore a vision of a lost unity. It is also the approach of Rousseau, where the ideal of community expresses a longing for harmony among persons. Foucault characterises such an approach in one article as representing "the Rousseauist dream" of:

> [a] transparent society, visible and legible in each of its parts, the dream of there no longer existing any zones of darkness, zones established by the privileges of royal power or the prerogative of some corporation, zones of disorder. It was the dream that each individual, whatever position he occupied, might be able to see the whole of society, that men's hearts should communicate, their vision be unobstructed by obstacles, and that the opinion of all reign over each. (Foucault, 1980, p. 152)

In *The Archaeology of Knowledge* (1972, p. 114), Foucault explains this critique of unitarism, which he sees as having implications for totalitarianism, as being a "central theme". His concern was to uncouple the linkage that existed within systems of thought such as Hegelianism, as has preoccupied writers in both the liberal and continental traditions of thought, between metaphysical holism and terror. By so doing, Foucault attempts to salvage a pluralist political approach premised upon a holist onto-epistemology and a conception of the historical and social constitution of subjects, both as individuals and as collectivities. In this, Foucault's historical–critical approach is an experimental one. It rejects "radical and global" forms of analysis based upon an aspiration to restore a perfect, unified future, as:

> we know from experience that the claims to escape from the system of contemporary reality so as to produce the overall programs of another society, of another way of thinking, another culture, another vision of the world, has led only to the return of the most dangerous traditions. (Foucault, 1984b, p. 46)

Rather than seek to explain all phenomena in relation to a single centre, Foucault is interested rather to advance a polymorphous conception of determination in order to reveal the play of dependencies in the social and historical process. Hence, in opposition to the themes of totalising history, Foucault substitutes what he calls a "differentiated analysis":

> Nothing, you see, is more foreign to me than the quest for a sovereign, unique and constraining form. I do not seek to detect, starting from

diverse signs, the unitary spirit of an epoch, the general form of its consciousness: something like a Weltanschauung. Nor have I described either the emergence and eclipse of formal structure which might reign for a time over all the manifestations of thought: I have not written the history of a syncopated transcendental. Nor, finally, have I described thoughts or century-old sensitivities coming to life, stuttering, struggling and dying out like great phantoms—ghosts playing out their shadow theatre against the backdrop of history. I have studied, one after another, ensembles of discourse; I have characterised them; I have defined the play of rules, of transformations, of thresholds, of remanences. I have established and I have described their clusters of relations. Whenever I have deemed it necessary I have allowed systems to proliferate. (Foucault, 1978, p. 10)

While this entails an important theoretical point in reference to Foucault's rejection of theories of totality, as long as the qualifications posited above are kept in mind, Foucault accepts that a consensus model can operate in politics as a form of "critical principle". The issue was put to him put to him in 1983 by a group of interviewers, including Paul Rabinow, Charles Taylor, Martin Jay, Richard Rorty, and Leo Lowenthal:

Q. If one can assume that the consensus model is a fictional possibility, people might nonetheless act according to that fiction in such a way that the results might be superior to the action that would ensue from the bleaker view of politics as essentially domination and repression, so that although in an empirical way you may be correct and although the utopian possibility may never be achievable, nonetheless, pragmatically, it might in some sense be better, healthier, freer, whatever positive value one uses, if we assume that the consensus is a goal still to be sought rather than one that we simply throw away and say it's impossible to achieve.

M. F. Yes, I think that is, let us say, a critical principle ...

Q. As a regulatory principle?

M. F. I perhaps wouldn't say regulatory principle, that's going too far, because starting from the point where you say regulatory principle, you grant that it is indeed under its governance that the phenomenon has to be organised, within limits that may be defined by experience or the context. I would say, rather, that it is perhaps a critical idea to maintain at all times: to ask oneself what proportion of nonconsensuality is implied in such a power relation, and whether that degree of nonconsensuality is necessary or not, and then one may question every power relation to that extent. The farthest I would go is to say that perhaps one must not be for consensuality, but one must be against nonconsensuality. (Foucault, 1984a, p. 379)

Foucault's pluralism shows that it is in fact not necessary to dispense with a conception of the good so long as it is complexly mediated and democratically structured to allow respect for difference. The good as conceptualised in Greek ethics saw virtue as an ultimate end, or objective form, as "that to which reason apprehends", as "the agent's interest well understood" (Larmore, 1996, p. 21). This was both an essentialist and teleological conception. The good must be represented constructively rather than teleologically, however, more in the sense of Martha Nussbaum's (1995, p. 457) "thick, vague conception", which can be construed to represent the real needs and requirements of humans, such as the need to eat, the need for emotional sustenance, the need for shelter, and so on.[14] While these have certain effects on individuals which constrain their wishes and desires, and their ethical choices, they are not incompatible with diversity or difference. While people have needs for food and shelter, they will satisfy these in countless different ways, although there will also be certain common principles that all must respect, such as the principle of non-interference. Such a conception is not incompatible with democracy, however, and Foucault's (1991) working assumption of the equalisation of power relations[15] as the principle by which "self-creation" (Foucault, 1986) and *parrhēsia* (Foucault, 2001) are made possible gives pride of place to democracy as rule by which order and freedom are able to operate.

7   Reconceptualising Utopianism Post-9/11

While liberal strictures regarding too great an emphasis on consensus may well be heeded, it would seem to me that there is no *necessary connection* between such utopian models and totalitarian politics. Utopia need not be equated with unity, or with perfection. In this, it need not be defined as liberal philosophers defined it but, rather, it can be conceptualised to represent merely a model of how society ought best be structured for the good of all. This, it might be argued, is especially so in a global world where forms of philosophical monism centring on the nation are no longer so probable. Indeed, utopian models need not be undemocratic; neither must they be based on forms of philosophical monism, or absolute idealism. What is clear from examining liberal criticisms is that they are concerned not with utopias in general, but only with a specific type of utopianism—a form that emerged first in the Renaissance and became justified in the late 18th century in terms of philosophical monism and absolute idealism. Rather than point to the substantive content of political philosophies that contributed to totalitarianism, what is more relevant today in accounting for authoritarian political relations is that lack of theoretical work on democracy and the absence of democratic mechanisms and processes in the institutional structures of societies. What causes totalitarianism, to put it bluntly, is simply *an absence of democracy*. An absence, firstly, at the level of institutionalisation, and, secondly, at the level of theoretical and intellectual production.

In my view, given the changing concerns relating to security and freedom in the world post-9/11, utopian models offer a unique methodological vehicle for redesigning the balance between individual freedom and the needs of community. Accepting the argument that there is an "ideal" or "utopian" element to all thought, utopian models offer us a bulwark against totalitarianism in that they enable values such as freedom, equality, justice and security to be retheorised in the context of an "imagined" community rather than considered atomistically as a series of analytical relations. Although totalitarian or authoritarian politics is an ever-present danger and has taken various monstrous forms in the last 100 years, the view I want to suggest is that outside of the "Cold War" frame of reference, we must consider the power distortions that generate totalitarian rule to constitute a potential danger in all types of societies. Whether it is the bold action of a particular state governor, or private company, or of national leaders who illegally commit their countries to war (as in the war on Iraq, for example), the undemocratic misuse of power, which takes various forms, is an ever-present danger in all societies. As Foucault (1994, pp. 535–536) has observed, for instance:

> Of course fascism and Stalinism expanded their effects to hitherto unknown dimensions, and it is, if not to be rationally expected, at least to be hoped, that we never see their like again. They are therefore unique phenomena, but it cannot be denied that, in many respects, fascism and Stalinism simply extended a whole series of mechanisms that already existed in the social and political systems of the West. After all, the organization of great parties, the development of political apparatuses, and the existence of techniques of repression such as labor camps, all that is quite clearly the heritage of liberal Western societies, and all Stalinism and fascism had to do was to stoop down and pick it up.

In order to combat such forces, both the monstrous forms of fascism and Stalinism, as well as all other less serious abuses of political power, the best answer, in my view, must be sought in the strengthening or *deepening of democracy*, both nationally and globally, and envisaging *new forms of democracy* as a means of achieving this.

In this process, utopian modelling can be more useful than liberal philosophising. As Kenneth Keniston (1970, p. 300) says, the poverty of liberalism is that it constitutes a "privatization of utopia". Further (1970, p. 301):

> The deflection of the Utopian Spirit ... leads to a withdrawal of idealism from the areas of our shared lives that most need a Utopian vision.

As a consequence liberalism cannot constitute grounds for guiding political action in a global age. Freed from the spell of illusion and dreams they fall prey to political paralysis and nihilism. In Spragens's (1981, p. 5) view there has been an "incapacity of liberalism's deepest assumptions—ontological, epistemological and anthropological—to sustain its finest aspirations and ideals". The upshot of all of its theorising on the subject is an opposition to any form of positive or regulatory state at all. Any form of regulation in the interests of equality or justice is cast down the slippery slope to serfdom, rejected in relation to the bogey of totalitarianism.

Central to its own "repressed" utopian vision is the individualism of its epistemology, its ideal of a single language and a unified vision for all the sciences, the rationalism of its philosophical approach, distinct limits on the role of theory and imagination, its commitment to the uncritical pursuit of a narrowly conceived freedom, an image of man that is too rationalistic, as well as a peculiar form of social amnesia, which cuts people off from both past and community. Both Descartes and Locke warrant a reliable foundation for knowledge of "clear and distinct" ideas to be taken as "self-evident" truth. Although Descartes saw the *Cogito*, and Locke *experience*, as the starting point, in both cases direct simple ideas constituted the atomic components of reliable knowledge in thoroughly individualistic terms. Yet such an epistemology gave rise to a new philosophical dualism of its own. It was now divided into "us vs. them", "reliable concrete knowledge vs. ideology", "practice vs. theory", "individual vs. community". As Spragens (1981, p. 45) puts it:

> We might characterise this dominant paradigm ... as epistemological manicheanism. In its relation to the human understanding the world was divided into two. On the one side lay the kingdom of light, the land of the intelligible. In it, all was transparent and comprehensive with certitude. On the other side lay the kingdom of darkness, the land of the unintelligible. In it all was impenetrable to the best efforts of the human mind.

In the 17th century such views could also be seen as progressive and utopian. In this sense they were related to politics, for they believed, says Spragens (1981, p. 48), that the "triumph of reason would lead to the relief of man's estate. Like Plato, the adherents of the new rationalism offered their knowledge as a crucial resource for political regeneration". As Spragens (1981, p. 57) continues:

> The political benefits from the new epistemology were expected to be direct as well as indirect. The spread of enlightenment, it was hoped, would produce some crucially important, specifically political dividends. The miscarriages of politics had been caused by distortions in man's beliefs about himself and the world.

Although liberalism thus provided a convenient epistemology for the development and spread of science over several centuries, the contradictions between its ontological and epistemological principles, on the one hand, and its aspirations, on the other, were to become progressively apparent. In a global era, its failure to be able to theorise or accommodate the collective dimensions of life becomes a major weakness. In relation to politics, as Spragens (1981, p. 7) tells us, liberals naively conceptualise power "sustained by the happy faith that the hand of nature could produce an optimum social equilibrium". In a similar way liberals are too frequently naive concerning the political implications of economic forces. The conception of the role of the state they are left supporting, as the only one that is safe in terms of democracy, is a minimal form of laissez-faire. Stuck within an individualist ontology, they are unable to account for, or accommodate, the collective dimensions of life. The conception of democracy that they advocate is a purely formal one, one that is compatible with individualistically conceived liberty, which avoids questions concerning the sharing of resources or the benefits of the world's wealth. In such a model, as Spragens (1981, p. 10) says, "liberal premises are a stumbling block to liberal aspirations". Such a model, although *formally* democratic, as represented by contemporary liberal and conservative theorising, is not *deeply* democratic. In addition, it allows inequalities to develop unchecked, and as we enter the 21st century it becomes increasingly dominated by powerful and pervasive transnational interests. Such a world, post-9/11, confronts the erosion of traditional liberal values such as privacy and freedom, as it becomes preoccupied with the new "imperatives" of security. And it becomes culturally and environmentally unsustainable, and personally unrewarding. In this context structures of the social and the public sphere become more deeply privatised.

It is no coincidence that in this context utopian theorising has once again assumed popularity. Given the widespread "nihilism of our times", as Judith Green (1999, p. VII) argues, there is a need to deepen our understanding of democracy, moving beyond liberal fears. Utopian models, while they may harbour dangers, may also enable us to understand how a deeper conception of democracy might be possible. As I have written elsewhere (Olssen et al., 2004), what is necessary today is to understand democracy as a *comprehensive discourse* premised upon a reconstructed public sphere. Such a conception is in keeping with Dewey's sentiment, as Green (1999, p. IX) expresses it, that "the cure for the ailments of democracy is *more democracy*". Democracy as conceptualised in such a model is not simply a justification, but a *transformative ideal* that can always be improved, or deepened still further (Green, 1999, p. X). In my own account, democracy as a comprehensive discourse includes: (1) *safety and security*; (2) *freedom and autonomy*; (3) *inclusion and participation*; (4) *fairness and justice*; and (5) *equality of resources and capabilities*.

Safety and security express themselves in children's telephone helplines, women's refuges, or human rights accords for the treatment of ordinary citizens, or prisoners, and so on. *Inclusion* warrants that no one is excluded from democratic entitlement and constitutes the basis on which safety and security can be assured in the development of a reconstructed public sphere. *Freedom* incorporates freedom *from* domination and freedom *for* the development of capabilities. *Justice and fairness* promise treatment in a public arena according to publicly stated criteria embodied in constitutional laws and rules. *Equality* of resources and capabilities ensures opportunities and conditions for development for all. In that treating people fairly and reasonably on the basis of respect minimises terrorism and increases the chances for survival, democratic justice based on an equalisation of power and non-domination becomes an objective good. It is in the interests of both the individual and the collectivity. In an age of terrorism, where a global *Leviathan* is clearly an unsavoury possibility, *a comprehensive discourse of democracy becomes the best answer to the Hobbesian problem of order.*

Such a conception requires institutions committed to conflict resolution, ongoing debate and communication, as well as the mutual survival of different traditions. Such a democratic conception is not utilitarian but presupposes rights and entitlements which are universally given to all. Rights in this conception are not natural but are given by the state as the collective expression of the will of the people. Such rights are necessary to self-creation and constitute recognition that a space of autonomy is necessary to self-development of both individuals and groups. The events of 9/11 may hopefully reintroduce a concern for rights, and other themes within liberal constitutionalism, as fundamental to the emancipatory and progressive concerns of a genuinely democratic world order. Such a conception of democracy also underpins multicultural rights by recognising different group aspirations yet underpinning them with a rights culture. Unlike liberal conceptions of democracy, it is not insensitive to diversity and does not seek cultural homogeneity through the uniform application of a single standard or rule.

8   Conclusion

If post-9/11 makes democracy of more pressing concern; a concern with utopian modelling as a way of deepening democracy can move well beyond a narrow formal theory of liberal and conservative theory. If at the level of theory, our conception of democracy posits certain general principles, which allow for a degree of diversity and pluralism, our procedural view of democracy is as a multifaceted array of mechanisms and processes instituted to ensure the *inclusion, security* or *safety* as well as *development* and *opportunities* of all individuals and groups. In this respect research on utopia needs to focus of the means of *deepening* democracy to satisfy these goals. As a way of concluding this article, it might look to include research on all or any of the following themes:
– *The concern with equality*: the development of any conception of democratic justice must seek to deal with rather than avoid issues to do with distribution of resources and life chances. Given a rejection of the classical liberal fiction regarding entitlement to property based on a model of pre-social, possessive individuals who "owe nothing to society", it is important to theorise the implications of a social ontological framework of community for considerations of democratic justice as it pertains to distributional ethics. Community in this sense is definable as an all-encompassing arena without fixed borders or unity, which comprises an assortment of values, norms and institutions that enable life to be lived. Such a conception of community recognises social ties and shared values, as well as practices of voluntary action and public institutions like education which constitute the conditions for stability and reproduction of society. Although neoliberal philosophers like Nozick (1975) have shifted political philosophy away from a concern with issues of distributive justice in recent years, my own view is similar to the 19th-century social democrat L. T. Hobhouse (1911), who held that one's entitlement to rewards and gain must be balanced by one's obligation to society. What liberal conceptions of democracy obscured, in Hobhouse's view, was the interdependence between individuals and the social structure or for the social and moral obligation of the society (acting through the vehicle of the

state) to assist in arranging the social futures of each rising generation. As he argued in his book *Liberalism* (1911, pp. 189–190), in his justification for redistributive policies of progressive taxation, the state has an obligation to enforce reasonable conditions of equality on the basis that while a society should provide the conditions for enterprise, all individuals are correspondingly indebted to society for the conditions and structures provided, and, on this basis, individuals should contribute in direct proportion to the luck or good fortune they experience.

- *The role of the state*: The role of the state should be concerned with guaranteeing both negative freedom and positive freedom. Negative freedom involves the state's responsibility for ensuring the universal entitlements to safety and reasonable autonomy for all. The trade-off in respect to privacy will be necessitated to the extent that these obligations are threatened. To the extent that greater surveillance is deemed necessary, the proposals must be themselves subject to democratic processes that ensure visibility, openness, deliberation and debate. The state's obligations as regards positive freedom involve it in developing opportunities based on people's rights to inclusion and the development of their capacities. This obligation gives the state a role in the provision of social services, healthcare, and education. In brief, the role for the positively geared state lies in relation to socially directed investment decisions, to provide for the general conditions for all species' needs and development, including education and training, and to create and maintain quality infrastructure such as schools, hospitals, parks and public spaces.

- *The development of civil society*: a vibrant civil society can constitute a check on the powers of government. Civil society refers to that sector of private associations relatively autonomous from the state and economy, which spring from the everyday lives and activities of communities of interest. Clearly, one principle of democracy is the idea of multiple centres of power, and of their separation, as suggested by writers like Montesquieu and de Tocqueville. More recently, it can be gleaned from Foucault's work that democracy consists in an "equalisation" of power relations. Another principle of democracy is the right to contest, challenge or oppose. Institutions of civil society, as writers like Paul Hirst (1995) have maintained, can be seen to constitute an important powerful network of quasi-independent associations, which can strengthen democratic rule through checking the power of the state. If democracy is rule by the people, the ability, and opportunity to contest power, as Philip Pettit (1997) has put it, or of *parrhēsia*, or speaking the truth to power, as Michel Foucault (2001) has put it, is itself one of democracy's crucial rights, indeed its very condition. According to Cohen and Arato (1992), civil society strengthens democracy in both a defensive and offensive sense. The defensive aspect refers to the way that associations and social movements develop forms of communicative interaction that support the development of people's identities, expand participatory possibilities and create networks of solidarity. The offensive aspect refers to how associational networks and institutions come to exert influence on, and constitute checks to, the state, and to each other.

- *The role of education*: the role of education is crucial for democracy, as educational institutions, whether compulsory or post-compulsory, intersect with, and therefore mediate between, institutions like the family and those of the state and the economy. Although formal institutions of education have been in the main public institutions, there is an important sense in which they are semi-autonomous from the state. This is not the neoliberal sense, where management and administration are devolved to the local school, but the sense in which the schools are located in, and represent local community groups. In this sense, schools are important as democratic organisations, through the particular way that they are connected to communities, through their ability to empower families, and involve minority groups in participatory projects. Education is also crucial as the central agency responsible for the production of democratic norms such as trust and political decision making. This is to say, as Mill (1910) recognised in *Representative Government*, educational institutions are important as sites where democracy and self-government are learned. Deliberative democracy is especially complex, for it involves not just norms and procedures of debate but norms and procedures of contestation, inclusiveness, tolerance, compromise, solidarity with others, generosity, care, the operations of forums, and of checks and balances, the use of sanctions and screens, and the separation of powers. In the republican tradition, schools are instrumental in the development of civic virtue and habits of good citizenship. This is what signals the real importance of the "knowledge economy". For education is essentially important in its role of constructing democratic civic norms, and this must become one of the central aims of government policy in this regard. It is not a case of "brainwashing" or "socialisation" but of teaching skills and establishing models of civic conduct based on tolerance, deliberation, conflict resolution, give and take, and trust. While educational processes depend upon fairness of political processes, and in the distribution of economic resources, education is necessary to construct the network of norms that permit both the market and democracy to function. As Philip Pettit (1997, p. 255) puts it, education represents a "stark choice between the invisible hand and the iron hand: between a strategy of marketing and a strategy of management". It is this reason of course why education should ideally be *public, universal, compulsory* and *free*. For if education is vital in constructing norms that nurture the market, it cannot be itself subject to the market's disorganising effects.

Acknowledgement

This chapter originally appeared as Olssen, M. (2003), Totalitarianism and the "repressed" utopia of the present: Moving beyond Hayek, Popper and Foucault, *Policy Futures in Education*, *1*(3), 526–552, https://doi.org/10.2304/pfie.2003.1.3.6. Reprinted here, with minor edits, with permission from the publisher.

Notes

1 Thomas More, *Utopia* (1516).
2 Johan Eberlin von Günzburg, *Wolfaria* (1521).
3 Anton Francesco Doni, *Il mondo savio e pazzo* (1552).
4 Tommaso Campanella, *La città del sole* (1602).
5 Johann Valentin Andreae, *Christianopolis* (1619).
6 Robert Burton, *A Utopia of Mine Own* (1621).
7 Francis Bacon, *New Atlantis* (1624).
8 See, for instance, Gray (1984), Hindess (1990), Tomlinson (1990).
9 Hayek's argument against early communist regimes which sought to replace markets with state planning are indeed valid, but accepting this argument, which was relevant only at the time Hayek wrote, does not logically or empirically coerce a view that planning in all forms should be (or indeed could be) done away with.
10 Such an analysis would take substantial space, and would be beyond the scope of an article such as this.
11 My own conception of democracy, introduced below, extends this insight, except I will represent it as a comprehensive discourse which protects all, not just against leaders, but against all, through the rule of law. It is therefore a discourse which ensures rights, entitlements, security and freedom.
12 Most of the philosophical viewpoints criticised by liberals, e.g., Rousseau's, were, *in their own terms*, specifically democratic formulations, intended to address problems or weaknesses within existing philosophical theories. The liberal critique is, in this sense, directed against the *effects* that liberals interpret these theories to have, rather than to deliberate arguments against democracy by the philosophers concerned. Of course, some (e.g., Plato) did maintain antidemocratic views.
13 In nearly all liberal philosophical accounts there is no mention of local factors specific to the countries involved, or to the rise of such discourses as eugenics throughout the Western world.
14 Her list also comprises such things as the requirements of practical reason and cognitive development. Nussbaum's conception is perfectionist in that it specifies an objective con-

ception of the good, which comprises the core human capabilities consisting of "the most important functions of human beings in terms of which human life is defined" (1995, p. 457). Such a conception is not metaphysical in that it does not claim to derive from a source exterior to human beings in history. Rather, she says (1995, p. 457), it is "as universal as possible" and aims at "mapping out the general shape of the human form of life, those features which constitute life as human wherever it is".

15 In his interview "The Ethic of Care for the Self as a Practice of Freedom", Foucault (1991) suggests that liberty and ethics are not possible where domination strategies are fixed and oppressive (p. 3), and that the ideal situation for self-creation is where "games of power can be played with a minimum of domination" (p. 18). I have interpreted and argued that this supports a broad normative principle of "the equalisation of power relations", which can be extracted from Foucault's analysis (see Olssen, 2002).

References

Beiser, F. C. (2002). *German idealism: The struggle against subjectivism, 1781–1801*. Harvard University Press.

Berlin, I. (1969). *Four essays on liberty*. Oxford University Press.

Cohen, J. L., & Arato, A. (1992). *Civil society and political theory*. MIT Press.

Dahrendorf, R. (1967). *Society and democracy in Germany*. Doubleday and Co.

Eliav-Feldon, M. (1982). *Realistic utopias: The ideal imaginary societies of the Renaissance 1516–1630*. Clarendon Press.

Foucault, M. (1972). *The archaeology of knowledge*. Tavistock.

Foucault, M. (1978). Politics and the study of discourse (C. Gordon, Trans.). *Ideology and Consciousness, 3*, 7–26.

Foucault, M. (1980). The eye of power (C. Gordon, Trans.). In C. Gordon (Ed.), *Power/knowledge: Selected interviews and other writings 1972–1977* (pp. 146–166). Harvester Press.

Foucault, M. (1984a). Politics and ethics: An interview (C. Porter, Trans.). In P. Rabinow (Ed.), *The Foucault reader* (pp. 373–380). Pantheon.

Foucault, M. (1984b). What is enlightenment? (C. Porter, Trans.). In P. Rabinow (Ed.), *The Foucault reader* (pp. 32–50). Pantheon.

Foucault, M. (1986). *The history of sexuality, volume 3: The care of the self* (R. Hurley, Trans.). Pantheon.

Foucault, M. (1991). The ethic of care for the self as a practice of freedom: An interview (J. D. Gauthier, Trans.). In J. Bernauer & D. Rasmussen (Eds.), *The final Foucault* (pp. 1–20). MIT Press.

Foucault, M. (1994). La philosophie analytique de la politique. In D. Defert & F. Ewald (Eds.) with J. Lagrange, *Dits et écrits, 1954–1988* (4 Vols., Vol. 3, No. 232, pp. 534–551). Éditions Gallimard

Foucault, M. (2001). *Fearless speech* (J. Pearson, Ed.). Semiotext(e).

Gray, J. (1984). *Hayek on liberty*. Blackwell.

Green, J. M. (1999). *Deep democracy: Community, diversity, transformation*. Rowman & Littlefield.

Hayek, F. A. (1944). *The road to serfdom*. Routledge & Kegan Paul.

Hayek, F. A. (1945). The use of knowledge in society. *American Economic Review, 35*(4), 519–530.

Hayek, F. A. (1952). *The sensory order*. Routledge & Kegan Paul.

Hayek, F. A. (1960). *The constitution of liberty*. Routledge & Kegan Paul.

Hayek, F. A. (1967). *Studies in philosophy, politics and economics*. Routledge & Kegan Paul.

Hayek, F. A. (1973). *Law, legislation and liberty, volume 1*. Routledge & Kegan Paul.

Hayek, F. A. (1976). *Law, legislation and liberty, volume 2: The mirage of social justice*. Routledge & Kegan Paul.

Hayek, F. A. (1979). *Law, legislation and liberty, volume 3: The political order of a free society*. Routledge & Kegan Paul.

Hegel. G. W. F. (1942). *The philosophy of right* (T. M. Knox, Trans.). Clarendon.

Heyman, S. (1992). Positive and negative liberty. *Chicago-Kent Law Review, 68*(1), 81–98.

Hindess, B. (1990). Liberty and equality. In B. Hindess (Ed.), *Reactions to the Right* (pp. 7–31). Routledge.

Hirst, P. (1995). Can secondary associations enhance democratic governance? In J. Cohen & J. Rogers (Eds.), *Associations and democracy* (pp. 101–112). Verso.

Hobhouse, L. T. (1911). *Liberalism*. Williams & Norgate.

Hoffer, E. (1951). *The true believer*. Harper & Row.

Keniston, K. (1970). *The uncommitted*. Dell.

Larmore, C. (1996). *The morals of modernity*. Cambridge University Press.

Martell, L. (1992). New ideas of socialism, *Economy and Society, 21*(2), 152–172.

Mill, J. S. (1910). *Representative government*. Everyman.

Montgomery McGovern, W. (1946). *From Luther to Hitler: The history of Fascist-Nazi political philosophy*. George Harrap.

Noddings, N. (1996). On community, *Educational Theory, 46*(3), 245–267.

Notturno, M. A. (2003). *On Popper*. Thompson/Wadsworth.

Nozick, R. (1975). *Anarchy, state, utopia*. Blackwell.

Nussbaum, M. (1995). Human functioning and social justice: In defence of Aristotelian essentialism. In D. Tallack (Ed.), *Critical theory: A reader* (pp. 449–472). Harvester Wheatsheaf.

Olssen, M. (2002). Michel Foucault as "thin" communitarian: Difference, community, democracy. *Cultural Studies/Critical Methodologies, 2*(4), 483–513. https://doi.org/10.1177/153270860200200403

Olssen, M., Codd, J., & O'Neill, A.-M. (2004). *Education policy: Globalization, citizenship & democracy.* Sage.

Pettit, P. (1997). *Republicanism: A theory of freedom and government.* Oxford University Press.

Popper, K. R. (1945). *The open society and its enemies* (2 Vols.). Routledge & Kegan Paul.

Popper, K. R. (1961). *The poverty of historicism.* Routledge & Kegan Paul.

Popper, K. R. (1992). *The lesson of this century* (Interview by G. Bosetti). Routledge.

Spragens, T. A. (1981). *The irony of liberal reason.* University of Chicago Press.

Talmon, J. L. (1952). *The origins of totalitarian democracy.* Mercury Books.

Tomlinson, J. (1990). Market socialism: A basis for socialist renewal? In B. Hindess (Ed.), *Reactions to the Right* (pp. 32–49). Routledge.

Wright, E. O. (1995). Preface: The Real Utopias Project. In J. Cohen & J. Rogers (Eds.), *Associations and democracy* (pp. ii–xxii). Verso.

CHAPTER 18

Wittgenstein and Foucault

The Limits and Possibilities of Constructivism

Abstract

James Marshall (1995) once argued that Wittgenstein's social constructivist view of mathematics is not "idealistic", "relativistic" or "subjectivistic" but rather is "non-idealistic and objective". Wittgenstein is not idealistic because he attacks the prioritizing of mental states over linguistic accompaniments of those internal states. What he emphasizes is not intuition or mental process but the use of language. This, says Marshall, is an objective criterion, for although mathematics is "invented" rather than "discovered", the manner of its invention is in the form of discursive construction and in this sense it is independent of the individuals who use it as are the criteria of the truth and falsity of its propositions. It is thus non-foundational in the Russellian/Fregian senses. Rather, its objectivity is guaranteed by understanding mathematical objects within a formal language system. Truth in this sense depends on correct derivation in terms of the rule structure of the "language game" relative to a "form of life". Truth is thus "internal to a scheme".

1   Introduction

In this article I compare Wittgenstein to Foucault with respect to the issues of idealism, scepticism and language to highlight some of the main issues which seem to me central to any serious consideration of the limits and possibilities of social constucivism.[1] These relate to (1) the central differences between radical constructivism and social constructionism, and (2) the extent to which the problem of relativism is overcome by Wittgenstein and Foucault making comparisons between the two thinkers. In completing these tasks, I will also consider some of the contributions of Foucault to the constructionist debate.

2   Social and Individual Constructions

The distinction between "individual" and "social" is clearly central to the difference between radical constructivism and social constructionism. Radical constructivism's model of society (if we can speak of such) is simply an aggregation of individuals, there being no recognition of distinctions between the individual and the collective, or between structure and agency. In the radical constructivist view of knowledge acquisition there is then no recognition of the structural dimensions of knowledge development. Rather, each individual is seen as constructing their knowledge themselves. This is a far cry from the model of society adopted by the so-called "social constructionists", amongst whom Wittgenstein is one, and Vygotsky, Foucault and Gramsci could be considered others. This group do not share the ontological, methodological or epistemological individualism of radical constructivism. For these writers there is agreement that explanations about individuals cannot be solely in terms of statements about individuals. Rather, they maintain a commitment to a model of society based on a distinction between structural processes and individual agents, and they would argue that a varied list of structural factors, including "society", "forms of life", "history", "discursive formation" or even "mode of production" constitute important dimensions of social reality.[2] Methodologically they tend to be holists as opposed to individualists, seeing the explanation of any event or process as dependent on its social, historical or cultural location and seeing society in some senses as more than the sum of its parts.[3] The consequences of ontologically privileging society over the individual include (1) that the contents of an individual's mental representations are social in origin, and (2) that an individual's cognitive functioning could not be fully explained in terms of purely individualistic mental constructions.

3   Idealism

Wittgenstein is clearly not an idealist in the classical sense of the term characteristic of Berkeley and the German idealists who articulate a thesis of the primacy of mind, which is to say they see perception as guided through divinely directed or constituted minds, and which understands physical objects in the world, in this sense, as "mind dependent". In this sense, Wittgenstein clearly differs from Kant, who while he acknowledged that some sort of physical stuff was there in the external world, saw the form and intelligibility of its existence as imposed through a priori categories of the cognition. As these a priori categories included such central dimensions of space and time, there is a very important and clear sense in which Kant was an idealist. Wittgenstein clearly differed from this sort of view in a very marked way. Mental concepts for him were not derived directly or indirectly from God, nor were they a part of an individuals' cognitive makeup. For Wittgenstein, intuitivism or approaches to learning based on internal mental constructions neglect the importance of language as a socially objective structure. In their turn, these socially objective structures of language were relative to a "form of life". The focus upon language, which is related to a "form of life" in one important sense reframes ideation and mental perception in terms of material processes in the sense that languages and forms of life are linguistic and/or cultural systems which develop and change in the course of history. In an important sense, then, they are historically generated. As long as Wittgenstein can hold, which quite possibly he can, that such cultural phenomena arise themselves from historical events and developments, which themselves are originally constituted from physical and chemical processes, then he is freed from the sorts of idealism that afflicted many thinkers, all the way back to the ancient Greeks.

The hard-nosed critic of idealism may raise an important objection here. They could argue that thought is simply pushed back one stage, beyond discourse, which doesn't exactly get rid of thought nor of the problems traditionally associated with idealism. They could maintain that Wittgenstein, and Foucault, too, adhere to a version of the thesis that the real develops, if not inside thought, then certainly inside discourse. For to go beyond or try to conceive of an existence which is outside discourse, and therefore, outside thought, is to posit a noumenal "thing in itself" which discourse and thought somehow reflect. What Wittgenstein and Foucault could say here, quite plausibly I suggest, is that to say that language, discourse, or mind (individual or group) is a necessary medium through which all knowledge claims are made is not to say that they constitute the *prius* of all things in the sense that they constitute those things or even that they have greater reality than those things, or that they constitute the only reality. Indeed, to say that we can only know the world through discourse, is not to say that the world is not there independent of discourse. The issue is not one of ontology, it is one of epistemology. We can grant that this was the error of Hegel, who took the view, now widely discredited, that because objective reality can exist only in thought, reality itself must reside in an Absolute Idea (God). The silent transition or "jump" from the *act of conceiving* to *what is conceived*, i.e., objective being, encapsulated in Hegel's identification of the ideal (thought) and the real (objective reality, God) is certainly not made by Wittgenstein or Foucault. While they agree that a thing is only conceivable through discourse, language and thought (or minds) relative to these, nothing is presupposed about the reality of that which is conceived. For them, the matter of how knowledge is rendered reliable would work, not through introspection, digging further down into thought, or through transcendence whereby minds can link with a unified spiritual intelligence (God), but by working outwards to the objects represented through discourses, language systems and minds, despite the difficulties. The methodological task would become how we can best legitimate our knowledge claims given the frequent and uncertain lack of synchronization between discursive and non-discursive, as well as the distorting relativities associated with social structures, "forms of life", discourses, and individual and collective "minds", in history. Although I am not intending to do justice to such a defence here, they may have recourse to various forms of argument, of which the following two types strike me as potentially fruitful but of which neither would overcome the problems associated with uncertainty and relativism in any total sense. Firstly, both may presuppose transcendentally the necessary existence of the non-discursive objects of existence as a condition for our being able to think and know in the first place, related to survival and existence. Secondly, as with naturalists, positivists and empiricists, they could conjecture that some sort of either reliable or unreliable knowledge accrues through the methodological triangulations of multiple forms of checking and testing in history. Developing projects and technologies that appear to work would seem to constitute an indirect validation of knowledges developed. Gaining intersubjective agreement is another. It would seem initially plausible also that the twin methods of coherence and correspondence could both be fruitful in this process. What may be the outcome of such an approach, one might conjecture, is the confidence or certitude one might be able to claim in the knowledge banks we store up in history.

While this sort of defence, then, avoids the central traps and snares of classical idealism, their more discursive approach is possibly open to being criticized in relation to yet a different form of idealism. This criticism might be called discursive idealism, or linguistic idealism. It is often made by Marxists against Wittgenstein and consists in the notion that language is prioritized over the material forms of reality such as technology, labour, or production, things, or, as a Marxist might say, that "cultural superstructure is being given priority over the economic base". A similar criticism to this has also been directed at Michel Foucault, especially in relation to his earlier writings where discourse was considered as an autonomous realm separate and largely unaffected by material practices. In *The Order of Things* (1970), as Ian Hacking (1979, pp. 41–42) summarizes it, Foucault maintained that systems of thought were "anonymous, autonomous and rule governed" elaborating a view of the "production of things by words" (Barrett, 1988, p. 130). During the later 1970s when he wrote *Discipline and Punish* (1977) and *The History of Sexuality* (1978), Foucault sought to address the criticisms that discourse was considered in isolation from practice. In the later works, where he was interested specifically in the processes of institutional surveillance and control, he sought to de-emphasize the autonomy of discourse and emphasize its relation to material practices in the world. As he explained in an interview:

> I believe one's point of reference should not be the great model of language and signs but that of war and battle. This history which bears and determines us has the form of a war rather than a language: relations of power, not relations of meaning. (Foucault, 1980, p. 114)

Foucault's increasing interest in the relations of discourse to practice paralleled his increasing recognition in the late 1960s of the importance of *power* as it affects the development of discursive formations, meaning that all knowledge structures (or "language games") are systems of "power/knowledge":

> There is no power relation without the correlative constitution of a field of knowledge nor at the same time any knowledge that does not presuppose and constitute at the same time power relations. (Foucault, 1977, p. 27)

By progressively becoming concerned to explicate how material practices constrained discursive systems, Foucault sought to avoid charges of "cultural idealism". He never, however, disavowed a certain autonomy to the discursive but developed conceptions of strategy and power and tactics in order to express how subjects in history negotiated, sidestepped, overcame, or were thwarted by, these constraints of the physical material world. In dispensing with any notion of the "outside" and subscribing to a model of "internal history" at the end of the 1960s, he became acutely aware that an unresolved issues concerning scepticism that arose in relation to the difficulty of how one separated power and knowledge, or discourse, from truth when there is no point external to history by which neutral and objective judgements might be made. It is notable with reference to this, for instance, that in *The Archaeology of Knowledge* he acknowledges that he is "avoiding the ground upon which [his studies] could find support" (1972, p. 205). What was evident, however, is that discursive systems are often out of synchronization with underpinning material realities, and given that the world is always discourse-dependent in the sense that any claim about the world is mediated through discourse, the issue of how discursive and non-discursive interrelate, and how reliable judgements and assessments could be made, was for Foucault, as for Wittgenstein, an important matter.

4 Objectivity, Truth and Relativism

For Wittgenstein, mathematical propositions are "objective", and truth criteria are unambiguous in the sense that there is a correct way of proceeding, and correct and incorrect answers to be obtained. These are internal to the language system and the form of life of the culture. Yet the notions of objectivity and truth here are simply *conventional* and this itself is not uncontentious. Truth, in this sense, depends simply on the correct derivation from the syntax of the system, or, in Donald Davidson's phrase, it is "truth relative to a scheme" (Davidson, 1985). So too with "objectivity"—it is an objectivity guaranteed by a formal system. The important question which remains unanswered, however, is what guarantees the rationality of the formal system. This is a question to which I believe Wittgenstein has no real answer. Truth and objectivity are secure but only "relative to a scheme" and the central problem of historical relativism is not overcome.

Can such a problem be overcome with reference to Foucault? For Foucault, like Wittgenstein, all knowledge structures are socially and historically constructed. What distinguishes the two approaches, however, is that, while Foucault's approach is also inherently anti-foundational, he demonstrates a greater appreciation of the importance of history and power and of the messy interactions between social structure and discourse than did Wittgenstein. Objectivity is largely a function of power relative to the instantiation of a discourse within a particular social-historical formation. In this sense, while objectivity is guaranteed by a rule ordained by the hegemonic code, Foucault's analysis too can be criticized on the grounds of relativism for it is unable, on the surface, to provide any extra-historical conception of rationality capable of grounding a particular discourse, or "language game" or "form of life" or "regime of truth". As truth itself is always internal to discourse, the extent to which such truth is indeed *the truth* (i.e., in an eternal or ahistorical sense), remains effectively and theoretically unresolved. Whether Wittgenstein and Foucault should be criticized for this is uncertain. At one level, they could claim that while there may well be eternal truths that exist, within our own location in history and life, it is never possible to know these truths in any absolute sense. Only an all-knowing God could know them. They might also say that the history of science, full of wrong turnings, blind alleys and false starts, as it has been, is living testimony to this. The status of our knowledge must remain tentative and revisable. There are many senses that this matter remains one of the central conundrums of philosophy and is one which mobilizes many different types of practice and enquiry, from policy dilemmas to science to clairvoyance, all aimed at bracketing the distorting social, personal and historical lens that interfere with and frustrate our claims to know.

Like all historicists Foucault's approach attempts to describe history while denying the existence of historical laws, of a constant human nature, of subject-centred reason or of any absolute or transhistorical values. Building on the epistemological work of Gaston Bachelard and Georges Canguilhem, Foucault is interested in explaining the discontinuities, breaks, and ruptures that signal fundamental changes in discursive systems. While truth, especially as it manifests itself in terms of practical consequences, constitutes one such factor, issues such as what works, what best sustains life in the current milieu, as well as issues of power and privilege, all play a role. He is thus also interested in the interrelations and entanglements between discursive formations and the various political, economic, social and ideological practices that go to make up the social structure and which distort or frustrate our ability to see clearly. Foucault approaches ideas and values not in terms of absolute norms of truth and good but as the expression of a specific age, culture or people. If such values, ideas, or knowledge systems are functions of historical conditions in which they emerge, then they may change with changes in those conditions, and no possible evaluation of their value or truth in general is possible.

The apparent relativism of such an anti-foundational view is a problem which Foucault sought to address in his later writings. In his interviews published in 1980, he puts the view that not all discipline-based knowledge can be assessed in the same way and suggests that the epistemological "armature" of a discipline can mature and become more objective in history. This notion parallels his later views on "the self", which he maintained could gain increased "objectivity" and "detachment" by progressively extricating itself from the developing social structure in the course of its development (Foucault, 1986; Deleuze, 1988, pp. 106–107).

In my view, while Wittgenstein presents a more analytically orientated assessment of semantics and language use than does Foucault, Foucault's approach suggests a more *historically grounded* concept of objectivity than is present in Wittgenstein. When Foucault compares medicine to psychology, for instance, he states that "medicine has a much more solid scientific armature, … but it too is profoundly enmeshed in social structures" (cited in Rabinow, 1984, p. 51). The natural sciences like theoretical physics or organic chemistry also have "solid scientific armatures". Although they are also affected by power relations in the larger society, Foucault recognizes that the relations between social structure and the discipline "can be difficult to untangle" (ibid.). With respect to forms of knowledge like psychiatry, however, Foucault maintains:

> the question is much easier to resolve, since the epistemological profile is a low one and psychiatric practice is linked with a whole range of institutions, economic requirements and political issues of social regulation. (Foucault, 1980, p. 109)

5 The Centrality of Language and Discourse

Both Foucault and Wittgenstein maintain a similarity of approach in terms of a central focus on language. While Foucault focuses on serious formal statements in order to accurately chart the historically constituted discursive frame, Wittgenstein, at least in his later work, concentrated on ordinary language and common sense as a form of life.[4] For Wittgenstein, as for Foucault, language is not seen as an expression of "inner states", but as a historically constituted system, which is social in its origins as well as in its uses. In abandoning the phenomenological subject, the dualism of mind and world is surpassed, as well as the intractable difficulties as positing the world as a product of mind. The rules of language were themselves seen as a bundle of interactional and public norms. Meaning is generated within the context of the frame of reference (for Wittgenstein, a game; for Foucault a discourse). Hence to understand an individual we must understand the patterns of their socialization, the nature of their concepts, as well as the operative norms and conventions that constitute the context for the activity and the origin of the concepts utilized. If mind operates, not as a self-enclosed entity, as Descartes held, attaching words to thoughts, as if they were markers, but rather operated in terms of publicly structured rule systems, then meanings are in an important sense public.[5]

It is related to the discursive nature of meaning and the publicity of language that practices can be seen to be intelligible only in relation to existence as communal. Existence is communal in the sense that meanings are public. A communal context defines a group of beings collectively adapting public resources for their use. Yet, the implications of this are far reaching. If meanings are linguistic, and language is public, and being public relates to individuals together, i.e., in communities, then as Hacking (2002, p. 131) says, "we are not talking only about language, but about high politics, about the person and the state, about individual rights, about the self, and much else". The thesis here is that the social nature of practices defines a community context in one very important sense, a sense which is fundamentally inescapable. Such a theoretical revolution, which has largely developed in the 20th century, has rendered the liberal conception of the autonomous self-interested individual as obsolete. Todd May, in his discussion of the work of Jean-Luc Nancy, expresses the sense in which a conception of the social nature of practices presupposes a conception of community:

> An instance of a single-practice community would be people working in a particular political campaign. They are engaged in a common task,

> recognize their compatriots as being so engaged, and are bound by this engagement, this recognition, and the norms of their practice. Everyday talk reflects the use of term "community" in this way: we speak of political, religious, and even economic communities in referring to communities comprising specific practices. (May, 1997, p. 57)

In most cases, however, May explains that it is multiple, or what he calls "overlapping practices" that constitute a community (p. 57). May notes that in the Continental tradition, Michel Foucault, Gilles Deleuze and Jean-François Lyotard represent such a social theory of practice. In Anglo-American philosophy, Wittgenstein, Wilfred Sellars and Robert Brandom (p. 51). The central claim is that "a community is defined by the practices that constitute it" (p. 52). This defines, he says, what it means to be in community. Practice, he defines as "a regularity or regularities of behaviour, usually goal directed, that are socially and normatively governed" (p. 52). While, in this sense, practices are "rule governed", such rules need not be formal, or even explicit. A second feature of practices is that their normative governance is social, which is to reject the idea of a private language. This is to say that not only is the *governance* of practices social, but the *practices* are also social. Even solitary practices, like diary writing, are social in this sense. May says as such (p. 53): "the concept of practice lies at the intersection of individuality and community". Thirdly, he says, "practice … involves a regularity in behaviour. In order to be a practice, the various people engaged in it must be said to be 'doing the same thing' under some reasonable description of their behaviour" (p. 54). As a consequence of these three definitions, says May, practices must be seen as discursive, meaning that they involve the use of language. (p. 55). This entails:

> some sort of communication between participants in order that they may either learn or coordinate the activities that the practice involves. … Moreover, this communication must be potentially accessible to non-participants, since without such accessibility the practice would cease to exist when its current participants dropped out. The communication required by a practice, then, must be linguistic. The idea of linguistic communication can be broadly constructed here, needing only a set of public signs with assignable meanings. (p. 55)

Such a theory of practice, says May (p. 55) "is akin to Wittgenstein's idea that language games are central components of forms of life". The central theoretical point concerning practices is that they embody actions organized according to rules which are both linguistic and cultural. As Theodore R. Schatzki

(2001a, p. 48) points out, "practices are organized nexuses of activity", and constitute "a set of actions ... constituted by doings and sayings". In this sense, he says (p. 45), "the social order is instituted within practices". Schatzki defines the social order as "arrangements of people, and the organisms, artefacts, and things through which they coexist" (p. 43). They coexist within what Schatzki (2001b, p. 2) calls "a field of practices" which constitutes "the total nexus of interconnected human practices". Such practices are "embodied, materially mediated arrays of human activity centrally organized around shared practical understanding". Referring to Foucault, Schatzki (p. 2) notes how "bodies and activities are 'constituted' within practices". It can be said, further, echoing Foucault in *The Archaeology of Knowledge*, that the practices that make up the social order comprise both "discursive" and "extra-discursive" elements. In this way, the idea of practices highlights "how bundled activities interweave with ordered constellations of nonhuman entities" (p. 3). In this sense, says Schatzki, "practice approaches promulgate a distinct social ontology: the social is a field of embodied, materially interwoven practices centrally organized around shared practical understandings" (p. 3).

A similar thesis is made at the level of language by J. L. Austin (1962) and John Searle (1969, 1995), who note the "performative" dimensions of language use within a community.[6] As performative, language is also constitutive and derives its meaning in relation to a "form of life". It is in this sense that possible language usage is never constrained by the actual system of rules that operate. Such a model allows for the possibility of contingency and novelty. Building on Wittgenstein in the *Philosophical Investigations*, we can say that language does not have a "fixed and unequivocal use" (1953, p. 37) at all times and places. Names, thus, do not have fixed meanings but depend on their *use*. This recalls the principle of contingency where things are not determined by prior causes, in the natures of things, but depend on context, and are historical, and hence, in classical parlance, *could have been otherwise*. As Wittgenstein (1953) says:

> the application of a word is not everywhere bounded by rules. ... What does a game look like that is everywhere bounded by rules? Whose rules never let a doubt creep in, but stop up all the cracks where it might? (s. 4, p. 39)

Austin's speech act theory both drew on and further developed a broad system of philosophical pragmatism building on a tradition, including William James, Charles Horton Cooley, John Dewey, George Herbert Mead, Charles Sanders Pierce, and Alfred Schultz, all who introduced in different but related ways notions of the relative autonomy of language and the interactional character of self and society.[7]

6 Foucault as Constructivist

As Foucault told Claude Bonnefoy, "language is what we use to construct and absolutely infinite number of sentences and utterances" (Foucault & Bonnefoy, 2011, pp. 65–66). Moreover, says Foucault, "the body itself … is like a language node" (p. 26). His constructivist approach to the autonomy of language was already clear in 1963 in his radio lecture, "Mad Language", where he says:

> Words, their arbitrary encounter, their confusion, all their protoplasmic transformations are sufficient in themselves to bring into being a world that is both true and fantastic. (Foucault, 2015, p. 28)

The nature and extent of Foucault's constructivist claims vary according to the specific propositions being made. In relation to the social sciences, the constructivist claims are stronger than in relation to the natural sciences. Foucault not only is prepared to make distinctions between different disciplines, but he clearly sees some as having more "solid armatures" and of being more "mature" in their development than others.

In relation to disciplines like psychiatry, Foucault makes strong constructionist claims. Disciplines like psychiatry can, in Foucauldian terms, be represented as discourses which, rising in the 19th and early 20th centuries, defined new ways of relating to the world, new means of administrative control, and new ways of defining and talking about people. They produced new boxes to put people in, new labels, new categories and classifications which became inscribed in the practices of daily life and in the organizational and institutional structures of society. Although the emergence and development of such a discursive system was made possible by the material conditions of early modern society, in relation to providing a context of conditioning and limiting factors, Foucault is also of the view that a degree of happenstance and the aleatory were responsible for movements in one rather than another direction. In addition, as new developments in technology produced new ways of addressing social problems, new patterns of normalization and new bases for social authority were established. The very emergence of the knowledge discipline, says Foucault, became implicated in producing the conceptions of normality they claimed to uncover. Hence the human sciences formulate ways of organizing the world and, in doing so, position people in relation to the categorizations and classifications theory construct. Foucault considers that the human sciences, "the dubious sciences" (Foucault, 1973), although contributing little knowledge about human beings, have attained massive importance and power in society, a fact that itself needs to be explained. In his conception they have become complex strategic constructs and forms of domination.

In making strong constructivist claims, as he did in his earlier writings, Foucault held that the objects of which the discourse spoke were themselves constituted by the discourse, that once distinctions were made, new realities effectively came into being; that is, that the types of objects of a domain "were not already demarcated prior to the discourse but came into existence only contemporaneous with the discursive formations that made it possible to talk about them" (Rouse, 1994, p. 93).

In his later writings and interviews, Foucault sought to qualify the general nature of his constructionist claims in relation to the issue of realism (see Foucault, 1980, pp. 108–110). Not only were distinctions introduced between different disciplines and between knowledge claims within disciplines, but in that disciplines constructed knowledge, they did so only within distinct boundaries and limits. Foucault became ever more sensitive to the independent status and autonomy of material practices (Foucault, 1977, 1978, 1980; Smart, 1983; Poster, 1984).

Foucault's constructionism is thus similar to what Ian Hacking (1986, p. 236) calls "dynamic nominalism". It is a constructionism that, while recognizing the generative potential of discourses in its relation to the world, also recognizes the variations that may exist in relation to different domains of enquiry and different knowledge forms, recognizes as well the existence of real-world structures and practices and the limits and boundaries within which constructions can take place, and yet also recognizes that there are numerous kinds of knowledge claims (about types of human beings, for instance) that come into being hand in hand with our invention of the categories labelling them.

With reference to this last type of knowledge claim, Ian Hacking (1986) looks at the issue, central to the constructionist's heart, of "making up people", and examines, using Foucauldian insights, some of the different ways, and different theories, by which people in different ages have been constituted as types. Starting with Arnold Davidson's observation that there were no perverts before the latter part of the 19th century, Hacking goes on to consider the constitutive categories of "multiple personality" (invented, he claims, in 1875), "split personality" (invented in the same period) and "possession" (a common form of Renaissance behaviour that died long ago but still survives in a few German villages). While these are different ways of "making up people", and indicate the pertinence of the constructivist thesis when considered in a sociological sense, it cannot be asserted in any unproblematic sense that individual people simply choose to become "splits" or "multiples" or "possessed" (although in some instances conceivably they could do so). These are social categories, and in any period the hegemonic form will constitute the dominant code. As the criteria of truth and falsehood are internal to the scheme, making comparative evaluations between "splits" or "possessed" is not possible for they are terms from different "discursive formations", "language games", frameworks, etc.

While no readily apparent solution to this historical relativism is suggested by either Wittgenstein or Foucault, it seems to me that the only progress out of this impasse can be made if one asks how discursive formations relate to the real world, and whether discourses do not survive or die depending upon their usefulness to particular societies at particular times. I do not mean by this suggestion to license a "whig" conception of history in the sense that whatever has survived must have done so because it is useful and therefore better, for it may well not be useful tomorrow, or it may have already outlived its functional importance and thus constitute a residual and disappearing category. What is being suggested is a point I have taken from Ian Hacking, that discourses are in a constant process of testing themselves in terms of practice in history, and further that the mere existence of "discourses" or "language games" does not necessarily therefore suggest relativism. As Hacking puts it:

> It has taken millennia to evolve systems of reasoning. ... Some of our once favoured styles of reasoning have turned out to be dead ends and others are probably on their way. However, new styles of reasoning will continue to evolve. (Hacking, 1986, p. 150)

Looked at in this way, the historicity of our own styles of reasoning in no way makes them less objective or less rational. Rationality and objectivity are related to context. Discursive systems have histories. Some work better than others, are more useful etc., or continue "to deliver the goods". Moreover, while the truth claims associated with any discipline (e.g., mathematics) may be internal to the formalized structure, this does not mean that human beings cannot exercise rational judgement related to their being in the world. Hacking believes this when he says:

> There are good and bad reasons for propositions about nature. They are not relative to anything. They do not depend on context. (Hacking, 1985, p. 151)

It would seem to me that this form of simple realism about straightforward claims could also be maintained by both Wittgenstein and Foucault. This is a similar claim to that Gramsci makes when he distinguishes between "good sense" and "folklore" as being the two elements of "common sense". By such a distinction Gramsci attempted to resolve the impasse of a blunt-edged relativism in the context of historicist and anti-foundational conceptions of the emergence and development of knowledge. For Gramsci, "good sense" was the criterion of evaluation generated by experience, whereas "folklore" was knowledge handed down from generation to generation simply based on custom or tradition. The task of educators was to instil "good sense" and eradicate "folklore" through utilizing the critical faculties.

Some commentators believe that Foucault was approaching a similar conception of the relation between discourse and practice in his later writings (see Deleuze, 1988; Gutting, 1989, 1994). Certainly, in his later writings, as I have stated above, he moderated the general nature of his constructivist claims and became more sensitive to the constraining nature of the real world and to the overall complexity of the interrelationships between discourse and the practice. In his later work, *Care of the Self*, notably, it is evident that while changes in material context over the period of the Roman Empire were determinant of the range and limits of behaviours enabled, they still established a range of possibilities enabling freedom of choice. Discourse in this sense had a constructive potential although changes within social structure would open and limit possibilities. What distinguishes Foucault's constructivism and differentiates his position from empiricism and positivism is that whereas those perspectives assume the possibility of an immediate pre-given correspondence between discourse and the world, Foucault, while not denying such a possibility, problematizes it. He became increasingly sensitive to the way in which knowledge became untied from its condition of origin or from the practices it pertains to and claims to explain. Such a non-correspondence has been described by Barry Smart (1983, p. 94) as a routine feature of positive significance requiring analysis in each instance. A similar point is made by Gordon, who summarizes Foucault's position in the following way:

> Our world does not follow a programme, but we live in a world of programmes, that is to say in a world traversed by the effects of discourse whose object ... is the rendering rationalizable, transparent and programmable of the real. (Gordon, 1980, cited in Smart, 1983, p. 95)

For Foucault, not only is the discipline structure of knowledge constructed in history, but that discourse has a "constructive potential" in bringing new realities into existence. Just as labelling theories and "social problem" perspectives once maintained that social realities are conditioned and even created by the labels we apply, Foucault claims that many of our categorizations, including those concerning our own subjectivity, are constructed in history. Giving names to things is one aspect of this process of constitution. As Foucault says:

> We should try to discover how it is that subjects are gradually progressively, really and materially constituted through a multiplicity of organisms, forces, energies, materials, desires, thoughts, etc. (Cited in Hacking, 1986, p. 226)

With relation to the constitution of subjectivity, Foucault advances, a strong constructivist programme which can be distinguished from the "weak" constructivist programme of labelling theories and "social problem" perspectives. In his strong claims as they relate to the subject, Foucault takes objects like the body and focuses on how conceptions of subjectivity are created or invented in history. His claims have influenced many researchers advancing constructivist theses, some whom it may be considered, go a little too far. Hence, David Armstrong's *The Invention of Infant Mortality* (1986); Sarah Nettleton's *Inventing Mouths* (1994), where she advances a strong constructivist position, arguing that "the mouth with teeth is not a pre-existent entity but an object that has been realized through the discourse of dentistry"; or Nikolas Rose's *Governing the Soul* (1990) where he examines the constitution of persons or subjects by the psy-professions in various political contexts.

It is clear that Foucault has inspired many new types of research, and that the social constructivist dimension to knowledge production is important. In many senses the discourse does create the reality—the body analysed for "humours" will contain "humours", a body analysed for "organs and tissues" will contain "organs and tissues", a body analysed in terms of "psychological functioning" is a "psychological object", a body analysed for "intelligence" will contain "intelligence"—and these are important senses in which the "gaze" or "perspective" constructs the object. While this need not deny that outside of discourse, something exists, it is to highlight the role that discourse plays is giving form to and framing the way the world is understood, i.e., constructed. To focus, as Foucault does, on how the domains of the body become possible objects of positive knowledge and to expose the biomedical roots of modern knowledge as expressions of power/knowledge is surely his lasting contribution. None of Foucault's claims should offend our realist sensibilities. To the extent that some of his followers appear to do so, in that they speak of the "invention of mouths", or of "infant mortality", etc., the ambiguities are resolved once the propositions being advanced are clearly expressed.

7 Conclusion

In conclusion, I would agree that Wittgenstein's social constructivist view of mathematics avoids idealism and subjective mental state constructivism. While anti-foundational, Wittgenstein is also not sceptical about objectivity or truth criteria. The larger problem of relativism, I claim, has not been entirely overcome, however. By turning to Foucault, we can see more clearly the different dimensions of this problem and how it might be overcome, although my suggestions should only be regarded as tentative. It is claimed, finally, that Foucault recognizes the discursive construction of knowledge and of subjectivity without completely giving up on realism, and he is prepared to alter his claims according to different fields of knowledge. This could perhaps be called "dynamic constructivism".

Acknowledgement

This chapter originally appeared as Olssen, M. (2017), Wittgenstein and Foucault: The limits and possibilities of constructivism, in M. A. Peters & J. Stickney (Eds.), *A companion to Wittgenstein on education* (pp. 305–320), Springer, https://doi.org/10.1007/978-981-10-3136-6_20. Reprinted here, with minor edits, with permission from the publisher.

Notes

1 I will use the terms "constructivism" and "constructionism" in this chapter interchangeably. While I take them to mean much the same thing, to the extent that there is any difference it seems to me that constructivism is more relevant to the epistemological dimension of the thesis whereas constructionism pertains more generally as a descriptor for an entire approach or paradigm.

2 In using the word "holism" here, I would differentiate it from traditional senses of the word as characterised for instance in Hegel's philosophy, but utilise it more in the sense of what might be termed "relational holism" or even "pluralistic holism". This is the sense that writers like Avital Simhony speak of "relational organicism". For various complex reasons, mainly to do with the usage of the concept historically, I prefer to use the concept of "relational holism". While holist theories were anachronistic with individualist epistemologies and ontologies from the 17th to the late 19th centuries, the rise of quantum theories and of complexity sciences from the mid-20th century once again reinstated versions of holism, albeit of a very different sort, as central approaches in science.

3 The whole is more than the sum of its parts in some senses but not others. In complexity physics this is recognised in relation to concepts such as "downward causation". Societal structures are constituted by emergent processes and maintain some degree of efficacy and

derivative autonomy in relations to parts. It is also in the sense that wholes conceptualised as open and incomplete structures are non-reducible to parts.
4 I have in mind the *Philosophical Investigation*, not the *Tractatus*, nor the *Philosophical Grammar*.
5 Although meaning systems are public, the agent can be seen as active and volitional in relation to the fact that life is independent of the discursive, and appropriates, utilizes, and manipulates existing discursive options specific to the concerns and purposes of life in particular times and places. Unlike the systems theorists, for Foucault the structures of life, labour and language operate in history as coterminous with the environment.
6 Austin's key distinction was between "locutionary acts", "illocutionary acts" (which are performative), and "perlocutionary" effects of actions (which are also performative).
7 The possible list could be extended, and could include systems theorists like Luhmann, as well as writers like Garfinkel (1989), Bakhtin (1998), Putnam (1997), and many more.

References

Armstrong, D. (1986). The invention of infant mortality. *Sociology of Health and Illness, 8*, 211–232.
Barrett, M. (1988). *The politics of truth*. Polity.
Davidson, D. (1985). On the very idea of a conceptual scheme. In J. Rajchman & C. West (Eds.), *Post-analytic philosophy* (pp. 183–198). Columbia University Press.
Deleuze, G. (1988). *Foucault* (S. Hand, Trans.). University of Minnesota Press.
Foucault, M. (1970). *The order of things*. Tavistock.
Foucault, M. (1972). *The archaeology of knowledge* (A. Sheridan, Trans.). Pantheon.
Foucault, M. (1973). *Madness and civilization: A history of insanity in the age of reason* (R. Howard, Trans.). Vintage/Random House.
Foucault, M. (1977). *Discipline and punish: The birth of the prison* (A. Sheridan, Trans.). Penguin.
Foucault, M. (1978). *The history of sexuality, vol. 1: An introduction*. Vintage.
Foucault, M. (1980). Truth and power (C. Gordon, Trans.). In C. Gordon (Ed.), *Power/knowledge: Selected interviews and other writings 1972–1977* (pp. 109–133). Harvester Press.
Foucault, M. (1986). *History of sexuality, vol. 3: The care of the self* (R. Hurley, Trans.). Pantheon.
Foucault, M. (2015). Mad language. In M. Foucault, *Language, madness, and desire: On literature* (P. Artières, J.-F. Bert, M. Potte-Bonneville, & J. Revel, Eds.; R. Bononno, Trans.; pp. 25–39). University of Minnesota Press.
Foucault, M., & Bonnefoy, C. (2011). *Speech begins after death* (R. Bononno, Trans.; P. Artières, Ed.). University of Minnesota Press.
Gutting, G. (1989). *Michel Foucault's archaeology of scientific reason*. Cambridge University Press.

Gutting, G. (Ed.). (1994). *The Cambridge Companion to Foucault*. Cambridge University Press.

Hacking, I. (1979). Michel Foucault's immature science. *Nous, 13*, 39–51.

Hacking, I. (1985). Styles of scientific reasoning. In J. Rajchman & C. West (Eds.), *Post-analytic philosophy* (pp. 145–165). Columbia University Press.

Hacking, I. (1986). Making up people. In T. C. Heller, M. Sosna, & D. E. Wellbery (Eds.), *Reconstructing individualism: Autonomy, individuality and the self in Western thought* (pp. 222–236). Stanford University Press.

Marshall, J. D. (1995). Wittgenstein and Foucault: Resolving philosophical puzzles. In J. Marshall & P. Smeyers (Eds.), *Philosophy and education: Accepting Wittgenstein's challenge* (pp. 205–220). Kluwer Academic.

Nettleton, S. (1994). Inventing mouths: Disciplinary power and dentistry. In C. James & R. Porter (Eds.), *Reassessing Foucault: Power, medicine and the body* (pp. 73–90). Routledge.

Poster, M. (1984). *Foucault, Marxism, history: Mode of production vs mode of information*. Polity.

Rose, N. (1990). *Governing the soul*. Routledge.

Rose, N. (1994). Medicine, history and the present. In C. James & R. Porter (Eds.), *Reassessing Foucault: Power, medicine and the body* (pp. 48–72). Routledge.

Rouse, J. (1994). Power/knowledge. In G. Gutting (Ed.), *The Cambridge companion to Foucault* (pp. 92–144). Cambridge University Press.

Simhony, A. (1991). Idealist organicism: Beyond holism and individualism. *History of Political Thought, 12*(3), 515–535.

Smart, B. (1983). *Foucault, Marxism, critique*. Routledge.

Wittgenstein, L. (1953). *Philosophical investigations* (3rd ed., G.E.M. Anscombe, Trans.). Macmillan.

CHAPTER 19

Invoking Democracy

Foucault's Conception (with insights from Hobbes)

Abstract

Although Foucault advanced no overarching theory of democracy, this article asks which of his ideas and formulations are relevant for a theory of democracy. My approach is premised on the fact that while Foucault showed little interest in, and indeed some distaste for, normative political theorizing, I have no such inhibitions. My tactic will be to piece together the fragments of a theory of democracy, to show how Foucault approached democracy as a set of historically contingent practices, and to reveal the latent normative conceptions and suggestions within his texts. My argument and conclusion will be that Foucault *suggests* a theory of democracy and also suggests a series of conceptions of democracy that takes us beyond our current models and practices.

1   Introduction

William Connolly (1998) has suggested that:

> Foucault does not articulate a vision of democracy. His early objections against political ideals such as prisons militates against it; and his later cautious affirmation of a positive political imagination never takes this form. But numerous comments in the context of his participation in public protests and demonstrations are suggestive on this score. It seems to me that a series of correspondences can be delineated between the ethical sensibility cultivated by Foucault and an ethos of democracy they invoke. (p. 120)

It is in this spirit of the ethos of democracy invoked by Foucault that my article takes root. Like Connolly, I will supplement Foucault with ideas and thoughts that extend beyond him, until I create a picture coherent enough to satisfy. I will of course differentiate Foucault's thought from the extensions and supplementations I provide. To the extent that Foucault advanced no overarching theory of democracy, the questions become, which of his ideas and formulations are relevant for a theory of democracy; how might he have problematized existing conceptions and formulations; and what lines of argument might he suggest for future explorations. My approach is premised on the fact that while Foucault showed little interest in, and indeed some distaste for, normative political theorizing, I have no such inhibitions.[1] My tactic is to piece together the fragments of a theory of democracy, to show how Foucault approached democracy as a set of historically contingent practices, and to reveal the latent normative conceptions and suggestions within his texts. My argument, and conclusion, will be that Foucault *suggests* a theory of democracy and suggests a series of conceptions of democracy that takes us beyond our current models and practices.[2] I endeavor to outline what such a conception might look like. The basis for such an argument stems from Foucault's later writings on ethics and self-creation, liberty, autonomy and rights. More specifically, I will consider the following areas of his thought:

- A relational and dialogical conception of ethics with implications for agency, liberty, autonomy and interdependence
- A conception of liberty as nondomination or as involving an equalization of power relations
- A pragmatic political principle that would necessarily oppose government policies that conflict with or inhibit the cultivation of the self
- A critique of philosophical and political monism and an argument for political pluralism
- A historico-political discourse on rights
- Insights derived from his writings on power and resistance
- An advocacy of *parrhēsia* or speaking the truth to power

2   Liberty, Ethics and Domination

Foucault's conceptions of liberty and ethics can be seen to presuppose a democratic context. Although historically democracy has been associated, as Weber argued, with an expanding hierarchical bureaucracy and as a form of technical expertise as ends in themselves, Foucault would see these tendencies as contingent historical episodes and challenges to be surmounted rather than as the necessary consequences of the expansion of the democratic process.

Foucault's conceptions of liberty, ethics and more broadly in relation to his writings on the cultivation and constitution of the self presuppose several normative themes related to democracy. In his later two volumes of *The History of Sexuality*, and in a variety of articles and interviews, Foucault develops a conception of the self which while avoiding liberal humanist conception of the autonomous chooser, incorporates a sense of agency and freedom. In this newfound concern with an active subject, there is on the surface a shift in relation to Foucault's interest away from knowledge as a coercive practice of subjection to being a practice of the self-formation of the subject. Yet, this positing of a more active, volitional subject does not involve a radical break with his earlier work, nor is it inconsistent with it. As Foucault states in his essay "The Concern for Truth" (1989, p. 296) whereas in *Madness and Civilization*, it was a matter of knowing how one "governed" "the mad"; in his later two works, it is a matter of how one "governs" "oneself". In addition, in another essay he says:

> If now I am interested ... in the way in which the subject constitutes himself in an active fashion, by the practices of the self, these practices are nevertheless not something that the individual invents by himself. They are patterns that he finds in his culture and which are proposed, suggested and imposed on him by his culture, his society and his social group. (Foucault, 1991, p. 11)

Cultivating the self is the basis of ethical work. Ethical work, says Foucault, is the work one performs in the attempt to transform oneself into an ethical subject of one's own behavior, the means by which we change ourselves in order to become ethical subjects. Such a history of ethics is a history of aesthetics. In his interview "On the Genealogy of Ethics", Foucault (1984b) explains that there is:

> another side to the moral prescriptions, which most of the time is not isolated as such but is, I think, very important: the kind of relationship you ought to have with yourself, *rapport à soi*, which I call ethics, and which determines how the individual is supposed to constitute himself as a moral subject of his own actions. (p. 352)

Ethics, as such, is part of morality, but rather than focus exclusively on codes of moral behavior, it concentrates on the self's relationship to the self, for the way we relate to ourselves contributes to the way that we construct ourselves and form our identities, as well as the way we lead our lives and govern our conduct.

Foucault's understanding of ethics and liberty invoke a particular form of community. Hence, Foucault's conception of ethics is not the narrow individualist conception of Western modernity. Rather it refers to what Kant termed *Sitten*—customs or practices. Hence, ethics for Foucault is not intended in the Kantian sense, as Ian Hacking (1986) puts it, as "something utterly internal, the private duty of reason" (p. 239), but more in the sense of ancient Greece, where ethics was concerned with the good life. As Foucault (1991) states it:

> The Greeks ... considered this freedom as a problem and the freedom of the individual as an ethical problem. But ethical in the sense that Greeks could understand. *Ethos* was the deportment and the way to behave. It was the subject's mode of being and a certain manner of acting visible to others. One's *ethos* was seen by his dress, by his bearing, by his gait, by the poise with which he reacts to events, etc. For them that is the complete expression of liberty. (p. 6)

Foucault's understanding of the care of the self involves a politically active subject acting in a community of subjects, involving practices of the self that require governance as well as the problems of practical politics. Foucault speaks for instance of liberty as implying complex relations to others and self. Ethical action is not for Foucault an individual affair but presupposes a certain political and social structure with respect to liberty. For liberty or civic freedom to exist, there must be a certain level of liberation conceived as the absence of domination. Thus, the subject's activity is intrinsically mediated through power, which coexists with freedom in that relationships of power are changeable relations that can modify themselves. But where states of domination result in relations of power being fixed "in such a way that they are perpetually asymmetrical [then the] margin of liberty is extremely limited" (Foucault, 1991, p. 12). Foucault (1991) gives the example of the traditional conjugal relation in the 18th and 19th centuries:

> We cannot say that there was only male power; the woman herself could do a lot of things: be unfaithful to him, extract money from him, refuse him sexually. She was, however, subject to a state of domination, in the measure where all that was finally no more than a certain number of tricks which never brought about a reversal of the situation. (p. 12)

Invoking democracy, the normative inference is the counterfactual: resistance should oppose domination wherever it finds it. Such an inference suggests that domination is an imbalance of power, it is one of many structurings of power, and what resistance aims at is an "equalization"; and rather than a concentration, it suggests a disbursement. The emphasis on "minimizing domination" appears again in his remarks on Habermas. Criticizing Habermas for advocating a form of "utopian" thinking, whereby communicative action operates in a powerless vacuum, Foucault (ibid.) says:

> I don't believe there can be a society without relations of power. ... The problem is not of trying to dissolve them in the utopia of perfectly

> transparent communication, but to give oneself the rules of law, the techniques of management, but also the ethics, the *ethos*, the practice of self, which would allow these games of power to be played with a minimum of domination. (p. 18)

In this sense:

> liberty is itself political. And then it has a political model, in the measure where being free means not being a slave to one's self and to one's appetites, which presupposes that one establish over one's self a certain relation of domination, of mastery, which was called *arche*—power, authority. (p. 6)

When one practices liberty, one is engaged in moral conduct, which is to say that liberty must be practiced ethically. As Foucault (1991) puts it: "Liberty is the ontological condition of ethics. But ethics is the deliberate form assumed by liberty" (p. 4). This means that the "care for the self" involves liberty and ethics, which presumes a certain form of social structure: a certain degree of liberation.

In this sense, ethical action also takes place in a community, in that care for the self involves care for others. In Foucault's words:

> The care for the self always aims at the good for others. ... This implies also a relation with others to the extent that care for self renders one competent to occupy a place in the city, in the community or in interindividual relationships. ... I think the assumption of all this morality was that one who cared for himself correctly found himself, by that very fact, in a measure to behave correctly in relationship to others and for others. A city in which everyone would be correctly concerned for self would be a city that would be doing well, and it would find therein the ethical principle of its stability. (1991, p. 7)

Such a community is both *borderless* and *complexly differentiated*. These are the two essential conditions of what I have called elsewhere (Olssen, 2002) a "thin community". In such a conception difference and unity are balanced. Thin communities are linked to other communities and to the global order. Foucault's rejection of Hegelianism and forms of monist communitarianism establish difference as an important political principle, which ensures and safeguards pluralism, globalism, democracy and inclusion. In such a conception, democracy is the protection of difference. For Foucault, the principle of difference underpins his approach to the political as well as his global conception of citizenship. It is the theory of difference that establishes relationality and diversity as fundamental social and political attributes. It is also his conception of difference that establishes the character of Foucault's communitarianism as "thin", and which regulates the legitimate sphere of state and group actions vis-à-vis individual and group discretion.

Democratic tactics comprise a multifaceted range of mechanisms and processes. Its advantage for a Foucauldian politics is not simply that it enables the participation and approval of concerns by the entire collectivity and of all the major groups within it, but more importantly, it permits continued debate, modification, rejection, or revision of agreed decisions while enabling a maximum of freedom and autonomy, an ongoing possibility of negotiation and dialogue, and the most effective opposition possible to abuses of power. Government is important for Foucault, as Mitchell Dean (1999) says, "according to whether it allows rather than inhibits the 'self-directed use and development of capacities'" (p. 184). There is an obvious sense in which democracy is the form of government best suited to these ends.

In his "unfashionable interpretation of Michel Foucault",[3] James Johnson (1997) maintains that Foucault's commitment to concepts and principles such as those cited in the quotations above suggest a normative analysis of power contra the fashionable postmodern interpretations of his work. Johnson further supports his case by tracing similar references to canonical works such as *Discipline and Punish* as well as in Foucault's articles and interviews. In *Discipline and Punish*, Foucault (1977, p. 222) speaks of institutions such as prisons and schools as having the role of "introducing insuperable asymmetries and excluding reciprocities". Here Foucault talks of the disciplines as being "essentially nonegalitarian and asymmetrical" (p. 222). Johnson accepts the view contra the postmodern interpretations of Foucault, "that disciplinary power is *normatively objectionable* [for Foucault] precisely *because* it imposes unequal, asymmetrical, nonreciprocal relations and *because*, in doing so, it obliterates the sorts of extant communicative relation that, potentially at least, could produce social relations characterized by equality, symmetry and reciprocity" (1997, p. 572). Hence, says Johnson, power relations for Foucault are "objectionable because they subvert relations of communication, relations of the sort that—if more fully specified—might sustain the vision of political agency that is implicit in his commitment to resistance or dialogical ethics" (p. 572).

As against totalizing approaches, such as Marxism, Hegelianism, and liberalism, the normative emphasis of Foucault's position is that all power relations must be characterized by *openness* (i.e., not be "set", "congealed", "nonegalitarian", "asymmetrical" or "nonreciprocal"). Consequently, such principles give a normative basis to a conception of democratic justice, while at the same time recognizing that justice will require different things at different times and places. Although principles, of varying degrees of importance and weight, will relate to all aspects of conflicts in local situations, such principles will always underdetermine any actual ethical dilemma, and hence never fully resolve issues internal to such conflicts. While power relations must remain dialogically open, and be normatively skewed toward power equalization,[4] they must also be context-sensitive to the specific contingencies of historical circumstance.

3 Rights as a Historico-Political Discourse

I want now to look at three practices of democracy, or better tactics or strategies that can be called *democratic*: rights; contestation; and deliberation. A genealogy of democracy would trace the historical descent and emergence of the multiple processes, strategies, mechanisms, and tactics that societies instantiate as discourses of protection against war and conquest. That is, it would trace the shifting historically contingent conceptions of what constituted democracy in different societies at different times. Rather than government "by the people" in any direct or unmediated sense of "pure" democracy,[5] as in Greek society, or in 18th-century Europe and North America, or as in the later "representative" traditions, Foucault would see practices of democracy more broadly as representing "historico-political" discourses, comprising an assortment of tactics, strategies and mechanisms.

What are such tactics, strategies and mechanisms aimed at? In Foucault's view, the discourse of rights is a "historico-political discourse" aimed at the protection of lives. As he puts it (2003):

> The jurists of the seventeenth century and especially the eighteenth century were, you see, already asking this question about the right of life and death. The jurists ask: when we enter into a contract, what are individuals doing at the level of the social contract, when they come together to constitute a sovereign, to delegate absolute power over them to a sovereign? They do so because they are forced to by some threat or by need. They therefore do so in order to protect their lives. (p. 241)

Thus, viewing the development of rights in relation to "mechanisms, techniques and technologies of power" (p. 241), they assumed prominence because, "in the seventeenth and eighteenth centuries we saw the emergence of techniques of power that were essentially centered on the body" (ibid.). In this, rights constituted:

> devices that were used to ensure spatial distribution of individual bodies (their separation, their alignment, their serialization, and their surveillance) and the organization around those individuals of a whole field of visibility. They were also techniques that would be used to take control over bodies. (p. 241)

Rights are part of the "individualizing–totalizing" disciplinary technology. They were juridical technologies charged with protecting the *pluribus* while promoting the *unum*. Although rights constituted individualizing technologies of power, a new form emerged at the end of the 18th century, which also applied to rights in that it enabled individuals to be monitored, counted, compared, processed, treated equitably:

> This technology of power does not exclude the former, does not exclude disciplinary technology, but it does dovetail into it, integrate it, modify it to some extent, and above all, use it by sort of infiltrating it, embedding itself in existing disciplinary technologies. ... So after a first seizure of power over the body in an individualizing mode, we have a second seizure of power that is not individualizing, but, if you like, massifying, that is directed not at man-as-body, but man-as-species. ... What I would call a "biopolitics" of the human race. (p. 242)

Hobbes is, in this sense, the father of rights, for he saw the issue was security. As Foucault (2003) notes:

> Leviathan's strategic opposite number is, I think, the political use that was being made in political struggles of a certain historical knowledge pertaining to wars, invasions, pillage, dispossessions, confiscations, robbery, exaction, and the effects of all that, the effects of all these acts of war, all these feats of battle, and the real struggles that go on in the laws and institutions that apparently regulate power. ... Leviathan's invisible adversary is the Conquest. (p. 98)

It was a fear of the Conquest that led Hobbes to stress the role of the state:

> Hobbes may well seem to shock, but he is in fact being reassuring: he always speaks the discourse of contracts and sovereignty, or in other

words, the discourse of the State. After all, philosophy and right, or philosophico-juridical discourse, would rather give the State too much power than not enough, and while they do criticize Hobbes for giving the State too much power, they are secretly grateful to him for having warded off a certain insidious and barbarous enemy. (pp. 98–99)

Rights crystallize whatever given imbalance of power and wealth exists in a society. In the 17th century, natural rights theories were developed by conservative thinkers in the defense of property and competition and other bourgeois values. A system of rights constituted part of a historico-political *settlement*. A settlement can be represented, in Rawls's (1996) sense, as a *modus vivendi*, which is to say, a treaty, or alliance of diverse interests, which may at times constitute an overlapping consensus. In situations of war the settlement collapses and rights mean nothing. In this sense, the concept of settlement, although not explicitly used by Foucault, is useful in that it attests to the historical character of rights as they are embodied in broader discursive arrangements at a particular time.[6] Rights are a *war-preventing* strategy. They constitute a system of universal regulation of what is due whom and what is owed.

In this sense, what is to be made of Hart's (1955) claim that rights are natural? And, if there are no natural rights, is the discourse of rights redundant? What Hart failed to see is that moral rights may be built on a historically constituted settlement, and they will reflect the injustices and iniquities built into that settlement. In this sense, the existence of moral rights does not mean there must exist a natural right of liberty amongst men.[7] For Foucault, rights systems take effect as a settlement against war. They are a technology fixing the relation of the individual to the society; they differentiate; they are one of the "dividing practices". Foucault (2003) cites and endorses the views of Boulainvilliers, who argues that the idea of a natural right is "no more than a useless abstraction" (p. 156). In Boulainvilliers's view you can study history for as long as you like but you will never discover any natural rights. Behind the existing divisions between groups or strata in society are wars and struggles. Freedom, specifically, is not natural, for freedom is only conceivable if there are no relationships of domination between the individuals concerned. Freedom for Boulainvilliers is essentially the freedom to trample on the freedom of others. In this sense, freedom is the direct opposite of equality. Whatever the relation between the two, it is something that is decided and enjoyed according to "difference, domination, and war, thanks to a whole system of relations of force" (ibid., p. 157). In these relations, any laws of nature, if indeed they do exist, are weaker than the "nonegalitarian law of history":

It is therefore natural that the egalitarian law of nature should have given way—on a permanent basis—to the nonegalitarian law of history. It was because it was primal that natural right was not, as the jurists claim, foundational; it was foreclosed by the greater vigor of history. The law of history is always stronger than the law of nature. This is what Boulainvilliers is arguing when he says that history finally created a natural law that made freedom and equality antithetical, and that this natural law is stronger than the law inscribed in what is known as natural right. The fact that history is stronger than nature explains, ultimately why history has completely concealed nature. When history begins, nature can no longer speak, because in the war between history and nature, history always has the upper hand. There is a relationship of force between nature and history, and it is definitely in history's favor. So natural right does not exist, or exists only insofar as it has been defeated: it is always history's great loser, it is "the other". (2003, pp. 157–158)

A further point Boulainvilliers suggests is that "war is both the starting point for an analysis of society and the deciding factor in social organisation" (Foucault, 2003, p. 158). What is meant here is that wars and struggles determine the form of the relation of force between freedom and equality in the settlements or agreements that separate wars and contain struggles. The nature of military institutions, or the problem of "who has the weapons" is crucial to the maintenance of order between wars. The "problem of who has the weapons" is bound up, says Foucault (2003) "with certain technical problems, and it is in this sense that it can provide the starting point for a general analysis of society" (p. 159). He continues:

> History now looks essentially like a calculation of forces. ... Once the strong become weak and the weak become strong, there will be new oppositions, new divisions, and a new distribution of forces: the weak will form alliances among themselves, and the strong will try to form alliances with some and against others. ... For his part Boulainvilliers makes the relationship of war part of every social relationship, subdivides it into a thousand different channels, and reveals war to be a sort of permanent state that exists between groups, fronts and tactical units as they in some sense civilize one another, come into conflict with one another, or on the contrary, form alliances. There is no more multiple and stable great masses, but there is a multiple war. In one sense, it is a war of every man against every man, but it is obviously not a war of every man against

every man in the abstract and—I think—unreal sense in which Hobbes spoke of the war of every man when he tried to demonstrate that it is not the war of every man against every man that is at work in the social body. With Boulainvilliers, in contrast, we have a generalized war that permeates the entire social body and the entire history of the social body; it is obviously not the sort of war in which individuals fight individuals, but one in which groups fight groups. (p. 161)

The upshot of this conception is that war is a "disruption of right" (ibid., p. 163). Here, says Foucault:

War turns the very disruption of right into a grid of intelligibility, and makes it possible to determine the force relationship that always underpins a certain relationship of right. Boulainvilliers can thus integrate events such as wars, invasions, and change—which were once seen as simply naked acts of violence—into a whole layer of contents and prophecies that covered society in its entirety. ... A history that takes as its starting point the fact of war itself and makes its analysis in terms of war can relate all these things—war, religion, politics, manners, and characters—and can therefore act as a principle that allows us to understand history. (p. 163)

Citing and summarizing Foucault in his account of Boulainvilliers here brings to the fore the functions of democratic practices and tactics—not simply rights, but also the others—contestation, deliberation, the rule of law, parliamentary elections, forms of representation—as part of the settlement against war and chaos.[8] In this sense, rights may recognize, preserve and legitimate the existing unequal relation of forces in society, as they did in the 17th century, in consolidating bourgeois relations of property and class.[9] Or they may, in other periods, conceivably extend from the political to the economic domains, seeking to challenge unequal relations and forces. In this sense, rights to life, to a certain minimum level of sustenance and property, to walk the streets in day or night, to speak, to contest, can be endorsed, exchanged, surrendered, or exempted. What is clear, however, is that for Foucault, democracy is the alternative to war, for democracy is nothing but the tactics adopted to resolve conflict, ensure more or less peaceful transitions of power, and to permit each individual their legitimate arena or space, whereby rights—both passive and active—can be exercised and maintained. In this sense, by invoking the normative in Foucault, we can see that democracy is the containment and management of war. Democracy is politics, and "politics", as Foucault (2003) says, inverting Clausewitz's famous aphorism, "is the continuation of war by other means" (p. 15).

Hobbes, rather than Locke, is the preferred starting point for a social conception of rights, for the juridical tradition that passes through Hobbes is more compatible with the priority of the social over nature and, in this sense, of the "triumph of the will" (Rials, 1994, p. 168). For Locke, the law restores natural right and is subservient to it, which is the basis, ultimately, for Locke, of giving citizens the right to rebel against the state. For Hobbes, the situation is more complex. Although, in *Leviathan* (1885, pp. 65–66) there is a "right of nature" (*jus naturale*) which resides in "the liberty each man hath to use his own power, as he will himself, for the preservation of his own nature, that is to say his own life", a state wherein "every man has a right to everything". Hence a state where "there is no security" (p. 66), it would be a mistake to confuse this abstract and unqualified "right of nature" with the modern notion of subjective rights based upon the idea of an individual power. As Rials (1994) notes:

> Hobbes does not think that the "right of nature" dissolves, despite his ambiguous phrasing, into the "natural rights" of individuals. Right is constituted only once the individual "powers" or "forces" come together to constitute a societal machine, the "artificial man" (Leviathan) whose strength is the sum of all prior individual forces that have made him sovereign. This is the difference between Hobbes and the teachers of the modern natural-right school. If there are no natural rights while the social contract is in the making, there surely are none once it is made. In the contract, the "right of nature" gives way entirely to the "civil right", which is the fruit of law's exaltation. With Hobbes one already has voluntarist positivism. (p. 168)

4   Contestation and Deliberation

Foucault's writing on rights, as summarized above, from his February 11th, 1976, lecture at the Collège de France show his serious consideration in relation to the themes of war, peace, and security. Such considerations also give substance to his political work on behalf of prisoners and other marginalized groups. In June 1984, *Libération* carried his brief article "Confronting Governments: Human Rights", where he states:

> There exists an international citizenship that has its rights and its duties and that obliges one to speak out against every abuse of power, whoever

its author, whoever its victims. After all, we are all members of the community of the governed, and thereby obliged to show mutual solidarity. (2001, p. 474)

The conception of rights here invoked seems to be one beyond both sovereignty and discipline; one which Foucault (1980b) hinted at towards the close of the second lecture on power (January 14th, 1976), where he said:

> If one wants to look for a non-disciplinary form of power, or rather, to struggle against disciplines and disciplinary power, it is not towards the ancient right of sovereignty that we should turn, but towards the possibility of a new form of right, one which must indeed be anti-disciplinarian, but at the same time liberated from the principle of sovereignty. (p. 108)

A conception of right not subject to normalization, and not legitimating the interests of the monarch might then exist in contestation as is entailed in Foucault's discussions of resistance to power. Such resistance occurs wherever domination occurs. It is present also in relation to his later discussions concerning *parrhēsia*, which has a range of meanings and uses, the main one of which functions in relation to democratic institutions and means essentially speaking truth to power. Foucault (2001a) points to an ancient tradition revolving around free speech, as embodied in *parrhēsia*, which he defines as "frankness in speaking the truth" (p. 11).[10] Ordinarily translated into English as "free speech", *parrēsiazomai* or *parrhēsiazesthai* is to use *parrhēsia*, and the *parrhēsiastes* is the one who uses *parrhēsia* (i.e., the one who speaks the truth). But someone is said to use *parrhēsia* "only if there is a risk or danger for him in telling the truth ... the *parrhēsiastes* is someone who takes a risk" (2001a, p. 16). In addition:

> The function of *parrhēsia* ... has the function of criticism. ... *Parrhēsia* is a form of criticism, either towards another or towards oneself, but always in a situation where the speaker or confessor is in a position of inferiority with respect to the interlocutor. The *parrhēsiastes* is always less powerful than the one with whom he speaks. (2001a, p. 16)

Finally, "in *parrhēsia*, telling the truth is regarded as a duty" (p. 16). Foucault (2001a) draws the various elements together. Thus:

> *Parrhēsia* is a kind of verbal activity where the speaker has a specific relation to truth through frankness, a certain relationship to his own life

through danger, a certain type of relationship to himself or other people through criticism ... and a specific relation to moral law through freedom and duty. More precisely, *parrhēsia* is verbal activity in which a speaker expresses his personal relationship to truth and risks his life because he recognizes truth telling as a duty to improve or help other people (as well as himself). In *parrhēsia*, the speaker uses his freedom and chooses frankness instead of persuasion, truth instead of falsehood or silence, the risk of death instead of life and security, criticism instead of flattery, and moral duty instead of self-interest and moral apathy. That, then, quite generally, is the positive meaning of the word *parrhēsia* in most of the Greek texts ... from the fifth century BC to the fifth century AD. (pp. 19–20)

In relation to Greek uses, *parrhēsia* was potentially seen as dangerous to democracy. As Foucault explains:

The problem very roughly put was the following. Democracy is founded on *politeia*, a constitution, where the *demos*, the people, exercise power, and where everyone is equal in front of the law. Such a constitution, however, is condemned to give equal place to all forms of *parrhēsia*, even the worst. Because *parrhēsia* is given even to the worst citizens, the overwhelming influence of bad, immoral, or ignorant speakers may lead the citizenry into tyranny, or may otherwise endanger the city. Hence *parrhēsia* may be dangerous to democracy itself. (Ibid., p. 77)

Thus, Foucault cites the third book of Plato's *Republic* (Book VIII, 557a-b), where Socrates tells Adeimantus that: "When the poor win the result is democracy. They kill some of the opposite party, banish others, and grant the rest an equal share in civil rights and government, officials being usually appointed by lot" (pp. 83–84). Socrates goes on to enquire as to what people are like in a democracy: First of all, they are free. Liberty and free speech (*parrhēsia*) are rife everywhere; anyone is allowed to do what he likes. That being so, every man will arrange his own manner of life to suit his pleasure. Plato's concern here, says Foucault (2001a) is that in a democracy there is:

no common *logos*, no possible unity, for the city. Following the Platonic principle that there is an analogous relation between the way a human being behaves and the way the city is ruled, between the hierarchical organization of the faculties of the human being and the constitution makeup of the polis, you can see very well that if everyone in the city behaves just as he wishes, with each person following his own opinion, his own will or desires, then there are in the city as many constitutions, as many small autonomous cities, as there are citizens doing whatever they please. And you can see that Plato also considers *parrhēsia* not only as the freedom to say whatever one wishes, but as linked with the freedom to *do* whatever one wants. It is a kind of anarchy involving the freedom to choose one's own style of life without limit. (p. 84)

Plato's treatment occludes difference, or rather, fails to allow for difference within unity. *Parrhēsia* is not condemned because all citizens are given rights to influence the city, or to have a say. For Plato, it is because of this very quality that it is opposed. Yet, within the context of security and war, this democratic right (*parrhēsia*) becomes the condition on which peace is maintained. *Parrhēsia* contributes to the democratic settlement against war that constantly threatens to erupt or become uncontainable. Such insights are potentially continuous with the republican tradition in political theory, where rights of contestation are prior to consent, and where public decisions are legitimate so long as they are capable of withstanding group and individual contestation under procedures agreed by all. In this sense, contestation is a hedge against arbitrariness in decision making. Essentially, contestation, preferably augmented by universal education, introduces the fundamental idea of democracy as "self-rule".

If *parrhēsia* could contribute to an ideal of democracy within the law, according to the constitutional rules that limit its scope, in talking about moving beyond sovereignty and discipline, Foucault seems to acknowledge a more fundamental right to *resistance* when power becomes damned up, resulting in domination. Thus, in his interview "Truth and Power", he (1980a) speaks of *strategies of resistance* taking effect when surveillance and oppression become "unbearable" (p. 122). In this sense, it would constitute a right, not because it relates back to nature, but in that it becomes the condition on which war and chaos are avoided and survival and life continuance assured. While such strategies don't guarantee the avoidance of war, they become its best hope, and its minimum condition. Let us say, without such a right, war, which is really the suspension of all rights, all security, becomes almost certain. Resistance—short of war—becomes a condition of pluralist democracy, which is itself a strategy for the avoidance of war.

Strategies of contestation are linked to deliberation, which requires the fostering of institutions in which political action, with all its limitations, can be pursued. Deliberative democracy acknowledges that viewpoints and preferences will conflict, and allows therefore for an uncoerced or open context as essential to the arrival at an agreed outcome. Such strategies for Foucault are essentially group based where the views of individuals are transformed in the process. Deliberative democracy thus counts to insure against open conflict.

In the Foucauldian sense, deliberation recognizes and tolerates differences to a much greater sense than in Habermas's understanding. Habermas's post-Kantian conception of a transcendent communicative consensus, embodied through the ideal speech situation is replaced by a much looser context of shared agreements, more of the character of Rawls's (1996) *modus vivendi* than a consensus reached based on epistemological grounds of the force of the better argument alone. As a *modus vivendi* is simply a loose treaty, or agreement, it is based sometimes on nothing more than a shared interest in survival. The aim of deliberation is not epistemic consensus, pace Habermas, but rather, a new concordance, or settlement, based on a workable balance between different views, a pragmatic consensus of sorts, based on epistemic factors, conceptions of justice, as well as a range of pragmatic factors, such as the priorities for peace and stability at a particular moment in time.

5   Extending Foucault and Democracy Post-9/11

If a settlement is a historically contingent accord or agreement which constitutes a system of rules whose function is the containment of conflict and prevention of open hostilities, in the Hobbesian sense, it is motivated by the quest for security. In his essays in *Society Must Be Defended*, Foucault clearly accepts such a view, but whether he would accept Hobbes's skepticism in international relations is more doubtful. The standard view of international relations accords with the Westphalian model of free independent states, organized and run on the basis of autonomy and non-interference. Such a view represents an extrapolation from Hobbes views about individuals in the state of nature to ethical skepticism concerning relations between states in the international arena. For Hobbes there were no *effective* moral principles in the state of nature.[11] The fact that one individual cannot trust another individual to abide by a moral rule or norm, makes it pointless acting in such a way oneself—which is why life in the state of nature is "solitary, nasty, brutish and short". In the international system of states, ethical skepticism means that there are no moral restrictions on a state's interpretation of its own interests. Hence, as moral rules would be inappropriate, the system is seen as "anarchic".

Kant rejected such a conception, as did Grotius and Pufendorf before him. Rather than support an anarchic conception of international relations based on individual state interests, they supported an ethical view of the role of the state acting in accord with an objective moral rule.[12] Initial plausibility of such a view can be seen in the existence of human rights accords, international charters, and initiatives towards international peace, which would seem to suggest that some conception of international morality does exist, and does influence states in their actions towards each other. Before the Peace of Westphalia, Grotius had defined international relations as a moral community of states.[13] Pufendorf also developed a conception of the "morality of states", interpreting international relations from within a natural law tradition.[14]

Globalization, terrorism and weapons of mass destruction make such a model, based on an "ethical" conception of the global order, more of a necessity than a plausible option in the 21st century. The rise of international terrorism and weapons of mass destruction, as well as phenomenon like climate change, SARS, MERS, AIDS, avian flu, Ebola, COVID-19, alters the "equation", for they make individual and collective survival an important ethical concern. The possibilities of nuclear terrorism, together with the democratization of knowledge and of access to nuclear knowledge and technology, make the challenges facing humanity even more formidable. In this situation, survival constitutes a new imperative, a "final settlement", to justify a global law of morality amongst nations. Acting according to principles becomes compelling if by so doing acts of terrorism are *minimized*, and the possibilities for survival are *enhanced*. Similarly, the possibility of acts of terror or of violence, or unintended developments like climate change, AIDS or avian flu, COVID-19, increases the need for a discourse of safety and security. We may not agree with Hobbes on very much, but the priority of *security* over *freedom*, was indeed a profound insight. Globalization and terrorism raise the issue of "survival" both for individuals and nations.

Such a thesis would argue that given these new realities of acts of terror and weapons of mass destruction, the *self-interest* of states, like the *self-interest* of individuals, is a poor basis for action and ethics. Indeed, actions calculated in terms of short-term interests may not be realized as in the long-term interests of either. The interests of survival are normative in that they impose requirements of action in the interests of all. The self-interests of humanity cannot be calculated based on the interests of each, however, but must involve a collective consideration. This necessitates a conception of democracy, as Beitz (1979) puts it, which expresses a "moral point of view":

> The moral point of view requires us to regard the world from the perspective of one person among many rather than from that of a particular self with particular interests, and to choose courses of action, policies, rules, and institutions on grounds that would be acceptable to any agent who was impartial among the competing interests involved. ... From the

moral point of view ... one views one's interests as one set of interests among many and weighs the entire range of interests according to some impartial scheme. (p. 58)

This principle of democracy is *non-foundational* but *universal*. It is not based upon any fixed conception of human nature, or of a premise, as with Habermas, of universal rationality, but rather purely on a principle of a *mutual interest in universal survival. In an age of terrorism democracy is the condition upon which survival can best be assured*. Such a conception is universal to the extent that it is *willed*. The inspiration is Nietzschean rather than Kantian. It is also, I think, Foucauldian, in the sense that it constitutes *a universalism of democracy as a contingent discourse of open protection and facilitation in a world of dangers*.[15]

Although survival may justify democracy, as an end or goal it is too thin to be fully adequate, of course, for mere survival cannot possibly satisfy a complete account of life's ends and aims. And it may not be universally agreed to, if we mean by universal "agreed to by all", for there are no doubt some, including "suicide bombers", for whom it holds no sway at all. Ultimately, that is the choice of course, and certainly it focuses the concentration. For if democracy is the *precondition* of survival, then it requires a democratic mandate to be effective, even so.

Beyond this, it is possible to build a much richer conception of democracy on this basis. If survival is a final justification, and focuses our attention as to why democracy is important, survival with dignity resonates of a more traditional concern with *ends*. This of course is the classic conception of democracy as a doctrine based on the ultimate worth and dignity of the human being, as espoused in the republican tradition. Thus, it is not the narrow "realist" theory of democracy that has been articulated and advocated by postwar American political science, commonly associated with the writings of Joseph Schumpeter, *Capitalism, Socialism and Democracy* (1976), which refers to a narrow system of representative government and a means of changing governments through a system of elections. Rather, if safety, dignity, and survival are to be possible, democracy must be deepened, once again, to refer to a substantive end which is something more than mere utility, but encompasses the well-being and safety "of each and all". Such a conception must once again entail a certain idea of participation, equality, inclusion, social justice, and freedom as well. Democracy must in this light be seen as a comprehensive discourse of (1) safety and security, (2) freedom and autonomy, (3) inclusion, (4) fairness and justice, (5) equality of resources and capabilities. In an age of terrorism, where a global *Leviathan* is feared, *a comprehensive discourse of democracy becomes the best answer to the Hobbesian problem of order.*

While some political theorists might sense a resonance here with Rousseau's general will, this would be mistaken. The model suggested here is, in the sense of Foucault, not a totalizing one, which presupposes unity between individual and collective, but a *detotalizing* one that is based on the notion of general well-being, while recognizing the diversity and differences between cultures and people. In terms of social ontology such a conception could possibly be reconciled with Martha Nussbaum's (1995) "thick, vague conception" (p. 456) of the good. Nussbaum advances "a soft version of Aristotelian essentialism" (p. 450) which incorporates a "determinate account of the human being, human functioning and human flourishing" (p. 450). While in formal terms it recognizes that all individuals and cultures have certain developmental and lifestyle needs, this "internal essentialism" is "an historically grounded empirical essentialism" (p. 451). As such, it is purely empirical, for within this broad end, and subject to the limits necessary for its realization and continuance, it permits and recognizes a multitude of identities and projects and ways of life.

Of course, in that Nussbaum claims to be influenced by Aristotle, there is a clear difference with Foucault, who was more influenced by Nietzsche. Thus, Foucault would reject the essentialist teleological conception of the subject as "realizing" their *ends* or *destiny*, in preference for a more constructivist Nietzschean emphasis on "self-constitution". But beyond this, it can be claimed that self-constitution presupposes certain "capabilities" in the ways Nussbaum claims. Also, the models of social relations, and specifically of the ontological priority of the social to the individual, are similar in both traditions. It should also be noted that Nussbaum has been challenged on her dependence on Aristotle (see Arneson, 2000; Mulgan, 2000). In defense of locating herself in an Aristotelian tradition, she maintains that she is inspired by the basic ontological postulates, but not the detailed arguments, of Aristotle, and she admits that her identification as "Aristotelian" has a great deal to do with her own biography and early philosophical commitments and training (see Nussbaum, 2000).

Nussbaum's conception of the good is concerned "with the overall shape and content of the human form of life" (p. 456). Such a conception, she says, is "vague, and this is deliberately so ... for it admits of much multiple specification in accordance with varied local and personal conceptions. The idea is that it is better to be vaguely right than precisely wrong" (p. 456). Such a conception is not metaphysical in that it does not claim to derive from a source exterior to human beings in history. Rather, it is as "universal as possible" and aims at "mapping out the general shape of the human form of life, those features that constitute life as human wherever it is" (p. 457). Nussbaum calls this her "thick, vague conception ... of the human form of life" (p. 457). Hence, her list of factors constitutes a formal list without substantive content, allowing for difference or variation within each category. Amongst the factors are (1) mortality: all human beings face death; (2) various invariant features of the human body, such as "nutritional, and other related requirements" regarding hunger, thirst, the need for food and drink and shelter; (3) cognitive: "all human beings have sense perception ... the ability to think"; (4) early development, (5) practical reason, (6) sexual desire, (7) affiliation with other human beings, and (8) relatedness to other species and to nature (pp. 457–460).

As purely formal factors or generic species characteristics, which can admit to cultural and historical variation, Foucault, in my view, could be rendered consistent with the general tenor of Nussbaum's list, although he may wish to enter qualifications or caveats on specific features (sexual desire?). Foucault himself says that universal forms may well exist. In "What Is Enlightenment?", Foucault (1984) suggests there may possibly be universalizing tendencies at the root of Western civilization, which include such things as "the acquisition of capabilities and the struggle for freedom", as "permanent elements" (pp. 47–48). Again, more directly, in the preface to *The History of Sexuality, Volume 2*, Foucault (1984a) says that he is not denying the possibility of universal structures:

> Singular forms of experience may perfectly very well harbor universal structures; they may well not be independent from the concrete determinations of social existence. ... [T]his thought has a historicity which is proper to it. That it should have this historicity does not mean it is deprived of all universal form, but instead that the putting into play of these universal forms is itself historical. (p. 335)

Like Nussbaum, the factors he recognizes as invariant do not derive from any "extra historical metaphysical conception" (Nussbaum, 1995, p. 460). Also, Foucault's conception is very much in keeping with Nussbaum's "thick, vague conception" in that it is concerned to identify "components that are fundamental to any human life" (p. 461). Of course, the recognized features of human life should be seen as largely in relation to *general form* rather than *actual substance*, for Foucault would be skeptical that any essential properties of a human being could be distinguished from the accidental, contingent properties, in that human beings and their needs are historically constituted in the process of history.[16]

Richard Bernstein (1994) notes Habermas's criticism that when critique is totalized it is caught in a contradiction as it has no standard. Thus, as Habermas

(1987) put it, genealogy "is overtaken by a fate similar to that which Foucault had seen in the human sciences" (pp. 275–276). Yet, Bernstein seeks to defend Foucault's position by relating critique to the exigencies of the environment, not in terms of truth, but in terms of the ever-present dangers in which people in history face. What is dangerous is that "everything becomes a target for normalisation".[17] What is dangerous is that war and violence destroy the possibilities of *any* form of human order of life. What is at issue is survival itself. In this sense, Foucault's "archaeological–genealogical analyses of problematiques are intended to specify the changing constellation of dangers" (Bernstein, 1994, p. 227). For as Foucault (1984b) said, "everything is dangerous", and "if everything is dangerous, then we always have something to do" (p. 343).

Acknowledgement

This chapter originally appeared as Olssen, M. (2007), Invoking democracy: Foucault's conception (with insights from Hobbes), in M. A. Peters & T. A. C. Besley (Eds.), *Why Foucault? New directions in educational research* (pp. 205–226), Peter Lang. Reprinted here, with minor edits, with permission from the publisher.

Notes

1 I am not suggesting that Foucault could not have justified his own position, but simply indicating that my own interest is in deriving normative inferences from his analysis. Foucault's reasons for rejecting normative theory, while interesting, are beyond the scope of this paper.
2 In claiming that Foucault "suggests" a theory of democracy, I seek only to selectively link certain social and ontological fragments in Foucault's thinking to assess their implications for a normative conception of democracy. My claims are of a distinctly limited and exploratory nature in relation to both Foucault scholarship, as well as democratic theory. I am quite aware that I am selectively picking out certain themes and emphases in Foucault to assemble my own conception, and that the conception offered is somewhat speculative and far from complete. It is also acknowledged that Foucault on his own provides only limited value in respect to generating normative principles of democracy and that insights from writers like Heidegger, Nietzsche and Spinoza are needed to flesh the picture out and make it coherent. Such an enlarged perspective is beyond the scope of this inquiry, however.
3 This is the subtitle to his 1997 article in *Political Theory*.
4 Such an emphasis on equalization, or equilibrium of powers has potentially interesting affinities to Montesquieu's theory in *The Spirit of the Laws*. The jurist Charles Eisenmann (1933) maintains that the representation of Montesquieu's thesis as a "separation of powers" thesis is a myth, and that Montesquieu was really advancing a thesis concerning the equilibrium of powers, where the concern was with "balance" or "combination" rather than separation.

Although interesting as a future area of enquiry, it is not possible to explore such affinities in this paper.
5   Government "by the people" was a term used by Tom Paine.
6   The concept of "settlement" in that it suggests a contingent assemblage of elements at a particular time is consistent with historicist theories like Foucault's. It would constitute a form of "discursive apparatus". In that Foucault did not himself use this concept, I appreciate that I am "extending" Foucault's frame of reference somewhat.
7   For Hart says, "if there are any moral rights, it follows that there is at least one natural right, the equal right of all men to be free" (p. 175). For Hart, natural rights are clearly non-conventional and pre-political.
8   Although he doesn't necessarily concur with everything writers like Hobbes or Boulainvilliers says, it is the function of rights as a historically specific strategy against war and chaos that Foucault extracts from their writings as a central theme.
9   Foucault's point here seems to be that the discourse of rights can serve to both protect individuals and crystallize power and wealth simultaneously. In this sense, rights can have multiple functions.
10 Writers like Nancy Fraser (1989) and Jürgen Habermas (1987) accuse Foucault of "crypto-normativism" by which they partly mean that he invokes liberal arguments while critiquing liberalism. The concept of *parrhēsia* might count in this sense being indistinguishable from the right to free speech. But Foucault would easily respond to such a charge for while he clearly agrees with many liberal ideals and values, he would maintain that the ontological and epistemological basis of liberalism is incapable of supporting them. Part of his quest can be seen as the search for a different type of philosophical support for such ideals.
11 Hobbes did maintain there were natural principles and proposes 19 laws of nature (see Hobbes, 1885, chapters 14 and 15). The trouble in international relations, as in the state of nature, is the difficulty in being sure that others would act on them.
12 For contemporary work in this tradition, see the English School of Martin Wright (1992) and Hedley Bull (1977).
13 Grotius's was a "pre-liberal" conception, and notably, he argued against the principle of "non-interference", arguing that it is sometimes justifiable (see Beitz, 1979, p. 71).
14 Although he argued against Hobbes, as Beitz (1979, p. 60) notes, he produces similar conclusions about the weakness of moral rules in international relations.
15 My view is that survival is a better basis to justify democracy than the idea of a founding or original "social contract". Survival is an end that comprises two aspects: self-preservation (individually and collectively) and well-being. It is not grounded in human nature but constitutes a choice which must be enacted. The inspiration here is more Spinozian than Foucauldian, although I would claim that they are not inconsistent with Foucault's approach.
16 Such a reconciliation between Foucault and Nussbaum would require far greater effort than is possible here. There is some point to the argument that Nussbaum's focus on survival and well-being would only be fruitful if re-packaged in a more constructivist frame of reference influenced by Nietzsche and Spinoza.
17 Bernstein is citing Hiley (1988, p. 103).

References

Arneson, R. J. (2000). Perfectionism and politics. *Ethics*, *111*(1), 37–63.

Beitz, C. (1979). *Political theory and international relations*. Princeton University Press.

Bernstein, R. J. (1994). Foucault: Critique as a philosophical ethos. In M. Kelly (Ed.), *Critique and power: Recasting the Foucault/Habermas debate* (pp. 211–242). MIT Press.

Bull, H. (1977). *The anarchical society*. Columbia University Press.

Connolly, W. (1998). Beyond good and evil: The ethical sensibility of Michel Foucault. In J. Moss (Ed.), *The later Foucault: Politics and philosophy* (pp. 108–128). Sage.

Dean, M. (1999). *Governmentality: Power and rule in modern society*. Sage.

Eisenmann, C. (1933). *L'esprit des lois et la séparation des pouvoirs*. Mélanges Carré de Malberg.

Foucault, M. (1977). *Discipline and punish: The birth of the prison* (A. Sheridan, Trans.). Pantheon.

Foucault, M. (1980a). Truth and power (C. Gordon, Trans.). In C. Gordon (Ed.), *Power/knowledge: Selected interviews and other writings 1972–1977* (C. Gordon, Trans.; pp. 109–133). Harvester Press.

Foucault, M. (1980b). Two lectures (K. Soper, Trans.). In C. Gordon (Ed.), *Power/knowledge: Selected interviews and other writings 1972–1977* (pp. 78–108). Harvester Press.

Foucault, M. (1984a). Politics and ethics: An interview (C. Porter, Trans.). In P. Rabinow (Ed.), *The Foucault reader* (pp. 373–380). Pantheon.

Foucault, M. (1984b). On the genealogy of ethics: An interview of work in progress. In P. Rabinow (Ed.), *The Foucault reader* (pp. 340–372). Pantheon.

Foucault, M. (1984). What is enlightenment? (C. Porter, Trans.). In P. Rabinow (Ed.), *The Foucault reader* (pp. 32–50). Pantheon.

Foucault, M. (1989). The concern for truth. In S. Lotringer (Ed.), *Foucault live: Interviews, 1966–84* (pp. 293–308). Semiotext(e).

Foucault, M. (1991). The ethic of care for the self as a practice of freedom: An interview (J. D. Gauthier, Trans.). In J. Bernauer & D. Rasmussen (Eds.), *The final Foucault* (pp. 1–20). MIT Press.

Foucault, M. (2001a). *Fearless speech*. J. Pearson (Ed.). Semiotext(e).

Foucault, M. (2001b). Confronting governments: Human rights. In J. D. Faubion (Ed.), *Essential works of Foucault, 1954–1984, vol. 3: Power* (R. Hurley et al., Trans.; pp. 474–476). Penguin.

Foucault, M. (2003). *Society must be defended: Lectures at the Collège de France, 1975–76* (D. Macey, Trans.). Allen Lane/Penguin.

Fraser, N. (1989). *Unruly practices: Power, discourse and gender in contemporary social theory*. Polity.

Habermas, J. (1987). *The philosophical discourse of modernity* (F. Lawrence, Trans.). MIT Press.

Hacking, I. (1986). Self-improvement. In D. C. Hoy (Ed.), *Foucault: A critical reader* (pp. 235–240). Basil Blackwell.

Hart, H. L. A. (1955). Are there any natural rights? *The Philosophical Review, 64*(2), 175–191.

Hiley, D. R. (1988). *Philosophy in question: Essays on a Pyrrhonian theme*. Chicago University Press.

Hobbes, T. (1885). *Leviathan*. George Routledge and Sons.

Johnson, J. (1997). Communication, criticism, and the postmodern consensus: An unfashionable interpretation of Michel Foucault. *Political Theory, 25*(4), 559–583. https://doi.org/10.1177/0090591797025004004

Mulgan, R. (2000). Was Aristotle an "Aristotelian social democrat"? *Ethics, 111*(1), 79–101.

Nussbaum, M. (1995). Human functioning and social justice: In defense of Aristotelian essentialism. In D. Tallack (Ed.), *Critical theory: A reader* (pp. 449–472). Harvester Wheatsheaf.

Nussbaum, R. (2000). Aristotle, politics, and human capabilities: A response to Antony, Arneson, Charlesworth, and Mulgan. *Ethics, 111*(1), 102–140.

Olssen, M. (2002). Michel Foucault as "thin" communitarian: Difference, community, democracy. *Cultural Studies/Critical Methodologies, 2*(4), 483–513. https://doi.org/10.1177/153270860200200403

Olssen, M. (2003). Structuralism, post-structuralism, neo-liberalism: Assessing Foucault's legacy. *Journal of Education Policy, 18*(2), 189–202. https://doi.org/10.1080/0268093022000043047

Paine, T. (1989). *Thomas Paine: Political writings*. Cambridge University Press.

Rawls, J. (1996). *Political liberalism*. Columbia University Press.

Reid, J. (2003). Foucault on Clausewitz: Conceptualizing the relationship between war and power. *Alternatives, 28*(1), 1–28.

Rials, S. (1994). Rights and modern law. In M. Lilla (Ed.), *New French thought: Political philosophy* (pp. 164–177). Princeton University Press.

Schumpeter, J. (1976). *Capitalism, socialism and democracy*. Allen and Unwin.

Wright, M. (1992). *International theory: The three traditions*. Holmes and Meier.

Printed in the United States
by Baker & Taylor Publisher Services